SOCIOLOGY

ACADEMIC REVIEWERS FOR THE SECOND EDITION

We would like to express special thanks to the following people, who gave generously of their time and expertise in reviewing all or various parts of the book for the second edition.

Michael Bassis,
University of Rhode Island

Aubrey Bonnett,
Hunter College

Ruth Brown,
Oscar Rose Junior College

Walter Buckley,
*University of
New Hampshire*

John Dudley,
*Virginia Polytechnic
Institute*

Susan Eckstein,
Boston University

Joe Feagin,
University of Texas

William Feigelman,
Nassau Community College

William Foster,
Oregon State University

Don C. Gibbons,
Portland State University

Richard Gigliotti,
University of Akron

Louis Wolf Goodman,
*Social Science Research
Council*

David Grafstein,
University of Toronto

Gerald Handel,
City University of New York

Joan Huber,
University of Illinois

Theodore Kachel,
Earlham College

Irwin Kantor,
Middlesex County College

Mark Kassop,
Bergen Community College

Lewis Killian,
University of Massachusetts

Patrick McNamara,
University of New Mexico

Katherine Meyer,
Ohio State University

Marshall Meyer,
*University of California,
Riverside*

Robert Mitchell,
*Pennsylvania State
University*

Charles O'Connor,
Bemidji State University

Anthony Orum,
University of Texas

Ira Reiss,
University of Minnesota

Frank Roberts,
San Antonio College

William Stacey,
*University of Texas,
Arlington*

John Strength,
San Antonio College

Caryl Utigard,
Highline Community College

Pierre Van den Berghe,
University of Washington

Joann Vanek,
Queens College

Dennis Wrong,
New York University

SOCIOLOGY

SECOND EDITION

Donald Light, Jr.
City College of the City University of New York

Suzanne Keller
Princeton University

Alfred A. Knopf  New York

Second Edition
987654321
Copyright © 1975, 1979 by Alfred A. Knopf, Inc.

Library of Congress Cataloging in Publication Data

Light, Donald, 1942–
    Sociology.

    Includes bibliographies and indexes.
    1. Sociology.   2.   United States—Social
conditions.   I.   Keller, Suzanne Infeld, 1927–
joint author.   II. Title.
HM51.L52 1979   301   78-11922

ISBN 0–394–32031–x

Manufactured in the United States of America
Composed by New England Typographic Service, Inc., Bloomfield, Ct.
Printed and bound by Rand McNally & Co., Indianapolis, Ind.
Picture research by Abigail Solomon
Cover design by Meryl Sussman Levavi
Cover art: Naum Gabo. *Linear Construction in Space, Number 4.* (1958).
Plastic and stainless steel. 40 x 21 x 21 inches.
Collection of Whitney Museum of American Art.
Gift of the Friends of the Whitney Museum of American Art.

Acknowledgments

Chapter-opener photos: Ch. 1: George Hall/Woodfin Camp & Associates; Ch. 2: J. Cooke/Photo Researchers, Inc.; Ch. 3: Mike Mazzaschi/Stock, Boston; Ch. 4: Camilla Smith; Ch. 5: Norman Lerner/Photo Researchers, Inc.; Ch. 6: Andy Mercado/Jeroboam; Ch. 7: Owen Franken/Stock, Boston; Ch. 8: Stella Gosman; Ch. 9: © Bernard Guillot; Ch. 10: Owen Franken/Stock, Boston; Ch. 11: Erik Anderson/Stock, Boston; Ch. 12: Dan McCoy/Rainbow; Ch. 13: Frederick P. Bodic/Stock, Boston; Ch. 14: David Krasnor/Photo Researchers, Inc.; Ch. 15: Sylvia Johnson/Woodfin Camp & Associates; Ch. 16: Sylvia Johnson/Woodfin Camp & Associates; Ch. 17: Ellis Herwig/Stock, Boston; Ch. 18: George Hall/Woodfin Camp & Associates; Ch. 19: Frank Wing/Stock, Boston; Ch. 20: Oliver Rebbot/Woodfin Camp & Associates; End matter: Joseph Crilley.

(Continued on p. xviii following the Subject Index.)

PREFACE

The second edition of this textbook was a challenge: we wanted to maintain the characteristics that we strove for in the first edition, while making changes and improvements that seemed called for by events in the outside world as well as by feedback from students and professors. We feel hopeful that we have succeeded.

Updating: Every effort was made to keep the book as current as possible, in terms of both sociology and current events. This involved using the latest statistics available and incorporating the most recent sociological research.

New topics: Major sections have been added on economics and the environment, and many smaller sections were added on such topics as occupational socialization (in the Socialization chapter); informal social control (in the Deviance and Social Control chapter); college life (in the Education chapter); and technological change as illustrated by the computer (in the Social Change and Technology chapter).

Organization: We have made several changes in the sequencing of chapters. The chapter on Organizations and Bureaucracy now follows the chapter on Social Groups. The chapter on Deviance and Social Control and the chapter on Power, Politics, and Economics were moved up in the book.

Integration of chapters: To meet the request that chapters be integrated more closely, we added an Epilogue (chapter 20) that shows how many of the topics covered in the text apply directly to the student's present and future life. We also added part introductions that give a brief overview of what will be covered within the chapters in each part.

Use of examples: Wherever possible we tried to add more of the kind of teaching examples that characterized the first edition. Thus in framing a new section on group dynamics, we used a series of excerpts from William Golding's popular *Lord of the Flies,* a novel whose vivid scenes of interaction among a group of boys readily illustrate the sociological points critical to an understanding of the group dynamics process.

Illustrations: Where possible, we tried to improve the integration of illustrations and captions with the text. We also added many full-color illustrations.

New boxes: We added a series of new boxes, with the theme Common Sense and Sociology, which highlight the value of the sociological point of view. The In-the-News boxes that appeared in the first edition were completely updated, and we also added many new boxes on current research studies.

Careers appendix: A Careers in Sociology appendix was added to describe the various careers for which a degree in sociology prepares a student, as well as the value of the study of sociology for almost any occupation.

As with every revision, students and professors who provided comments and suggestions enabled us to chart a preliminary course in making changes that would improve the book. To them we are grateful, as we are to the academic reviewers listed opposite the title page. We would like to thank Romaine Lindsey for her research assistance in updating the book. We are also indebted to writers Ann Levine, Neil Gluckin, and Roberta Meyer for shaping our ideas into the words that appear on the printed page. Our special thanks go to several members of the Random House staff: Deborah Drier, who supervised the entire art program and carried the book through production; Kathy Grasso, who coordinated and supervised all stages of production; Brenda Kamen, designer; Dorchen Leidholdt, Leslie Strand, and John Sturman, who provided valuable editorial assistance; and above all, Helen Greer, who advised us in the difficult selection of what materials to add and what to retain, and who edited the chapters into their final form.

All these people helped us to achieve the goals we set. If we fell short, the responsibility, of course, is ours.

DL, Jr.
SK
Princeton, N.J.

CONTENTS

LIST OF BOXES   xvii

Part 1   THE SOCIOLOGICAL PERSPECTIVE   2

Chapter 1   The Sociological Eye   4

USING THE SOCIOLOGICAL PERSPECTIVE   6
     Social Facts   7
THE DEVELOPMENT OF SOCIOLOGY   11
THEORETICAL ORIENTATIONS   12
     Structural-Functionalism   13
     Conflict Orientation   14
     Symbolic Interaction   15
THE USES OF SOCIOLOGY   15
     Sociology and Other Disciplines   15
     Sociology and Public Policy   17
     summary   18
     glossary   19
     references   20
     for further study   21

Chapter 2   Science and Methods in Sociology   22

THE NATURE OF SCIENCE   24
     The Scientific Method: Émile Durkheim's Study of Suicide   24
SCIENCE AND SOCIOLOGY   28
THE METHODS OF SOCIOLOGY   30
     Survey Research   30
     Experiments   33
     Participant Observation   35
     Interviewing   36
     Interpreting Data   38
VALUES, ETHICS, AND USES OF SOCIOLOGY   42
     The Myth of Value-free Sociology   42
     Professional Ethics   43
     summary   45
     glossary   46
     references   47
     for further study   48

Chapter 3 Social Structure   **50**

LEVELS OF SOCIAL STRUCTURE   52

     The Micro-level   52

     The Macro-level   54

COMPONENTS OF SOCIAL STRUCTURE   55

     Status   55

     Roles   56

     Groups   60

     Institutions   61

THE PATTERNS OF SOCIAL RELATIONSHIPS   62

     Exchange   62

     Cooperation   63

     Conflict   65

     Competition   67

THE IMPACT OF SOCIAL STRUCTURE: PRISONERS OF SOCIETY?   68

     Society in People: The Structuralist Position   68

     Innovation and Improvisation: The Symbolic Interactionist Position   69

     summary   73

     glossary   75

     references   76

     for further study   76

Part 2   BECOMING A SOCIAL BEING   78

Chapter 4 Culture   **80**

THE EVOLUTION OF CULTURE   82

THE ELEMENTS OF CULTURE   82

     Norms   83

     Values   86

     Symbols   89

     Language   90

UNITY IN DIVERSITY   92

     Cultural Universals   93

     Adaptation, Relativity, and Ethnocentrism   93

     Cultural Integration   95

AMERICAN CULTURE   95

     Basic American Values   96

     Subcultures   98

CULTURE AGAINST PEOPLE 101
    summary 103
    glossary 105
    references 105
    for further study 106

Chapter 5 Socialization **108**
  BIOLOGY, CULTURE, AND SOCIALIZATION 110
    Biological and Cultural Interaction 110
  SOCIALIZATION AND IDENTITY 112
    Charles Horton Cooley: The Looking-glass Self 112
    George Herbert Mead: Taking the Role of the Other .. 113
    Sigmund Freud: The Psychoanalytic View 115
    Erik H. Erikson: The Eight Ages of Man 117
    Jean Piaget: Cognitive Development 119
    Lawrence Kohlberg: Moral Development 122
  AGENTS OF SOCIALIZATION 123
    The Family 123
    The Media 125
    Peer Groups 128
  ADULT SOCIALIZATION 131
    Marriage and Parenthood 133
    Occupational Socialization 134
    Growing Old 135
    summary 137
    glossary 138
    references 139
    for further study 140

Chapter 6 Sex Roles **142**
  HOW DIFFERENT ARE THE SEXES? 144
    The Biological Evidence 144
    Gender Identity and Socialization 145
  THE SOCIOLOGY OF GENDER: SEX ROLES AND SOCIETY . 148
    Cross-cultural Variation 148
    Subcultural Variation 150
  SEX ROLES IN AMERICA 151
    The American Woman 154
    The American Man 162
  THE FUTURE OF AMERICAN SEX ROLES 165
    summary 169
    glossary 170
    references 171
    for further study 173

Part 3   ORGANIZING SOCIAL LIFE   174

Chapter 7   Social Groups   176
WHAT ARE SOCIAL GROUPS?   178
GROUP STRUCTURE   179
   Boundaries   179
   Group Size: Dyads and Triads   183
GROUP DYNAMICS   185
   How Groups Work   186
   Group Leadership   188
   Group Decision-making   189
PRIMARY AND SECONDARY GROUPS   191
   Primary Groups   191
   Secondary Groups   192
   From *Gemeinschaft* to *Gesellschaft*   193
THE SEARCH FOR INTIMACY AND COMMUNITY   196
   The ''Singles Industry''   196
   Religious Movements   198
   summary   198
   glossary   199
   references   200
   for further study   201

Chapter 8   Organizations and Bureaucracy   202
FORMAL ORGANIZATIONS   204
THE RISE OF MODERN BUREAUCRACIES   205
   Weber's Model   206
   The Reality of Bureaucracies   208
   Formal Versus Informal Structure   211
ORGANIZATIONS: PEOPLE SOLVING PROBLEMS   214
   The Process of Organizing   214
   Adaptation to the External Environment   215
   Shaping the Internal Environment: Recruitment and
      Socialization   216
   Total Institutions   219
THE FUTURE: WILL ORGANIZATIONS RUN OUR LIVES?   221
   Warnings   221
   Countertrends   222
   From X to Y: Humanizing Organizations   223
   Conclusion   224
   summary   225
   glossary   227
   references   228
   for further study   228

Chapter 9   Deviance and Social Control   **230**
  THE NATURE AND FUNCTIONS OF DEVIANCE   232
    What Is Deviance?   232
    The Social Functions of Deviance   235
  EXPLANATIONS OF DEVIANCE   236
    Biological Explanations   237
    Psychological Explanations   238
    Sociological Explanations   239
  LABELING AND DEVIANT CAREERS   243
    The Labeling Process   243
    Who Gets Labeled?   244
    Consequences of Labeling: Stigma and the Deviant Career   245
    Limitations of Labeling Theory   245
  SOCIAL CONTROL   247
    Informal Social Controls   247
    Formal Social Controls   249
    Prisons   253
    summary   257
    glossary   258
    references   259
    for further study   260

Part 4   POWER, WEALTH, AND STATUS   262

Chapter 10   Social Stratification   **264**
  THE DIMENSIONS OF STRATIFICATION   266
    Income and Wealth   267
    Power   272
    Prestige   274
    Classes in America   277
  TWO THEORIES OF SOCIAL STRATIFICATION   279
    Functionalist Theory   279
    Conflict Theory   281
  LIFE CHANCES   284
    Nutrition and Health   284
    Housing   284
    Criminal Justice   285
  THE LAND OF OPPORTUNITY: AN EVALUATION   286
    Social Mobility   286
    Reducing Inequality   290
  THE PERSISTENCE OF INEQUALITY   292
    summary   295
    glossary   296
    references   297
    for further study   299

Chapter 11   Racial and Ethnic Minorities   **300**

ETHNIC DIVERSITY IN AMERICA   302
  Black Americans   302
  Jews   305
  Mexican-Americans   306
  Puerto Ricans   307
  American Indians   307
  Chinese- and Japanese-Americans   309
  White Ethnics   309
RACE, PREJUDICE, AND DISCRIMINATION   311
  What Is Race?   311
  Racial Myths   312
  Prejudice and Discrimination   313
PATTERNS OF ETHNIC RELATIONS   315
  Patterns of Acceptance   315
  Patterns of Rejection   318
  Minority Responses   319
PROTEST AND PROGRESS   321
  Where Do We Stand?   322
OBSTACLES TO FULL EQUALITY: INSTITUTIONAL RACISM   325
  Zoning   325
  Affirmative Action   325
  Busing   327
  Prospects   328
  summary   328
  glossary   330
  references   331
  for further study   332

Chapter 12   Power, Politics, and Economics   **334**

WHAT IS POWER?   336
THEORIES OF POWER   338
  Marx: An Economic Theory of Power   338
  Pareto and Mosca: The Elitist View   338
  C. Wright Mills: The Power Elite   339
  The Pluralist View   340
POWER IN THE ECONOMIC SYSTEM   341
  The Organization of the American Economic System   342
  Who Controls the American Economy?   347
POWER IN THE POLITICAL SYSTEM   350
  Power and the State   350
  Political Power in America   352
  summary   361
  glossary   362

references 363
for further study 364

Part 5   SOCIAL INSTITUTIONS   366

Chapter 13   The Family   368
DEFINING THE FAMILY 370
    The Family as a Biological and Social Unit 370
CROSS-CULTURAL PERSPECTIVES 372
    The Nayar, the Dani, and the Israeli Kibbutzim 372
    Origins of Different Family Forms 374
    The Nuclear Family as an Ideal 376
THE AMERICAN FAMILY 378
    Family Types 378
    Social Class Differences 381
    Love and Marriage 384
    Divorce 385
THE CHANGING AMERICAN FAMILY 388
    Child-rearing 388
    Women in the Work Force 388
    Alternative Forms of Marriage 390
    summary 395
    glossary 396
    references 397
    for further study 398

Chapter 14   Education   400
THE SOCIAL FUNCTIONS OF EDUCATION 402
    Schools as Agents of Political and Social Integration 402
    The Hidden Curriculum 403
    Schools and Learning 406
    Selecting Talent: The Screening Function 408
THE SOCIAL STRUCTURE OF HIGHER EDUCATION 412
    The College Experience 412
    Junior and Community Colleges 417
THE FUTURE OF EDUCATION 418
    Infant Education 418
    Lifelong Learning 419
    summary 420
    glossary 421
    references 422
    for further study 423

Chapter 15   Religion   **424**
     THE BASIC ELEMENTS OF RELIGION   426
          Émile Durkheim: The Sacred and the Profane   426
          Beliefs   428
          Rituals   428
          The Community of Worship   430
     THE FUNCTIONS OF RELIGION   431
          Social Functions   431
          Individual Functions   433
     RELIGION AND SOCIAL CHANGE   435
          Repressing Change: Marx   435
          Inspiring Change: Weber   436
     FORMS OF RELIGIOUS EXPRESSION   438
          Church and Sect   439
          Invisible or Private Religion   440
          Civil Religion   440
     TRENDS IN RELIGION   442
          Secularization   442
          Trends in the Major Faiths   443
          The Fundamentalist Revival   446
          The Rise of Mysticism   448
          summary   450
          glossary   451
          references   452
          for further study   453

Part 6   CHANGING SOCIETY   454

Chapter 16   Population and Health   **456**
     STUDYING POPULATION   458
          Counting Population   458
          Population Growth   458
     THE POPULATION EXPLOSION   466
          The Demographic Transition   466
          The Burdens of High Birth Rates   469
          Bringing the Birth Rate Down   473
     POPULATION GROWTH IN AMERICA   474
          Contraception   474
          Abortion   475
          The Birth Dearth: Will It Last?   476
     HEALTH IN AMERICA   477
          The Diseases of Affluence   477
          Health of the Disadvantaged   478

Health Care in America   478
Future Trends   482
summary   482
glossary   483
references   484
for further study   486

Chapter 17   Urban Life and the Environment   488
THE URBAN TRANSFORMATION   490
The Birth of the City   490
World Urbanization   491
MODERN URBAN LIFE   493
Is the City Alienating?   494
Life in the Suburbs   495
Urban Ecology   497
Megalopolis   500
THE URBAN CRISIS   501
"Unslumming" the City   505
THE ENVIRONMENT   508
The Ecosystem: How Much Will It Sustain?   508
Environmental Problems in Sociological Perspective   512
summary   515
glossary   516
references   517
for further study   518

Chapter 18   Collective Behavior and Social Movements   520
COLLECTIVE BEHAVIOR: AN OVERVIEW   522
Preconditions of Collective Behavior   522
CROWD BEHAVIOR   524
Mobs   524
Explanations of Crowd Behavior   527
SOCIAL MOVEMENTS   529
Women's Liberation: A History and an Explanation   529
Professional Movements   533
COMMUNICATION AND COLLECTIVE BEHAVIOR   534
Rumors   534
Public Opinion   535
Manipulating Public Opinion   536
summary   538
glossary   540
references   541
for further study   542

Chapter 19 Social Change and Technology — **544**

APPROACHES TO SOCIAL CHANGE — 546
The Evolutionary Perspective — 546
The Cyclical Perspective — 547
The Equilibrium Perspective — 548
The Conflict Perspective — 549
SOURCES OF CHANGE — 550
Internal Sources of Change — 551
External Sources of Change — 554
MODERNIZATION — 555
Strains and Adjustments — 558
TECHNOLOGY AND WORK — 560
Technology and the Occupational Structure — 560
Industrialization and Alienation — 562
Are Workers Alienated Today? — 562
What Makes Work Satisfying? — 562
CHANGING WORLD DIRECTIONS — 565
summary — 568
glossary — 569
references — 569
for further study — 571

Chapter 20 Epilogue — **572**

"FINDING THE HANDLE" — 575
Organizations — 575
Deviance — 575
Groups — 575
Social Stratification — 576
PREPARING FOR CHANGE — 576
The Family — 578
Sex Roles — 579
Education — 579
Religion — 580
Population — 580
references — 581

Appendix — **582**

CAREERS IN SOCIOLOGY — 582
Advanced Degrees in Sociology — 583
Sociology and Your College Career — 584

Glossary — i

Name Index — iv

Subject Index — x

Acknowledgments — xviii

BOXES

Chapter **1** Welfare: Myths and Realities 16

2 Research into Institutional Racism 26
An Attitude Scale 31
Classifying Data: Mode, Mean, and Median 38
How to Read a Table 39

3 IN THE NEWS Social Roles and Growing Old 58
Face-saving at the Singles Dance 70

4 IN THE NEWS Nine-to-What? Japanese Business Comes to
America 84
The Russians: One Man's View 88
Jargon and Subculture 99

5 IN THE NEWS Most Children Are Happy at Home but Fear
World 126
Shaping Adolescent Life Styles: The Effects of
Socialization 130

6 Common Sense and Sociology: Work and the Working-class
Wife 152
IN THE NEWS The New Masculine Ideal 166

7 Tokenism 180
IN THE NEWS Lifelines to Others 197

8 Sociology and Common Sense: The Unfeeling
Bureaucrat 210
IN THE NEWS Tailoring Schedules to Suit Workers 217

9 Corporate Crime and Irresponsibility 250
IN THE NEWS Prison Prevention 254

10 Blue-collar Aristocrats 287
IN THE NEWS Growth and Greater Equality Meet in
Taiwan 293

11 Roots: The Importance of Origins 304
IN THE NEWS Becoming American 316

12 Michels's "Iron Rule of Oligarchy" 339
Poor People's Movements 358

13 Raising Children in a Changing Society 380
Puzzle: Measuring Divorce 387
IN THE NEWS Living Alone—and Liking It 392

14 IN THE NEWS Racism Persists on Campus 414

15   From Ritual to Popular Expression: Modern and Religious
      Change in India   436
      IN THE NEWS Converting to Health   447

16   The Census: A Continuous Count   459
      IN THE NEWS Blacks Move South Again   464

17   IN THE NEWS Families May Leave, but the City Still
      Thrives   502
      The Plight of the Cities: Who Is Responsible?   506

18   Keeping the Faith or Pursuing the Good Life   530

19   IN THE NEWS Amish Farmers Resist Modernization   559
      The Artist's Shifting Image   561

SOCIOLOGY

The Sociological Perspective

Sociology is not simply a collection of facts, figures, and theories. It is a special way of looking at the social world in which we live.

Chapter 1 introduces this perspective through presentation of the social "facts of life." Many of our most private experiences are shaped by social forces that are beyond the individual's control. From the beginning sociologists have sought to explain these forces, to understand the patterns that transcend particular historical moments, societies, and people. Sociologists have approached this task from different angles, from different theoretical perspectives, each of which contributes part of the answer. Taken as a whole, the sociological perspective has changed the way other social scientists, government policy makers, and the public at large view trends and events. And this may be the primary use of sociology.

Chapter 2 shows just how sociologists go about their work. The application of the scientific method to the investigation of social patterns requires special techniques, including surveys, laboratory experiments, and field work. The data sociologists collect do not speak for themselves; they must be interpreted. A science of human behavior is bound to be controversial, and sociology is no exception.

Chapter 3 begins on a street corner in Washington, D.C., to show how rules of social interaction pattern everyday behavior. The chapter then moves to an analysis of larger social forces—the institutions that in a society serve as a master plan for social action. Here you will see the sociological perspective in action.

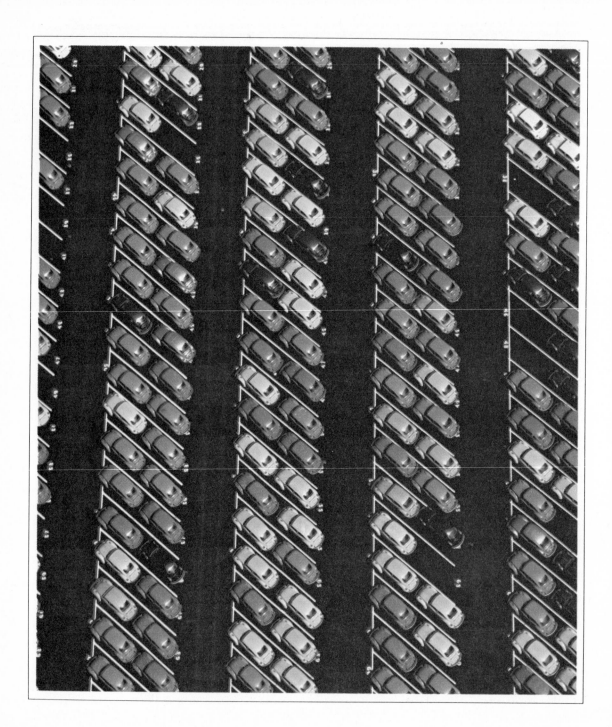

CHAPTER 1

The Sociological Eye

A black student is bused to a school in a white neighborhood clear across town and finds himself the subject of unwanted controversy. An urban middle-class couple with a five-figure income is shocked to discover they can't afford to buy a house within commuting distance of the city. A bank employee who embezzled thousands of dollars by programming a computer to divert pennies to his account is caught but given only a suspended sentence. Liberal, free-thinking parents are bewildered when their son joins a fundamentalist religious sect. "Why?" they ask themselves.

We tend to think that what happens to us is the result of something we did or something "they" did to us, ignoring the social forces that shape us. In different ways, all of these individuals are caught up in sociological events that are beyond their direct control. But these forces are not beyond understanding. It takes what C. Wright Mills called "sociological imagination" to perceive the larger forces that shape our lives—and to stop blaming ourselves or others for our frustrations.

The sociological eye looks beyond individual psychology and unique events to the predictable patterns and regular occurrences of social life. A sociologist would be more interested in the effects of marijuana on teen-age dating behavior than in the habits of one individual who smokes. A sociologist would be more interested in how best-selling novels come to be published, how they are circulated, and which groups read them and why than in what merits or flaws a particular novel has. A sociologist would be more interested in the similarities and differences among families that produce a schizophrenic child than in the case history of a particular child.

There is nothing mysterious or cold-blooded about the sociological perspective. It is one way of examining our social lives in order to make sense and meaning out of the forces that shape our individual destinies. It complements the perspectives and angles of vision we already have at our command. In this first chapter, we will discuss how the sociological perspective is used and the meaning of social facts. We will also consider the main theoretical orientations in sociology, the origins of sociology, its relations to other disciplines, and its uses in contemporary society.

USING THE SOCIOLOGICAL PERSPECTIVE

Before starting a new course, students may know who is teaching it and what other students have said about the instructor and the subject. During the first class they will be interested in learning who else is in the class, what the professor looks and sounds like, what is on the reading list, how many papers are required, and whether and when exams are given. Throughout the course, students will assess the lecturer's knowledge, personality, and skill as an instructor. In short, a student's evaluation of a class is based on a *personal* reaction to a particular professor and subject.

A sociologist looking at this classroom would study social relationships rather than individual behavior. (Owen Franken/Stock, Boston)

A sociologist looking at the same college classroom would analyze it somewhat differently, focusing on social relationships rather than on individual behavior or on the specific course content. Some of the things a sociologist might focus on would be power relations, rules of conduct, and class characteristics.

There is an unequal distribution of power in the classroom: the teacher has control over the topics of conversation and directs the flow of class discussion by determining who will talk when. The teacher also has the ultimate power to determine grades. There are many social supports for this unequal distribution of power. The instructor gets paid for being in the classroom, while the students must pay. The teacher stands at the front of the group and can fully observe all of the students, while the students' desks are lined up in rows and each student can thus make direct contact with only a few other students. The instructor has access to each student's work and thereby has the full

power of comparison and judgment, while each student sees only his or her own work.

Teachers have a variety of institutional supports at their command: they can delay returning reserve books to the library without paying a fine; they can examine each student's academic record; and they can have any student physically expelled from the classroom. All of these factors contribute to a teacher's power. On the other hand, the teacher's power is not absolute. If the students refuse to come to class, refuse to pay attention in class, refuse to do the work, or complain to the administration about the quality of teaching, the teacher's power will be curtailed. These power relations in the classroom operate without regard to any particular student or any particular teacher. The classroom has a sociological power structure all its own, which can be analyzed in its own right without consideration for individual habits, histories, personality traits, or desires.

The sociologist will also analyze the rules of conduct in a classroom. These are the unspoken rules everyone more or less follows, the expectations everyone pretty much fulfills. For example, people rarely rip off their clothes during class time; everyone shows up pretty much on time; the teacher talks about material relevant to the course and not about his or her hobbies or sports interests; people don't speak all at once, but take turns speaking; everyone (except perhaps the teacher) sits during the class time; the class period has a designated beginning and ending that are observed. Again, these rules belong to the accepted order of things in the classroom and can be discussed without any reference whatsoever to particular students or particular teachers.

As a unit the class has characteristics of its own that are not properties of any individual in the class. For example, the class meets in a certain room, is of a certain size, has a specific average age of students and a specific number of men and women, and so on. Each of these characteristics belongs to the *class* as a whole; they are not the characteristics of each individual in that class.

All of these observations about the college classroom are sociological observations. They concern patterns and regularities that will occur regardless of the individuals who occupy that classroom. The sociological perspective clearly differs from other perspectives one might use for observing a classroom. An architect, for example, might pay attention to the size of the space, the comfort of the furniture, the arrangement of the desks in relation to the space, the quality of the acoustics. A doctor might consider the physical condition of the class members, including skin tone, eye brightness, or manifestations of fever or disability. And a painter or photographer might notice the quality of the light in the room, the variety of poses assumed by class members, the anatomical differences between various students, and the colors of their clothing.

Whenever we attempt to make sense of the world around us, we must make choices about which details we will attend to in constructing our meanings. The *sociological perspective* trains us to pay attention to regular and patterned details, those details that are not unique to a particular situation or to particular people in those situations.

Social Facts

Those of us brought up to believe in our individual worth and uniqueness sometimes find it difficult, if not infuriating, to hear ourselves talked about as if our individual histories, biographies, and feelings were of no consequence. Since all of us feel ourselves to be unique and special, we may resent being chucked into categories for the convenience of a sociologist. But we all use categories and abstractions much of the time. How often have you used or heard the terms "the older generation," "hippies," "dope addicts," "feminists," "blacks," "jocks," "Wasps"? These are all categories of people who have something in common, but who as individuals have a great deal that is unique. And yet these terms are useful for explaining and giving meaning to the things in the world we try to understand.

Despite our resistances to categorization, there are certain things about human social life that simply can't be explained by reference to individual feelings or behavior. Émile Durkheim (1858–1917), a pioneering French sociologist of the nineteenth century, pinned down this truth when he posited the existence of something called a *social fact*, which is an entity in its own right, different from the elements (or individuals) of which it is composed. Durkheim compared the uniqueness of the social fact to the uniqueness of the human body: although the human body is made up of cells, a person who examined the human body cell by cell would never discover the properties or capacities of the human body. In short, the whole is greater than the sum of its parts. "It is very certain that there are in the living cell only molecules of crude matter. But these molecules are in contact with one another, and this association is the cause of the new phenomena which characterize life, the very germ of which cannot possibly be found in any of the separate elements" (Durkheim, 1938).

The same part-whole relationship is true for individuals and social facts. There are properties of social life that simply cannot be explained by reference to the activities, sensibilities, or characteristics of any individual. We need only look at our own lives to realize how inescapable this conclusion is. For example, consider a few social facts that make

modern urban life less than pleasant—crime rates and bureaucratic red tape.

Crime Rates   When we walk down a big city street late at night most of us are, to say the least, wary. Is this wariness purely a psychological trait of ours? Can we explain it by exploring our childhood experiences? No, our uneasiness stems from the social fact of crime rates. If we compare the rates of crime in different localities at different hours of the day, we find that crime rates are highest in urban areas at night. Our private fears as we hurry down the street are thus attributable not to psychological quirks but to social facts. Even the crime rates themselves, although composed of the sum of individual acts, are social realities that surpass the activities of any one criminal. Thus, our fear as we walk down a deserted city street after dark is not prompted by our knowledge of individual criminals nor by our own psychological obsessions but rather by our knowledge of a social fact—a crime rate—that surpasses both us as individuals and criminals as individuals.

Red Tape   When we find ourselves entangled with large bureaucratic organizations, such as government agencies, and we experience the frustrations of "red-tape runaround," are those frustrations attributable to our own inabilities to get things done quickly? Are they the fault of the receptionists and secretaries who shuttle us around and have us fill out forms in triplicate? Of course the frustrations are no one's fault. Simply by virtue of their size large organizations require complicated record-keeping procedures, ordered hierarchies, and many separate departments. The unpleasantness of bureaucratic procedures can only be explained by a social fact—the size of the organization. Since the larger an organization is, the more division of labor there will be, the more clear cut the hierarchy will be, and the more divisions and departments there will be (Blau and Meyer, 1971), we can understand our personal experiences of frustration only in terms of an impersonal reality. The size of an organization is a property of that organization and not of any of the individuals involved in it, and we must therefore look to a social reality to explain a very individual experience. These two examples suggest that Durkheim was right: ''Society is not a mere sum of individuals. Rather, the system formed by their association represents a specific reality which has its own characteristics'' (Durkheim, 1938).

But the existence of social facts that have characteristics and properties of their own is not the only reason for adopting the sociological perspective. There is another even more compelling reason. Every experience that a human being has, no matter how private it may seem, is somehow touched and shaped by social forces that are not of that person's making. While this statement may seem overly dramatic, by examining a few of our most private experiences we can see just how important social conditions are in determining the course of our inner lives.

Being Sick   Surely, it would seem, being sick is an entirely private experience. When we are lying in bed with fever, aches, and pains, absorbed in our own personal miseries, how can there be any social forces at work on us? There can be, and there are. How do we know that what we are feeling is sickness? In some societies fever, aches, and pain are symptoms of spirit visitations. The individual plagued with these discomforts is not treated as a sick person but as a person possessed. In our society, however, we treat these symptoms as manifestations of treatable diseases. When we experience these symptoms, we have learned from our culture to call ourselves sick. A pulled muscle, a broken

finger, or a poison-ivy rash may make us just as uncomfortable as symptoms of a cold or flu virus, but we do not call them sicknesses. Thus, how we know when we are sick is something we have learned from our social world; it is not a property of the physical discomfort itself.

The society we live in also has a widely understood set of rules about how we behave when we are sick. For certain illnesses we are entitled to stay in bed, free from all obligations that might sap our strength. For others, we are expected to continue our daily round of activities. Thus, if your sociology lecturer didn't show up for a scheduled class one day, sending word that he or she was absent because of a stubbed toe or an infected hangnail, class members would be rightfully indignant at the lecturer's irresponsibility (''rightfully'' because we have all learned that these are not debilitating illnesses). On the other hand, if the lecturer showed up for class despite a raging fever, he or she would have been responsible beyond the call of duty—that is, beyond the expectations of our society about sickness behavior (Jaco, 1972).

Rules about behavior during illness govern not only how much activity the sick person is excused from, but also how the sick person is to conduct his or her recovery. In our society a sick person who isn't terminally ill has an obligation to behave in a way that will lead to full recovery. He or she is expected to follow the doctor's instructions concerning medication, rest, exercise, and interaction with others. An individual who does not follow these instructions, and thereby prolongs the illness, is termed a ''malingerer,'' an ''attention seeker,'' a ''self-destructive person,'' or a ''downright burden.'' When we are sick we assume a specific role, that of the ''sick person,'' and thereby incur a set of obligations and rights that have been carefully defined for us by our society's ''sickness rules.''

The sickness rules also tell us who is qualified to heal us. In American society we are supposed to be healed by a qualified medical doctor. We don't go to medicine men, witch doctors, spiritual exorcists, or mediums for cures (as is done in other societies) but to a man or woman who's had a certain amount of certified education and training and who the society says is qualified to heal people.

Thus, being sick is far from a purely private experience. While, again, there is a great deal of room within the confines of the sick role for individual performances, the general outline of the role is *socially* and not individually defined.

Being sick may seem to be a private experience, independent of social forces. However, our society imposes certain expectations upon the sick person, such as seeking treatment from trained physicians. (Robert Foothorap/Jeroboam)

Suicide   One final example, involving the seemingly most private act of all, should convince us that no part of our inner lives is unaffected by social forces. Comparisons of suicide rates of different groups have shown that certain social factors influence an individual's chances for self-destruction (Durkheim, 1951). Details of Durkheim's study of suicide are described in chapter 2, so for the present we need only note that suicide rates are higher for single people than for married ones, higher during periods of economic inflation or depression than during times of economic stability, higher among urbanites than among rural dwellers. In fact, certain social conditions that have nothing to do with the individuals who are the subjects of their results operate to create "suicide currents" within a population, and these currents "are just as real and just as much external to the individual as are the physical and biological forces that produce death by disease" (Barnes, 1948:510). Thus, even the

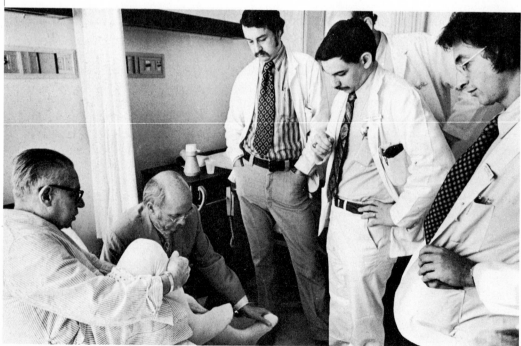

lonely moments of self-obliteration may be rooted in the larger context of the social order.

If, then, we recognize that individual experiences can only be understood with reference to larger social forces, how are we to go about understanding those forces? How, in short, are we to *do* sociology?

THE DEVELOPMENT OF SOCIOLOGY

The history of doing sociology in a systematic, recognizable manner is a very short one. Although attempts to develop patterned social codes to enhance the social order date back to 2000 B.C., it was not until the end of the eighteenth century that social philosophy (philosophical *ideas* about how the world does or might run) gave way to social science (systematic *studies* of how the world does in fact run). The roots of the scientific approach to the study of society were established early in the seventeenth century with the arrival of the Age of Reason, when men like Francis Bacon and René Descartes argued that observation, experimentation, and reason must replace philosophy, religion, and moral musings. But it was not until the French philosopher Henri de Saint-Simon (1760–1825) imagined a "political science" that the discipline as we now know it achieved a recognizable form (Saint-Simon, 1964). When Saint-Simon's celebrated student and colleague Auguste Comte (1798–1857) changed the name of this new discipline to *sociology*, the sociological enterprise was officially under way.

Comte theorized that human intellectual development was an evolutionary process based on scientific progress. He believed that *positivism*—the use of experimentation and observation—was crucial for encouraging and maintaining the natural process of progress. If human beings were to create a more satisfying social world, they would have to advance the natural process of progress toward that goal through the exercise of scientific discipline (Comte, 1915).

Once sociology had been officially baptized by Saint-Simon and Comte, the science of society became a tool for those who were trying to deal with the vast social problems that were arising everywhere in Europe as a result of the changes brought by the Industrial Revolution. Social thinkers all over Europe began turning to sociology or to the sociological perspective for solutions to the misery and confusion left in the wake of urbanization, industrialization, and bureaucratization. But the solutions these thinkers arrived at were not always the same or even compatible.

Herbert Spencer (1820–1903), for instance, an Englishman who wrote during the late nineteenth century and who during that period was extremely influential in both Europe and America, believed that society developed through natural processes. It was he (and not Charles Darwin) who coined the phrase "survival of the fittest." By this he meant that through natural selection societies would work out the optimum social arrangements. Spencer believed, for example, that national governments should not make legislation concerning social progress because such legislation would interfere with the natural order of societal development. Thus, such public policies as public education, public health care, and work laws should not be legislated, because those who were fittest would be able to fend for themselves. Furthermore, to interfere with the success of the fittest would be to interfere with the progress of natural societal growth. For Spencer, what *was* in the world was synonymous with what *ought* to be there (Spencer, 1898).

This view was vehemently opposed by Karl Marx (1818–1883), who believed that revolution and not evolution was the key to Europe's ills. Marx felt that differentiation in society comes about not through natural selection of the fittest but through the consolidation of groups of people who have similar economic interests and experiences. The structure of society, for Marx, was based on economic foundations: people's relationship to the means of production determines their position in the society, and this position heavily influences values, attitudes, and behavior. Since the different groups, or classes, had different economic interests, they would inevitably be antagonists. For Marx, the only means by which the economically oppressed classes could convince the economically advantaged classes to relinquish some of their supremacy was through revolution. After the revolution, it would be possible to create a classless society in which everyone labored according to ability and everyone received according to need. Thus, Marx believed that social change would come about by planned social action (Marx, 1955, 1967), while Spencer suggested that if you leave the world alone it will eventually cure its own ills.

Although both these theorists believed they were describing the world as it really was, neither of them drew upon strictly scientific methods to document their observations convincingly. What was needed now were innovative research techniques that would be suitable for the scientific study of society. The first major step toward the development of these techniques was taken by Émile Durkheim. He collected statistics from several European countries on the incidence and preconditions of suicide and organized these statistics in such a way that they empirically documented his theories about social organization.

Durkheim's empirical approach, the giant step between social philosophy and social science, has been adopted with particular enthusiasm by American sociologists. As in Europe, American sociology first focused on the formidable social problems of the day, including crime and poverty, social disorder and deviance. But early in the development of American sociology, sociologists began to adopt the scientific perspective, placing heavy emphasis on observation and scientific measurement. However, the scientific approach has always been tempered by the realization, first fully elaborated by Max Weber (1864–1920), that human beings are not inanimate objects that can be manipulated and studied like rocks, minerals, or cells. Human beings have feelings, thoughts, consciousness, attitudes, and values that are best reckoned with and accounted for by empathy, or *Verstehen*, as Weber called it (1964). The scientific study of human beings must include elements of insight and empathy if it is to stay true to the actual conditions of human life.

Today sociology reflects the change from social philosophy to social science (tempered with insight and empathy), and ''schools'' of sociology have come to emphasize one or the other of the approaches put forth by the founders of the field.

THEORETICAL ORIENTATIONS

The first and most crucial step in the exploration of any unknown phenomenon is the formulation of questions about that phenomenon. The questions we ask strongly influence the explanations we arrive at. So it is when sociologists try to explain human social behavior. Depending on how they formulate their questions, they often come up with different explanations for the same phenomena. The different types of questions that a sociologist is likely to ask reflect his or her theoretical orientation. An old joke about a pessimist and an optimist perfectly illustrates this. Pointing to a glass containing some water, the pessimist will say, "That glass is half empty." The optimist will respond, "No, it's not; it's half full." Although both pessimist and optimist have observed the same phenomenon, their explanations of what they saw differ because they have different orientations. In sociology, as in all scientific disciplines, there are several different theoretical orientations, each of which has its ardent admirers and detractors. In America the most prevalent is *structural-functionalism*.

Structural-Functionalism

Sociologists with a structural-functional approach study the way each part of a society contributes to the functioning of the society as a whole. Social balance is emphasized. Since sociologists with the structural-functional orientation view society as a system of interrelated parts, they are mainly interested in the contributions these parts make to, or the purposes they serve in, the maintenance of ongoing social life. For example, in trying to explain why all human societies have a family system, the structural-functionalists will ask: What function (need) does the family system fulfill for the larger society? The answers to this question will all highlight the contributions that family systems make to the ongoing life of societies. For example, families ensure that someone will be responsible for the care of dependent infants. Or take the case of political machines, which continue to flourish in American cities despite periodic condemnations of them by important members of American society (Merton, 1968). Structural-functionalists would say that these machines serve positive (though unrecognized) functions for some

members of society. For example, they provide a political voice for new immigrants and minority groups.

By looking at the social world through a structural-functionalist perspective, sociologists often develop convincing explanations for the existence of social phenomena that would otherwise be puzzling or incomprehensible. For example, one of the most influential functionalists, Kingsley Davis, once asked these questions: "What is there about the nature of human society that causes it to give rise to, and maintain [prostitution] while at the same time it condemns the practice? What functions does prostitution serve that are not served by other institutions in the society?" (Davis, 1937). As a result of this line of questioning, Davis came up with some innovative and convincing answers. For example:

1. Prostitution provides a sexual outlet for those who cannot at the moment find permanent or stable partners (for example, traveling salesmen, sailors, businessmen at conventions).

2. Prostitution provides a sexual outlet for those who do not have the energy or will to pursue more elaborate forms of courtship.

3. Prostitution provides a source of sexual satisfaction during times when more stable relationships are temporarily out of kilter (for example, during separation, divorce, or widowhood).

4. Prostitution provides an outlet for sexual perversions that can't be expressed in long-term enduring relationships, thus helping to preserve those relationships.

5. Prostitution provides partners for those men who for whatever reason are unable to compete in the ordinary sexual marketplace (for example, the disfigured, handicapped, or impotent).

While Davis's analysis makes sense, it provides only a limited explanation for the existence of prostitution, and this limitation is imposed by the very questions he asks in the beginning: ''What functions does prostitution serve that are not served by other institutions in the society?'' (Note that Davis is viewing society from the male perspective alone.) One could ask other questions about prostitution, but these would probably come out of a different theoretical orientation.

Conflict Orientation

A second orientation—and one that stands in opposition to the functional approach—focuses on social conflict and opposition rather than on social balance. This approach has several contemporary proponents, whose objections to the functionalists are echoed in the following statement: ''[In functionalism] there is much concern with social order and norms, little with social discord and power, opposition and oppression. The functional orientation introduces a conservative bias into sociological analysis . . . in the specific sense that it directs attention to system maintenance and stability and diverts attention from conflict and change'' (Blau, 1972).

A sociologist with the *conflict orientation* would ask questions about who benefits and who is systematically deprived by certain social patterns. They would ask about the overall conditions of society that would even allow certain phenomena to be functional at all. For example, a sociologist with a conflict orientation would ask the following questions about prostitution:

1. If prostitution has arisen and flourished to accommodate the restless male, why hasn't it also arisen to accommodate the restless female?
2. What are the costs of prostitution to society? These include the costs of creating an outcast group, the prostitutes themselves, and the

costs for men, in hypocrisy, deception, and *self*-deception.
3. What are the contradictions in the laws of society that create legal institutions (monogamous marriage) and at the same time allow for the violation of these institutions?
4. How can changes in the practice of prostitution be brought about?

These questions will clearly give rise to different answers about the nature of prostitution—its causes and consequences—than resulted from the functionalist approach. While neither approach is right or wrong, each provides a distinctive explanation for

Encounter between a man and two prostitutes. The structural-functionalist would analyze the underlying causes of this encounter; the conflict-oriented sociologist would examine who benefits and who suffers in the transaction; and the symbolic interactionist would study the specific behaviors involved. (Hap Stewart/Jeroboam)

the same social phenomenon, and sociologists of one orientation must be aware of the questions that someone with a different perspective might ask.

Symbolic Interaction

A third and increasingly popular orientation to studying social phenomena is the *symbolic interactionist* approach. Sociologists with this perspective focus their attention not on large social structures and institutions but on the day-to-day communication that occurs when people interact in face-to-face situations. The emphasis is on the meaning of social life as it is interpreted by individuals going about their daily business. Regarding prostitution, an interactionist would be less interested in why it exists or why it generally is practiced by women than in *how* people actually go about contracting for sexual services. The interactionist would ask such questions as:

1. What kinds of interactions take place between purchaser and purchased?
2. How are the signals arranged between a prostitute and her "john" so that each knows the other as a potential temporary partner?
3. What do the prostitute and her customer make of their interaction; what meaning does it have for each?
4. How are the rules of the interaction established, and what are the understood codes of behavior?

The answers to these questions would tell us more about the process of prostitution and its meaning for the participants than about its consequences for the larger social system.

Using any one of these perspectives we would come to understand something about the ubiquitous social phenomenon prostitution, but we would learn different things as a result of orientation. In studying or doing sociology we must always remain aware of the underlying orientation so that we will be alert to the questions that have not been asked and to the biases underlying those that have been.

THE USES OF SOCIOLOGY

Whatever a sociologist's orientation, his or her task will always be the same: to understand and interpret events and patterns that transcend particular individuals, cultures, and historical moments. Unlike the psychologist, who is concerned with specific individuals in specific situations, the sociologist tries to uncover basic truths about human social behavior in general. "Know thyself" becomes, for the sociologist, "Know thy social being." But what good does it do to know the social being? Have sociologists simply devised a new vocabulary for personal introspection? Not really.

Sociology and Other Disciplines

Sociological concepts and findings have been used for many purposes beyond self-revelation. For example, under the influence of sociology, history has become less elitist. Historians used to focus on the lives of great men (and sometimes women), in the belief that individuals make history. However, sociological research prompted historians to look at ordinary people, family life, work arrangements, and the patterns of daily life in times gone by. Historians now seek to find out what social forces shaped specific eras and how men and women in these periods coped with these forces. Quantitative methods borrowed from sociology have helped to provide answers (Liebenstein, 1976).

WELFARE: MYTHS AND REALITIES

TRUE or FALSE: Most people on welfare are loafers who could support themselves if they had to.
TRUE or FALSE: Once people become poor, they remain poor.
TRUE or FALSE: Poor black people leave the South for places like New York and Detroit because the welfare payments are larger there.

Each of these statements is false, yet millions of Americans persist in believing they are true. Sociologists can't force people to change their minds about welfare and poor people, but they can present hard evidence proving that many stubbornly held "truths" are in fact myths.

Researchers at the Rand Corporation found, for example, that "of the 11.2 million people who receive basic welfare payments under the program of Aid to Families with Dependent Children, fewer than 150,000 are men. Eight million are children of school age or younger, and the others are their mothers." Those without small children are "substantially underschooled, undertrained and underskilled." Welfare recipients are therefore not people who could support themselves if they wanted to.

Data also disprove the notion of a long-enduring group of poor people. In fact, the poor population changes every year: about 10 million people move above the poverty line, and another 10 million move below it.

Finally, researchers have found that Southern blacks are lured North not by the promise of fatter welfare checks but by the hope of finding work. A demographer at the United States Census Bureau analyzed six Northern cities with large black populations and found that "Southern blacks who had migrated there were less likely to be on welfare than were blacks who had been born in the cities."

SOURCE: David E. Rosenbaum, *The New York Times*, May 22, 1977, Section 4, p. 3.

Political scientists, too, have incorporated the sociological perspective. They have begun to focus on such sociological issues as: How do different people acquire political views? What is the relationship between the political attitudes of parents and those of their children? How does the process of formal education contribute to political opinions? These are sociological questions that until the last few decades have been overlooked by most political scientists.

Economics, the most prestigious of the social sciences, used to be based on rather simple models of human behavior that made sense on paper and generated elegant theories but led to predictions that rarely came true. The new economics incorporates data and theories on the social dimensions of the marketplace.

Sociology has also been useful in exploding unexamined popular myths (see the box on welfare, p. 16). For example, the work of sociologists has led to the realization that most of the people who are incarcerated in state mental hospitals are not psychotic or dangerous (Scheff, 1966). Due in part to this work the laws permitting involuntary commitment to mental hospitals have been made stricter, and civil rights are gradually being restored to mental patients. The mental hospital was also the site of the remarkable finding by sociologists that when mental patients become psychotic on the ward, sometimes they are responding not so much to inner erratic impulses as to tension generated by the staff when it is in conflict over patient care (Stanton and Schwartz, 1954).

Recently, in response to increasing interest in a negative income tax (which would provide extra income to those who earn less than a certain minimum), social scientists studied the ways in which poor people spend additional income. They demonstrated with hard evidence that poor people, like people everywhere, spend the money to free themselves from menial tasks and to provide their children with niceties (Mathematica, 1974). If and when Congress does consider some proposal for a negative income tax, sociologists will be ready with data on how such extra income would be spent, allaying the fears of cautious congresspersons that the poor will "squander" the extra funds.

Sociology and Public Policy

Not only has sociology been useful in enriching its fellow disciplines, but it has also had a unique impact on public programs and policy. As early as 1883, American sociologist Lester Ward set the tone by stating that sociology was not an ivory-tower discipline but a science to "benefit mankind." Sociologists and psychologists were cited in the famous Supreme Court decision on the case of *Brown* v. *Board of Education*, which made deliberate racial segregation in schools (once a matter of policy) illegal on the grounds that it did irreparable damage to both black and white children. Since then, many sociologists have contributed policy research to such projects as the presidential commissions on pornography, population growth, the prevention of violence, and law enforcement.

Of course, once politicians have solicited and been given recommendations, they are under no obligation to act on what they have learned. The Commission on Obscenity and Pornography found no proof that exposure to explicit sexual materials leads to crime and delinquency and recommended the repeal of laws prohibiting the distribution of pornography to adults. Congress declared the report "irresponsible"; President Nixon called it "morally bankrupt"; the Supreme Court turned decisions over to local communities. Similarly, no action was taken on the Commission of Population Growth and the American Future's recommendation that teenagers be given contraceptive information and materials (see Komarovsky, 1975).

On the other hand, sociologists' findings were used in the design of programs to solve such thorny problems as how to provide better health care for low-income families (Rainwater, 1968; Dreitzel, 1971) and how to demobilize soldiers without provoking anger and resentment in those left behind (Shils, 1961). Awareness that sociology is useful in informing people about the nature of social life, in providing data on important issues, and in analyzing the causes of social problems is growing at all levels of government.

One of the newest and perhaps most ambitious undertakings of sociologists concerned with applied rather than theoretical work has been the attempt to develop *social indicators*. Every January the Council of Economic Advisers issues detailed reports on the nation's economy, as measured by statistics on growth, employment, inflation, and the Gross National Product (GNP). But until quite recently there has been no parallel attempt to monitor the *quality* of life in this country.

As Harvard professor Raymond Bauer told a Senate subcommittee on social planning in 1971, ''While we could reduce hunger, we do not know just who is hungry. While we could reduce crime, our knowledge of even how many crimes of what type are committed is highly imperfect. While we could improve the quality of life, we do not know what our citizens value in their lives'' (Bauer, in Melville, 1973: 13).

In the last five to ten years sociologists and other social scientists have begun to develop a system of social indicators comparable to our existing system of economic indicators. These social indicators are designed to measure such seeming intangibles as aspirations and levels of satisfaction in health, work, friendship, family, marriage, and community. A decade ago we could only guess about the number and kinds of crimes that were never reported to the police. The National Crime Survey now questions households and businesses directly. We knew how many children went to school, how regularly they attended, and how much different schools had budgeted for their education. But we did not know what children actually learned in school. The National Assessment of Educational Progress now administers standardized tests of knowledge, understanding, and skills to a nationwide selection of young people. The Annual Housing Survey collects data not only on such things as the cost of housing, the number of people per room, and the plumbing, but also on people's feelings about their surroundings— what pleases, bothers, or frightens them.

The goal of all these studies is to develop a set of social indicators that will give policy makers a sense of what it is like to live in America during a certain year or period. If the quality of life at any particular moment can be accurately assessed and compared with the quality at another time, policy makers will have a factual and realistic foundation on which to base their decisions about social programs. The social-indicators movement is one of the first large-scale attempts to put sociological knowledge to practical use. As the public begins to gain more confidence in sociological approaches and methods, surely there will be others. In the next chapter, we discuss several of the methods sociologists use in doing research.

SUMMARY

Sociology invites us to set aside our personal view of the world in order to see with greater clarity and objectivity the forces that shape and control our lives. It attempts to understand the social nature of things—in particular, the patterns and regularities of behavior people exhibit as they go about their daily lives. The *sociological perspective* focuses on those details that are regular and patterned, details not unique to a particular situation or to particular people in that situation.

A compelling reason for using the sociological perspective is that human experience—no matter how private and individual it may seem—is touched and shaped by social forces not made or controlled by individuals. Being sick and committing suicide are two seemingly personal experiences that, when viewed sociologically, turn out to be affected by social forces.

The sociological perspective is not a rigid, singular way of looking at society; there are several different theoretical orientations. The most prevalent orientation in America is the *structural-functional* approach. The emphasis in this approach is on society and the interrelationships of its components, rather than on groups or individuals as such. Structural-functionalists try to discover the social function something serves in society. They often develop convincing explanations for the existence of phenomena that would otherwise be puzzling or incomprehensible. *Conflict orientation* focuses on conflict and opposition rather than on positive functions. The proponents of this approach feel that the structural-functionalists introduce a conservative bias into sociological analysis by directing attention toward maintaining the system as it is and away from conflict and change. A third and increasingly popular orientation is loosely labeled *interactionist*. Attention is focused on the day-to-day communication that takes place when people interact face to face. Emphasis is on the meaning of social life as it is interpreted by individuals going about their daily business, rather than on large social structures and institutions. Each of these orientations influences the results of a sociological inquiry, for the type of questions a sociologist asks, and the answers he or she receives, reflects his or her theoretical orientation.

No matter what his or her orientation, every sociologist always tries to understand and interpret events and patterns that transcend particular individuals, cultures, and historical moments. The sociologist tries to uncover basic truths about human social behavior. Sociological concepts and findings have been used for many purposes. The study of history has been affected: it has begun to use sociological techniques to explore everyday life in the past. Political science, too, has been influenced; it now explores such issues as: How do different people acquire political values? What is the relationship between the political attitudes of parents and those of their children? Economists now build sociological data into their models.

Sociology has also had an impact on public programs and policy. The findings of sociological studies have been applied to such diverse issues as school segregation and pornography. One of the newest undertakings of sociologists concerned with applied rather than theoretical work is the attempt to develop *social indicators*, which measure the quality of life. If the quality of life at any particular moment can be accurately assessed and compared with the quality of life at another time, policy makers will have a factual and realistic basis on which to reach their decisions about social programs.

GLOSSARY

conflict orientation a theoretical perspective that emphasizes conflict, opposition, and change within a society.

social indicators measures of the quality of life, including such seeming intangibles as aspirations and levels of satisfaction in health, work, friendship, marriage, family, and community.

sociological perspective a way of observing social life that focuses on regular and patterned details, aspects that are not unique to a particular situation or to individuals in that situation.

sociology the scientific study of social phenomena. The sociologist is interested in broad patterns and regular occurrences, rather than in the unique peculiarities of a specific individual or incident.

structural-functionalism a theoretical perspective that emphasizes the way each part of a society contributes to the functioning of the society as a whole. A structural-functionalist tries to discover the social function something serves in society.

symbolic interactionist orientation a theoretical perspective that focuses on the day-to-day communication that takes place when people interact in face-to-face situations, rather than on the large social structures and institutions.

REFERENCES

Harvey Averech et al., *How Effective Is Schooling?* Princeton, N.J.: Princeton University Press, 1972.

Harvey Elmer Barnes, *An Introductory History of Sociology.* Chicago: University of Chicago Press, 1948.

Peter Blau, "Dialectical Sociology: Comments." *Sociological Inquiry*, vol. 42 (Spring 1972): 17–22.

_____ and Marshall W. Meyer, *Bureaucracy in Modern Society.* New York: Random House, 1971.

James Coleman et al., *Equality of Educational Opportunity.* Washington, D.C.: U.S. Government Printing Office, 1972.

Auguste Comte, *The Positive Philosophy*, trans. and ed. Harriet Martineau. London: Bell, 1915.

Kingsley Davis, *Human Society,* New York: Macmillan, 1937.

_____, "The Sociology of Prostitution." *American Sociological Review*, vol. 2 (1937): 744–755.

Hans Peter Dreitzel, ed., *The Social Organization of Health.* New York: Macmillan, 1971.

Émile Durkheim, *The Rules of Sociological Method.* Chicago: University of Chicago Press, 1938.

_____, *Suicide: A Study of Sociology* (1897), trans. J. A. Spaulding and G. Simpson. New York: Free Press, 1951.

Eliot Freidson, *Profession of Medicine: A Study of the Sociology of Applied Knowledge.* New York: Dodd, Mead, 1970.

E. Gartly Jaco, ed., *Patients, Physicians, and Illness,* 2nd ed. New York: Free Press, 1972.

Mirra Komarovsky, ed., *Sociology and Public Policy: The Case of Presidential Commissions.* New York: Elsevier, 1975.

Harvey Leibenstein, *Beyond Economic Man.* Cambridge, Mass.: Harvard University Press, 1976.

Karl Marx, *Capital*, ed. Friedrich Engels. New York: International Publishers, 1967.

_____ and Friedrich Engels, *The Communist Manifesto*, ed. Samuel H. Beer. New York: Appleton, 1955.

Mathematica and the Institute for Research on Poverty, "Final Report of the New Jersey Graduated Work Incentive Experiment." Princeton, N.J., and Madison, Wis., unpublished report, June 1974.

Keith Melville, "A Measure of Contentment." *The Sciences*, vol. 13 (December 1973): 12–15.

Robert K. Merton, *Social Theory and Social Structure.* New York: Free Press, 1968.

Talcott Parsons, *The Social System.* New York: Free Press, 1951.

Lee Rainwater, "The Lower Class: Health, Illness, and Medical Institutions," in Irving Deutscher and E. Thompson, eds., *Among the Poor.* New York: Basic Books, 1968.

Henri de Saint-Simon, *Social Organization: The Science of Man*, trans. and ed. Felix Markham. New York: Harper & Row, 1964.

Thomas J. Scheff, *Being Mentally Ill.* Chicago: Aldine, 1966.

Edward Shils, "The Calling of Sociology," in Talcott Parsons et al., eds., *Society*. New York: Free Press, 1961.

Herbert Spencer, *The Principles of Sociology*. New York: Appleton, 1898.

Alfred H. Stanton and Morris S. Schwartz, *The Mental Hospital*. New York: Basic Books, 1954.

Max Weber, *The Theory of Social and Economic Organization*, trans. A. N. Henderson and Talcott Parsons. New York: Free Press, 1964.

FOR FURTHER STUDY

The Sociological Perspective.   As a basic orientation to sociology, we can recommend two small books written for the beginning student: Peter Berger's popular *Invitation to Sociology* (Garden City, N.Y.: Doubleday, 1963) and Alex Inkeles's *What Is Sociology?* (Englewood Cliffs, N.J.: Prentice-Hall, 1964). Many students will be interested in *The Humanities as Sociology,* edited by Marcello Truzzi (Columbus, Ohio: Merrill, 1973). A whimsical and interesting approach to social life is represented in a book edited by Marcello Truzzi, *Sociology and Everyday Life* (Englewood Cliffs, N.J.: Prentice-Hall, 1968). One of the finest books by a sociologist who saw social life largely in terms of power and conflict is *The Sociological Imagination* by C. Wright Mills (New York: Oxford University Press, 1967). One sociologist who has criticized the social sciences for their pretensions and deceptions is Stanislav Andreski, in *Social Sciences as Sorcery* (New York: St. Martin's, 1973).

Theoretical Orientations.   An interesting description of the classical theorists and their ideas is *Masters of Sociological Thought: Ideas in Historical and Social Context* (New York: Harcourt Brace Jovanovich, 2nd ed., 1977) by Lewis A. Coser. Another excellent examination of major theorists is Raymond Aron's *Main Currents in Sociological Thought,* vols. 1 and 2 (New York: Basic Books, 1965). Jonathan H. Turner's *The Structure of Sociological Theory* (Homewood, Ill.: Dorsey Press, 2nd ed., 1978) is a good overview of contemporary sociological theory.

The Development of Sociology.   To understand how sociology developed as a discipline, we recommend Robert W. Friedrichs's *A Sociology of Sociology* (New York: Free Press, 1972) and Nicholas Mullins's *Theories and Theory Groups* in *Contemporary American Sociology* (New York: Harper & Row, 1973). Robert E. Faris gives an account of the early formative years of sociology in the United States in *Chicago Sociology* (Chicago: University of Chicago Press, 1967).

The Uses of Sociology.   One development in sociology of interest to students is its use as a tool in social reform. Gary Marx's book, *Muckraking Sociology: Research as Social Criticism* (New Brunswick, N.J.: Transaction, 1972) provides many examples. *Sociology and Public Policy: The Case of Presidential Commissions* (New York: Elsevier Scientific Publishing, 1975), edited by Mirra Komarovsky, describes the experiences of four sociologists who served on presidential commissions concerned with obscenity, violence, population growth, and law enforcement. Arthur Shostak's *Sociology in Action* (Homewood, Ill.: Dorsey Press, 1966) discusses some practical uses of sociology.

CHAPTER 2

Science and Methods in Sociology

On February 26, 1972, a twenty-foot wall of churning mud and debris broke through a dam in Buffalo Creek, West Virginia, scouring a valley that had been home for some 5,000 families. Assessing the damage to property was difficult. But how could one assess the damage to individuals' lives? to neighborhoods and communities?

This was the challenge the law firm representing the survivors presented to sociologist Kai Erikson (1977). Erikson spent a year reviewing some 40,000 pages of testimony, studying legal and historical documents, and visiting the valley to conduct interviews and administer questionnaires. He concluded that the survivors were suffering not only from individual trauma (a sudden blow to the psyche they could not deal with effectively) but also from collective trauma ("a blow to the basic tissues of social life"). Always poor, the valley people had valued neighborliness above all else; then suddenly their neighborhoods were demolished and their neighbors gone.

Erikson came to know and respect the people he was studying. They had been the victims of so many forces beyond their control that he hesitated "to imprison them once again between the cold parentheses of a theory." This is a problem central to all sociological research: translating human experiences into measurements without oversimplifying the situation.

The key is the scientific method. The main goal of this chapter is to describe the application of the scientific method to the study of society. It also explores some of the basic questions that confront all sociologists. Is sociology truly a science? How do sociologists work? Is it ethical to experiment with people? We begin with the most fundamental question: What is science?

THE NATURE OF SCIENCE

Essentially, science is a *method* for collecting and explaining facts. Scientists confine their investigations to phenomena that can be observed and measured, and to statements about the relationships among phenomena that can be verified by independent observers. Empirical proof is the basis of all science. Researchers are expected to approach their work in a detached way and to report their findings accurately. Other scientists then retest to make sure these findings hold up. In the words of one of the characters in C. P. Snow's novel *The Search*, "Now if false statements are to be allowed, if they are not to be discouraged by every means we have, science will lose its one virtue, truth. The only ethical principle which has made science possible is that the truth shall be told at all times" (281). Scientists seek the truth and attempt to eliminate, or at least minimize, personal bias and error by applying the scientific method to their research.

The Scientific Method: Émile Durkheim's Study of Suicide

The publication of Émile Durkheim's *Suicide* in 1897 marked the beginning of a revolution in thinking about social behavior. In Durkheim's time suicide was thought to be an individual act caused by mental illness or inherited suicidal tendencies, or was explained as the effect of climate on reasoning. If these really *were* the causes, then why did suicide rates vary from period to period? If suicide is caused by forces within individuals, why should the suicide rate be higher in one country than in another? Durkheim decided to find out why by conducting one of the first scientific studies of social behavior.

Émile Durkheim, the Frenchman whose scientific research on the causes of suicide was a breakthrough in the development of modern sociology. Durkheim identified marital status, religious beliefs, and economic and political stability as factors having a substantial effect on suicide rates. His work led him to conclude that a society is not merely a collection of people but a distinct and powerful force, which influences the actions and attitudes of its members. Durkheim's study also laid the groundwork for future scientific exploration of social phenomena. (The Bettmann Archive)

Defining the Problem Defining terms and concepts in a precise way is often more difficult than you might think. For example, what is suicide? If a person dies because he or she miscalculates danger or fails to take a necessary precaution, has he or she committed suicide? Examining the different implications of this word, Durkheim concluded that the term *suicide* refers to "all cases of death resulting directly or indirectly from a positive or negative act of the victim himself, which he knows will produce this result" (44).[1] Durkheim decided to use official records for his study, even though he realized that many suicides went unreported.

The next problem was to define the factors to be studied in some concrete way. When scientists study such abstract concepts as prejudice, religiousness, or economic stability, for example, they must define each idea in terms of measurable variables. This is called an *operational definition.* For purposes of study the scientist may define religious beliefs in terms of membership in religious organizations, or economic stability in terms of fluctuations of the stock market. In *Suicide*, Durkheim decided to use statistics on religious affiliation, marital status, military involvement, and economic and political stability as measures of the social causes of suicide.

Reviewing the Literature Durkheim's next step was to check existing theories against the facts. A preliminary review of official records revealed that suicide rates were highest in countries that had the lowest rates of mental illness, suggesting that insanity alone did not explain suicide. And while more women than men were confined to mental asylums, more men than women committed suicide. This observation suggested to Durkheim that suicide is not related to heredity, for if it were, men and women would be af-

fected equally.[2] Nor did the facts support the climatic theories of suicide. All that remained was the fact that suicide rates varied from one social group to another.

Forming a Hypothesis Using this fact as a base, Durkheim concluded: "We have shown in fact that for each social group there is a specific tendency to suicide explained neither by the organic-psychic construction of the individuals nor the nature of the physical environment. Consequently, by elimination, it must necessarily depend upon social causes and be itself a collective phenomenon . . ." (1951: 145).

At this point Durkheim had formulated a proposition: suicide has some relationship to social causes. A philosopher might stop here, having shown by the logical process of elimination that suicide is related to social causes. But logical deduction is not enough; scientists demand empirical proof. The first step toward obtaining such proof is to translate the problem into a hypothesis, a statement worded in terms that can be tested.

A *hypothesis* predicts how two or more variables will affect one another. It is phrased in such a way that it can be proved or disproved empirically. For example, the statement "God exists" is simply an assertion: it can be neither proved nor disproved. The statement "People who attend church regularly believe in God" can be tested (by interviewing people who attend church and people who do not), and it is therefore a hypothesis. A *variable* is some attitude, behavior pattern, or condition that is subject to

---

[1] By "positive act" Durkheim meant such things as shooting oneself or jumping off a bridge. By "negative act" he meant such things as failing to take necessary medicine or not getting out of the path of a moving vehicle.

[2] Both of these conclusions are questionable. Criteria for mental illness vary from culture to culture, and the number of people confined in asylums is not necessarily a good indicator of the number of people who are depressed or disturbed. Moreover, the question of whether suicidal tendencies are inherited still remains unanswered.

RESEARCH INTO INSTITUTIONAL RACISM

For many years Émile Durkheim's study of suicide has been considered a classic example of the scientific method. A hypothesis led to data collection and analysis followed by an explanation. But it is misleading to suggest that Durkheim's approach is the only road to sociological truth.

Because of his subject—suicide—Durkheim had to rule out the personal interview or questionnaire as a means of gathering data. With no living subjects to interview, he was forced to construct his hypothesis from statistics about suicide rates. Since Durkheim's time, most sociological research has focused on living subjects, and today's sociologist spends at least as much time collecting data from live subjects as he does gathering information from sources in the library.

For example, Sanford Dornbusch was interested in understanding a problem that has challenged social scientists for years. Namely, why do black students get low grades in school? (This stage in a research study is called *defining the problem*.) Dornbusch and his colleagues *reviewed the literature* and found that previous research had eliminated such possible explanations as low IQ, parents' lack of interest in students' schoolwork, or low self-esteem among black students.

Clearly, a new approach was needed, and the researchers formulated a *hypothesis*: black students get low grades because they are misled into thinking they are doing well when they are not, and they therefore do not work hard enough to get good grades.

To test this hypothesis the Dornbusch team devised a *research design* around a questionnaire for students. They chose a random sample of students from eight San Francisco high schools; to encourage the more alienated students to respond, the researchers paid each subject $2. But this did not solve all the

change. Durkheim hypothesized that suicide rates would vary: for Catholics, Protestants, and Jews; for married and unmarried people; for soldiers and civilians; in times of economic and political stability and unrest. In his study, religious affiliation, marital status, and so on were the independent variables, the factors thought to affect the suicide rate; the suicide rate was the dependent variable, the factor expected to change in relation to the independent variables.

In any scientific study the *independent variable* is a quality or factor that influences the dependent variable. The *dependent variable* is a quality or factor that is affected by one or more independent variables.

Choosing a Research Design   Once his terms were defined and his hypotheses formulated, Durkheim had to decide how to collect data that would prove or disprove the hypotheses. This involved selecting the group or groups to be studied, evaluating various sources of information, and deciding how to measure the variables. Depending on the problem being investigated, a researcher might de-

problems. Some students could not read the questions, so the researchers read them aloud to small groups. The research design also called for *gathering data* about grades, truancy, and other aspects of the students' behavior, so school files were checked for each subject.

They then *analyzed the data* and found that as a group black students had the lowest academic performance, but they also most often rated the teachers as friendly, warm, and personally interested in them. Black students worked the least bet rated themselves highest of any group on their effort. This led to the crucial question: "How is it possible for this situation to exist in the schools—that black students are allowed to kid themselves on their level of effort *and* future expectations, given their low academic achievement and grades?" (8)

The *explanation* the Dornbusch team suggested was that teachers systematically praise black students who are actually not doing good work. The researchers called this "institutional racism," because they suspect this pattern is less a matter of teachers being clever racists than a matter of the schools putting them in a position of teaching poorly educated students they have no time to bring up to par. So the teachers smile and let the poor work continue.

Actually, this explanation of the data is itself only a hypothesis. There is no direct evidence of teachers acting this way; all the data come from students' opinions. But one study leads to another. The next step is to study the teachers themselves, and that is what one of Professor Dornbusch's students is doing.

SOURCE: Grace Carroll Massey, Mona Vaughn Scott, and Sanford M. Dornbusch, "Racism Without Racists: Institutional Racism in Urban Schools," *The Black Scholar*, vol. 7 (November 1975), pp. 1–11.

sign an experiment, conduct interviews, spend time observing the way people interact in certain settings, or examine records. (A researcher may actually use several of these data-collection methods.) Durkheim chose to use official records on suicide from a number of European nations.

Analyzing the Data Examining these records, Durkheim found that more Protestants than Catholics and more Catholics than Jews committed suicide. Single people committed suicide most often, and married people with children least often. Soldiers were more prone to suicide than civilians. Durkheim also discovered that suicide rates rose during periods of sharp economic reversals (inflations or depressions), but fell during periods of political instability. These findings had to be interpreted. Why, for example, do suicide rates vary with religious affiliation?

The answer was not obvious. Certainly religious beliefs didn't explain the variations Durkheim found. The Catholic church teaches that suicide is a sin, while Jewish doctrine is vague on the subject. Yet Jews had the lowest suicide rates. Durkheim resolved this paradox by looking beyond specific religious beliefs to the *social impact* of different faiths. Protestantism emphasizes skepticism and individualism; Catholicism and Judaism stress tradition and authority while at the same time demanding that a person become involved in the religious community. Similarly, married people (particularly parents) are involved with other people in a way that single people are not.

Explaining the Results From this analysis, Durkheim concluded that suicide rates rise when people's social bonds to significant groups are weakened and fall when they are strengthened. The stronger the ties people have to social groups, the more they depend on these groups and the more likely they are to take other people into account when making decisions. People who have few ties to their community are more likely to take their own lives than people who are deeply involved with their community.

In drawing this conclusion, Durkheim had formulated a general theory about social bonds and individual behavior. We often use the word "theory" to mean abstract ideas, as in the sentence "That may be true in theory, but not in fact." In science, however, a *theory* explains the relationship between major concepts. The function of a theory in science is to summarize and order information in a meaningful way, to suggest new ways of looking at phenomena, and to stimulate new research. The test of a theory is whether or not the hypotheses derived from it can predict what will happen.

Critical Assessment Like other communities, the scientific community is governed by certain values and norms. These norms include making results available to everyone and analyzing one another's work according to preestablished impersonal criteria. The accuracy of the findings of a particular scientific study is determined by an assessment of the study's validity and reliability. *Validity* is the degree to which a scientific study measures what it attempts to measure. *Reliability* is the degree to which a study yields the same results when repeated by the original researcher or by other scientists. The value of a scientific study lies partly in the information the researcher collects and partly in the new investigations the study stimulates.

The norms of the scientific community have been applied to Durkheim's work on suicide. Some sociologists have questioned his data, asking whether official records are an accurate measure of suicide rates. Not only do people cover up suicides, but they may do so in systematic ways that would affect and distort the patterns Durkheim analyzed. For example, records revealed that Protestants had a higher suicide rate than Catholics. But what if Catholics simply concealed more suicides than Protestants did? But the heart of *Suicide* is its theory not its data. Never before had a private, psychological act like committing suicide been explained in terms of social forces. Sociologists have built on Durkheim's ideas to explain a range of actions—from stealing a car to falling in love—in terms of group affiliations and social pressures.

SCIENCE AND SOCIOLOGY

[T]here can never be, and has never been, "disinterested" research in the social field, as there can be in the natural sciences. Valuations are, in fact, determining our work even if we manage to be unaware of it. And this is true, however much the researcher is subjectively convinced that he is simply observing and recording the facts. (Myrdal, 1973: 9)

The question of whether sociology is a science comparable to physics, biology, and astronomy has never been completely resolved. Auguste Comte, the French philosopher and founder of positivism, believed that all aspects of social life could be measured, analyzed, and explained with the tools of natural science. He also believed that sociologists would ultimately be able to cure social ills, just as medical scientists have learned to cure many physical ills. In contrast, Max Weber, the German sociologist and political economist, emphasized the *subjective* elements of social behavior. He argued that empathy and insight are as valuable to the sociologist as hard facts, that to understand social phenomena, the researcher must "get inside" them.

This debate continues today, with some sociologists emphasizing the need to replace insight with hard facts, and with others arguing that sociology cannot and should not imitate the natural sciences because they are fundamentally different. Quite simply, people cannot be manipulated like atoms: people can and do change their minds, talk back, or answer questions dishonestly. People are also more complex than bacteria or the smaller organisms natural scientists work with, because human genes do not predetermine most of human behavior.

Nor do social variables remain constant over time and place. The law of gravity and the composition of water are the same everywhere, the same today as they were yesterday. But no two families are exactly alike, and ideas about what the family should be vary enormously from one culture to another. In the words of Swedish social scientist Gunnar Myrdal:

The really important difference between [social scientists] and our natural science colleagues is that we never reach down to constants—like the speed of light or sound in a particular medium, or the specific weights of atoms or molecules. We have nothing corresponding to the universally valid measurements of energy, voltage, ampere, etc. The regularities we find do not have the firm general validity of "laws of nature." (1973)

Perhaps most significant, the sociologist's relation to his or her subject is quite different from the astronomer's relation to the stars or the physicist's relation to energy. Objectivity is a major problem for all social scientists. As Herbert Spencer wrote nearly a hundred years ago:

To cut himself off in thought from all his relationships of race, and country, and citizenship—to get rid of all those interests, prejudices, likings, superstitions, generated in him by the life of his own society and his own time—to look on all the changes societies have undergone and are undergoing, without reference to nationality, or creed, or personal welfare; is what the average man cannot do at all, and what the exceptional man can do very imperfectly. (1877: 74)

Does this mean that sociology is merely masquerading as a science, or does it mean that sociologists should confine themselves to collecting hard facts, to conducting surveys, and to other forms of information gathering in which personal bias can be minimized? Not necessarily. It means, first, that it's essential for sociologists to recognize their biases and assumptions and to state them explicitly, and, second, that sociologists should combine the quantitative (or hard) and qualitative (or soft) approaches to the study of social behavior. In both the natural and the social sciences, we must not forget that insight, hunches, and creative moments are vital.

Durkheim's study of suicide illustrates this last point. By collecting data he was able to prove that suicide rates vary with religious affiliation, marital status, military involvement, and economic and political stability. But it was insight that enabled him to perceive the underlying variable—the degree of involvement in social groups.

THE METHODS OF SOCIOLOGY

Having described how Durkheim used scientific methods to analyze suicide rates, we now examine the procedures and techniques—both objective and subjective—that sociologists use to study social behavior.

Survey Research

Surveys composed of questionnaires, interviews, or some combination of the two enable sociologists to gather information about how large numbers of people think, feel, or act. Surveys can be used to make predictions about how people will behave (for example, election polls), to test hypotheses, and to measure public opinion.

The validity of a survey depends on the care with which the researcher constructs questionnaires or structures interviews and on the selection of a representative sample. Theoretically, a sociologist who's interested in the attitudes of American college students concerning politics or sex or any other issue could hire an army of interviewers to contact every student in the country. However, the cost and time involved in such a venture would be prohibitive. For these very practical

reasons, sociologists generally question only a sample of the population. In this context, *population* refers to all the people with the characteristics the researcher wants to study—all American college students, for example. A *sample* is a limited number of people selected from the population.

Choosing a Sample   There are several ways to choose a sample, and the method used depends on what the researcher is studying. One form is the *random sample*. The researcher in effect puts the names of all people in the population in a barrel, blindfolds himself, and picks as many names as he needs, leaving the selection to chance. The more sophisticated and more usual technique is to assign each person in the population a number and to pick a sample from a table of random numbers. With a random sample each person in the population has an equal chance of being selected; researcher bias is eliminated.

Most people think a big sample provides more accurate results than a smaller one, but this is not necessarily true. The real key to accuracy is polling a true cross section of the population being studied. The attempt to predict the winner of the 1936 presidential election is a famous example of this. A popular magazine, *Literary Digest*, sent post-card ballots to 10 million people chosen from telephone directories and auto-registration lists. The *Digest* predicted, on the basis of 2 million returns, that Alfred Landon would beat Franklin D. Roosevelt by a landslide. Meanwhile, a young man named George Gallup sampled 312,551 people and correctly predicted that FDR would win. The editors of the *Literary Digest* were stunned by the election results. How could their giant survey have been so wrong? The key to accuracy was not the *number* of people polled but their characteristics. During the depres-

AN ATTITUDE SCALE

Sociologists may construct questionnaires that allow them to distinguish degrees of difference in attitudes among respondents. Rather than asking respondents to rate their own attitudes, the interviewer asks several questions and assigns a numerical value to each answer. The total is used to place the person's attitude on a scale of favorable to unfavorable to the particular topic. Scales may be used to determine such attitudes as degree of confidence in authority, political liberalism or conservatism, or support for or opposition to social policies.

The following example shows part of a scale (there were originally six items) constructed to determine belief in the "work ethic," or the idea that hard work leads to the worthwhile goal of individual success.

1. If a close relative of yours who had a job he disliked inherited enough money to live comfortably without working, would you encourage him to continue working full time, to cut back to part time, or to quit working altogether?

		Value
A.	continue full time	3
B.	part time	2
C.	quit work	1

2. Some people say that if a man is working full time and is still not earning enough to stay out of poverty, he should be encouraged to seek welfare or relief. Others feel that no one should be encouraged to seek welfare or relief. What do you believe?

		Value
A.	encouraged	1
B.	not encouraged	2

3. Some people say that in America the road to success is equally open to all; others disagree with them. How do you feel?

		Value
A.	agree	2
B.	disagree	1

A score of 7 indicates strong support for the work ethic. A score of 3 indicates weak support for the work ethic. Scores between 7 and 3 indicate moderate degrees of support.

SOURCE: John B. Williamson, "Beliefs About the Motivation of the Poor and Attitudes Toward Poverty Policy," *Social Problems*, vol. 21, no. 5 (June 1974), p. 637.

"That's the worst set of opinions I've heard in my entire life." (Drawing by Weber; © 1975 The New Yorker Magazine, Inc.)

sion years, only middle- and upper-class people could afford telephones and automobiles, and a disproportionate number of middle- and upper-class people were Republicans. As it turned out, the less well off, who voted heavily for Democrat Franklin Roosevelt, decided the election (Labovitz and Hagedorn, 1971: 33; Hennessy, 1971: 79–81). The staff of the *Literary Digest* had incorrectly assumed that the more people they contacted, the better their chances would be of accurately predicting the outcome of the election.

Gallup's success was not a matter of luck—he had polled a scientific cross section that accurately represented the proportion of Republicans and Democrats in the *entire* population of voters. Selecting a sample that accurately reflects the proportions of different groups in the population being studied is called *stratified random sampling*.

Designing the Questionnaire The accuracy of a survey also depends on the way questions are worded. A survey is meaningless if respondents don't understand the questions, if they don't answer truthfully, and if their answers can be interpreted in different ways. With mailed questionnaires, it is difficult to judge whether or not respondents take the survey seriously, and the information collected may not really reflect actual beliefs, habits, and preferences.

There is also a danger of middle-class bias. It is generally easier to get answers from middle-class respondents than from welfare clients, who have reason to be suspicious of official-looking papers and of strangers who ask questions. Moreover, in face-to-face interviews, people tend to give the socially acceptable response. For example, when Richard Carter asked Bowery bums if they were married, a surprising number said no. However, when he asked instead, "Where is your wife?" many more gave truthful answers, without stopping to think about the implications of desertion in a yes response (Carter, in Hennessy, 1971: 110).

In addition, researchers face the problem of translating responses into statistics. If a pollster asks a hundred different people what they think of a specific administration, he or she may get a hundred different answers. How, then, can the results be presented? Because of this problem, researchers use structured questions wherever possible—that is, questions that can be answered yes or no, true or false; multiple-choice questions; and rating questions, where a respondent indicates the extent (on a scale of one to five) to which he or she agrees or disagrees with a statement.

Experiments

Sociologists conduct experiments when they want to study cause-and-effect relationships. In simplest terms, sociological *experiments* consist of exposing subjects to a specially designed situation and systematically recording their reactions. The advantage of experiments over other methods is that they allow the researcher to study the impact of only one or two variables, which is hard to do in real-life situations.

Examining Prison Life For example, Philip Zimbardo wanted to study the impact of prison life on both guards and inmates. He could have studied actual prisoners and guards in their natural setting, but he would have had to follow prison rules, and his findings would have been complicated by such variables as differences in individual background. Instead, he ran an experiment using student volunteers (Zimbardo, 1972). By using people who were neither guards nor prisoners, Zimbardo was able to study the effects of social roles on behavior. In actual prisons he would not have been able to separate the actors from their roles as easily. (See chapter 3 for a more complete discussion of social roles.)

Zimbardo began by constructing a prison in the basement of the psychology building at Stanford University. Twenty-four normal college and graduate students ("normal" according to accepted psychological tests) were divided into two groups—"guards" and "prisoners." The two groups were matched for socioeconomic background, ed-

ucation, and race. One night, without warning, the prisoners were collected in a simulated arrest. All were given uniforms and numbers and were confined in the basement jail. The guards were dressed appropriately and instructed on their responsibility for maintaining order. Two days after the experiment began, rumors of a prisoner rebellion began to spread. The guards reacted with surprising brutality, to which the prisoners submitted with little resistance. These normal students got so deeply involved in their make-believe prison roles that Zimbardo had to stop the experiment before it was completed. Zimbardo concluded that the behavior of real guards and prisoners is determined much more by the institutional structure of prisons than by the personalities of the people involved. (We will discuss the ethical problems raised by this controversial experiment later in the chapter.)

Studying Obedience Stanley Milgram's experiments on obedience were equally controversial (1965; 1973). Milgram recruited subjects by advertising in a local paper; the ads called for volunteers for an experiment on learning. Over a period of several years, more than a thousand people from all walks of life participated. When a subject arrived at the lab, he or she was introduced to two people. The first, who wore a lab coat, was the experimenter; the second, dressed in street clothes, was supposedly another volunteer. In reality, however, this second person was part of the experimental team. Milgram explained that he was conducting a test of the effects of punishment on learning, and asked the subject to play the role of "teacher." The second person was asked to be the "student"; he or she was strapped to a chair and wired with electrodes. The teacher was given a seat at an impressive-

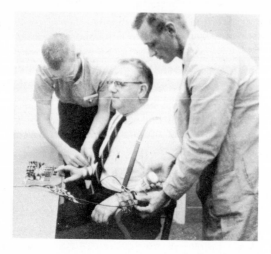

Stanley Milgram's controversial experiments tested the extent to which people will obey an authority figure. Here, the "student," actually a member of the experimental team, is wired with electrodes. The subject, or "teacher," will ask him questions and administer increasingly strong shocks for each wrong answer. (Stanley Milgram)

looking shock machine and was told to ask the student a series of questions and to administer increasingly higher doses of electric shock for each wrong answer. The shock board was labeled from 15 volts (SLIGHT SHOCK) to 450 volts (DANGER—SEVERE SHOCK).

As the experiment proceeded, the student gave a number of wrong answers. He began to complain when the shocks reached 175 volts, and by 285 volts he was emitting agonized screams, pleading to be released. Nearly all of the teachers became troubled when the student complained; when they turned to the experimenter for advice, they were told to continue. In reality, the shock machine was a fake and the students were acting, but the teachers did not know this.

Nevertheless, two-thirds of the subjects continued to press the shock button, right up to 450 volts.

Limitations of Experiments The chief drawback with experiments is that a laboratory is one step removed from real life, and the setting itself may influence the way people behave. For example, Milgram's subjects may have obeyed the experimenter because they believed he was a doctor, and presumably doctors don't harm people.[3] For this reason, researchers may run two tests with two matched groups. One group, the *experimental group*, actually undergoes the experiment. The other, the *control group*, is brought to the lab and exposed to everything *but* the independent variable. The experimenter then compares the responses of the two groups.

Field Experiments Still, the question of whether observations made in a laboratory apply to real-life situations remains. Some researchers avoid this problem by conducting experiments in the field. One of the most famous field experiments in sociology was conducted by Elton Mayo at Western Electric Company's Hawthorne plant in Chicago (Roethlisberger and Dickson, 1939). Mayo wanted to learn how variations in factory conditions affected worker output. Management felt sure that employees would work harder if they were paid in proportion to what they produced; management also thought that coffee breaks would improve morale. But Mayo and his colleagues found that

---

[3]   Milgram tested this contingency by performing a second series of experiments in an unimpressive office building that was identified as a commercial research organization; the results were much the same.

every change they made increased output. Employees worked faster when management increased or *decreased* the number or length of coffee breaks. Mayo concluded that it wasn't lighting or coffee breaks or even salary incentives that raised productivity, but rather the attention the employees were getting. The positive impact that an experiment has just because the researchers are giving people extra attention is known as the *Hawthorne effect*. Sociologists may try to eliminate the Hawthorne effect by using hidden tape recorders and other ''unobtrusive measures'' (Webb et al., 1966), but there is growing doubt about the ethics of experimenting on people without their knowledge.

Participant Observation

One of the oldest yet most controversial research methods in sociology is *participant observation*. Participant observers deliberately involve themselves in the activity, group, or community they are investigating in order to gain an insider's view. William Foote Whyte (1955), for example, moved into a low-income Italian-American community that was uncharted territory in the late 1940s. Before Whyte's study, street-corner residents were known to the outside world primarily as clients of social workers, as defendants in criminal trials, or simply as the masses (xvii). Whyte met Doc, the leader of the Norton gang, through a social worker. Doc then introduced him to the other residents, and for eighteen months Whyte shot pool, played cards, bowled, dated, ''chewed the fat,'' and most important, watched his subjects. In time he became a fixture on the street corner, a trusted friend who was able to learn how these people conducted their daily lives. Like Herbert Gans, author of a similar study (*The Urban Villagers*, 1962), Whyte ''tried to describe the way of life of [these] people as they might describe it themselves if they were sociologists'' (x). This is the primary goal of participant observation: to obtain firsthand knowledge of a way of life. In effect, the investigator uses himself as a research instrument. He knows how the people he is studying feel because he feels the same way. Even in the computer age, participant observation continues to be a popular and important research method. Recent studies discussed in this book include Liebow's book on poor urban blacks (*Tally's Corner*, 1967); Erikson's insights into an Appalachian community (*Everything in Its Path*, 1977); and Judah's observations of the Hare Krishna movement (*Hare Krishna and the Counterculture*, 1974).

Participant observation requires exceptional self-discipline. The first problem a field worker faces is gaining access to the group he or she wants to study and establishing rapport with its members.[4] If researchers reveal their intentions, they risk putting their subjects on guard; if they conceal their motives, they must live with pretense and duplicity for the duration of the study. Participant observers must develop techniques for recording their observations faithfully and systematically without influencing the way people act. They must become involved in the group life without allowing themselves to be blinded by their own emotions.

An important advantage of participant observation is that it is extremely flexible. Whyte found, for example, that ''as I sat and

---

[4] Gans never was able to win the confidence of the young single men who frequented West End bars; Whyte's success depended largely on his informant and collaborator, Doc.

listened, I learned the answers to questions that I would not even have had the sense to ask'' (303). Skilled field workers observe behavior in its natural setting; they can see behind individuals' public selves and discern the relationships between what people say and what they do. However, even good participant-observational studies have problems. The observations of the researcher may or may not accurately represent the group as a whole. There is always some danger that the field worker will rely on information gained from the more articulate and outgoing members of the group, or that he or she will misinterpret the significance of certain events. Moreover, in participant observation the sample is necessarily small.

For these reasons, participant-observational studies are generally used to uncover relationships that can then be tested more systematically. But despite the limitations of such studies, many of the classic works of sociology rest on observational research that uncovered significant aspects of social life. For example, Whyte found that low-income neighborhoods are highly structured communities—not the chaotic places they appear to be to outsiders; Gans argued that residents of Boston's West End were not ''frustrated seekers after middle-class values'' (x) but had a culture of their own. Both of these ideas were radical in their time.

A *case study* is an intensive observational study supplemented by formal interviews, surveys, data gathered from official records, and whatever other information may seem relevant. The researcher attempts to learn everything there is to know about a particular group, community, or incident. Examples are the Lynds' profiles of Middletown, U.S.A. (1929;1937); Clifford Shaw's life history of a juvenile delinquent (1966); and Hadley Cantril's anatomy of a lynching in Leeville, Texas (1963).

Interviewing

Interviewing people is a vital social-research skill that can be used in surveys, experiments, and participant observation. In an interview the researcher is face to face with his or her subject. The best interviewers are good listeners. They accurately hear what someone is saying and are sensitive to other people's feelings and to their own. Is he upset? Why is she talking in circles? Why am I getting bored? Good interviewers know their emotions and use their personal reactions as signals.

To conduct a profitable interview, the interviewer also needs good questions, questions that are *focused, clear,* and *neutral.* A question such as ''Do you think the government needs to be more efficient and effective?'' lacks all three qualities. It is so open to interpretation that focused questions concerning various government programs at various levels must follow. Because it is double-barreled, it is not clear; it must be split into two questions, one concerning the government's efficiency and one concerning its effectiveness. Finally, the phrase ''needs to be more efficient'' is biased. A neutral, clear revision of the original question would be ''How efficient do you think the government is?'' ''And how effective do you think it is?''

The Structured Interview In doing surveys and experiments, sociologists generally use the *structured interview,* an interview with carefully phrased questions—often with multiple-choice answers—to be asked in a strict order. For example, the question ''Do you think homosexuals should teach in public schools?'' has the possible answers ''Yes/No/Indifferent/No Opinion.'' Such careful structuring makes the data obtained systematic and comparable: each person is asked the same question and each answer is one of the four alternatives. But the structured interview also poses problems. If someone answers, "It depends on whether the teacher flaunts his homosexuality or keeps his sexual life to himself and acts like a professional," the researcher has no way to classify the response. Even well-phrased questions in a tightly structured interview will probably be more meaningful to some people than to others. Sociologists have found that if you ask people a question they will usually give you an answer even if they don't really care or know much about the subject.

The Unstructured Interview If the real goal is not to ask specific questions but to understand a certain aspect of social life, such as how people cope with retirement or how college affects students' relations with their parents, it may be better to use an unstructured interview, in which neither the questions nor the answers are predetermined. The unstructured interview allows the interviewer to explore a subject in terms of what the respondent finds important and meaningful. But the answers from several unstructured interviews may be difficult to compare.

One solution to the problems of both structured and unstructured interviews is the *semi-structured interview*. Here the interviewer works out in advance what areas or even what specific issues will be covered (structured), but lets the respondent talk about them in the terms most meaningful to him or her (unstructured). Which technique is used in any particular investigation depends, of course, on what kinds of information the researcher is seeking.

Time: The Hidden Variable An important variable in much sociological research is *time*. Changes in people and institutions often occur too slowly to be observed easily. Sociologists deal with this problem in one of two ways. The first is the *cross-sectional study*, which simultaneously looks at different groups of people at different stages of change. For example, a survey may sample the political opinions of adolescents, their parents, and their grandparents in order to see how aging affects political ideology. This is a quick and economical method, but it has its dangers. It assumes, for example, that the adolescents sampled today will become like their parents in twenty years and like their grandparents in forty years. In fact twenty years from now the young people of today may *not* have adopted their parents' attitudes; they may think very differently.

The second possible solution, a *longitudinal study*, is a more accurate research tool because it follows the same people over a number of years. No assumptions about people becoming like other people are necessary. In one well-known longitudinal study, T. M. Newcomb analyzed the effect of Bennington College on students' political attitudes. Newcomb questioned the same group of graduates over a twenty-year period, and found that, years after they had left college, Bennington alumnae were still unusually liberal for people of their socioeconomic class (1943; 1963). One problem with longitudinal studies is that they are expensive and slow. Americans are often so eager for quick results that such studies are rare in American sociology, although they have been done more often in Europe.

Sometimes the problem is not slow change but change so rapid that an event is over before we can begin to study it. Then the sociologist has no choice but to do an *ex post facto study*. In such studies, variables that could not be measured while an event was taking place can be analyzed statistically

CLASSIFYING DATA: MODE, MEAN, AND MEDIAN

Frequently researchers summarize data on a given population by calculating central tendencies, or averages. There are three ways to do this.

The *mode* is the figure that occurs most often in the data. For example, a researcher studies seven families and finds that their yearly incomes are

$3,000	$11,000
$3,000	$15,000
$7,500	$90,000
$9,000	

The modal income in this group of families is $3,000 a year. The mode does not give any indication of the range in data, and it is useful only when a researcher wants to show which statistic appears most often.

The *mean* is what is commonly referred to as the average. To calculate the mean you simply divide the sum of all the figures by the number of items. The mean or average income for the families above is $19,786 ($138,500 ÷ 7). Researchers frequently calculate the mean because it reflects all the available data. However, as the example here illustrates, the mean can be misleading: the fact that one of the families in this group has an income of $90,000 a year obscures the fact that six of the seven families have incomes of less than $19,786 a year. The mean is most useful when the range of figures is narrow.

The *median* is the number that falls in the middle of a series of figures—in this example, $9,000 a year. The median is useful because it does not allow extremes (here, $3,000 and $90,000) to hide the central tendency. Frequently researchers calculate both the mean and the median in order to present an accurate impression of their findings.

after the fact. The numerous government studies of civil disorders, initiated after the riots of the late 1960s, are ex post facto studies.

Interpreting Data

Politicians, advertisers, and journalists are so fond of quoting statistics that it sometimes seems as if they believe there's magic in numbers. Many people take statistics as gospel; "You can't argue with the facts," they say. Others believe you can use numbers to prove or disprove almost anything, and automatically stop listening when they hear the phrase "Statistics indicate . . ." The truth lies somewhere in between these two points of view.

The data a researcher collects in a survey, experiment, or observational study does not speak for itself. Data must be classified and trends and relationships identified for a study to be meaningful. For example, a list con-

HOW TO READ A TABLE

The following steps for interpreting the accompanying table are general guides that can be applied to any chart or table.

1. Read the title to find out what kind of information is in the table and how it is presented. In this table, the data are presented in terms of percent of the total responses, but this is not true of all tables. Some tables present their data in thousands.
2. Look for headnotes and footnotes that may explain how the data were collected, why certain variables were studied, and whether data were collected differently for some of the categories. In the accompanying table, a slightly different category was used on one of the dates in the survey (see footnote 1). Some tables have a footnote explaining how the data were collected; this provides one way of assessing the validity of the data. This table has no such explanation, and moreover, it does not tell how large the sample was. The source of the data, usually given at the bottom of a chart or table, is another measure of validity. For example, the organization that did this survey (the Gallup polls) is well known for the quality of its research. The source note is also a clue as to whether the researchers were objective or biased.
3. Read the labels for each column and row to learn exactly what data appear in the table. Here, the column labels indicate that the researchers broke the totals down by sex and community size. Four different-sized communities were surveyed, and people were asked whether they are afraid to walk alone at night. The possible answers were "Yes," "No," or "Can't say." The row labels at the left tell us that responses over a ten-year period, from 1965 to 1975, are being compared.
4. Look at the data and find the highest, lowest, and average rates. Then compare these with the other data in the table. In this table the totals in the first three columns give you an idea of the overall response. The percentage of people saying they were afraid to walk alone at night rose markedly after 1968.
5. Draw conclusions about the information in the table and consider what other questions it raises. Here, note how the totals break down by sex. Male response differs greatly from female response, which shows how grand totals can hide important differences in the data. Women are two and a half times as likely to answer yes to this question. Also, note the difference community size makes. The percentage of frightened people increases with community size, the sharpest increase coming between the first and second categories. It seems, then, that people in cities with populations from 2,500 to over 500,000 tend to be afraid of walking alone on the streets at night more than people in smaller towns. Further research might reveal the influence of other variables, such as age, income, race, and education.

table 2:1   PERSONS AFRAID TO WALK ALONE AT NIGHT, 1965–1975
By sex and community size (by percent)

Year (Month)	Total			Male			Female			Under 2.000			2.500 to 49.999			50.000 to 49.000			500.000 and over		
	Yes	No	Can't Say	Yes	No	Can't Say	Yes	No	Can't Say	Yes	No	Can't Say	Yes	No	Can't Say	Yes	No	Can't Say	Yes	No	Can't Say
1965 (April)[1]	34	63	3	17	80	3	49	47	4	21	77	2	29	67	4	41	54	5	48	49	3
1968 (September)	35	62	3	19	79	2	50	47	3	24	74	2	23	65	2	42	53	5	41	56	3
1972 (December)	42	57	1	22	77	1	61	39	—	28	71	1	40	69	1	51	49	—	48	51	1
1975 (June)	45	54	1	26	73	1	63	36	1	28	72	—	45	55	—	50	48	2	56	43	1

— Represents zero.

[1]The category "Don't know" was used instead of "Can't say."

SOURCE: American Institute of Public Opinion, Princeton, New Jersey.

taining the age of every American is useless unless this information is divided into categories—that is, the percentage of the American population under twenty-five, between twenty-six and forty, between forty-one and sixty-four, or sixty-five and over. The most common and useful methods of classifying statistics are explained in the accompanying boxes.

Once a researcher has organized his or her findings, a decision must be made about what the facts mean. A few simple examples illustrate the hazards of interpreting data. Suppose a researcher who is interested in the relationship between literacy rates and income collects data on Spain, Israel, and Kuwait. He or she discovers that per capita income is highest in Kuwait, where literacy rates are lowest, and concludes that the less literate a people are, the more money they earn. This researcher has made the common error of relying on grand averages, or very general statistical data, which often conceal significant patterns. For although Kuwait is a rich *nation*, the vast majority of its *people* are extremely poor. If the researcher had exam-

ined literacy rates for different *income groups* within each country instead of literacy rates for entire nations, he or she would have discovered that there is a direct relationship between literacy and income.

Data on crime and deviance are notoriously misleading. Statistics on mental illness, drug use, and homosexuality are nothing more than a count of the people who happen to come to the attention of police, social workers, and other public officials. These data do not include drug users who escape detection, or those people who are wealthy enough to afford private treatment for mental illness. Most people assume that crime is a lower-class phenomenon, whereas in fact many more dollars are lost through such white-collar (or middle-class) crimes as fraud and embezzlement than through such lower-class crimes as muggings and burglaries. Similarly, most people believe the crime rate has risen sharply during the last decade. While the crime rate may indeed have risen, some of this increase is due simply to improved methods of reporting and recording crimes (although exactly how much is diffi-

Statistics may be deceptive. Although Kuwait has an extremely high per capita income, its wealth is concentrated among only a few citizens. Most Kuwaitis are very poor. (Top and Bottom, Marc Riboud)

cult to say). In short, the way researchers analyze and interpret their data is as important as the care they take in collecting it.

VALUES, ETHICS, AND USES OF SOCIOLOGY

Sociology is founded on the belief that it is possible to apply the scientific method to the study of social behavior. Yet if sociology has proven anything in its brief history, it is that people are cultural animals, and that separating them from their social moorings is impossible. Thus sociologists find themselves in the awkward position of striving for objectivity on the one hand and recognizing the importance of subjectivity on the other. Can this dilemma be resolved?

The Myth of Value-free Sociology

For generations sociologists have labored under the eleventh commandment, "Thou shalt not commit a value judgment." Every textbook and every lecturer stress this point. But what exactly is meant by this commandment? Should sociologists never express opinions about issues that lie outside their sphere of competence? Should they be indifferent to the moral implications of their work? Should they never speak out on the probable consequences of public policy? Should they never attempt to correct popular beliefs, such as the notion that certain races or ethnic groups are inferior? Should they never express their values in their role as teachers?

In Alvin Gouldner's view, sociologists must stop pretending that their field can or should be value-free. Sociologists, like everyone else, are products of their times, and they cannot divorce themselves from their values and beliefs. In choosing an area for study, in deciding how to research a particular question, the sociologist inevitably makes certain assumptions about what is significant. For sociologists to deny their predispositions and biases, writes Gouldner, is absurd.

> If truth is a vital thing, as Weber is reputed to have said on his deathbed, then it must be all the truth we have to give, as best we know it, being painfully aware that even as we offer it we may be engaging in unwitting concealment rather than revelation. If we would teach students how science is made, really made rather than as publicly reported, we cannot fail to expose them to the whole scientist by whom it is made, with all his gifts and blindnesses, with all his methods and his *values* as well. (1962: 212)

Gouldner agrees with Gunnar Myrdal (1969) that sociologists can counteract bias only by explicitly stating their theoretical assumptions and values.

Howard S. Becker carries this argument a step further. He contends that sociologists always take sides, not only because they have the sympathies and likes and dislikes of all people, but also because investigating one point of view requires them to temporarily disregard another (1967). For example, the researcher who talks to inmates after a prison riot will arrive at one picture of the incident; the researcher who talks to guards and wardens will obviously arrive at another. Which is correct? For the sociologist, both are true, both relevant. Even interviewing both guards and inmates doesn't solve the problem, because the researcher will still analyze the data according to her or his theoretical orientation (see chapter 1).* Social realities are always complex; there is always more than one side to a story. Only by including these different perspectives can sociologists gradually approach all the facts and thus arrive at an accurate assessment of social reality. Becker acknowledges that this is a long-term solution.

> What do we do in the meantime? . . . We take sides as our personal and political commitments dictate, use our theoretical and technical resources to avoid the distortions that we might introduce into our work, limit our conclusions carefully, recognize the hierarchy of credibility for what it is, and field as best as we can the accusations and doubts that will surely be our fate. (1967: 247)

Becker cautions, however, that in giving some rein to their sympathies sociologists must resist the desire to suppress unpleasant findings and the temptation to disregard what they do not like seeing.

Professional Ethics

The debate over objectivity in sociology spills over into a number of complex ethical questions. Sociology is not a self-supporting enterprise. Like most researchers, sociologists depend on grants from public and private institutions for financial support. While these organizations do not dictate what researchers should find in their studies, they do exercise indirect control over the choice of topics by funding research in some areas but not in others. Intentionally or not a discipline may adjust its priorities to match those of the agencies which fund it.

Often there is a fine line between obtaining funds from and working *for* the government or special-interest groups. This is why

Project Camelot, for example, became so controversial. This project was conceived in the Special Operations Research Organization (SORO) of the U.S. Army. Its purpose, as described in a recruiting letter, was to devise procedures for "assessing the potential for internal war within national societies" and to "make it possible to predict and influence politically significant aspects of social change in the developing nations of the world" (Horowitz, 1965: 4). In other words, the army wanted to learn what circumstances sparked revolutions in underdeveloped nations, and what the governments of these nations could do to prevent them—hence the name "Camelot," which the director of the project felt connoted "a stable society with peace and justice for all."

The army backed its interest with an allocation of $6 million and successfully recruited some of the most respected social scientists in this country. Enthusiasm was high; participants believed Project Camelot would be an opportunity to influence government policy directly and to "educate" the army. As far as they could tell, military officials had no intention of interfering with their work.

The project was abruptly terminated when Chilean officials protested to the State Department, and the Chilean press began to publish stories about academic spies. Neither the State Department nor the Senate was willing to jeopardize our friendly relations with Latin American nations for the sake of gathering data, and there was some question as to the army's true motives.

Although Project Camelot never got off the ground, it did raise numerous questions during its brief history. Is it ethical for social scientists to work for the military? Many American sociologists thought not. But Project Camelot was an opportunity to study political order and disorder in depth. Would the project have become so controversial if it had been launched with funds from nongovernmental sources? After all, there is nothing to prevent military strategists from using (or misusing) research financed by private sources.

Equally problematic are questions about sociologists' responsibilities toward the people they study. Does a researcher have the right to deceive people about his or her intentions, to risk exposing and hurting them in the name of scientific inquiry? Stanley Milgram, for example, recruited subjects for his experiment by lying to them. It is difficult to estimate what impact participation in Milgram's experiment had on the subjects: one man told Milgram his wife had said, "You can call yourself Eichmann" (1973). Philip Zimbardo's techniques have also been questioned. The "prisoners" hadn't been told that they would actually be arrested, and they didn't know where they were being taken. During the experiment, three prisoners became so hysterical or depressed that they were released after two days, and the entire study was canceled after six days, although it was originally planned to run six weeks.

George Ritzer (1972) suggests that we ask the following questions in evaluating research:

1. Did the researcher harm the subjects he or she studied?

2. Did the researcher affect the subject's behavior and thereby invalidate his or her conclusions?

We would add a third question:

3. Could the researcher have obtained the same data without deceiving people and injuring their self-esteem?

The question of whether sociologists should actively participate in the political arena also involves ethical issues. Many believe that sociologists should remain neutral, that taking a stand would contaminate the discipline. But as Robert Lynd suggested in *Knowledge for What?:*

> Somebody is going to interpret what the situation [the facts] means. . . . When the social scientist, after intensive study of a problem, avoids extrapolating his data into the realm of wide meaning, however tentatively stated, he invites others presumably more biased than himself—e.g., the National Association of Manufacturers, the American Federation of Labor, the advertising man, the American Legion and so on—to thrust upon the culture their interpretations. (1939: 185–186)

In short, Lynd and many other sociologists argue that social scientists should suggest social policies because if they don't, others with their own special interests at heart will.

SUMMARY

Science is a method for collecting and explaining facts, involving the following procedures: (1) defining the problem to be studied; (2) reviewing the literature; (3) forming a hypothesis; (4) choosing a research design; (5) analyzing the data; (6) explaining the results.

Émile Durkheim was a pioneer in applying the scientific method to the study of social behavior. Durkheim believed that mental illness, heredity, or climate did not explain variations in suicide rates. In describing the problem, he focused on social factors, which he defined operationally in terms of religious affiliation, marital status, military involvement, and economic and political stability. He then formulated the *hypothesis* that suicide rates would vary according to religious affiliation, marital status, and so on. Examining official records, he found that suicide rates did indeed vary along these dimensions. Through a combination of statistical analysis and insight, he reached the conclusion that suicide rates vary in relation to the strength of social group ties (to families, religious organizations, and so forth). Building on this observation, Durkheim theorized that society has a determining influence on the way people think and act. His study has been subjected to the norms of the scientific community and assessed critically in terms of its validity and reliability, the impersonal criteria scientists use to evaluate one another's work.

Sociologists cannot put human beings under a microscope or weigh social behavior in imitation of physical scientists. Sociologists deal with meanings as well as facts, with change as well as constants, and they must count themselves as variables in any research they do. This does not mean that sociology is not a science, but rather that studying social behavior is very complex and requires both quantitative and qualitative data.

Sociologists collect their data in three basic ways: through *survey research, laboratory experiments,* and *field studies,* including *participant observation.* A *survey* is a collection of facts, figures, and/or opinions. The validity of a survey depends on the care with which the researchers construct their questions and on the selection of a representative sample. In *random samples,* every member of the population being studied has an equal chance of being selected. *Stratified random samples* re-create the proportions of significant groups in a population. In an *experiment,* researchers can control the variables they are studying, but their very presence may influence the results. In order to gain an insider's view, participant observers deliberately involve themselves in the activity, group, or community they are investigating. *Interviewing* is a technique that can be used in conjunction with all the other methods of data collection.

Despite methodological precautions against error and bias, sociologists find themselves in the awkward position of striving for objectivity on the one hand, while recognizing the importance of subjectivity on the other. Can sociology be value-free? This may be an unrealistic goal, since sociologists are as culture bound as all people; they inevitably take sides. Rather than pretend to absolute objectivity, sociologists must make their values and assumptions clear. Should sociologists work for the government? Is it ethical for sociologists to conceal their true objectives from the people they study? Would it contaminate the field if sociologists used their expertise to influence politicians and other decision-makers? All sociologists must face these questions.

GLOSSARY

case study an intensive observational study, in which the researcher attempts to learn everything there is to know about a particular group, community, or incident.

control group in an experiment, the subjects who are not exposed to the independent variable, giving the experimenter a basis for comparison with subjects who are exposed to it.

cross-sectional research a quick way to study long-term changes by studying people in different phases of change all at the same point in time. This research method can be misleading.

dependent variable a quality or factor that the researcher believes is affected by one or more independent variables.

experiment a research method that exposes subjects to a specially designed situation. By systematically recording subjects' reactions, the researcher can assess the effects of several different variables.

experimental group in an experiment, the subjects who are exposed to the independent variables and observed for changes in behavior.

ex post facto research a form of research in which variables that could not be measured at the time of an event can be analyzed after the fact.

hypothesis a proposition about how two or more factors or variables are related to one another.

independent variable a quality or factor that the researcher believes to affect one or more dependent variables.

interview a face-to-face discussion, which may be more or less structured, between a researcher and a subject.

longitudinal research studies that use the same sample over time.

mean statistical average calculated by dividing the sum of a series of figures by the number of items in the series.

median the number that falls in the middle of a series of figures.

mode the figure that occurs most often in a group of data.

participant observation a method in which researchers join and participate in the groups they plan to study in an effort to gain firsthand knowledge of a way of life.

population in a research study, all the people an investigator wants to learn about.

random sample a sample that gives every member of the population being studied an equal chance of being selected. In this way, experimenter bias is eliminated.

reliability the degree to which a study yields the same results when repeated by the original researcher or by other scientists.

sample a limited number of people selected from the population being studied.

social indicators statistics that provide a measure of the quality of life in a society.

stratified random sample a sample that reflects the proportions of different groups in the population being studied.

survey a set of questions administered to groups of people in order to learn how they think, feel, or act. Good surveys use random samples and pretested questions to ensure high reliability and validity.

theory a comprehensive explanation of apparent relationships between or underlying principles of certain observed phenomena.

validity the degree to which a scientific study measures what it attempts to measure.

variable an attitude, behavior pattern, or condition that is subject to change.

REFERENCES

Stanislav Andreski, *Social Sciences as Sorcery.* New York: St. Martin's, 1973.

Solomon E. Asch, "Opinions and Social Pressure." *Scientific American,* vol. 193 (November 1950): 408.

Bernard Barber, *Science and Social Order.* New York: Collier, 1962.

Raymond A. Bauer, *Social Indicators.* Cambridge, Mass.: MIT Press, 1966.

Howard S. Becker, "Whose Side Are We On?" *Journal of Social Problems,* vol. 14 (Winter 1967): 239–247.

Hadley Cantril, *The Psychology of Social Movements.* New York: Wiley, 1963.

Émile Durkheim, *Suicide: A Study of Sociology* (1897), trans. John A. Spaulding and G. Simpson. New York: Free Press, 1951.

Kai Erikson, *Everything in Its Path.* New York: Simon & Schuster, 1977.

Amitai Etzioni, "Policy Research." *American Sociologist,* vol. 16 (1971): 8–12.

James Fennessey, "Some Probabilities and Possibilities in Related Research." *Social Science Research,* vol. 1 (December 1972): 359–383.

Herbert J. Gans, *The Urban Villagers.* New York: Free Press, 1962.

William J. Goode and Paul K. Hatte, *Methods in Social Research.* New York: McGraw-Hill, 1952.

Alvin W. Gouldner, "Anti-minotaur: A Myth of a Value-free Sociology." *Journal of Social Problems,* vol. 9 (1962): 199–213.

Bernard Hennessy, *Public Opinion,* 2nd ed. North Scituate, Mass.: Duxbury, 1971.

Irving Louis Horowitz, "The Life and Death of Project Camelot." *Transaction,* vol. 3 (November–December 1965): 3–7.

Thomas Ford Hoult, *Dictionary of Modern Sociology.* Totowa, N.J.: Littlefield, Adams, 1969.

J. Stillson Judah, *Hare Krishna and the Counterculture.* New York: Wiley, 1974.

Thomas S. Kuhn, *The Structure of Scientific Revolutions,* 2nd ed. Chicago: University of Chicago Press, 1962.

Sanford Labovitz and Robert Hagedorn, *Introduction to Social Research.* New York: McGraw-Hill, 1971.

Elliot Liebow, *Tally's Corner.* Boston: Little, Brown, 1967.

Robert S. Lynd, *Knowledge for What?* Princeton, N.J.: Princeton University Press, 1939.

————, *Middletown in Transition: A Study in Cultural Conflicts.* New York: Harcourt Brace, 1937.

———— and Helen M. Lynd, *Middletown.* New York: Harcourt Brace, 1929.

Keith Melville, "A Measure of Contentment." *The Sciences,* vol. 13 (December 1973): 12–15.

Robert K. Merton, *Social Theory and Social Structure.* New York: Free Press, 1957.

William Michelson, "The Reconciliation of 'Subjective' and 'Objective' Data on Physical Environment in the Community." Sixty-eighth Annual Meeting of ASA, August 27–30, 1973.

Stanley Milgram, "Some Conditions of Obedience and Disobedience to Authority." *Human Relations,* vol. 18 (1965): 57–76.

————, *Obedience to Authority: An Experimental View.* New York: Harper & Row, 1973.

Kewal Motwani, *A Critique of Empiricism in Sociology.* New York: Allied, 1967.

Gunnar Myrdal, "How Scientific Are the Social Sciences?" *Bulletin of Atomic Scientists,* vol. 29 (January 1973): 31–37.

————, *Objectivity in Social Research.* New York: Pantheon, 1969.

T. M. Newcomb, *Personality and Social Change.* New York: Holt, Rinehart and Winston, 1943.

————, "Persistence and Regression of Changed Attitudes: Long-range Studies." *Journal of Social Issues,* vol. 19 (1963): 3–14.

George Ritzer, *Issues, Debates and Controversies: An Introduction to Sociology.* Boston: Allyn & Bacon, 1972.

F. J. Roethlisberger and William Dickson, *Management and the Worker.* Cambridge, Mass.: Harvard University Press, 1939.

Clifford R. Shaw, *Jack-Roller: A Delinquent Boy's Own Story.* Chicago: University of Chicago Press, 1966.

Julian L. Simon, *Basic Research Methods in Social Science.* New York: Random House, 1969.

Gideon Sjoberg, ed., *Ethics, Politics, and Social Research.* Cambridge, Mass.: Schenkman, 1967.

C. P. Snow, *The Search.* New York: Scribner's, 1958.

Herbert Spencer, *The Study of Society.* New York: Appleton, 1877.

Samuel A. Stouffer, *Communities, Conformity and Civil Liberties.* New York: Doubleday, 1955.

Eugene Webb et al., *Unobtrusive Measures: Nonreactive Research in the Social Sciences.* Chicago: Rand McNally, 1966.

William Foote Whyte, *Street Corner Society: The Social Structure of an Italian Slum,* rev. ed. Chicago: University of Chicago Press, 1955.

Philip G. Zimbardo, "Pathology of Imprisonment." *Society,* vol. 9 (April 1972): 4–8.

FOR FURTHER STUDY

Understanding Science. Although most beginning students will not want to pursue the details of different methods, some may be interested in the basic questions of how we know that something is true, and how we go about explaining the way things are. In *The Conduct of Inquiry* (San Francisco: Chandler, 1964), Abraham Kaplan explores these fundamental problems of science in a clear and intelligent way. One serious alternative to the usual approach to these questions is to be found in *Discovery of Grounded Theory: Strategies for Qualitative Research* (Chicago: Aldine, 1967) by Barney Glaser and Anselm Strauss, two sociologists who use mainly participant observation for their research. Stephen Cole's *The Sociological Method,* 2nd ed. (Chicago: Rand McNally, 1976) is a good example of how one may apply the scientific method to the analysis of human behavior.

Doing Sociology. Formulating a good sociological problem worthy of one's efforts is not an easy task, as Robert K. Merton explains with great clarity in his essay, "Notes on Problem-finding in Sociology," in Robert K. Merton, Leonard Broom, and Leonard S. Cottrell, Jr., eds., *Sociology Today: Problems and Prospects* (New York: Basic Books, 1959). Fourteen sociologists write about their actual research experiences, including false starts and wrong turns, in *Sociologists at Work: Essays on the Craft of Social Research* (New York: Basic Books, 1964), edited by Phillip E. Hammond. An excellent guide for carrying out participant observation is provided by *Issues in Participant Observation: A Text and Reader* (Reading, Mass.: Addison-Wesley, 1969), edited by George J. McCall and J. L. Simmons. One fine example of this approach, discussed in the next chapter, is *Tally's Corner* (Boston: Little, Brown, 1967) by Elliot Liebow, who discusses his experiences as a participant observer in an urban ghetto. An excellent step-by-step guide for doing survey research is provided by Charles H. Backstrom and Gerald D. Hursh's *Survey Research* (Evanston, Ill.: Northwestern University Press, 1963).

Ethics in Sociology.   The uses and abuses of sociology are not only interesting in themselves but are becoming increasingly important as the social sciences gain influence in shaping social policy. One of the clearest and most thoughtful books on this subject is by Robert Lynd, with the appropriate title *Knowledge for What?* (Princeton, N.J.: Princeton University Press, 1969). *The Use and Abuse of Social Science:* (New Brunswick, N.J.: Transaction, 1972), edited by Irving L. Horowitz, discusses the ethical problems of sociological research. An actual case is described by Professor Horowitz in *The Rise and Fall of Project Camelot: Studies in the Relationship Between Social Science and Practical Politics* (Cambridge, Mass.: MIT Press, 1967). Another fine volume containing case studies that highlight this problem is *Ethics, Politics, and Social Research* (Cambridge, Mass.: Schenkman, 1967), edited by Gideon Sjoberg. A number of essays have been written on the influence of public policy on sociological research, on the internal structure of the sociological community, and on the values of the investigators. These have been collected in *The Sociology of Sociology,* edited by Larry T. Reynolds and Janice Reynolds (New York: McKay, 1970).

CHAPTER 3

Social Structure

Nobel-prize-winning author Alexander Solzhenitsyn has described a vast system of prison camps—"a country within a country"—that existed in Russia under Stalin. Although most of the Russian people didn't know this system existed, to those in the camps its structure was all too clear. Everyone had a position—ordinary prisoner, gang boss, clerk, or guard. And each had a particular role to fill: the "special prisoner" got the privileged job of mopping the floor (rather than working outside in subzero weather in meager clothing); the guard locked people up for getting out of bed late. Not only individuals but groups, too, had a function in the system. The group to which a locked-up prisoner belonged couldn't save him by speaking out, but they supported him in the only way they could—by keeping his breakfast for him. Individuals and groups in turn were both part of a larger institution—the secret prison system.

While it is easy to perceive the structure of a distant and self-contained society such as the prison-camp system, the fact is that every society has structures. *Social structure* refers to the orderly, patterned ways individuals or groups of people re-

late to each other in a society or in one of its parts. One familiar example is the university: every year a group of seniors leaves and a new class of freshmen enters; some faculty members are replaced; a few new classes are added to the curriculum. Yet despite changes in personnel and policy, some things remain unchanged. Faculty members still design their courses and assign work to students; students still carry out their teachers' assignments and take exams. The ways in which individual faculty members and students perform their roles vary, but the *general patterns* are much the same and fit together into an overall structure we call a college. Although the structure itself remains invisible, it silently shapes our actions. Thus, analyzing the form and influence of social structure gives sociology a distinctive power in understanding human affairs.

In this chapter we will examine the levels of social structure; the components of social structure, including statuses, roles, groups, and institutions; the patterns of social relationships; and the impact of social structure on our everyday lives. We begin in Washington, D.C., on Tally's corner.

LEVELS OF SOCIAL STRUCTURE

A pickup truck drives slowly down the street. The truck stops as it comes abreast of a man sitting on a cast-iron porch and the white driver calls out, asking if the man wants a day's work. The man shakes his head and the truck moves on up the block, stopping again whenever idling men come within calling distance of the driver. At the Carry-out corner, five men debate the question briefly and shake their heads no to the truck. The truck turns the corner and repeats the same performance up the next street. In the distance, one can see one man, then another, climb into the back of the truck and sit down. In starts and stops, the truck finally disappears.

What is it we have witnessed here? A labor scavenger rebuffed by his would-be prey? Lazy, irresponsible men turning down an honest day's pay for an honest day's work? . . .

Let us look again at the driver of the truck. He has been able to recruit only two or three men from each twenty or fifty he contacts. To him, it is clear that the others simply do not choose to work. Singly or in groups, belly-empty or belly-full, sullen or gregarious, drunk or sober, they confirm what he has read, heard and knows from his own experience: these men wouldn't take a job if it were handed to them on a platter. (Liebow, 1967: 29–30)

Why are these men hanging around on street corners? And why are many others like them hanging around on corners in urban ghettos across the country?

Sociologists answer these questions in two ways. One is by examining the *micro-level* of social structure—that is, the pattern of personal interactions that characterizes everyday life. This would mean investigating in-terpersonal relationships between these men on the street corners to learn how they see themselves and relate to others in face-to-face situations, how they balance their values and aspirations with their experiences.

The second approach is to focus on the *macro-level* of social structure—that is, the large social patterns that shape an entire society. These patterns are beyond any one person's control, yet they play a powerful role in shaping our lives. For example, the hierarchy of jobs and rewards, national patterns of prejudice and discrimination, and the stereotypes concerning appropriate behavior for each sex are macro-forces that strongly influence the lives not only of street-corner men but of all of us.

The Micro-level

From all appearances the truck driver who feels the street-corner men "wouldn't take a job if it were handed to them on a platter" is correct. But appearances can be misleading, as Elliot Liebow demonstrates in *Tally's Corner* (1967).[1] In fact, most of the men who refused the driver's offer already have jobs. Sweets, for example, works nights in office buildings, hotels, and other public places, "cleaning up middle-class trash"; Tally, a laborer, has the day off because bad weather stopped construction where he was working. Irregular hours and irregular jobs such as these are the rule in the ghetto. Other men on the street refused work because they were disabled. (Accidents occur more often on construction sites and in factories where

---

[1]   Elliot Liebow spent over a year as a participant observer on the streets of a ghetto in Washington, D.C., only blocks from the Capitol. During this time he came to know the two dozen or so men who frequented a neighborhood carry-out shop that was a popular social center.

Social forces, not laziness, explain why these men and many others spend their days on urban street corners. The hierarchy of jobs and rewards and national patterns of racial discrimination are two such forces. (Leo Stashin / Rapho / Photo Researchers)

unskilled laborers work than in offices.) Some of the men are drawing nearly as much or more money from unemployment compensation than they could earn as laborers. A few are working quite hard at illegal activities—"buying and selling sex, liquor, narcotics, stolen goods, or anything else that turns up" (33). And Tonk is on the corner because he's afraid that if he goes to work his wife will disgrace him by taking the opportunity to be unfaithful.

Actually, only a handful of the men linger-

ing on the street fit the truck driver's image of them: Arthur has no intention of looking for a job; Leroy is playing pinball instead of reporting to work; last week Sea Cat quit a job without giving notice; and over the weekend Richard drank away his entire paycheck. Why aren't these men out looking for work or working? Many people think that the poor don't want to work, that somehow they have never absorbed the work ethic.

The street-corner man, many believe, lives from moment to moment, indulging his whims "with no thought for the costs, the consequences, the future" (64). Working regularly, saving, accepting responsibility for a wife and children, and planning for the future are supposedly alien to him. He doesn't care about being respectable; in fact, he makes fun of those who are. He lives in a world of gambling, liquor, and drugs, fancy cars and clothes (when he can get them), "fancy women," fast talk and fast money. Liebow rejects this. He argues that to understand why these men have the attitudes they do and why they fail to look for work or why they hold the kinds of jobs they do, we have to look beyond the street corner to the macro-level of social structure.

The Macro-level

Moving back from the close-up view, Liebow analyzes the position of Tally and his neighbors in the American economic system, and shows that this position shapes not only their jobs but also their feelings about themselves. Our economic system is competitive and profit-oriented. And poverty is profitable— for those on top. The fact that some people live in poverty enables others to live in luxury. The poor do society's dirty work (such as scrubbing floors); free the well-off from menial tasks; provide a market for substandard services and goods (such as day-old bread); and create jobs for others (such as social workers) (Gans, 1973). Tally and his cohorts perform these functions.

Typical jobs available to these men include those of unskilled laborer, janitor, dishwasher, elevator operator, bus*boy,* and delivery *boy.* Not one of these occupations pays enough to enable a man to support a family. Not one has any future. "The busboy or dishwasher who works hard becomes, simply, a hardworking busboy or dishwasher. Neither hard work nor perseverance can conceivably carry the janitor to a sit-down job in the office building he cleans up. . . . [T]he job . . . is a dead end" (63). More important, none of these jobs offers any prestige.

Neither the streetcorner man who performs these jobs nor the society which requires him to perform them assesses the job as one "worth doing and worth doing well." Both employee and employer are contemptuous of the job. The employee shows his contempt by his reluctance to accept it or to keep it, the employer by paying less than is required to support a family. Nor does the low-wage job offer prestige, respect, interesting work, opportunity for learning or advancement, or any other compensation. (58)

There are several reasons why Tally and the other men Liebow observed find themselves in unstable and unrewarding jobs. Most obviously, they lack the education or training that would qualify them for better jobs. More subtly, they lack the contacts in the business world that middle-class people establish while they are growing up. Being black, Tally and his neighbors have been victims through the years of *institutionalized racism,* a social phenomenon wherein habits of discrimination become fixed into the social structure. Thus, without being "prejudiced," institutions merely by functioning in certain established ways continue to discriminate. American society, for example, is structured so that blacks and members of other minority groups have trouble getting into the lucrative trade unions. Because school budgets usually are linked to the tax base of the surrounding neighborhood, the educational opportunities of ghetto children are often limited, with poor education leading to poor jobs, and so on. In recent years things have begun to change and opportunities are opening up. Yet racial prejudice, manifest in many ways, still sets distinct boundaries around the opportunities available to Tally and his friends.

In summary, an analysis of only the micro-level of social structure—the way a group of men and women conduct their lives on a day-to-day basis—does not explain poverty and unemployment. The larger aspects of social structure—including the hierarchy of jobs and rewards, the educational system, and a pattern of racial discrimination—must all be taken into account.

COMPONENTS OF SOCIAL STRUCTURE

How are the men on Tally's corner drawn into the social structure? The best way to explain how social structure works is to break it down into its component parts. At the micro-level of organization, individual behavior is patterned by *statuses* and *roles*. This sets the stage for the formation of small and large, formal and informal *groups*. Groups in turn link the micro-level of social structure to the macro-level, where we find such *institutions* as the economic system, the political system, and the family. In this way, expectations about how this or that person will behave are transformed into relatively stable and orderly patterns of life that provide social structure.

Status

Ordinarily we use the word "status" to mean prestige. However, sociologists use the term somewhat differently. In sociology, *status* refers to a position in the social structure—any position, high or low—that determines where a person fits into the society and how he or she is expected to relate to other people. For example, at the time of Liebow's study, Tally was a thirty-one-year-old black man, a school dropout (who could neither read nor write), a construction worker, and an estranged husband and father. All of these statuses affected Tally's life. People

would have related to him differently if he had been fifteen instead of thirty-one, a concert pianist rather than a laborer. As this example illustrates, each individual occupies a number of statuses at any given time. Tally was not only a construction worker but also a husband, father, and so forth.

Ascribed and Achieved Status Within a social structure, some statuses are ascribed and some achieved. An *ascribed status* is one that is assigned to a person at birth or at different stages in the life cycle—for example, being male or female, a Mexican American, a Rockefeller, a teen-ager, a senior citizen. To be born a Rockefeller in our society guarantees one a high social position; even today to be born poor and black ensures that one will face obstacles and restrictions. An *achieved status* is a position a person attains largely through personal effort. Physician, politician, artist, or teacher, the town drunk or the Boston Strangler—each of these is an achieved status. (Once a person attains a deviant status, he or she may be marked for life. We will discuss this problem in chapter 9.) Thus Tally's age, race, and sex are ascribed statuses; the level of education he has reached, his occupation, and his marital position are achieved statuses.

Master Status When one of a person's statuses largely determines his or her social identity, it is called a *master status*. This may be an occupation that takes up most of a person's time and uses up most of his or her energy (such as the presidency), or it may be a position of particular symbolic significance. For children in our society, age and sex are the most salient statuses; for example, a child will identify herself as a seven-year-old girl, or himself as a five-year-old boy. For adults, occupation is usually most significant. However, a master status may also be

Body builders display a unique form of achieved status. (Abigail Heyman/Magnum)

an ascribed status such as handicapped, ugly, or beautiful. Today a great effort is being made by groups such as women and the handicapped—people with an ascribed master status—to weaken the dominance of this status over their lives.

Roles

Every status carries with it socially prescribed *roles*—that is, expected behavior patterns, personality traits, obligations, and privileges. We learn how to perform a role by observing and interacting with others who know the ropes—a process known as socialization (see chapter 5). From the age of five, for example, American children are taught the role behaviors that are associated with their status as

students. Raising hands, doing homework, and studying for tests are all aspects of the role that students are expected to play.

One status typically involves several roles. For example, a medical student fills one role in relation to his or her teachers and others in relation to fellow students, to nurses, and to patients. Similarly, an actor or actress relates somewhat differently to each of the following: other actors, the director, stagehands, the audience, the press. The complex of roles that accrues to a single status is a *role set* (Merton, 1968: 422–423).

Roles and the Individual   Roles provide the social setting and script for individuals to express themselves in their own distinctive way. No two people who occupy the same status perform their roles identically. Individuals differ in what they believe is expected of them. For example, one professor may feel her role is to challenge students, to make them doubt and question established

figure 3:1   Statuses and roles

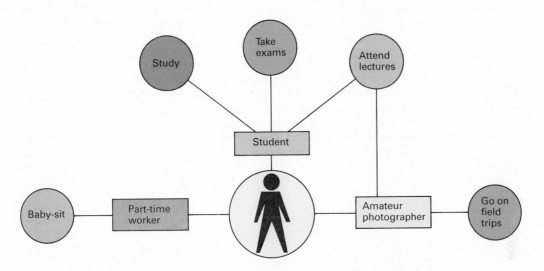

*Of the many statuses each of us has (to this person's list we would surely add "son"
or "daughter" and possibly "brother" and "sister"), one may be a* master status, *as
"student" is here. Each status has at least one role attached to it, and some have
several. Sometimes a role—like "attend lectures"—will draw on more than one status.*

theories; another may see his role as dis-
pensing knowledge. Whether or not individuals live up to their roles is still another
question. A father who feels his role is to be a
pal to his children may actually relate to
them in a formal and rather distant way; a
policeman who thinks his role is to enforce
the law may actually break the law in his
eagerness to apprehend criminals.

Although playing a new social role at first
may involve acting and pretense, people
tend to *become* what they play at being:

One feels more ardent by kissing, more humble by kneeling and more angry by shaking
one's fist. That is, the kiss not only expresses
ardor but manufactures it. Roles carry with
them both certain actions and emotions and

attitudes that belong to these actions. The
professor putting on an act that pretends to
wisdom comes to feel wise. The preacher
finds himself believing what he preaches.
The soldier discovers martial stirrings in his
breast as he puts on his uniform. In each
case, while the emotion or attitude may have
been present before the role was taken on,
the latter inevitably strengthens what was
there before. In many instances there is
every reason to suppose that nothing at all
anteceded the playing of the role in the
actor's consciousness, in other words, one
becomes wise by being appointed a professor, believing by engaging in activities that
presuppose belief, and ready for battle by
marching in formation. (Berger, 1963: 96)

Roles, then, transform both the action and
the actor.

IN THE NEWS

Social Roles and Growing Old

"One out of three people dies within a year of entering a nursing home." Certainly this figure reflects the poor health of people who enter nursing homes, but it also may tell us something else. Sociologists have found that, for many elderly people, just living in a nursing home is an important factor in precipitating illness and death. And Dr. Zachary T. Bloomgarden has documented this finding.

Dr. Bloomgarden is concerned about the way the social structure of nursing homes affects a person's self-image. Attesting to the powerful way in which social structure shapes the roles we assume, Bloomgarden writes:

[A person] does not merely live in the nursing home—he becomes a patient, profoundly dependent on the medical personnel around him. Gradually and progressively, there is a somaticization of many psychic troubles until he becomes entirely submerged in this role.

Becoming a patient doesn't just happen—the social structure of the nursing home helps the transformation along. As in other institutional settings, residents are expected to leave their individuality behind and conform to the rules of the establishment. And the rules are deadening.

Most of [the] residents must share a small bedroom with others, must eat their mass-prepared high-carbohydrate meals in a large, linoleum-floored dining room with others, watch television in a communal room with others. From bedroom to dining room to television, several times daily, the residents spend their lives.

In this setting, nurses do most of the supervising, a practice that encourages residents to become "patients" whether or not they are sick. Medication is distributed four times a day, and physicians regularly provide "orders" for medicine, diet, and activities.

Dr. Bloomgarden contends that for many elderly people, this "medical structure" is not necessary. Nursing homes aren't really designed to help old people, but to serve those who wish to put the elderly away. Instead, Dr. Bloomgarden thinks we should adapt the larger social structure to meet the needs of the elderly. With a little help, most old people could live in their own communities—alone, with relatives, or with each other. Social centers, accessible transportation, and home visits by medical personnel could turn the role of many old people from being patients back to being individuals who happen to be old.

SOURCE: Zachary T. Bloomgarden, M.D., "The End of the Line," *The New York Times*, January 18, 1977, p. 31.

Role Strain and Role Conflict ''People generally want to do what they are supposed to do'' (Goode, 1960: 485), but it isn't always easy or even possible. Sometimes people experience difficulty in meeting the demands of a role. *Role strain* may occur when conflicting demands are built into a role. For example, one part of a foreman's role is to maintain good relations with the people working under him. At the same time, he is expected to act as a representative of management, enforcing decisions from above. Robert Merton suggests that such conflicting patterns of expectation, which he calls *structural ambi-*

valence, are built into many roles in our society (1976).

Role strain also occurs when people can't meet the demands of their role. For example, Liebow found that most street-corner men had married early, with high hopes of becoming good husbands and fathers. But most failed—at first financially, then emotionally. ''Where the father lives with his own children, his occasional touch or other tender gesture is dwarfed by his unmet obligations. No matter how much he does, it is not enough'' (87).

Role conflict occurs in situations in which the fulfillment of one role automatically results in the violation of another. A classic example is the situation of the black policeman. As a black man he knows the system is weighted against black people; as a policeman, however, he is acting as an agent of

The black policeman may struggle with role conflict. As a black, he is aware of society's inequities; as a policeman, he enforces its laws. (Jeffrey Foxx / Woodfin Camp & Associates)

that very same system.[2] Soldiers may experience intense role conflict. Young men who have been brought up to feel that killing is wrong are expected to fire guns and drop bombs. Many try to resolve this conflict by not using their weapons. Writing after World War II, S. L. A. Marshall estimated that even when being fired upon, only 25 percent of the soldiers fired back (1947: 50).

Systematic expectations about how people should behave—organized in terms of statuses and roles—are the foundation of social structure. The strain and conflict people experience as they play their parts suggest how powerful status and role are.

Groups

A *group* is a set of people with interrelated statuses and roles—for example, a family or the men who hang out on Tally's corner. Members of a family interact as husband/wife, parent/child, brother/sister. The men on Tally's corner support one another's efforts to fill the roles of breadwinner, father, husband, lover, and friend; some actually call each other "brother."

Groups may be based on similar roles (for example, students getting together for a party or tenants organizing for a rent strike) or on complementary ones (for example, a surgical team or an opera company). Some are small (a doctor and a patient, with their complementary roles, constitute a group); some large (thousands of young and old people who try to block construction of a nu-

clear power plant and are arrested together). Groups may be formal (for example, a board of directors whose members have specific titles and responsibilities and meet regularly) or informal. Liebow writes of the street-corner group:

> There is nothing to join, no obligations. . . . [E]ach man comes here mainly because he knows others will be here, too. He comes to eat and drink, to enjoy easy talk, to learn what has been going on, to horse around, to look at women and banter with them, to see "what's happening" and to pass the time. (22–23)

Whatever their composition, *all* groups are organized in terms of related statuses and role relationships. Even an informal group like that on Tally's corner has structure. There are leaders and followers, troublemakers and peacemakers, and so on. Tally was a leader, a status that derived in part from the belief that he had once been a professional fighter. "When asked to affirm or deny his status, Tally merely grins, assumes the classic stance of the boxer, and invites the questioner to 'come on.' No one does." (23) It was largely thanks to Tally that Liebow—an inquisitive white middle-class social scientist—was able to penetrate the street-corner man's world. If Tally thought he was okay, others figured he must be okay.

In a sense, groups are the link between the micro- and macro-levels of social structure. Take, for example, the family. Each man on Tally's corner wanted to maintain a family, a reflection of what he saw happening in the larger society—at the macro-level. Yet at the micro-level, all these men had problems doing this. Liebow suggests that many families fell apart because the men were unable to cope with the fact that they couldn't fill the traditional male family role as breadwinner.

---

2   Peter L. Berger notes that one response to role conflict is increased zealousness. "The theologian who doubts his faith will pray more and increase his church attendance, the businessman beset by qualms about his rat-race activities starts going to the office on Sundays too, and the terrorist who suffers from nightmares volunteers for nocturnal executions" (1963: 97).

Walking out was easier than facing evidence of failure day after day.

In sum, the family tradition permeates all levels of society. As a specific *group*, the family plays a central role in an *individual's* life (at the micro-level of social structure). As a vital cluster of statuses and roles—what sociologists call an *institution*—the family plays a central role in the life of *society* (at the macro-level of social structure).

Institutions

Much of social life and social structure centers around certain basic needs that confront all societies: (1) organizing activities so that people obtain the goods and services they need to live, while the society maintains a balanced relationship with the environment; (2) protecting people from external threats, such as military invasions, and from internal threats, such as crime; (3) replacing people who die or migrate; (4) transmitting a knowledge of statuses and roles, and the skills needed to fill them, to new members (children and immigrants); and (5) motivating people to perform their roles by giving meaning and purpose to social activities. These needs must be met in order to ensure the survival of both the people who make up a society and their way of life.

Sociologists use the term *institution* to describe the widely accepted relatively stable clusters of roles and statuses, and the meanings attached to them, that develop around these basic needs of a society. An example we have already cited is the *family*. The family is one solution to the problems of regulating sexual activity, replenishing the population, assigning responsibility for children and for initiating them into the ways of a society, defining relationships between people in a community (the kinship system), and settling economic questions (such as inheritance). Religion and law sanctify and protect the family. It is one of the "natural" facts of life that people take for granted. To be sure, not everyone in our society grows up in the traditional nuclear family (a mother, a father, and their children all living together), and not everyone grows up wanting to marry and have children of their own. Still, the traditional idea of the family carries considerable moral weight.

The more technologically advanced a society, the more interdependent its members. Few American families or communities produce everything they need for themselves. *Economic* institutions deal with the problems of producing and distributing goods and services. When these institutions fail to provide some people—Tally and his neighbors, for example—with the basic goods, people turn to other—often illegal—means. As the problem grows, the macro-structure develops new institutions, such as welfare, to meet pressing needs.

Our economy requires people with varied technical and managerial skills, flexibility, and a competitive spirit. *Educational* institutions solve the problem of training people for new and future roles in this system.

Institutions, however, actually perform two kinds of functions: those they are openly and specifically set up to perform *(manifest functions)* and those that are unintended by-products *(latent functions)*. Often, latent functions also go unrecognized. Our educational system, for example, has the manifest function of providing opportunity for education to all. But because of differences between schools and selective admissions policies, it has had the latent function of perpetuating discrimination and actually denying some people access to certain opportunities. Our economic system is also based on the manifest function of equal opportunity for all—we speak of "free enterprise" and "open competition." But in fact the capitalist system serves to maintain many gross inequalities.

Thus, the family, the economic, political, and educational systems, religions, and other institutions channel human experience and activity in much the same way as instincts channel animal behavior (Berger, 1963: 87). They are the basic social structures, the ideas and customs around which life in a society is organized. This is not to say that institutions are always rigid and unyielding. To be useful, they must be flexible. For example, an increasing number of people remain single for some or all of their adult lives; this relatively new development will undoubtedly produce changes in our institution of the family and will also lead to new institutions to meet the needs the family once served.

THE PATTERNS OF SOCIAL RELATIONSHIPS

Like statuses, roles, groups, and institutions, regular, predictable patterns of interaction are a part of social structure. Liebow found that the men on Tally's corner devote much of their time to "the construction and maintenance of personal relationships" (161). When Liebow describes the kinds of behavior that make or break friendships, certain patterns emerge. For example, close friends (men who "go for brothers") automatically help one another out financially. Failure to assist a "brother" who is in trouble, to share a windfall, or to repay a loan brings friendship to an end. Similar patterns are found in other groups and in other settings.

In the following pages we will discuss four basic patterns of social relationships, patterns common to individuals as well as to whole societies: *exchange, cooperation, conflict,* and *competition.*

Exchange

Gratitude is like mercantile credit. The latter is the mainstay of business; and we repay our debts, not because it is right that we should discharge them, but in order more easily to borrow again.
—La Rochefoucauld, The Maxims

When a person or a group assists another for the express purpose of obtaining some material or emotional reward—and both parties understand this—they are engaged in an exchange, not in exploitation. *Social exchange* is based on the principle of reciprocity—that people should both help and not injure people who have helped them. By extension, giving a gift or performing a service creates an obligation on the part of the recipient—one that may be repaid in kind or simply with gratitude. As Georg Simmel wrote, "Often the subtlest as well as the firmest bonds among [people] develop from this feeling" (in Nisbet, 1977: 58).

Exchange is the most basic form of social interaction. Social exchange can be observed everywhere once we are sensitized . . . to it, not only in market relations but also in friendship and even in love . . . as well as in many social relations between these extremes in intimacy. Neighbors exchange favors; children, toys; colleagues, assistance; acquaintances, courtesies; politicians, concessions; discussants, ideas; housewives, recipes. (Blau, 1964: 88)

These reciprocal transactions serve the function of binding individuals and groups together with ongoing networks of mutual obligations and gratitude (Blau, 1975: 229).

Of course, social exchange is not always equal; love or respect may be one-sided. If one group in a society controls most of that society's resources, it may exercise unlimited power. Similarly, a person who extends assistance to someone who cannot reciprocate (but who does not refuse aid) places himself or herself in a superior position (Blau, in Nisbet, 1970: 66). But equal or unequal, exchange creates social bonds—between king and peasant, man and wife, the senator from Maine and the senator from Texas, officer and enlisted man, nation and nation. These links are crucial for the simple reason that many (if not most) of the things people need and value are scarce. And perhaps even more important, many are beyond the reach of individual effort.

Cooperation

Cooperation is one of several solutions to the problem of scarcity: people who recognize a common objective join forces to achieve their goal and share in the rewards. The scarcity of meat led East African tribes like the Ik to form a wide arc of up to a hundred people moving across the plains with nets attached to poles. From a position far out in front of the net arc, women and small children would begin beating the grass to force the game toward the trap. Men and boys would wait with spears and bows and arrows—some within the next arc, some behind to catch the animals that escaped. Each member of the hunt shared equally in the day's catch (Turnbull, 1972: 24–25). Net hunts were a tradition among the Ik; they had hunted this way for as long as anyone could remember.

Nisbet distinguishes this kind of *traditional cooperation*, which carries the weight of custom, from directed, contractual, and sponta-

neous cooperation. By *directed cooperation* he means the kind of joint activity people in authority force on those beneath them (1977: 61). For example, an officer commands enlisted men to take a hill; a teacher insists that children share the baseball diamond; the federal government directs American citizens to pay taxes. Deutsch (1949) directed cooperation when he divided a class of psychology students into five-member teams for a six-week course in problem-solving. He informed half the teams that individual grades would depend on what the *team* accomplished as a whole. Members of the other teams were graded for individual achievement, the more common practice in American education. Deutsch found that the students were more productive when they cooperated than when they competed with one another—at least on the tasks he assigned. But to generalize from this to the idea that cooperation is better than competition would be simplistic. We return to the question later in the chapter (in the section on conflict).

Contractual cooperation is a limited preplanned agreement to join forces in specific ways, for a specific period of time, to achieve specific goals. Unlike traditional cooperation, which is woven into a group's entire way of life, contractual cooperation is strictly utilitarian. According to exchange theorists, *all* cooperation is implicitly contractual, because the questions underlying all cooperation are "What am I getting out of this? What am I giving?"

Of course, the oldest, most natural, and most widespread form of cooperation is neither directed nor preplanned: it arises *spontaneously* when a situation seems to call for joint action. For example, when one of the street-corner men was arrested for manslaughter, Tally and his friends collected bail money, visited the man's family, and recruited Liebow to help prepare the defense.

Traditional cooperation. For generations, the men and women of this Ghana village have gathered to haul in their fishing nets from the Atlantic. This custom originated because the weight of the nets requires a community effort. The villagers divide their catch among themselves and sell any surplus. (Peter Buckley)

This is not to say that crises always inspire cooperation. During the 1960s, for example, the Ik were forced off their game-rich plains (which were designated national parks and reserves) into the arid mountains above the plains. Threatened with starvation, they became extremely individualistic. No one shared food any more; children were left to forage on their own; people literally took food from the mouths of the old and the sick. In his somewhat controversial analysis of the "sociology of survival" among the Ik, Colin Turnbull suggests that cooperation, brotherhood, and even love can exist only where people enjoy at least a minimal standard of living. Whether or not this is true, spontaneous cooperation does depend on three basic things: the norms of reciprocity, the capacity to imagine oneself in another's role, and a shared definition of the situation (Nisbet, 1977: 60–61).

Conflict

Rather than joining forces to share in the rewards, people in *conflict* "struggle with one another for some commonly prized object or value" (Nisbet, 1977). Conflict may be physical, as in wars, or symbolic, as when combatants fight with threats and insults.

Promoting Cooperation Common sense suggests that conflict is inherently disruptive and should be avoided at almost any cost. This is a logical assumption, to be sure, but a sociologically inaccurate one. In fact, one of the primary functions of conflict is the stimulation of *cooperation* within opposing groups (Simmel, 1955). Struggles with outsiders invariably bring insiders closer together. As Georg Simmel notes, France owes its unity to the wars with England; Spain, to its battles against Moorish invaders; this country, originally to the War of Independence (101). Similarly, students begin to think and act as a group when the administration suddenly raises tuition; families tend to draw together when one member is attacked.

Defining Problems and Values Conflict may also define problems and revitalize norms and values that have fallen into disuse. For example, in the early 1950s relatively few white Americans were conscious of the extent to which blacks were being denied even the most basic civil rights: "[T]he shock of recognition, the jolt of conscience, occurred only when the Negroes, through by-and-large nonviolent action in the South and through increasingly violent demonstrations in the North, brought the problem forcibly to the attention of white public opinion and the white power structure" (Coser, 1967: 86). Similarly, singer Anita Bryant *helped* gay activists by campaigning *against* a bill to guarantee homosexuals equal rights. The bill was defeated, but the struggle called attention to the fact that homosexuals are denied civil liberties—something most people didn't know.

On a more personal level, conflicts may revitalize relationships. "It has been said . . . that intimate relations, such as love and friendship, need occasional quarrels in order to be reminded of the happiness by the contrast with the discord they suffered; or in order to interrupt the closeness of the relationship—which, after all, has something coercive and enclosing for the individual—by an alienation which removes this pressure" (Simmel, 1955: 110–111).

Promoting Social Change Conflict may also act as a catalyst for needed social change. After the race riots of the late 1960s, both the McCone Commission appointed in California and the Kerner Commission appointed by President Johnson described the riots as more or less justified expressions of black outrage, and went on to recommend a "reordering of priorities" in America. Many sociologists believe that conflict is inherent in modern society, with its increasing bureaucracies on one hand, and its emphasis on individual freedom and personal indulgence

Tension in Northern Ireland has run high because of both physical conflict—bombings and bloodshed—and symbolic conflict, such as this young girl's taunting of British soldiers. (Jim Anderson/Woodfin Camp & Associates)

on the other (Lipset, 1975: 195). In this sense, conflict can serve as a safety valve, bringing issues to the surface before they explode on a massive scale.

Resolving Conflict How are conflicts ended? They end when one party defeats the other; when both calculate that the costs of continued antagonism exceed the possible benefits of success and agree to a compromise; or when a sudden change in circumstances gives the two parties reason to forget their differences and join ranks. Surrender is always based on the assumption that the victors will discontinue their attacks (Turner, 1969: 823). For example, even though the Catholics in Northern Ireland live in constant danger, they have not surrendered because they don't believe the government would (or could) bring exploitation of the Catholic community to a halt.

Achieving a compromise is an even more complex process. By definition, conflicts involve irreconcilable goals and/or groups. As Ralph Turner writes, "agreement on [the] issues does not erase the injury that each has done to the other in the course of the conflict" (823). In essence, compromise depends on the willingness of each antagonist to act as if "the other did not fully mean what he said, that his threats were not really meant to be carried out, and that his insults did not express his most enduring feelings and views" (824). There is an element of irrationality in compromise and accommodation, "something like a denial of what existed a moment before" (Simmel, 1955: 117). Soon after World War II, for example, the people we had been killing—the Germans and the Japanese—became our close allies.

Surrender or compromise is unnecessary if by chance or design two irreconcilable parties suddenly find they have an enemy or a problem in common. Muzafer Sherif (1958) demonstrated this in a famous experiment at a summer camp for boys. He divided the campers into two teams, and by setting up competitions in which only the winning team got prizes, by tricking one team into thinking the other had spoiled its food, and by employing other means, he created an extremely volatile situation. (In fact, Sherif and his colleagues found it difficult to prevent as real a war as ten-year-olds are capable of waging!) However, when the camp's water supply was cut off and when a group of boys from another camp were brought in for a day of sports, the teams forgot how much they hated each other and joined forces. Larger goals may thus turn enemies into collaborators, who then direct their energies against a new enemy.

Competition

Competition is one special form of conflict, although it differs from conflict in the extent to which all parties agree to the "rules of the game" and confine their conflict within

America's oil companies engage in competition through advertising. Their sales pitches vary, but only within narrow limits. (Adam Woolfitt/Woodfin Camp & Associates)

them. In other words, competition, like co-operation, has its rules and limits. For example, oil companies compete for customers by advertising how many services their local stations provide. But, with rare exceptions, they avoid so-called price wars; when one company raises prices, the others also raise them. Only when environmentalist groups began to exert pressure did the oil and auto companies begin to run ads about their concern for ecology—and, again, they acted together. In other words, they compete only within certain well-defined narrow limits. If this agreement breaks down, other more basic forms of conflict arise.

As the examples in this section indicate, patterns of exchange, cooperation, conflict, and competition structure relationships at both the micro- and macro-levels of society.

THE IMPACT OF SOCIAL STRUCTURE: PRISONERS OF SOCIETY?

Discussions of social structure inevitably lead to questions about free will. Patterns of social interaction are regular and predictable, as if the way we behave were predetermined. Institutions shape our aspirations; groups have an existence of their own that is relatively independent of individual members; people tend to become what they play at being. Are we, then, prisoners of society?

To deny the impact of social structure on our attitudes and behavior would be foolish. At the same time, however, people *feel* that they are free, that they make decisions, that they are the authors of their own lives. Is this feeling of self-determination a delusion? So-

ciologists would agree that to some extent it is. People tend to lose their awareness of the impact of social pressure (if they were ever conscious of it at all). There is much debate within sociology as to how free we really are. In this section we present that debate.

Society in People: The Structuralist Position

Peter L. Berger has few qualms about unmasking our most cherished beliefs, including our ideas about love.

> In Western countries, and especially in America, it is assumed that men and women marry because they are in love. There is a broadly based popular mythology about the character of love as a violent, irresistible emotion that strikes where it will, a mystery that is the goal of most young people and often of the not-so-young as well. As soon as one investigates, however, which people actually marry each other, one finds that the lightning-shaft of Cupid seems to be guided rather strongly within very definite channels of class, income, education, racial and religious background. (1963: 35)

In other words, a person usually "falls in love" with someone who is sociologically and culturally similar to him or her. When people don't, the relationship is less likely to endure. Berger goes on to describe the courtship ritual as a couple proceeds from movie dates to meeting the family, from holding hands to "what they originally planned to save for afterwards," from planning evenings to planning a future, and to the decisive scene in the car, under the moon, when one or the other proposes. He writes, "Neither of them have invented this game or any part of it. They have only decided that it is with each other, rather than with other possible partners, that they will play it." Otherwise the rituals and stages of courtship are socially structured. While there is room for innovation and improvisation, "too much ad-libbing is likely to risk the success of the whole operation" (86).

Is Berger just being cynical? No, he is expressing a point of view shared by many students of human behavior. One of America's great social theorists, Robert K. Merton, has explained how people acquire the attitudes of society and come to think of them as their own (1938). In Merton's view, conforming and nonconforming behavior alike are the results of social pressure. Individuals construct a self-image by comparing themselves to members of groups they belong to, to members of groups with which they want to be affiliated, and to those people they want to disassociate themselves from. In the process, individuals assimilate rules and values that direct their behavior. For example, American society teaches that it is right and legitimate—perhaps even mandatory—to seek love and marriage by courting a member of the opposite sex in prescribed ways. The feelings of free choice, spontaneity, and passion that accompany the chase only indicate the extent to which these goals and means have been internalized.

> Society . . . is not only something "out there," . . . but it is also something "in here," part of our innermost being. . . . Society not only controls our movements, but shapes our identity, our thoughts and our emotions. The structures of society become the structures of our own consciousness. (Berger, 1963: 121)

It seems, then, that to call ourselves prisoners of society is misleading. While we may feel restricted by social pressures at any one time, it is only within their confines that we can take shape as individuals.

Innovation and Improvisation: The Symbolic Interactionist Position

The idea that people simply act out the roles society has prescribed, without thinking or reflecting, strikes many sociologists as an exaggeration. In attempting to describe and fix the patterns of everyday life, we may slip into the mistaken notion that the patterns create the behavior—an idea roughly equivalent to saying the game plays the person. Moreover, critics of the structuralist view argue that it underplays the ambiguity in face-to-face encounters. Only on the stage is the outcome of a meeting of two people predetermined.

Symbolic interactionists stress the situational character of social behavior. They argue that people don't interact according to a blueprint of social instructions. Instead, when two people meet, they constantly evaluate each other's behavior and react accordingly (Blumer, 1966). The symbolic interactionists see social interaction as a very delicate and complex process. Even the statement "I love you" may evoke several reactions.

> If a man says "I love you," to a woman, she may wonder whether he means it, whether he loves her only, how much he loves her, whether he will love her next week or next year, or whether this love only means that he wants her to love him. She may even wonder whether his love includes respect and care, or whether his love is merely physical. "I love you" is surely an ambiguous message. . . . Everything depends on who says what to

FACE-SAVING AT THE SINGLES DANCE

If ever there was a situation ripe for the observation of managing impressions, it is the singles dance. In big cities, where young men and women often find it hard to meet one another, attending a dance for singles seems like a good idea. Where else can one find so many potential dates all in one place? But there is a major drawback. Like "lonely-hearts clubs," singles dances have a decided stigma attached to them.

The stigma probably comes from the public nature of singles dances: you have to be invited to a party, but *anyone* can go to a singles dance. Just being at a singles dance is embarrassing, because it says to everyone there, including you, that you are needy. And what makes things even worse is the fear of being rejected by other people at the dance. Faced with this double threat to self-esteem, what do people do?

Sociologist Bernard Berk set out to answer this question. Like Erving Goffman, Berk was interested in the way people present themselves. More specifically, he wondered how they cope with "social rejection or discrediting" (530). The setting for Berk's participant-observation research was the singles dance. With a group of assistants, he attended over seventy dances and subsequently interviewed patrons about their experiences. What he discovered strongly supports Goffman's theories about managing impressions and saving face.

The organizers of a singles dance seem to know that their event bears a stigma, which they try to minimize by managing the setting. Holding the dance in a well-known hotel or club and appealing to "young professionals" or to "alumni" lends "prestige by association" (532). Dim lighting not only creates a romantic setting but also masks defects and permits illusions.

These organizational strategies may help bring people to a singles dance, but once they are there, presentation of self is still a major task. Berk discovered a variety of techniques people use to improve their social image. Arriving with a friend indicates popularity in spite of being at the dance. And arriving late implies that one is "not too eager." An aloof or "holier-than-thou" posture broadcasts a similar message. By seeming to be above it all, "the aloof player remains independent and protected." Berk describes two such women:

whom and how he says it, and human beings scan each other's utterances to see what lies behind the words. (Henry, 1965: 191)

W. I. Thomas, like Max Weber before him, pointed to the subjective quality of reality when he said, "If men define situations as real, they are real in their consequences" (1928: 572). Thomas meant that reality, like beauty, lies in the eye of the beholder. By itself, a symbol or a gesture—for example, hitting one's hands together—is meaningless. It becomes significant only when people invest it with meaning—in this case, it becomes applause. When two people meet, they bring their own meanings, their own

> Two attractive females were observed sitting talking with each other, and in the course of an hour over forty males attempted to approach them with requests to dance. They did not acknowledge any male's request with even a turn of the head. (536)

If you reject all advances, you can't be rejected in turn.

The most frequently used defense against the singles-dance stigma is the "sad tale," or "why I am here" story. People often claim that they have been "dragged there" by a friend, or that they have only recently gone through the break-up of a romance; these alibis are designed to set the person apart from others at the dance.

People want to feel apart at a singles dance, but only on their own terms—no one wants to feel rejected by others. Everyone at a dance faces this problem, and everyone has a way of coping with it. Some people tend to move around a lot so that they don't seem "wiltingly available." Complaints like "I'm tired tonight" or "I've worked very hard today" are good excuses for not having found someone at the dance (540). A man who asks a woman to dance and is refused might soften his rejection by calling the woman a loser; more likely, he will retreat to a far corner of the room. A common defense is to downgrade those who downgrade you, and friends often help each other with this face-saving strategy:

> A male asked a female for a dance and was refused. He left the situation immediately and returned to his friend for solace. Together they re-interpreted the situation, his friend telling him that "she was a dog," who if seen in the light would never have merited a request to dance. (540)

Through studies like this, Goffman, Berk, and other sociologists identify the ways people structure their everyday life and their relations with others. At the close of his paper, Berk raises an interesting question. Is the management of impressions strictly for individuals, or, he wonders, do whole societies use such tactics to bolster national images "and problems similar to loss of face"? (543)

SOURCE: Bernard Berk, "Face-saving at the Singles Dance," *Social Problems*, vol. 24, no. 5 (June 1977), pp. 530–544.

definition of the situation. Social order exists to the extent that people approach one another with similar understandings and expectations and share a common definition of the situation.

"The Presentation of Self" For sociologist Erving Goffman, many of our daily activities can be explained as our self-conscious effort to manage (that is, control) the impression we make on others. Like actors following scripts written by society's expectations, we behave in part to keep up appearances and save face, in part to get what we want from situations. Examples of this abound. College athletes wear their team practice shirts to classes and social gatherings; girls living in dormitories often don't come to the phone until after they've been paged several times, so that everyone within earshot knows they received a call (Waller, in Goffman, 1959: 4). Practically no one answers the phone on the first ring—it would appear overanxious. At the beginning of a semester students generally try to impress professors with how bright they are. After exams, during the grading period, they may try to appear harried or even sick to evoke sympathy. In short, the way people act in public has an ''onstage'' quality to it.

At the beginning of a romance, when both the man and the woman are a little unsure about how the other person perceives him or her, impressions become very important. In the following passage from Sylvia Plath's *The Bell Jar* (1971), Esther Greenwood, a shy, studious freshman, receives her first kiss from Buddy Willard. Ecstatic, she strives to appear nonchalant.

> I stood pretending to admire the lights behind the chemistry lab while Buddy got a good footing on the rough soil. While he kissed me I kept my eyes open and tried to memorize the spacing of the house lights so I would never forget them.
>
> Finally, Buddy stepped back . . . ''Wow, it makes me feel terrific to kiss you.''
>
> I modestly didn't say anything.
>
> ''I guess you go out with a lot of boys,'' Buddy said then.
>
> ''Well, I guess I do.'' I thought I must have gone out with a different boy every week for a year.
>
> ''Well, I have to study a lot.''
>
> ''So do I,'' I put in hastily. ''I have to keep my scholarship after all.''
>
> ''Still, I think I could manage to see you every third weekend.''
>
> ''That's nice.'' I was almost fainting and dying to get back to college and tell everybody. (67–68)

In most cases, the person or persons one tries to impress—the audience—will act as if the performance were real. There is an unspoken pact: you support my act and I will support yours. Violations by actor or audience lead to hostility and ostracism. Occasionally a person will try to create a negative or antisocial, eccentric impression, but more often people strive to live up to socially accepted ideals of behavior.

Discovering the Rules: Ethnomethodology

Some sociologists have become interested in uncovering the implicit understandings and expectations that guide social behavior. *Ethnomethodology* refers to the study of the rules that underlie ordinary daily activities. (*Ethnos* is the Greek word for ''people.'')

A leading ethnomethodologist, Harold Garfinkel, has devised a technique for uncovering these rules. His method is to discover the rules by *breaking* them (1967). For example, Garfinkel asked some of his students to pretend to be guests when they returned home to their families. For fifteen minutes to an hour, the students maintained the polite distance of guests—speaking only when spoken to, using formal modes of address (''Mr. Jones'' instead of ''Dad''), avoiding personal exchanges. Two of the forty-nine families thought the students were joking; one ignored the student's behavior; the remainder were upset and annoyed. ''Family members demanded explanations: What's the matter? What's gotten into you? Did you get fired? Are you sick? What are you being so superior about? Why are you mad? Are you out of your mind or just being stupid?'' (47–48). In one way or another, the students' families tried to restore ''normal'' relations and in the process made explicit certain hitherto-unstated assumptions about family life.

In other experiments, Garfinkel's students "made trouble" by attempting to bargain for items in a store (something Americans generally do not do); by breaking the rules in a game of tic-tac-toe (erasing the opponent's first move); and by closing in during a conversation so that they were nose to nose with the unsuspecting subject. Each of these violations of the rules of interaction produced confusion and often anxiety (in the students as well as in the ''victim'') and anger.

Garfinkel and the symbolic interactionists, then, affirm that there are patterns in the ways people relate to one another, but they emphasize that ''the established patterns of group life do not carry on *by themselves*'' (Blumer, in Wallace, 1969: 237, italics added). Patterns exist because people bring similar meanings to situations, because they repeat behavior that has ''worked'' in the past, and because it is generally easier to live within norms than to violate them. Social guidelines and habits free people from the impossible task of reviewing alternatives and making decisions every minute of their lives. The micro-, interpersonal structure of society emerges from this process of defining situations, interpreting the acts of others, and adjusting one's own behavior accordingly.

In summary, sociologists disagree about the impact of social structure on individuals. Structuralists maintain that we are shaped by forces beyond our control, and often beyond our conscious awareness. Symbolic interactionists emphasize our ability to use shared ideas about statuses and roles to define and create each situation, each relationship, anew. Goffman goes a step farther. He describes us as self-conscious actors following social scripts, each with a ''backstage'' or ''off-camera'' self we selectively reveal to other people.

SUMMARY

Social structure refers to the pattern of collective rules, roles, and activities in a society. There are several ways to examine this. One is to study the *micro-level* of social structure, the pattern of personal interactions that characterizes everyday life. Another is to look at the *macro-level*, the large social patterns that shape an entire society. In our examination of *Tally's Corner,* we concluded that while an analysis of the micro-level of street-corner society showed us how Tally and his friends related to one another and how they viewed themselves and their positions in life, it did not really explain their poverty and unemployment. For that kind of analysis and understanding, the larger aspects of social structure—including the educational system, the hierarchy of jobs and rewards, and racial discrimination—must all be taken into account.

We can also understand how social structure works by breaking it down into its component parts: individual statuses and roles, groups, and institutions. Status and roles are the translation of social structure at the personal level. A *status* is a position in the social structure that determines where a person fits in the community and how he or she should relate to other people. A status may be *ascribed* (assigned at birth or at different stages in the life cycle), or *achieved* (attained through personal effort). People generally have several statuses; common statuses include a person's age, race, and sex, and his or her educational, occupational, and marital positions. When one status determines a person's social identity, it is called a *master status*. Status affects an individual's actions and how others act toward him or her because of the roles associated with each status. Social *roles* are the expected behavior patterns, obligations, and privileges that are linked to a status. *Role strain* may occur when conflicting demands are built into one role. *Role conflict* may occur when meeting the demands of one role automatically results in the violation of another.

Individuals in societies gather into *groups*, sets of people with interrelated statuses and roles. Groups may be large or small, formal or informal; they may be based on similar or on complementary roles. All groups have a structure of some kind based on related statuses and role relationships. At the micro-level of society, an individual family is a group.

At the macro-level, all societies have certain basic needs: distributing goods and services among the people; protecting people from external and internal threats; replacing people who die or migrate; transmitting knowledge to new members; and motivating people to perform their roles. We use the term *institution* to describe the widely accepted relatively stable clusters of roles and statuses and the meanings attached to them that develop to meet these basic needs. At the macro-level of social structure, the family is an institution. Institutions perform both *manifest* (intended) and *latent* (unintended) functions.

Relationships between individuals, groups, institutions, and whole societies follow four basic patterns: exchange, cooperation, conflict, and competition. *Exchange* occurs when a person, group, or society assists another for the express purpose of obtaining some material or emotional reward. Another basic social relationship is *cooperation*, in which those who recognize a common objective join forces to achieve their goal and share rewards. *Conflict* results when two parties conclude that the only way to obtain a contested goal is to struggle with each other, either physically or symbolically. Conflict may prove destructive, but it may also increase cohesion within a group, revitalize norms, or provoke needed change. Enemies may even become collaborators when they encounter a common enemy. *Competition* is a special form of conflict in which parties agree to rules and limits within which they confine their struggle.

The existence of a social structure raises the question of how free people in a society actually are. Peter Berger and Robert Merton, expressing the *structuralist* point of view, insist that people's actions are largely the result of social pressure. We construct a self-image by comparing ourselves to members of groups we belong to, to members of groups with which we would like to be affiliated, and to people we want to dissociate ourselves from. *Symbolic interactionists* stress the situational character of social behavior, and view social interaction as a delicate process in which people constantly evaluate one another's behavior and react accordingly. Social order exists to the extent that people approach one another with similar understandings and expectations and share a common definition of the situation.

Symbolic interactionists focus on the way people behave in the course of everyday life; they try to discover the shared pattern of expectations that guide social behavior. For Erving Goffman, many of our daily activities can be explained as our self-conscious effort to manage (that is, control) the impressions we make on others. Sociologists such as Harold Garfinkel seek explanations through *ethnomethodology,* the study of the rules that underlie ordinary activities. Garfinkel tries to uncover these rules by breaking them and observing how people react when the behavior patterns they have come to take for granted are disrupted.

Sociologists, it is clear, disagree about the impact of social structure on individuals. Structuralists think we are shaped by forces beyond our control. Symbolic interactionists emphasize our ability to use a foundation of shared ideas to define and create each situation and relationship anew. Ethnomethodologists such as Goffman think we are self-conscious actors following social scripts, who selectively reveal ourselves to others.

GLOSSARY

achieved status a social position that a person attains through personal effort.

ascribed status a social position that is assigned to a person at birth or at different stages in the life cycle.

competition a special form of conflict in which parties agree to rules and limits within which they confine their struggle.

conflict a social relationship in which two parties struggle with each other, physically or symbolically, to obtain a contested goal.

contractual cooperation a limited preplanned agreement to join forces in specific ways for a specific period of time in order to achieve specific goals.

cooperation a social relationship in which people recognize a common objective and join forces to achieve their goal and share in the rewards.

directed cooperation the kind of joint activity people in authority impose on those beneath them.

ethnomethodology the study of the rules that underlie everyday behavior.

exchange a social relationship in which a person or a group assists another for the express purpose of obtaining some material or symbolic reward.

group a set of people with interrelated statuses and roles.

institutions the widely accepted relatively stable clusters of norms and values that develop around the basic needs of a society.

institutionalized racism habits of discrimination that persist in social patterns of housing, education, and employment regardless of conscious or deliberate prejudice.

latent functions the unintentional and often unnoticed functions of an institution or social pattern.

macro-level of social structure the large social patterns that shape an entire society, including the hierarchy of jobs and rewards, patterns of prejudice and discrimination, and the educational system.

manifest functions the apparent and deliberate goals or roles of an institution or social pattern.

master status the status that largely determines an individual's social identity.

micro-level of social structure the pattern of personal interactions that defines everyday life.

role expected behavior patterns, obligations, and privileges that are attached to a particular status.

role conflict a term used to describe situations where fulfillment of one role automatically results in the violation of another.

role set the complex of roles that accrues to a single status.

role strain personal difficulties that result when conflicting demands are built into a role.

social structure the pattern of collective rules, roles, and activities in a society.

spontaneous cooperation an unplanned, immediate group response to a specific situation.

status a position in the social structure that determines where a person fits in the community and how he or she is expected to relate to others and to act.

traditional cooperation a community effort to reach a shared goal that has become an integral part of a society's customs, conventions, or mores.

REFERENCES

Peter L. Berger, *Invitation to Sociology*. New York: Doubleday, 1963.

Peter Blau, *Exchange and Power in Social Life*. New York: Wiley, 1964.

———, "Parameters of Social Structure," in Peter M. Blau, ed., *Approaches to the Study of Social Structure*. New York: Free Press, 1975.

Herbert Blumer, "Sociological Implications of the Thought of George Herbert Mead." *American Journal of Sociology*, vol. 17 (March 1966): 534–548. (Also in Wallace, 1969.)

Lewis A. Coser, *Continuities in the Study of Social Conflict*. New York: Free Press, 1967.

Morton Deutsch, "An Experimental Study of the Effects of Cooperation and Competition upon Group Process." *Human Relations*; vol. 2 (1949): 199–231.

Herbert Gans, *More Equality*. New York: Pantheon, 1973.

Harold Garfinkel, *Studies in Ethnomethodology*. Englewood Cliffs, N.J.: Prentice-Hall, 1967.

Erving Goffman, *Presentation of the Self in Everyday Life*. New York: Doubleday, 1959.

William J. Goode, "A Theory of Role Strain." *American Sociological Review*, vol. 25 (1960): 483–496.

Jules Henry, *Pathways to Madness*. New York: Random House, 1965.

Elliot Liebow, *Tally's Corner: A Study of Negro Streetcorner Men*. Boston: Little, Brown, 1967.

Seymour Martin Lipset, "Social Structure and Social Change," in Peter M. Blau, ed., *Approaches to the Study of Social Structure*. New York: Free Press, 1975.

S. L. A. Marshall, *Man Against Fire*. New York: Morrow, 1947.

Robert Merton, "Social Structure and Anomie." *American Sociological Review*, vol. 3 (1938): 672–682. (Also in Wallace, 1969.)

———, *Social Theory and Social Structure*. New York: Free Press, 1968.

———, *Sociological Ambivalence and Other Essays*. New York: Free Press, 1976.

Robert Nisbet and Robert G. Perrin, *The Social Bond*, 2nd ed., New York: Knopf, 1977.

Sylvia Plath, *The Bell Jar*. New York: Harper & Row, 1971.

Muzafer Sherif, "Superordinate Goals in the Reduction of Intergroup Conflict." *American Journal of Sociology*, vol. 63 (1958): 349–356.

Georg Simmel, *Conflict and the Web of Group Affiliations*. New York: Free Press, 1955.

William I. Thomas and Dorothy Swaine Thomas, *The Child in America*. New York: Knopf, 1928.

Colin M. Turnbull, *The Mountain People*. New York: Simon & Schuster, 1972.

Ralph H. Turner, "The Public Perception of Protest." *American Sociological Review*, vol. 34 (1969): 815–830.

Walter A. Wallace, ed., *Sociological Theory: An Introduction*. Chicago: Aldine, 1969.

FOR FURTHER STUDY

The Micro-Structure. Sociologists have done considerable work on the micro-structure of social life, and since this level of analysis involves people directly interacting with one another, the perspective of the authors tends to be symbolic interaction. One of the greatest modern observers of micro-structure is Erving Goffman. See his books *The Presentation of Self in Everyday Life* (Garden City, N.Y.: Doubleday, 1959) and *Behavior in Public Places* (New York: Free Press, 1963). Another book discussing social interaction is *Queuing and Waiting: Studies in the Social Organization of Access and Delay* (Chicago: University of Chicago Press, 1975) by Barry Schwartz. Finally, two collections of essays on micro-structure are *Sociology and Everyday Life,* edited by Marcello Truzzi (Englewood Cliffs, N.J.: Prentice-Hall, 1968), and *People and Places: Sociology of the Familiar,* edited by Arnold Birenbaum and Edward Sagarin (New York: Praeger, 1973).

The Macro-Structure. On the macro-level, social scientists have identified several different types of societies, and some think that the comparative analysis of whole societies is the only way to develop powerful concepts in sociology. Research restricted to one country, they argue, is bound to mistake particular features for general patterns. Gerhard Lenski has recently analyzed differences between societies ranging from hunting and gathering groups to industrial social structures in *Human Societies* (New York: McGraw-Hill, 1974). Another analysis of macro-structures is Robert Marsh's *Comparative Sociology* (New York: Harcourt Brace, 1967).

The Conflict Perspective. Two important explanations of conflict theory are Lewis A. Coser's *The Functions of Social Conflict* (New York: Free Press, 1956) and Ralf Dahréndorf's *Class and Class Conflict in Industrial Society* (Stanford, Calif.: Stanford University Press, 1959). Some vivid examples of conflict theory in action include Eliot Freidson's *Professional Dominance* (New York: Atherton, 1970), which describes the conflict between doctors and the people they are supposed to serve, and *Being Mentally Ill* (Chicago: Aldine, 1966), Thomas Scheff's account of the conflict between society's effort to protect itself from insane people and the individual rights of people accused of being insane. An excellent example of combining functional analysis with a conflict perspective is Herbert J. Gans's "The Positive Functions of Poverty," *American Journal of Sociology,* vol. 78 (September 1972): 275–289.

Becoming a Social Being

Chapter 3 raises the question of whether we are prisoners of society unconsciously acting out the roles we are given. In part two you will learn, in more detail, why we raise that possibility. Humans are by nature social beings. Becoming a member of a particular society and a participant in a particular culture are a basic part of growing up human.

All of a people's shared customs, beliefs, values, and artifacts are integrated into what we call a culture, the subject of chapter 4. By examining our own culture and comparing it to others we see that we are both the creators and the creations of our way of life.

Chapter 5, on socialization, shows how culture and biology interact to transform a helpless infant into a functioning adult with the physical, mental, and social skills needed to survive, and with both a psychological and a social identity.

The close examination of the acquisition of sex roles in our culture in chapter 6 is a particularly good illustration of the process of socialization. You will see how traditional myths and stereotypes create a sense of inevitability or naturalness about certain social patterns—and also how these stereotypes can be broken.

CHAPTER 4

Culture

I remember watching a blind student several years ago walking across the campus of a large state university. He guided himself with a cane, tapping it against the sidewalk which ran in spokes from building to building. Although he knew the campus well, on that particular occasion he became distracted for a moment and wandered onto the grass, where he immediately lost all sense of direction. His movements became disorganized as he searched hopelessly for a bit of cement. He became visibly panicked until a passing student came up and led him back to the appropriate path. Once again he was able to continue toward his class unaided.

I was struck by the similarity of this situation to the situation of all human beings who have grown up within a particular social milieu. Out of an incredibly large number of possible ways of living successfully, all normal human beings operate within a narrow framework of convention. This convention is sometimes limiting and perhaps to certain individuals unsatisfying, but it provides a set of rules which act as guidelines for action. One learns not

only how to behave in given situations, but also what to expect from others. In addition, one learns how to act in relation to the physical environment [that is, how to survive]. Man's existence as a social animal is conditioned by these rules, and no human group could operate without them. These conventions, which are in many ways so similar to the sidewalk for the blind student, make up what the [social scientist] calls culture. Culture is essentially a set of rules for behaving in a human way (Alland, 1973: 227–228).

All of the customs, beliefs, values, knowledge, and skills that guide a people's behavior along shared paths are part of their culture (Linton, 1947: 10). We begin this chapter with a brief discussion of the evolution of culture. We then focus on the seen and unseen elements of culture and consider reasons for the almost infinite variety of cultural expressions. We will see how culture is the complement to social structure, giving style and texture to the statuses, roles, groups, and institutions in society. We will also discuss the ways in which culture works for and against people, with particular attention to American culture.

THE EVOLUTION OF CULTURE

The story of human evolution is also the story of cultural evolution. Dependence on language and learning, tools and traditions sets humans apart. Whereas other species adapt to their environments biologically, humans adapt to their environments culturally. For example, animals that live in the Arctic have evolved thick coats of fur to protect them from the cold; humans who live in the Arctic *make* thick coats. The adults of other species of animals are biologically prewired to engage in courtship behavior when females are in heat. A man and a woman engage in elaborate, culturally shaped courtship rituals designed to capture each other's heart and labor as well as each other's reproductive services.

In effect, then, culture plays the role in human behavior that instincts play in other animals' behavior. When you use the words "my instincts tell me," you usually mean "my cultural upbringing tells me." The advantage of culture over instincts is flexibility. Within limits, humans can change their traditional patterns of behavior.

How did we come to be "cultural animals"? The first signs of a distinctively human way of life appear in the archaeological record of some 2 to 3 million years ago, on the savannas of East Africa. But the essentials of culture were present 500,000 years ago. Already our ancestors had come to depend on tools to acquire and prepare food and to defend themselves. This suggests that they had a division of labor: very likely women specialized in gathering wild vegetables and fruits, men in hunting. This degree of cooperation in turn suggests that they may have been able to speak. Not only is language the primary means of creating and transmitting culture, but the capacity to produce and use language is one of the things that makes human beings unique. Whether 500,000 years ago our ancestors had begun to "tame" the world by creating myths to explain natural phenomena and rituals to control them is a matter of speculation. But eventually they would. (Jolly and Plog, 1976: 155)

It may seem as though the emergence of culture freed humans from the constraints of biological evolution. In reality, the two are interconnected. For example, early humans couldn't have made stone tools if they hadn't had five mobile fingers, good hand-to-eye coordination, and complex brains. In this instance, biological evolution made cultural development possible. Once humans began preparing food with stone tools and, later, fire, they no longer needed powerful teeth. Our teeth are smaller and softer than our ancestors' were. In this instance, cultural developments influenced biological evolution. Thus we are at once the producers and the products of culture.

THE ELEMENTS OF CULTURE

Culture can be divided into material aspects (the products of a people's arts and technology) and nonmaterial aspects (a people's customs, beliefs, values, and patterns of communication). In this chapter, we are focusing on nonmaterial culture.

Much of what we know about nonmaterial culture comes from field studies of people whose ways of life are different from our own. There are two basic reasons why studies of "exotic" ways of life interest sociologists. First, it is only by learning that other groups of people think and act differently that we realize how much of our own behavior is governed by cultural rules. Second, comparative studies reveal that although beliefs and practices vary widely, the forms culture takes are familiar. We can describe any human culture in terms of sets of norms and values.

Norms

In *Games People Play* (1964), Eric Berne describes the greeting ritual of the American:

"Hi!" (Hello, good morning.)
"Hi!" (Hello, good morning.)
"Warm enough forya?" (How are you?)
"Sure is. Looks like rain, though." (Fine. How are you?)
"Well, take cara yourself." (Okay.)
"I'll be seeing you."
"So long."
"So long." (37)

This brief exchange is conspicuously lacking in content. If you were to measure the success of the conversation in terms of the information conveyed, you would have to give it a flat zero. Nevertheless, both people involved leave the scene feeling quite satisfied. They have said no more and no less than the situation (a meeting of co-workers, neighbors, or acquaintances) required. Each behaved quite properly,[1] in accord with accepted social norms.

Norms are the guidelines people follow in their relations with one another; they are shared standards of desirable behavior. Not only do norms indicate what people should or should not do in a given situation, but norms also enable them to anticipate how others will interpret and respond to their words and actions. Norms vary from society

to society, from group to group within societies, and from situation to situation. Behavior that is the height of propriety in one society may be disgraceful in another. For example,

> Among the Ila-speaking peoples of Africa, girls are given houses of their own at harvest time where they may play at being man and wife with boys of their choice. It is said that among these people virginity does not exist beyond the age of ten. [In contrast] among the Tepoztlan Indians of Mexico, from the time of a girl's first menstruation, her life becomes "crabbed, cribbed, confined." No boy is to be spoken to or encouraged in the least way. To do so would be to court disgrace, to show oneself to be crazy or mad. (Ember and Ember, 1973: 318)

A generation ago in this country, virginity was highly prized; today, in marked contrast, virgins of twenty-two or twenty-three probably try to hide their inexperience, and may even wonder if something is wrong with them.

Some norms are situational—that is, they apply to specific categories of people in specific situations. We consider it appropriate for a person to pray to God in church, or to speak to people who have long since "gone to the other side" during a séance (even if we think the séance is phony). But a person who addresses God or invokes spirits during a dinner party or in a subway train will probably be considered insane. (See Goffman, 1959: 75–79, on occult involvement.)

Social norms govern our emotions and perceptions. For example, people are *supposed* to feel sad and act depressed when a member of their family dies. The jury in Camus's novel *The Stranger* condemns Meursault to death primarily because he went to a movie (even worse, a comedy) on the day his mother died—certain proof that

---

[1] Berne calls this type of ritual exchange *stroking*.

IN THE NEWS

Nine-to-What? Japanese Business Comes to America

In American businesses, the nine-to-five workday is sacrosanct. Non-executive employees who work longer hours expect to be paid for overtime, and a boss who consistently asks his secretary to stay late may soon find himself without one. For Japanese businessmen this is a striking contrast to what they are used to. In Japan, employees leave when they have finished the day's work, regardless of the hour. And for executives, a fourteen-hour day is routine.

As more and more Japanese companies set up branch offices in the United States, the differences between the two countries' business norms have become more obvious.

In Japan for example, businessmen seldom make definite appointments to see one another. When a visitor arrives, they take time.

The quantity of correspondence in the United States is another surprise. "Americans send too many letters," said Toshitaka Okazawa, a representative here for the Kirin Brewery. "It is like a contractual society. . . . In Japan, we trust each other." There is no need to put things in writing because a verbal commitment is enough. (1, 14)

The American custom of changing jobs several times during a career is also not the Japanese way.

Japanese spend their lives with a single company, and they are expected to be steady performers rather than super-stars. . . . flashy results are not encouraged. The policy of Sumitomo Shoji America, a trading company, is typical: "To look for speculative profit is, in no case, allowed." (14)

While Japanese executives in the United States continue to carry on business much as they would at home, their children are becoming Americanized. So when the families return to Japan (as all expect to do some day), it is the children who will face cultural barriers. Japanese executives are concerned about this. For one thing, the Japanese educational system is fiercely competitive, and a child who is not fluent in Japanese is at a disadvantage. For another, language and educational inadequacies can make it harder for young girls to find husbands. One Japanese businessman who has lived in the United States for eight years expressed deep concern for his children's future: "They are Americans," he said. "Someday they must make a home in a land they know nothing about."

SOURCE: Pamela G. Hollie, *The New York Times*, October 23, 1977, Section 3, pp. 1, 14.

he was ''inhuman'' (Henry, 1965: 15). Similarly, people are supposed to pay attention to certain things but not to others. For example, we consider it bad taste to gawk at a couple who are quarreling bitterly or to eavesdrop on an intimate conversation (particularly if the conversation is about the eavesdropper).

What is so interesting about social norms is how most people follow them automati-

The hand-shake is not a ''natural'' greeting, but is a social norm in most Western societies. In traditional Japan, bowing is the customary way of exchanging hellos. (Top, Barbara Alper/Stock, Boston. Bottom, René Burri/Magnum)

cally; alternatives never occur to them. This is particularly true of unspoken norms that seem self-evident, such as responding to a person who addresses you. People conform because it seems right; because to violate norms would damage their self-image (or "hurt their conscience"); and because they want approval and fear ridicule, ostracism, and in some cases, punishment.

Folkways and Mores Norms vary in intensity—that is, some are more important to people than others.

The term *folkways* refers to everyday habits and conventions people obey without giving much thought to the matter. For example, Americans eat three meals a day and call other food "snacks." We have cereal for breakfast but not for other meals; we save sweets for the end of a meal. Even though we could very easily begin dinner with cherry pie, we don't. Similarly, we expect people to cover their mouths when they yawn, to shake hands when introduced, to close zippers on pants or skirts, *not* to wear evening clothes to class. People who violate folkways may be labeled eccentrics or slobs, but as a rule they are tolerated.

In contrast, violations of mores provoke intense reactions. *Mores* are the norms people consider vital to their well-being and to their most cherished values. Examples are the prohibitions against incest, cannibalism, and child abuse. People who violate mores are considered unfit for decent company and may be ostracized, beaten, locked up in a prison or a mental hospital, exiled, or executed. (Most people would not condemn an individual who gave a child molester a severe beating.)

Laws In some cases, societies give norms the formal status of *law*. Punishments are fixed in advance and enforced by political authorities. Laws may formalize folkways (as traffic regulations do) or back up mores. In general, the laws that are most difficult to enforce are those that are not grounded in norms—for example, laws against gambling or the use of marijuana.

Values

The Tangu, a people who live in a remote part of New Guinea, play a game called *taketak*, which in many ways resembles bowling. The game is played with a top that has been fashioned from a dried fruit and with two groups of coconut stakes that are driven into the ground (more or less like bowling pins). The players divide into two teams. Members of the first team take turns throwing the top into the batch of stakes; every stake the top hits is removed. Then the second team steps to the line and tosses the top into their batch of stakes. The object of the game, surprisingly, is not to knock over as many stakes as possible. Rather, the game continues until both teams have removed the *same* number of stakes. Winning is completely irrelevant (Burridge, 1957: 88–89).

In a sense, games are practice for "real life"; they reflect the values of the culture in which they are played. *Values* are the general ideas people share about what is good or bad, right or wrong, desirable or undesirable. Unlike norms, the rules that govern behavior in actual relations with other people, values are broad, abstract concepts; indeed, they are the foundation for a whole way of life. The Tangu, for example, value equivalence: the idea of one individual or group winning and another losing bothers them, for they believe winning generates ill will. In fact, when Europeans brought soccer to the Tangu, they altered the rules so that the object of the game was for two teams to score

figure 4:1   Changes in student values, 1970–1976

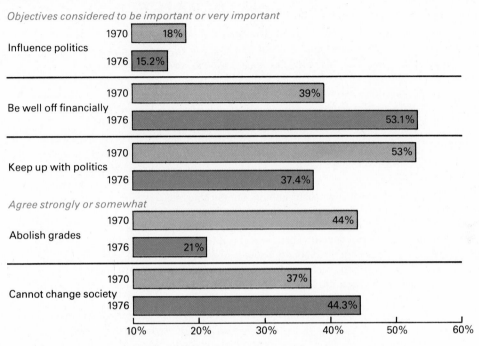

Objectives considered to be important or very important

Influence politics
- 1970: 18%
- 1976: 15.2%

Be well off financially
- 1970: 39%
- 1976: 53.1%

Keep up with politics
- 1970: 53%
- 1976: 37.4%

Agree strongly or somewhat

Abolish grades
- 1970: 44%
- 1976: 21%

Cannot change society
- 1970: 37%
- 1976: 44.3%

10% 20% 30% 40% 50% 60%

SOURCE: American Council on Education, *National Norms for Entering Freshmen, Fall 1970, ACE Research Reports*, pp. 42–43; and (with the University of California Graduate School of Education, Los Angeles) *The American Freshman: National Norms for Fall 1976*, pp. 55 and 60.

The concerns of college freshmen changed considerably between 1970 and 1976, as the influence of the counterculture values of the sixties waned. Students became less inclined to keep up with politics, as they felt less able to influence the political scene or to change society as a whole. The goal of financial success increased in importance, in part as a result of the recession and depressed job market of the 1970s.

the same number of goals. Sometimes their soccer games went on for days! American games, in contrast, are highly competitive; there are *always* winners and losers.

The Relation Between Norms and Values   Norms, then, derive from values, but there is no one-to-one correspondence: any given value can support several norms. Thus the American value of free enterprise can

allow for a variety of behaviors (norms), from the rampant cutthroat style of capitalism in the nineteenth century to government regulation and the social responsibility of business in the twentieth. We believed then and we believe now in free enterprise, but the rules governing behavior in the marketplace have varied over time. More than one value may also be operating in a given situation. If being honest also means being unkind to

THE RUSSIANS: ONE MAN'S VIEW

For three years, American journalist Hedrick Smith worked as *The New York Times* bureau chief in Moscow. He and his wife traveled extensively, visiting schools, farms, factories, and universities, and talking with people wherever they went. The result of Smith's years in the U.S.S.R. is a book—*The Russians*. In it, Smith describes his impressions of Russian life, mixing his own observations with the views of Russian citizens. What emerges is a picture of a culture in which, as in our own, ideals and reality don't always coincide.

Although economic egalitarianism is one of the major values of Soviet society, an elite group knows the value of *blat*—influence. Prominent political figures and those at the top of the Communist Party form a privileged class that is no secret from the rest of the country. Most people must wait in lines for two hours or more to buy poorly made, unstylish clothing, but the elite receives personal service and imported fashions. While most people live in cramped apartments, the elite enjoy several large homes. And though owning the humblest car is beyond the reach of the average factory worker, the privileged ride in chauffeured limousines. Russians seem to accept the disparity between the egalitarian ideal and the reality of an elite. As one young man told Smith, ''People don't want to change that part of the system, they want to beat it. . . . They don't say the system is wrong. They want exceptions made for them personally'' (52).

If the ideal of economic egalitarianism isn't always achieved, another Russian value, economic security, is more easily met. In a government-controlled economy, saving money is unnecessary, and people never worry about unemployment. This is quite different from the high value Americans place on free competition and noninterference by the government.

Russians also differ in the value they place on hard work. Whereas the ''work ethic'' still has a strong hold on Americans, Smith observed that ''sustained hard

another person, we are caught in a conflict of values. Telling a white lie in such a situation means choosing kindness over honesty.

Similar and more serious conflicts of values are bound to occur as we gain the ability to alter genes. The ability to modify unborn children's genes so that they grow up to be taller or darker or even smarter than their parents lies in the not very distant future. Scientists already have made genetic copies of carrots and frogs. This is done by *cloning*, a process that creates a duplicate organism from a single cell. What is there to prevent people from seeking immortality through one or more facsimiles of themselves? And if artificial wombs are perfected, will parents decide to reject their offspring on delivery if the child does not live up to their expectations? Tampering with life may go against our cultural grain, but self-improvement is very strongly favored. The conflict between the two could create serious dilemmas.

work is not a national characteristic [in the Soviet Union]" (222). Despite the mechanistic Soviet Economic Plan, the Russians themselves are not known for their efficiency. In fact, the Russian language has no word for efficiency.

Soviet culture also has little use for American-style rugged individualism, and Russians learn the value of conformity at an early age. As one Soviet author wrote: "The greatest offense a child can commit in kindergarten is to be different" (Leonid Vladimirov in Smith: 159). If a group of five-year-olds each makes a clay rabbit, every rabbit looks alike. In the upper grades, "the emphasis [is] on drill, drill, drill and straight memory work, often unchanged for generations" (165). The university curriculum also reflects the value of conformity over individual expression. Smith described it as "a system geared toward inculcating technical skills rather than being concerned with such liberal arts intangibles as learning to think or personal growth and self-expression" (191). In return for adherence to strict patterns, however, Soviet university graduates are guaranteed jobs in their chosen field.

This deemphasis on individuality differs sharply from the value Americans place on self-expression, but perhaps the greatest difference between these two peoples is in their attitudes toward authority and power. For centuries, Russians lived under the autocratic rule of the czars. Institutions designed to protect the individual from the power of the state simply did not exist. Where Americans are inclined to mistrust authority, Russians embrace it. As one Russian told Smith, "Under the czars we had an authoritarian state and now we have a totalitarian state, but it still comes from the roots of the Russian past" (250).

SOURCE: Hedrick Smith, *The Russians*, New York: Quadrangle, 1976.

Symbols

The study of the meanings people attach to the things they do and to the things they make is central to the study of culture, as our discussion of values indicated. These meanings may be stored in such *symbols* as the cross, the flag, or even the kiss.

A *symbol* is an object, gesture, sound, color, or design that represents something *other than itself*. For example, a circle is nothing more than a closed curve, all points of which are at an equal distance from a point at the center. But for the Oglala Sioux, the circle represents all that they know and feel and believe about the universe.

The Oglala believe the circle to be sacred because the great spirit caused everything in nature to be round except stone. Stone is the implement of destruction. The sun and the sky, the earth and the moon are round like a shield, though the sky is deep like a bowl. Everything that breathes is round like the stem of the plant. Since the great spirit has caused everything to be round mankind should look upon the circle as sacred, for it is the symbol of all things in nature except stone. . . .

For these reasons the Oglala make their *tipis* circular, their camp-circle circular, and sit in a circle at ceremonies. (Walker, 1968: 304)

Symbols are *arbitrary*—they do not necessarily look, sound, or otherwise resemble what they stand for. In some cultures, black is the color of mourning; in others, white or red suggests grief. These colors, like all symbols, derive their meanings from tradition and consensus, not from any qualities inherent in the colors themselves.

Symbols are *collective creations*—people in a society must agree on their meanings if they are to be understood. A gold band worn on the third finger of someone's left hand tells us that he or she is married *only* because in our culture it is a commonly recognized symbol for marriage. Of course, even though a wedding band is commonly understood to mean the wearer is married, the way the wearer and each of us interprets that condition has become quite flexible. For some, marriage means a lifelong partnership and absolute fidelity; for others, a greater measure of sexual and emotional freedom may be implied. Symbolic interactionists (see chapter 3) argue that the heart of social life is the sharing, the conflict, and the manipulation of symbols.

Because symbols are arbitrary, they are highly *flexible*: the meaning of words and gestures can and does change. For example, two fingers held in a V was once a rude gesture. When Churchill used it (palm forward) during World War II, it came to stand for victory; in the 1960s it was revived as a symbol for peace; this symbol in turn became a standard form of greeting among young people. Five years ago a man's opening a door for a woman or lighting her cigarette was a sign of respect; today these gestures often signal that a man doesn't accept women's liberation wholeheartedly.

Language

A *language* is a system of verbal and, in many cases, written symbols, with rules for putting them together. It is impossible to overestimate the importance of language in the development, elaboration, and transmission of culture. Language enables people to store meanings and experiences and to pass this heritage on to new generations. Through words, we are able to learn from the experiences of others and from events at which we were not present. In addition, language enables us to transcend the here and now, preserving the past and imagining the future; to communicate with others and formulate complex plans; to integrate different kinds of experiences; and to develop abstract ideas.

The study of different languages has yielded numerous insights into culture. For example, the number of words available to describe an object, event, or concept in a language indicates how important it is to a people. Arabs, for example, have hundreds of words to describe camels and camel trappings, and almost as many words to describe different kinds of horses. Similarly, Americans distinguish between sedans, station wagons, fastbacks, sports cars, convertibles, and compacts, suggesting the importance of automobiles in our culture. These words sensitize the individual Arab or American to subtle variations that a person from a different culture might not even notice.

Symbols, such as color, may be used to communicate emotion. Many Americans wear black to show grief for their dead. These New Guinea women paint themselves white. (Top, Wayne Miller / Magnum. Bottom, Philip Jones Griffiths / Magnum)

Language and Reality: The Sapir-Whorf Hypothesis Cross-cultural studies led Edward Sapir and his student Benjamin Lee Whorf to theorize that language doesn't simply reflect culture, but actually *shapes* our thoughts and directs our interpretation of the world.

> [L]anguage is not merely a reproducing instrument for voicing ideas but rather is itself the shaper of ideas, the program and guide for the individual's mental activity, for his analysis of impressions, for his synthesis of

his mental stock in trade. . . . (Whorf, in Carroll, 1956: 212–213)

Whorf based this theory on his comparison of the way Hopi Indians and English-speaking people think and speak about time. The Hopi language has no tenses and no nouns for times, days, or years. As a result, the Hopi tend to think in terms of continuous movement, of becoming. In contrast, the English language provides numerous ways of marking or counting time, as if hours and days were things or objects. The necessity to choose one of several tenses makes English-speaking people acutely conscious of the passing of time. English-speaking people think in terms of linear progressions.

In our own culture, the line is so basic, that we take it for granted, as given in reality. . . . We *trace* a historical development, we *follow the course* of history and evolution, *down to* the present and *up from* the ape. . . . And we . . . follow a *line* of thought, a *course* of action or the *direction* of an argument . . . we *bridge* a gap in the conversation, or speak of the *span* of life or of teaching a *course*, or lament our *interrupted* career. (Lee, 1968: 334–335)

In short, culture influences all areas of life. The things that people take for granted as right and good and as valuable and possible and the way that they respond emotionally and intellectually to their lives ultimately depend on the culture in which they live.

UNITY IN DIVERSITY

What is more "natural" than for a man and woman who love one another to be possessive and jealous? Eskimo men traditionally offered their wives to guests and friends as a gesture of hospitality; both husband and wife felt extremely offended if the guest turned down the offer (Ruesch, 1951: 87–88). The Banaro of New Guinea believe it to be disastrous for a woman to conceive her first child by her husband and not by one of her father's close friends, as is their custom.

The real father is a close friend of the bride's father. . . . Nevertheless the first born child inherits the name and possessions of the husband. An American would deem such a custom immoral, but the Banaro tribesmen would be equally shocked to discover that the first born child of an American couple is the offspring of the husband. (Haring, 1949: 33)

The Yanomamö of northern Brazil, whom social scientist Napoleon A. Chagnon (1968) named the "fierce people," encourage what we would consider extreme disrespect. Small boys are applauded for striking their parents in the face. The Yanomamö would laugh at our efforts to curb aggression in children, much as they laughed at Chagnon's naïveté when he first came to live with them.

The variations between cultures are startling, yet all peoples have customs and beliefs about marriage, about the bearing and raising of children, about sex, and about hospitality—to name just a few of the universals social scientists have discovered in their cross-cultural explorations. But the *details* of cultures do indeed vary: in this country, not so many years ago, when a girl was serious about a boy and he about her, she wore his fraternity pin over her heart; in the Fiji Islands, girls put hibiscus flowers behind their ears when they are in love. The specific gestures are different, but the impulse to symbolize feelings, to dress courtship in ceremonies, is the same. How do we explain this unity in diversity?

Cultural Universals

Cultural universals are behavior patterns and institutions that have been found in all known cultures. Social scientist George Peter Murdock identified over sixty cultural universals, including a system of social status, marriage, body adornments, dancing, myths and legends, cooking, incest taboos, inheritance rules, puberty customs, and religious rituals (Murdock, 1945: 124).

The universals of culture may derive from the fact that if they are to survive, all socie-

Cooking is a cultural universal, but it varies in detail from society to society. In the New Hebrides, a man with a flower in his hair prepares a meal. (Kal Muller / Woodfin Camp & Associates)

ties must perform the same essential functions—including organization, motivation, communication, protection, the socialization of new members, and the replacement of those who die. In meeting these prerequisites for group life, people inevitably arrive at similar—though not identical—patterns for living. As Clyde Kluckhohn once wrote, "All cultures constitute somewhat distinct answers to essentially the same questions posed by human biology and by the generalities of the human situation" (1962: 317).

The way in which a people express cultural universals depends in large part on their physical and social environment—that is, on the climate in which they live, the materials they have at hand, and the peoples with whom they establish contact. For example, the wheel has long been considered one of humankind's greatest inventions, and social scientists were baffled for a long time by the fact that the great civilizations of Latin America never discovered it. Then researchers uncovered a number of toys with wheels. Apparently the Aztecs and their neighbors did know about wheels; living as they did in a mountainous environment, they simply didn't find wheels useful.

Adaptation, Relativity, and Ethnocentrism

Taken out of context, almost any custom will seem bizarre, perhaps cruel, or just plain ridiculous. To understand why, for example, many tropical societies have strong taboos against a mother having sexual intercourse with a man until her child is at least two years old, you have to try to see things through their eyes. As a Hausa woman explains:

> A mother should not go to her husband while she has a child she is suckling . . . if she only

sleeps with her husband and does not become pregnant, it will not hurt her child, it will not spoil her milk. But if another child enters in, her milk will make the first one ill. (Smith, in Whiting, 1969: 518)

Why do Hausa women behave in a way that seems overprotective and overindulgent to us? In tropical climates protein is scarce. If a mother was to nurse more than one child at a time, or if she was to wean a child before it reached the age of two, the youngster would be prone to *kwashiorkor*, an often fatal disease resulting from protein deficiency. Thus, long postpartum (after childbirth) sex taboos are *adaptive*, because they enhance the capacity for survival. In a tropical environment, a postpartum sex taboo and a long period of breast-feeding solve a serious problem (Whiting, 1969: 511–524).

In modern societies, parents and others try to discourage young lovers from marrying before the man (if not the woman) is twenty or older. Most people in the world consider the years fourteen to twenty the flowering of adulthood and sexuality. No doubt they think people in modern societies are less potent than they are or are slow to mature. Young lovers also find the custom of late marriage unreasonable. But postponing marriage is adaptive in societies that need people with advanced education and offer few economic opportunities to teen-age husbands. The high rate of divorce among teen-age couples is not due to "immaturity" alone: our norms and folkways make it hard for young couples to succeed.

As these examples suggest, no custom is good or bad, right or wrong in and of itself. Each custom must be examined in light of the culture as a whole and evaluated in terms of how it works in the context of the entire culture. Social scientists call this *cultural relativity*. Although this way of thinking about culture may seem self-evident today, it is a lesson that the missionaries and merchants who often preceded social scientists to remote areas learned the hard way, by observing the effects they—with the best of intentions—had on peoples whose way of life was quite different from their own.

Ethnocentrism is the tendency to see one's own group's way of life, including behaviors, beliefs, values, and norms, as the only right way of living. Robin Fox points out that "any human group is ever ready to consign another recognizably different human group to the other side of the boundary. It is not enough to possess culture to be fully human, you have to possess *our* culture" (1970: 31).

Accounts of the first European contacts with sub-Saharan Africa are a study in ethnocentrism. The letters and journals of fifteenth- and sixteenth-century explorers, merchants, and missionaries overflowed with lurid descriptions of cannibalism, incest, and "unbridled lust." Religion, law, and government, reported the Europeans, were unknown. Any evidence of the great Sonniki dynasty in Ghana, founded in the second century A.D. (to name just one of the empires that flourished in African history), was overlooked. The following description is typical:

The majority of them . . . are entirely savage and display the nature of the wild beast . . . and are as far removed as possible from human kindness to one another; and speaking as they do with a shrill voice and cultivating none of the practices of civilized life as these are found among the rest of mankind, they present a striking contrast when considered in light of our own customs. (quoted by George, 1968: 25)

These accounts tell us more about how culture-bound "sophisticated" Europeans were than about how "beastly" Africans appeared. Surveying the fifteenth- and sixteenth-century literature on Africans, Katherine George found only one favorable report, written by a Dutch visitor to South Africa.

> I am astonished that . . . those half-truths that are spread about our [sic] Africans should have reached even your ears. I found this people . . . living in harmony with nature's law, hospitable to every race of men, open, dependable, lovers of truth and justice, not utterly unacquainted with the worship of some God, endowed . . . with a rare nimbleness of mother wit, and having minds receptive of instruction. . . . [I]t is through the faults of our own countrymen . . . that the natives have been changed for the worse. . . . From us they have learned . . . misdeeds unknown to them before, and, among other crimes of deepest die, the accursed lust for gold. (quoted by George, 1968: 32)

The history of race relations in this country suggests how far ahead of his time this observer was.

Cultural Integration

A people's customs, beliefs, values, and technology are *interdependent*. Changes in one area invariably affect other areas, sometimes throwing the entire system off balance. For example, missionaries succeeded in converting large numbers of Madagascans to Christianity. The result? Theft, which was practically unknown in the pre-Christian days, became commonplace; people stopped caring for their homes and villages. The reason? "The fear of hell and the police are a poor substitute for the fear of ancestral ghosts who know everything and punished the evil doer with sickness on earth and exclusion from the ancestral village in the hereafter" (Linton, 1947: 357).

Similarly, the introduction of steel virtually destroyed the highly integrated Stone Age culture of aboriginal societies in Australia. To the Europeans who brought them, steel axes were clearly an improvement over stone implements. But to the aborigines the ax was more than a tool: relations between families and tribes were based on the ceremonial exchange of cherished stonework (Arensberg and Niehoff, 1964: 50).

Cultural integration refers to the degree of internal consistency within a culture. In a well-integrated culture, there are few contradictions between the way people think and the way they act; established traditions enable them to make efficient use of the environment and to carry out the daily business of living with minimal inner conflicts. Yet, as Linton notes in *The Study of Man* (1947), a highly integrated culture, where religious, economic, and family life are all of one piece, is extremely vulnerable. The Madagascans, as we have seen, were unable to absorb Christianity into their existing cultural patterns without upheaval to their whole system. On the other hand, the Comanche, precisely because their traditions were comparatively weak, were able to adjust to the ways of the white conquerors more easily than were other Indian tribes (364–365). Linton writes that "cultures, like personalities, are perfectly capable of including conflicting elements and logical inconsistencies" (358). We needn't go very far to illustrate this point, for American culture is truly a study in paradox.

AMERICAN CULTURE

Attempting to write the definitive profile of American culture is trying to do the impossible. This country is unquestionably one of the most heterogeneous nations on earth. No pattern we can identify is ever without exceptions and contradictions. In fact, nothing about our culture suggests consistency or stability. One of its dominant themes is *change*; it is Americans who have spread the gospel of progress around the world. Almost anything we say about American culture today will seem outdated next year. Nevertheless, certain basic orientations do emerge, and certain forces from the past are still active today. The description that follows outlines these basic patterns and highlights the variations and contradictions in American culture.[2]

Basic American Values

We begin with the sacred triad American children learn in first grade: *freedom, equality,* and *democracy.* Americans are far more likely than people of other nationalities to mention freedom and "our system of government" when asked what they are proud of in their country, and the majority believe this *is* the land of opportunity (Williams, 1970: 478, 491).

Freedom By freedom, Americans generally mean freedom *from* external controls and freedom *to do* something in a manner they see fit (to pursue happiness, success, and so on). The emphasis is on noninterference and autonomy. There is a tendency "to think in terms of rights rather than duties, a suspicion of established (especially personal) authority, a distrust of central government, a deep aversion to acceptance of obvious coercive

restraint. . . . " (Williams, 1970: 480). This aversion can be seen in President Eisenhower's warnings about the military-industrial complex, in the vilificaton of the Establishment during the 1960s, in the culture of personal fulfillment ("doing your own thing") in the 1970s, and in Jimmy Carter's successful campaign against "big government."

Equality On one level, having equality as an ideal connotes a belief in the inalienable rights of all, in the inherent dignity of all people. The belief in the average person runs deep in America: a person will say, "I'm just an average, run-of-the-mill guy," with a hint of pride. A strong tradition of humanitarianism (for example, helping people recuperate from natural disasters) and a tendency toward generosity, gregariousness, and informality are linked to the belief in equality. On the other hand, Americans have never interpreted the word "equality" to mean equality of condition: the idea of equal distribution of wealth, for example, arouses a fear of governmental control. Rather, Americans take equality to mean that every individual has (or should have) an equally good position at the starting gate. The fact that some horses start the race lame has usually been ignored.

Racism, which surely is as American as apple pie, is problematic for just this reason. Americans in general are highly ethnocentric—both in the sense of seeing the United States as "bigger and better" and in the sense of clinging to their "own kind" within the country. At the same time, however, they go to considerable lengths to *deny prejudice* and discrimination. This conflict between equality and discrimination is but one of the contradictions built into American culture (see Myrdal, 1944).

Democracy The word *democracy* is con-

---

[2] Many of the ideas here are drawn from Robin Williams, *American Society* (1970), chapter 11, "Values in American Society."

spicuously missing from the Constitution; nevertheless, this document symbolizes democracy to most Americans and to people all over the world. The protection of individual rights (principally from government infringement) and of private property, rule by law (as distinguished from personal rule), and faith in the electorate are all part of the democratic creed. Yet the results of a national survey indicate that six out of ten young Americans believe this society is democratic in name only, with most of the power residing in special-interest groups (Yankelovich, 1973).

This triad of values—freedom, equality, and democracy—can thus support very different norms for patriotism. On the one hand, there are those who, believing this country has been good to them, call all criticism and protest ''un-American'' (by which they mean treasonous). On the other side, there are those who see unquestioning loyalty as antithetical to freedom and democracy and count criticism and protest among the citizen's moral obligations.

Success ''The business of America is business,'' said Calvin Coolidge, and, indeed, Americans value success the way other people value holiness, family, or military prowess. Success is our primary measure of self-worth. The persistence of organized crime and the relative toleration of white-collar crime—not to mention such expressions as ''business is business''—indicate the extent to which Americans suspend other values in their admiration of people scrambling for success. In addition to its practical significance, wealth has symbolic significance in this country, for it is one of the only measures of personal merit.

The rugged individualism of American culture finds its fullest expression in occupational competition. We still enjoy rags-to-riches stories; the idea that anyone who works hard and takes advantage of his opportunities can make it to the top dies hard. The problem is, of course, that in reality there is not much room at the top, and the myth that any boy who tries can grow up to be president implies that there is something *wrong* with those who don't.[3] In American culture, whether one succeeds or fails is believed to be due largely to one's own efforts; the individual who doesn't rise above his or her origins feels he or she has only himself or herself to blame. To be sure, many Americans are content with their work and their standard of living, but many others are haunted by a sense of personal inadequacy.

The Value of Work Closely related to the achievement syndrome is the belief that work is a good thing in and of itself.[4] According to a poll conducted in 1964, 80 percent of laborers said they would continue working even if they were able to maintain their current standard of living without a job (Williams, 1970: 461). During the 1960s, student protests, hippie attire, sexual freedom, and the call for new life styles led many people to conclude that American youth were abandoning traditional values, including the work ethic. But the results of a nationwide survey of attitudes and values among American youth, conducted by Daniel Yankelovich in 1973, present a less clear cut picture: 79 percent believe that commitment to a meaningful career is very important, but 30 percent would welcome less emphasis on working hard.

---

[3] We purposely refer only to boys here. For girls, the American dream has been to marry the man at the top.
[4] Again, we must qualify this by saying that no one places much value on menial jobs such as street or house cleaning.

Games reflect cultural values. In America, we strive to win and are ashamed to lose. (UPI)

Progress Americans value innovation and efficiency—which has often meant ''single-minded attainment of a goal or accomplishment of a task, with minimal attention to attendant costs, injuries, or disruptions outside the narrow zone of immediate attention'' (Williams, 1970: 466). The pollution of our air and water in the name of progress testifies to this. However, it would be foolish to ignore the positive effects of pragmatism—in such areas as medicine, for example.

The cult of progress is closely intertwined with the idea that science can and eventually will overcome all natural and man-made difficulties—an extraordinarily optimistic position, if you stop to think about it. The idea that some natural, social, and psychological phenomena are beyond rational comprehension, that some things happen for no reason at all, disturbs most Americans. Witness, for example, the numerous task-force reports commissioned by the federal government.

We said earlier that values are what people consider right or wrong, good or bad. It is likely, then, that the value conflicts between social conscience and competitiveness, between equality and racism, between the myth of opportunity and the realities of stratification—to name just a few—all contribute to a restless undercurrent in U.S. culture.

Subcultures

Another reason for the inconsistencies and exceptions in American culture is that our system includes a wide range of subcultures. When the perspective and life style of a

JARGON AND SUBCULTURE

People who engage in activities that are unusually demanding, isolating, unconventional, rebellious, or highly specialized often invent a language of their own—a *jargon* or argot. Jazz musicians are no exception:

I'm standing under the Tree of Hope, pushing my gauge. The vipers come up, one by one.

First Cat: Hey there, Poppa Mezz, is you anywhere?

Me: Man, I'm down with it, stickin' like a honky.

First Cat: Lay a trey on me, ole man.

Me: Got to do it, slot. (*Pointing to a man . . .*) Gun the snatcher on your left raise—the head mixer laid a bundle his ways, he's posin' back like crime sure pays.

First Cat: Father grabs him. I ain't payin' him no rabbit. Jim, this jive you got is a gasser. I'm goin' up to my dommy and dig that new mess Pops laid down for Okeh. I hear he rifled back on Zakly. Pick you up at The Track when the kitchen mechanics romp.

Translation:

I'm standing under the Tree of Hope, selling my marijuana. The customers come up one by one.

First Cat: Hello, Mezz, have you got any marijuana?

Me: Plenty, old man, my pockets are full as a factory hand's on payday.

First Cat: Let me have three cigarettes (fifty cents' worth).

Me: I sure will, slotmouth [a private interracial joke]. Look at the detective on your left—the head bartender slipped him some hush money, and he's swaggering around as if crime *does* pay.

First Cat: I hope he croaks [dies], I'm not paying him even a tiny bit of mind. [Literally, "Father grabs him" suggests that the Lord ought to snatch the man and haul him away; and when you "don't pay a man no rabbit," you're not paying him any more attention than you would a rabbit's butt as it disappears hurriedly over the fence.] Friend, this marijuana of yours is terrific. I'm going home and listen to the new record Louis Armstrong made for the Okeh company. I hear he did some wonderful playing and singing on the number "Exactly Like You." See you at the Savoy Ballroom in Harlem on Thursday. [That is, the maid's night off when all the domestic workers will be dancing there.] (187, 316)

In-words and usages, as the passage above suggests, serve multiple purposes: they pin down ideas that are only vague in everyday language; describe events and experiences for which no words exist in the mainstream language; promote in-group solidarity; and keep outsiders out. Interestingly, much hip talk has found its way into mainstream slang; most Americans know what "square" and "bread" mean. Other hip words, however, have remained in-words—for example, "ofay," which means white and comes from the pig Latin for "foe."

SOURCE: Mezz Mezzrow and Bernard Wolfe, *Really the Blues*, New York: Random House, 1972.

group's members are significantly different from those of other people in their culture, and when they define themselves as different, we say they belong to a *subculture*. Members of a subculture share a set of norms, attitudes, and values that gives them a distinct identity within the dominant culture. Subcultures may develop out of occupational groups, ethnic or religious groups, socioeconomic groups, or age groups. Adolescents, for example, build a private world out of their peculiar position as not-quite-adults and no-longer-children; medical students share common experiences, goals, and problems, and hence a common viewpoint. Subcultures grow among a group of people who find themselves isolated together outside the conventional world—isolated physically (adolescents in school, inmates in prison, soldiers on a base, or poor people in a ghetto), or isolated by what they do and think, by their world of meanings.

Professional baseball players are a good example of an occupational subculture: they share a world different from that of other people because of what they do. They travel and live together for long periods of time; their careers are relatively short; and they are regarded as an elite to which large numbers of people aspire.

They are, in fact, a symbol of American values. Baseball is our national sport, and it reflects some of the dominant values of our culture—equality, individuality, and success. The major leagues are open to anyone who has talent, and they have thus traditionally been an avenue of upward mobility for minorities. Although a player is a member of a team, he does strive for individual stardom. Baseball players also make a lot of money and become famous figures in their own right—in other words, they achieve success as it is defined in American society. Reggie Jackson, for example, the superstar of the

1977 season, signed a million-dollar three-year contract; endorsements of commercial products and personal appearances guarantee him many thousands of dollars of additional income.

Yet the ballplayer lives in an uncertain world where, in the end success or failure may have little to do with his own skill. For one thing, professional baseball is a business as well as a sport, so a club is governed by two layers of management: field management (coaches, trainers, managers), whose goal is winning games; and office management (the general manager and the front of-

Professional baseball players, such as pitcher Bob Gibson, share one of the many subcultures that give American society its complexity and diversity. (Marvin E. Newman / Woodfin Camp & Associates)

fice staff), who are oriented toward making profits. Players are in close and daily contact with field management, from whom they seek evaluation and approval; these sport professionals are competent to judge how a player is doing and to help him improve. Yet decisions about success or failure—about staying with the team or being sent down to the minor leagues or traded away—are made by office management, often for reasons unknown to the player and unrelated to his actual performance (Ball, 1976).

Other uncertainties are a part of the game itself. For example, a beautiful hit may be caught one day (for an out) or missed another day (for a triple). Players cope with such uncertainty by developing rituals, taboos, and fetishes, which they use in situations where outcomes depend on chance and where the emotions of hope and fear predominate, as opposed to situations in which outcomes are reliable and under the control of rational methods (Malinowski, quoted in Gmelch, 1971). George Gmelch (1971), a ballplayer turned social scientist, found that pitchers and hitters developed rituals, taboos, and fetishes to try to control performance. Gmelch himself, for example, once ate pancakes before a game in which he struck out four times; the same thing then happened several weeks later: "The result was a pancake taboo in which from that day on I never ate pancakes during the season" (41). He also adopted this ritual at one point: "In hopes of maintaining a batting streak, I once ate fried chicken every day at 4:00 P.M., kept my eyes closed during the national anthem and changed sweat shirts at the end of the fourth inning each night for seven consecutive nights until the streak ended" (40).

We are all accustomed to seeing pitchers go through peculiar gyrations on the mound, but most people are not aware that these rituals are as important as throwing the ball or winning the game. One pitcher reached into a back pocket and touched a crucifix, straightened his cap, and clutched his genitals after every pitch (Gmelch, 1971: 40). Another organized his pitching day in the following way for three months during a winning season:

> First, he arose from bed at exactly 10:00 A.M. and not a minute earlier or later. At 1:00 P.M. he went to the nearest restaurant for two glasses of iced tea and a tuna fish sandwich. Although the afternoon was free, he observed a number of taboos such as no movies, no reading and no candy. In the clubhouse he changed into the sweat shirt and jock he wore during his last winning game, and one hour before the game he chewed a wad of Beechnut chewing tobacco. (41)

All these activities, and the circumstances of their lives, set ballplayers apart. Like jazz musicians with their colorful jargon (see the box on jargon and subculture, p. 99), teenagers with their special codes of dress and behavior, or ethnic groups with their special foods and festivals, baseball players help give American culture its complexity and its heterogeneous quality.

CULTURE AGAINST PEOPLE

We began this chapter by saying that humans are animals who depend on culture the way other species depend on instincts. Thus the phrase "culture against people" would seem to be a contradiction in terms. How can culture be against the people who create it, who live in and by it? Sigmund Freud believed that discontent was built into the human condition, that the conflict between the individual and society would never be completely resolved. He questioned the possibility of people ever finding satisfaction. Freud argued that by nature people are egocentric, irrational, and antisocial: without coercion, we would never consent to the "instinctual sacrifices" that are necessary in any social order (1961: 6–7). However, he believed that overcivilization—the complete subjection of the self to social demands—was destructive. People can become neurotic when they give up too many of their desires and impulses.

In *The Pursuit of Loneliness* Philip Slater contends that American culture in particular doesn't meet three basic human needs: for community, for engagement, and for dependence (1976: 8–37). In Slater's view, the high value Americans place on individualism and competition works against the basic human desire for community—"the wish to live in trust, cooperation, and friendship with those around one." We are a lonely people who consider it bad form to ask something of another person unless we are desperate.

We are also prone to escaping, evading, and avoiding—to what Slater calls the Toilet Assumption, the notion that "unwanted matter, unwanted difficulties, unwanted complexities and obstacles will disappear if they are removed from our immediate field of vision" (21). We talk about cleaning up the environment, cleaning out city hall, clearing slums, wiping out poverty, mopping up wars—removing rather than solving problems. As a result, we have little experience with the realities of our world. Our basic desire for engagement—"the wish to come directly to grips with one's social and physical environment," the need to understand and feel able to cope with the world we live in—is not satisfied.

From early childhood, we are trained to exercise self-control: Americans believe that each individual is responsible for his or her own destiny. In other societies, individuals do not carry the burden of making important decisions and choices alone; going against family or clan in the choice of a career or a marriage partner is unthinkable. Nor is the individual expected to control his or her impulses all of the time: the group provides external controls. In a dispute, for example, the combatants can give full vent to their anger because they know their friends or family will keep the situation from getting out of hand. Lacking stable communities, living among strangers, constantly moving, Americans can't count on outside intervention or support. So the desire for dependence—"the wish to share responsibility for control of one's impulses and the direction of one's life"—is not satisfied.

In short, Slater sees our emphasis on individualism, on avoidance of difficulties, and on self-control as contrary to certain basic human needs. Yet he also sees evidence that Americans are recognizing the necessity for accommodating these aspects of our humanity. They are striving to become reconnected to one another and to their physical environment (1976: 215–221). The number of groups on the right and the left that for a variety of reasons are "taking the law into their own hands" is evidence of a move toward decentralization. The search for roots suggests the recognition that democracy, which we value so highly, depends on stable community bonds and opportunities for people to lean on one another: the pace of life is decelerating. In addition, certain forms of specialization are breaking down: we are moving toward depolarization. The women's movement, for example, has attacked the specialization that kept women in bedroom communities, detached from larger issues, and men in outside workplaces, detached from emotional concerns and interpersonal relations.

Yet while Slater laments our individualism, Bruno Bettelheim, in a study of life on the kibbutz (1969), finds that people living in a communal society sometimes decide to leave because their need for individualism is frustrated.

In the Israeli kibbutz, children, who are raised by the community rather than by their parents, form strong ties with the members of their peer group. The group nurtures and supports the individual, and great emphasis is put on comradeship and caring. The whole community, for example, works to help mentally retarded and brain-damaged children to function within the kibbutz (279–280). The same is true for the aged: "Those who grow old in the kibbutz are never alone. They remain as before in the middle of things, feeling needed. . . . there is as much for them, or as little, of importance to be done as they wish" (318).

The kibbutz therefore satisfies needs for community, engagement, and dependence—but not those for individualism and autonomy. Those who leave often speak of leaving as gaining personal maturity: "Whenever I'm in the city I feel grown up, but as soon as I return to the kibbutz, I feel again as if I were a child. So much is decided for me, so few decisions do I have to make on my own, so guilty do I feel if I do differently from what in kibbutz terms I am supposed to think, do, and feel" (272).

It would seem, then, that perhaps Freud was right—we are simply never satisfied with what we have, never content to follow our particular set of cultural rules. It is also probably true that *every* culture satisfies some human needs and doesn't satisfy others. Perhaps too, what causes us to question American values at this point in time is that the imbalance among needs has become too great: where once our lives had both individual (work, mobility) and collective (neighborhood, friends) aspects, now we seem to have been left with only our individualism.

SUMMARY

The customs, beliefs, values, knowledge, and skills that guide a people's behavior along shared paths are part of their *culture*. Human dependence on culture is a product of evolutionary forces. We believe the essentials of culture—tools, a division of labor, speech, myths, and rituals—evolved hundreds of thousands of years ago, influencing and influenced by biological evolution.

Social scientists distinguish between material and nonmaterial culture. The elements of nonmaterial culture include norms, values, symbols, and language.

Norms are the cultural guidelines people follow in their relations with one another. Norms vary in intensity from *folkways* (everyday conventions) to *mores* (rules considered vital to social life). Some norms are codified in *laws*.

Values are the general ideas people share about what is good or bad, right or wrong, desirable or undesirable. One way of examining values is to study the games that people in a society play, for the games reflect the values of the culture. Values are abstract; norms, which derive from values, are concrete. And because a value is a general idea, any single value can support several different and perhaps conflicting norms.

A *symbol* is an object, gesture, sound, color, or design that represents something other than itself. Much human behavior, and nearly all human communication, is symbolic. Symbols have significance in a culture only if their meaning is commonly and widely agreed upon.

Studying the language of a people can yield many insights into their culture. For example, if there are a number of words available to describe an object, event, or concept, this is a clue to its importance in the culture. Language can also tell us about a people's view of reality. Sapir and Whorf have theorized that language doesn't simply reflect culture but actually *shapes* our thoughts and directs our interpretation of the world.

Although the details of culture vary from society to society, social scientists have identified many *cultural universals*—behavior patterns and institutions that are found in all cultures. Cultural universals exist because all societies must fulfill the same basic functions to survive. But the way in which these cultural universals are expressed depends on the society's physical and social environment. Culture is adaptive—it provides people with a means of adjusting to the physiological needs of their own bodies and to their physical, geographical, and social environments.

When social scientists study culture, they evaluate customs and beliefs in light of the entire culture in which the customs and beliefs occur and in terms of how they work in that context. This way of thinking about culture is called *cultural relativity*. In contrast, *ethnocentrism* is the tendency to see one's own group's ideas, beliefs, and practices as being the only right way of living. *Cultural integration* refers to the degree of internal consistency within a culture. A people's customs, beliefs, values, and technology are interdependent, and changes in one area invariably affect other areas.

American culture is riddled with inconsistencies and exceptions even in terms of the basic values we hold. Our core values of freedom, equality, and democracy contain contradictions that can lead to much confusion and disquiet. The disparities between social conscience and competitiveness, between equality and racism, and between the myth of opportunity and the realities of economic and social stratification all contribute to a restless undercurrent in American society. One reason for the variations in American culture is the wide range of *subcultures*—groups whose perspective and life style are significantly different from the cultural mainstream, and who define themselves as different. Members of a subculture share a set of norms, attitudes, and values that gives them a distinctive identity.

Culture can also, it seems, work against people in the sense that it sometimes frustrates basic human needs. Freud believed it was a characteristic of humans never to be content. Philip Slater believes American culture is in a state of disarray because the accent on individualism and competitiveness frustrates needs for community, engagement, and dependence. But in his study of the communal kibbutz culture of Israel, Bruno Bettelheim found that there the emphasis on the group led some people to leave because their desire to act as autonomous individuals was frustrated. It is probably true that every culture meets some human needs and fails to meet others; it may also be true that we feel American culture is in crisis because the imbalance among needs has become too great.

GLOSSARY

cultural integration the degree of internal consistency within a culture.

cultural relativity the doctrine of examining a custom in light of the entire culture in which it occurs and of evaluating it in terms of how it works in that context, not in terms of right and wrong.

cultural universals the behavior patterns and institutions that have been found in every known culture.

culture the customs, beliefs, values, knowledge, and skills that guide a people's behavior along shared paths.

ethnocentrism the tendency to see one's own group and way of life, including behaviors, beliefs, values, and norms, as superior to other groups and ways of life.

folkways everyday habits and conventions.

jargon a language invented by people who engage in activities that are unusually demanding, isolating, unconventional, rebellious, or highly specialized.

language a system of verbal and, in many cases, written symbols, with rules for putting them together.

laws norms to which a society has given a formal status.

mores norms people consider vital to their well-being and to their most cherished values.

norms the guidelines people follow in their relations with one another; shared standards of desirable behavior.

subculture a group whose perspective and life style are significantly different from those of the cultural mainstream, and who define themselves as different; members share norms, attitudes, and values.

symbol an object, gesture, sound, color, or design that represents something other than itself.

values the general ideas people share about what is good or bad, right or wrong, desirable or undesirable.

REFERENCES

Alexander Alland, Jr., *Evolution and Human Behavior*, rev. ed. Garden City, N.Y.: Doubleday Anchor, 1973.

Conrad M. Arensberg and Arthur H. Niehoff, *Introducing Social Change*. Chicago: Aldine, 1964.

Donald W. Ball, "Failure in Sport." *American Sociological Review*, vol. 41 (August 1976): 726–739.

Howard S. Becker, *The Outsiders: Studies in the Sociology of Deviance*. New York: Free Press, 1963.

Eric Berne, *Games People Play: The Psychology of Human Relationships*. New York: Grove Press, 1964.

Bruno Bettelheim, *Children of the Dream*. New York: Macmillan, 1969.

Kenelm O. L. Burridge, "A Tangu Game." *Man*, vol. 57 (1957): 88–89.

John B. Carroll, *Language, Thought, and Reality: Selected Writings of Benjamin Lee Whorf*. Cambridge, Mass.: MIT Press, 1956.

Napoleon A. Chagnon, *Yanomamö: The Fierce People*. New York: Holt, Rinehart and Winston, 1968.

Alan Dundes, ed., *Every Man His Way: Readings in Cultural Anthropology*. Englewood Cliffs, N.J.: Prentice-Hall, 1968.

Carol R. Ember and Melvin Ember, *Anthropology*. New York: Appleton-Century-Crofts, 1973.

Harold Finestone, "Cats, Kicks, and Color." *Social Problems,* vol. 5 (1957): 3–13.

Robin Fox, "The Cultural Animal." *Encounters,* vol. 35 (July 1970): 31–42.

Sigmund Freud, *Civilization and Its Discontents.* New York: Norton, 1961.

Katherine George, "The Civilized West Looks at Primitive Africa: 1400–1800, A Study in Ethnocentrism," in Alan Dundes, ed., *Every Man His Way: Readings in Cultural Anthropology.* Englewood Cliffs, N.J.: Prentice-Hall, 1968.

George Gmelch, "Baseball Magic." *Transaction,* vol. 8 (June 1971): 39–41, 54.

Erving Goffman, *Presentation of the Self in Everyday Life.* New York: Doubleday, 1959.

Douglas Haring, ed., *Personal Character and Cultural Milieu,* rev. ed. Syracuse, N.Y.: Syracuse University Press, 1949.

Jules Henry, *Culture Against Man.* New York: Vintage, 1965.

Clifford Jolly and Fred Plog, *Physical Anthropology and Archeology.* New York: Knopf, 1976.

Clyde Kluckhohn, "Universal Categories of Culture," in Sol Tax, ed., *Anthropology Today: Selections.* Chicago: University of Chicago Press, 1962.

Dorothy Lee, "Codifications of Reality: Lineal and Nonlineal," in Alan Dundes, ed., *Every Man His Way: Readings in Cultural Anthropology.* Englewood Cliffs, N.J.: Prentice-Hall, 1968.

Ralph Linton, *The Study of Man.* New York: Appleton, 1947.

George Peter Murdock, "The Common Denominator of Cultures," in Ralph Linton, ed., *The Science of Man in World Crisis.* New York: Columbia University Press, 1945.

Gunnar Myrdal, *An American Dilemma.* New York: Harper & Row, 1944.

Hans Ruesch, *Top of the World.* New York: Harper & Row, 1951.

Philip E. Slater, *The Pursuit of Loneliness: American Culture at the Breaking Point,* rev. ed. Boston: Beacon Press, 1976.

J. W. M. Whiting, "Effects of Climate on Certain Cultural Practices," in W. H. Goodenough, ed., *Explorations in Cultural Anthropology.* New York: McGraw-Hill, 1969.

Robin Williams, *American Society,* 3rd ed. New York: Knopf, 1970.

Daniel Yankelovich, *Yankelovich Youth Study.* Copyright © 1973 by the JDR, 3rd Fund.

FOR FURTHER STUDY

American Culture. A land of immigrants, the United States has considerable cultural diversity. One major attempt by a sociologist to encompass this diversity is Robin Williams's book, *American Society,* 3rd ed. (New York: Knopf, 1970). An astute analysis of our culture today has been written by Godfrey Hodgson, and is entitled *America in Our Time* (New York: Doubleday, 1977). A more opinionated but still very interesting book on American culture is *The Americanization of the Unconscious* by John Seeley (New York: Science House, 1967). Another sociologist, Philip Slater, has written powerfully about the pathologies of American culture in *The Pursuit of Loneliness,* rev. ed. (Boston: Beacon Press, 1976). Finally, the drive to achieve is at the center of American life, and Richard M. Huber analyzes its influence on American history in *The American Idea of Success* (New York: McGraw-Hill, 1971).

Subcultures. This country is filled with subcultures that are fascinating to explore. For example, in *Whiz Mob* (New Haven, Conn.: College and University Press, 1964), David

Maurer describes the world of pickpockets and their trade through firsthand interviews. Laud Humphreys reports on life among some kinds of homosexuals in *Tearoom Trade* (Chicago: Aldine, 1970). Another fine book on a subculture is *The Professional Thief* (by a professional thief), interpreted by Edwin H. Sutherland in 1937 (Chicago: University of Chicago Press, 1972). Claude Brown provides a disturbing account of life in a black ghetto in *Manchild in the Promised Land* (New York: Macmillan, 1965).

Cultural Conflict.   Important features of two societies or subcultures are brought out by cultural conflict. In the United States, Indians have been fighting the ways of white men ever since the Europeans arrived. The following books describe Indian conflicts with Europeans. *Custer Died for Your Sins* by Vine Deloria, Jr. (New York: Macmillan, 1969) provides an overview of Indian-white conflicts. More specific works include Hal Borland, *When the Legends Die* (New York: Bantam, 1972); Barbara Bonham, *The Battle of Wounded Knee* (Chicago: Reilly & Lee, 1970); and Oliver La Farge, *Laughing Boy* (New York: New American Library, 1971). A careful study of Indian-white relations that applies symbolic interactionism and conflict theory is *Indian and White: Self Image and Interaction in a Canadian Plains Community* (Stanford, Calif.: Stanford University Press, 1975) by Niels Winther Braroe.

CHAPTER 5

Socialization

Infants come into this world with a helplessness that is unequaled in the animal kingdom. No other creature is quite so dependent for quite so long as the human infant. Babies may grow up to be da Vincis or Einsteins—but first they must be *taught* to sit up, to walk, to feed themselves, to talk, to know where danger lies, to live among people who expect certain kinds of behavior from them. In short, children must *learn* to be human.

The process of acquiring the physical, mental, and social skills that a person needs to survive and to become both an individual and a member of society is called *socialization.* It is this initiation into culture that makes social life possible.

> Without this process of molding, which we call socialization, the society could not perpetuate itself beyond a single generation and culture could not exist. Nor could the individual become a person; for without the ever-repeated renewal of culture within him [or her] there could be no human mentality, no human personality. Both the person and society are alike dependent on this unique process of psychic amalgamation whereby the sentiments and ideas of the culture are somehow joined to the capabilities and needs of the organism. (Davis, 1948: 195)

We will begin our discussion by considering the interaction of biology and culture in human development. Then we will discuss the ways in which self-image is affected by socialization—how the growing child learns to think of himself or herself. Next, we will focus on the people and institutions that socialize the child. In the last section of this chapter, we will look at the process of socialization during adulthood.

BIOLOGY, CULTURE, AND SOCIALIZATION

Ideas about the origins of human nature are a story in themselves. Once the nineteenth century overcame its initial shock at the idea that people and apes shared some distant ancestors, it accepted the ideas of Charles Darwin (1809–1882) with all the fervor of true believers. Once people recognized that human beings are animals, they then reasoned that, like other animals, humans must be born with instincts, or innate predispositions toward certain kinds of behavior. The herding instinct was used to explain the fact that people everywhere lived in societies; the maternal instinct explained mothering; the acquisitive instinct, the desire for and pursuit of private property; the aggressive instinct, war; and so on. A similar kind of reasoning was used to explain individual differences. Why did one person become a thief, another a saint? Because the first, it was held, inherited criminal tendencies (just as he or she inherited brown eyes and a crooked nose), while the second inherited holiness. The notion that human behavior is biologically determined dominated nineteenth-century thought.

Then, near the end of the century, a Russian physiologist named Ivan Pavlov (1849–1936) called attention to the fact that much behavior, even among the so-called lower animals, is *learned*. A hungry dog salivates instinctively when it sees food, but Pavlov showed that a dog could learn to associate the ringing of a bell with food and to salivate whenever it heard the bell, whether or not it saw food at the same time. With this experiment, Pavlov cast a shadow of doubt over the instinct theory of human behavior. Grad-

ually, over time, the idea that the infant is a tabula rasa (blank slate) and that people are *products* of their environment gained a considerable following. Nowhere is this position better stated than in psychologist John B. Watson's (1878–1958) manifesto:

> Give me a dozen healthy infants, well-formed, and my own specific world to bring them up in and I'll guarantee to take any one at random and train him to become any type of specialist I might select—a doctor, lawyer, artist, merchant chief, yes even a beggarman and thief, regardless of his talents, penchants, tendencies, abilities, vocations, and the race of his ancestors. (1970: 104)

Today, the vast majority of social scientists reject both biological *and* environmental determinism (Clausen, 1967). Neither heredity nor environment (learning) *alone* can explain the behavior patterns that distinguish one person from another, and the members of one society from those of another. The key to individuality is socialization, where biology and culture meet.

Biological and Cultural Interaction

Socialization begins with the people who care for an infant, attending to the child's many needs. A long period of dependency is one of our biological givens. Totally incapable of providing for themselves, newborn humans must be fed and sheltered. But food and shelter are not enough: infants also need to be handled and loved.

The Effect of Isolation   In his famous experiments with rhesus monkeys, psychologist Harry F. Harlow demonstrated the need for body contact. Harlow took infant monkeys away from their mothers and raised them in isolation. Each was given two wire "mothers," one equipped with a bottle, one covered with soft terry cloth. Surprisingly, the young monkeys became attached to the cloth "mothers" rather than to the "mothers" with bottles. Clinging to something soft meant more to them than food. Most significant, however, was the fact that *none* of the animals raised in isolation developed normally. When given the chance to associate with others of their species, all were frightened and hostile (Harlow and Zimmerman, 1959).

For obvious reasons, no similar experiments have been performed with human infants. However, we do know of at least one child who was raised in near-total isolation. Anna was the illegitimate child of a farmer's daughter. After unsuccessfully trying to place the child in a foster home or an institution, Anna's mother finally brought her home as a last resort. No one in the family was very proud of the new member; in fact, her grandfather refused even to acknowledge her existence. To avoid his violent disapproval, the mother put Anna in an attic room, where she remained for nearly six years. Except for feeding the child just enough to keep her alive, the mother ignored her.

When social workers discovered Anna, she could not sit up or walk, much less talk. In fact, she was so apathetic and uncommunicative that they assumed she was deaf, mentally retarded, or possibly both. However, the progress Anna made once she was placed in a special school indicated that she was capable of coordinating her body, communicating, and learning. With help, she began to talk and eventually learned to care for herself, to walk and run, and to play with other children. What Anna proved in the four and a half years between the time she was discovered and her premature death was that practically none of the behavior

we associate with human beings arises spontaneously (Davis, 1948: 204–205).[1]

Biological Traits and Socialization This brings us to another point about biological givens—each human being comes into the world with a unique genetic make-up. In large part, one's morphology (form and structure), facial features, and rate of physical and sexual development are genetically determined.[2] Differences in temperament are also apparent at birth; some infants like to be handled and cuddled, while others kick and scream whenever they are picked up. These characteristics influence socialization in several ways.

A person's size and strength will limit the activities he or she chooses and the roles for which he or she is recruited. A frail person can't realistically expect to participate successfully in activities that demand strength—for example, rowing against stiff currents or playing professional football. In addition, most, but not all, people still distinguish between activities appropriate for males and those suitable for females.[3] More subtly, a child's disposition, appearance, and rate of development affect the way parents and others respond to him or her. If the community into which a boy is born val-

---

[1] Studies of institutionalized children support this conclusion. Even with the best physical care—good food, regular diaper and clothing changes and baths, clean sheets, bright and airy nurseries—infants who are not handled and played with develop slowly, if at all. Mortality rates in orphanages are alarmingly high (Spitz, 1951; Bowlby, 1973). Yet love, trust, and satisfaction of a baby's needs can take as many forms as there are cultures.

[2] To date, studies of the relative influence of heredity and environment on intelligence are inconclusive. For a look at the controversy surrounding this topic, see the *Harvard Educational Review*, vol. 39 (1969). We will discuss this question more fully in chapter 11.

[3] Sex roles will be discussed in depth in chapter 6.

ues aggressive men, a male infant who energetically explores his surroundings and struggles vigorously, resisting any sort of constraint, will please his parents: "He's a go-getter," they will proudly conclude. A placid baby boy, on the other hand, will cause his parents to wonder whether he will be able to keep up with the others. Similarly, if a community expects young people to assume adult responsibilities at the age of twelve or thirteen, the child who matures slowly will be considered a misfit.

The point is that all communities project *meaning* onto any number of physical characteristics. People respond differently to bright and slow, homely and attractive, frail and robust children, and these responses subtly shape a child's self-image. In the next section we will focus on these influences to show how the child develops a sense of self and a feeling for her or his place in a community.

SOCIALIZATION AND IDENTITY

In the course of growing older, people develop a kind of amnesia about their early years. Perhaps a few incidents stand out, such as being taken to a strange place full of strange children and suddenly realizing your mother intends to leave you there. But how many people actually remember being put on a toilet and having no idea what it was for, or banging a spoon on a highchair tray, or lying in a crib watching a toy circle overhead and feeling pleasant inside?

One reason why these early memories fade is that infants are fundamentally different from the people they become as they grow up. As adults we find it almost impossible to recall not being able to talk or being uncoordinated and unselfconscious. For the

first month or two of life, babies don't distinguish between their own bodies and actions and the people and objects around them. Infants cry spontaneously when they are wet or hungry or cold. Only gradually do they realize that they are making these sounds, that they can turn crying on and off, that turning it on brings someone running, and much later, that crying is "baby stuff." The emotions, thoughts, and sense of identity that adults take as givens emerge gradually during the process of socialization.

Various social scientists have looked at this process from different points of view, but in ways that enhance one another. The analyses of socialization that we examine in this section all focus on interaction—on the dialogue between children and the people around them. Cooley, Mead, Freud, and Erikson focus on the emergence of a sense of self; Piaget examines cognitive (intellectual) development; and Kohlberg looks at moral development.

Charles Horton Cooley: The Looking-glass Self

Charles Horton Cooley (1864–1929) won a permanent place in the annals of sociology with his insights into the ways in which people establish and maintain a sense of personal identity. Adults take the words "I" and "me" for granted; we experience ourselves as distinct persons, separate from all others. But can there be an "I" without a corresponding "they"? Cooley thought not. The self, he believed, is a social product that emerges as the child interacts with other people. He used the image of a looking-glass to explain how others influence the way we see ourselves:

Each to each a looking-glass
Reflects the other that doth pass.

By this, Cooley meant that we gain a feeling about ourselves by imagining what others think about the way we look and behave. For Cooley, the *looking-glass self* has three main elements: the way we imagine we appear to others; the way we imagine others judge that appearance; and the way we feel about those judgments.

In Cooley's view, a person's self-image and self-esteem depend heavily on the feedback he or she receives as a child, a student, a worker, a parent, and so on. Without the social mirror, there can be no sense of self.

George Herbert Mead: Taking the Role of the Other

Taking his cue from Cooley, George Herbert Mead (1863–1931) traced the development of self-awareness back to the interaction between mother and child.[4] At a very early age, children begin to realize that they depend on other people (usually their mothers) to keep them comfortable, and that their behavior influences the way these important other people act toward them. Infants learn that crying brings food, smiles bring cuddling, and so on. Gradually, as they explore different ways of arousing desired feelings and responses in others, they acquire a vocabulary of *significant symbols*—that is, conventionalized gestures (smiles, screams, and words) that people around them understand. Mead believed that symbols are the foundation of social life. Symbols guide feelings and experiences into standardized channels. In learning to communicate symbolically, children learn to think about themselves and their behavior in much the same way as the people around them do.

---

[4] This discussion is based on George Herbert Mead's *Mind, Self, and Society*, part 3 (Chicago: University of Chicago Press, 1934).

Mead was among the first to conceive of individual psychology in social terms. He believed the self was composed of two parts: the active, spontaneous, idiosyncratic self, which he called the "I," and the social self (the internalized social expectations and demands), which he called the "me." The "I" is the product of individual distinctiveness; the "me," the product of socialization. Without the "me," orderly social interaction couldn't occur; without the "I," social interaction would be mechanical and monotonous. With these two complementary parts, we are able to reflect on our own behavior and develop a sense of inner continuity, or identity. "The self is something which has a development; it is not initially there, at birth, but arises in the process of social experience and activity, that is, develops in the given individual as a result of his relations to [the social] process and to other individuals within that process" (1934: 135).

By the time children begin to walk and talk, they have already acquired strong impressions about the world around them—impressions they work out in play. Two-, three-, and four-year-olds spend much of their time in the world of make-believe. For hours on end they play at being mothers and fathers, mail deliverers and doctors—often embarrassing adults with the accuracy of their imitations. Mead called this form of play "taking the role of the other." In effect, the child becomes one of the people who figure importantly in his or her social world, whom psychiatrist Harry Stack Sullivan called *significant others*. Exploring various roles firsthand, children learn how different activities look from someone else's perspectives. One minute the child is a father demanding his dinner; the next, a mother saying she is too busy to cook. By so doing, children learn to look at themselves through the eyes of other people. Children at this age seem especially

By acting out adult roles, children begin to see the world from perspectives other than their own. (Bill Stanton/Magnum)

fond of playing mothers fussing at babies who have wet themselves, and at lecturing other children on their behavior.

In time the characters children pretend to be become part of their internal landscape. They learn to imagine how people will respond to them without actually having to act out the situation. Thus, a five- or six-year-old will stop with her hand halfway to the cookie jar and say to herself, "No, you will spoil your appetite." Mead conceived of thinking as an internal conversation between the self and others who have become part of the self. The individual becomes aware of himself or herself, Mead wrote, "not directly or imme-

diately . . . [but] only by taking the attitudes of other individuals toward himself within a social environment or context of experience and behavior in which he and they are involved" (138).

Gradually, as children move from their families out into the world of other children and adults, they begin to develop a generalized impression of what people expect from them and of where they fit in the overall scheme of things—what Mead called the *generalized other*. The generalized other embodies the attitudes and viewpoints of society as a whole—the rules of group life. It provides a basis for developing one's self-concept on the one hand, and a guide for behavior in social situations on the other. Mead believed the generalized other emerges when a child is around eight or nine, roughly the age at which children leave the land of make-believe for the world of games. In effect, children learn to play for real. Mead explained this transition by calling attention to the complexity of organized games. To play baseball, for example, a child must understand the rules of the game—anticipate what will happen if the batter slugs a ball into right field—and must behave accordingly. Similarly, to "play the game of life"—that is, to participate in the social world of the community—children must be able to understand their position in terms of the community as a whole. The values and attitudes of the community become an integral part of the child's personality.

A number of contemporary sociologists have suggested that our social self depends to a great extent on the context. For example, we would think it very odd for a man to treat his colleagues as he does his children. Thus from this point of view the "generalized other" refers to the role set one happens to be in at the moment. If you carry this position to its logical extreme, the inevitable conclusion is that there is no stable "core" personality—only a *situational self* which varies with the role one is playing at a given time (Brim, 1960). Although this view may be extreme, we definitely do behave differently in different contexts.

Sigmund Freud: The Psychoanalytic View

No discussion of socialization would be complete without some mention of Sigmund Freud (1856–1939), Cooley and Mead's famous contemporary. Although the number of orthodox Freudians in psychology today is relatively small, Freud's work did represent a turning point in our conceptualization of human behavior and personality. Throughout his life Freud's primary concern was to establish a science of the mind that compared with the physical sciences. He assumed that every aspect of human behavior could be explained rationally, in terms of cause and effect. He felt rational explanations could even be found for seemingly accidental slips of the tongue and for the most bizarre dreams and hallucinations. His clinical work led him to conclude that childhood experiences have a determining effect on personality.

Besides being the father of modern clinical psychiatry, Freud was also interested in the relationship between the individual and society. He believed that every society has to channel and repress people's primitive drives. Society to him was a necessary compromise between individuals' basic drives and the social need for people who would work together in a community.

Freud's description of socialization begins with amoral, egocentric, aggressive, pleasure-seeking infants. In the first years of life all of a child's energies are directed toward oral gratification (sucking and eating), the pleasurable release of tension in defecation, and the joys of masturbation. Freud used the word *id* to describe not only sexual and aggressive urges, which he believed were inborn biological givens, but also all bodily pleasure. Society—by way of parents—interferes with children's pleasure-seeking: their demands for food are met only at certain times; they are forced to regulate their bowel movements; and they are punished for masturbating. As children struggle to accommodate to these and other social demands, what Freud called the *ego* begins to develop. The ego is the rational part of the self that interprets information obtained through the senses and that finds realistic ways of satisfying biological cravings. However, the pleasure-seeking infant is not yet "tamed."

Four- and five-year-old children still have

In our society, we are taught from infancy that gratification of physical urges must be regulated. According to Freud, as children adapt to these social demands—becoming toilet trained, for example—the ego, or rational part of the self, begins to develop. (Peeter Vilms / Jeroboam)

powerful desires, but their fears are also very strong. Realizing that their parents have enormous power over them, they fear violent reprisals for their sexual and aggressive impulses. Striving to be what their parents want them to be is one way of protecting themselves. The *superego*, or conscience, develops during this period. Children begin to internalize their parents' ideas of right and wrong, including their parents' moral ideals. Children learn to repress socially unacceptable desires and, ideally, to redirect their energies into approved channels. For a time,

during what is called the latency stage, children seem to be asexual. This is not to say, however, that sexual and aggressive impulses disappear; the id has simply been forced underground. The desires and fears of childhood, which are stimulated by the re-emergence of sexuality during adolescence, remain active in the unconscious, influencing the way a person behaves lifelong.

Freud's view of the process of human development is thus radically different from Cooley's and Mead's. Where they saw socialization as the gradual, complementary merger of individual and society, Freud argued that socialization was forced on small children very much against their will. Freud's is a *conflict* theory of socialization. For this reason Freud believed that socialization is never complete. The id continues to press for gratification. The ego's function is to control these lustful and antisocial drives, while at the same time modifying the unrealistic demands of the perfection-seeking superego. Driven one way by biology, the other by society, we are—in Freud's view—eternally discontent (see *Civilization and Its Discontents*, 1930).

Erik H. Erikson: The Eight Ages of Man

During the late 1940s and early 1950s, Erik H. Erikson, one of Freud's students, began to expand both the scope and content of his teacher's theory of human development. One of Erikson's most significant contributions to the study of socialization is his vivid description of the problems of adolescence and young adulthood; in fact, he gave us the

now-familiar term "identity crisis." But this concept is only a small part of Erikson's comprehensive theory of human development, which brings Cooley, Mead, and Freud together, integrating the physiological, psychological, and social elements of socialization. Erikson does this by focusing on the ego in its role as mediator between the individual and society.

Erikson's central concern is with the feelings people develop toward themselves and the world around them. He described socialization as a lifelong process, one which begins at birth and continues into old age. In *Childhood and Society* (1950), Erikson describes eight stages of human development. Each stage constitutes a crisis brought on by

figure 5:1 Erikson's eight stages of life

Age	Psychosocial crisis
Infancy	Basic trust vs. mistrust
Early childhood	Autonomy vs. shame and doubt
Four to five (Play stage)	Initiative vs. guilt
Six to twelve (School age)	Industry vs. inferiority
Adolescence	Identity vs. role confusion
Young adulthood	Intimacy vs. isolation
Young adulthood and middle age	Generativity vs. stagnation
Old age	Integrity vs. despair

SOURCE: Adapted from Erik Erikson, *Identity, Youth and Crisis* (New York: Norton, 1968).

physiological changes and new social environments, to which the growing person must adapt. Although Erikson distinguishes between positive and negative responses to these crises, he emphasizes that most people combine both types of response. When things go well, the maturing ego works out solutions to these crises that build up to a stable identity. We will look at five of these stages in detail.

Trust Versus Mistrust (Infancy) During their first year children are totally dependent on adults, primarily their mothers. Even their own sensations of comfort and discomfort are unfamiliar and unpredictable. Children whose mothers respond warmly and consistently to their needs begin to develop feelings of basic trust. Comfort becomes what Erikson calls an inner certainty, and such children come to believe that the world is reliable. If a mother is erratic about caring for her child, the child may grow afraid to let the mother out of his or her sight, fearing that she might never return. The quality of maternal care during this first year shapes infants' basic orientation toward themselves and other people.

Autonomy Versus Shame and Doubt (Early Childhood) For the first two years of life, children spend endless hours trying to make their bodies do what they want them to do. By the age of three, their muscles and nerves have developed to the point where they are capable of grasping, reaching, walking, controlling their bowels, and so on—delightful accomplishments from their point of view. However, while these accomplishments bring new autonomy, they raise new doubts. A child walks around the corner to another room, then realizes he is alone and cries out. Besides the doubts involved with going it alone, the child sometimes experiences the

shame of losing control, as when a toilet-trained toddler wets a neighbor's rug.

Erikson suggests that to develop self-confidence, children should be encouraged to "stand on their own feet," but that they must also be protected from experiences of shame and doubt.

Initiative Versus Guilt (The Play Stage) At four or five, children begin to extend their mastery over their own bodies to the world around them (if, that is, they have developed some sense of autonomy). They enjoy attacking and conquering the material world; in their play and fantasies they begin to act out adult roles, transforming (and hence mastering) the world in their imagination. Most important, in Erikson's view, children begin to initiate purposeful activities on their own. Earlier, their play consisted mostly of imitating others and exploring.

Children's feelings of self-worth grow if their parents and others who are important to them respect their efforts. Ridicule and disinterest make children wonder about the value of their actions and goals; they may punish themselves for their failures. There is a danger, then, of children at this age developing more or less permanent guilt feelings about any self-initiated activities.

Industry Versus Inferiority (School Age) The social setting now shifts from home to school and the larger community. As they begin to acquire the skills and technology of their society, children "learn to win recognition by producing things" (1950: 259). Ideally, they come to take pride in industry. However, if they fail to do well in school, if they find that their race or family background or looks or even the way they dress automatically disqualifies them in other people's eyes, their experience will be negative. At this stage, some children develop a deep sense of inferiority, a fear of being required to perform and failing. In trying to compensate for feelings of inadequacy, some overcommit themselves to the sphere of work and may later become "workaholics."

Identity Versus Role Confusion (Adolescence) With childhood drawing to a close and adulthood looming ahead, adolescents become preoccupied with the question of identity and often experience an identity crisis. It's not that they don't know who they are before this time, but rather that they've been changing and shaping themselves in many different ways. The time has come to draw together all the various elements that have made up their lives, to give a more permanent shape to who they are and where they are going as adults. What Erikson means by *identity* is being able to derive a sense of continuity about one's past, present, and future, coordinating feelings about the self with the image reflected in the social looking-glass. There's also the danger, however, that a person won't be able to integrate his or her various roles into a clear identity. This role confusion makes a person less socially integrated and less able to form intimate relations with significant others—problems which many college students face.

The last three of Erikson's stages of development occur during the period of adulthood: the intimacy versus isolation of young adulthood, when close relationships are formed; the generativity versus stagnation of middle age, whose theme is the need to be needed; the integrity versus despair of old age, when one comes to terms with death by assessing the life one has lived. (For another view of adult development, see figure 5:2.)

In describing the "eight ages of man," Erikson focuses on the potential for negative as well as positive developments in each stage. He also emphasizes that the growing person's adjustment in one stage affects his or her orientation in the next. Thus, for example, gaining a sense of initiative aids a person in being industrious, though the sequence is not rigid. Erikson believes that the concerns of every stage are present throughout a person's life, though each pair has its time of prominence. This means that a person can overcome an early sense of shame or mistrust by working at it later, or that through great strain later on in life a person can lose an early strength like initiative. Erikson's theory complements those of Cooley and Mead by emphasizing symbolic interaction and role learning. Unlike Freud, he pictures the social order as growing out of (and therefore in harmony with) developmental stages. As people work out the solutions to developmental problems, the solutions become institutionalized in the culture and are thereby available to future generations.

> The underlying assumptions . . . are (1) that the human personality in principle develops according to steps predetermined in the growing person's readiness to be driven toward, and be aware of, and to interact with, a widening social radius; and (2) that society, in principle, tends to be constituted as to meet and invite this succession of potentialities for interaction and attempts to safeguard and to encourage the proper rate and proper sequence of their unfolding. (270)

This interrelationship between personal crises in growth and the social structure is the most striking part of Erikson's theory, which he has applied to studies of Hitler, Martin Luther, Gandhi, and others.

Jean Piaget: Cognitive Development

Among the basic processes of socialization are learning to talk, to think, and to reason;

figure 5:2   Levinson's model of adult development: The novice phase

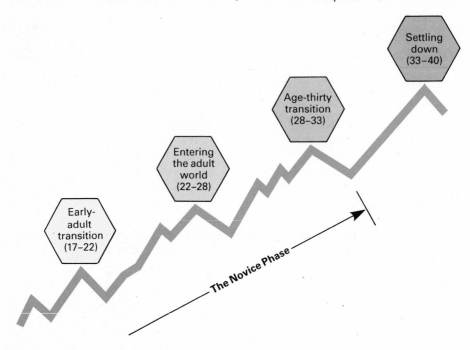

SOURCE: Adapted from Daniel J. Levinson, *The Seasons of a Man's Life* (New York: Knopf, 1978), chapters 5–6.

When Daniel J. Levinson of Yale University decided to study the midlife decade (ages 35–45) in men, he and his colleagues interviewed forty persons—ten novelists, ten biologists, ten executives, and ten laborers. Levinson found that a man's ability to adjust during this crisis period is largely dependent upon his development during his early adulthood (roughly the ages 17–33). Levinson grew particularly interested in this formative stage, which he has termed the novice phase. *He has broken the period down into three subdivisions: the early-adult transition (17–22), entering the adult world (22–28), and the age-thirty transition (28–33). During the novice phase, the young man has four major challenges: (1) to develop and delineate his Dream—the ideal or goal that he will strive for; (2) to form a mentor relationship with an older person, who may act as a teacher, friend, or example to guide him; (3) to translate his interests and abilities into a satisfying occupation; and (4) to enter into intimate relationships, primarily marriage and parenthood. These challenges are similar for women as well. If they are met successfully, then the young man will move into the next stage in Levinson's model—settling down.*

together they constitute *cognitive development*. The child psychologist Jean Piaget was one of the first to recognize that cogni- tive development is a social as well as a psy- chological phenomenon. The four stages he outlines complement and reinforce Erikson's and Mead's theories of personality development and add a new dimension to our picture of socialization.[5]

In Piaget's scheme, very young children gradually acquire *motor intelligence*—that is, a physical understanding of themselves and their world. They discover *object permanence*: the child realizes that his or her parents, toys, and other objects don't dissolve when they leave his or her range of vision. The child also begins to distinguish his or her own body from the environment. This cognitive development parallels the emotional development of trust in Erikson's first stage. The next step is the acquisition of language, which enables children to communicate with other people, to think, and to represent the external world, the past, and the future. Children can carry out mental experiments and evaluate themselves (by taking the role of the other), although they cannot consider more than one point of view, and therefore are not yet cognitively able to recognize Mead's generalized other. For example, J. L. Phillips, Jr. (1969), asked a four-year-old boy if he had a brother. The child said yes, he did have a brother named Jim. "Does Jim have a brother?" Phillips then asked. After pausing a moment, the child replied, "No."

During Piaget's third stage (which is equivalent to Erikson's age of industry versus inferiority), children's thinking matures markedly. As children learn to manipulate the tools of their culture (what Erikson calls industry), they begin to understand the rule of cause and effect. They also learn to consider other people's points of view, and most important, to coordinate others' viewpoints with their own (the stage at which, as G. H. Mead pointed out, children begin to play

Piaget argues that intelligence develops in stages. This child, aged seven, is thinking about whether a given quantity of water becomes "more" if it is poured into a taller glass. (The New York Times)

games). In this stage, children are extremely concrete: they think in terms of real objects and situations that they can handle physi-

---

[5] For a more detailed discussion of Piaget, see Furth (1969).

cally. This concreteness in part explains the susceptibility to feelings of inferiority that Erikson described. At eleven or twelve, children begin to think in terms of abstract concepts, theories, and general principles. Whereas younger children test their ideas by trying them out, adolescents can formulate hypothetical problems in their heads. The development of abstract or formal thinking explains adolescents' ability to reflect on their self-image and future hopes. Trying to combine personal desires and social demands, adolescents strive to develop an identity, as Erikson suggested.

Is the development of abstract reasoning (and, by extension, an identity crisis) inevitable? Lawrence Kohlberg, who has devoted much of his career to investigating Piaget's theories empirically, found that "the adolescent revolution is extremely variable in time, [and] that for many people it never occurs at all" (Kohlberg and Gilligan, 1971: 1065). He estimates that perhaps 50 percent of Americans never develop formal reasoning. Kohlberg is mainly interested, however, in questions of judgment and the development of moral thinking. Along with psychological and cognitive growth, moral development adds a third dimension to the process of socialization.

Lawrence Kohlberg: Moral Development

A man's wife is dying and there is only one drug that can cure her, but the small dose that is needed costs $2,000. Unable to raise the money, the man asks the druggist to let him pay part now, the rest later. The druggist refuses, and in desperation the man breaks into the drugstore and steals the medicine. Is the man's action right or wrong? Lawrence Kohlberg has presented such moral dilemmas to children from the United States, China, Malaysia, Turkey, and Mexico. He concluded that there are universal ways people think about moral issues, and that these ways develop in stages as children gain experience in the world.

At first, children do as they are told solely because they fear punishment. Then they begin to realize that certain actions bring rewards, but they view human relations in terms of a marketplace, of reciprocity. Malaysian boys at this stage, for example, thought the man in Kohlberg's story "should steal the medicine because he needs his wife to cook for him." As children grow, they become increasingly concerned about what other people think of them and their behavior becomes largely other-directed. Gradually, ideas about right and wrong develop. For example, a child at this point in self-development might say that the man in the story should not have broken into the drugstore because it's always wrong to steal.

Then, as children begin to associate with people whose ideas may be different from their own, they begin to recognize moral conflicts. For example, they understand why the man decided to break into the drugstore, but wonder what would happen if everyone decided to steal. As the conflicts between individual needs and the need for social order, between the values adults profess to believe in and those they actually live by become clearer to them, children begin to sense strong feelings of good and evil within themselves. At this point, they are becoming self-directed: gradually, they develop "universal principles of justice, of the reciprocity and equality of human rights, and of respect for the dignity of human beings as individual persons" (Kohlberg and Gilligan, 1971: 1068).

AGENTS OF SOCIALIZATION

Growing up in the modern world takes sixteen, twenty, and sometimes even more years—primarily because there is so much to learn. The separation of work and family, specialization, social mobility, the lack of fixed traditions, proliferating subcultures, and the generation gap all contribute to the complexity of modern life. A person must learn to play many roles, and socialization has become a lifelong process. A person's family, schools, peers, lovers and spouses, children (if the person has children)—all play a part.

The Family

Sometimes people have children because they want to watch a young person grow, or to perpetuate the family name, or to prove their virility or femininity. Some people hope that a child will fill some vacancy in their own lives, perhaps by realizing their own frustrated dreams; others have children because they assume all *normal* people marry and raise families, or perhaps because their method of birth control failed (Stone and

From an early age, children learn what their families value most. Like most middle-class children, this little girl will be encouraged in her curiosity about the world. Since her father is a concert violinist, she also is likely to develop a special interest in and respect for music. (Gene Maggio)

Church, 1973: 145). The motives people have for becoming parents—subtly communicated in the way mothers hold their newborn infants, satisfy their needs, respond to their first explorations—make a difference to their children. Parents are, for the first few years at least, the whole world to children; they are the mirror in which children begin to see themselves, and the source of ideas about what does and does not matter. It is from parents and family that children learn values and prejudices.

The Impact of Social Class   The behavior adults encourage and discourage and the ways in which they discipline children affect the basic orientation of the child toward the world. But values and styles of child-rearing vary from family to family. One explanation for the differences, presented in a study by Melvin Kohn (1969), suggests that social class influences how children are raised, although there is in fact much variation within classes as well as between them. The working-class parents Kohn studied value obedience, neatness, cleanliness, and respect. They want their children to conform to traditional standards of behavior; they demand that children do as they are told. Focusing on the immediate consequences of a child's actions, they tend to enforce discipline with physical punishment. Middle-class parents, in contrast, are more concerned about the child's motives and intentions than with his or her actions per se. Usually, they attempt to reason with the child, trying to make him or her understand why he or she should or should not do this or that. Why? Because they value curiosity, happiness, and above all, self-control. They want the child to be self-directed. However, middle-class parents often use the withdrawal of their love and emotional support as a form of psychological punishment.

Kohn suggests that these different approaches to the raising of children are directly related to the parents' occupations, particularly to three aspects of the job experience: how closely supervised the person is, how routine the job is, and how complex it is (Kohn, 1976: 112). Whereas most white-collar jobs require some measure of initiative and independence, as well as an ability to get along with people and to manipulate ideas, blue-collar jobs usually consist of carrying out a supervisor's directions. Success in the blue-collar world depends on following rules and orders, and working-class parents train their children to follow orders. Similarly, middle-class parents try to prepare children for the social reality they know. (In the next chapter we will consider how children learn other social roles—being male or female—and how this affects them throughout life.)

Authoritarian and Permissive Parenting   Discussions of the relative merits of authoritarian parenting (forcing a child to obey) and permissive parenting (giving a child more or less free rein) tend to take on moral overtones. Allport (1954) argues that authoritarian parents give children the impression that ''power and authority dominate human relationships—not trust and tolerance.'' Moreover, children who are taught not to have tantrums and not to masturbate learn to mistrust their impulses—and, by extension, to ''fear evil impulses in others.'' [6] In contrast, ''the child who feels secure and loved *whatever he does* . . . develops basic ideas of equality and trust'' (italics added).

Diana Baumrind (1966) disagrees. The

---

[6]   Other critics of a stern upbringing argue that authoritarian parents may provoke antisocial behavior and rebellion with their sternness, or on the other hand, may generate passivity and dependence, as the child simply gives in (Baumrind, 1966).

permissive school of child-rearing is based on the idea that by not interfering with the child, parents communicate their approval and respect for him. But isn't it possible that the child experiences noninterference as indifference? Baumrind suggests that permissiveness handicaps the child in two ways: first, by depriving the child of the chance to learn the costs of nonconforming behavior; second, by not giving the child opportunities to argue and rebel, thereby formulating his or her own positions. In Baumrind's view, parents should be authoritative, not authoritarian—enforcing their own rights as well as the child's "in a rational, issue-oriented manner" so that the child learns how to balance responsibility and freedom.

Of course, the best intentions and the soundest theories may fall by the wayside in the day-to-day interaction of parent and child. Parents learn to be parents "the hard way, by practicing on their first-born" (Stone and Church, 1973: 146). Research by I. Hilton and others indicates that new mothers are more anxious, and therefore more attentive and interfering, than experienced mothers. The behavior of new mothers is more extreme. By the time a second or third child arrives, the mother is more relaxed: she knows what to expect and how to handle most problems. Experienced mothers tend to rely on the child to express his or her needs and make his or her way; they do not fuss so much. Thus no two children, not even two members of the same family, are socialized in exactly the same way.

In modern societies the school is the primary agent for weaning children from home and introducing them into the larger society. Life at school is a drastic change from life at home. In the family, relations are built around emotional ties ("I'm spanking you because I love you"). At school, children are expected to obey not because they love their teachers or depend on them but because rules are rules and they exist to be obeyed.

In most schools, every moment of the students' day is planned and scheduled for them. Students don't participate in decision-making about rules or curricula or other issues that affect their lives; they don't even have the right to speak up, move around, or go to the bathroom without permission. An extensive study of today's schools concluded:

> [There] is no more firmly rooted tradition than the one that holds that children must sit still at their desks without conversing at all, both during periods of waiting, when they have nothing to do, and during activities that almost demand conversation. Yet even on an assembly line, there is conversation and interaction among workers, and there are coffee breaks and work pauses as well. (Silberman, 1971: 128)

The avowed purpose of school, of course, is to teach young people technical and intellectual skills and cultural values and attitudes, to prepare them for their roles as adults in a subordinate position in an office or factory. As work and authority relations change in modern society, schools are changing too, and in chapter 14 we examine more fully just what functions education serves today.

The Media

Competing with school for the child's attention are the media: movies that depict life as a series of disasters, violent encounters, and sexual adventures; the radio, which broadcasts romanticized notions of interpersonal relations, in the form of popular songs, twenty-four hours a day; and television, which may avoid explicit sex but popularizes violence.

For many American children, TV has become a major agent of socialization (see the box). Recent data indicate that children under five watch television for an average of 23.5 hours a week. By the time they graduate from high school they will have spent 15,000 hours in front of the "tube" (more time than they devoted to any other activity except sleep), seen 350,000 commercials, and witnessed 18,000 fictional murders (*Newsweek*, February 21, 1977).

What effect does the routine portrayal of violence on television have on growing children? Numerous experiments and field studies suggest that a child who has watched a violent video sequence is more likely to engage in subsequent aggressive acts than one who has not (Cater and Strickland, 1975: chapters 4 and 5). According to one study, a preference for violent TV shows is a more accurate predictor of aggressiveness than socioeconomic background, family relationships, IQ, or any other single factor (Cater and Strickland, 1975: 50). It is difficult to say

IN THE NEWS

Most Children Are Happy at Home but Fear World

Most of the nation's grammar school-age children are happy with their family lives but fearful of the world at large—two-thirds are afraid that "somebody bad" might get into their houses; a quarter are afraid that when they go outside somebody might hurt them.

These startling findings emerged as the result of a 1976 survey the Foundation on Child Development conducted of a cross section of 17.7 million American children. The children, who ranged in age from seven to eleven years old and who came from various economic and geographic backgrounds, were questioned on their feelings about their lives, homes, neighborhoods, and selves. Most of the children gave answers that indicated they were happy at home but that they harbored many fears, the most important of which was the fear of violence. Their fears differed from the usual childhood fears of ghosts and bogeymen in that they seemed to be justified by actual instances of being bothered in the neighborhood or by realistic portrayals of such instances, as viewed on television.

Why are children so afraid? Childhood socialization can be marred by any number of negative influences. Some of these influences are not as obvious as others, and sometimes effects may surface so gradually that the original cause is forgotten or overlooked. Besides the fear of strangers, the survey gave indications of other childhood concerns.

Although generally content with their families, and themselves, the majority of children said they felt afraid when their parents argued and were angry when they were ignored at home.

When marriages were described as

which comes first, the aggressive disposition or the preference for violent shows, but the relationship between the two stands. A steady diet of TV assaults and murders may also make kids numb. One eleven-year-old said, "You see so much violence that it's meaningless. If I saw someone really get killed, it wouldn't be a big deal. I guess I'm turning into a hard rock" (*Newsweek*, February 21, 1977, p. 67).

In addition to violence, television tends to promote sex-role stereotypes. According to one survey, there are six times as many men as women on adventure shows. Although men are shown taking responsibility for a wide range of activities, women are often depicted as "amusingly" incompetent housewives (particularly in ads) (Miles, 1975).

More subtly, children who spend much of their free time in front of the TV are likely to become jaded. Compared to what they see on television, real life may seem dull, passé. In the words of one child, "I'd rather watch TV than play outside because it's boring out-

"not too happy" by mothers or where the spouses had separated, the effects tended to show up in the children—for instance, such children were more likely to fight at school.

Many children desired more contact with their parents, nearly half wishing their fathers would spend more time with them and more than a third wishing their mothers would.

And, once again, the controversy over violence on television, as a negative influence on childhood socialization, came to the forefront. Survey results showed that

nearly a quarter of the children said they felt afraid of "TV programs where people fight and shoot guns," in an apparent link between TV watching

and fear. And heavy watchers—four or more hours a weekday—were twice as likely to feel "scared often."

Results of the survey were unclear on whether heavy television watching was the cause of the children's fear or whether it was the result of children staying indoors because they feared the outside. Nevertheless, the survey director, Dr. Nicholas Zill, felt the results of the survey indicated a need for a much closer look at the effect television violence has on children. He felt that the problem called for a much stronger remedy than Sesame Street and the "family hour," and he urged the Federal Communications Commission to zero in on this area of concern.

SOURCE: Richard Flast, "Survey Finds That Most Children Are Happy at Home but Fear World," *The New York Times*, March 2, 1977, p. 12.

side. They always have the same rides, like swings and things'' (*Newsweek*, February 21, 1977: p. 67). Television creates the illusion of having been places one hasn't been and having done things one hasn't done, and thus promotes spectatorship: watching instead of doing. For many children, watching TV has supplanted such traditional activities as playing outdoors, making models, collecting, reading, and perhaps even talking. (Television replaces the ''what did you do today'' hour in many households.) Television may teach youngsters that most problems can be solved in thirty or sixty minutes.

On the positive side, TV can be instructive and challenging. For example, the 1977 broadcast of *Roots* to an estimated audience of 130 million undoubtedly contributed to this country's understanding of race relations. Experiments show that just as watching violent shows facilitates aggression, watching shows that emphasize sharing, cooperation, and self-discipline (such as *Mister Rogers*) encourages social behavior (Cater and Strickland, 1975: 51). Indeed, television may be a major source of stimulation and instruction for deprived children in impoverished environments. Why children watch ''prosocial'' or antisocial shows, and which type has more impact, are open questions.

Peer Groups

Power in the family and the schoolroom is one-sided; parents and teachers can force children to obey rules they neither understand nor like. But peers are relatively equal. By virtue of their age, sex, and rank (as child and as student), peers ''stand in the same relation to persons in authority'' and therefore ''see the world through the same eyes'' (Davis, 1948: 217). Among their equals, children learn the true meaning of

exchange and cooperation. Peers share forbidden knowledge, information about such matters as sex and ways to evade and manipulate parents and teachers.

The importance of the peer group increases as children grow older, reaching its peak when they become adolescents. While society and adults are anxious to socialize a new generation in adult roles, adolescents are determined to gain independence from the adults. In a sense, adolescents have recently been gaining ground in this perennial conflict. As first described by David Riesman in *The Lonely Crowd* (1950), large social forces have been working to shift the center of socialization from the family to the peer group. One of these forces is the rapidity of change. Knowledge parents have gained through experience, which at one time would have been considered wisdom, is now seen as irrelevant (Elder, 1975: 10).

While peer groups are important to all adolescents, they are especially influential when parents don't give guidance, affection, and attention (Elder, 1975: 11). As Baumrind found (see the box on pp. 130–131), alienated and delinquent adolescents, as well as those she calls ''social victims'' and ''antihumanists,'' are more deeply affected by their peers than are their complementary types, the ''traditionalists,'' ''socialized,'' ''social agents,'' and ''humanists.''

In peer groups, young people can defend themselves against the ambiguities of adolescence. In most traditional societies, children win adult status early by undergoing rites of passage. When they emerge from such ceremonies, boys are men and girls are women, with all the rights and responsibilities accompanying adult status. In our society, adolescence is a no man's land.

Just when [they are at their] peak sexually, adolescents must remain celibate; just when

During adolescence, peer groups play a strong role in shaping the values, attitudes, and style of young people. (Margot Granitsas / Photo Researchers)

greatest, they are denied the right to participate in society's decision-making. (Boroson, 1971: 86)

By aligning themselves *with* peers and *against* adults, young people who are still financially dependent on their parents (and who may remain so for years if their parents finance college and graduate education), who are still practicing instead of participat-

they have the most strength and energy, they are given no productive, satisfying work to do; just when they are at their intellectual height, and when their need for power is

SHAPING ADOLESCENT LIFE STYLES:
THE EFFECTS OF SOCIALIZATION

Between 1960 and 1970 the arrest rate for youths under eighteen more than doubled (Davids and Engen, 1975: 343). Since then, the rate has continued to rise, and in 1976, 1,196,391 people under eighteen were arrested, including 794 who were arrested for murder.

Juvenile crime is not the only problem worrying observers of today's youth. The ''dropping out'' phenomenon of the early 1970s, often coupled with heavy drug use and deep feelings of alienation, disturbed many social scientists. Some found explanations in the materialism of American culture and in the Vietnam War. But these factors alone can't explain why millions of young people became hippies, while millions more did not. To understand why some adolescents become delinquents or heavy drug users or suffer from extreme alienation while others participate in movements for social change or set traditional career goals for themselves, social scientists look beyond the larger culture to the influences of the family.

One such researcher, interested in discovering how parent/child relationships influence adolescent life styles, is Diana Baumrind. Baumrind has identified eight ''adolescent prototypes,'' which she then links to childhood experiences. These prototypes or life styles can be grouped into two main categories, either high or low on the scale of social responsibility. For Baumrind, social responsibility implies friendly, cooperative behavior, both with other children and with adults. Adolescents low in social responsibility are described as social victims, alienated, delinquents, or antihumanists; those high in social responsibility are seen as social agents, traditionalists, socialized, or humanists.

Adolescents in the low social responsibility categories have much in common, and so do their parents. The main problem in these families is a lack of both consistency and a principled moral code. Values preached on Sunday may be disregarded on Monday, so children grow up feeling that anything goes. And in the families of delinquents, discipline is arbitrary, too: it is either absent or overly harsh. As a result, explains Baumrind, delinquents ''expect to be treated unjustly'' (129).

ing in the work of society, can achieve some sense of autonomy.

In the last decade, peer groups have become important agents of socialization during postadolescence, as growing numbers of people consider ''singlehood'' as a way of life, not just as a temporary condition. (*Newsweek* [July 16, 1973: 52] reported that 12.7 million Americans between the ages of twenty and thirty-five are single, an increase of 50 percent over the last ten years.) Many single men and women live in a subculture of their own, one built around clubs and apartment complexes, transitory relationships, and the continuing search for identity (as opposed to the traditional search for a mate). To some degree, the peer group—the people who frequent a club or bar, the group that works or plays together—becomes an extended family.

In the homes of alienated youths, the problem is not parental harshness but frustration. The parents of alienated adolescents are often disillusioned people with deep feelings of despair and *anomie* (the absence of a firm set of moral guidelines or internalized norms). In one study sons and daughters described their parents as "insufficient to the challenge of rearing children and as indecisive, depressed people whom [they] did not wish to emulate" (128). Adolescents from such families have a "Who cares?" attitude about others and about their own futures as well. Rejecting the main values of society and lacking "a sense of the world as orderly and supportive of realistic aspirations," these young people are adrift.

At the high end of the social-responsibility scale we find a very different set of attitudes. Anomie gives way to commitment; concern for others replaces indifference, and self-confidence supplants feelings of worthlessness. Interestingly, adolescents from traditional families don't experience the identity crisis that so many other young people suffer through. They select an occupation and a set of values consistent with their parents' standards and thereby feel a sense of continuity and social belonging rather than of confusion and anomie.

What kind of child-rearing practices do traditionalists' parents follow? In these families discipline is firm, but it is accompanied by strong affectional ties. Children are punished whenever they do something wrong, but they are also warmly loved and are praised whenever they do something right. Parents also point to external supports for their authority in the home, citing both religious and patriotic values (126). In short, parents of traditional adolescents adhere to what are commonly thought of as values. In her analysis of the child-rearing practices of these families, Baumrind concludes: "[W]ithin American society, families who maintain a strong belief system and a traditional family structure seem best able to shield their youth from drug use and anomie" (127).

SOURCE: Diana Baumrind, "Early Socialization and Adolescent Competence," in Sigmund E. Dragastin and Glen H. Elder, Jr., eds., *Adolescence in the Life Cycle*, New York: Halsted Press, 1975.

ADULT SOCIALIZATION

Socialization doesn't end when a person is nineteen or twenty. Entering the work force, moving into one's own apartment, marrying, becoming a parent, changing jobs or neighborhoods or spouses, and growing old all require learning new roles. For example, when a couple move in together, they are still the same people they were the week before when they lived apart. Yet there are changes. One may find it difficult to reassure the other that wanting some time alone is not a rejection—a problem that may never have come up before. Arguments take on a new significance—they can't go home to cool off for a while any more. Similarly, when a couple decides to separate, each has to relearn the role of being single. After six or eight

table 5:1 PROPORTIONS OF CREATIVE OUTPUT PRODUCED IN EACH DECADE OF LIFE

FIELD	NUMBER OF MEN	NUMBER OF WORKS	20s	30s	40s	50s	60s	70s
Scholarship								
Historians	46	615	3	19	19	22	*24*	20
Philosophers	42	225	3	17	20	18	*22*	20
Scholars	43	326	6	17	*21*	*21*	16	19
Means			4	18	20	20	*21*	20
Sciences								
Biologists	32	3,456	5	22	*24*	19	17	13
Botanists	49	1,889	4	15	*22*	*22*	*22*	15
Chemists	24	2,120	11	21	*24*	19	12	13
Geologists	40	2,672	3	13	22	*28*	19	14
Inventors	44	646	2	10	17	18	*32*	21
Mathematicians	36	3,104	8	*20*	*20*	18	19	15
Means			6	17	*22*	21	20	15
Arts								
Architects	44	1,148	7	24	*29*	25	10	4
Chamber musicians	35	109	15	*21*	17	20	18	9
Dramatists	25	803	10	27	*29*	21	9	3
Librettists	38	164	8	21	*30*	22	15	4
Novelists	32	494	5	19	18	*28*	23	7
Opera composers	176	476	8	30	*31*	16	10	5
Poets	46	402	11	21	*25*	16	16	10
Means			9	23	*26*	21	14	6

Note: Maximum values are shown in italics. Total output in each field = 100.

SOURCE: Wayne Dennis, "Creative Productivity Between the Ages of 20 and 80 Years," *Journal of Gerontology*, vol. 21 (January 1966): 2. Data gathered by analyzing published biographies of contributors to the fields listed above.

Declining productivity and old age do not necessarily go together. Much of the total contribution to scholarship, science, and art made by men who live to old age comes in their later years. For the men represented in the above table (all of whom lived to age seventy-nine and over) 20 percent of their output in scholarship, 15 percent in the sciences, and 6 percent in the arts was made during their seventies.

years of marriage, dating again may make a person feel as awkward as an adolescent.

Adult socialization builds on the norms, values, and habits learned in childhood and adolescence. For an adult, learning new roles is largely learning new ways of expressing existing values. For example, if a woman who has spent many years being a wife and mother and working for the PTA and various charities becomes active in women's liberation groups, she is still seeking the pleasures of belonging to an organization, still working for a cause in the hope of making things better. Of course, she may seem quite different to her family and friends and even to herself, but adult socialization is largely a reshaping of existing orientations.

Marriage and Parenthood

Not too long ago, marriage was a step into the unknown—very few couples lived together before their wedding. In many cases, one or both were virgins. Today, most couples know a great deal more about each other than did their parents when they got married. This is not to say that learning to be married is easier now than it was then. On the contrary. In the past, people got married because they wanted a respectable sexual relationship and a family. Today marriage is not a prerequisite for sex or respectability, and the population explosion makes having children a questionable choice, so there is less reason to get married in the first place.

Premarital sex surely makes wedding nights less awkward and embarrassing. On the other hand, contemporary couples may be more self-conscious about their sex lives than their parents were. They expect more. A great many couples think something must be wrong if they do not make love as often as they did when they were first together, or if they do not experiment, as they have read others do. In some circles, the husband or wife who resents his or her spouse's extramarital activities finds little support. In addition, the traditional roles of wife/homemaker/mother and husband/breadwinner/father are no longer givens. Although more and more people today accept that women have a right to pursue a career, we have not, as a society, resolved the question of who is going to take care of the children. Finally, with divorce becoming more common and more acceptable, marriage itself is not the final commitment it once was.

So to a large extent today, the absence of clear models forces couples to define their roles as husband and wife on their own. Some people welcome this freedom, but others find it trying.

The process of defining roles begins anew when a child is born and the family of two becomes three. Having worked out a routine for living with each other, the couple now must learn how to deal with a young child. In a very real sense, their life is not their own any more (they can no longer just pick up and go). Relationships in the family continue to change as the children grow up; the couple faces middle age; the children leave

As a result of such forces as the breakdown of traditional sex roles and the rising divorce rate, modern adults—this young father for one—must increasingly define marriage and parenthood in their own terms. (Owen Franken/Stock, Boston)

home and Mom and Dad learn to be a couple again; one spouse dies. Each change brings new roles to be learned. (We will explore these ideas further in chapter 13.)

Occupational Socialization

When a person takes a job, he or she becomes a new member of an organization. Inevitably, there is a period of initiation, during which the person learns the skills and vocabulary of his or her new position, the formal and informal pecking order of the organization, and its written and unwritten rules. For the organization, socializing new members means breaking them in. It is an opportunity for the boss to test neophytes (who might one day become competitors) and to reassert his or her own power. For recruits, socialization into an organization means adjusting expectations to reality, learning the system, establishing new loyalties, and discovering their own strengths and countervailing power.

Corporate Careers Sociologists who have studied America's corporations have found that companies select certain kinds of individuals for managerial positions, and nurture certain of their personality traits.

During the 1950s and early 1960s, businesses sought men[7] who wanted the security of working for somebody else. Other-directed and content with the status quo, they avoided ''rocking the boat.'' The hidden message in executive training programs was ''Be loyal to the company and the company will be loyal to you.'' This admonition

influenced a man's choice of wife—indeed, his entire life style. These executives were company men through and through. Dwight D. Eisenhower, who led the country down a safe, dull path and smoothed away troubles with his smile, typified the company man.

During the late 1960s and 1970s, however, corporations began looking for adventuresome, dynamic men who loved change and wanted to direct it. Superstars who inspired their teams to victories, this new breed of executives is motivated by the desire to be known as winners. They conceive of projects, relationships, and their careers in terms of possibilities and options, as if they are playing a game. John F. Kennedy was a gamesman (Maccoby, 1977).

Gamesmen tend to avoid deep personal involvements and commitments. They are perpetual adolescents who never outgrow their compulsion to score. Corporations value them because they are willing to take the risks necessary in an unstable economy.

The Process of Occupational Socialization Whereas corporate careers build on (and even exaggerate) existing qualities, other careers (such as medicine—psychiatry in particular—law, the military, and police work) require *resocialization*. Training programs are consciously and unconsciously designed to strip away the self-images and perspectives that have resulted from previous socialization, and to replace them with a new outlook and self-image. Resocialization occurs gradually over a period of time. The experience varies from profession to profession, and from individual to individual. However, it is possible to identify six stages through which most initiates go.

In the first stage, recruits are made to feel different. For example, psychiatric residents, who had learned to see themselves as competent young doctors, are told they will go

---

[7] In the 1950s and 1960s corporations did indeed choose men for managerial positions, to the exclusion of women. This pattern is only beginning to change. Hence we used the word ''men'' advisedly in this section.

slightly crazy. Rookie cops are viewed by veteran police as novice outsiders who must prove themselves (Van Maanen, 1976).

The second stage involves being discredited. Military inductees are given haircuts, uniforms, and numbers (on dog tags), and are generally stripped of their civilian identities. Veterans tell rookie cops to forget everything they learned at the police academy; it will be useless on the streets. Discrediting serves the dual purpose of breaking down the recruits' image of themselves as ready and near-competent, and of destroying preconceptions about the career so that *re*socialization can take place.

Typically, a period of conflict and confusion follows. Nursing students mutter that school isn't what they expected (Davis, 1968). Psychiatric residents wonder if senior staff members really mean that they should try not to cure patients but to understand them. They feel morally uncomfortable with the message that they should give priority to patients they can learn from. Rookie cops find their ideas of right and wrong attacked. Most neophytes don't realize that others are experiencing the same conflicts.

The combined effects of feeling different, discredited, and confused lead to despair. The novices are unable to maintain their old sense of self under the onslaught of conflicting norms and values. At this point, some consider dropping out. Others muddle through. They stop trying to understand or justify what's going on and just do what is expected. In short, they stop resisting.

The more individuals play at being what they hope to become (whether nurse, psychiatrist, or cop), the more sense the new moral order makes. Resocialization occurs in this stage. Nursing students begin to align themselves with their teachers (who conceive of nursing in broad, theoretical terms), against ward personnel (who see nursing in

terms of specific tasks). Rookie cops begin to dissociate themselves from the general public on the one hand, and from the police establishment (represented by the "desk jockeys") on the other. Your only friends are gonna be other cops 'cause they're the only ones who have been there and know the score'' (Van Maanen, 1976: 53).

A period of self-affirmation follows. Finally, the individual internalizes the world view of the career, and accepts its norms and values as his or her own. Ex-recruits reevaluate past experiences in the new terms, with some amusement about how naïve they were at the onset. The rookie has become a cop; the resident, a psychiatrist; the recruit, a soldier.

Growing Old

On the day he turns sixty-five, the president of General Motors becomes just another one of our 17 million "old people"; on the day her husband dies, the renowned hostess becomes a widow. Both have, between one day and the next, lost the major social roles of their adult lives—and in American society, a large part of their identities.

Yet despite the fact that the proportion of the American population sixty-five and older has increased five times since 1900, while the total population has increased only two and a half times, and that by 1990 about 20 million people over sixty-five will be 10 percent of the population, for most who grow old in our society, socialization to the final years of life is socialization to withdrawal (see Riley et al., 1968).

Because so few people are self-employed, most—even the president of a giant corporation—cannot choose when to retire: companies and unions make the rules. And the provisions of the social security laws penalize the older person for earning much in addition to the benefits he or she receives. So even the productive, active person is virtually forced to withdraw from the labor force. In our society, women also live longer than men; by age seventy-five, there are 100 women for every 75 men, thus minimizing the chances for the kind of social life to which adults in American society are accustomed.

Zena Blau's study, *Old Age in a Changing Society* (1973), points up the fact that retirement and widowhood are ''exits'' from major social roles, sudden discontinuities in the pattern of life rather than a movement from one stage to another (14, 15). The demoralization that results is often extreme:

> What am I doing on this earth? What good am I here? . . . Not having learned how to play or having formed any kind of hobby in almost fifty years of hard work, I now find myself at a loss to know what to do with the life I must continue to live.
>
> Since I retired, it seems I am living in a different world. My old . . . associates don't know that I am still in this world. . . . I know there is something wrong with me . . . but I can't seem to solve my problem. . . . (26, 27)

Yet there are many ways to counteract this loss and isolation. Blau shows that an active social life or just one intimate friend is enough to maintain morale, and both Blau and the anthropologist Margaret Mead (1971) contend that useful work—a second

Through their riding club, these Icelandic women keep themselves active and involved, proving that the experience of old age needn't be lonely or demoralizing. (© Robert Weinreb 1975)

career, civic service, continuing education—can allow people to minimize loneliness and despair and society to utilize their skills and experience. Other societies have roles for older people; there is no reason why our society can't also provide a place for them.

SUMMARY

Socialization is the process of acquiring the physical, mental, and social skills that a person needs to survive and become both an individual and a member of society. During the early twentieth century, two schools of thought concerning human development predominated: the Darwinians, who believed that human nature was biologically determined, and the Pavlovians, who felt that people were simply products of their environment. Today social scientists recognize that the key to individuality is socialization, where biology and culture meet.

The interaction of culture and biology during the socialization process affects a child's development in many ways. Although we know that socialization should begin with mutual trust between parent and child, every society has ideas about the right and the wrong ways to satisfy an infant's basic needs. Furthermore, each parent interprets society's child-rearing norms in his or her own way; and the unique genetic make-up of each child influences the way he or she will be treated. Facial features, rate of physical and sexual development, and differences of temperament, size, and strength can all affect the way parents and others respond to an infant. The way in which they respond is influenced by the meaning communities project onto any number of physical characteristics. The responses and expectations of the people in a child's world subtly shape the youngster's self-image.

Many students of social behavior have contributed to our understanding of the process of socialization. Charles Horton Cooley used the image of a looking-glass to explain how others influence the way we see ourselves. The self is a social product, which emerges as the child interacts with other people, and a person's self-image depends on the feedback he or she receives as a child, a student, a worker—throughout life. George Herbert Mead expanded Cooley's theory. He argued that by "taking the role of the other" in play, children learn to imitate others in their lives (those Harry Stack Sullivan called *significant others*). They learn to see themselves through other people's eyes. Gradually, children develop a generalized impression of what people expect from them and of where they fit in the overall scheme of things (what Mead called the *generalized other*). Mead believed that the self was composed of two parts: the "I" (the active, spontaneous, idiosyncratic self) and the "me" (the social self).

Whereas Cooley and Mead viewed socialization as the gradual merger of individual and society, Sigmund Freud argued that socialization is thrust upon the child against his or her will, and that socialization is never complete. For Freud, an essential aspect of socialization is the taming of the *id*, the repository of innate sexual and aggressive urges. The *superego*, or conscience, begins to develop, and the child starts to internalize his or her parents' ideas of right and wrong. Socially unacceptable desires are gradually repressed in favor of meeting socially acceptable goals. Gradually the child develops an *ego*, the conscious part of the self that seeks socially acceptable ways to satisfy biological cravings. Throughout life the ego mediates between the id and the superego. Driven one way by biology, the other by society, we are, in Freud's view, eternally discontent. Erik Erikson, a student of Freud, has described human emotional development in terms of eight stages ranging from infancy to old age. Erikson's central concern is with the feelings people develop toward themselves and the world around them. In many ways he brings Cooley, Mead, and Freud together, integrating the physiological, psychological, and social elements of socialization.

Jean Piaget adds another dimension to the process of socialization with his analysis of the stages of *cognitive development*. He showed that there are very real differences in the *way* children think at different ages. Piaget concludes that the stages of cognitive development do not unfold automatically but are the result of each child's interaction with the world. Lawrence Kohlberg has added much to our knowledge of *moral development*. He has concluded that the way people think about moral issues is not simply a reflection of their culture but, like emotional growth and cognitive skills, is something that develops in stages as the child gains experience in the world.

Socialization is a lifelong process in which family, schools, peers, lovers, and children all play a part. Families inculcate their values in their children—values that, as Melvin Kohn has suggested, are influenced by the parents' social class. School socializes young people to society's values and to the organizational life they will experience as adults, as do the media. Peer groups also play a large role in socialization. Among their friends, children can test ideas and share knowledge that may not easily be discussed at home. Peer groups allow young people to defend themselves against the ambiguities of adolescence by aligning themselves *with* each other and *against* adults. To some extent, peer groups become an extended family. Adult socialization builds on the norms, values, and habits learned in childhood and adolescence. Learning new roles through work, marriage, parenthood, and old age is largely a matter of learning new ways of expressing existing values.

In our society socialization to old age is, for many, socialization to withdrawal. Zena Blau and Margaret Mead suggest that old people can keep up their morale and play useful roles in society by using their experience in second careers, civic service, and continuing education. Society must, however, institutionalize meaningful social roles for old people.

GLOSSARY

cognitive development   the gradual maturation of a child's ability to reason and think in abstract terms.

ego   Freud's term for the conscious part of the self that finds socially acceptable ways of satisfying the biological cravings of the *id*.

generalized other   a child's generalized impression of what other people expect from him or her.

id   Freud's term for the innate collection of sexual and aggressive urges, as well as for all bodily pleasure.

identity   a sense of continuity about oneself, derived from one's past, present, and future, from what one feels about oneself, and from the image reflected in the social looking-glass. This sense of continuity is formed during what Erikson has termed the *identity crisis*.

identity crisis   Erikson's term for the period in a person's life during which confirmation of self is sought by selecting, among many and often conflicting possibilities, a life goal and direction.

looking-glass self Cooley's term to explain how others influence the way we see ourselves. We gain an image of ourselves by imagining what other people think about the way we look and behave.

motor intelligence Piaget's term for children's physical understanding of themselves and their world.

object permanence a child's realization that objects exist even when they are not within his or her range of vision.

significant others when young children play at taking adult roles, they in effect become the people who figure importantly in their social world. Psychiatrist Harry Stack Sullivan termed these people *significant others*.

significant symbols according to Mead, the conventionalized actions and words acquired by infants in interactions with their parents, especially their mothers, by means of which they arouse desired responses in those responsible for their care.

socialization the process of acquiring the physical, mental, and social skills that a person needs to survive and to become both an individual and a member of society.

superego Freud's term for the conscience, the part of personality that internalizes society's views of right and wrong.

REFERENCES

Gordon W. Allport, *The Nature of Prejudice*. Reading, Mass.: Addison-Wesley, 1954.

Diana Baumrind, "Effects of Authoritative Parental Control on Child Behavior." *Child Development*, vol. 37 (1966): 887–907.

Zena Smith Blau, *Old Age in a Changing Society*. New York: New Viewpoints, 1973.

Warren Boroson, "In Defense of Adolescents," in Glen A. Newkirk, ed., *Contemporary Issues*. Glencoe, Ill.: Scott, Foresman, 1971.

John Bowlby, *Separation: Anxiety and Anger*. New York: Basic Books, 1973.

Orville G. Brim, Jr., "Personality Development as Role-Learning," in Ira Iscoe and Harold Stevenson, eds., *Personality Development in Children*. Austin: University of Texas Press, 1960.

Douglass Cater and Stephen Strickland, *TV Violence and the Child: The Evolution and Fate of the Surgeon General's Report*. New York: Russell Sage Foundation, 1975.

John A. Clausen, "The Organism and Socialization." *Social Behavior*, vol. 8 (1967): 243–252.

Charles Horton Cooley, *Human Nature and the Social Order*. New York: Schocken, 1964.

———, *Social Organization: A Study of the Larger Mind*. Glencoe, Ill.: Free Press, 1956.

Fred Davis, "Professional Socialization as Subjective Experience: The Process of Doctrinal Conversion Among Student Nurses," in Howard S. Becker et al., eds., *Institutions and the Person*. Chicago: Aldine, 1968.

Kingsley Davis, *Human Society*. New York: Macmillan, 1948.

Glen H. Elder, Jr., "Adolescence in the Life Cycle: An Introduction," in Sigmund E. Dragastin and Glen H. Elder, Jr., eds., *Adolescence in the Life Cycle: Psychological Change and the Social Context*. New York: Halsted Press, 1975.

Erik Erikson, *Childhood and Society*. New York: Norton, 1950.

———, *Identity: Youth and Crisis*. New York: Norton, 1968.

Hans G. Furth, *Piaget and Knowledge*. Englewood Cliffs, N.J.: Prentice-Hall, 1969.

Harry F. Harlow and R. Z. Zimmerman, "Affectional Responses in the Infant Monkey." *Science*, vol. 130 (1959): 421–432.

Lawrence Kohlberg and Card Gilligan, "The Adolescent as a Philosopher: The Discovery of the Self in a Postconventional World." *Daedalus*, vol. 100 (Fall 1971): 1051–1086.

Melvin L. Kohn, *Class and Conformity: A Study in Values*. Homewood, Ill.: Dorsey, 1969.

———, "Occupational Structure and Alienation." *American Journal of Sociology*, vol. 82 (July 1976): 111–130.

George Herbert Mead, *Mind, Self and Society*. Chicago: University of Chicago Press, 1934.

Margaret Mead, "A New Style of Aging." *Christianity and Crisis*, November 15, 1971, pp. 240–243.

Michael Maccoby, *The Gamesman*. New York: Simon & Schuster, 1977.

Betty Miles, *Channeling Children: Sex Stereotyping in Prime-time TV*. Princeton, N.J.: Women on Words and Images, 1975.

Talcott Parsons, "The School Class as a Social System: Some of the Functions in American Society." *Harvard Educational Review*, vol. 29 (Fall 1969): 297–318.

J. L. Phillips, Jr., *The Origins of the Intellect: Piaget's Theory*. San Francisco: Freeman, 1969.

David Riesman, *The Lonely Crowd*. New Haven, Conn.: Yale University Press, 1950.

Matilda White Riley et al., *Aging and Society*, vol. 1, *An Inventory of Research Findings*. New York: Russell Sage Foundation, 1968.

Charles E. Silberman, *Crisis in the Classroom*. New York: Random House, 1971.

R. A. Spitz, "The Psychogenic Diseases of Infancy: An Attempt at Their Etiological Classification." *Psychoanalytic Study of the Child*, vol. 6 (1951): 255–275.

L. Joseph Stone and Joseph Church, *Childhood and Adolescence: A Psychology of the Growing Person*, 3rd ed. New York: Random House, 1973.

John Van Maanen, "Rookie Cops and Rookie Managers." *The Wharton Magazine*, vol. 1 (Fall 1976): 49–55.

John B. Watson, *Behaviorism* (1925). New York: Norton, 1970.

Lenore J. Weitzman et al., "Sex Role Socialization in Picture Books for Preschool Children." *American Journal of Sociology*, vol. 77 (May 1972): 1125–1150.

FOR FURTHER STUDY

The Biosocial Perspective. A growing number of sociologists think we underestimate the degree to which biological forces interact with social ones to make us the people we are. Among them is Pierre Van Den Berghe, author of *Man in Society: A Biosocial View* (New York: Elsevier, 1975). This excellent overview is complemented by a broad selection of readings in *Personality: Biosocial Bases*, edited by David R. Heise (Chicago: Rand McNally, 1973). One major force is sex; how much does it shape socialization? In his controversial book *The Inevitability of Patriarchy*, Steven Goldberg (New York: Morrow, 1974) argues that male dominance has a biological base.

Becoming a Doctor. Many students aspire to be physicians or to work with them in related careers. They will find fascinating details about such careers in sociologists' studies of medical students and will understand better what physicians go through. The classic studies are *Boys in White* by Howard S. Becker et al. (New York: Irvington, 1961) and *Student-Physician*, edited by Robert Merton et al. (Cambridge, Mass.: Harvard University Press, 1970). But the heart of medical training is now in residencies, which Rue Bucher and Joan G. Stelling have studied in their new book entitled *Becoming Professional* (Beverly Hills, Calif.: Sage, 1977).

Enduring Law School. Professional socialization into the law is no less grueling than socialization into medicine, as a number of studies have shown. The question for a sociologist is what impact these socialization experiences have on the values and organization of professional work. See Barrie Thorne's overview in *Education for the Professions of Medicine, Law, Theology, and Social Welfare*, edited by Everett C. Hughes et al. for the Carnegie Commission on Higher Education (New York: McGraw-Hill, 1973). To get an inside feel for socialization in law school, read Scott Turow's *One L* (New York: Putnam, 1977).

Old Age. Is it a contradiction to say that socialization can occur in old age? With the rising numbers of old people, this area has received more attention. In *Socialization to Old Age* (Berkeley: University of California Press, 1975), Irving Rosow examines these questions with thoughtful care. Zena Smith Blau's survey entitled *Old Age in a Changing Society* (New York: New Viewpoints, 1973) gives us a clear, immediate sense of what old people think and what experiences they have. A more comprehensive study of aging is the volume edited by Matilda Riley and Anne Foner, *Aging and Society*, vol. 1 (New York: Russell Sage Foundation, 1968).

Socialization for the Future. It has been said that society changes so fast that we can't socialize our children for the future. If that is true (are there not timeless qualities to human relations?), the problem is made worse because we can't help but be socialized by the past—that is, by the previous generation. The following works provide fascinating ideas and information about the future. In *Posthistoric Man* (Chapel Hill, N.C.: University of North Carolina Press, 1950), Roderick Seidenberg discusses the implications of technology for human values and social life. The same themes are pursued by Lewis Mumford in *The Myth of the Machine* (New York: Harcourt Brace, 1970). Mumford also provides great empirical detail of how human relations have changed. More optimistic is Robert J. Lifton, who wrote the famous essay entitled "Protean Man," which predicts a new, flexible, and open human being. Others who see social freedom as a fruit of technology are Marshall McLuhan, *Understanding Media* (New York: New American Library, 1970) and *Culture Is Our Business* (New York: Ballantine, 1972); Marshall McLuhan and Quentin Fiore, *War and Peace in the Global Village* (New York: Bantam, 1971); and Thomas Hanna, *Bodies in Revolt* (New York: Holt, Rinehart and Winston, 1970).

CHAPTER 6

Sex Roles

Much has changed in the period between a small meeting in Betty Friedan's apartment in 1966 that marked the founding of NOW and the National Women's Conference in Houston in 1977 that drew 10,000 delegates from all over the country. Women now hold one in four seats in law and medical schools. Forty million American women have jobs—including over half of all married women with school-aged children. This has affected the home as well as the office and the factory. Women who work outside the home inevitably gain confidence in their own abilities and acquire friends and independent interests. Apparently men are adjusting to this. According to a 1977 *New York Times / CBS News* poll, Americans of both sexes believe a marriage in which husband and wife share the tasks of breadwinner and homemaker is a more satisfying way of life than a traditional marriage, in which the woman is a full-time wife and mother and the man is the sole provider.

Thus it seems that rigid sex roles are breaking down and that American society is moving steadily toward equality for women. But is this really the case? Large, outspoken segments of the population (particularly those who oppose abortion and gay rights) are fighting equality. They believe that a woman's place is in the home, and that supporting the family is a man's responsibility. Despite great strides in some fields, women are still vastly outnumbered by men in others. For example, less than 5 percent of the members of the House of Representatives are women, and there is only 1 woman senator.

Women are still underpaid. On the average, women who work full time earn only two-thirds of men's salaries.

This chapter explores male and female biology, the acquisition of sex-typed behavior, attitudes, and interests, and the changing meaning of gender. How different are the sexes, and in what respects? Are any of these differences universal? What roles have been set aside for men and women in different societies? In America? How are these roles changing in the late twentieth century?

HOW DIFFERENT ARE THE SEXES?

For centuries people assumed that the differences between the sexes were inborn or ''natural,'' that biology decreed different interests and abilities for women and men. Men were thought to be instinctively aggressive; a woman caring for a child was supposedly fulfilling her ''maternal instinct.'' Generations of husbands told their wives not to worry their ''pretty little heads'' about politics or business, and gallantly protected the ''weaker sex'' from education. It was not until researchers discovered societies in which men are passive and vain and women domineering, and societies in which there are few differences between the way men and women behave, that people began seriously to question the biological basis of masculinity and femininity. Anatomy was not destiny after all. Feminists especially, but male thinkers as well, began to argue that the differences in behavior between males and females were learned, not innate. Little girls are given dolls, little boys trucks and guns, and few of us escape the ''blue and pink'' tyranny (Reuben, 1972). Rather quickly people divided into two camps: those who maintained that sex differences were innate (the ''nature'' argument), and those who argued emphatically that they were not (the ''nurture'' argument). We are beginning to learn that the truth lies somewhere in between and is more complex than the nature and/or the nurture arguments suggest.

The Biological Evidence

Human beings are divided biologically into male and female by *sex*. Besides the obvious anatomical distinctions between males and females, differences are apparent in the unequal sex ratio at conception (about 106 males are conceived for every 100 females), in the higher rates of prenatal mortality for males, and in chromosomes and hormones. Every human being has twenty-three pairs of *chromosomes,* threadlike bodies in each cell that carry within them the determiners of hereditary characteristics. Each pair is alike except one—the pair of sex chromosomes. Female cells have two X chromosomes, male cells an X and a Y. When sperm cells are produced, half of them have an X chromosome, half a Y. If an ovum (which always has an X chromosome) is fertilized by a sperm with an X chromosome, the child will be a female (XX); an ovum fertilized by a Y-carrying sperm produces a male (XY).

During the first twelve weeks, however, the fetus is sexually undifferentiated (Scarf, 1972: 102). Differentiation depends on *hormones,* chemical substances that stimulate or inhibit vital chemical processes. The major sex hormones are estrogen and progesterone (secreted by the ovaries in females) and testosterone and the androgens (secreted by the testes in males). These hormones initiate sexual differentiation in the fetus, and activate the reproductive system and the development of secondary sex characteristics in puberty. At some point, the male fetus begins to produce testosterone, which inhibits the development of female characteristics.[1] If testosterone is not produced, a female is born. A female fetus given testosterone will develop malelike genitalia; a male castrated before puberty won't develop secondary sex characteristics (such as a beard)

---

[1] Alfred Jost demonstrated this in the late 1940s when he castrated a male rabbit *in utero;* when born, the animal had female genitalia, despite his chromosome pattern (Jost, quoted in Scarf, 1972: 102).

or genital sexuality. In other words, biological sex differentiation is multidimensional: genetic sex, fetal and pubertal hormones, and internal and external anatomy do not necessarily coincide. There is much variation within the sexes, as well as between them (Money and Ehrhardt, 1972).

Do sex hormones influence behavior? Every so often something goes awry during prenatal development and an infant is incorrectly classified as female or male at birth, creating a "natural experiment." The parents accept the doctor's sex identification and raise the child as a boy or girl—whichever they've been told. The child grows up to be, in his or her own mind, this sex—sometimes despite evidence to the contrary. John Money and Anke Ehrhardt studied matched pairs of hermaphrodites (children born with the internal organs of both sexes) who were biologically identical but had been assigned to different sexes. The contrasts between those raised as females and those raised as males were so complete, "the ordinary person meeting them socially or vocationally has no clues as to the remarkable contents of their medical history." Money and Ehrhardt (1972: 18) conclude that a major part of *gender differentiation*—the psychological identification of the person as "masculine" or "feminine"—takes place after birth.

Gender Identity and Socialization

The differentiation and identification of *gender*, the psychological characteristics associated with femininity or masculinity, begin in infancy and continue into adolescence, with its biological changes and fumbling discoveries, and into adulthood.

Infant Care In large part, infant care is not gender-bound. All infants must be fed, bathed, diapered, cuddled, and rested. There is no sex typing in these basic activities, but there is some evidence that parents respond differently to male infants than they do to female ones (Lewis, 1972). Parents tend to handle infant girls more warmly and affectionately than they do infant boys, and to be more tolerant of assertiveness and physical aggression in infant boys.

Gender Training When the child reaches the age of two or three, what were at first casual, half-conscious distinctions become

These children are old enough to be aware of their gender identity, which they will continue to develop into adulthood. Whether they will feel required to adopt conventional sex roles, however, will depend upon information they receive from their parents, teachers, peers, and the media. (Jennifer Fearon/Photo Researchers, Inc.)

explicit lessons. Parents begin to address the child as "Daddy's little girl" or "Mommy's big boy" and to actively discourage (or at least ignore) behavior they consider inappropriate. In some ways the change is greater for boys than for girls. Boys are expected to outgrow dependency and clinging, whereas this kind of behavior is acceptable from girls (Bardwick and Douvan, 1971). A mother may begin to ignore a boy's whimpering. If he persists, she may ask him, "Did you ever see your father cry? Do you think Joe Namath or Muhammad Ali cries? Of course not." Gradually boys learn that only girls are supposed to cry. A little girl finds that her parents are genuinely angry when she uses a "nasty" word, but chuckle if her brother does. The message is clear. All children develop concrete notions of girl and nongirl, boy and nonboy even before they understand the facts of life. Girls are supposed to be pretty, clean, neat, sweet, and popular; boys should be clever, strong, and fearless. For most children, striving to live up to these ideals is the path of least resistance.

Of course, parents are not children's only source of information on how they are supposed to act; brothers and sisters, other children, teachers, television, and books provide additional models. Lenore J. Weitzman and Deborah Eifler (1972) found that nearly all prize-winning children's books present highly stereotyped and unrealistic images of girls and boys, men and women. Although 51 percent of the population is female, the ratio of pictures of males to pictures of females was eleven to one; and one-third of the books involved *males only*.

When girls did appear in the children's books, they were nearly always indoors, helping, watching, or loving the book's hero. The one exception to this statement was a book about a little girl named Sam who convinced a boy to act out her mischievous fan-

tasies. One set of books, called *Mommies and Daddies*, was not very complimentary to mothers: "Daddies," the author wrote, "know you're big enough and brave enough to do lots of things that mommies think are much too hard." Not one of the books mentioned mothers who work outside the home or showed fathers helping around the house; not one dealt with death or divorce or any of the real-life problems that might trouble children.

Prime-time TV programs and commercials also reinforce sex-role stereotypes, as a recent study concludes:

> Children "see, overall, more men than women on their television screens; on the exciting adventure shows, they see nearly six times as many men." More men are shown in diverse breadwinner roles and more men are shown as competent, authoritative and dominant, whereas women are shown as incompetent and lacking in authority. (Miles, 1975: 29–30)

Sex roles—the behavior patterns expected of males and of females in a society—are also taught in school. On a typical day at the Educational Alliance Child Care Center in New York City, a visitor can find little girls busily hammering and sawing, and little boys rocking doll cradles and setting tables. This day-care center is exceptional. (The very thought of boys playing with dolls would strike terror into the hearts of many parents.) The teachers, who were participating in a demonstration project to combat sex stereotypes, had to make their own books containing pictures of women working and fathers cooking, cleaning, and caring for children. The teachers' biggest problem, however, was learning to identify their own unconscious biases. Even the children, though only four or five years old, resisted innovation. The girls shied away from building blocks—until, that is,

Not only boys like woodworking; not only girls like babies. Both these children are learning skills that will make them more flexible men and women. (Top, Gene Maggio. Bottom, Globe Photos)

they visited a construction site where a woman was working as an engineer (*The New York Times,* April 19, 1974, p. 40).

In most schools, boys and girls are segregated in sports (for example, hardball for boys, softball for girls) and in such classes as shop and home economics. The irony in keeping girls out of shop is that women who become housewives need to know how to use tools as much as or more than their husbands do, because their husbands may not be home when things break.

Since the early 1970s, parents around the country have organized to combat sexual discrimination in curricula and teaching materials. But it is difficult to say whether teaching children of both sexes the same skills in the same classes alters the personality/attitude dimension of gender training. Harriet Holter (1970) believes that by the time children reach school, such personality traits as emotional expressiveness, self-reliance, or competitiveness may be relatively fixed.

Gender identity, then, does not develop naturally and inevitably as a by-product of physical maturation; it is acquired gradually through experience (Stoller, 1968; Money and Ehrhardt, 1972; Money and Tucker, 1975). It involves an awareness of physical distinctions (anatomy and appearance); a consciousness of sex-specific activities, skills, and modes of self-preservation; and covert feelings of liking or disliking for the interests reserved for one's sex (Kagan, 1964).

In our society, discrepancies between gender assignment and the behavior associated with it are strongly disapproved of and even punished. Homosexuality, for example, was for a long time illegal in most states; it was considered a sign of deviance and treated as a mental illness. This demonstrates that society has a stake in how individuals perform their roles as men and women and that social agents such as parents, teachers, and other authorities will try to dictate the social script outlining each individual's behavior.

THE SOCIOLOGY OF GENDER: SEX ROLES AND SOCIETY

> Why, generally, do European actresses present multi-dimensioned personalities while our American stars flatten out like uncorrugated cardboard? . . . We caricature screen heroines . . . we categorize . . . overplay . . . overdress. Our women slide into easy character niches. . . .
>
> But European movie makers don't give us such easy signals . . . in the course of the films their women often reveal themselves as rich, complex human beings. . . . Nothing stagnates, and no one is readable at a glance. (Rosen, 1973: 352)

Why do Swedish or French women behave differently from American women, both on and off the screen? As the preceding discussion suggested, we won't find the reason by examining their genes, hormones, or bodies; all these women are biologically female. The reason lies, rather, in culturally patterned expectations about what is appropriate for women or for men. This is what we mean by sex roles: they are guidelines for gender-appropriate appearance, dress, interests, skills, and self-perception; models of what men and women should be like.[2] Perhaps the best way to illuminate sex roles is to contrast our standards with those of other cultures.

---

[2] It is important to remember that roles are models of ideal behavior, not descriptions of how people really act. Obviously, for example, not all women are compassionate and maternal (although most may think they should be), and men can and do cry.

Cross-cultural Variation

When social scientist Margaret Mead left for New Guinea in 1931, she "shared the general belief in our society that there was a natural sex-temperament which at most could be distorted or diverted from normal expression" (1950: xvi). After she lived with and studied the Arapesh, the Mundugumor, and the Tchambuli, her attitude changed, and she explained why in *Sex and Temperament in Three Primitive Societies* (originally published in 1935).

The Arapesh   The mountain Arapesh are a very mild-mannered people. They regard competitiveness and aggression as aberrations. An Arapesh may fight to defend a relative, but he or she would be ashamed to show anger on his or her own behalf. What interested Margaret Mead most about this tribe was that they have no notion of any temperamental difference between men and women. They expect all people to be gentle and home-loving; they believe men and women are equally inclined to subordinate their own needs to the needs of those who are younger or weaker, and to derive personal satisfaction from the giving of themselves. No Arapesh can bear to hear an infant cry; the nearest man or woman rushes to cuddle and feed an unhappy child. Often, relatives borrow a youngster for the sheer pleasure of participating in his or her upbringing. In short, they are what we would call a maternal tribe. "To the Arapesh, the world is a garden that must be tilled, not for one's self, not in pride and boasting, not for hoarding and usury, but that the yams and the dogs and the pigs and most of all the children may grow" (109).

The Mundugumor   The neighboring Mundugumor are as fierce as the Arapesh are gentle. The Mundugumor assume that hostility between members of the same sex is natural; relations between sexes are only slightly less mistrustful. "The Mundugumor man-child is born into a hostile world, a world in which most of the members of his own sex will be enemies, in which his major equipment for success must be a capacity for violence, for seeing and avenging insults, for holding his own safety very lightly and the lives of others even more lightly" (146–147). The birth of a child is an ambiguous event among the Mundugumor. If the child is a boy, the father considers him a rival. Members of this tribe obtain brides by exchanging sisters and daughters, and a father and his son have an equal claim on the females that are their daughters and sisters, respectively. If the child is a girl, the mother begins worrying that the father will exchange this daughter for a new, rival bride. Often a couple will offer one or another of their children for adoption. The children they keep receive only minimal attention and are expected to fend for themselves as soon as they can walk, while their parents plot and scheme ways to satisfy their lust for power, position, and revenge. The aggressive, combative Mundugumor ideal applies to *both* sexes. Both men and women exhibit what we might call exaggerated *machismo*.

The Tchambuli   Members of the third tribe Mead studied did believe the sexes are temperamentally different, but the roles they prescribe for men and women are the exact opposite of our sex roles. Tchambuli women are "solid, preoccupied (with practical matters), powerful, with their shaven unadorned heads." Every dawn they set out for the lagoons to fish and trap, returning at mid-morning to work on the crafts they exchange with other tribes. Tchambuli men drift about the fringes of the women's circle, hoping for an approving word, an invitation, a gift. It is the women who pull the economic strings in Tchambuli society, and the men who devote their lives to self-adornment and the arts of "languishing looks and soft words"; men bicker and pout, exhibiting the emotional ups and downs and employing the wiles we call feminine. Mead says Tchambuli women have an attitude of "kindly toleration and appreciation" toward Tchambuli men; they don't take men terribly seriously.

Commenting on these surprising discoveries, Mead concludes that strange as it may seem "to a civilization that in its sociology, its medicine, its slang, its poetry, and its obscenity accepts the socially defined differences between the sexes as having an innate basis," the characteristics we tend to regard as belonging to one sex or the other are "mere variations of human temperament to which members of either or both sexes may, with more or less success in the case of individuals, be educated to approximate" (xvi).

Women in Russia   If we were to insist that men are *born* with interests and talents different from those of women, how do we account for the fact that 76 percent of the physicians in the Soviet Union but only 6 percent of their American counterparts are female (Sullerot, 1971: 151)? Marx, Engels, and other communist thinkers equated the subjugation of women with the oppression of the workers: under capitalism, women were chattel. In the early days of the Soviet experiment, women were seen as natural allies of men in the struggle, and their role in the Russian Revolution was idealized. In fact, ideology coincided with need in Russia. War had created a shortage of manpower; if the country was to modernize, women had to work. Indeed, women were doubly valuable—as workers and as mothers, who in bearing children would contribute needed additions to the population.

But although today a Russian woman who chooses not to work is stigmatized as a kept woman, a parasite, Marx's intentions have not been realized. Russian men consider housework degrading; as a result, Soviet women are housewives as well as workers. And although women have entered many professions (the Soviet Union had the first female astronaut), they are underrepresented in executive and managerial positions in industry and in the Communist party (Field and Flynn, 1970). In addition, such professions as teaching and medicine, where women are most heavily represented, are at the bottom of pay and status scales (Smith, 1976). Nevertheless, the large number of female physicians, engineers, and the like in the Soviet Union and in a few other countries shows clearly that society, not biology, determines what women can do.

The comparative study of sex roles challenges the implicit equation between women's biological make-up and their worldly achievements. In single-society research, the sociological determinants of achievements predominantly linked with one or the other sex often remain hidden, tempting researchers to attribute differences between the sexes to genetic or hormonal endowment. Cross-cultural data show that this assumption is false. The different rates of women's participation in professional and public life can hardly be attributed to biology, which, as far as we know, does not vary nationally.

Subcultural Variation

Even within a single society, norms for masculinity and femininity vary from one subculture to another. For example, in American society the ideal that men should be bread-winners and women homemakers is realized primarily in middle-class settings, although it is believed in most strongly by working-class wives, who are themselves more likely to have to work to help support the family. Nor does the image fit the upper class, where neither spouse may have to work, or both may prefer to work. Homebound and child-oriented (at least in principle), middle-class wives do many chores that upper-class women leave to servants. Not surprisingly, these different milieus present differing definitions of femininity to little girls growing up in them. In one case, it means scrubbing floors, washing, ironing, and cooking three meals a day; in the other, it means supervising the people who do such work.

Mirra Komarovsky's *Blue-Collar Marriage* (1967) highlights the differences between working-class and middle-class (college-educated) gender ideals. Komarovsky found that many working-class men and women got married because they were unhappy living with their parents or because they thought it was time to settle down (marriage being a symbol of adulthood). Middle-class men and women, many of whom leave home before they marry, cite a desire for companionship and intimacy as motivations for marriage. Although some working-class wives are troubled by the low levels of communication in their marriages, most feel that if a husband is a good provider and a wife a good homemaker neither has any grounds for complaint. After all, they told Komarovsky, men and women are different:

"When I was first married, half of the time I didn't know what she was driving at, what it was all about," confessed a 23 year-old grade school graduate. "Sometimes I'd think I'd got her all figured out and then I don't make her out at all. The women in her bunch understood her pretty well though," he added. "They seemed to understand her better than I did sometimes. They'd tell their husbands about her and the fellows would tell me." His 22 year-old wife remarked, "Men are different. They don't feel the same as us."

"You're supposed to tell your husband everything," said one young wife, "but you don't. Nobody can tell you what you ought to tell him. Sometimes you can tell him just the little old nothings and it is as wrong as it can be. And sometimes you tell him something you think will bring the roof down and he won't even bat an eyelash." (33)

Working-class wives tend to confide in their female relatives and friends, husbands in their men friends; on social occasions, men and women separate into two groups. Middle-class couples do not make so sharp a distinction between the world of men and that of women. Interestingly, however, working-class mothers were less likely than their middle-class counterparts to feel guilty about taking a job. Working-class mothers who took jobs explained that they needed the money or that they simply wanted to get out of the house (see box).

Regional variations in attitudes concerning appropriate behavior for either sex are also apparent. Why, for example, did Wyoming grant women the right to vote fifty years before the country as a whole saw fit to do so? The diversity of state laws on marriage, divorce, alimony, employment, and health standards all attest to the existence of special subcultural and subgroup definitions of masculinity and femininity.

SEX ROLES IN AMERICA

There is no doubt that sex roles are changing in this country. In the past several years television, magazines, and the other media have begun presenting alternatives to the man who gets a job, marries, fathers two children, and settles into the comfortable respectability of being a hard worker and a good provider, and the woman who, having had the wedding of her dreams, devotes her life to her husband, her children, and her home. Indeed, as we suggested earlier, these stereotypes never really applied to many lower- and upper-class people.

Nor are these stereotypes true for all periods of history.[3] In colonial times, for instance, women had a very conspicuous degree of economic power partly because they were in short supply but chiefly because it was up to them to produce many of the commodities needed by the family. There was no "breadwinner" per se, since the work performed by both men and women was essential to the maintenance of a household, and on the frontier, to survival itself. The advent of industrialism gradually weakened the financial partnership that had formerly existed between husbands and wives. In an economy based increasingly on money and on wage labor, it was typically the husband who worked, and it was his paycheck—occasionally supplemented by children's wages—that supported the family. Long hours of work now separated husbands from wives, and during their leisure hours, men were likely to spend their time at a tavern or a gambling parlor. The result was that women gained greater control over domestic matters because they were the ones who were always at home. During the Victorian Era, segregation of the sexes was almost complete. The woman's role was primarily that of caretaker of the children.

If anything, modern times intensified this polarity. As jobs came to require increasing mobility, fathers were often absent from the

---

[3]   The following discussion is based on Elizabeth Pleck (1974): 11–19.

COMMON SENSE AND SOCIOLOGY:
WORK AND THE WORKING-CLASS WIFE

Ask several people if a middle-class college-educated woman would be happy as a full-time housewife. The answer will probably be no. Then ask the same question about working-class wives with high school educations. You'll probably hear more yeses. Conventional wisdom has it that educated women work outside the home because it is stimulating, but working-class wives seek jobs only to earn extra money. But in fact, like a lot of other common-sense conclusions, this is simply not true.

Curious about working-class women's attitudes toward housework and outside employment, sociologist Myra Marx Ferree interviewed 135 women living in a blue-collar community near Boston. All of these women had school-aged children, so child care was only a part-time activity. "Slightly more than half of the women worked outside the home, and their jobs represented the typical occupations of women: most were supermarket and department-store clerks, waitresses, factory workers, typists, and nurse's aides, along with a few bookkeepers, bank-tellers, and beauticians" (76).

These are not glamorous or exciting jobs, yet the wives who held them were happier than full-time housewives. In Ferree's sample, "[almost] twice as many housewives as employed wives said they were dissatisfied with their lives (26 percent to 14 percent) and believed their husbands' work was more interesting than theirs (41 percent to 22 percent)" (76).

Ferree was puzzled by these findings. Why should tallying grocery prices or carrying trays of food and dirty dishes be more satisfying than taking care of one's own home? As she talked with the women in her sample, two reasons came up over and over again. Unlike a paying job, which has clear responsibilities and rewards, housework can be never-ending and is generally unappreciated. Husbands often accuse full-time housewives of "doing nothing all day," and over half of the women themselves "felt they were not very good at [housework]" (78). Full-time housework, then, often leads to low self-esteem.

It also leads to isolation, the second major complaint of full-time housewives. Previous generations of working-class wives were likely to live near close relatives who offered companionship and relief from the demands of child care and housework. But in recent decades, the increasing mobility of American families coupled with the growing number of women who have returned to work have made "housewife networks . . . difficult to maintain" (78). As a result, the full-time housewife leads a lonely life. "Staying home all day, said one woman 'is like being in jail'" (78). Indeed, among the working wives Ferree spoke to, "getting out and seeing other people" was a strong motive in their decision to get a job.

Ferree concludes that we need to modify the common-sense view of working-class wives. They work for the same reasons everyone else does—"for the money, to be sure, but also for the pleasure" (80).

SOURCE: Myra Marx Ferree, "The Confused American Housewife," *Psychology Today*, September 1976, pp. 76–80.

Sex roles have begun to change in America. Slowly but surely, more women are joining the work force as doctors, architects, carpenters, and in many other capacities. (Architect, Ray Ellis / Rapho / Photo Researchers, Inc. Doctor, Bruce Roberts / Rapho / Photo Researchers, Inc. Carpenter, UPI)

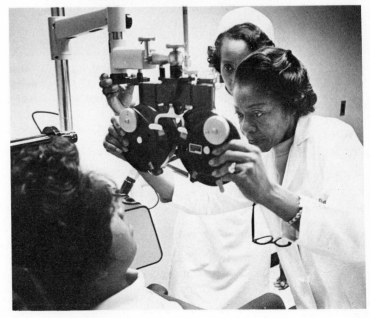

family while women took care of the children and did the housework. Once a center of production, the home became a center of consumption; it was often equipped with advanced technological devices like dishwashers, refrigerators, and vacuum cleaners that kept women busy—but also kept them isolated from the public world of paid employment. Not until significant numbers of women began to enter the work force were the essentially Victorian values that predominated even questioned. The situation of American women today is ambiguous, and that ambiguity is reflected in the law: for example, legislation that removes barriers to women's equality exists side by side with other laws or court decisions that seek to protect women as though they were still the "weaker sex." The continued existence of the latter rulings serve as reminders that in many areas Victorian ideals concerning the proper roles for men and women still prevail, despite realities such as those discussed in the section on subcultural variations.

Indeed, even though we can discern some important changes in sex roles, it is still possible to identify certain basic beliefs about men and women that have widespread approval and official (legal) support and that affect all Americans to some degree, even though these core values are often not reflected in reality.

The American Woman

What have Americans traditionally believed about the capacities and destinies of women? Popular wisdom has held that all "normal" women want to marry and have children, and that whatever other interests they may pursue are secondary. Women who don't want to marry or mothers who don't enjoy their children are thought to be

unusual or strange. Until quite recently, having children was in itself an honorable occupation, and was one of the chief ways for a woman to validate her femininity and fulfill herself as a person. What happened to a woman after her children were grown was not important (see Bernard, 1971: 80–81).

On the whole, a woman's status depends on the men in her life (first her father, then her boyfriends, husband, and sons). Taking her father's name at birth and her husband's name after marriage symbolizes this dependency. (For this reason, many women are now keeping their maiden names after marriage.) We still consider it perfectly legitimate for a woman to depend entirely on her husband for support. Indeed, many a husband still feels that if his wife takes a job it somehow reflects on his masculinity.

Women have traditionally been urged to share the triumphs and sorrows of their husbands and children, rather than to pursue their own goals. Although "the pursuit of self-interest is almost a virtue in the world men inhabit," a woman is still expected to put her family's needs before her own (Bernard, 1971: 26). Displays of self-assertiveness or aggression are considered more masculine than feminine—unless a woman is defending her home and family, in which case she is allowed to be ferocious. Similarly, women are discouraged from taking direct initiatives in sexual relations.

A capacity for sympathy, caring, love, and compassion (exemplified in such occupations as nurse and teacher) is central to the female role in America. Women are associated with nurturant and life-preserving activities, such as bearing children and taking care of the helpless and the ailing. Stroking—building up another person's ego by downplaying one's own talents—is one of woman's chief functions (Bernard, 1971: 88–94). Whereas men are expected to be achievement-

figure 6:1   Qualities most admired in the sexes

Ideal attributes for a man

As seen by men:	intelligence self-control humor sensitivity leadership frankness	As seen by women:	intelligence sensitivity humor gentleness self-control ability to express feelings

Ideal attributes for a woman

As seen by men:	intelligence gentleness sensitivity humor self-control sex appeal	As seen by women:	intelligence sensitivity humor self-control gentleness ability to express feelings

SOURCE: *The Virginia Slims American Women's Opinion Poll,* vol. 3, *A Survey of the Attitudes of Women on Marriage, Divorce, the Family and America's Changing Sexual Morality,* conducted by The Roper Organization Inc. (Spring 1974), pp. 18–19, 24.

This chart illustrates those qualities most admired in each sex by each sex as reported in a national survey of a cross-section of 3,000 women and 1,000 men conducted in 1974 by The Roper Organization. Note that intelligence is the highest rated quality in all four lists. It is interesting to note that women's standards transcend gender borders— for women, the qualities they rate highest in themselves are virtually identical with those they most admire in men. Women, then, perceive an ideal person, but men ascribe quite different ideals to themselves and to women.

oriented, women have traditionally been raised to be people-oriented, to place personal loyalty above other considerations. For example, a woman is not condemned for protecting her child, even if the child is a criminal. Finally, women are encouraged to cultivate beauty and sex appeal and to be concerned with personal adornment (traits that not incidentally have the latent function of stimulating consumption, as well as men). All these supposedly feminine characteristics have led Americans to treat women dif-

ferently from men (Bernard, 1971: 26).

To be sure, there are more and more exceptions to this expected pattern. Career women, working wives, and working mothers have defied the "rule" that women should be economically dependent on men. Many unmarried women, lesbians, and call girls have rejected being sexually dependent on men. (Call girls, of course, depend on men, but not on one man.) The women's movement (which we discuss in chapter 18) has questioned the entire system of female/male relations. And while many women still conform to the conventional ideals of femininity, a growing number do not.

The Benefits of the Female Role

With all the talk about sexism and discrimination against women these days, it is easy to forget that the traditional woman's role does have its benefits as well as its liabilities (and vice versa for the male role). What are some of these benefits or privileges?

Although increasingly large numbers of women are entering the work force all the time, many women are not obliged to work thirty-five or forty hours a week all their lives to provide for others. Furthermore, they have the legal right to claim support from their husbands. In many states, a man is liable for his wife's debts, but she is not responsible for his. Until recently men couldn't sue for alimony or child support (in the rare case where a divorced man was awarded the custody of his children), but women could. Of course, women do work; but employment, though perhaps an economic necessity, is not yet a *moral* duty for most women.

Nor do women suffer from the same pressures to achieve that haunt men in our society. Although a woman may strive to reach the top of her profession, there is little shame in failure or in achieving only moderate success. Most women do not suffer from the career syndrome. Philip Slater elaborates:

> When we say "career" it connotes a demanding, rigorous, preordained life pattern, to whose goals everything else is ruthlessly subordinated—everything pleasurable, human, emotional, bodily, frivolous. . . . Thus when a man asks a woman if she wants a career . . . he is saying, are you willing to suppress half of your being as I am, neglect your family as I do, exploit personal relationships as I do, renounce all spontaneity as I do? Naturally, she shudders a bit. (1970: 72)

Women also have more emotional freedom than men, in that they are permitted to express their doubts and vulnerabilities and that they have more outlets for tension and anxiety. The sphere of intimacy and close human contact is more accessible to women; the expression of nurturance, warmth, and sympathy, which is to some extent denied men in our society, can be its own reward. The fact that women rarely participate in the "rat race," and that they aren't required to inhibit their emotions, may partially explain why women live longer than men and have fewer heart attacks, ulcers, and other health problems related to tension and stress. But women are treated and institutionalized for mental illness more often than men are, perhaps because women must repress their hostile and assertive feelings more; because housework doesn't provide many rewards for educated women; and because the role of housewife is unstructured and unsung, leaving much time for brooding—especially when the children have grown up and left home (Gove and Tudor, 1973; see also Chesler, 1972).

The area of beauty and erotic love is largely woman's domain. Arousing admiration is an intrinsically satisfying and creative experience for some women. For others, however, being a sex object—or not being one—is dehumanizing. Moreover, the glamour-girl ideology involves the notion that once a woman is past the age of twenty-five, everything is downhill. This brings us to the liabilities of the woman's role.

The Costs of the Female Role

Women are denied autonomy in most spheres of American life. To channel small girls' talents into domestic/maternal areas, parents put more restraints on their daughters than they do on their sons. Girls are not supposed to be independent or adventuresome, and the economic dependency they experience as grown women may lead to passivity, timidity, and weakness. (For example, a woman who has no profession or trade and who hasn't worked in ten or fifteen years will think twice before she decides to get out of an unhappy marriage.) This taboo on self-development and self-assertion has been especially trying for independent, highly motivated women who are not content with the traditional female role.

In her article entitled "Fail: Bright Women" (1969), Matina Horner argues that many women consider success and femininity to be mutually exclusive, and that bright women especially are afraid of success. This conclusion was based on a study of male and female undergraduates. The women were asked to write a four-minute story about Anne, a woman who at the end of her first term of medical school was at the top of her class. Over 65 percent of the women wrote stories about Anne losing her friends or feeling guilty and unhappy, and some even denied that such a person existed (they suggested that Anne was a code name for a group of students). Only 9 percent of the male subjects wrote negative stories about John (the male counterpart of Anne) being at the top of his class. Horner then gave women

"I just want you to know, R. B., how much I admire the way you out-maneuvered Allied on that takeover without losing your femininity." (Drawing by Lorenz; © 1974 The New Yorker Magazine, Inc.)

who showed a high "fear of success" two anagram tests, one to be done alone and one involving "mixed-sex competition." Thirteen of the seventeen women who took the tests did better working alone.

Not surprisingly, this study attracted a great deal of popular and professional attention; the idea that women fear success seemed so right. But Horner's study is far from conclusive. First, it is unscientific to generalize from a sample of less than 200 undergraduates to the entire female population, as many people have. (*Ms.* magazine reported: "Psychologists found women's data indicated a hopeless will to fail.") Horner didn't study the women whose stories indicated they did *not* fear success; she also failed to study the *men* who feared success. (Other studies have found that as many or more men than women fear success and that a substantial percentage of male students associate high grades with "endless drudgery and premature coronaries" [Prescott, 1971; Robbins and Robbins, 1973].)

David Tresemer, who reviewed the many studies on this topic (1974, 1976), found that the percentage of women who wrote stories that suggested a fear of success varied from 11 to 88 percent; the variation in the percentage of men who wrote such stories was similar—from 14 to 86 percent. His own study of high school students indicated that students wrote different themes for different success stories, mixing positive and negative responses with little consistency. Thus, Tresemer questions Horner's definition of success. Citing another definition—"He has achieved success who has lived well, laughed often, and loved much"—he asks whether solving anagrams with ease or being first in your class in medical school is truly an indication of success. He argues that one question about a woman's being number one in her class at medical school is simply too limited a test.

Educational Aspirations In a survey of 21,000 college students conducted by the Educational Testing Service (Baird, Clark, and Hartnett, 1973), researchers found some striking differences between the aspirations of college men and those of college women.

Holding grade averages constant, men generally had higher aspirations than women; for example, of the students with B+ or A averages, 59 percent of the men expected to obtain Ph.D.s, but only 23 percent of the women did. Although the percentages of female and male students planning graduate study in the arts and sciences were about equal, twice as many men as women planned to enter professional schools (for example, in business, law, medicine, and engineering).

In a follow-up study (Baird, 1976), the Educational Testing Service researchers analyzed the patterns of activities of men and women one year after their college graduation. Here, too, they found marked differences. For example, women were working more both full and part time than men were, reflecting the fact that women in general were less likely to pursue graduate or professional study than men (25.4 percent of the women vs. 37.9 percent of the men). In schools of business, law, and medicine, far fewer women than men were enrolled.

In the context of long-term trends, however, these statistics may be somewhat misleading. For while the relationship between sex and educational and career decisions can still be seen, it appears to have changed considerably over the past quarter of a century or so. Between 1965 and 1976, for instance, the number of women in graduate schools has increased markedly. In 1964 to 1965, females represented less than 34 percent of all master's degree recipients; in 1975 to 1976, the women accounted for 46 percent. Similarly, while women earned only 11 percent of the Ph.D. degrees granted in 1964 to 1965, a decade later the share of women receiving Ph.D.s had climbed to 23 percent (National Center for Education Statistics, 1978). The percentage of women earning professional degrees has also been rising. Only 7 percent of the students entering medical schools in 1959 were women, compared to about 25 percent in 1976 (Etzel, 1977). In law schools, the story has been much the same, with the proportion of women receiving law degrees growing from a little over 3 percent in 1964 to 1965 to 19 percent in 1975 to 1976.

The career aspirations of women have been changing too. In a number of traditionally male areas—such as architecture, accounting, geology and physics, and engineering—the proportion of women earning bachelor's degrees began to increase noticeably in the late 1960s and early 1970s. That this trend is likely to continue is suggested by the career plans of first-year college women belonging to the class of 1978: these students intended to enter fields like business, medicine, engineering, law, science, and college teaching in far greater numbers than their counterparts in the class of 1970 (Freeman, 1976: 179).

Patterns of Work The percentage of women jobholders has risen steadily over the years. In 1977, almost 49 percent of women over sixteen were employed (up from 34 percent in 1950). The entry of middle-aged women into the labor force accounted for the increase in female employment between 1950 and 1965. Since 1965, women under thirty-five have been largely responsible for the increase (U.S. Department of Labor, Bureau of Labor Statistics, 1977).

Female college graduates have made the most progress in the job market. Between 1969 and 1974, income increased 49 percent for women with four years of college who were employed full time and year-round, versus 33 percent for men with the same background. In the twenty-five to thirty-four age category, the income of women college graduates rose 37 percent, as opposed to 24 percent for men with the same education (Freeman, 1976: 171). The realities behind those percentages, however, tell a slightly different tale, for even with their improved wages and salaries, female graduates who were employed year-round and full time were earning a median annual income of $12,109 in 1976, compared to $19,338 for male graduates (U.S. Bureau of the Census, 1977).

Although women are entering the work force in larger numbers, they are still overrepresented in low-paying jobs, and they still aren't earning equal pay for equal work. In fact, over the past two decades the median annual earnings of female workers in comparison to those of male workers actually dropped. In 1955, the average female worker earned 64 percent of the earnings of the average male worker; in 1976 she earned only 60 percent.

Perhaps half of this differential can be explained in terms of unequal experience. Often women drop out of the labor force to raise children, reentering a very different job market when they are in their late thirties or early forties. But this still leaves the other half of the differential unexplained. It may be due to employers treating women as a "fair weather" labor reserve that is tapped when the economy is expanding and is ignored the rest of the time. This makes it difficult, if not impossible, for women to develop coherent ideologies or programs to improve their earning power through group effort. That

figure 6:2   Median weekly earnings of full-time wage and salary workers by sex and industry groups, May 1976

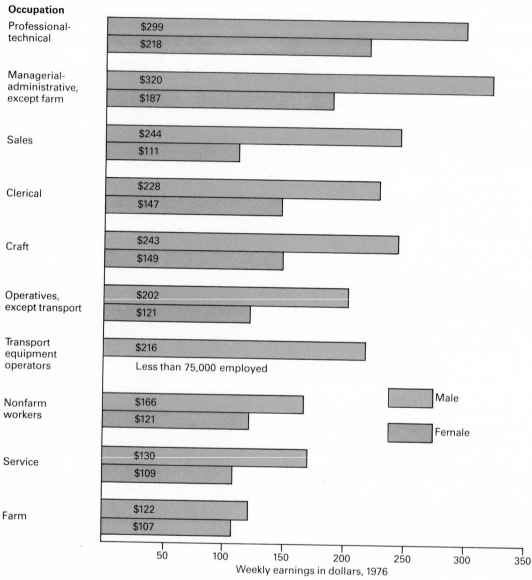

Occupation

Professional-technical: $299 (Male), $218 (Female)

Managerial-administrative, except farm: $320 (Male), $187 (Female)

Sales: $244 (Male), $111 (Female)

Clerical: $228 (Male), $147 (Female)

Craft: $243 (Male), $149 (Female)

Operatives, except transport: $202 (Male), $121 (Female)

Transport equipment operators: $216 (Male), Less than 75,000 employed

Nonfarm workers: $166 (Male), $121 (Female)

Service: $130 (Male), $109 (Female)

Farm: $122 (Male), $107 (Female)

Male

Female

Weekly earnings in dollars, 1976

SOURCE: U.S. Department of Labor, Bureau of Labor Statistics, *U.S. Working Women: A Databook* (Washington, D.C.: U.S. Government Printing Office, 1977), p. 34.

women are less well trained than men has contributed to their being treated as a marginal group of workers who join the labor force only when they want extra money (Waldman, 1970; Gubbels, 1968; Griffiths, 1972; Huber, 1976).

Far more significant in explaining this differential, however, is occupational segregation by sex: "When earnings are adjusted for occupational differences, the gap between the sexes is almost removed. . . . As recently as 1970, 73 percent of all female workers were in occupations where women were grossly over-represented. . . . [And] the figure was virtually identical ten years earlier—72 percent" (Vanek, 1977: 7). A 1975 Conference Board study of occupational patterns predicts that although more women will be performing such blue-collar jobs as bus driver or TV repairer by 1985, nearly three-fifths will still be in clerical and service jobs, and a staggering 98.6 percent of secretaries and 93.2 percent of typists will still be women (*The New York Times,* November 29, 1977, p. 28).

The evidence we have contradicts the theory that women who take jobs are only working for "extras." In reality, three-fourths of working women are either single or married to a man who earns less than $7,000 a year. Strangely, the tax laws penalize working wives (a working couple pays higher taxes than a one-worker family with the same income). The reasoning seems to be that a woman may stop working at any point (after all, she is only working for "extras") or may become pregnant. Indeed, the biological capacity to bear children is an economic liability for American women. In many states a pregnant women can't draw unemployment insurance even if she is laid off for reasons other than pregnancy. And of course housewives and mothers aren't paid for their work. If they were, according to one estimate, each full-time mother/housewife would be worth $14,000 in hired help. Such economic restrictions as no pay or low pay without the ability to get a loan tend to make women permanent minors not only in their own eyes but also in the eyes of society.

Patterns of Influence This is not to say, however, that American women are powerless. Many observers take the formal dependency and subordination of women rather too literally, overlooking the possibilities women have for exercising power behind the façade of male supremacy. The literature on Jewish, Italian, and black mothers and the jokes about henpecked husbands attest to the fact that women do dominate in some spheres. Housewives exercise power by running households, dominating kinship networks, arranging a couple's social life, making demands on husbands, supervising their children's lives, and managing the family budget. Indeed, housewives may resent intrusions on their territory.

> The traditional woman's self-esteem would be seriously threatened if her husband were to play a role equal to her own in the lives and affections of her children or in the creative or managerial aspect of home management. . . . The lesson is surely not lost on her daughter, who learns that at home father does not know best, though outside the home men are bosses over women. (Rossi, 1964: 15)

The difference is that women's influence is often personal, indirect (covert and perhaps manipulative), and emotional (women today cry, much as their grandmothers fainted). But the female role does not, as is often claimed, preclude the exercise of power.

Role Conflicts Finally, a number of conflicts are built into the female role. Women are supposed to depend on men but to be resourceful in times of crisis, to be domestic and also glamorous, to be faithful to one man but to make themselves irresistible to many. Not surprisingly, a growing number of women are fighting for the eventual elimination of distinct sex roles. But some respond to these conflicts by clinging to the customs and beliefs that make the sexes separate and unequal. So do some men.

The American Man

The male role is as deeply tied to the family as is the female role, although the connections are not always so obvious. First and foremost a man is expected to be a good provider for his wife and children. Financial independence is a prerequisite for manhood in our society; respect goes to men who are reliable, hard-working, and achieving. Americans don't think it odd for a man to sacrifice his leisure hours, his time at home, even his health to a career. His accomplishments and property are indications of his worth. Initiative, ambition, and strength are all part of the "masculine mystique." We say a man is mature if he accepts obligations for dependents, takes the necessary risks, makes decisions, and provides security and protection for those in his care.

It is no wonder, then, that so many American fathers encourage their sons to excel in sports (sometimes ignoring the fact that a boy is not interested in or built for athletics). Sports are not an end in themselves: very few boys will go on to become professional athletes, and few fathers expect them to. But team sports teach a boy to be assertive, aggressive, and competitive—all of which are thought to be essential masculine qualities. These qualities are also, it turns out, some of those necessary for corporate success at the managerial level. As Hennig and Jardim point out in *The Managerial Woman* (1977), football, baseball, and basketball help boys develop personal skills important to a later career: how to compete to win; how to cooperate with those you would not choose as friends to get a job done; how to win and

how to lose; how to take risks; how to take criticism; and how to bend the rules. These sports also make boys aware of the necessity for goals and plans and the need for a leader. The ground rules of team sports become the basis for life in the corporation. And they are rules and skills that women, who tend to participate in one-on-one sports such as tennis, swimming, or skating never learn.

Most elementary school teachers are female and most fathers spend relatively little time at home, so contact with and acceptance by male peers are especially important to a boy. To a large degree, boys depend on one another for information about the male role. The "locker-room culture" of adults (nights out with the guys, drinking, playing cards, going to a ball game) is reminiscent of youthful team sports. As Joseph Pleck suggests, "It seems hard to get a group of men together for very long without someone suggesting a competitive game" (1972: 10).

Sports provide many object lessons in self-reliance and stoicism. Weakness, doubt, and compromise are signs of failure for men, who are raised to conceal or deny such feelings. The taboo on expressing emotions and self-doubt explains the American stereotype of the strong, silent type. The 100 percent American he-man is happiest when he is with his buddies or alone with his horse. Courteous to women, he is also detached and prefers dealing with them on a "man-to-man" basis. He is impervious to pain as well as to feelings, is rugged and resourceful, and enjoys going up against overwhelming odds. John Wayne, of course, is the prototype for this "ideal man." In recent years the cowboy has been resurrected as the playboy: suave, urbane, shrewd—in a word, cool—who treats women like consumer products, never becoming emotionally involved with them (Balswick and Peek, 1971).

Heterosexual prowess is also essential to

Team sports have traditionally taught boys to be assertive, aggressive, and competitive, qualities regarded as masculine. In addition, the experience these high school football players will gain in cooperating and competing with others will help prepare them to succeed in the corporate structure. Girls, who are generally excluded from team sports, do not receive this valuable training. (Jeffrey Foxx / Woodfin Camp & Associates)

American manhood. Men are expected to have a nearly unlimited appetite for sexual adventure and to enjoy sex for its own sake (unlike women, who are thought to require at least some romantic feelings). Far more stigma is attached to effeminate behavior from a boy than to masculine behavior from a girl, who can play the role of tomboy. A woman who shows little interest in hetero-sexual relationships may be labeled prissy or frigid; a man is assumed to be homosexual. And there is no worse insult to an American man—except perhaps the imputation that someone is ''trespassing on'' his woman.

Benefits of the Male Role Like the female role, the male role has mixed effects. American men have access to the pinnacles of institutional power; men (white men, that is) control the nation's government, churches, corporations, professions, universities—even theaters and art galleries. Men are free to exercise legal and social powers denied to women and children. With the notable exceptions of the now-defunct draft law and alimony statutes, neither law nor custom discriminates against or restricts men solely on the basis of their sex. Men have more opportunities than women to develop their talents and to acquire special skills and knowledge useful for coping with the world. (If a family has only enough income to send one child to college, in all likelihood it will choose the son. Men are overrepresented in all the professions.) In general, men earn more than women performing similar kinds of work, and are more likely to be promoted to powerful and lucrative executive positions (where they enjoy the ministrations of secretaries, who are nearly always women). The fact that men are encouraged to display initiative and independence from the time they are small must also be counted among the benefits of the male role. Finally, the pervasive myth of male supremacy cannot but buoy the male ego.

It's important to remember, however, that although these potentialities are built into the male role, they are not available to all men. Opportunities for training, economic self-support, and power are clearly more accessible to men at the top of the social pyramid than to those at the bottom. To generalize from the privileged few to the struggling many distorts the actual situation for the vast majority of men, who are not in control of their lives nor anywhere near the seats of economic and political power.

Costs of the Male Role   The responsibilities attached to the male role in America can be a source of great stress and anxiety as well as a source of satisfaction and pride. Being in a position to make decisions is fine if a person knows what he is doing, but it may seem less of a privilege to a man who is uncertain of himself. Complicating this is the fact that men are supposed to maintain the impression of strength and courage at all times. Fear of inadequacy and failure is the dark side of the pressure on men to prove themselves. What's more, the emphasis men place on strength, toughness, initiative, and superiority can have unintended conse-

quences, such as the need to test or prove these attributes by engaging in violent exchanges with other men, or by "taking what is man's due" through, for example, rape, which is really less a sexual act than a hostile assertion of power.

Equally costly is the competitive syndrome that asks men to consider all other men as either inferiors or rivals and requires substantial mobilization of psychic aggression. Well known as the idea of male solidarity is, male friendships are not necessarily easy relationships.

> When stripped of male sex role "props," such as baseball scores, automobiles, and masculine sex boasting and fantasy, many men find great difficulty in relating to other men. A man in a group said, "You know, I have a pretty good idea of what I can get in a relationship with a woman; but I just don't know what I could get from a man. I just don't know." (Pleck, 1972: 8–9)

In very concrete terms, men do not live as long as women and suffer more heart attacks. In 1975, average life expectancy at birth was 68.7 for men and 76.5 for women, a difference of eight years (U.S. Department of Health, Education, and Welfare, 1977). Men also have more psychosomatic diseases, such as ulcers, spastic colons, asthma, and migraine. The male suicide rate is triple the female rate, and men are fourteen times as likely to become alcoholics. Moreover, men commit 95 percent of all violent crimes and eight times as many murders as women do. Men also have to fight the wars other men make.

Role Conflicts   Finally, as with the female role, a number of conflicts are built into the male role. Men are supposed to be single-minded in the pursuit of success but not neglectful of their families; they should be simultaneously interested and disinterested in women; and they must be strong and self-reliant, yet require the care of a nurturant wife.

As a result, masculinity is in many ways a rather vulnerable and precarious status. The male role is demanding and difficult and the "failure" rate is high even in the best of times. In American society, as in other industrial societies, few men can in fact achieve the wealth, power, and positions of leadership that are held out as ideals for all. *Machismo,* or compulsive masculinity, may be a last resort for men who accept the traditional masculine role but cannot fill it. Overtly, machismo consists of a show of strength and sexual prowess as well as the denigration, exploitation, and often brutalization of women. Covertly, this display masks fears and doubts about self-worth. In an effort to convince other men, women, and above all himself that he is truly all-male, a man uses machismo as a front for insecurity, self-doubt, and worldly failure (Aramoni, 1972: 69–72).

Serious doubts and anxieties about masculine identity and purpose are bound to occur as many women forgo the need for male protection and successfully compete with men in spheres previously considered off-limits to them. For example, 30 percent of the male undergraduates in one study experienced some conflict between the desire for female intellectual companionship and the notion that as men they should be intellectually superior (Komarovsky, 1973).

Some men have begun to see these changes in the female role as a welcome liberation from the burdens of traditional masculinity. These men seek a new male ideal, less geared toward competition and dominance. Men will be better off, they argue, if they can learn to acknowledge their human vulnerability and limitations and escape the posturing and pretense of the male role. However, others see change as a dethronement from a previously privileged status. The more they feel they have to lose, the more likely men—and women—are to resist change. The days ahead will not be easy for those who are wedded to traditional gender ideals. Anger, conflict, and misunderstandings are bound to develop as traditional roles change for both men and women.

THE FUTURE OF AMERICAN SEX ROLES

Social necessity has always been a prime agent for change. During both world wars, for example, American women suddenly became capable of performing work they were thought unsuited for a year or two earlier: they "manned" the nation's defense plants. In the past, most religions emphasized the procreative role of both men and women. After all, life was precarious, and many children did not survive infancy. Except for priests and other celibates, family and sex roles were interdependent. The moral/religious formula read: female = potential wife and mother; male = potential husband and father. However, the threatening possibility of standing room only on this planet and the easy availability of reliable birth-control devices have diminished the importance and desirability of reproduction. Procreation is no longer an imperative. And while sexual relations are still necessary for conception (although artificial insemination can now be used), the reverse is less and less true: conception is no longer the typical outcome of sexual relations.

Other changes are also apparent. Women are breaking into occupations that used to be labeled "men only" (such as the priesthood),

IN THE NEWS

The New Masculine Ideal

During the last ten years, the feminist movement has had great impact on how women perceive themselves and their possibilities. Just as importantly, the movement has effected men and how they view themselves and their sex role. More and more, men are concerned with the "rethinking of male personality" and are considering how they can achieve intimate relationships with women that will accommodate both the new female and male roles. Even the movies, which are usually slow to present original visions, are beginning to reflect a new masculine ideal as The New York Times *reports:*

In what may be an emerging genre in the movies—the post-feminist romance—there appears a character who expresses in his personality and relations with the heroine a new ideal of masculinity. He might be described as the emotionally competent hero. Alan Bates plays him in "An Unmarried Woman"; Jon Voight plays him in "Coming Home." He is the man to whom women turn as they try to change their own lives: someone who is strong and affectionate, capable of intimacy, unthreatened by commitment, masculine without being dominating.

Compared to the archetypal, old-fashioned hero exemplified by John Wayne or Gary Cooper or Cary Grant, the current figure of romantic imagination is less wooden, more emotionally articulate. Unlike the intensely emotional heroes that Marlon Brando and James Dean portrayed in the fifties, he is at ease with himself; he's more mature and less troubled. Nor is he the kind of anti-hero played by Dustin Hoffman or Jack Nicholson in movies of the last decade—small, estranged, in Nicholson's case often cynical and debauched. The hero in the post-feminist romance, although not

and men are entering areas once dominated by women (such as nursing and teaching in elementary schools). New attitudes toward sex and innovative family styles are also chipping away at the traditional roles. Of late we have seen men winning paternity leaves and alimony suits, and numerous changes in the laws concerning adoption and people's attitudes about divorce.

Both to those who applaud them and to those who deplore them, these changing styles and attitudes are symbolized by the equal rights amendment, better known as the ERA, a piece of legislation first written in 1923 and finally approved by the House in 1971 and by the Senate a year later. The ERA, which would be the Twenty-seventh Amendment to the Constitution, states that "Equality of rights under the law shall not be denied or abridged by the United States or

overpowering, is a firm and clear-headed fellow, possessed of a calm intensity of feeling, a capacity for unneurotic expressiveness.

In these films, the more coventional male is usually portrayed by the heroine's husband and the "new man" is epitomized by her lover. The husband is self-absorbed, aggressive, and emotionally distant from his wife, while the lover is tender, considerate, responsive, and easygoing.

The husband in these new films is virile enough, even athletic. . . . The husbands' problem isn't impotence: He can respond physically, but he can't respond emotionally. The new man is more responsive, softer, in some ways more domestic.

Ideals of male identity go through periods when they become more "masculine" or more "feminine." . . . Whereas earlier in this century we were in a "masculinizing" period—of which Lawrence and Hemingway and the cult of the "real man" were an expression—today we are in a period when masculinity is being softened. . . . Feminism and economic independence have encouraged women to make greater emotional demands of men not to put up with the distant self-absorption of the competitive male primarily involved with his career. These new characters on screen embody many of the qualities of responsiveness and intimacy now sought by women. They are the idealized response to a real change in social life.

SOURCE: Paul Starr, "Hollywood's New Ideal of Masculinity," *The New York Times*, July 16, 1978, pp. 1 and 26.

by any state on account of sex." As of July 1977, thirty-five state legislatures of the thirty-eight needed for the amendment's passage had ratified the ERA. However, three of those thirty-five—Tennessee, Nebraska, and Idaho—followed their decision to ratify with a decision to rescind their ratification (a move that, some said, the U.S. Constitution did not permit). Indeed, even before the amendment's fate was decided, the ERA had already served to highlight the profound ambivalences, uncertainties, and misunderstandings that surround the issue of sexual equality in the United States. But despite its political future, ERA has changed American culture. As Martha Weinman Lear wrote in 1976, at the height of the ERA controversy, "Today, even people who call themselves antifeminist insist upon equal pay for equal work. It has passed into the

figure 6:3   College and noncollege women's beliefs about sex roles

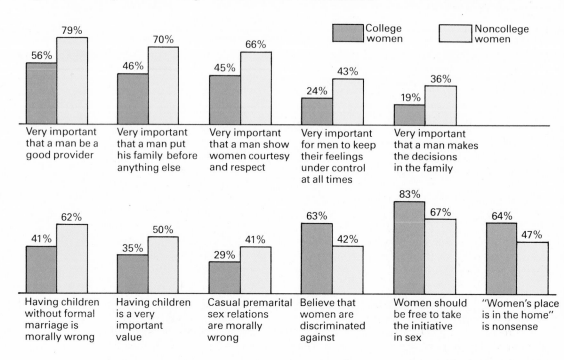

SOURCE: Daniel Yankelovich, *Changing Youth Values in the 70's,* Copyright © 1974 by the JDR 3rd Fund, Inc.,
pp. 34–35.

national consciousness as a basic principle, not of feminism—as it clearly was [in the early 1960s]—but of pure justice'' (*The New York Times,* April 11, 1976, p. 120).

But what are the far-reaching consequences of the changes in sex roles that have been occurring in recent decades? The gains of women have reached into every aspect of life: new laws and regulations govern pay, promotions, and job qualifications, as well as marital property and divorce. Even the mass media have altered their messages somewhat so that women in television serials now play other roles besides those of homemaker and mother. The other side of this new awareness in society is resistance to it. In general, earnings of women continue to be far lower than those of men, and the highest ranks of business and politics, despite the token admission of a few women, are still virtually all-male preserves. The traditional stereotypes of women as mothers and wives first, and of men as worker-breadwinners, persist. For many women, this means they must graft new responsibilities onto the old, becoming not more equal, only more tired.

Today sexual stereotypes and traditional attitudes coexist alongside the new, emerging patterns. Whether the old beliefs will change even more profoundly in the near future, or whether we will stand still for a while to evaluate recent changes, will reflect the capacity and desire of our society to change some of its most fundamental values.

SUMMARY

The traditional assumption that men and women are born with different abilities and temperaments which make them naturally suited for different social roles is no longer a statement to be accepted or denied with confidence. Nor is the opposite position, that sex differences have nothing to do with biology. We are beginning to learn that the truth lies somewhere in between and is more complex than the nature and/or the nurture arguments suggest. Although genes and hormones determine *sex* (that is, male or female biology), they do not determine *gender* (the psychological characteristics associated with femininity and masculinity). Even the biological differences between the sexes are not as clear-cut as most people would imagine. The discovery that children who have been assigned the wrong sex at birth grow up believing in the assignment substantiates this conclusion.

Gender differentiation—the psychological identification of oneself as ''masculine'' or ''feminine''—begins at birth and continues through adolescence into adulthood. Small children are given both subtle and direct clues to sex-appropriate behavior and feelings. Parents actively discourage or at least ignore behavior they consider inappropriate; children's books depict boys as bright and adventurous, girls as quiet, helpful, and doll-like. *Sex roles*—the behavior patterns expected of males and of females in a society—are taught in school as well as at home and in the media. Schools have traditionally segregated the sexes for physical education, home economics, and shop; guidance counselors have steered girls in certain directions, boys in others.

Cross-cultural studies show beyond any doubt that sex roles are socially and not biologically determined. Margaret Mead studied two tribes in New Guinea that didn't differentiate between the sexes with regard to temperament: all members of one were encouraged to be what we would call feminine, while all members of the other were exaggeratedly masculine. A third tribe reversed our traditional sex roles. Occupational opportunities for women differ from one industrial nation to the next; this underlines the social nature of male and female roles. In the Soviet Union, for example, 76 percent of physicians are women.

Even within a single society, norms for masculinity and femininity vary from one subculture to another. The ideal that men should be breadwinners and women homemakers, for example, is realized primarily in middle-class settings and is not a pattern typical of the lower or upper classes; yet it is believed in most strongly by working-class wives who themselves must often hold a permanent job. In addition, reasons for marriage and patterns of communication within marriage vary widely from subculture to subculture.

There is no doubt that sex roles are changing in American society, and that the stereotypes, which themselves date only from Victorian times and were not true of, for example, colonial America, are changing as well. Yet certain basic beliefs about men and women still have widespread acceptance and legal support, and these beliefs continue to influence all Americans to some degree. Women are expected to want marriage and a family and to put the family first; to depend on their husbands, financially and socially; to live vicariously through their husbands and children; to be passive and self-sacrificing, rather than aggressive and self-assertive; to be loving and sympathetic; and to be glamorous.

Certain benefits attach to the female role, as well as certain costs. Women are exempted from the moral obligation to support themselves and others and from the pressures of the business world. They also have more emotional freedom than men, and greater chances to reap the rewards of intimacy and close human contact. But the costs are lack of autonomy in most spheres of life and a tendency toward passivity, timidity, and weakness, toward what psychologist Matina Horner has called a ''fear of success.'' Women are not given equal opportunity and encouragement for self-development through education, and in the work force, despite the fact that nearly half of all women now work for most of their adult lives, they are segregated into lower-paying dead-end clerical and service jobs. These educational and work patterns are beginning to change, but not enough has changed yet to make a real difference in comparisons between men and women in terms of position and pay. Women are not, however, without any influence in American society—but that influence is often personal, indirect, and emotional.

American men, on the other hand, are expected to be good providers and to be competitive, achieving, self-reliant, and less emotional. They have access to the pinnacles of institutional power and are specifically trained, particularly through competitive team sports, to succeed in business and institutional life. They are granted more autonomy as children and adults; they are freer in the eyes of the law, earn more than women for equal work, and can bask in the pervasive ideology of male supremacy. But the responsibilities that attach to the male role, the pressures on men to succeed, and the competitive atmosphere in which they live are distinct liabilities. In concrete terms, American men do not live as long as American women; they suffer from more psychosomatic diseases, commit suicide three times as often as women, and are fourteen times as likely to become alcoholics. Moreover, only a few men are actually in a position to exercise self-determination; *machismo,* or compulsive masculinity, is often a sign that a man accepts the traditional masculine role but cannot fill it, rather than an indication of success. Recently, some men have begun to argue that traditional masculinity is not worth the costs and that sex roles should be more flexible.

Sex roles are changing because society is changing. The availability of reliable birth control and the threat of overpopulation means that procreation is no longer a moral imperative. Housekeeping and mothering are becoming less gratifying and necessary roles for women. Innovative family styles are chipping away at traditional roles, as are changing educational and professional goals for women and the increasing participation of women in the work force. Today, sexual stereotypes and traditional attitudes coexist alongside new patterns. What the results will be—more change or a period of evaluation and consolidation—will depend on whether or not we wish to alter fundamental values.

GLOSSARY

chromosome   the material in a cell that carries the determiners of hereditary characteristics.

gender   the psychological characteristics associated with femininity or masculinity.

gender differentiation   one's psychological identification as feminine or masculine.

hormones   chemical substances that stimulate or inhibit vital chemical processes.

machismo compulsive masculinity, evidenced in posturing, boasting, and an exploitative attitude toward women.

sex male or female biology.

sex role the behavior patterns expected of males and of females in a society, including appearance, interests, skills, and self-perceptions.

REFERENCES

Aniceto Aramoni, "Machismo." *Psychology Today,* vol. 5 (January 1972): 69–72.

Leonard L. Baird, "Entrance of Women to Graduate and Professional Education," paper presented at the American Psychological Meeting, Washington, D.C., September 1976.

———, Mary Jo Clark, and Rodney T. Harnett, *The Graduates.* Princeton, N.J.: Educational Testing Service, 1973.

Jack O. Balswick and Charles W. Peek, "The Inexpressive Male: A Tragedy of American Society." *The Family Coordinator,* vol. 20 (October 1971): 363–368.

Judith M. Bardwick and Elizabeth Douvan, "Ambivalence: The Socialization of Women," in Vivian Gornick and Barbara K. Moran, eds., *Women in Sexist Society.* New York: Basic Books, 1971.

Simone de Beauvoir, *The Second Sex.* New York: Knopf, 1953.

Jessie Bernard, *Women and the Public Interest: An Essay on Policy and Protest.* Chicago: Aldine-Atherton, 1971.

Phyllis Chesler, *Women and Madness.* New York: Doubleday, 1972.

Sylvia I. Etzel, "Medical Education in the United States." *Journal of the American Medical Association,* vol. 238 (December 26, 1977): 2761–2866.

Mark G. Field and Karin I. Flynn, "Worker, Mother, Housewife: Soviet Women Today," in Georgene H. Seward and Robert C. Williamson, eds., *Sex Roles in Changing Society.* New York: Random House, 1970.

Richard B. Freeman, *The Over-educated American.* New York: Academic Press, 1976.

Betty Friedan, *The Feminine Mystique.* New York: Dell, 1963.

———, "The Problem That Has No Name," in

Elsie Adams and Mary Louise Briscoe, eds., *Up Against the Wall, Mother . . .* Beverly Hills Calif.: Glencoe Press, 1971.

Walter R. Gove and Jeannette F. Tudor, "Adult Sex Roles and Mental Illness," in Joan Huber, ed., *Changing Women in a Changing Society.* Chicago: University of Chicago Press, 1973.

Martha W. Griffiths, "Can We Still Afford Occupational Segregation? Some Remarks." *Signs,* vol. 1 (Spring 1976): 7–14.

Robert Gubbels, "Characteristics of Supply and Demand for Women Workers in the Labor Market," *Employment of Women,* Regional Trade Union Seminar, Paris, November 26–29, 1968 (Paris, France: OEEC and D, 1970).

Margaret Hennig and Anne Jardim, *The Managerial Woman.* Garden City, N.Y.: Anchor Press/Doubleday, 1977.

Harriet Holter, *Sex Roles and Social Structure.* Oslo: Universitets Forlaget, 1970.

Matina S. Horner, "Fail: Bright Women." *Psychology Today,* vol. 3 (November 1969): 36ff.

———, "Toward an Understanding of Achievement-related Conflicts in Women." *Journal of Social Issues,* vol. 28 (1972): 157–175.

Joan Huber, ed., *Changing Women in a Changing Society.* Chicago: University of Chicago Press, 1973.

———, "Toward a Socio-Technological Theory of the Women's Movement." *Social Problems,* vol. 23 (April 1976): 371–388.

Jerome Kagan, "Acquisition and Significance of Sex Typing and Sex Role Identity," in M. Hoffman and L. W. Hoffman, eds., *Review of Child Development Research,* vol. 1. New York: Russell Sage Foundation, 1964.

Suzanne Keller, "The Family in the Kibbutz:

What Lessons for Us?'' in Michael Curtis and Mordecai S. Chertoff, eds., *Israel—Social Structure and Change*. New Brunswick, N.J.: Transaction Books, 1973.

Mirra Komarovsky, ''Cultural Contradictions and Sex Roles: The Masculine Case,'' in Joan Hul er, ed., *Changing Women in a Changing Society*. Chicago: University of Chicago Press, 1973.

————, *Blue-Collar Marriage*. New York: Vintage, 1967.

Michael Lewis, ''Culture and Gender Roles: There's No Unisex in the Nursery.'' *Psychology Today*, vol. 5 (May 1972): 54–57.

Karen Oppenheim Mason, John Czajka, and Sara Arber, ''Change in U.S. Women's Sex-role Attitudes, 1964–1974.'' *American Sociological Review*, vol. 4 (August 1976): 573–596.

Margaret Mead, *Male and Female*. New York: New American Library, 1950.

————, *Sex and Temperament in Three Primitive Societies* (1935). New York: Morrow, 1963.

Betty Miles, *Channeling Children: Sex Stereotyping in Prime-Time TV*. Princeton, N.J.: Women on Words and Images, 1975.

John Money and Anke Ehrhardt, *Man and Woman, Boy and Girl*. Baltimore Md.: Johns Hopkins Press, 1972.

John Money and Patricia Tucker, *Sexual Signatures*. Boston: Little, Brown: 1975.

National Center for Education Statistics, Washington, D.C., unpublished data, 1978.

Elizabeth Pleck, ''Sex Roles in Transition: The Historical Perspective,'' in Dorothy G. McGuigan, ed., *New Research on Women and Sex Roles*. Ann Arbor: University of Michigan Center for Continuing Education of Women, 1974.

Joseph Pleck, ''Male Sex Role and Personality: Toward a Research and Clinical Perspective,'' paper given at Harvard University, February 1972.

D. Prescott, ''Efficacy-related Imagery, Education, and Politics,'' unpublished honor thesis, Harvard University, 1971.

David Reuben, *Any Woman Can*. New York: McKay, 1972.

Lilllian and Edwin Robbins, letter. *The New York Times Magazine*, February 4, 1973, p. 56.

Marjorie Rosen, *Popcorn Venus*. New York: Coward, McCann, and Geoghegan, 1973.

Alice S. Rossi, ''Equality Between the Sexes: An Immodest Proposal.'' *Daedalus*, vol. 93 (Spring 1964): 607–652.

Maggie Scarf, ''He and She: The Sex Hormones and Behavior.'' *The New York Times Magazine*, May 7, 1972, pp. 30ff.

Philip Slater, *The Pursuit of Loneliness*. Boston: Beacon Press, 1970.

Hedrick Smith, *The Russians*. New York: Quadrangle/The New York Times Book Co., 1976.

Robert Stoller, *Sex and Gender*. New York: Science House, 1968.

Evelyn Sullerot, *Women, Society, and Change*. New York: McGraw-Hill, 1971.

David Tresemer, ''Fear of Success: Popular but Unproven.'' *Psychology Today*, vol. 7 (March 1974): 82–85.

————, ''Do Women Fear Success?'' *Signs*, vol. 1 (Summer 1976): 863–874.

U.S. Bureau of the Census, ''Money Income and Poverty Status of Families and Persons in the United States: 1976,'' Series P-60, no. 107 (September 1977).

U.S. Department of Health, Education, and Welfare, Statement by Dorothy P. Rice before the Senate Health Subcommittee, United States Senate, March 31, 1977.

U.S. Department of Labor, Bureau of Labor Statistics, *U.S. Working Women: A Databook*. Washington, D.C.: U.S. Government Printing Office, 1977.

Joann Vanek, ''The New Family Equality: Myth or Reality?'' paper presented at the annual meetings of the American Sociological Association, September 8, 1977.

Elizabeth Waldman, ''Changes in the Labor Force Activity of Women.'' *Monthly Labor Review* (June 1970): 10–18.

Leonore J. Weitzman and Deborah Eifler, ''Sex Role Socialization in Picture Books for Preschool Children.'' *American Journal of Sociology*, vol. 77 (May 1972): 1125–1144.

FOR FURTHER STUDY

Historical Debate.   The social implications of sex differences have been discussed by philosophers, theologians, and novelists. A famous and impassioned book on women's rights, originally published in 1792, is Mary Wollstonecraft's *Vindication of the Rights of Women* (New York: Norton, 1967). Almost a century later, in 1869, another English writer, the philosopher John Stuart Mill, presented the case against the oppression of women in his penetrating book *The Subjection of Women* (London: Oxford University Press, 1966). In this century Virginia Woolf, in *A Room of One's Own* (New York: Harcourt Brace, 1929), brilliantly argues the costs to women—and men—of women's lack of autonomy and self-reliance. A comparison of these three books, which range over two centuries, will reward the reader.

Socialization of Sex Differences.   One controversy concerns the nature versus nurture argument regarding sex differences. Proponents of the first argue that sex differences are genetically or hormonally programmed. Supporters of the second argue that sex differences in interests, skills, and personality develop through learning, imitation, and selective reinforcement. Some important research has been collected in the following works: Jerome Kagan, ''Check One: Male/Female,'' *Psychology Today,* vol. 3 (July 1969): 39–41; and Patrick C. Lee and Robert S. Stewart, eds., *Sex Differences: Cultural and Developmental Dimensions* (New York: Urizen Books, 1976).

Cross-cultural Studies of Sex Roles and Gender.   The most famous book is Margaret Mead's *Sex and Temperament in Three Primitive Societies* (New York: Morrow, 1963). Here the student can learn how differently societies define the roles we assume to be universal. One type of cross-cultural study is historical, for comparisons across the centuries permit us to see contrasting ways of organizing sex differences. A fascinating book drawing on myths, artifacts, and religious rituals is Wolfgang Lederer's *The Fear of Women* (New York: Harcourt, Brace and World, 1968). Finally, there is the instructive comparison of other contemporary modern societies. In ''Thailand: Equality Between the Sexes,'' in Barbara E. Ward, ed., *Women in the New Asia* (Paris: UNESCO, 1963), Lucien M. Hanks, Jr., and Jane Richardson Hanks describe a contemporary society in which the sexes are hardly differentiated by temperament and skills. *Women of the Forest* by Robert F. and Yolanda Murphy (New York: Columbia University Press, 1974) is a husband/wife team's study of the role of women and of sex typing among the Mundurucó culture of Brazil. In *Women and Men: An Anthropologist's View* (New York: Holt, Rinehart and Winston, 1975), Ernestine Friedl shows how the mode of subsistence technology in hunting and gathering and horticultural societies affects patterns of sex stratification.

Homosexuality and Departures from Normative Sex Roles.   The recent front-page treatment of gay liberation has raised many questions about homosexuality and whether it should be considered a perfectly normal human response, which is repressed in most people, or a pathological aberration. Some readings to help clarify one's thinking on these issues are Edward Sagarin, *Odd Man In: Societies of Deviants in America* (Chicago: Quadrangle Books, 1969), and Robert Stoller, *Sex and Gender* (New York: Science House, 1968). In *Conundrum* (New York: Harcourt Brace Jovanovich, 1974), Jan Morris describes her change from a celebrated male journalist named James to a woman journalist named Jan.

Organizing Social Life

Put five or ten people together, give them a task or the opportunity to do whatever they like, and the first thing they will do is "get organized." Each of the chapters in part three deals with the process of organizing social life.

Much of the drama of human existence is played out in the context of social groups, beginning with our families. Indeed, we are so accustomed to group life that we rarely, if ever, stop to ask precisely what a group is and how groups affect their members' behavior. Sociologists do ask these questions, as you will see in chapter 7.

Chapter 8 examines formal organizations; turns to that peculiarly modern (and often annoying) phenomenon, the bureaucracy; then looks ahead to new directions in organization for the accomplishment of the complex tasks of the late twentieth century.

Any form of organization—be it a family, a business, or an entire society—requires some degree of conformity from its members. But the very processes that encourage conformity also inspire, or create, deviance. We will explore this paradox in chapter 9.

CHAPTER 7

Social Groups

Put thirty boys—any thirty boys—alone on a tropical island. Some will try to get organized, to reestablish the discipline adults imposed at home and at school, hold meetings, and delegate responsibility for chores. Some will band together in "war parties," taking advantage of their freedom from adult surveillance to act out their wildest fantasies. Some will whimper for their homes and families, and will look for someone to fill the role of older brother. Leaders will emerge, weld together cliques, and vie for power. The group may divide into hostile camps. The boys may get carried away, find themselves swept by group momentum, and do things they might never have imagined on their own. This is what happens in William Golding's novel *Lord of the Flies*, a book to which we shall return later in the chapter.

A central theme in *Lord of the Flies* is that although we like to think we are fully in command of our private behavior, we are in fact influenced to a remarkable degree by our group experiences. None of us lives alone on an island. Social groups provide the vital link between our private lives and the larger society. Not only do they offer us security and support, but they shape our values, attitudes, and behavior as well, because in groups we are directly exposed to the opinions of others, who often matter greatly to us. Thus in order to understand the external forces that mold our experiences, we must pay close attention to the nature of social groups and to the impact they have on our private lives.

Because group life is so essential to human survival and to the individual's sense of well-being, a vast amount of research has been devoted to understanding the varieties of human groups and to exploring how groups influence individual experience. In this chapter we will consider the nature of social groups and the way groups are formed and work. We will also look at how modern urban society has changed the quality of social relationships, and at how people search for community in modern life.

WHAT ARE SOCIAL GROUPS?

Although each of us is a unique individual, we owe much of what we are to groups: to our families; to the relatives that gather on special occasions to dote on members of the next generation, advise, and lecture; to classmates and neighborhood friends who include us in pranks and secrets; to the team or club that gave us a chance to play the role of captain or old reliable sidekick; to organizations that involved us in community politics; to cliques that gather in the cafeteria or office, over the back fence or on the corner, to gossip and bolster one another's egos; to an intimate friendship that anchors us to one special person in our own and other people's minds. We feel we belong with these people, at least on certain occasions or for certain purposes. (Nothing is more depressing than spending a holiday alone, for example.) We expect things from them that we don't expect from outsiders. And others recognize us as members of a particular group (Merton, 1968: 339–340).

As distinguished from people who just happen to be together, a *social group* consists of people who identify and interact with one another in a structured way based on shared values and goals. Groups may be formal or informal, large or small, task-oriented or fun-oriented. Not every group, of course, possesses all four traits that characterize social groups completely: members may share only some values or may agree on some goals and disagree on others. But every group must display the following four characteristics to some degree, as the example most familiar to us, the family, shows.

Identity   Members of social groups feel a sense of belonging: they identify with one another and the group. To some extent, they define themselves in terms of the group. Being a member is part of their identity, their concept of themselves. A family may invite a friend for an extended visit and allow that friend to share their home and meals, joys and problems. But the visitor doesn't become a member of the family. After a time, both guest and host feel it is time for the visit to end.

Shared Values and Goals   Members of a group agree to some extent on values and goals. Parents and their offspring may argue heatedly about how to spend a vacation, each trying to convince the other that their plan is best. But all are agreed on spending the holiday in a way that will satisfy all of them; they all value collective decision-making. Otherwise they would not be arguing.

Interaction   A group is composed of individuals who interact and communicate with one another. Often interaction is based on membership. For example, cousins may have few interests in common. The only reason they get together is that they are members of the same family. But interaction on family occasions gives them shared experiences they may use to build a closer relationship.

Structure   Finally, a group has a structure of statuses and roles. In a family, one member usually emerges as the person who coordinates domestic life, another as the major source of financial support. Members agree in general terms about the relationships between them. Structure sets groups apart from *aggregates* (individuals who happen to be in the same place at the same time, such as theater audiences) and *categories* (individuals who have common characteristics but do not interact, such as old people, smokers, bicycle riders, or voters). Aggregates and categories lack structure.

GROUP STRUCTURE

Boundaries

One of the structural properties of a group is its boundaries. Without boundaries there would be no way of setting groups off, no way of distinguishing members from non-members, those inside the group from those outside of it. A fraternity pin is a symbolic but tangible social boundary: those who own one are members, those who do not are non-members. When a "brother" (note the symbol of closeness) gives his pin to a woman, he symbolically extends the group boundary to include her. A college decal on a car window is a social boundary; it publicly differentiates insiders from outsiders. Skin color can be a boundary, as can ethnic or religious background.

These Swiss nuns belong to a clearly defined group. They share values and goals—piety, chastity, and devotion to the Church, they live and work together in their convent, and they adhere to an age-old hierarchical stucture. Their distinctive dress, called habit, reinforces their group identity by creating a social boundary between the nuns and the outside world. (Porterfield-Chickering/Photo Researchers, Inc.)

In-groups and Out-groups   The terms "in-group" and "out-group" were first used in 1906 by American sociologist William Sumner in his attempt to describe the feelings of "we" and "they" generated by group membership. The notion of an *in-group* as a circle of people in which a person feels at home has been in common usage ever since. In-groups breed a consciousness of kind. They are typified by families, friendship cliques, social clubs, and religious and ethnic groups.

The members of an in-group usually de-

TOKENISM

A male employee at "Indsco" was discussing his feelings about ambitious women in his company: " 'It's okay for women to have these high-level jobs,' " he said, " 'as long as they don't go zooming by *me*' " (in Kanter, 1977: 218). This man is not a chauvinist pig, trying to put women down. According to sociologist Rosabeth Moss Kanter, he is simply reacting as a member of the dominant group who feels threatened by a token minority member—in this case a woman.

At Indsco—Kanter's name for a large industrial supply corporation—the proportion of women to men is very small. No women report to corporate officers; only five women could be called executives; and out of three hundred salespeople, only twenty are women. When outnumbered to this extent, women "become *tokens*: symbols of how-women-can-do, stand-ins for all women" (207). In any group where the majority makes up at least 80 percent of the membership, the remaining group members are tokens. And being a token has its consequences.

Continuing in the tradition of Georg Simmel, Kanter found that the lives of a group's token members are deeply affected by group structure. "Regardless of the category from which the tokens come," she writes, three characteristics of minority/majority group relations generate special pressures for tokens. These are visibility, contrast, and stereotyping.

Visibility. Like all tokens, the women at Indsco get a lot of attention—they stand out. But visibility has its drawbacks. "If it seems good to be noticed, wait until you make your first major mistake," one upper-level woman complained (213). Another recalled that she had once used some swear words in an Atlanta hotel while going to have drinks with colleagues. A few days later, in Chicago, she was being called a "radical." Visibility tends to cramp a woman's style. Where majority members can openly criticize the company, women feel they can't. What they say or do is too noticeable.

Tokens are also sensitive to doing better than the dominants. Indsco women worry about making the men "look bad." Many are even afraid to excel. And, Kanter found, there are grounds for this fear. One man "revealed a central

velop their sense of "we-ness" as a result of sharing common experiences. In one of the most thoroughgoing sociological studies, conducted between 1927 and 1932 in a Western Electric plant, investigators observed in detail the social dynamics of a small group of factory workers whose job it was to prepare banks of wires for telephone switchboards (Homans, 1950). This group of men developed their own rules about how much work each man should produce, and despite the fact that all the men were paid according to the number of units the whole group completed, overproduction ("rate

principle for the success of tokens in competition with dominants: to always stay one step behind, never exceed or excel'' (218).

Contrast.   If members of the majority group feel threatened by tokens, closing ranks is one way of dealing with the threat. Kanter calls this ''contrast, or exaggeration of the token's differences from dominants'' (221). At Indsco, the men drew the lines in the battle of the sexes. Around women, men would tell war stories and engage in sexual teasing. ''They highlighted what they could do, as men, in contrast to the women'' (223).

Sometimes contrast led to isolation, adversely affecting women's careers. Left out of the informal ''buddy network,'' women didn't know they were being criticized by higher management until it was too late to improve. Again, under-representation in the group puts women at a disadvantage.

Stereotyping.   Finally, as tokens, women are subject to stereotyping. Domi-nant-group members have fantasies about what tokens ''must'' be like. This happens in any skewed population because there are so few representatives of the token's type. Stereotyping sharply limits the roles tokens may comfortably assume. At Indsco, for example, ''[women] were often taken for secretaries; on sales trips they were often taken for wives or mistresses; with customers, they were first assumed to be temporarily substituting for a man'' (231). Tokens, then, must spend time correcting mistaken impressions, and ''establishing ac-curate . . . role relations'' (231). The effects of stereotyping are so far-reaching that even when men *knew* that women weren't secretaries, they would still treat them as if they were.

Kanter's book does more than itemize the special problems of women in a man's world. It reflects ''the experiences of people of any kind who are rare and scarce: the lone black among whites, the lone man among women, the few foreigners among natives'' (207). What matters in groups is ''how many of one social type are found with how many of another. As proportions begin to shift, so do social experiences'' (207).

SOURCE: Rosabeth Moss Kanter, *Men and Women of the Corporation*, New York: Basic Books, 1977, pp. 206–238.

busting'') was as much discouraged as un-derproduction (''chiseling''). The sense of togetherness among the workers was en-hanced by an elaborate system of controls they designed to keep outsiders from secur-ing information about the group's activities. These factory workers had a strong sense of ''we-ness,'' and they clearly defined people who were not members of the group as out-siders.

An *out-group*, then, is a circle of people to which a person feels he or she does not be-long. Out-groups surround us everywhere. If we are drug users, the out-group is the straight world; if we don't use drugs, users are the out-group. To the rich, the out-group is the middle class; to the middle class, both the rich and the poor are out-groups. All those groups of individuals who differ from us in significant ways comprise our out-groups.

Group Conflict   Once we recognize that all groups have boundaries, we can begin to ask questions about how these boundaries are established. One of the most effective ways of creating and maintaining group boundaries is through conflict with outsiders. A common enemy helps draw people together, and through confrontation with out-groups, insiders begin to develop a sense of "we-ness." As Georg Simmel, the great sociologist who studied group conflict, suggested: "A state of conflict [with outsiders] pulls the members . . . tightly together. . . . This is the reason why war with the outside is sometimes the last chance for a state ridden with inner antagonisms to overcome these antagonisms" (Simmel, in Coser, 1956: 87).

Lewis Coser, an American sociologist who elaborated on Simmel's writings about conflict, suggests that white Southerners at the turn of the century exaggerated stories of black crimes against whites to tighten their ranks. Blacks actually committed very few crimes against whites, but stories of rapes, murders, and imminent race wars abounded. As Coser says, "Fear of the Negro, far from deriving from the Negro's actual behavior, is a means of keeping the status system intact, of rallying all members of the white group around its standard" (1956: 109).

Of course, no amount of conflict with outside groups can sustain a group that isn't a going concern. Unless a group has *some* basis for cohesion and consensus, it will fall apart and not be able to rally under external pressure. During the Great Depression in America, for example, close families became

closer and stronger as they united against their troubles, but weak families disintegrated (Komarovsky, 1971).

Like conflict with outsiders, *internal* conflict and its eventual resolution may help to define and strengthen a group's boundaries. When a group successfully expels its "enemies from within," it publicly reaffirms its boundaries. During the Vietnam War, for example, draft resisters presented American society with an acute problem of internal conflict: if individuals were allowed to follow their own consciences and not the edicts of the draft board, how could the nation remain

These demonstrating Japanese students use flags and slogan-bearing helmets as identifiable group boundaries. (Paolo Koch/Rapho/Photo Researchers, Inc.)

unified in the face of conflict with outside groups? America's solution to this threat of internal dissension was to close its ranks against the dissenters. Draft resisters were sent to jail or fled the country in self-imposed exile. Both "solutions" maintained the cohesion necessary to continue the war. Through expulsion of the dissenters, American society established its boundaries as the type of social group that would not (or could not) tolerate in its midst men who refused to fight when they were called. (Eventually resisters were granted *conditional* pardons.)

Of course, internal conflict is not always so threatening to group cohesion that the dissenter must be expelled in order for group unity to be restored. If a group is secure in its own basic cohesion, in its common value system, it can tolerate and adjust to relatively large amounts of dissension. In fact, this very tolerance often allows members to let off steam before so much pressure builds up that the whole system explodes. It is the rare family that sends its dissenting adolescents packing, and it is the rare professional organization that ejects its challenging members.

Reference Groups   These are the groups to which we consciously or unconsciously refer when we try to evaluate our own situations in life.

When a student receives a B on an exam, he or she can feel either terrific in comparison to the C students or inadequate compared to the A students. A basketball player six feet four inches tall may feel gigantic in comparison with average players but short in comparison with many professionals. When a woman becomes a general practitioner (M.D.), she can feel either accomplished in relation to most women or inferior in relation to neurosurgeons. The groups we refer to in evaluating ourselves, but to which we do not necessarily belong, are called *reference groups*. Depending on what groups we select

to compare ourselves with, we either feel deprived or privileged, satisfied or discontented, fortunate or unfortunate.

Our feelings about ourselves are very much determined by what groups we choose as reference groups. Even our thoughts and beliefs can be molded by our real (or imagined) perceptions about the acceptable thoughts and beliefs of our reference groups. We often change reference groups in college as we change our sense of self. In a classic study of Bennington College, for example, Theodore Newcomb (1958, 1967) found that the liberal faculty replaced conservative parents as a reference group for the students. The longer students stayed at Bennington, the more liberal they became, except for students who continued to lean on their families for guidance.

Group Size: Dyads and Triads

Although we rarely think about it, the size of a group very much affects our behavior and feelings in that group. A person's sense of security can be greatly altered by group size. In a family, for example, the first child often resents the birth of a second. Similarly, the addition of a third friend can create uncertainty for the original two. (Consider how often couples quarrel about the amount of time one or the other spends with a best friend.)

The differences between *dyads* (two-person groups) and *triads* (three-person groups) are striking. The very existence of a dyad depends on the participation of both members. If either withdraws, the group ceases to exist. A three-person group, however, can survive the loss of a member. Participants in a dyad cannot "pass the buck." If, for example, two people are living together and one of them finishes off the last piece of cake, both know with certainty who did it. When three or more people live in the same

Dyads and triads are strikingly different. Dyads depend upon the participation of both members, who share an intimate and private bond. Triads allow for shifting alliances, majority and minority opinions, and mediation of disputes. (Top, Bruce Roberts / Rapho / Photo Researchers, Inc. Bottom, Kent Reno / Jeroboam, Inc.)

house, only the person who ate the cake knows for sure. Thus a member of a dyad "is much more frequently confronted with All or Nothing than is the member of a larger group" (Simmel, 1950: 135).

In groups of three or more, one member can reconcile conflicts between other members. If members of a dyad disagree, there is no insider to act as a mediator. But dyads don't have to deal with the problems of intruders or spectators. Neither of the two needs to perform for the benefit of a third party; they don't have to worry about giving a third party "air time." All of these factors, which are entirely due to the properties of size, have an enormous impact on private experiences.

Triads also have special qualities. A majority or minority and a coalition are impossible in a dyad. However, a number of coalitions are possible in a triad, as Theodore Caplow suggests in a book aptly titled *Two Against One* (1969). If A is more powerful than B, and B has the same power as C, then the possibilities for winning coalitions exist between A and B versus C; B and C versus A; and A and C versus B. The potential for new alliances prevents triads from becoming static. "In most triads members tend to switch coalitions from one disagreement to another simply to maintain solidarity and avoid permanent exclusion of one member" (Hare, 1962: 242).

Adding a fourth member to a triad again changes things drastically. It opens up new possibilities for coalitions (for example, two vs. two; three vs. one). As the size of a group grows, the number of possible relationships increases geometrically. (See table 7:1.)

table 7:1	**INCREASE IN POTENTIAL RELATIONSHIPS WITH AN INCREASE IN GROUP SIZE**

SIZE OF GROUP	NUMBER OF RELATIONSHIPS
2	1
3	6
4	25
5	90
6	301
7	966

SOURCE: A. Paul Hare, *Handbook of Small Group Research* (Glencoe, Ill.: Free Press, 1962), p. 229.

From this very brief discussion we can see how important size is in determining our seemingly personal and unique experiences in different groups. Size, like boundaries, is a structural property of groups, and it influences the behavior of members regardless of their individual psychological makeup.

GROUP DYNAMICS

William Golding's novel *Lord of the Flies* (1955) takes place in hypothetical times. During a war, a plane full of British schoolboys is shot down over an uninhabited tropical island. The pilot is killed in the crash, and the boys are alone. Piggy, a fat, clumsy, Mama's boy with asthma who is virtually blind without his spectacles, finds a fair-haired, athletic twelve-year-old named Ralph on the beach.

At Piggy's suggestion, Ralph uses a conch shell, which becomes a symbol of power, as a trumpet to call the survivors together. Faces materialize at the edge of the jungle. Small boys, clutching the remnants of school uniforms, clamor around the trumpeter. Like a mirage, a group of choirboys appears on the beach, "marching approximately in step in two parallel lines," their bodies covered from throat to ankle in black robes. As they gather on the beach, the boys slowly begin to realize that they have to create a group life of their own, without any help from adults.

The boys' struggle to form and maintain a group illustrates some of the basic principles of *group dynamics*, the study of relationships within small groups. Conformity to norms, the quest for status, the emergence of leaders, and the process of collective decision-making are the "sociological glue" that holds this ragtag collection of youngsters together.

figure 7:1   A sociogram

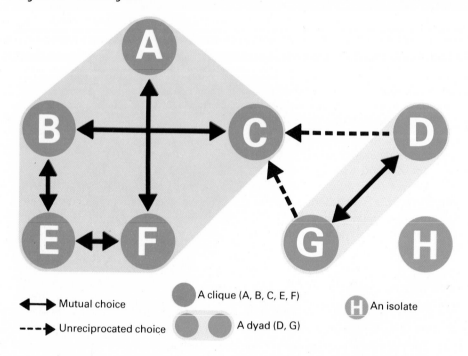

Mutual choice

Unreciprocated choice

A clique (A, B, C, E, F)

A dyad (D, G)

An isolate

Some years ago, J. L. Moreno devised a technique for describing relationships within a group. The researcher questions each member of the group on his or her personal preferences. For example, he might ask each person: Whom would you like to work with on this project? Whom do you enjoy spending time with after hours? Whom do you consider to be your best friends? These preferences are then transcribed to a diagram. Each circle stands for one person. The resulting sociogram enables the researcher to identify popular and influential individuals, cliques, dyads or triads, and isolates at a glance. Sociograms are extremely useful in clarifying communication networks and decision-making patterns in small groups.

How Groups Work

In his classic study *The Human Group* (1950), George Homans reveals three basic principles of group dynamics that involve the links between norms, interaction, and status.

Norms   From the beginning, Ralph and another boy, Jack, stand out because more than any of the others, they conform to schoolboy norms and ideals. Both are brave, agile, and adventuresome—everything the "littluns" look up to in a "bigun." In contrast, Piggy is fearful, myopic, asthmatic, and fat—a worrier and complainer.

There [grew up] tacitly among the biguns the opinion that Piggy was an outsider, not by accent, which did not matter, but by fat, and ass-mar, and specs, and a certain disinclination for manual labor. (81)

figure 7:2 Group dynamics as seen in terms of balance theory

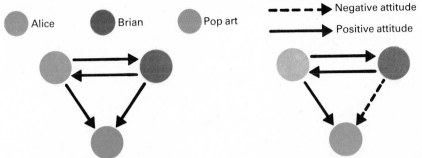

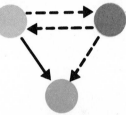

Negative attitude

Positive attitude

Suppose two art history majors, Alice and Brian, like each other, and both of them like pop art. Their relationship is then in a state of balance.

Suppose, however, Alice and Brian like each other, but Alice likes pop art while Brian prefers impressionism. Their relationship becomes imbalanced and strained.

Imbalance may be resolved in one of three ways:

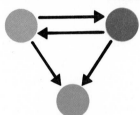

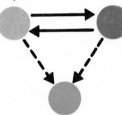

Alice and Brian discuss pop art, and Brian is persuaded that it is genuinely innovative.

Alice and Brian discuss pop art, and Alice decides that it is superficial and fraudulent.

Alice and Brian discuss pop art, and both retain their original attitudes. Alice decides, however, that Brian is a conservative bore, and Brian concludes that Alice is a faddist snob.

SOURCE: Adapted from T. M. Newcomb, *The Acquaintance Process* (New York: Holt, Rinehart and Winston, 1961).

Social scientists have approached the question of how groups work from perspectives other than Homans's. T. M. Newcomb, for example, has developed balance theory, or the ABX theory of attraction, in which A and B represent two individuals and X is an object, concept, or third person toward which each has a certain attitude. According to Newcomb, we can directly relate the attraction between people to the attitudes they hold toward specific objects.

Piggy's outcast status illustrates Homans's first principle: conforming to group norms increases a person's status. People who fail to conform, for one reason or another, are left out.

Interaction Ralph and Jack are rivals. Still, they are drawn to one another (rivals often are), and when, on that first day, the boys climb a mountain to light a fire to attract a passing ship, they "discover" each other.

. . . Ralph found himself alone on a limb with Jack and they grinned at each other, sharing this burden. Once more, amid the breeze, the shouting, the slanting sunlight on the high mountain, was shed that glamour, that strange invisible light of friendship, adventure, and content.

"Almost too heavy."

Jack grinned back.

"Not for the two of us." (51)

Homans's second principle is that interaction breeds friendship. We all know that friends interact more, but we sometimes overlook how people who are thrown together tend to become friendly as a result.

Status   According to Homans, individuals who enjoy high status initiate interaction with other members more often than people of low status.[1]

Ralph exemplifies this principle of group dynamics. No one pays much attention to Piggy or to Simon, a quiet, introspective boy whose mystic insights leave the others baffled. Piggy and Simon are outsiders. But Ralph's easy self-assurance earns him the respect of these boys. They applaud when Ralph is elected chief. His concern for the littluns allays their fears of a "beast" lurking somewhere on the island. Ralph is the only one who recognizes Piggy's intelligence and befriends him. He includes Simon in his plans, even though he can't quite understand him. The ability to interact with all kinds of boys gives Ralph the initiative (for the first half of the book). The boys look to him to call meetings, establish rules, and assign tasks.

---

[1]   Here all three dimensions come together. Observing norms increases status, and higher status leads to more interaction, which in turn widens one's circle of friends.

Group Leadership

A power struggle that arises between Ralph and Jack (and that ultimately turns into an all-out war) illustrates some important points about leadership. Who becomes leader, and what needs of the group a person meets as leader, depend a lot on circumstances.

Leadership Depends on the Situation   Leadership emerges from group interaction. Golding suggests at first that Ralph has *charisma*, a special quality that causes others to accept a person's authority.

> None of the boys could have found good reason [for wishing Ralph to be chief]; what intelligence had been shown was traceable to Piggy while the most obvious leader was Jack. But there was a stillness about Ralph as he sat that marked him out: there was his size, and attractive appearance; and most obscurely, yet most powerfully, there was the conch. (30)

However, as the story unfolds, it becomes increasingly clear that in large part circumstances forced this role on Ralph—his being a bit older and abler than most of the others, his desire for order, his happening to be the one who first blows the conch. Far from being a natural leader, he is uncomfortable with the attention and the responsibility and is often at a loss as to what to do next. Research supports the view that leadership depends more on the situation than on the person. Attempts to distinguish natural leaders from natural followers on the basis of personality traits alone have consistently failed (Secord and Backman, 1974: 344–346).

Leadership Roles: Task and Emotional Support   By carefully observing groups from the moment they start, Harvard professor Robert

Bales and his students have observed that leadership is needed in two areas: in getting the job done and in providing support to group members (Secord and Backman, 1974). On the island, the boys elected Ralph their overall leader, just as in most groups one person at first is the source of both ideas and group support. But as generally happens, two people are soon needed to meet these two separate group needs, and Ralph appoints Jack as task leader to get food.

Sociologists refer to the role of directing a group toward its goals as *task leadership*; to the role of maintaining good spirits and relations in a group as *social-emotional leadership*. Ralph has the qualities of a good socio-emotional leader: he values harmonious, democratic social relations, and he protects Piggy and other underdogs and listens to everyone's ideas and needs. But he is so intent on keeping a smoke signal going that he neglects the socio-emotional needs of the group.

> "Look at us. How many are we? And yet we can't keep a fire going to make smoke. Don't you understand? Can't you see we ought to—ought to die before we let the fire out?"
> There was a self-conscious giggling among the hunters, Ralph turned on them passionately. . . .
> "And another thing."
> Someone called out.
> "Too many things." . . .
> There was a row immediately. Boys stood up and shouted and Ralph shouted back. (101)

Jack, who glories in excitement, tests of strength and bravery, and violent conquest, is greedy for power. He senses the unmet needs of the group and changes from being the task leader, hunting for food, to being the socio-emotional leader, offering fun and adventure to those who will leave Ralph, who because of his focus on keeping the fire alive has become something of a taskmaster.

> "Bollocks to the rules! We're strong—we hunt! If there's a beast, we'll hunt it down! We'll close in and beat and beat and beat____!"
> He gave a wild whoop and leapt down to the pale sand. At once the platform was full of noise and excitement, scramblings, screams and laughter. (114)

Thus leadership roles on the island get reversed, but at all times the group needs and finds both task and socio-emotional leaders.

Group Decision-making

The boys on Golding's island have no idea why events take the course they do. Things just happen; decisions get made. However, sociologists who have studied group interaction have identified certain regularities in communications among group members. Whatever the group's composition or the task at hand, the group goes through four distinct stages in arriving at decisions (Bales and Strodtbeck, 1951).

A scene early in the novel illustrates the decision-making process. The first stage is devoted to orientation. Members analyze the task before them, exchange data, and offer possible solutions. In the second stage, the group evaluates the information it has collected. Individuals offer opinions and weigh other members' suggestions.

> Ralph cleared his throat.
> "Well then."
> All at once he found he could talk fluently and explain what he had to say. He passed a hand through his fair hair and spoke.
> "We're on an island. We've been to the mountain-top and seen water all around. We

Toward the end of Golding's Lord of the Flies, *the rivalry between the leaders—democratic Ralph and authoritarian Jack—reaches a state of severe imbalance, and the two boys break irrevocably. Conflict between their respective groups has become inevitable, and Jack and his hunters terrorize the enemy camp. (The Museum of Modern Art / Film Stills Archive)*

saw no houses, no smoke, no footprints, no boats, no people. We're on an uninhabited island with no people on it. . . . This is our island. It's a good island. Until the grownups come to fetch us we'll have fun."

Jack held his hand out for the conch.

"There's pigs," he said. "There's food; and bathing water in that little stream along there—and everything." (42–45)

Tension mounts as the group moves toward the third stage and a decision (in this case, to put aside childish fears and concentrate on making the best of things and creating their own society). Once a decision is made, the group moves toward the fourth stage and the restoration of equilibrium. A period of joking and informal banter draws dissenters into the fold. In various ways, members stress the importance of group solidarity.

Ralph lifted the conch again and his good humor came back as he thought of what he had to say next. . . .

"This is what I thought. We want to have fun. And we want to be rescued."

The passionate noise of agreement from

the assembly hit him like a wave and he lost his thread. He thought again. . . .

"We want to be rescued; and of course we shall be rescued."

Voices babbled. . . .

"There's another thing. We can help them to find us. If a ship comes near the island they may not notice us. So we just make a fire on top of the mountain. We must make a fire."

"A fire! Make a fire!"

At once half the boys were on their feet. Jack clamoured among them. . . .

"Come on! Follow me!" (48–49)

And the boys are off.

PRIMARY AND SECONDARY GROUPS

We have looked at what groups are and how they work. Now we will look at another facet of groups: the kinds of relationships members have to one another. Sociologists have categorized social groups into two types according to the degree of closeness and involvement of their members, and have called these types *primary* and *secondary* groups.

Primary Groups

Charles Horton Cooley (1909) characterized *primary groups* as those based on

> intimate face-to-face association and cooperation. They are primary in several senses, but chiefly in that they are fundamental in forming the social nature and ideals of the individual. The result of intimate association, psychologically, is a certain fusion of individualities in a common whole, so that one's very self, for many purposes at least, is the common life and purpose of the group. Perhaps the simplest way of describing this wholeness is by saying that it is a "we"; it involves the sort of sympathy and mutual identification for which "we" is the natural expression. (23)

Breaking Cooley's definition down into a list, we find five interconnected features:

1. continuous face-to-face interaction
2. permanence
3. ties of affection
4. multifaceted relationships
5. non-task-oriented relationships

The nuclear family, at least in theory, is the primary group par excellence. Members of the family are frequently in face-to-face interaction; the unit is enduring (even after members move away from the main body of the family, they are still considered part of it); family members are bound together by love and affection; family members have many kinds of relationships with one another (ranging from exchange of services—"You set the table, I'll wash the dishes"—to emotional support and physical protection); and the family is a unit because it *is* a family, not because it is trying to accomplish something. (Of course, not all families live up to the ideal.)

Primary groups also develop in other settings, as Roger Little (1970) discovered. Little was interested in finding out why a soldier will risk his life in a foreign war. He found that after fifteen months with a rifle company in Korea, soldiers tended to be suspicious of bravery, courage, heroism, and other so-called manly virtues.

What matters most to soldiers is staying alive. This primary concern with survival links every soldier to every other soldier with whom he eats, sleeps, and fights. Cut off from civilian life, soldiers begin to think of their platoons as families; buddies even speak of one another as brothers. During World War II, said one soldier, "The men in my squad were my special friends. . . . We bunked together, slept together, fought together, told each other where our money was pinned in our shirts. . . . If one man gets a letter from home, the whole company reads it. Whatever belongs to me belongs to the whole outfit" (Shils, 1950: 18). Soldiers obey orders that involve risking their lives not only for love of country, devotion to cause, and allegiance to the army, but to support and protect the close-knit group that now sustains and defends them.

Secondary Groups

In contrast to primary groups, secondary groups as an ideal type have the following characteristics:

1. limited face-to-face interaction
2. nonpermanence
3. ties of exchange, not of affection
4. limited relationships
5. task-oriented relationships

An example of a secondary group would be a high-pressure task force organized within a large corporation. Members of a task force meet infrequently, and for only a few hours at a time. They don't have opportunities to get to know one another in a variety of situations, as family members do. They get together for an explicit purpose, and too many digressions from this task will be met with impatience and hostility. Although members may hold similar attitudes and values, their basic ties are intellectual and not emotional. (Of course, friendships may form even under the most adverse conditions.)

The intense primary-group relations ob-

served in World War II and to some extent in Korea did not develop in Vietnam. Charles C. Moskos (1975), who conducted in-depth interviews with soldiers while they were in Vietnam and after they'd returned home, has suggested why. In combat situations, soldiers face more than just threats to their lives; they also have to contend with such routine physical stresses as tasteless food, lack of sleep, intense heat or cold, rain, mud, and insects. Keeping well is as much of a struggle as staying alive. All soldiers, in Moskos's view, are motivated by "individual self-concern."

The rotation system used in Vietnam reinforced individualism. Instead of being assigned to a single combat group for the duration of hostilities, as soldiers were in World War II, each man was given a twelve-month tour of duty. This meant that the rate of turnover was extremely high, preventing the development of close, enduring primary relations. Each soldier had his own arrival and departure date. "The end of the war was marked by the individual's rotation date and not by the war's eventual outcome—whether victory, defeat, or negotiated stalemate" (31). In effect each soldier was fighting a very private war—for his own survival.

However, Moskos notes that the development of a protest movement within the army led to the formation of at least temporary primary groups. Protest broke down the barriers of individual self-interest. Army records contain hundreds of accounts of "fragging"—group attacks on white officers who were perceived as racists, on army drug enforcement officials, and on gung-ho officers who risked their subordinates' lives.

As this discussion suggests, the distinction between primary and secondary groups is not absolute: relationships in a family may turn cold and utilitarian, while friendship or love may develop in the most impersonal

settings. These concepts, however, are extremely useful in analyzing the characteristics of group life across time as well as at any given point in time. They have, in fact, been used in just this way (but have been given different names) by Ferdinand Tönnies and Émile Durkheim in an attempt to understand the changes in group life that have taken place as a result of modernization and the transition from village to urban life.

From Gemeinschaft to Gesellschaft

If we think of the vast differences between life in a tribal village and life in a big city, we can begin to grasp the wide range of possibilities for organizing our social-group experiences. In a tribal village, all members may relate to one another every day. They

Members of a combat platoon generally form a group so tightly knit that men will risk their lives to preserve it. In Vietnam, however, such intense primary relationships were the exception rather than the rule because of the individual rotation system. Here, soldiers carry the body of one of their buddies from the battlefield. (UPI)

share a common ancestry, as well as common goals, values, aspirations, and traditions. Everyone in the tribe is involved with the survival and welfare of the whole. In addition, each member of the tribe has a fixed position in the social order, one usually assigned at birth. Geographic mobility is as limited as social mobility; a tribe member often lives and dies in a very restricted geographic area. Such expressions of individuality as clothing, work aspirations, leisure activities, and friendship circles are all highly circumscribed by the rights and obligations of tribe members. The entire web of each person's relationships is interconnected and predetermined at birth. Since every aspect of an individual's life meshes with every other aspect (family, co-workers, neighbors, and friends are all the same people), a tribe member's entire social identity is involved in each relationship. Personal, social, and economic life are all rolled up in one, and the notion of self is virtually indistinguishable from the notion of one's own tribe.

Among these Brazilian Indians, personal, social, and economic relationships overlap, and notions of "myself" and "my tribe" are virtually identical. Such communities display characteristics of primary groups, Gemeinschaft, and mechanical solidarity. (Claudia Andujar / Rapho / Photo Researchers, Inc.)

We need hardly mention the dramatic differences between this type of primary-group life and the kind we are so familiar with in our own urban, industrial society. For the mid-twentieth-century city dweller, social life is much more fragmented. Relatives may live far away, friends may live across town, fellow workers may live in a different town altogether, and an individual may not know any of his or her neighbors. With no one group, except perhaps the immediate nuclear family, do we have regular, continuous, face-to-face interaction. Those who live around us may come from very different backgrounds and have very heterogeneous histories, so we don't necessarily share common goals, values, aspirations, and traditions with them. The survival and well-being of one group is often antithetical to the survival and well-being of another (think of labor unions and management; taxi drivers and bus drivers; industrialists and ecologists). And unlike

tribe members who spend their entire lives in one village, we are so mobile that one out of every ten Americans moves each year. We also move socially, leaving old friends behind as we make new ones.

Between these extremes lies the whole range of possibilities for human social organization. We have learned to take both ends of the spectrum for granted, but in earlier times, particularly during the nineteenth and early twentieth centuries, when the world was undergoing breathtaking changes as a result of modernization (industrialization, urbanization, and bureaucratization), the switch from stable, intimate villages (typified by rural agrarian communities) to fragmented, heterogeneous cities was a source of great dismay, fear, curiosity, and wonder.

In trying to make sense of these changes, early sociologists often resorted to extremes of comparison between what was in the past and what would be in the future. The first of these commentators was Ferdinand Tönnies (1855–1936), a German sociologist, who distinguished between relationships in what we now call primary and secondary groups. Tönnies (1957) elaborated on the contrast between *Gemeinschaft,* or community, and *Gesellschaft,* or society. *Gemeinschaft* is characterized by close, intimate, overlapping, and stable relationships (as in tribal villages). *Gesellschaft* is characterized by the pursuit of self-interest, fewer personal attachments, and more abstract bonds holding people together.

Mechanical Versus Organic Solidarity   Emile Durkheim (1947) was also concerned with the nature of social relationships within these two contrasting types of societies. But he described the kinds of social bonds that hold people together in terms of mechanical solidarity and organic solidarity. *Mechanical solidarity* is Durkheim's term for the primary relationships that link members of small, stable communities.

In such societies there are relatively few specialized roles; social bonds develop in the process of sharing many common activities and roles with the same people. This can lead, as Tönnies said, to deep friendship, personal loyalty, and a sense of community. But Durkheim emphasized that it can also lead to a person's feeling trapped or confined.

By contrast, *organic solidarity* rests on having many interdependent roles (secondary relationships) with different people. Just as the parts of the body differ dramatically from one another in appearance, substance, and function, and yet depend completely upon one another for survival, so the segments of an organically linked society differ drastically from one another, yet depend on one another for survival. One is tied to a much larger number of people—shopkeepers, service people, and civil servants who make the daily routine possible. But the tie to any one of these people is specialized. While you may know the waiter in your favorite restaurant, you probably don't see him in any other context. This may lead, on the one hand, to a sense of fragmentation and impersonality. On the other, organic solidarity leaves each person largely free to form close relations with whomever he or she chooses.

Consequences of Gesellschaft   The consequences of the drastic shift in human relations brought about by modernization have both fascinated and frightened many social observers, and the total eclipse of human community has been forecast with gloom and doom for at least a century now. But while no one would deny that the shifts from farm to factory and from village to city have brought about great changes in human social organization, the initial alarm has been tempered by the discovery that modern relationships are not wholly isolating and alienating and that traditional relationships were not wholly intimate, supportive, and integrating. Even when families are separated by great spaces and different value systems, they still stay in contact and help one another (think of how many college students go home for vacation; receive gifts on holidays; keep their parents informed of their whereabouts). Even in large urban centers, people still make friends at work, in their neighborhood, through their children's schools. Even in the most bureaucratic organizations, work groups and friendship cliques form. While these relationships are clearly not as all-consuming as the relationships in a tribal village, they often have their own merits.

Erich Fromm has suggested that modern society promotes greater independence and self-reliance (1941: 124). What he means is that in a society where people have substantial freedom to select their friends, their jobs, and their leisure activities, they are more able to create their *own* identities, rather than being tied to the social roles into which they were born. But this type of freedom does often leave us bewildered and confused by the choices at hand: ''The structure of modern society affects man in two ways simultaneously; he becomes more independent, self-reliant, and critical, and he becomes more isolated, alone and afraid'' (Fromm, 1941: 124).

THE SEARCH FOR INTIMACY AND COMMUNITY

Because the great forces of modernization have led to important changes in the nature of human social organization, many people long to return to the intimacy and safety of earlier communities. Attempts to bring people closer together range from two-hour ''human growth'' groups to permanent, enduring communes. Interestingly, American society has generated a number of secondary groups whose main purpose is to foster primary relationships. The ''singles industry'' and the religious movements of the 1970s are examples.

The "Singles Industry"

American society is designed for families and couples. With the break-up of traditional communities, people who have reached adulthood without marrying (or whose marriages have been disrupted) are no longer incorporated into families as maiden aunts or bachelor uncles. Urban life is not conducive to extended-family living, if only because space is so limited in high-density apartment houses, and the break-up of small communities has robbed people of the protection and sustenance of a community that assumes responsibility for its members. And although most people meet friends and mates through schools and jobs (Walton and Carns, 1977), there is still a need to meet people in other ways. How, then, do isolated individuals in a society geared to family units create or locate a community for themselves?

In his book entitled *The Mating Trade* (1973), John Goodwin explores the many and diverse institutions that have sprung up to service the never-wed, separated, deserted, divorced, and widowed millions in America. Goodwin estimates that there are some 36 million single adults in America, and with the break-up of traditional communities, which often provided meeting places for the unwed, the singles industry has flourished as a means of bringing together

IN THE NEWS

Lifelines to Others

There's an old song that goes, "Be my life's companion, and you'll never grow old." According to several studies, this promise is not as far-fetched as one might think. At least two scientific studies, one conducted by Lisa Berkman at the Human Population Lab in 1977 and the other conducted by James Lynch at the University of Maryland Medical School in 1961, have concluded that loneliness can kill. According to Lynch,

The bachelor who hops from one singles bar to another, the middle-aged divorced man who spends his nights watching television, the elderly widow who seeks companionship from her poodle—all are likely to die from illnesses aggravated by the same disease: their feelings of isolation.

Lisa Berkman found that people with few friends and few close relatives face two to four times the risk of dying from illness than those with many such human links. The lack of social ties is also a very important factor in most suicides, in that those who take their lives usually don't have strong social networks established. A major reason for living, that of human relationships, is missing.

Most socially isolated and lonely people develop such poor habits as smoking, overating, drinking, and not exercising, all of which may lead to fatal diseases. James Lynch even found statistical correlation between death from heart disease and isolation.

—Of white males per 100,000 population, 176 married men die of heart disease compared to 362 single men.

—Of nonwhite males per 100,000 population, 142 married men and 298 divorced men died of heart disease.

—Of white females per 100,000 population, 44 married women died of heart disease as opposed to 67 widows.

—Of nonwhite females per 100,000 population, 83 married women and 165 widows died of heart disease. Lynch says that for every listed cause of death—cancer, suicide, cirrhosis of the liver, rheumatic fever, pneumonia, diabetes, tuberculosis, syphilis—the single, widowed and divorced had significantly higher death rates than did married people, both white and nonwhite and of both sexes.

Both scientists maintain that dialogue, both verbal and nonverbal, is, as Lynch states, "the elixir of life," without which people rapidly progress toward death.

Lynch concludes that

we must evolve a medicine that moves beyond science. . . . We have to treat humans as more than man-machines that can be fixed up with pills and technology. We must realize that feelings cause disease.

SOURCE: Harry Nelson, "Study Links Social Ties, Mortality Rate," *Los Angeles Times*, December 11, 1977, p. 38; "We Can Die of Loneliness, Doctor Says," *Los Angeles Times*, December 11, 1977, Part 4, p. 4; song "Be My Life's Companion" by Hillard and Delugg, Edwin H. Morris Company.

unattached adults. There are singles bars, singles clubs, singles magazines, singles parties, singles weekends, singles cruises, single-parent groups, and on and on.

These secondary-group structures fill a need for primary-group relations (a community of singles, and perhaps a mate). The computerized dating services, which Goodwin calls "electronic cupids," are "nothing less than the automation of the hallowed ritual of Boy meets Girl" (1973: 79). But that hallowed ritual, particularly for men and women cast adrift in urban settings, is working with decreasing effectiveness, and a modern world is turning to modernized means for filling the gaps that are created by the decline of long-lasting primary communities.

Religious Movements

The religious movements that have attracted so much attention in the seventies—Reverend Sun Myung Moon's Unification Church, the Hare Krishna movement, and others—combine elements of primary and secondary groups. In most cases, individuals join these groups to get away from the impersonality of modern society. They are looking for a community, engagement (the opportunity to do something about interpersonal and social problems), and dependence (shared responsibility for guiding one's life) (Slater, 1976). In other words, they are looking for primary-group relationships. At the same time, joining either of the movements mentioned above means becoming a member of a large, complex, nationwide organization with its own schools, housing, and even industries. Unlike members of other older religious communities (such as the Amish), "Moonies" and Krishna people work in urban settings, on the streets, delivering their message to shoppers, sports fans, and others. People who seek a smaller, more traditional world are thus seeking—and apparently finding—it by remaining in the modern, more impersonal one.

SUMMARY

Groups play a central role in all our lives. A *social group* is a number of people who feel a sense of identity, share values and goals, and interact within a structure of roles and statuses. These four characteristics distinguish groups from categories and aggregates.

Boundaries are the structural components of groups that create feelings of "we" and "they."

An *in-group* is a circle of people in which a person feels at home. It develops from shared experiences that breed a sense of "we-ness." An *out-group* is a circle of people to which a person feels he or she does not belong. Out-groups are by necessity implied by the existence of in-groups and may be largely a result of stereotyping. Another category of groups is *reference groups:* groups to which we refer and compare ourselves but to which we do not necessarily belong. The choice of a reference group strongly affects a person's feelings about himself or herself.

Each group, then, defines itself and sets itself apart from others. One effective way to create and maintain group boundaries is through conflict, for it brings the group together in the face of a common enemy. In this way a sense of unity and "we-ness" is attained, as well as a sense of who the outsiders are. The effects of conflict vary with group size, however, as a comparison of dyads and triads illustrates.

Selections from Golding's *Lord of the Flies* highlight basic principles of group dynamics. First, conforming to group norms increases a person's status. Second, interaction breeds liking. Third, individuals with high status initiate interaction more often than people with low status. Leadership emerges from group interaction. At first groups welcome an effective task leader, but they need socio-emotional leadership as well.

Although they may not realize it at the time, groups go through four stages in designing a plan for action: orientation, evaluation, making the decision itself, and restoring equilibrium.

Groups can also be characterized by the kinds of relationships that bind their members. *Primary groups* are characterized by several interconnecting features: continuing face-to-face interaction, permanence, ties of affection, multifaceted relationships, and non-task-oriented relationships. *Secondary groups* have the following characteristics: limited face-to-face interaction; nonpermanence; ties of exchange, not of affection; limited relationships; and task-oriented relationships. Primary groups developed under fire in Korea, but not in Vietnam, where soldiers were rotated and each fought his own private war.

The concepts of primary and secondary groups can also be used to understand changes and differences in group life across time, in particular the shift from village to urban life. Ferdinand Tönnies, a nineteenth-century German sociologist, described the contrast between *Gemeinschaft*, a community characterized by intimate, overlapping, and stable relationships, and *Gesellschaft*, a society characterized by impersonal attachments, an emphasis on efficiency and progress, and the pursuit of self-interest. Émile Durkheim drew upon Tönnies's distinctions to examine the social bonds that existed in each type of society. He called the link that binds members of simple societies together *mechanical solidarity:* relationships that are characterized by personal, stable, intertwining emotional attachments. *Organic solidarity,* which binds people in complex, industrialized societies, is characterized by relationships that are impersonal, transient, fragmented, and rational.

Modern society has produced yearnings in many people for a return to the more intimate communities of the past. To ease their feelings of loneliness and alienation, people have tried various solutions. The singles industry, the aim of which is to bring unmarried people together for entertainment and living, is one example. Religious movements are another. Both combine elements of primary and secondary groups in modern solutions to interpersonal and social problems.

GLOSSARY

aggregate a set of individuals who happen to be in the same place at the same time.

category a set of individuals who have common characteristics but do not interact.

charisma a special quality that causes others to accept a person's leadership.

dyad a two-person group.

Gemeinschaft Tönnies's term for small, traditional communities characterized by intimate, overlapping, and stable relationships.

Gesellschaft Tönnies's term for societies characterized by impersonal attachments, an emphasis on efficiency and progress, and the rational pursuit of self-interest.

group dynamics the study of relationships within groups.

in-group a group in which an individual feels at home and with which he or she identifies.

mechanical solidarity Durkheim's term for the stable social bonds, based on sharing many activities and roles with the same people, characteristic of simple societies.

organic solidarity Durkheim's term for the transient and fragmented social bonds, based on interdependence, that characterize complex industrialized societies.

out-group a group to which an individual feels he or she doesn't belong, and with which he or she doesn't identify.

primary group a group characterized by continuous face-to-face interaction, permanence, ties of affection, and multifaceted and non-task-oriented relationships.

reference group a group or social category that an individual refers to in evaluating himself or herself.

secondary group a group characterized by limited face-to-face interaction; nonpermanence; ties of exchange, not of affection; and limited and specifically task-oriented relationships.

social-emotional leadership leadership with the function of maintaining good morale and relations in a group.

social group a set of people who identify and interact with one another in a structured way based on shared values and goals.

task leadership leadership with the function of directing a group toward its goals.

triad a three-person group.

REFERENCES

Robert F. Bales and Fred L. Strodtbeck, ''Phases in Group Problem Solving.'' *Journal of Abnormal and Social Psychology*, vol. 46 (1951): 485–495.

Theodore Caplow, *Two Against One: Coalition in Triads*. Englewood Cliffs, N.J.: Prentice-Hall, 1969.

Charles H. Cooley, *Social Organization* (1907). New York: Scribner's, 1929.

Lewis Coser, *The Functions of Social Conflict*. New York: Free Press, 1956.

Émile Durkheim, *The Division of Labor in Society* (1893), trans. George Simpson. Glencoe, Ill.: Free Press, 1947.

Erich Fromm, *Escape from Freedom*. New York: Avon, 1941.

William Golding, *Lord of the Flies*. New York: Coward-McCann, 1955.

John Goodwin, *The Mating Trade*. New York: Doubleday, 1973.

A. Paul Hare, *Handbook of Small Group Research*. New York: Free Press, 1962.

George Homans, *The Human Group*. New York: Harcourt Brace, 1950.

Mirra Komarovsky, *The Unemployed Man and His Family: The Effect of Unemployment upon the Status of the Man in Fifty-nine Families* (1940). New York: Arno Press, 1971.

Roger W. Little, ''Buddy Relations in Combat Performances,'' in Oscar Grusky and George A. Miller, eds., *The Sociology of Organizations*. New York: Free Press, 1970.

Robert K. Merton, *Social Theory and Social Structure*. New York: Free Press, 1968.

Charles C. Moskos, Jr., ''The American Combat Soldier in Vietnam.'' *Journal of Social Issues*, vol. 31 (Fall 1975): 25–37.

Theodore Newcomb, ''Attitude Development as a Function of Reference Groups: The Bennington Study,'' in G. E. Swanson, T. M. Newcomb, and E. L. Hartley, eds., *Readings in Social Psychology*. New York: Holt, Rinehart and Winston, 1958.

_____ et al., *Persistence and Change: Bennington College and Its Students After 25 Years*. New York: Wiley, 1967.

Paul F. Secord and Carl W. Backman, *Social Psychology*, 2nd ed. New York: McGraw-Hill, 1974.

Edward A. Shils, "Primary Groups in the American Army," in R. K. Merton and P. F. Lazarsfeld, eds., *Continuities in Social Research*. New York: Free Press, 1950.

Georg Simmel, *The Sociology of Georg Simmel*, trans. and ed. Kurt H. Wolff. New York: Free Press, 1950.

Philip Slater, *The Pursuit of Loneliness*, rev. ed. Boston: Beacon Press, 1976.

William Graham Sumner, *Folkways*. Boston: Ginn, 1906.

Ferdinand Tönnies, *Community and Society* (1887), trans. and ed. Charles A. Loomis. East Lansing, Mich.: Michigan State University Press, 1957.

John Walton and Donald E. Carns, *Cities in Change*, 2nd ed. Boston: Allyn & Bacon, 1977.

FOR FURTHER STUDY

Groups and Social Psychology.   A. Paul Hare's *Handbook of Small Group Research,* 2nd ed. (New York: Free Press, 1976), organizes findings on all facets of this fascinating subject: how groups develop, the individual versus the group, kinds of leadership, and communication networks in groups. A good broad text in social psychology is Paul Secord and Carl Backman, *Social Psychology,* 2nd ed. (New York: McGraw-Hill, 1974).

Gemeinschaft *and* Gesellschaft.   Sociologists have been studying communities in America for a long time, and from these studies one can see what Maurice Stein called the *Eclipse of Community* during this century (Princeton, N.J.: Princeton University Press, 1971). But what are the crucial elements of a successful community? In *Commitments and Community* (Cambridge, Mass.: Harvard University Press, 1972), Rosabeth Kanter analyzes dozens of utopian communities to determine why most failed and what allowed a few to succeed. An important portrait of how communities of immigrants around Chicago fought the anonymity of the big city is drawn by Richard Sennett in *Families Against the City* (Cambridge, Mass.: Harvard University Press, 1970). Finally, some readers might enjoy reading how we try to recapture a sense of *Gemeinschaft* through personal intimacy, described in sensitive detail in Murray Davis's *Intimate Relations* (New York: Free Press, 1973).

Being a Soldier.   Few civilians have a clear idea of the soldier's life and the group pressures that affect it. Since the pioneering study by Shils and Janowitz in *Public Opinion Quarterly,* vol. 11 (Summer 1948): 280–315, a number of sociologists have made excellent studies of the modern soldier. A major work about officers is *The Professional Soldier* by Morris Janowitz (New York: Free Press, 1960). Sanford Dornbush, once a West Point cadet, wrote a report critical of that institution entitled "The Military Academy as an Assimilating Institution," *Social Forces,* vol. 33 (May 1955): 316–321. The life of the ordinary American soldier in recent years has been studied and described by Charles Moskos in his book *The American Enlisted Man* (New York: Russell Sage Foundation, 1970).

CHAPTER 8

Organizations and Bureaucracy

"You wish there was a better system. A lot of money is held up and the grantees want to know why they can't get it. Sometimes they call and get the runaround on the phone. . . .

"A lot of times the grantee comes down to our audit department for aid. They're not treated as human beings. Sometimes they have to wait, wait, wait—for no reason. The grantee doesn't know it's for no reason. . . .

"They send him from floor to floor and from person to person, it's just around and around he goes. Sometimes he leaves, he hasn't accomplished anything. I don't know why this is so." (Diane Wilson, process clerk, quoted in Terkel, 1974: 348)

Maddening as they are—to both the people who work in them and the people who need their services—bureaucracies are an integral and necessary part of our lives.

Many of the things we value most would be unattainable without large organizations: higher education (made available through large university systems); information and entertainment (provided by the media—radio, television, newspapers, and movies); government services (from mass elections to street cleaning); and even health care (delivered by doctors who trained at universities and who depend on laboratories, hospitals, and drug companies to confirm diagnoses and provide treatment).

No one will deny that large organizations also create waste and encourage thoughtless routine. Incorrect bills, red tape, and incomprehensible income tax forms, as well as petty clerks who give you the runaround, police officers who don't care *why* your car is double-parked, standardized TV shows, and government inertia, are brought to you by large bureaucratic organizations.

One of the major problems of our times is balancing the benefits of large organizations (how *they* serve *us*) with their costs (how they affect the people who work in them, and how they threaten to limit our freedom, as individuals and as a society). In this chapter we will look at how organizations develop and work to see what effect they have on the way we live today and the way we will live in the future.

FORMAL ORGANIZATIONS

A drive down a typical American highway reveals how prevalent organizations have become in everyday life. The hamburger stand is a McDonald's, one of many links in a nationwide fast-food chain. The typical gas station is an Exxon, connected to a company that drills for and refines oil and gas and sells its products all over the world. The roadside boardinghouse has been replaced by a Holiday Inn, and the little chicken farm where a woman in a straw hat used to sell fresh eggs by the dozen has turned into a gigantic "factory" that produces and sells thousands of eggs every month.

Why have large-scale organizations become as pervasive as they are? What makes them so well suited to the performance of such a variety of tasks, from selling eggs to putting men on the moon? The key is planned coordination: in organizations, the work of a number of people is consciously structured and coordinated to meet some specific goal. There is virtually no limit to the range of goals that organizations can pursue. Selling hamburgers, pumping gasoline, and providing rooms for travelers are all organizational goals.

A *formal organization*, then, is a group whose activities are deliberately coordinated for the achievement of specific goals or purposes. Work within organizations is broken down into tasks or routines according to the principle of division of labor. Activities are governed by explicit rules and regulations that are designed to make work and behavior predictable. And the various jobs and members of an organization are arranged in a hierarchy of authority and responsibility.

In contrast to the social groups we examined in the preceding chapter, organizations tend to be self-perpetuating. Their procedures and goals do not change whenever an old member leaves or a new one arrives; members are usually expected to fit themselves into a structure. Organizations thus develop an existence apart from their members. They do not arise casually or spontaneously like social groups, but generally are set up to achieve a specific goal. And organizations are secondary groups, which means that face-to-face interaction may be limited, that ties between people are based on exchange rather than affection, and that relationships will be task-oriented and nonpermanent. The term "formal organization" reflects the fact that roles and relationships are arranged in an explicitly defined pattern.

As we will see in this chapter, organizations include not only profit-making associations such as corporations but also police departments, schools, hospitals, prisons, and tenants' associations. One type of organization that is currently growing in popularity in the United States is the *voluntary association*, a formal organization people join primarily out of personal interest, because they share the organization's goals and norms. Members of such fraternal organizations as the Elks or the Masons, for instance, engage in social activities and also undertake philanthropic projects; such a group will sponsor a youth club, for example, or will conduct a fund drive for some local hospital or charity.

Voluntary associations have long been a part of the American scene. During the early nineteenth century, the French writer Alexis de Tocqueville visited the United States and remarked on both the wide variety of voluntary associations he saw and on the broad range of personal needs that such associations seemed able to meet. Many Americans all over the country now seem to be rediscovering voluntary associations as a means of controlling aspects of their own lives or environments that previously appeared un-

Voluntary associations, such as the Shriners, have a long tradition in the United States. Members join out of personal interest, engaging in social activities and undertaking philanthropic projects. Today, there are also voluntary associations that promote reformist causes and self-help. (John Running/Stock, Boston)

preservation of historic sites and properties, and tenants' rights (to name just a few).

A number of these new voluntary associations are self-help groups—self-governing, self-regulating, and self-supporting entities whose members share some common condition or experience. Such organizations do have a formal structure, but it is neither elaborate nor rigid. In general, what they offer is a one-to-one "fellowship network" for coping with particular problems of living; what they demand from members is intense commitment and responsibility. Alcoholics Anonymous is perhaps the oldest and best known of the self-help groups, and has many imitators. Prison Families Anonymous, for example, is designed to meet the emotional problems of families of prisoners; Families Anonymous is directed toward relatives and friends of juveniles with behavior problems; Parents Without Partners is aimed toward single parents.

But when most of us hear the term "organization," we tend to think of the large, impersonal bureaucracy—a many-leveled, widely spread collection of offices and functions such as General Motors or the major agencies of the federal government. To understand how and why organizations work as they do, we need to understand the modern bureaucracy and the ideas of Max Weber, the sociologist who first analyzed the phenomenon.

controllable. The present trend can be traced back at least to the early 1960s, when the civil rights movement and organizations such as the Peace Corps offered people a way to work for social change. Today, voluntary associations pursue not only such traditional goals as recreation and philanthropy but also such reformist causes as feminism, environmental protection, wildlife conservation,

THE RISE OF MODERN BUREAUCRACIES

Many people living in ancient times wouldn't have been puzzled by the idea of a giant bureaucratic organization. The pyramids of ancient Egypt, monuments to mighty rulers, are also monuments to a mighty organization. The fact that in Julius Caesar's day all roads actually did lead to Rome was a reflection of the Roman Empire's vast and sturdy administrative structure. But when we talk about the pervasiveness and power of bureaucracies, we are talking about a uniquely modern development. The "Age of Bureaucracy" dawned during the late nineteenth century when the strong wind of industrialization began to sweep through the nations of Europe.

Throughout the eighteenth century, the image of the machine exerted a peculiar fascination on Western minds. God was likened to a watchmaker, and the world to a clock that kept perfect time. By the end of the nineteenth century, there was no longer a need for fanciful images: machines like the cotton gin, the steam engine, and the locomotive were speaking noisily for themselves, and for the enormous power of mechanization—a power that would allow humankind to transform the world. According to the proponents of the machine, where miseries once abounded, peace and social justice would soon appear.

Looking back, we can easily understand the enthusiasm people felt for mechanization. It offered seemingly limitless possibilities and supported the new faith in reason and progress. It gave people the sense that they could control the environment and plan the future. To the advent of mechanization we can trace our own high standard of living, our jet travel, our global communication networks, and even our ability to feed, clothe, and provide medical care for every person on earth (if we wanted to). But mechanization is only part of the story; an equally important influence on the shape of modern life has been the spread of bureaucracy.

Weber's Model

The fully developed bureaucratic mechanism compares with other organizations exactly as does the machine with non-mechanical modes of production. (Weber, in Gerth and Mills, 1946: 214)

A machine is "an apparatus consisting of interrelated parts with separate functions, used in the performance of some kind of work" (*Random House Dictionary of the English Language*, 1967). Substitute the word "organization" for "apparatus," and we have a basic definition of bureaucracy: an organization consisting of interrelated parts with separate functions, designed to perform some kind of work. The key terms are "interrelated" and "separate functions." Or, put another way, bureaucracy represents the application of mechanical principles to the organization of work.

Max Weber's analysis of bureaucratic structure—written long before "red tape" became an acknowledged social problem and the word "bureaucrat" an uncomplimentary term—remains the classic work in the field. Weber traced the development and spread of bureaucracies to large-scale production and advances in technology in the nineteenth century. Although he recognized and regretted its dehumanizing side effects, he believed bureaucracy to be *technically* superior to other forms of social organization as a means of coordinating the activities of a number of people toward specific objectives. "Precision, speed, unambiguity, knowledge of files, continuity, discretion, strict subordination, reduction of friction and of material and personal costs—these are raised to the optimum point in the strictly bureaucratic administration" (Weber, in Gerth and Mills, 1946: 214). To emphasize the differences between bureaucracies and other organizations, Weber defined bureaucracy in terms of five characteristics and tried to show how each of them functions to further the goals of

Max Weber, whose analysis of bureaucratic structure remains the classic work in the field. Weber traced the development of bureaucracies to the technological advances of the late nineteenth century. In fact, he regarded bureaucracy as the application of mechanical principles to the organization of work. Weber outlined five characteristics—specialization, a hierarchy of offices, rules and regulations, impartiality, and technical competence—which the ideal bureaucracy possesses and against which actual bureaucracies can be measured. Although he believed bureaucracy was a technically superior form of organization, Weber was aware of its dehumanizing side effects. (The Granger Collection)

the organization. Together, these characteristics make up an ideal type or model, against which the realities of actual bureaucracies can be measured.

1. *Specialization*: Bureaucratic organization is based on the precept that the most efficient way to do complex work is to divide production up into small tasks, and to have people specialize in performing one or another of these tasks. The reasoning behind this idea becomes quite clear if we consider the fact that it is impossible for one person to learn every step in the production of an airplane or all there is to know about medicine. In a bureaucracy, workers in each area are familiar with and responsible for only one part of the bureaucracy's administration or its production process.

2. *A hierarchy of offices*: Once production has been broken down into a number of separate activities, the entire operation must then be integrated; the gears of the machine must mesh. If they don't, experts in one department might design a bolt that is one-eighth of an inch larger than the nut designed in another department (Blau and Meyer, 1971:8). The solution is to organize workers in a *hierarchy*, with each person responsible to the person directly above in the chain of command, and responsible for the actions of those below.

   Organizational hierarchies consist of positions or offices, not of people. Each office carries with it specific duties, responsibilities, and privileges, as well as a specific salary. Authority rests in the office, not in the person who occupies it.[1] In addition, the authority of bureaucratic officials is clearly defined and

---

[1] Weber called this *rational-legal authority*, to distinguish it from the links of authority one finds in older, more traditional societies. We will return to this distinction in chapter 12.

limited. While they have the power to recommend that individuals be promoted or fired, supervisors have no formal authority over the personal lives of their subordinates (unlike the head of many a family business).

3. *Rules and regulations*: Activities and relationships among officers in a bureaucracy are governed by explicit rules and regulations. In this way, each bureaucrat knows (at least in general terms) what is required of him or her in the way of performance, and how his or her decisions will be carried out. Rules make the workings of even the most complex bureaucracy orderly and predictable.

4. *Impartiality*: Weber argued that because personal emotions impede efficiency, they have no place in a bureaucracy. Impartiality toward both co-workers and those who do business with the organization assures that all will be treated equitably and that personal considerations will be subordinated to organizational goals. If officials make a practice of promoting subordinates because they are friends, or of awarding contracts to companies owned by relatives, the organization will eventually suffer.

5. *Technical competence*: Positions in a bureaucracy are awarded on the basis of technical qualifications (as measured by tests or other standardized procedures), and people are paid for their work. Weber also felt that people should be guaranteed a job as long as they perform their duties adequately. Promotions and raises handed out on the basis of merit and/or seniority were seen by Weber as essential not only to motivate individual effort but also to keep up a bureaucracy's *esprit de corps*. Weber maintained that the more complicated and specialized work became, the greater would be the need of a bureaucracy of "personally detached and strictly 'objective' experts."

The Reality of Bureaucracies

Does an equivalent of Weber's model of bureaucracy exist in reality? Not entirely. Studies of business firms in 150 societies and an analysis of 10 organizations in this country suggest that the 5 bureaucratic traits don't always appear together (Udy, 1959; Hall, 1963–1964). Wide variations were found in degree of specialization, in hierarchical organization, and in adherence to rules and regulations, both within and between companies. The fact that an organization relied on specialization did not mean that employees were arranged in a hierarchy or that their relationships were impersonal. Moreover, professionals within organizations may possess a degree of authority—based on their expertise—not necessarily indicated by their position in the hierarchy.

As we suggested earlier, therefore, Weber's model is an ideal type that calls attention to significant characteristics by emphasizing, and perhaps overstating, trends. It was not meant to fully describe reality. "The ideal-type bureaucracy may be used much as a twelve-inch ruler is employed. We would not expect, for example, that all objects measured by the ruler would be exactly twelve inches—some would be more and some would be less" (Gouldner, 1950: 53–54).

In fact, while bureaucracy may be the solution to some problems, it is often the cause of many others. Modern research has shown that many of Weber's most cherished assumptions—that rules always help organizations achieve their goals, for example, or that job security promotes expertise and efficiency—must be taken with a grain of salt. The bureaucratic structure also has some side effects on workers that Weber didn't consider important or simply didn't consider.

"Grow, industry, grow, grow, grow," sing these employees each morning at a Matsushita television factory in Japan. Identical work-stations signal the regularity of tasks performed in the row at the right. (Fred Ward/Black Star)

Let's examine a few of these side effects more closely.

Ritualism Do rules and regulations facilitate rational decision-making and maximize efficiency, as Weber suggested? In a famous essay on the bureaucratic personality, Robert Merton (1968) came to the conclusion that when people become devoted to procedures, as bureaucrats tend to do, they lose sight of why those procedures were established in the first place and end up performing them simply as *rituals*. Such rigid adherence to established procedures prevents people from recognizing and dealing with new conditions and problems. Officials become inflexible. Merton describes the bureaucrat as a person who feels totally satisfied if he or she does everything exactly as the rules specify, regardless of the consequences. Under such circumstances, organizational efficiency and goals often go up in smoke.

Protection of the Inept Weber believed that bureaucratic organizations would make the best possible use of available talent, weeding out deadwood as a matter of course. Recent research indicates, however, that bureaucra-

SOCIOLOGY AND COMMON SENSE:
THE UNFEELING BUREAUCRAT

To be called a "bureaucrat" is a kind of insult. The label carries with it the image of a cold, elusive, and unpleasant person, more preoccupied with rules than with individuals. Maligned as bureaucrats are, a recent study revealed that, surprisingly, they are not so bad.

A group of researchers at the Institute for Social Research of the University of Michigan were curious about the public's attitude toward bureaucrats and toward government agencies in general. They surveyed people who had contacted government service agencies in search of a job, workmen's compensation, unemployment compensation, public assistance, hospital care, or retirement benefits. Among the questions the researchers posed to their sample were the following:

How satisfied were you with the way the office handled your problem?
Was it hard to find an office or official who could handle your problem?
How much effort did the people at the office make to help you?
How efficient did you think the office was in handling your problem?
Do you feel you were treated fairly or unfairly by the office?

The answers to these questions contradict just about all the stereotypes of bureaucrats and government agencies. Two-thirds of the respondents were satisfied with the way their problem was handled, not at all consistent with most people's unpleasant expectations. The researchers also found that bureaucrats are hardly elusive, inefficient "goof-offs." Ninety percent of the people surveyed found the right person or agency to deal with; 60 percent were satisfied with the amount of work that agency personnel had done to help them; and 72 percent gave the agency high marks for efficiency. Seventy-five percent felt that they had been treated fairly (114). (Fairness and efficiency are two major advantages of bureaucracy identified by Weber.)

The researchers then went beyond the respondents' personal experiences to ask how these people felt *generally* about government agencies, and what they found shows that personal experience doesn't always destroy stereotypes. For example, only 30 percent of the people surveyed felt that government agencies are good at solving problems; 50 percent saw the government as inefficient; and only 40 percent thought people are treated fairly by government agencies. These figures show that even though people had good personal experiences with government bureaucrats, they retained their negative stereotypes about government bureaucracies.

SOURCE: Daniel Katz, Barbara A. Gutek, Robert L. Kahn, and Eugenia Barton, *Bureaucratic Encounters*, Survey Research Center, Institute for Social Research, Ann Arbor, University of Michigan, 1975.

cies may be safe places for the inept. Given the fact that the boss has the power to promote or fire subordinates, it is in the employees' interest to conceal problems and withhold information from supervisors. And William Goode (1967) calls attention to the fact that companies, for their part, are usually reluctant to demote or otherwise discredit incompetent employees. Thus, people who do not meet company standards in one position may be "kicked upstairs" to a less responsible but still prestigious job, or may be fired but provided with glowing recommendations.

The Peter Principle There are other disadvantages associated with advancement on the basis of merit. When a supervisor needs to fill a position, he or she will naturally choose a person who is good at his or her present job. If people who have been moved up then prove capable of handling the new assignment, they will be advanced again and again—until they finally reach their level of *in*competence! A very good teacher, for instance, may not make a good principal. But a good teacher who becomes a good principal might then be promoted to district superintendent. If this same teacher performs poorly at that level, that is where he or she will remain, with unhappy consequences. For instance, people who know their performance is substandard often try to alleviate their anxiety by burying themselves in rules and regulations, which further decreases the quality of their work (Blau and Meyer, 1971: 104).

The process we have been describing is so widely in evidence that it has become something of a household word, the *Peter Principle*: "In a hierarchy, every employee tends to rise to his [or her] level of incompetence" (Peter and Hull, 1969: 25). But if there were no exceptions to the Peter Principle, our or-

ganizations wouldn't work at all. Lane Tracy has suggested a provocative and not necessarily far-fetched qualification. Tracy argues that organizations are able to function as well as they do because of an oppressed minority—secretaries—who cannot rise to their level of incompetence (Tracy, 1972: 65–66).

Waste-making Writing when he did, Weber could not have foreseen all the possible ramifications of ever-increasing size. For example, in principle, people hire assistants when they feel they can no longer handle all their work alone. In practice, however, people may request additional staff to increase their prestige in the organization. Suppose a bureaucrat hires two assistants (two being safer than one, who might become a competitor). In all likelihood, he will reserve the power to make decisions for himself, thereby adding supervision to his original workload. If all goes well, however, in a year or two his assistants will need assistants, and there will be five or even seven people to do the work of one. But the ritual of shuffling paper back and forth among seven people will by itself keep them all *demonstrably* busy. This is the essence of *Parkinson's Law:* "Work expands to fill the time available for its completion" (Parkinson, 1957).

Formal Versus Informal Structure

All organizations seek to define members' responsibilities and regulate their activities. The explicit rules defining each person's duties, written or unwritten organizational charts, and a system of rewards and punishments (for example, promotions and demotions) constitute the organization's *formal structure*. However, any time people join forces to accomplish a task, friendships and power relationships develop, and with them come cliques, grapevines, and the like.

figure 8:1   A formal organization chart

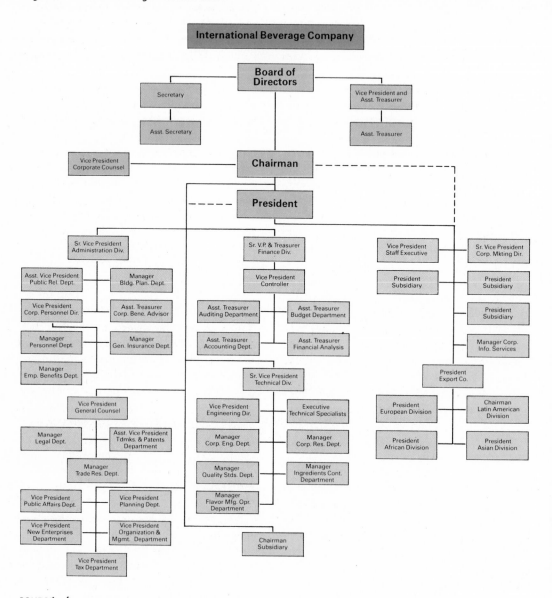

SOURCE: *Corporate Organization Structures* © 1973 The Conference Board, p. 37.

This chart shows the hierarchy of offices in an international beverage company. By following vertical lines to their source, you can see who reports to whom. Generally, the position of an employee's supervisor is an indication of his or her own power in the hierarchy. Note, for example, that even though the vice president of the Tax Department is at the bottom of the chart, he or she reports directly to the chairman.

Some people wield more influence—and others less—than their job title indicates. Thus there evolves alongside the formal structure an *informal structure*: procedures that enable people to solve problems not covered by the formal regulations, to eliminate unpleasant or unnecessary work, and to protect their own interests. Informal structures emerge in part because of the values of our society at large. "In a democratic culture," write Peter M. Blau and Marshall W. Meyer (1971: 58), "where independence of action and equality of status are highly valued, detailed rules and close supervision are resented." Thus workers will often organize their own informal groups and establish strict standards and procedures to which they adhere. "A striking contrast exists between the rigorous discipline employees willingly impose upon themselves because they realize that their work requires strict operating standards, and their constant annoyance at being hamstrung by picayune rules that they experience as being arbitrarily imposed upon them" (Blau and Meyer, 1971: 58).

Informal structures often emerge as a means of dealing with problems or situations not covered by organizational rules or procedures. Consider the police officer on patrol duty. While he or she is the lowest-ranking member in the organizational hierarchy, the patrol officer is nevertheless called upon to exercise more discretion and to do more individual decision-making in the day-to-day line of duty than any of his or her superiors. Put yourself in the shoes of the police officer who one night discovered the nearly nude and thoroughly drunk daughter of a prominent citizen staggering down a suburban street. According to law, everyone who is seen committing an offense or who can be reasonably suspected of having done so should be arrested. In this instance, however, the police didn't arrest the girl. Instead, they took her to the station house, photo-graphed her, and turned the picture over to her parents to convince them of the seriousness of the problem (Wilson, 1974: 220).

This incident is not unusual. Police forces have developed a special code for handling their discretionary role: "with respect to routine police matters the normal tendency of the police is to underenforce the law" (Wilson, 1974: 48–49), to make substantially fewer arrests than observed citizen behavior warrants. Why? Among the possible explanations are (1) the fact that patrol officers resent fellow officers who work harder than they do, and thus exert an informal pressure to conform, and (2) the fact that members of the police organization, almost all of whom started out on patrol duty, believe that the public would not tolerate a policy of full enforcement of all laws all the time.

The Negotiated Order In a variety of complex organizations such as psychiatric hospitals, formal and informal arrangements are often tried simultaneously in the handling of novel or unexpected situations. A constant process of bargaining, diplomacy, and give-and-take whereby people at various levels of an organization together solve work-related problems is called a *negotiated order* (Strauss et al., 1964). In their study of one hospital, Anselm Strauss and his colleagues discovered many kinds of negotiations taking place. Doctors often had to negotiate to get their patients into certain wards, and to get cooperation and information from nurses and aides; nurses had to bargain with the doctors to get certain treatments for patients instituted or changed; and the patients devoted considerable effort to haggling for privileges, drugs, placement in certain wards, and information concerning the length of their stay and their progress in the hospital. Many students of organizations are increasingly coming to believe that the distinction between formal and informal patterns may be less important than the fact that *both* can be seen as attempts to solve specific problems.

ORGANIZATIONS: PEOPLE SOLVING PROBLEMS

The formal patterns that emerge as an organization evolves represent, as Weber maintained, an attempt to solve the problem of *efficiency*. But if we ask why an organization seeks efficiency one way instead of another, we come up against the larger problem of survival. All organizations must cope with the external environment—physical, social, and political—within which they exist; each organization must also devise ways to cope with its own internal environment—the activities and attitudes of its own members. Because these environments are constantly changing, every organization that wishes to survive must maintain a balance between stability and flexibility, between concentration on its own goal and awareness of what is happening in the world outside of it.

Sociologists have therefore begun to look at organizations not as unchanging structures but as people continually solving problems, continually organizing. In this section we will look at this process of problem-solving in the context of how organizations interact with their environments. We will also look at the total institution, a type of organization that attempts to solve the problem of survival by sealing itself off from the world.

The Process of Organizing

"We were by no means agreed as to the kind of institution we wanted," recalled economist Alvin Johnson in describing how he and a number of associates set about founding a school where academic freedom would take priority over all other considerations (Johnson, 1952: 273). At first the founders couldn't even agree upon a name for their institution, but they finally came up with a compromise: the New School for Social Research. Then they decided that the school should offer, at least to begin with, a lecture program addressed specifically to adults. At the same time, they had to find a location for the school, decide on a financing plan, appoint a board of trustees, apply for a charter, and set up an administrative staff.

The story of the New School is, in a sense, the story of most organizations: they are put together step by step. First, people get together with a goal in mind. Then they work out a way of accomplishing their purpose. Of course it's not usually that simple. As the organization matures, original goals often change or are supplemented by new ones; sometimes, as was the case with the New School, even after the organization has gotten off to a good start, the founders still can't agree on what its true goals should be. The New School opened its doors in New York City in 1919, and it succeeded immediately in attracting a high caliber of adult student and faculty members. But some of the founders were dissatisfied. Why was there so much emphasis on lectures? Where was the research implied by the school's name? Eventually three of the founders quit, leaving only Johnson. But by that point the school had already acquired a reputation; it had converted two unused buildings in Manhattan into a campus; it had a staff and a faculty. It had developed, in short, a number of stable roles and routines typical of formal organizations.

In many organizations in which roles and routines have been established, those elements tend to become fixed, especially after the originators are no longer on the scene. Their successors often forget that structures are made by people and can be changed by people. But in taking over as head of the New School, Johnson avoided this pitfall. He quickly saw the need for flexibility, and the actions he took amounted to a re-creation of the organization. The New School hired a publicist to help raise funds and attract students. It gave students a voice in school affairs, with the result that the institution's academic scope was broadened to include courses on psychoanalytic theory and modern art. In the 1930s Johnson brought European scholars endangered by Nazi persecution to the New School, and what began as a "university in exile" later became a graduate faculty of political and social science.

Thus, in many organizations, activities often precede goals; objectives are later formalized to perpetuate or justify changes that have already taken place—a practice that contrasts markedly with the traditional Weberian concept that goals always come first (Weick, 1969: 37).

Adaptation to the External Environment

Although organizations often appear to be self-contained entities, the truth is that they are all involved in more or less constant and two-way interaction with the *external environment*: those resources, other organizations, customers, transport systems, governments, and so on within which an organization operates. Some organizations must survive in and interact with several different environments simultaneously. For instance, many American firms do business in other countries. And—as the public has learned during the past few years—while giving bribes to improve business is considered an illegitimate form of interaction in the United States, in many foreign countries under-the-table payoffs are a time-honored custom.

The most threatening aspect of any external environment is its unpredictability. New technologies or products may appear; natural resources may run out; the market for a product may diminish, to name just a few typical unscheduled events. To survive in the face of these threats, organizations may change their strategies or even their shape, as the New School did to meet the changing needs of adult students.

To insulate themselves against competition, many organizations specialize, or narrow their range of strategies. The makers of Polaroid cameras, for instance, have avoided competing with the manufacturers of elaborate lenses and photographic systems by restricting themselves to the production of cameras that use the Polaroid process of instantly developing film. Organizations can also adapt to their environments by diversifying. When the surgeon general of the United States issued a report on the health hazards of smoking, for example, the Liggett-Myers Tobacco Company bought a dog-food business to decrease the risks of depending on customers in just one market.

An organization can adapt to its environment by gaining power over it. A cheap—perhaps the cheapest—way to acquire power is by gaining prestige (Thompson, 1967: 33). If an organization (and its products) comes to be held in high regard, it will more easily find qualified personnel, exert influence, and attract customers, investors, and clients. Beer companies that sponsor rock concerts, oil companies that help finance public television, and universities that devote great energy to building and maintaining nationally ranked football teams are all examples of organizations seeking to gain prestige.

ALL ROME THOUGHT HIM A FOOL, BUT HIS GENIUS WAS SURVIVAL

I, CLAUDIUS

SUNDAYS AT 9 PM
ON CHANNEL 26 PBS
BEGINNING
NOVEMBER 6
MASTERPIECE
THEATRE
Mobil

Prestige helps an organization to interact with its external environment—resources, government, other organizations, and the public. By financing public television, for example, Mobil Oil builds an image of concern for the arts, which attracts new personnel, customers, and investors. (Poster design and illustration Seymour Chwast/Push Pin Studios)

Growth can also bring increases in power. At an early point in their histories, most of the major American oil firms were refineries. As they grew, they sought to control more and more elements in their environment, which necessitated changes in organiza-

tional structure. They set up marketing divisions to create and promote products, retail divisions to sell those products, exploration divisions to find raw materials, and transport divisions to move supplies and finished products from one place to another.

The rise in our times of the immensely profitable *multinational corporation,* an organization with productive facilities in several countries, is an extreme example of how growth can insulate an organization against the unpredictability of the environment. A multinational can move tremendous sums of money around the world to take advantage of favorable—or to avoid unfavorable—conditions. Or it may, through advertising, create a market in a particular country for merchandise it can no longer sell anywhere else, such as outdated automobiles or television sets. (See chapter 12 for more discussion of multinationals.)

Shaping the Internal Environment: Recruitment and Socialization

No matter how well adapted it may be to the external environment, an organization won't survive for long if its members fail to perform their jobs adequately. An organization must therefore have control over its *internal environment*—over its members and the jobs they do. To achieve control, most organizations rely on a system of rewards and punishments, including such incentives as raises and promotions, on the one hand, and the ability to fire an ineffective worker, on the other. In addition, organizations attempt to regulate their internal workings through *recruitment*—selecting as members individuals who already meet some or all of the organization's requirements—and *socialization*—the education or training of members to fill organizational roles.

IN THE NEWS

Tailoring Schedules to Suit Workers

A special "mothers' shift" that allows mothers to see their children off to school and get home as soon as school is over has proven to be a profitable innovation for at least one organization. A large computer firm adjusted to its inner-city location in St. Paul, Minnesota, by gearing work schedules in its bindery plant to the needs of many mothers and students in the area. Unable to take on full-time jobs, mothers work for five hours in the middle of the day, during the time when their children are in school. The students then begin their three- to four-hour shift. Workers tend to be hired on the basis of need in this economically depressed area, and the arrangement has been working out well for both employer and employee:

Control Data, a computer and financial services conglomerate with 41,000 employees in 33 countries, initiated the bindery operation in a converted bowling alley seven years ago, following the urban riots of the late 1960's.

"It was our plan to provide the kind of employment most needed, in the place it was most needed," said James Bowe, vice president of Control Data.

On the other hand, he emphasized, the plant is "not a charitable operation. . . . We may have a jump on a lot of companies in thinking you can make money by solving social problems."

Last year, the bindery plant turned a profit of $20,000 and picked up 75 new customers. . . .

The bindery workers' hourly pay ranges from $2.71 to $3.12 (after a year) to $5, according to plant manager Richard Mangram. Employees earn on the average $80 week for 25 hours.

In addition to her wages, a mother employed at the plant might get an additional $270 monthly welfare grant (compared with $400 a month if she were unemployed), so that the job plus the welfare check means a boost in her income of perhaps $190 a month.

The company estimates that its payroll has saved almost $600,000 in local welfare costs over the past seven years.

Though the bindery jobs require little skill, the plant offers training and a chance to move into full-time work for women who want to do so. Mangram said about 150 employees so far have done that. . . .

Plant manager Mangram maintains that the plant is competitive because of its low overhead, low absenteeism and turnover, and its high productivity per worker. . . .

The Control Data executives are not sure why more firms have not followed their example. "The problems are solved, we're making money and yet we're still the only ones around [the inner city]," Bowe said.

By tailoring its work schedules to fit the needs of workers in the community, the plant meets its own needs as well—an opportunity seemingly overlooked by other companies.

SOURCE: *The Washington Post*, December 27, 1977, pp. Al, A6.

Recruitment   If a shoe factory hires a skilled cobbler, then it won't have to devote much effort to teaching him how to make shoes. By the same token, a university department head who hires a sociology instructor with some prior classroom experience won't have to acquaint her with the fundamentals of teaching. In fact, every organization has jobs or tasks that must be performed in a certain way. The more selective an organization is in recruiting people who possess not only the skills but also the attitudes that the organization feels are desirable, the less it will have to socialize its members to conform to organizational requirements.

Socialization   As we saw in chapter 5, every organization has a spoken or unspoken "system" that new employees must learn if they are to succeed. School prepares people for some of what to expect in the working world. For instance, schedules and deadlines, assignments or reports, and the pressure to adhere to such behavioral norms as being punctual and showing respect for one's superiors are features of the classroom that prepare us for similar demands in the office.

For the most part, however, formal schooling does not prepare men and women for *specific* occupational roles. Rather, college offers a general orientation to a wide range of careers, as well as experience with an organization—the university. Recognizing this fact, most large corporations conduct formal training programs. "Come graduation," writes William H. Whyte, Jr., in *The Organization Man* (1956: 69), seniors "do not go outside to a hostile world; they transfer." By this he meant not only that a college curriculum is often deliberately designed to prepare students for organizational careers, but also that many corporations

have tailored their training programs to university graduates by setting up corporate campuses and classrooms.

Ostensibly, corporation training programs are designed to teach newcomers the skills required of a manager, an accountant, or an engineer. However, all have an unspoken agenda—namely, teaching the "company way." As training proceeds, recruits realize that they are being rated for the way they conduct themselves and get along with others, as well as for their skills. Ideally, then, when trainees move from the program to formal positions in the organization, they have been sufficiently indoctrinated to fit in smoothly.

Organizations also use socialization to maintain the commitment of members whose careers have not been especially successful. Unless alternative definitions of success are available, those who have not reached at least the foothills of managerial power may consider themselves failures, may lose incentive to keep working effectively, and may eventually "opt out" of the system altogether.

One way to deal with this problem is to give status to those who haven't gained power by calling them "professionals." Strictly speaking, the term "professional" refers to people trained in a technical field such as engineering or science. But organizations use the term more widely to refer to personnel ranging from salespeople to members of the maintenance staff, in order to create the impression that such professionals are more committed to succeeding in their special areas of competence than to moving into managerial positions. "This professional identification," Fred H. Goldner and R. R. Ritti observe (1967: 500), "sustains many in a position of blocked mobility by providing them both with a reason for their lack of mobility and an alternative chance to advance within their 'profession'—on a plateau within the management organization.''

Total Institutions

The strategies we have been considering so far are used by organizations that are relatively open. The *total institution*, which we'll consider next, is an organization that deliberately closes itself off from the outside and creates and sustains its own internal environment in order to pursue its goals.

At first glance, prisoners, mental patients, monks, and soldiers may seem to have little in common. But in *Asylums* (1961), Erving Goffman argues that they all live in structurally similar institutions. A monk may take his orders voluntarily; he may wear a cassock instead of army drab or prison gray; he spends his hours in prayer or study, not in drills or therapeutic arts and crafts. But the structure of his life is much the same as that of a convict in a prison, an inmate in a mental hospital, or a recruit in the army—all of which are total institutions, or in Goffman's terminology, asylums. Goffman defines an *asylum* as a place where ''a large number of like-situated individuals, cut off from the wider society for an appreciable period of time, together lead an enclosed, formally administered round of life.'' In asylums, bureaucratic control over the internal environment is carried to its extreme.

Because they are extreme cases, asylums highlight certain features that are less visible in most other bureaucracies. The asylum's relation to its inmates is a *coercive* one, even if they volunteered to enter it. All organizations are coercive to some degree: schools coerce, though for fewer hours of the day, and corporations coerce employees into fol-

lowing company rules. But in total institutions, people lose all control over and all responsibility for their lives. Socialization, in other words, reaches into every corner of the member's life.

Total institutions try to control their internal environments by segregating their members as completely as possible—emotionally, mentally, even physically—from other environments. In time, the organization becomes the only, or at least the dominant, reality for its members. For instance, once a person is admitted to a total institution, the process that Goffman calls *mortification* begins. Individuals are methodically stripped of the clothes, adornments, and personal possessions people use to define themselves in everyday life. In exchange, they receive standard, nondescript, and often ill-fitting attire—a uniform or hospital robe. They may be disfigured as well—by a military or prison haircut, for example. The new member's spirit is mortified, too. The institution designs exercises to break the will: people are forced to perform meaningless acts, to submit to arbitrary and unreasonable commands as well as to personal abuse (verbal or physical). Finally, they are deprived of privacy, both physical (through a debasing physical examination) and social (they must sleep, shower, and eat with a group). They are under constant surveillance, with every moment of every day being planned by others. These procedures disabuse people of their feelings of self-worth and train them for deference. Individuals in total institutions are forced into a kind of regression; they are made to feel helpless and therefore dependent on the organization. At this point they are ready to be resocialized to a new role, one the organization has designed.

People may react to their confinement in one of three main ways. In hospitals, some

These prisoners are experiencing "mortification"—the stripping away of personal privacy, possessions, and self that characterizes life in total institutions. (Bruno Barbey/Magnum)

actively work to sabotage routines, but their rebellion is generally short-lived because the institution can isolate or drug the rebel. Moreover, the staff can withhold privileges, fail to communicate messages to a doctor, and the like. Another possibility is that inmates can simply withdraw, detaching themselves from their surroundings as much as possible. Finally, they can accept their subjugation, as many do.[2] For such individuals, the asylum becomes a home they don't want to leave. Indeed, some actively seek out curtailments of the self, so mortification is complemented by self-mortification, restrictions by renunciations. Attached to the simple, predictable routines and the security of the asylum, they resist being discharged. If by chance they are let out, many find ways to be readmitted.[3]

Goffman attributes the extremes of total institutions to the low status accorded inmates, to the fact that inmates greatly outnumber staff, and to the tendency for means to become ends for the staff. Finishing the day's work becomes more important than meeting the institution's goals, which are themselves only poorly defined. "Keeping the lid on" mental hospitals, prisons, and the military occupies hundreds of thousands of

[2] A full 40 percent in one hospital, according to Ailon Shiloh (in Wallace, 1971: 8–23).

[3] This phenomenon is widespread enough to warrant a psychiatric term, *"institutional transference."*

bureaucrats today and uses up vast financial and human resources.

THE FUTURE: WILL ORGANIZATIONS RUN OUR LIVES?

Organizations and bureaucracies have been remarkably successful in adapting to and manipulating their environments; they have indeed learned how to survive and flourish. The question now is, Have they learned too well? Have they grown so powerful that they and not we direct our society? Do huge and autonomous organizations control our resources, decide what work we can do, and collect information about every detail of our lives? The ultimate danger in such a society would be the eventual conquest of individuality and freedom by the bureaucratic values of conformity and authoritarianism. How real is this danger?

Warnings

By the 1870s, the first signs of the spread of bureaucratic values were clearly evident in the United States, particularly in industry; by the 1930s, the trend had culminated in the "organizational society," characterized by a concentration of large organizations in government and in the major economic sectors of society. So argues Robert Presthus in his book *The Organizational Society* (1962: 59). Within the next three decades, the spread of large, bureaucratic institutions extended into new areas, particularly newspapers and radio and television. One consequence of this spread, Presthus argues, was that the

mass media began to publicize the image of the successful organizational personality— someone who shares the bureaucratic goals of survival, growth, and power, and who accepts authority easily and is anxious to conform to the group—thus influencing the ways in which parents and schools were socializing their children to be functional members of society. Middle-class families in particular, says Presthus, "employ child-rearing practices that give their children the inside track by emphasizing striving, punctuality, and the suppression of unprofitable emotions. These attributes prove functional in big organizations, now the main sources of status and prestige" (1962: 133–134).

A recent study of 250 executives in 12 large corporations produced a composite portrait of the typical successful manager that bears out some of Presthus's observations. Highly intelligent and quick to learn, the "gamesman," as Michael Maccoby calls the dominant managerial type (1977), is competitive, well adapted to the turbulent environment of the 1970s, and deeply committed to winning the games he plays for the organization. At the same time, the gamesman has no time for personal problems, no time for altruism or deep involvement with his colleagues, and no compassion for losers. "The fatal danger for gamesmen," Maccoby points out, "is . . . never outgrowing the self-centered compulsion to score, never confronting their deep boredom with life when it is not a game, never developing a sense of meaning that requires more of them and allows others to trust them" (109).

For Presthus, the dangers inherent in an organizational society do not end with socialization. He warns that the organization's emphasis on structure, efficiency, security, prestige, and power leads to indifference and frustration on the part of workers, who no longer derive any real satisfaction from their

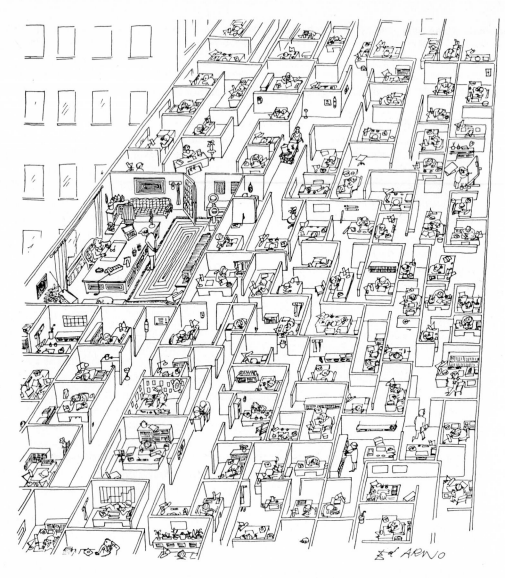

room for individual creativity and growth, they will usher in an age of unmotivated but cheerful robots (1962: 323).

Countertrends

jobs. Presthus concludes that if organizations don't change their logic and values to make

At the McDonald's headquarters in Oak Brook, Illinois, employees can retire to a cozy and private "think tank" whenever they feel the need to be by themselves; IBM has made it possible for workers to take time off, with pay, to participate in public works projects. Both of these are examples of a promising new movement aimed at restoring some of the autonomy and creativity Presthus feels is necessary if workers are to be satisfied. Some of the other innovations being tried at workplaces in the United States and abroad include giving people greater control over time, removing layers of supervision, and allowing workers at all levels to have more of a say in organizational decision-making processes (Dickson, 1975: 16–17).

What constitutes job satisfaction? A consistent relationship has been shown to exist between satisfaction and the amount of control a person can exercise in a work situation (Tannenbaum et al., 1974: 7). "Having some say in the affairs of the work situation contributes also to a member's sense of involvement in his work and in the organization, as well as to his identification, personal commitment, and feeling of responsibility on the job" (Tannenbaum et al., 1974: 7).

A study of hierarchies in organizations in five countries (Italy, Austria, the United States, Yugoslavia, and Israel) has shown that the closer a member is to the top, the greater his or her motivation and initiative are (Tannenbaum et al., 1974: 153). Similarly, in four of the countries, there was a positive correlation between position in the hierarchy and psychological adjustment. What these findings suggest is that in organizations in which a hierarchy is not sharply defined or heavily imposed on the members, overall satisfaction will be higher than in organizations with steep, all-pervasive hierarchies. And the researchers made another discovery: the highest degree of alienation and the strongest feelings of powerlessness, meaninglessness, social isolation, and the

like were found among workers in a rigidly hierarchical Italian industrial plant where members were allowed very little participation in decision-making; the least alienation, by contrast, was found among the members of an Israeli kibbutz, an organization based on common ownership and formal participation of members in setting organizational policies and goals. The *most* alienated workers in the kibbutz, in fact, were still more satisfied, on the whole, than the *least* alienated Italians. That job satisfaction may also have implications for physical health is suggested by the fact that the Italians also had the highest rate of ulcers.

From X to Y: Humanizing Organizations

"Theory X" and "Theory Y" were the anonymous-sounding names chosen by psychologist Douglas McGregor (in Dickson, 1975) to describe two radically different styles of organizational management. Theory X is based on the assumption that people hate work, seek to avoid responsibility, and must therefore be coerced into doing anything productive. By contrast, Theory Y sees people as anxious to be creative and to assume responsibility, and therefore as only too happy to work under the right circumstances. Both theories are somewhat exaggerated to portray an extreme, but they nevertheless apply to the problem we have been considering—namely, how can workers be given more control over their own occupational activities?

A famous group of Theory Y experiments have been initiated in Sweden by the arch-rival auto manufacturers SAAB and Volvo. The most striking innovation is the elimination of the assembly line, or at least of some of its worst parts, but the novelties do not stop there. At SAAB, for instance, workers finishing rough engines divide into teams of four, and each team decides for itself how to divide the work—that is, whether to work alone or in pairs or all together. Although the new system created certain complications in some factory processes and used more time to complete an engine than did the traditional method, SAAB's management expected several benefits, among them less absenteeism, higher overall quality of work, better worker attitudes, and better public relations. In 1974, less than two years after the new process was put into operation, the plant was meeting all its production targets and SAAB was firmly committed to the new system. Volvo's experiments have been just as revolutionary, and just as successful.

In the United States, the General Foods Corporation found itself with a golden opportunity to innovate when in 1968 it realized it would have to build a new plant in Topeka, Kansas, to meet the demand for its Gaines pet-food products. This was to be no ordinary factory: working with the architects were an experienced and imaginative plant manager and a behavioral scientist. The design that emerged was based on such unconventional considerations as the ego, social, and security needs of the people who would work in the plant. The final plan called for autonomous work groups that would each perform a complete function, with each job in the group requiring about the same degree of skill; supervisors who would be team members rather than bosses; the right of each team to make its own day-to-day assignments, to recruit and hire new members, and to set its own goals; and the use of machines to perform unpleasant tasks, with other menial chores divided equally among team members. The physical design of the factory reinforced the nonhierarchical concept: there were to be no reserved parking

places, everyone would enter and leave through the same door, the size of the office would be related to the work being done there rather than to the rank of the occupant, and the work-floor plan would make it easy for employees to get together during work hours. Such mingling was expected to be pleasant and also to help people learn about other jobs.

Employees were to be encouraged to learn as many jobs as possible; there would be no time clocks; plant rules would be made by the people working there; and workers would be kept informed not only about their own performances but also about the performance of the Gaines line, about how other dog foods were doing, and about how the factory fit into the overall General Foods scheme. Did it work? The plant went into operation in 1971. Before the year was over, General Foods reported high product quality, a very low absentee rate, and a productivity rate that was 10 to 40 percent higher per person than in similar operations elsewhere, despite the fact that as much as 30 percent of each person's day was devoted to training, meetings, and breaks. After eighteen months, the safety record at the plant was one of the best in the company, there were 92 percent fewer rejected dog-food batches than was normal in food processing, and the combined value of all the improvements was computed at $600,000 a year (Dickson, 1975: 156–160).

Conclusion

At the dawn of the Age of Organizations, as institutions based on bureaucratic principles evolved to meet the opportunities and problems of the Industrial Revolution, a philosophy similar to Theory X was considered valid. There was no empirical reason to consider it otherwise: organizations based on strict control of members, rigid hierarchies, and an implicitly negative view of the worker brought profits and prosperity on a scale unprecedented in history.

Today, Theory X coexists with Theory Y. Large organizations are, as we have seen, becoming more responsive to the needs and aspirations of those who work for them and those who benefit from them. Volvo and SAAB changed the assembly line; many West German firms allow office workers to set their own hours; stockholders sue managements to force greater social responsibility.

Yet as society and technology become more and more complex, the need for coordination is so great that organizations can't help but generate more and more rules and regulations. When a Kansas farmer's choice of crops can affect not only his livelihood but the country's balance of payments and the world food supply, the decision about what and how much to plant can't be his alone. When a huge corporation manufactures and markets hundreds of products in plants scattered across the country or the world, it must have standardized procedures and detailed plans to avoid destroying a state's or country's economy. So there are trends in both directions—X and Y. It is, in fact, in the process of accommodation between the two that the future of the large organization will be shaped.

SUMMARY

Formal organizations are groups whose activities are deliberately coordinated, by means of rules and a hierarchy of authority and responsibility, to achieve specific goals. Unlike other kinds of social groups, formal organizations are *self-perpetuating:* members may come and go, but procedures and goals remain. Relationships within formal organizations are based on exchange rather than affection.

People also may join an organization because they share the organization's goals and norms. Such groups—for example, feminist organizations or Alcoholics Anonymous—are called *voluntary associations.*

Most formal organizations have a bureaucratic structure—that is, they consist of interrelated parts with separate functions. Although bureaucracies are not a modern invention, the "Age of Bureaucracy" actually began during the nineteenth century, when the Western nations started to industrialize. Bureaucracy represents the application of mechanical principles to the organization of work. Max Weber identified the distinguishing characteristics of bureaucracy as (1) specialization (the division of production into small tasks); (2) a hierarchy of offices (with each individual being responsible to the person above him or her and for the people below him or her, and with authority vested in the office, not in the individual); (3) adherence to explicit rules and regulations; (4) impartiality (because emotions impede efficiency); and (5) technical competence (paying people for their work, and awarding raises and promotions on the basis of achievement and seniority). Weber described a model or ideal type; in reality, the completely bureaucratic organization does not exist.

Although Weber saw bureaucracy as promoting efficiency, others have pointed out how the bureaucratic model may lead to inefficiency. For example, Robert Merton asserts that the emphasis on rules results in *ritualism*—bureaucrats lose sight of goals and end up performing procedures simply as rituals. Others note that in hierarchies employees tend to protect inept co-workers. To designate another drawback of hierarchies, Lawrence Peter formulated the *Peter Principle:* "Every employee tends to rise to his [or her] level of incompetence." And the waste of time and money in vast hierarchies gave rise to *Parkinson's Law,* which is that "work expands to fill the time available for its completion."

Organizations have both a formal and an informal structure. The explicit rules defining each member's duties, organizational charts, and a system of rewards and punishments constitute the *formal structure.* The *informal structure* consists of a loose network of procedures that facilitate problem-solving, eliminate unnecessary work, and protect the interests of individual workers. The process of bargaining and give-and-take whereby people at various levels of an organization solve work-related problems is called a *negotiated order.*

But organizations don't exist in a vacuum: they must cope with their internal and external environments, both of which constantly change, in order to survive. Although the established roles and routines often come to seem unchangeable, in fact these elements can and do change, as the example of the New School for Social Research shows. That organization was almost re-created from within when outside pressures demanded flexibility.

In dealing with the external environment, the greatest problem the organization faces is unpredictability: necessary resources may suddenly become unavailable, customers may stop buying the product, governments may make demands or become uncooperative. Some organizations adapt to the environment by insulating themselves through specialization; others diversify and grow extremely large. Still others attempt to acquire power over the external environment by gaining prestige.

Control of the internal environment—members and the jobs they do—is another vital adaptation. Organizations achieve control by a system of rewards and punishments and through *recruitment* (selecting as members those who already meet some or all of the organization's requirements) and *socialization* (educating or training members to fill certain roles). *Total institutions* and *asylums* are terms Goffman uses to characterize organizations that are closed off from the outside world and that create and sustain their own internal environments in order to pursue their goals. Monasteries, prisons, mental hospitals, and military organizations are all examples of total institutions. They initiate members by *mortification* (stripping them of all outward signs of individuality), and they demand submission.

The question we face now is, Have organizations learned to adapt to and manipulate their environments so well that they and not we direct our society? Robert Presthus argues that by the 1930s bureaucratic values were so entrenched that America could be called an "organizational society," one characterized by a concentration of large organizations in government and in the major economic sectors. But there are countertrends, efforts to restore some of the autonomy and creativity Presthus believes is necessary for job satisfaction. The General Foods Gaines pet-food plant in Topeka, Kansas, is an example of this tendency to give people greater control over their time and work, remove layers of supervision, and deemphasize hierarchy.

"Theory X" and "Theory Y" are terms coined by Douglas McGregor to describe two radically different styles of organizational management that exist today. Theory X—that people hate to work, seek to avoid responsibility, and must be coerced into being productive—was once considered the only valid philosophy. Theory Y—that people are anxious to be creative and to assume responsibility, and therefore to work under the right circumstances—is now, as the General Foods and other experiments show, regarded as equally valid, and the two theories currently function as counterbalances in the evolution of the large organization.

GLOSSARY

bureaucracy an organization consisting of interrelated parts with separate and specialized functions, designed to perform some kind of work.

external environment for an organization, those resources, other organizations, customers, transport systems, governments, and so on within which it operates.

formal organization a group whose activities are deliberately coordinated for the achievement of specific goals or purposes.

formal structure in an organization, the elements of formal structure include the explicit rules defining each person's duties, organizational charts describing relationships among members, and a system of rewards and punishments.

hierarchy in bureaucracies, a chain of command, with each person responsible to the person directly above him or her and responsible for the actions of those directly below.

informal structure in an organization, the informal structure consists of the procedures that enable people to solve problems not covered by the formal regulations, to eliminate unpleasant or unnecessary work, and to protect their own interests.

internal environment for an organization, its members and the jobs they do.

mortification Goffman's term for the process of stripping a person of his or her civilian identity and physical integrity, in preparation for indoctrination into a new role.

multinational corporation An organization with productive facilities in several countries.

negotiated order the process of bargaining, diplomacy, and give-and-take whereby people at various levels of an organization together solve work-related problems.

Parkinson's Law Parkinson formulated his law to explain why bureaucratic employees often appear busier than they should be: "Work expands to fill the time available for its completion."

Peter Principle attempting to account for the incompetence characteristic of many bureaucratic employees, Peter and Hull suggest that "in a hierarchy, every employee tends to rise to his [or her] level of incompetence."

rational-legal authority Weber's term for authority that rests in the office, not in the person who occupies it.

ritualism Merton's term for following rules and regulations without regard for the original goals or the consequences of one's actions.

total institution an organization closed off from the outside in which inmates lose nearly all control over and responsibility for their own lives (Goffman).

voluntary association an organization people join because they support its goals and values.

REFERENCES

Peter M. Blau and Marshall W. Meyer, *Bureaucracy in Modern Society*, 2nd ed. New York: Random House, 1971.

Paul Dickson, *The Future of the Workplace*. New York: Weybright and Talley, 1975.

H. H. Gerth and C. Wright Mills, eds., *From Max Weber: Essays in Sociology*. Oxford: Oxford University Press, 1946.

Erving Goffman, *Asylums*. Garden City, N.Y.: Doubleday, 1961.

Fred H. Goldner and R. R. Ritti, "Professionalization as Career Immobility." *American Journal of Sociology*, vol. 72 (March 1967): 489–502.

William J. Goode, "The Protection of the Inept." *American Sociological Review,* vol. 32 (February 1967): 5–19.

Alvin Gouldner, *Studies in Leadership*. New York: Harper & Row, 1950.

Richard H. Hall, "The Concept of Bureaucracy: An Empirical Assessment." *American Journal of Sociology*, vol. 69 (1963–1964): 32–40.

Alvin Johnson, *Pioneer's Progress*. Magnolia, Mass.: Peter Smith, 1952.

Michael Maccoby, *The Gamesman*. New York: Simon & Schuster, 1977.

Robert Merton, *Social Theory and Social Structure*. Glencoe, Ill.: Free Press, 1968.

C. Northcote Parkinson, *Parkinson's Law*. Boston: Houghton Mifflin, 1957.

Laurence F. Peter and Raymond Hull, *The Peter Principle*. New York: Morrow, 1969.

Robert Presthus, *The Organizational Society*. New York: Knopf, 1962.

Anselm Strauss et al., *Psychiatric Ideologies and Institutions*. New York: Free Press, 1964.

Arnold S. Tannenbaum et al., *Hierarchy in Organizations: An International Comparison*. San Francisco, Calif.: Jossey-Bass, 1974.

James D. Thompson, *Organizations in Action*. New York: McGraw-Hill, 1967.

Lane Tracy, "Postscript to the Peter Principle." *Harvard Business Review,* vol. 50 (July–August 1972): 65–71.

Stanley H. Udy, Jr., " 'Bureaucracy' and 'Rationality' in Weber's Organizational Theory: An Empirical Study." *American Sociological Review,* vol. 24 (December 1959): 791–795.

Samuel E. Wallace, ed., *Total Institutions*. Chicago: Transaction/Aldine, 1971.

Max Weber, *The Theory of Social and Economic Organization*, trans. Talcott Parsons. Glencoe, Ill.: Free Press, 1947.

K. E. Weick, *The Social Psychology of Organizing*. Reading, Mass.: Addison-Wesley, 1969.

William H. Whyte, Jr., *The Organization Man*. New York: Simon & Schuster, 1956.

James Q. Wilson, *Varieties of Police Behavior*. New York: Atheneum, 1974. (Originally published by Harvard University Press.)

FOR FURTHER STUDY

Giant and Multinational Corporations.   No organizational form besides the government so shapes our lives and the fate of nations as do large corporations. Two important, exciting books are *Global Reach: The Power of the Multinational Corporations* by Richard Barnet and Ronald Müller (New York: Simon & Schuster, 1975), and *The Multinational Company* by E. Kolde (Lexington, Mass.: Lexington Books, 1974). Ralph Nader and his team have written *Taming the Giant Corporation* (New York: Norton, 1976), a provocative book about large companies in the U.S.A.

statement on how total institutions work and affect both
by Erving Goffman (New York: Doubleday, 1961). A
t is found in *Total Institutions,* edited by Samuel E.
ldine, 1971). A contrasting view is that inmates may
scussed by Goffman but more fully examined by B. M.
ness: The Mental Hospital as a Last Resort (New York:
The authors have persuasive evidence that at least in
ylums more than the asylum oppressed the inmates.

e organizations become so pervasive that this is an
is addressed in various ways by Robert Presthus in
rk: Vintage, 1962); by A. Ernest Fitzgerald in *The*
rton, 1972); and in *American Society, Inc.,* Maurice
0). Also see the appropriate readings in *Crises in*
me H. Skolnick and Elliott Currie, eds. (Boston:
e essay by Heilbroner.

study of organizations and their internal struc-
s in all of sociology. A good overview of bureau-
dern Society (New York: Random House, 1956).
Administrative Behavior, 3rd ed., by Herbert A.
valuable text in the field is Richard S. Hall's
d ed. (Englewood Cliffs: Prentice-Hall, 1977).

HAPPY
B-DAY, KID!

Just thought
I'd Let Ya
Know I was
thinkin' Of Ya!)

Love,

CHAPTER 9

Deviance and Social Control

Everyone knows about Saint Joan, the fifteenth-century French peasant girl who broke the siege of Orléans and crowned the dauphin at Rheims, only to be captured by the British, tried for heresy, and burned at the stake. In his play *Saint Joan* (1924), George Bernard Shaw suggests that Joan's execution was inevitable. She violated the established order by commanding her social ''betters'' to follow her, committed ''crimes against Nature'' by donning men's clothes and becoming a soldier, and defied the church on grounds of individual conviction. In Shaw's play a reluctant chaplain expresses doubts about Joan's culpability. The Inquisitor grows serious:

> Brother Martin. . . . Heresy begins with people who are to all appearances better than their neighbors. A gentle and pious girl may be the founder of a heresy that will wreck both Church and Empire if not ruthlessly stamped out. . . . [T]he woman who quarrels with her clothes, and puts on the dress of a man, is like the man who throws off his fur gown and dresses like John the Baptist: they are followed, as surely as night follows the day, by bands of wild women and men who refuse to wear any clothes at all. (144–145)

We no longer burn people at the stake, but we do execute some, isolate others in prisons and hospitals, and shun others whom we consider deviant. Sociologists are interested in understanding why some forms of nonconformity threaten to society, and why societies vary in their reactions to deviance. Why, for example, are people who hear voices, as Joan did, burned in one century and hospitalized in another? Why are people who aspire to roles that are traditionally reserved for the opposite sex ridiculed or ostracized?

In this chapter we will attempt to answer these questions. First we define deviance. Then we examine biological, psychological, and sociological explanations of deviance. We will also explore the social consequences for those caught breaking social rules and labeled deviant, focusing on who gets labeled and why. The last part of the chapter is concerned with the mechanisms of social control. We take a critical look at prisons and suggest directions for prison reform.

THE NATURE AND FUNCTIONS OF DEVIANCE

What Is Deviance?

One text on deviance and social control begins, "The subject of this book is knavery, skulduggery, cheating, unfairness, crime, sneakiness, malingering, cutting corners, immorality, dishonesty, betrayal, graft, corruption, wickedness, and sin . . ." (Cohen, 1966: 1). This description is only partly accurate, for as we have seen, even a saint may be considered deviant. *Deviance* is any behavior that violates social norms and expectations.

The sociology of deviance may have begun with Émile Durkheim's observation that behaviors which qualify one person for sainthood may condemn another to prison, a mental asylum, or the stake. His point, quite simply, was that no act is *inherently* deviant. Deviance is defined by social norms, and because norms are relative to time and place, so too is deviance. Even killing another person is considered normal and right if you are wearing a soldier's uniform and are fighting for your country. (We never say that a soldier *murdered* one of the enemy.) Thus one person may be honored and another sent to prison for committing the same act. What sociology teaches us is that in order to understand why a given act is considered deviant, we must know the context in which it occurs.

Even among those acts that are agreed to be deviant, some are considered more serious than others and incur more stringent penalties. Telling a lie to a friend violates an informal norm and creates bad feelings, but such an act will not result in your being thrown in jail. Different violations of the law also elicit different punishments: for speed-ing on the highway, one may have to pay a fine; for committing murder, the penalty may be death. Most of us are already aware of these facts. The process of becoming a member of society is in many ways synonymous with learning the limits of acceptable and unacceptable behavior.

Social control, the group of formal and informal mechanisms which ensure that society's rules are learned and followed, is the mirror of deviance: each kind of behavior considered deviant will be matched by a punishment of some sort. But deviance, as well as the mechanisms intended to control it, can change with the situation or over time. The use of marijuana is an interesting example. During the 1930s, a propaganda poster warned that marijuana was "a powerful narcotic in which lurks Murder! Insanity! Death!" By the end of that decade, use of the drug was illegal in every state and was also banned by federal law. During the 1960s, however, the reputation of the drug began to change, particularly on college campuses. A Gallup poll taken in 1967 found that 5 percent of the college population had tried "grass"; in a national survey done eight years later, the proportion of college students who had tried marijuana had risen to 64 percent. In the population at large, according to a 1977 Gallup poll, 24 percent of Americans had at least tried the drug, twice the level recorded in 1973 (Gallup Opinion Index, 1977).

Along with marijuana's increasing popularity came an increase in the pressure for a change in the law. By 1977, nine states had decriminalized the possession of small amounts of marijuana—replacing arrests and jail sentences with fines and citations resembling traffic tickets—and other states were preparing to follow suit. "In the last few years," a journalist wrote recently, "public attitudes toward marijuana have shifted sufficiently so that favoring its decriminalization

table 9:1 PERCENTAGE DISTRIBUTION OF PEOPLE IN EACH COUNTRY RESPONDING TO THE QUESTION, ''DO YOU THINK THIS ACT SHOULD BE PROHIBITED BY LAW?''

TYPE OF ACT	COUNTRY	RESPONSE[1]	
		Yes	No
Mugging a person for money	India	97.30	2.70
	Indonesia	99.20	.00
	Iran	97.90	2.10
	Italy (Sardinia)	100.00	.00
	U.S.A.	100.00	.00
	Yugoslavia	98.40	.40
Embezzlement from the government	India	96.60	1.20
	Indonesia	99.80	.20
	Iran	97.10	2.90
	Italy (Sardinia)	100.00	.00
	U.S.A.	92.30	7.10
	Yugoslavia	98.00	.00
Homosexuality in private between mutually consenting adults	India	74.10	25.00
	Indonesia	85.90	7.20
	Iran	90.30	9.70
	Italy (Sardinia)	86.50	12.50
	U.S.A.	18.30	66.90
	Yugoslavia	71.60	13.60
Use of illegal drugs	India	74.90	24.60
	Indonesia	93.30	2.40
	Iran	89.80	10.20
	Italy (Sardinia)	92.00	3.00
	U.S.A.	89.60	11.80
	Yugoslavia	89.20	4.20
Air pollution caused by a factory	India	98.80	1.20
	Indonesia	94.90	1.00
	Iran	97.70	2.30
	Italy (Sardinia)	96.00	3.50
	U.S.A.	96.40	3.00
	Yugoslavia	92.80	1.60
Public, nonviolent political protest	India	33.30	65.80
	Indonesia	72.30	20.90
	Iran	77.00	23.00
	Italy (Sardinia)	34.50	64.50
	U.S.A.	5.90	91.10
	Yugoslavia	46.20	38.40
Failure to help another person who is in danger	India	44.50	53.90
	Indonesia	67.70	24.40
	Iran	56.40	43.60
	Italy (Sardinia)	79.50	20.00
	U.S.A.	27.80	52.70
	Yugoslavia	76.60	12.20

[1] The category ''Don't know'' is not included in the percentages.

SOURCE: Adapted from Graeme Newman, *Comparative Deviance: Perception and Law in Six Cultures* (New York: Elsevier, 1976), table 4, p. 116.

This poster is one of many issued during the 1930s to warn against use of marijuana. Such propaganda led to legislation banning the drug. Today, "grass" has become widely accepted, and penalties for its possession have been relaxed. This reversal illustrates how social perceptions of deviance can vary over time. (The Morgan Love Company)

has become a politically safe position" (Goldstein, *The New York Times*, February 3, 1977). Indeed, so safe had that position become that after less than a month in the White House, President Jimmy Carter and his wife endorsed the removal of criminal penalties for the possession of small amounts of what had once been known as the "killer weed."

Deviance varies not only within a given

society but cross-culturally as well. In parts of the Near and Far East, for example, opiates are sold on a cash-and-carry basis in open markets, and people smoke marijuana and hashish publicly. Even in this country, attitudes toward drugs in general are extremely inconsistent. There is little or no stigma attached to taking tranquilizers, sleeping pills, or painkillers obtained with a doctor's prescription, to drinking large quantities of alcohol (at socially appropriate times), or to smoking tobacco, some of which pose clear health hazards.

Just as judgments about what is and what is not deviant vary, so do explanations of nonconforming behavior. At one time, almost all Americans considered homosexuality an expression of depravity, a sin, a ''crime against nature'' that made a person morally unfit for life among decent people. Then homosexuality ''became'' a mental illness, an unfortunate compulsion that might be cured through psychotherapy. But in 1974 the American Psychiatric Association voted to remove homosexuality from its catalogue of mental illnesses, declaring it to be a ''sexual orientation disturbance,'' not an illness.[1] Similarly, certain kinds of behavior were once thought to be a sign of possession by evil spirits or the devil, and people who exhibited such behavior were subject to exorcism or burning. During the twentieth century, these same sorts of behavior came to be considered symptoms of mental illness, and those behaving in such ways are treated by various kinds of therapies and drugs. Thus the definition of deviance always depends on

[1] Interestingly, Sigmund Freud anticipated this shift. In a ''Letter to an American Mother'' he wrote: ''I gather from your letter that your son is a homosexual. . . . Homosexuality is assuredly no advantage, but it is nothing to be ashamed of, no vice, no degradation, it cannot be classified as an illness; we consider it to be a variation of the sexual function'' (in Schur, 1965: 72).

what the prevailing norms are—and on who is doing the defining, a subject we'll explore later.

The Social Functions of Deviance

Although deviance is by definition behavior that poses a threat to the social order, at the same time deviance makes it possible to define what the social order actually is.

Deviance Defines the Social Order   In most societies, the boundaries between acceptable and unacceptable behavior are not clear-cut, and the limits are constantly being changed and reestablished. Deviance plays a double role in that process: first, in defining certain kinds of behavior as deviant, a group or a society also defines what behavior is acceptable; and second, in uniting in opposition to the deviant, that group or society comes together and reaffirms its common bonds. When people in a town in the old West formed a posse, when parents unite to fight school busing, or when citizens vote for a new, uncorrupt politician, they owe a debt to the outlaw, the judge who ordered the busing, or the corrupt politician for bringing them together. And usually they do more than reaffirm those values; they also strengthen other values, work together, and pour energy into shoring up the social order they believe in.

When Anne Hutchinson began to proclaim, for example, that Boston's ministers did not have the exclusive right to interpret the Bible, as they were doing around 1630, she drew large audiences, but she also angered the Puritan ministers who ruled colonial Boston. She was undermining church authority, they said, which was nearly synonymous with civil authority. Yet she was an upright and perfectly law-abiding citizen, and they therefore had no way to define her deviance. They finally wrote a law that made what she was doing illegal, found her guilty, and banished her from the colony. ''I desire to know wherefore I am banished,'' she said. Governor Winthrop gave her this answer: ''Say no more, the court knows wherefore and is satisfied.'' ''And that was exactly the point,'' writes Kai T. Erikson in his account of the peculiar controversy.

> The court *did* know why Mrs. Hutchinson had to be banished, but it did not know how to express that feeling in any language then known in New England. The settlers were experiencing a shift in ideological focus, a change in community boundaries, but they had no vocabulary to explain to themselves or anyone else what the nature of these changes were. The purpose of the trial was to invent that language, to find a name for the nameless offense which Mrs. Hutchinson had committed (Erikson, 1966: 100–101).

Thus, without realizing it, Anne Hutchinson helped the Massachusetts Bay Colony redefine the limits of acceptable religious beliefs. And somewhat ironically, she also contributed to the social solidarity of the community she left behind.

Deviance Stimulates Change   Deviants are often the leading edge of a new trend and therefore serve as agents of social change. For example, the unwillingness of blacks to comply with segregation laws—beginning with one woman's refusal to sit at the back of a bus—has given rise to a new legal and moral code. And during the past decade or so, efforts by women to achieve sexual equality have also involved behavior that initially appeared—or is still thought to be—deviant, such as the refusal, on ideological grounds, to give up one's own last name after getting married.

Perhaps nowhere else does deviance lead to such spectacular change as in science. During the 1960s an American biochemist, Howard Temin, announced that the order of DNA and RNA production in genes, which scientists had already worked out, could also be accomplished in the reverse order. Like many other scientists before him, Temin was widely attacked by his colleagues, because he threatened the prevailing theory in his scientific community. But by the 1970s, Temin's theory had profoundly changed the basis of cancer research, and in 1975, he and two other men won the Nobel Prize in Medicine.

What makes deviance in science particularly interesting is that science *depends* on new breakthroughs (a kind of deviance) to advance, and scientists are trained to challenge prevailing ideas. Nevertheless, the scientific community, like every other human group, adopts conventions (prevailing theory) that order its work. Because the very breakthroughs that advance knowledge threaten so much of the research going on at the time, they may be resisted and may even go unrecognized for years after they occur.

EXPLANATIONS OF DEVIANCE

In 1975, there were twenty-one serious crimes committed in the United States *every minute*. It is estimated that there was a murder every twenty-six minutes; a woman forcibly raped every nine minutes; a robbery every sixty-eight seconds; a burglary every ten seconds; and a theft of $50 or more every five seconds (Uniform Crime Reports, 1975). In all likelihood, these figures are underestimates, since not all crimes are re-

Scientific breakthroughs depend upon deviant research. Today, for example, experiments in genetic engineering are highly controversial. This frog is a clone, produced asexually by implanting a frog body cell nucleus into a foster egg. Since each of an organism's body cell nuclei seems to contain a complete and identical set of genes, the number of replicas that could be cloned from one parent frog is theoretically immense. Proponents of these experiments point out that cloning could be an invaluable means of increasing food supplies. But critics inside and outside the scientific community feel that interference with natural genetic processes is a threat to life as we know it. (J. B. Gurdon/Scientific American)

ported. But crime makes up only a part of the picture. The National Center for Health Statistics records illegitimacy, suicide, and mental illness rates. According to their figures, in 1975, of the approximately 3.1 million births registered in the United States, as many as 447,900 of them—14.2 percent—were illegitimate, up 7 percent from the year before. In 1974, there were 26,430 suicides, representing 1.4 percent of all deaths (in fact, suicide is now one of the top ten causes of death in America). Mental illness is also a form of deviance, and the extent of this problem is suggested by the fact that in 1973, there were 636,984 mental-hospital patients in the United States. Why do people deviate? As we will show in the pages that follow, the answer isn't at all obvious.

Biological Explanations

According to the nineteenth-century view of the world, humans were rational beings. They were supposed to act only in ways advantageous to themselves. "Crime does not pay," so how could someone be rational and yet be a criminal? Cesare Lombroso, an Italian criminologist, suggested an explanation—people could be *born* criminals (Lombroso, in Ferrero, 1911). He suggested that criminals were throwbacks, more nearly representative of our primitive and savage ancestors than of modern men and women. This flash hit Lombroso as he examined Villella, an Italian master criminal. He reported excitedly that

At the sight of that skull, I seemed to see all of a sudden, lighted up as a vast plain under a flaming sky, the problem of the nature of the criminal—an atavistic being who reproduces in his person the ferocious instincts of primitive humanity and the inferior animals. Thus were explained the enormous jaws, high cheekbones, prominent superciliary arches . . . found in criminals, savages, and apes. . . . (Lombroso, in Cohen, 1966: 50)

Lombroso and his students made dozens of measurements of the heads and bodies of scores of prisoners, and every criminal fit the "animalistic" pattern. But Lombroso did make one serious error—he measured only criminals. When Charles Goring, a British physician, measured ordinary citizens, he found that they were no different, at least physically, from criminals (Goring, 1913), and Lombroso's famous theory was dashed.

But the spirit of Lombroso, the belief in and search for a biological basis for deviant behavior, remains very much alive. Every year biological research into the causes of schizophrenia, manic depression, and other mental disorders grows more intense and produces increasingly credible results. Indeed, biological explanations of such socially stigmatized diseases as mental retardation and hemophilia have already won wide acceptance.

Could criminal behavior also have a genetic basis? Much attention has been paid recently to the so-called XYY syndrome, the possibility that the presence of an extra Y chromosome in some men might predispose them toward deviance. (A normal man has an XY chromosome pattern; a normal woman has an XX chromosome pattern.) When researchers found that a greater percentage of XYY men than normal men were in prison for crimes, it lent evidence to the idea that the extra Y chromosome makes a man more aggressive and therefore leads to

increased criminal behavior (cited in Witkin et al., 1976: 548). But like Lombroso's work, the sample studied was made up only of prisoners. A recent comprehensive study in Denmark found a significant difference between the percentage of XYY men and that of XY men who had been convicted of one or more criminal offenses (Witkin et al., 1976: 550), but little evidence linking criminality with increased aggressiveness. Instead, the researchers found that men with an extra Y chromosome were appreciably less intelligent than XY men, and might thus be easier for the police to catch—which would explain why more XYY men land in jail.

Psychological Explanations

Today, a more typical reaction to deviance is to look for some psychological explanation. When asked in a survey why people smoke marijuana, for example, most respondents said smokers were "insecure," "escapist," or "looking for kicks" (Simmons, 1965: 227). Though these judgments may be superficial, there is no reason to suppose that deviance can't be at least partially explained in psychological terms. In fact, psychologists have attempted to explain deviance in a number of ways.

Freudian psychologists maintain that all people have deviant impulses toward sexuality and aggression, but that in the process of growing up most of us learn to inhibit them. Freud argued that through identification with their parents, children acquire a superego, or conscience, that forbids deviant kinds of behavior, and an ego that enables them to deal realistically with internal drives and social demands (see chapter 5). Psychoanalytic theory suggests that acts of wanton cruelty and crimes committed without apparent motives may indicate an underdeveloped superego. Conversely, an *overdeveloped* superego may also lead to deviance. People who are repulsed by their own urges may commit deviant acts to receive the punishment they feel they deserve for hating their parents or for having sexual fantasies, for example (Cohen, 1966: 56–57).

Other psychologists argue that we simply learn from those around us. Albert Bandura and Richard H. Walters, for example, compared groups of delinquent and nondelinquent white boys from financially stable homes (1959). They found that continuously harsh physical discipline or overindulgence could lead to delinquency. Boys whose fathers often beat them tended to rely on external controls. They based decisions on the chances of being caught, not on inner feelings of right and wrong. On the other hand, boys who had their parents' uncritical approval grew up believing that anything they wanted to do was good—an assumption not always shared by the outside world.

Sociological Explanations

Although psychological theories of deviance provide insights into individual cases, they don't explain why *rates* of deviance (the number of deviant acts per unit of population) vary from group to group, from neighborhood to neighborhood. Sociological theories deal with this question. Sociologists have found that social environment influences many kinds of deviance—even something so psychological as psychosis and so personal as suicide (see chapter 2). The fact that there is more than one sociological theory of deviance may suggest that the "right answer" has not yet been found, but this is a false impression; each theory is useful because it provides us with a specific piece of a very complex puzzle.

Theories of Social Stress The essence of stress or strain theories is the assumption that when conformity to social norms fails to satisfy a person's legitimate desires, that person will eventually be forced to seek satisfaction through deviant means (Hirschi, 1969: 3). The concept of *anomie,* a state of deregulation or normlessness experienced when there is no meaning or stability in life because of sudden depression, prosperity, or rapid technological change, was originally proposed by Émile Durkheim (1897) to explain certain forms of suicide. Durkheim saw the aspirations of humans as having no limits; he thought that the collective order of norms and values established by society regulates human desires and keeps them within the bounds of realistic possibility (Gibbons and Jones, 1975: 84–85).

Robert K. Merton applied the concept of anomie in an American context as he sought to describe the different ways in which people adapt to the discrepancy between expectations and opportunities. He used stress theory to account for varying crime rates in different social classes (1957) and linked high rates of deviance to anomie. For example, people may expect to have a job, but the economy may not provide enough jobs to go around. Merton reasoned that to some degree all people internalize the goals considered worth striving for in their culture. Everyone also internalizes the norms governing proper and legitimate ways of striving for these goals. When opportunities for achieving highly valued goals (as the culture defines them) do not exist, people seek alternatives. Thus, "some social structures exert a definite pressure upon certain persons in the society to engage in nonconforming rather than in conforming behavior" (Merton, 1957: 132).

Merton defined *conformity* as seeking culturally approved goals by culturally approved means. He outlined four types of deviant behavior that may occur when social realities don't match cultural expectations. One type is *innovation*—pursuing culturally approved goals by deviant means. A thief, for example, is pursuing the same objectives as a working person—namely, money, the things it can buy, and the prestige it confers. Another way to resolve conflicts between goals and means is *ritualism*, adhering rigidly to norms at the expense of goals. A teacher who maintains order in the classroom and delivers lessons in the prescribed way regardless of whether students learn anything is a ritualist. Merton uses the term *retreatism* to describe giving up. Retreatists are people who have lost the desire to pursue certain cultural goals as well as the belief that following certain norms is intrinsically worthwhile. Drug addicts, alcoholics, many psychotics, drifters, and bums are examples. Finally, people who are alienated from both the goals and the standards of their culture may come up with new ideals and new rules for pursuing them. Merton calls this *rebellion*. The Weathermen and the short-lived Symbionese Liberation Army (SLA) are examples.

Since its publication in 1957, Merton's theory has been highly praised and widely criticized. For instance, Travis Hirschi (1969) argues that there is little empirical evidence to support the hypothesis that delinquency is a frustrated response to the success ethic and is therefore likely to be most prevalent among those least able to succeed (see the discussion of social-bond theory below). Other criticisms of Merton include the objection that he assumes everyone embraces the same ideals of "success" and that he fails to emphasize the effects of group interaction enough. "The unsuccessful individual who is surrounded by associates who have been successful in pursuing conventional goals by legitimate means may well react to his own situation differently from the person who is in contact with others who have gotten ahead by cutting corners or by using illegitimate means," according to Albert K. Cohen (1965).

Cultural Transmission of Deviance In the 1920s, Clifford Shaw and Henry McKay noted that high crime rates had persisted in the same Chicago neighborhood for over twenty years, even though different ethnic groups had come and gone. Obviously, ethnic traditions couldn't explain the crime rate. In one of the classic studies of deviance (1929), Shaw and McKay found that newcomers were continuously learning deviant ways from established residents, primarily in play groups and teen-age gangs. Once the newcomers had absorbed the neighborhood norms and values, they in turn passed them on to the next wave of immigrants.

Shaw and McKay's study was supported by the work of Edwin Sutherland, whose *Principles of Criminology* (1960) contains an explanation of how this *cultural transmission*—the process by which deviance is learned through the transmission of norms within a community or group—takes place. Sutherland points out that everyone is exposed to different and conflicting definitions of right and wrong. The standards people eventually adopt as their own are learned and depend on the timing, number, frequency, duration, and intensity of their contacts with deviant or nondeviant others—criminals or law-abiding persons, radicals or conservatives, homosexuals or heterosexuals. If those who matter most to a person (family, friends, peers) *devalue* conformity and/or practice deviant behaviors, that person is far more likely to learn techniques for committing deviant acts, as well as rationalizations for them.

Through the transmission of norms within a community or group, people can be socialized to the drug subculture, the homosexual subculture, the radical subculture, and so on. For just as some communities offer young people opportunities for education, role models of people who have achieved success by conventional means, and contacts with people who can help advance their careers, other communities offer opportunities for learning how to hustle and evade authorities, role models of people who have achieved success as gamblers or pimps, and contacts with the underworld. In the Harlem section of Manhattan, for instance, thousands of street-wise boys and girls between the ages of nine and sixteen are told that they can make a lot of money simply by selling little envelopes of heroin they are given by narcotics dealers. The inducements to become a "runner" are strong: by the time he was fifteen, one "runner" had earned himself enough money to buy a $12,000 car. The deterrents, on the other hand, are weak: as one girl told a reporter, "I was spending the money to help my family. Mom didn't care if I ever went back to school, so long as I brought in the money" (*The New York Times*, April 21, 1977).

Community norms and values have as strong an effect on youths growing up in a high-crime neighborhood as on youths being raised in conventional ones. Walter Miller, who did a three-year participant-observational study (1958), called these norms "focal concerns." For lower-class urban adolescent males, Miller found, these included *trouble* (with the law and with women); *toughness* (physical prowess and playing it cool); *smartness* (being able to outsmart and con others, as well as a respect for verbal quickness and ingenuity); *fate* (a sense that many forces are beyond one's control, that success is a matter of luck); and *autonomy* (a resentment of outside controls—"No one's gonna push me around"). Such delinquent acts as drinking or stealing cars, Miller concluded, are expressions of these important subcultural concerns; delinquency, he argued, can thus be seen as "a directed attempt . . . to adhere to forms of behavior and to achieve standards as they are defined in that community" (5).

Not only do subcultures bring their members into contact with others who share their perspective on life, but they also offer emotional support for a person who is having experiences that are not understood beyond the community's boundaries. Contact with the members of a subculture may help a person adopt a new and more fulfilling identity. For example, when a long-time lesbian with a working-class background finally encountered the gay community, she was afforded her first sustained exposure to people from classes above her own. As a result of her contact with the lesbian subculture, the woman became dissatisfied with her job and began training for one that paid more, required greater skill, and had greater prestige; her taste in music, art, and food also changed (Simon and Gagnon, 1970: 114). Subcultures serve another important purpose by providing members with a justification system—a pattern of beliefs—that explains why they are deviant. Homosexuals, for instance, believe that their persuasion is as natural for them as heterosexuality is for others (Simon and Gagnon, 1970: 127). Subcultures may even develop a public collective identity to fight against society's discriminatory ways: think of gay lib, and of the organizations dedicated to bettering the lot of ex-convicts or the aged.

Subcultures provide havens for those whom society regards as deviant. The lesbian subculture, for example, brings these women into contact with others who share their life style, supports them emotionally in crises that outsiders would condemn or fail to understand, and helps them to develop a more positive self-image. (Camilla Smith)

Social-bond Theory The two theories that we have examined so far both assume that people want to conform. According to stress theory, people try first to conform to the normal pattern of achieving success, and turn to illegitimate means only after the legitimate approaches have failed. Cultural-transmission theorists argue that even deviants conform, but that they conform to the norms of a deviant community or subculture. Social-bond theory, in contrast, is built on the as-

sumption that people are in conflict with social norms. According to this theory, when people do conform, it is only because they are forced to do so by social bonds. When those bonds weaken or dissolve (see the discussion of anomie earlier in this chapter), people are apt to become deviant, disoriented, or suicidal.

Some strong support for social-bond theory comes from the comprehensive study of delinquency conducted by Travis Hirschi (1969). The data in this study did not support the notion that deviance springs from the pressure of unfulfilled but legitimate desires, or from subcultural or group traditions and relationships. Rather, when Hirschi compared delinquents to nondelinquents, he found that delinquents were less attached to family, friends, or conventional goals. The delinquent, Hirschi concluded, was best described as ''a person relatively free of the intimate attachments, the aspirations, and the moral beliefs that bind most people to a life within the law.'' The weakness of social bonds, in other words, appeared to be the most conspicuous factor behind delinquent behavior.

Each of the theories of deviance offers valid insights into a phenomenon involving a wide range of forms, contexts, and social groupings. These insights are not mutually exclusive: the pressure that society places on its members to succeed; the role that a group can play in giving an individual a sense of identity; and the control that social rules and conventions can have over social action may *all* contribute to the rate of deviance in a group. Deviance among college students during the 1960s, for example, involved several related elements: among them were the existence of a sizable radical subculture and a sense of normlessness growing out of the conviction that society was being manipulated by a military-industrial complex. One theory of deviance, then, may offer the most apt explanation of a particular situation, but at the same time other theories illuminate factors important to our understanding of the situation as a whole.

LABELING AND DEVIANT CAREERS

In the late 1950s, some sociologists began wondering if they hadn't been asking the wrong questions about deviance. Virtually everyone breaks rules at one time or another. A survey of nearly 1,700 New Yorkers, for example, revealed that 99 percent had violated the penal code at least once. A random sample revealed that as many as one in every five residents of midtown Manhattan is severely disturbed, though none of them was hospitalized (Srole, 1975). And Kinsey found that 37 percent of American men reported having had one or more homosexual experiences. Most of these people are not considered to be deviants by others. Their nonconformity is simply one, perhaps secret, aspect of an otherwise respectable life. However, others who have performed the very same acts (or have been falsely accused of doing so) are branded criminal, psychotic, or ''queer'' for the rest of their lives. A key question, then, is why some people are *labeled* (assigned the status of) deviant, while others who commit the same acts are not. This leads to a fourth major explanation of deviance.

The Labeling Process

As Howard S. Becker suggests in *Outsiders* (1963), people perform deviant acts for various reasons. They may not even know they are doing anything wrong, or they may know they are breaking a rule, but rationalize their deviance away. They may simply have no reputation to maintain, no stake in appearing to be a normal and conventional person. Their fate depends *not* on whatever reason they may have for deviating but on whether they are caught and publicly *labeled* deviant.

A similar point is made by Edwin M. Lemert (1951), who distinguishes between primary and secondary deviance. *Primary deviance* occurs when someone violates a norm for any one of a variety of reasons—social, psychological, cultural, physiological—but does not consider himself or herself a deviant. *Secondary deviance* occurs when others react to a person's deviant behavior and label that person a deviant. That individual may accept the label and redefine himself or herself as deviant, or may refuse to accept it. The crucial act, argued Lemert, is not the original deviant behavior, for we all deviate at some time in our lives. What matters sociologically is who is labeled and what consequences the labeling involves—being ostracized, losing a friend, being arrested, being sent to a mental hospital. Secondary deviance can start a spiral of stigma, more deviance, harsher reactions, and eventually alienation. The labeling perspective, then, looks at social control from the deviant's point of view and assumes conflict between those who deviate and those who label.

Who Gets Labeled?

As the statistics at the beginning of this section indicate, only a fraction of the people who break rules are caught and publicly discredited. Sociologists are interested in discovering the kinds of people who *do* get labeled and the process by which this happens. In the 1960s, William J. Chambliss (1973) spent two years as a participant observer at ''Hannibal High School.'' During this period he became acquainted with the members of two gangs, the Saints and the Roughnecks. The eight members of the Saints came from upper-middle-class families; they were good students and were active in school affairs. On weekends and on days when they sneaked out of school (most days, Chambliss found), the Saints amused themselves with various forms of delinquency: heavy drinking, reckless driving, petty theft, vandalism, and games of ''chicken.'' A favorite pastime was removing the wooden barricades and lanterns from street repair sites and watching unsuspecting drivers cruise into the hole. Although the Saints' activities were hazardous, the people of the town considered them good boys who

were sowing a few wild oats. Stealing small items and breaking into empty houses were considered pranks. Not one Saint was arrested in the two years Chambliss spent at ''Hannibal High.''

In contrast, the six Roughnecks were constantly in trouble with the police, and the townspeople considered them good-for-nothings. The Roughnecks came from lower-class families and were not particularly good students. Most weekends they could be found hanging around the local drugstore, drinking from concealed bottles. Almost every month they got into a fight—usually among themselves. Like the Saints, they stole, more for profit than for thrills. Even so, Chambliss estimates that property damage done by the Saints cost the townspeople *more* than the Roughnecks' thefts. And although the Saints rarely fought, they endangered their own and other people's lives nearly every time they got behind the wheel of a car.

Why did townspeople excuse the Saints but condemn the Roughnecks as delinquents? One reason was that the Saints had cars and left the immediate community for their drinking bouts. The Roughnecks, too poor to own cars, were more visible. In addition, the police knew from experience that the Saints' upper-middle-class parents would cause trouble if their children were arrested, insisting their sons were just having fun and putting police on the defensive. The Roughnecks' parents lacked the power and influence to protect their children. Finally, the Saints dressed nicely, drove good cars, and spoke politely to teachers, police, and other authority figures. Anyone could see they were ''good boys,'' tomorrow's leaders. The Roughnecks were different: ''everyone agreed that the not-so-well-dressed, not-so-well-mannered, not-so-rich boys were heading for trouble'' (27). In short, the community's social structure protected the Saints but not the Roughnecks (recall the discussion or Talley's corner in chapter 3).

Consequences of Labeling: Stigma and the Deviant Career

Typically, people who are labeled criminals, declared mentally ill, or branded ''queer'' are excluded from conventional social life. A man convicted of a crime describes the experience:

> And I always have this feeling with straight people—that whenever they're being nice to me, pleasant to me, all the time really, underneath they're only assessing me as a criminal and nothing else. (in Goffman, 1963: 14)

According to the labeling perspective, deviant labels—''queer,'' lunatic, thief, junkie—become a master status (see chapter 3). They tend to wipe out whatever favorable impressions a person may create. One day he is the man next door, a good friend and neighbor. The next day people discover that he is not what he was supposed to be; instead, he is a homosexual. ''The question is raised: 'What kind of person would break such an important rule?' And the answer is given: One who is different from the rest of us, who cannot or will not act as a moral human being and therefore might break other important rules' '' (Becker, 1963: 33–34).

Deviant labels tend to become self-fulfilling prophecies; Chambliss found that with few exceptions, the Saints and Roughnecks lived up (and down) to community expectations. As Goffman has written, ''one response to this fate [being labeled deviant] is to embrace it'' (1963: 30). This is the final step toward a deviant career. Cut off, the addict begins to associate almost exclusively with other addicts, the prostitute with other prostitutes. (Often these associations are begun in prisons and in other institutions aimed at *correcting* deviant inclinations.) Gradually people develop new understandings and routines. They learn techniques for deviating from more experienced offenders. Equally important, career deviants learn rationalizations for deviant behavior. For example, prostitutes grow to regard their work as a social service and consider those who condemn sex for money as hypocrites. The deviant subculture begins to play an increasingly central role in the person's identity and life style. As one addict told a researcher, she realized she was addicted when she noticed that all her friends were junkies (Becker, 1963: 38). Thus in labeling certain people deviant and shutting them out of conventional life, society virtually *ensures* the behavior it is trying to prevent.

Limitations of Labeling Theory

While this description of the drift into deviant careers is compelling, in several ways it verges on ''liberal overkill.'' Labeling theorists imply that the people who fill the wards of mental hospitals, for example, are there because someone more or less arbitrarily decided to label them sick and subject them to the consequences. They tend to ignore the fact that most of the people in mental hospitals were unable to cope with their lives and their problems outside. Sociological studies have found that both families and authorities consider commitment to a mental hospital a very last resort, and exhaust all other alternatives before launching commitment proceedings (Gove, 1970).

Labeling theorists also tend to pay relatively little attention to the fact that not all

table 9:2 **PERCENTAGE DISTRIBUTION OF A CROSS-CULTURAL SAMPLE OF PEOPLE ANSWERING "YES" TO THE QUESTION, "DO YOU THINK THAT A PATIENT RELEASED FROM A MENTAL HOSPITAL, WHO HAD BEEN PROPERLY TRAINED, MAY BE TRUSTED IN THE FOLLOWING OCCUPATIONS?"**

OCCUPATION	DELAWARE (N = 479)	HAWAII (N = 404)	ENGLAND (N = 285)[1]
Farmer	92	96	92
Housekeeper	92	94	92
Painter (artist)	90	92	94
Salesclerk	90	86	95
Journalist	80	75	79
Foreman	66	58	55
Bus driver	60	52	35
Teacher	53	47	45
Lawyer	48	34	27
Police officer	36	22	23
Doctor	30	22	23
General	22	13	22

[1]N equals the number of individuals interviewed.

SOURCE: Adapted from Alexander Askenasy, *Attitudes Toward Mental Patients* (The Hague: Mouton, 1974), table 93, p. 208.

labeled people accept their stigma passively. Mentally retarded people who have been released from institutions, for instance, go to great lengths to hide their stigma not only from others but also from themselves: they often explain their period of institutionalization with such excuses (or other labels) as the need for surgery, treatment for "nerves," or even punishment for sex delinquency or for criminal behavior. And when retarded patients who have been released do acknowledge their general lack of competence, they blame it on the depriving experience of having been unjustly institutionalized (Edgerton, 1967: 144–171). It is also true that some labels can be shed. Many alcoholics, for example, have been able to de-label themselves by joining Alcoholics Anonymous, an organization that makes it possible for problem drinkers to replace their stigmatized deviant status with a socially acceptable "repentant role" (Trice and Roman, 1970).

This is not to say that labeling theory is "wrong," but that it only partly explains deviant careers. It does not explain why people violate rules in the first place or why some people are able to resist or overcome the stigma of deviance. The conflict perspective of labeling theory does, however, help us to focus on the social structure of power behind the rules. What really matters is who makes the rules and who has the power to make the labels stick. This is the underlying theme of social control.

SOCIAL CONTROL

In any community, the purpose of social control is to encourage conformity. The chapter on socialization partly answered the question of why most people conform. Sociologists use the term *internalization* to describe the process by which cultural standards become part of the growing child's personality structure. The result is that people have so thoroughly accepted certain norms and values that they take them for granted. They abide by these rules not because they fear being labeled and punished for nonconforming behavior but because socialization is so successful. Deviating from these norms makes most people feel guilty and disoriented. In an important sense, internalized norms and values are the basis of social order, for people police themselves. But socialization is never perfect: people may not internalize all the rules society considers "right." Many informal and formal social controls fill this gap.

Informal Social Controls

A crowded bus winding through a rain-soaked city stops at a corner to pick up a load of passengers. One of the people who gets on is a frail, elderly woman loaded down with parcels and bags, beads of water dripping from her plastic rain bonnet. She looks for an empty seat, but there is none. Shrewdly, she next looks for someone who might stand up so that she can sit down. The rest of the scene is easy to imagine: she makes her way with ostentatious difficulty to where a healthy-looking college student is sitting, and she plops her bags down right in front of him. The student knows what's expected,

but he's comfortable. Other people on the bus begin to eye him with disapproval. The woman sitting next to him clears her throat loudly. The student no longer feels comfortable. Reluctantly, but with a flourish, he surrenders his seat.

The situation offers a straightforward illustration of *informal social control*, unofficial pressure to conform to norms and values that are not fully internalized. All of us try to live up to the expectations of others, even in ways we don't always consciously recognize. The fear of ostracism, ridicule, verbal and physical threats, and other negative sanctions, and our desire for such positive sanctions as a smile, a pat on the back, or a kiss, influence the way we sit in class, the way we talk, the clothes we wear, and much else besides.

Disapproval as Control Often the mere anticipation of disapproval from family, friends, co-workers, or even strangers in a public place stops people from engaging in deviant activities. Indeed, disregard for public opinion—as when people talk to themselves or masturbate in public—is considered a primary symptom of mental illness (Goffman, 1963). Aside from indicating how we can gain the approval of others, informal social controls also satisfy our very basic need to be able to predict the behavior of others.

Informal social controls operate most directly within the setting of the primary group. Almost as soon as we are born, parents begin telling us what and what not to do. They respond positively when we learn to walk and talk, negatively when we learn to throw food on the floor, using not only verbal communication but also such nonverbal signals as hugs and smiles or frowns and spankings. With respect to who actually applies informal sanctions, however, not all cultures are alike. In the Soviet Union, for example, it is perfectly normal for total strangers to try to influence one another's behavior in a manner that, in the United States, is rarely seen between people who are not members of the same family. In a train station in Leningrad one cold night, *New York Times* correspondent Hedrick Smith (1976) watched two female railroad-car porters scold a middle-aged navy commander for starting to leave the train without an overcoat on. Although he was not, in fact, warmly dressed—he wore a warm-up suit, which serves most Russian train travelers as both a day outfit and pajamas—all he wanted was a quick breath of fresh air. But the women would not hear of it. '' 'You'll catch cold, comrade,' counseled the first. 'It's forbidden without a coat,' commanded the second.'' Eventually the Russian abandoned his plans with equanimity. While a Westerner, observes Smith, would probably have gone into the cold just to prove his or her independence, the Russian is more likely to submit to such controls, because he is used to external controls in many areas of life.

The Penalties of Ignoring Informal Control   No matter what the culture, the refusal to conform to informal controls can involve penalties ranging from mild disapproval to differential treatment with potentially painful consequences. In many instances, of course, the definition of nonconformity involves a question of degree. A prankster who shows up for class in a tuxedo once or twice may get people to laugh or ask "Hey, where are you going?" A person who wears that costume to class all the time is likely to earn an unflattering label. Still, norms governing personal appearance are relatively relaxed at most colleges. As many students are coming to realize, though, these norms get surprisingly strict when one heads from the campus to the office. In the competition for jobs after college, men whose hair is too long and women whose skirts are too short frequently lose out for no better reason than that they just didn't look right at their job interviews.

Informal controls even operate in hospitals, where patients who conform quietly with hospital norms and procedures are likely to get better care than those who interrupt well-established routines by arguing with staff members and by complaining excessively about pain and discomfort. The chief method of informal control doctors and nurses use to enforce conformity to "good patient" norms is the withholding of information, which serves to minimize criticisms and arguments. If a patient continues to deviate and earns the "problem" label, the result may be deliberate neglect, early discharge, or referral to a psychiatrist. Word about "problem" patients travels quickly through hospitals, and once the staff knows that a psychiatrist had to be called in for a certain patient, an explicit label will be applied. For the rest of that patient's stay, he or she will be regarded as neurotic or psychotic, and therefore as someone without legitimate complaints (Lorber, 1975: 223).

Backfire   Although they are intended to promote compliance with norms and values, informal controls sometimes work in the opposite direction, pressuring conforming individuals into deviant acts. For example, an adolescent may steal or take drugs to gain prestige among his or her peers, or adults may embezzle to maintain the standard of living people expect of them. The norms of family and friendship require people to protect deviants who are close to them—the words "tattletale," "fink," and "informer" are not terms of praise. As a result, modern societies depend heavily on institutionalized formal controls.

Formal Social Controls

Formal social controls are all those organizations and roles specifically designed to enforce conformity in a society, including police departments, courts, prisons, juvenile facilities, mental hospitals, drug rehabilitation centers, and settlement houses and other social-work agencies. Police officers, judges, and prison and hospital guards are the most obvious agents of social control, but psychiatrists, social workers, ministers, teachers, and lawyers are also in a position to enforce conformity. To get a fuller sense of how a chain of formal social controls works, we will focus on the processes for controlling crime.

Measuring Crimes and Corrections A national survey asked citizens whether they had been victims of a crime in the last year. The results showed that crime rates in the United States are about twice as high as those which the FBI draws from local police records (National Opinion Research Council [NORC], 1965/66). A similar poll conducted in Washington, D.C., revealed an even wider gap. Why do crimes go unreported? Most people told NORC interviewers that they knew the police couldn't do anything, so why bother? A smaller number said they didn't want to get the offender in trouble. (Eighty-eight percent of murders, 66 percent of rapes, and 75 percent of assaults are committed by family members or acquaintances [Mitford, 1973: 61].) Still others said they feared revenge.

The FBI statistics are published each year in the Uniform Crime Report, a compilation of national statistics on seven "crime index offenses": murder, rape, robbery, aggravated assault, burglary, larceny (theft of $50 or more), and auto theft. Of course, these figures represent only those crimes that came to the attention of the police. But adding on the estimated number of crimes that go unreported still doesn't produce a comprehensive picture of crime in the United States. In a sense, what the FBI statistics leave out is almost as informative as what they include. The omissions show that the criminal justice system in the United States is a highly selective one: many serious offenses are not defined as crimes, and only a very few of the people who commit crimes are prosecuted to the full extent of the law. (See figure 9:1 and the box on corporate crime.)

For instance, the FBI does not collect statistics on murders, assaults, and thefts committed by mine owners, slum landlords, construction companies, car manufacturers, and other corporations that violate health and safety codes (resulting in death and injury) and rob consumers through deceptive advertising and packaging (Mitford, 1973: 64). The Uniform Crime Report also doesn't include crimes committed by the police, who usually do not report themselves. Every day for seven weeks, Albert J. Reiss, Jr., and a team of thirty-six participant observers accompanied police officers in high-crime districts of Boston, Chicago, and Washington, D.C. Although the police officers knew they were being watched, one out of five committed crimes during the course of the study, the most common being stealing from drunks and "deviants," stealing from establishments that had been burglarized, and taking bribes. The Reiss team also observed forty-four police assaults, only seven of which could be characterized as provoked. Reiss concluded that police probably break even more laws when they do not have to modify their behavior for observers (1971).

How Much Deviance Is Controlled? How did the police and the courts handle the 11 to 12 million murders, forcible rapes, robberies,

CORPORATE CRIME AND IRRESPONSIBILITY

When a dam of coal wastes in the mining valley of Buffalo Creek, West Virginia, broke, flooding and burying the towns in its path under 40,000 tons of water and slag, the mine owners called it "an act of God." One hundred and twenty-five people were killed, and five thousand lost their homes. The survivors knew that God had nothing to do with the disasters, and found a law firm to prove it.

The "criminals" in this case will never appear in the FBI's files, and the crime they committed was not planned. The Buffalo Creek disaster resulted from corporate irresponsibility and greed. The Buffalo Mining Company, owned by the Pittston Corporation, worked eight mines in the vicinity of Buffalo Creek. Each day these mines churned out one thousand tons of refuse, or slag, which had to be disposed of. The company found a convenient, cheap dumping ground—a small stream that fed into Buffalo Creek. By February 1972, nearly a million tons of waste were damming up 132 million gallons of black water. Soaked by the winter rains, the slag heaps collapsed, unleashing a "mud wave" that tore down the valley and engulfed everything in its path.

You needn't be a civil engineer to know that a "dam" built out of slag with no foundation and no emergency spillways could not last forever. One company official admitted that no engineers had been consulted before the "dams" were constructed, and "no engineering calculations whatsoever [were made] on Middle Fork" (Stern: 161). Yet a senior executive in the Pittston Coal Group said, under oath, that his company had done nothing wrong. A West Virginia state commission disagreed. They found that "the Pittston Company, through its officials, [showed] flagrant disregard for the safety of residents of Buffalo Creek . . ." (Stern: 70).

By industry standards, Pittston had done nothing wrong. But after two years of litigation, the victims won a $13.5 million settlement. Pittston's slag dam had destroyed an entire community, leaving thousands of people rootless and suffering from the kind of anguish that no amount of money can alleviate. One elderly woman described the feelings of many of the survivors when she told sociologist Kai Erikson: "I just don't take no interest in nothing like I used to, I don't have no feeling for nothing, I feel like I'm drained of life" (Erikson: 194). "She was," writes Erikson, "reflecting a spirit still numbed by the disaster, but she was also reflecting a spirit unable to recover for its own use all the life it had signed over to the community" (194).

The court settlement is evidence of a new realization in our society: not just individuals, but corporations and other institutions, commit crimes. Until recently, toy companies made dangerous toys, the FBI condoned illegal practices as routine, and nearly every industry polluted the environment without a second thought. Today an increasing number of courts are judging as criminal corporate and governmental practices that were recently considered normal.

SOURCE: Kai T. Erikson, *Everything in Its Path*, New York: Simon & Schuster, 1976; Gerald M. Stern, *The Buffalo Creek Disaster*, New York: Vintage Books, 1976.

figure 9.1 The pyramid of crime

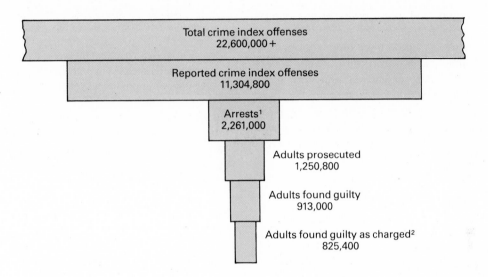

Total crime index offenses
22,600,000+

Reported crime index offenses
11,304,800

Arrests[1]
2,261,000

Adults prosecuted
1,250,800

Adults found guilty
913,000

Adults found guilty as charged[2]
825,400

[1] Juveniles account for about one third of the people who are arrested. Their cases are referred to the juvenile courts.
[2] The remainder are found guilty of lesser offenses.

SOURCE: Adapted from Federal Bureau of Investigation, *Uniform Crime Reports for the United States: Crime in the United States 1976* (Washington, D.C.: U.S. Government Printing Office, 1976), pp. 217–219.

The great majority of crime index offenses—murder, rape, robbery, aggravated assault, burglary, larceny, and auto theft—in the United States go unreported or unsolved. Furthermore, these statistics do not include corporate, "white collar" crimes, crimes committed by police officers, or other offenses.

aggravated assaults, burglaries, larcenies, and auto thefts that were reported in 1976? To begin with, 80 percent of the lawbreakers were not apprehended (UCR: 219). Thirty-three percent of the crime index offenders were under eighteen years of age and were referred to juvenile courts (216). (Juveniles accounted for a startling 53 percent of all auto-theft arrests and 51 percent of all burglary arrests [UCR: 33, 25]). Of the remaining adults, 83 percent were formally charged and held for prosecution in the courts; 66 percent were found guilty as charged, 7 percent were convicted of a lesser offense, and

27 percent were either acquitted or their cases were dismissed (215).

These statistics show not only that the percentage of offenders actually apprehended is small, but also that of the people who are arrested, a large percentage of them slip through the court system unscathed. Thirty-eight percent of all adult murder defendants were acquitted or won freedom through dismissal; 49 percent of all adult defendants in forcible rape cases were similarly released (vs. 42 percent found guilty as charged); and the comparable figures for robbery and aggravated assault were 36 percent and 35 percent respectively (UCR: 11–21). How many people who are arrested, prosecuted, and found guilty of one charge or another actually go to jail? In 1965, less than 3 percent of known serious crimes actually resulted in prison terms. Clearly, very few of the people who commit crimes are prosecuted to the full extent of the law. And the majority of these are young, male, poor, and in four cases out of ten, nonwhite (Mitford, 1973: 133). Prisoners, in other words, are selected.

The Control Process   In theory a police officer's job is to enforce the law. In practice, though, the police also decide *when* and *how* to enforce the law, because arresting all lawbreakers would be impossible. They rely on their own judgment (on "instincts" and experience) in deciding who is a danger to the community and who threatens police authority. In plain language, they arrest people whom they "know" to be potential or actual troublemakers.

This discretionary application of formal controls was clear in police harassment of the rough-mannered, back-talking Roughnecks and toleration of the smoother middle-class Saints, mentioned earlier. The screening process continues in the courts. Studies of bail hearings held shortly after a person is arrested indicate that judges tend to trust white middle-class offenders to appear for trial, but demand bail from the poor (white and black), who are least able to afford it (Bell, 1973). Why? The President's Commission on Crime (Katzenbach, 1967) reasoned:

> Most city prosecutors and judges have middle-class backgrounds and a high degree of education. When they are confronted with a poor, uneducated defendant, they may have difficulty judging how he fits into his own society or culture. They can easily mistake a certain manner of dress or speech, alien or repugnant to them but ordinary enough in the defendant's world, as an index of moral worthlessness. They can mistake ignorance or fear of the law as indifference to it. They can mistake the defendant's resentment against the social evils with which he lives as evidence of criminality. (317)

Despite the presumption of innocence written into our legal code, a defendant who cannot raise bail is held in jail, and in large cities many must wait a full year or longer to come to trial.

Copping a Plea   Ninety percent of the people arrested and charged agree to plead guilty to a lesser charge. By doing this, they avoid the risk of a more severe penalty. This practice is known as *plea bargaining,* or "copping a plea." The Supreme Court declared plea bargaining legal in 1969, acknowledging that it saves the state the expense of lengthy trials and lessens the already staggering burden on the courts.

Often it is the poor who lack the money for a good defense and who therefore must plead guilty to a lesser charge. Statistics indicate that defendants who insist on a trial, if found guilty, receive sentences that are on the average twice as long as those meted out to defendants who plead guilty (Mitford, 1973: 76).

Sentencing   Unless a state has prescribed mandatory penalties for specific crimes, sentencing is left to the judge's discretion. And, as with labeling and arrests, social status and power play a role. Nonwhites typically serve longer terms than whites found guilty of the same crime, but blacks who commit crimes against blacks serve shorter terms than blacks who commit crimes against whites (Bell, 1973). As a rule, white businessmen receive very light penalties. Because of the inherent unfairness of these discrepancies, a number of criminologists have recommended that judges impose fixed sentences for specific crimes.

Prisons

Prisons are a relatively modern invention. Two hundred and fifty to three hundred years ago, convicted criminals were killed, maimed, branded (for example, with a scarlet A for adultery), or deported (as often as not, to the New World). The idea of locking people up, which began to take hold during the mid-nineteenth century, was based on the assumption that isolation and hard work would make the sinner reconsider his or her errant ways and repent. But once prisons were established, they became institutionalized.

The Control Functions of Prisons What functions do prisons perform? Most obviously, they punish criminals for their wrongdoings. Clearly, prisoners do suffer, and most people consider this just. Prisons are also supposed to protect the public by taking known deviants off the streets. In addition, they are thought to act as a deterrent, discouraging those on the outside from breaking laws and those on the inside from committing crimes after they are released. Finally, there is much talk of prisons rehabilitating offenders through training programs and counseling, so that when they are released, they will approach life in a new, law-abiding frame of mind. These different goals present each prison warden with a difficult and conflicting mandate.

> Somehow [the prison warden] must resolve the claims that the prison should exact vengeance, erect a specter to terrify the actual or potential deviant, isolate the known offender from the free community, and effect a change in the personality of his captives so that they gladly follow the dictates of law— and in addition maintain order within his society of prisoners and see that they are employed at useful labor. (Sykes, 1958: 44–45)

Do Prisons "Work"? The cost of locking a person up for a year is between $6,000 and $10,000 (as critics of prisons note, this is enough to send a person to Harvard with a summer vacation in Europe). This amounts to nearly $12 billion annually (WNBC, 1974). What does this money buy?

Clearly, prisons don't protect the public. Only 3 percent of the people known to have committed crimes ever go to jail (only 1.5 percent if we include unreported crimes). Moreover, most prison officials estimate that, at most, only 15 to 25 percent of inmates are actually dangerous (Mitford, 1973: 285).

Nor do most prisons accomplish anything that might be called rehabilitation. After their release, at least a third of former prison inmates end up back in prison. Indeed, prisons may socialize people *to* deviance, as suggested earlier. Many observers consider them "schools for crime," where first offenders learn the tricks and rationalizations of deviant careers.

And there is little evidence that prisons act as a deterrent to potential lawbreakers. In 1961 the penalty for assault with a deadly weapon in California was one to ten years. In 1966 the California legislature raised the sentence for assaulting a police officer with a deadly weapon to five years to life. That year the rate of attacks on police was 15.8 per 100 officers, compared to 8.4 per 100 officers in 1961 (Mitford, 1973: 280–281).

Prison Reform Are there any alternatives to prisons as we know them? Efforts to reform

IN THE NEWS

Prison Prevention

Perhaps the toughest and most effective deterrent to a career of crime is the real-life example of someone confined to prison for life.

"Imagine being buried alive and knowing that there was no way out," the stern-faced prisoner told the 11 obviously frightened teen-agers who sat almost motionless on a long bench in front of him.

"Then imagine having to worry about whether this will be the day that someone runs a shank through you while your back is turned or that you have to fight, and maybe even kill, to prevent some guy from forcing you to have sex with him.

"That is the kind of thing you will have to face every day if you wind up in here."

This description was delivered by a man serving a life sentence at Rahway State Prison in New Jersey to fourteen- to sixteen-year-old delinquent youngsters who'd had minor brushes with the law. The program in which these youths were participating, which uses fear and guilt as its main ingredients, is called "Juvenile Awareness, Project Self-Help," and aside from rap sessions like the one quoted above, it utilizes tours of the worst areas of prisons as a means of frightening juveniles away from crime.

For nearly an hour and a half, seven "lifers" used brutal and explicit language to describe the humiliation, misery and terror of their existence.

They also spoke bitterly of the unhappiness they had caused their families.

Relentlessly, as the juveniles sat

prisons—whether motivated by humanitarian principles or by the desire to reduce crime—have centered around three general areas: work programs, conjugal visits, and group therapy (Bloch and Geis, 1970: 469–474). In this country, North Carolina has led the way with "work furlough" programs, where inmates are permitted to leave prison for up to sixty hours a week to work on the outside. More than thirty states launched similar programs during the 1960s, but usually on a small scale. In the Swedish penal system, widely regarded as the most enlightened in the world, providing prisoners with steady, useful jobs and requiring them to support themselves and their families, while paying restitution to their victims, are central to the rehabilitation effort (Durham, 1973).

Only a few prisons in this country allow conjugal visits, but many other nations permit spouses of prisoners to visit them, and some allow prisoners to visit their families for short periods. The idea behind conjugal visits

quietly with heads down on the lighted stage of the otherwise dark and cold prison auditorium, the prisoners ridiculed their misdeeds.

"It ain't glamorous in here the way it is pictured in the old Bogart and Cagney movies," a prisoner shouted. "It is like hell."

"You fight for everything you get, and you have to fight to keep it."

"And what is it all for?" another inmate asked. "All to prove yourself to your peers."

One teen-ager said he would not wind up in prison because he was too smart.

A prisoner responded that "most of the smart people, like us, are in jail."

"We all thought we were slick and that we were too smart to get caught," he said. "And here we are in this hell hole."

The program itself was conceived and designed by the "Lifers Group," which is made up of men serving a life sentence. Although the sessions, which are conducted approximately three times a week, are very taxing for the prisoners, they are felt to be a workable deterrent to crime. Of course the degree of success of such a program can only be determined with time, but of the 300 juveniles who have attended sessions so far, only four have been arrested on new charges—an encouraging recidivism rate. More importantly:

As evidence [the prisoners] read numerous letters from parents and juveniles saying they had helped set a new and positive course for the teen-agers.

SOURCE: Nathaniel Sheppard, Jr., "A Lesson in Prison Life, Taught by Experts," *The New York Times*, January 25, 1977, p. 39.

is that the people who are most likely to discourage a convict from continuing in a criminal career are his or her spouse and children.

Group therapy programs are difficult to assess. Nearly all forms of psychotherapy depend on uninhibited self-revelation and open expression of feelings. But the psychologists who run such programs in prisons are, after all, prison officials. A prisoner's parole may depend on his or her participation in a therapy program, thus making its voluntary nature problematical. The inmate is thus put in a double bind: total openness might well delay his or her parole, but self-concealment renders the program useless.

Undoubtedly the most radical approach to penal reform is to eliminate prisons altogether. Just such an approach was tried with juvenile offenders in Massachusetts: between 1969 and 1972, Dr. Jerome Miller, commissioner of the Department of Youth Services, reduced the population of juvenile prisons from about 1,350 to 90. Young lawbreakers were returned to their families or

Most American prisons require husbands and wives to visit across metal barriers. In newer prisons, such as the Illinois State Penitentiary pictured above, prisoners live in private rooms equipped with radio, desk, and bed. (Top, Cornell Capa/Magnum. Bottom, UPI)

placed in foster homes, in small unlocked residences, or in a few prep schools that ordinarily cater to middle- and upper-class youngsters. Officials helped older boys and girls find their own homes and jobs.

The goal of this program was first, to stop the process of labeling youngsters ''delinquent,'' and second, to help them to cope with life on the outside, rather than socializing them to the authoritarianism and brutality of prisons. The experiment was not a total success. The community-based care approach proved disorderly at first, and a public outcry arose for new institutions. As of 1977, the Massachusetts Department of Youth Services was operating nine juvenile corrections facilities, but was also firmly committed to the goal of helping young people adapt to a normal community rather than to an institution.

SUMMARY

Deviance is any behavior that violates social norms and expectations. Whether an act is considered deviant or not depends on who commits it, where, and when. Definitions and explanations of deviance—for example, of marijuana use and homosexuality—change with circumstances and time. They are ultimately a matter of tradition and social power; people who have the power to enforce their definitions decide what is proper and what is deviant. Deviance also serves several social functions: it defines what the social order actually is, the boundaries between acceptable and unacceptable behavior; it also stimulates change—as, for example, when groups whose culture or behavior is considered deviant press the larger society to accommodate to them, rather than vice versa.

In the nineteenth century, Lombroso argued that criminals were throwbacks to an earlier stage of evolution; more recently, the so-called XYY syndrome has been advanced as a genetic explanation of deviance. But although the possibility of a biological explanation remains, to date there is no proof that deviants are ''born that way.'' Some psychologists believe deviants haven't learned to inhibit inborn antisocial impulses; others argue that deviants learn that antisocial behavior is rewarded. But psychological profiles of deviants don't explain why rates of deviance vary from one social group to another. Sociologists focus on this problem.

Robert K. Merton used stress theory to account for deviance and linked rates of deviance to Durkheim's concept of *anomie*, a state of normlessness that occurs because of sudden depression, prosperity, or technological change. Merton identified four types of deviant adaptations: *innovation* (pursuing culturally approved goals by deviant means), *ritualism* (adhering to rules at the expense of goals), *retreatism* (abandoning culturally prescribed goals and means), and *rebellion* (substituting new goals and new means for pursuing them). A second explanation of deviance is the theory of *cultural transmission*, that people can be socialized to deviance. Shaw and McKay, in a classic study, found that in one Chicago neighborhood a high crime rate persisted over the years because newcomers learned deviant ways from established residents. Edwin Sutherland argues that this transmission takes place because the standards people adopt depend on the timing, number, frequency, duration, and intensity of their contacts with deviant or nondeviant others. Walter Miller suggests that delinquency, for example, can be seen as an attempt to conform to such subcultural standards as toughness, smartness, and autonomy. A third theory of deviance assumes that people do *not* want to conform; they do so only because they are forced to by *social bonds*. When these bonds break or are nonexistent, as Hirschi's study of delinquency shows, deviance results. Although each of these theories offers valid insights, no one alone is a complete or correct explanation.

Virtually everyone violates social norms occasionally, but only some of us are stigmatized as deviant. Some sociologists argue that the stigma results from a person's being caught and publicly *labeled* deviant. Lemert defines two kinds of deviance, *primary* and *secondary*, to distinguish between the deviant act and the deviant label. Chambliss's comparison of the Saints and Roughnecks suggests that people who come from influential middle-class families, and who speak politely and dress well, are able to resist deviant labeling. People from lower-class families are not: they lack the social power. Deviant labels, as this study showed, tend to function as self-fulfilling prophecies. The "offender" is isolated (socially if not physically), is denied opportunities to conform, and is thus pushed toward deviant subcultures that offer lessons in breaking rules. These subcultures socialize people for deviant careers.

Most people usually conform because socialization welds social norms to the child's sense of identity: breaking some rules becomes unthinkable. *Informal social controls* (disapproval, ridicule, the threat of exclusion) prevent people from violating norms they haven't internalized. But socialization is never perfect, and informal controls may promote as well as prevent deviance. Hence the need for *formal social controls,* such as police, the courts, and the penal system.

The control of crime is a good example of how the process of formal controls operates. Although incomplete, statistics on crime are the best measure of deviance we have. What happens to known lawbreakers? The police and courts exercise considerable discretion in applying the penalties available under the law; only a very small percentage of the people known to have committed crimes are arrested, tried, and sent to prison. The functions of prison include punishing lawbreakers, protecting the public, deterring others from breaking the law, and rehabilitating prisoners. Since at least a third of inmates eventually return to prison, it seems that prisons do punish offenders, but that they neither rehabilitate convicts nor deter potential criminals. Efforts to reform prisons center around work furloughs and conjugal visits (the mainstays of the Swedish penal system), group therapy, and the elimination of prisons as we know them (a solution Massachusetts has tried with juvenile offenders).

GLOSSARY

anomie Durkheim's term for the state of deregulation or normlessness experienced when there is no meaning or stability in life because of sudden economic depression, prosperity, or rapid technological change.

conformity seeking culturally approved goals by culturally approved means (Merton).

cultural transmission the process by which deviance is learned through the transmission of norms within a community or group.

deviance behavior that violates social norms and expectations.

deviant career the adoption of a deviant life style and identity within a supporting subculture that provides techniques for breaking rules and rationalizations for nonconformity.

formal social controls roles and institutions consciously designed to enforce conformity.

informal social controls disapproval, ridicule, the threat of ostracism, and other unofficial pressures to conform.

innovation pursuing culturally approved goals by deviant means (Merton).

internalization the process by which cultural standards become part of the growing child's personality structure.

labeling the assigning of a deviant status to a person, which then dominates his or her social identity.

plea bargaining in a criminal trial, a defendant's agreeing to plead guilty to a lesser charge rather than risk conviction and a more severe penalty.

primary deviance when someone violates a norm for any one of a variety of reasons—social, psychological, cultural, physiological—but does not consider himself or herself a deviant.

rebellion creating new goals and new means for pursuing them (Merton).

retreatism abandoning culturally prescribed goals and means (Merton).

ritualism adhering rigidly to norms at the expense of goals (Merton).

secondary deviance when others react to a person's deviant behavior and label that person a deviant. That individual may accept the label and redefine himself or herself as deviant, or may refuse to accept it.

social control the group of formal and informal mechanisms which ensure that society's rules are learned and followed.

REFERENCES

Albert Bandura and Richard H. Walters, *Adolescent Aggression*. New York: Ronald Press, 1959.

Howard S. Becker, *Outsiders*. New York: Free Press, 1963.

Derrick A. Bell, Jr., "Racism in American Courts." *California New Law Review*, vol. 61 (January 1973): 165–203.

Albert A. Bloch and Gilbert Geis, *Man, Crime and Society*, 2nd ed. New York: Random House, 1970.

William J. Chambliss, "The Saints and Roughnecks." *Society*, vol. 11 (December 1973): 24–31.

Albert K. Cohen, *Deviance and Control*. Englewood Cliffs, N.J.: Prentice-Hall, 1966.

———, "The Sociology of the Deviant Act: Anomie Theory and Beyond." *American Sociological Review*, vol. 30 (February 1965): 5–14.

Michael Durham, "For Swedes a Prison Sentence Can Be Fun." *Smithsonian*, vol. 4 (September 1973): 46–52.

Émile Durkheim, *Suicide: A Study in Sociology* (1897), trans. J. A. Spaulding and G. Simpson. New York: Free Press, 1951.

Robert B. Edgerton, *The Cloak of Competence*. Berkeley: University of California Press, 1967.

Kai T. Erikson, *Wayward Puritans*. New York: Wiley, 1966.

Gallup Opinion Index, Report no. 143 (June 1977).

Don C. Gibbons and Joseph F. Jones, *The Study of Deviance*. Englewood Cliffs, N.J.: Prentice-Hall, 1975.

Erving Goffman, *Behavior in Public Places*. New York: Free Press, 1963.

———, *Stigma: Notes on the Management of Spoiled Identity*. Englewood Cliffs, N.J.:

Prentice-Hall, 1963.

Charles Goring, *The English Convict.* London: His Majesty's Stationery Office, 1913.

Walter R. Gove, "Societal Reaction as an Explanation of Mental Illness: An Evaluation." *American Sociological Review,* vol. 55 (October 1970): 873–884.

Travis Hirschi, *Causes of Delinquency.* Berkeley: University of California Press, 1969.

Nicholas deB. Katzenbach, Chairman, *The Challenge of Crime in a Free Society.* Washington, D.C.: U.S. Government Printing Office, 1967.

Edwin M. Lemert, *Human Deviance, Social Problems, and Social Control.* New York: McGraw-Hill, 1951.

Cesare Lombroso, quoted in G. L. Ferrero, *Criminal Man.* New York: Putnam, 1911.

Judith Lorber, "Good Patients and Problem Patients: Conformity and Deviance in a General Hospital." *Journal of Health and Social Behavior,* vol. 16 (June 1975): 213–225.

Robert K. Merton, *Social Theory and Social Structure.* Glencoe, Ill.: Free Press, 1957.

Walter B. Miller, "Lower-class Culture as a Generating Milieu of Gang Delinquency." *Journal of Sociological Issues,* vol. 14 (Summer 1958): 5–19.

Jessica Mitford, *Kind and Usual Punishment.* New York: Knopf, 1973.

Albert J. Reiss, Jr., *The Police and the Public.* New Haven, Conn.: Yale University Press, 1971.

Edwin M. Schur, *Crimes Without Victims.* Englewood Cliffs, N.J.: Prentice-Hall, 1965.

Clifford R. Shaw and Henry D. McKay, *Delinquency Areas.* Chicago: University of Chicago Press, 1929.

J. L. Simmons, "Public Stereotypes of Deviants." *Social Problems,* vol. 13 (Fall 1965): 223–232.

William Simon and John H. Gagnon, "On Being in the 'Community,' " in Jack D. Douglas, ed., *Observations of Deviance.* New York: Random House, 1970.

Hedrick Smith, *The Russians.* New York: Quadrangle/The New York Times Book Co., 1976.

Leo Srole, "Measurement and Classification in Socio-Psychiatric Epidemiology: Midtown Manhattan Study (1954) and Midtown Manhattan Restudy (1974)." *Journal of Health and Social Behavior,* vol. 16 (December 1975): 347–364.

Edwin H. Sutherland and Donald R. Cressy, *Principles of Criminology,* 6th ed. Philadelphia: Lippincott, 1960.

Gresham Sykes, *The Society of Captives.* Princeton, N.J.: Princeton University Press, 1958.

Harrison M. Trice and Paul Michael Roman, "Delabeling, Relabeling, and Alcoholics Anonymous." *Social Problems,* vol. 17 (Spring 1970): 538–547.

Uniform Crime Reports, *Crime in the United States, 1975.* Washington, D.C.: U.S. Government Printing Office, 1976.

Herman A. Witkin et al., "Criminality in XYY and XXY Men." *Science,* vol. 193 (August 1976): 547–555.

WNBC, "The High Cost of Crime," a special program produced by the editorial services of WNBC, New York, N.Y., written for WNBC, New York, N.Y., by Ann Sternberg, copyright ©1974 National Broadcasting Company, Inc.

FOR FURTHER STUDY

Drugs and Social Control. To the individual, taking marijuana, cocaine, amphetamines, barbiturates, or heroin is a psychological and physiological experience. It is also an experience that involves group pressures and the organization of social control. The best studies of how society turns a drug into a social issue have been done on marijuana. See *The Marihuana Papers,* edited by David Solomon (New York: New American Library, 1968), especially the essay by Alfred Lindesmith. To gain perspective on the American approach to marijuana, see Andrew Skull's essay in *Theoretical Perspectives on Deviance,* edited by Robert A. Scott and Jack D. Douglas (New York: Basic Books, 1972). In regard to the individual level of becoming a marijuana user, Howard Becker has written two important essays that are available in his book *Outsiders* (New York: Free Press, 1963). On addicts, see the essay by Edwin Schur in *The Other Side,* edited by Howard Becker (New York: Free Press, 1964).

Several excellent books on the sociology of drug control are·*The American Connection* by John Pekkanen (Chicago: Follett, 1973); *Nark!* by reporter Joe Eszterhas (San Francisco, Calif.: Straight Arrow Books, 1974); and *The Drugged Nation* by John Finlator (New York: Simon & Schuster, 1974). Matthew Dumont has written a valuable overview entitled "The Politics of Drugs," *Social Policy,* vol. 3 (July 1973): 32–35.

Police. The most useful way to begin studying the police is to observe them firsthand. Albert J. Reiss has done this in *The Police and the Public,* 2nd ed. (New Haven, Conn.: Yale University Press, 1973). Another important field study of the police is by Aaron Cicourel, *The Social Organization of Juvenile Justice* (New York: Wiley, 1967), especially chapters 4–6. An important study of police corruption is *The Knapp Commission Report on Police Corruption,* with a foreword by Michael Armstrong (New York: Braziller, 1973). See also "A Typology of Police Corruption" by Julian Roebuck and Thomas Barker, *Social Problems,* vol. 21 (1974): 423–437, and George O'Toole's *The Private Sector* (New York: Norton, 1978), which explores the half of our police forces who are hired by private interests. An important case around which to focus sociological thinking about the police is reported by Roy Wilkins and Ramsey Clark in *Search and Destroy: A Report of the Commission of Inquiry into the Chicago Police Raid on the Black Panther Headquarters, December 4, 1969* (New York: Harper & Row, 1973).

Criminal Justice and the Sociology of the Courts. Although most acts of justice and injustice take place in or near a patrol car, the courts actually serve as the formal institutions of justice. Two sociological studies of how they work are Robert Emerson's *Judging Delinquents: Context and Process in Juvenile Courts* (Chicago: Aldine, 1969) and David Sudnow's article entitled "Normal Crimes," *Social Problems,* vol. 12 (Winter 1965): 255–275. For a critical overview, read *Criminal Justice in America,* Richard Quinney, ed. (Boston: Little, Brown, 1974). Bias in sentencing is the subject of Willard Gaylin's *Partial Justice,* a subtle analysis of how judges decide how to sentence people (New York: Random House, 1975).

Power, Wealth, and Status

At various points—the description of Tally's corner in chapter 3, the discussion of sexual inequality in chapter 6, the consideration of deviants in chapter 9—we've noted that some people and groups in our society have more power, wealth, and status than others. The question is, Why? Part four looks at this question.

Social stratification is multidimensional. Chapter 10 examines the disparities that exist in American society; the social structures that perpetuate inequality; and proposals for distributing the good things in life more evenly.

National origins have always played a major role in social stratification in the United States. Chapter 11 describes and explains changing patterns of racial and ethnic relations in our society. The phenomena of prejudice and discrimination are explored in detail.

Given this background, we can now ask, Who rules America? Who controls the economy? Do the two overlap? Are political and economic power one and the same? Chapter 12 addresses these controversial topics.

CHAPTER 10

Social Stratification

A sample list of annual salaries for a recent year (Reiss, 1976) reads in part like this:

Anderson, Warren	Corporate executive vice-president	$190,000
Aquilar, Nimio	Shoe repair operator	6,000
Barthelme, Donald	Professor	18,812
Blass, Bill	Clothing designer	250,000
Bridges, Harry	Corporate president and chief executive officer	460,000
Callahan, Dorene	National Park Service ranger	7,102
Chapo, Eliot	Orchestra concertmaster	47,500
Coe, Gail	Bank teller	7,100
Feingold, Dr. Milton J.	Physician	56,077
Ford, Rita	Store owner	50,000
Foyt, A. J.	Racing-car driver	355,662

Everyone knows that true equality is impossible to achieve. Still, we like to think people are rewarded on the basis of hard work and effort. Yet a long look at these salaries makes us wonder. Does a teacher really work any less hard than a clothing designer? Why is a sports figure near the top of the list, exceeded only by a corporation executive? Women are conspicuously absent in the highest-paying jobs, and the only Spanish surname is that of a $6,000-a-year shoe repair operator.

In fact, access to high-paying jobs in this country is determined as much by race, sex, and parents' occupation as by individual effort. And the different rewards society bestows reflect in large part which jobs we prize. Social stratification in modern society is multidimensional: how much money you earn and how much prestige and power you have are all involved.

In this chapter we look at several aspects of a broad and complex topic: first, who gets what in America; then, why such inequalities exist; next, what the consequences of these inequalities are; and finally, what has been and can be done about them.

THE DIMENSIONS OF STRATIFICATION

The Siriono of Bolivia come as close to being a classless society as any people we know of. Like most hunters and gatherers, the Siriono have very few possessions—at most, bows and arrows, crude knives, bones or sticks for digging roots, animal bladders in which to carry water, large shells that double as baskets and cradles, sandals, skins to hold all these things. Nomads, the Siriono live from day to day. When the hunt is successful, they gorge themselves (they can't store meat for more than two or three days); when game elude them and foraging yields little, they go hungry. But whether the band faces feast or famine, the available food is distributed equally among all its members. The Siriono expect those who have to share with those who have not; they do not tolerate hoarding. As a result, no individual or family has the opportunity to accumulate food and buy the services or deference of another. Economically, all are equals. But the Siriono *do* have a pecking order. Older people, skilled hunters, and those who exhibit a talent for magic occupy special positions in the band. And the respect and honor they earn through longevity or prowess spill over into political matters, where these individuals carry more than equal weight (Lenski, 1966: 102–112).

Even in the relatively simple structure of Siriono society, it is possible to see some of the chief dimensions of social *stratification*—the unequal distribution of rewards or resources that a society considers scarce (Lenski, 1966). Control over important resources constitutes the *economic* dimension. The Siriono are not economically stratified, since their most important resource, food, is distributed evenly. But not all Siriono are equal in terms of the *status* dimension,

which refers to the recognition, prestige, or deference accorded good hunters, powerful magicians, and others who possess special skills or talents. *Power* is also a dimension of social stratification: being in a position to lead, guide, or influence the making of important political decisions or social policies.

Max Weber considered these dimensions of stratification in his discussion of class, status group, and party (in Gerth and Mills, 1946: 180–195). Weber used the term *class* to refer to a collection of individuals occupying the same rung on the economic ladder, and thus having approximately the same amount or source of income. People who inherit large chunks of property, for example, constitute a class, and in a broad sense so do professionals like doctors, lawyers, or engineers, since their skills give them access to similar rewards. But people who belong to the same class don't necessarily think or act alike, Weber argued. He referred to individuals who share a social identity based on similar life styles or patterns of consumption as a *status group*. Members of the same status group treat one another as social equals: they intermarry, belong to the same clubs and associations, and participate in the same informal social activities (Mayer, 1955: 24). Weber used the term *party* to refer to a group of people who share certain interests and seek to further them by gaining access to political power.

Weber emphasized that while these three classifications often overlap, they don't necessarily coincide. Even in a typically capitalist society such as the United States, social stratification is not simply a question of wealth: money is not synonymous with prestige or power. There are obvious differences, for instance, between people who earn $50,000 by drawing a salary, by collecting interest from an estate (''clipping coupons''), by selling heroin, by winning a Nobel Prize,

by holding public office, or by winning the lottery.

In short, income contributes to but doesn't determine prestige. Family name, ethnic and religious background, age, sex, education, occupation, life style, club membership, neighborhood—even grammar—all influence a person's social ranking. As Weber argued, social stratification in complex modern societies is *multidimensional*. It involves the unequal distribution of power and prestige, as well as of wealth. In the pages that follow, we will examine these three dimensions of stratification—wealth, power, and prestige—in the United States.

Income and Wealth

Economic stratification depends on what people earn (income) and what they own (wealth). Two people may have similar incomes, but one individual's may come entirely from a salary and the other's may come from dividends on vast security holdings. The second person is wealthier than the first. Both income and wealth are distributed unevenly, but to different degrees.

Social stratification in modern societies is multidimensional—it takes more than money to earn power and prestige. The social status of the residents of this estate, for example, depends not only on their wealth and income, but also on their occupations, education, family background, connections, and other factors. (Bullaty Lomeo Photo / The Image Bank)

Income   By April 15 every year, the Internal Revenue Service demands an accounting from all adult Americans of what they earn. Although not always complete, these statistics suggest the range of income inequality.

In 1976, the median family income was

table 10:1 **MEDIAN ANNUAL EARNINGS OF YEAR-ROUND FULL-TIME WORKERS IN 1975, BY SELECTED CHARACTERISTICS**

ITEM	ANNUAL EARNINGS	
	WOMEN	MEN
Total, 16 years and over	$ 7,504	$12,631
White	7,514	12,884
Black	7,237	9,710
Spanish origin	6,431	9,413
Years of school completed		
Less than 12	5,682	10,040
12 only	7,103	12,260
16 or more	10,519	17,129
Occupation:		
Professional and technical	10,524	15,968
Managers and administrators, except farm	9,125	15,903
Clerical	7,562	12,136
Operatives, except transport	6,241	10,953
Service, except private household	5,414	9,491

SOURCE: Adapted from U.S. Department of Labor, Bureau of Labor Statistics, *U.S. Working Women: A Databook* (Washington, D.C.: U.S. Government Printing Office, 1977), p. 36.

$14,958 per year—about 50 percent more than in 1960.[1] Approximately 10.4 percent of American families earned $5,000 or less; 19.6 percent between $5,000 and $10,000; 52.2 percent between $10,000 and $25,000; and 17.8 percent over $25,000. Breaking the population down into fifths, we find that the poorest 20 percent of Americans earned 5.4 percent of all personal income— about one-fourth what their share would be if income were distributed equally in the United States. The wealthiest 5 percent earned 15.6 percent of all personal income, about three times their share.

Education and occupational differences explain these gradations in part. While the median income of family heads who had not gone beyond elementary school was $10,694 in 1976, the median income of high school graduates was $15,886, and that of college graduates $22,019. Although these figures suggest that education is an excellent investment, they are somewhat deceptive, since many of the people who go to college come from middle- and upper-class achievement-oriented families and would probably earn better-than-average incomes without advanced education. Still, the more education a person has, the better his or her chances are of working in a high-paying occupation. Self-employed professionals receive the highest wages in this country (a median income of $25,724 in 1976 for a full-time male year-round worker); male farm laborers earn the lowest ($6,114). Table 10:1

---

[1] Unless otherwise indicated, all data are from the 1977 edition of *Statistical Abstract of the United States*, or from the 1977 *Current Population Reports*, both of the U.S. Bureau of the Census.

shows the median income of white, black, and Hispanic Americans, and the median incomes for males and females working in different occupations. Clearly, race and sex influence a person's economic standing in the United States, as blacks, Hispanics, and women typically earn less than whites and men.

Wealth The rich and the super-rich derive only a small proportion of their incomes from wages and salaries. Whereas Americans who earned $20,000 or less in 1966 drew 87 percent of their income from wages and salaries, those in the over-$100,000-a-year bracket earned only 15.2 percent of their income from salaries, 13.3 percent from small businesses they owned, and 66.8 percent from stocks, bonds, real estate, and other capital (Tumin, 1973: 55). The government's profile of American "wealthholders" is shown in table 10:2.

Wealth—especially in the form of stocks and bonds—is concentrated even more than income. In principle, any person can "own a piece of America" by buying stocks or bonds. In reality, the wealthiest 1 to 2 percent of the adult population completely dominates the ownership of corporate stock (Anderson, 1974).

---

table 10:2 AMERICAN WEALTHHOLDERS,[1] 1972

NUMBER OF WEALTHHOLDERS

Male	7,810,000 (60.9 percent)
Female	5,010,000 (39.1 percent)
Total	12,820,000

SIZE OF ESTATE	NUMBER	PERCENTAGE
$ 60,000–99,999	4,938,000	38.5
100,000–499,999	7,234,000	56.5
500,000–999,999	425,000	3.3
1,000,000–9,999,999 } 10,000,000 +	222,000	1.7

ASSETS	AMOUNT (IN BILLIONS OF DOLLARS)	PERCENTAGE
Total	2,265.1	
Real estate	650.1	28.7
Bonds	146.7	6.5
Corporate stock	712.8	31.5
Cash	279.2	12.3
Notes and mortgages	86.4	3.8
Insurance equity	42.0	1.9
Other	347.9	15.4
Debts	304.4	13.4
Net worth (less deficit)	1,960.7	

[1] People whose tax returns showed gross assets of $60,000 or more.

SOURCE: U.S. Bureau of the Census, *Statistical Abstract of the United States, 1976* (Washington, D.C.: U.S. Government Printing Office, 1976), p. 425.

Taxes The federal income tax is supposed to be a *progressive tax*—that is, the more money a person earns, the higher his or her rate of taxation. In 1976 the income tax rate for an income of $2,000 or less was 14 to 15 percent; for $19,950 to $20,000, 26 percent; for $100,000 or more, 70 percent. Progressive taxes are designed to distribute the cost of public goods and services according to people's ability to pay, and to deprive the rich of some luxuries in order to provide the poor with necessities. The tax reform bill that President Carter proposed in January 1978 was designed to ensure that the federal income tax is truly progressive; while the bill would reduce the income tax for all levels of earning, the most substantial reductions would be for the lower- and middle-income brackets.

But does our tax system actually reduce income inequalities? To some extent, yes. The poor pay proportionately lower federal taxes than do middle- and high-income people, and they benefit more from *transfer payments* (welfare, Medicaid, workmen's compensation, unemployment insurance, and other government subsidies that are not drawn from a person's salary, as Social Security is). The federal government allocated $27 billion to poverty programs in 1974 alone.

But in many ways the tax laws favor the well-off. Interest earned from state and local bonds is tax-exempt; in recent years the tax code has also allowed exemptions on more than one-fifth of the income earned from the production of oil, gas, and other minerals, and on as much as half the income earned through capital gains (profits on stocks, real estate, and other property). If exemptions such as these were not allowed—if all earnings were taxed at federal income tax rates—the government would collect billions more dollars each year than it currently does. In addition, many of the taxes Americans pay

are *regressive:* when everyone is taxed at the same rate, regardless of income, the poor actually contribute a greater proportion of their income than middle- and high-income people do. The federal payroll (Social Security) tax, state and local taxes (including the sales tax), and property taxes are all regressive. This, coupled with tax laws that may be manipulated in favor of wealth- and property-owning people, ensures that the tax system will foster some gross inequalities. According to government figures released in the late sixties, 381 people with incomes of $100,000 or more a year didn't pay one penny in federal income taxes in 1968; and more than 1,000 people who earned $200,000 or more paid the same proportion of their incomes in taxes as did people earning $15,000 to $20,000 (Stern, 1970).

Regressive taxes and tax loopholes shift a substantial part of the tax burden *back* to poor and middle-income families. Benjamin Okner, a Fellow at the Brookings Institution, calculates that federal taxes (income and payroll) reduced income inequality in the United States by only 4 percent in 1966 (Rose, 1972: 162). Does this figure represent progress? Has poverty decreased?

The War on Poverty—Victory or Defeat? The government's definition of poverty is based on the Department of Agriculture's estimate of the minimal cost of living for a family of four.[2] In 1976, a nonfarm family with an annual income of less than $5,815 was considered officially poor. About 11.8 percent of Americans fell into this category. Poverty is most prevalent among female-headed

---

[2] This amount of money should provide a family of four with a minimum food plan, indoor plumbing, a double bed for every two people, eating utensils, and a few other essentials. However, it is not enough to buy much meat or many fresh fruits and vegetables. There is no allowance for dental care or entertainment, and very little for clothes.

households and black Americans. In 1976, 31.1 percent of black Americans earned less than $5,815, compared with about 9.1 percent of white Americans; 33.0 percent of female-headed households were poor, compared with 5.6 percent of male-headed households. However, almost 67 percent of America's poor are white, and over 50 percent live in male-headed households.

In 1964, President Lyndon Johnson declared "unconditional war on poverty" and created the Office of Economic Opportunity, which conducted such programs as a Job Corps for dropouts, a Neighborhood Youth Corps for unemployed teen-agers, and a Community Action program to secure participation of the poor in running the antipoverty effort. Between 1965 and 1970, the government spent nearly $10 billion on antipoverty programs. Table 10:3 shows that the number of poor Americans dropped from 40 million in 1960 (before the war on poverty) to 24

table 10:3   **POVERTY IN THE UNITED STATES, 1960–1976**

YEAR	NUMBER IN MILLIONS	PERCENTAGE OF POPULATION	POVERTY LINE	PERCENT OF MEDIAN INCOME	NATIONAL MEDIAN INCOME
		The Poor			
1960	39.9	22.2	$3,022	53.8	$ 5,620
1963	36.4	19.5	3,128	50.0	6,249
1966	28.5	14.7	3,317	44.2	7,500
1969	24.1	12.1	3,743	39.7	9,433
1971	25.6	12.5	4,137	40.2	10,285
1972	24.5	12.0	4,275	38.4	11,120
1973	23.0	11.1	4,540	37.7	12,051
1974	24.3	11.6	5,038	39.2	12,836
1975	25.9	12.3	5,500	40.1	13,719
1976	25.0	11.8	5,815	38.9	14,958
		The Near-Poor[1]			
1960	54.6	30.4	$3,778	67.2	(NA)[2]
1963	50.8	27.1	3,910	62.6	(NA)
1966	41.3	21.3	4,146	55.3	(NA)
1969	34.7	17.4	4,679	49.6	(NA)
1971	36.5	17.8	5,171	50.3	(NA)
1972	34.7	16.8	5,344	47.9	(NA)
1973	32.8	15.8	5,675	47.1	12,051
1974	34.6	16.5	6,298	49.1	12,836
1975	37.2	17.6	6,875	50.1	13,719
1976	35.5	16.7	7,268	48.6	14,958

[1] People earning less than 125 percent of the poverty-level income.
[2] (NA) Not available.
SOURCE: U.S. Bureau of the Census, *Statistical Abstract of the United States, 1977* (Washington, D.C.: U.S. Government Printing Office, 1977), table 732, p. 453; U.S. Bureau of the Census, *Current Population Reports*, Series P–60, no. 107 (Washington, D.C.: U.S. Government Printing Office, 1977), pp. 20 and 24.

million in 1969. Much of this dramatic decline, however, was probably a result of a general rise in prosperity.

As Edward Fried and his colleagues (1973: 45) suggest, more Americans are able to purchase the necessities of life today than was true in the past. But the *gap* between the poor and other Americans has not changed. There is a more equal distribution of income today than in 1929 during the Great Depression, but it hasn't changed greatly since 1944. (See also figure 10:1.)

Power

The presidency of the United States is generally conceded to be the most powerful of-

figure 10:1 Distribution of family income, 1936 and 1974

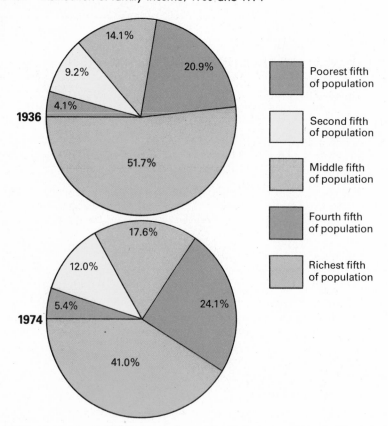

SOURCE: Courtesy of W. E. Brownlee; U.S. Bureau of the Census, *Current Population Reports,* Series P-60, no. 97 (Washington, D.C.: U.S. Government Printing Office, 1975); U.S. Bureau of the Census, *Statistical Abstract, 1975* (Washington, D.C.: U.S. Government Printing Office, 1975), table 636.

As a comparison of these two pie graphs shows, the overall distribution of income in the United States has remained relatively stable between 1936 and 1974. The gap between the very poor and the very rich remains.

fice in the world. The decisions the president makes are not like other people's: few of us think in billions of dollars, in millions of people, in terms of the risk of triggering a nuclear war. The view from the top of the American power structure is very different from the one from the bottom.

Basically, *power* is the ability to mobilize collective energies, commitments, and efforts or to set policies for others to follow. Personal power is the freedom to make choices affecting one's own destiny. Power may be formal or informal. By formal power, or *authority,* we mean the prerogatives that legitimately go with an office such as the presidency of a nation or company. By informal power, we mean *influence,* the know-how and the know-who to pull the strings behind the scenes. (We will explore the question of political power in greater depth in chapter 12.) The president of this country has a great deal of formal power; Martin Luther King, Jr., had enormous informal power. But how many others share this power in our society?

Is There a Power Elite?   Not surprisingly, this is one of the most hotly debated questions in sociology. C. Wright Mills argued that the heads of government, the military, and business in this country constitute a *power elite.* These are the people who make the decisions that determine how the rest of us will live. They are accountable only to themselves, and are relatively immune to public pressure and the public interest (Mills, 1956).

David Riesman (1953), among others, disagreed with Mills. Where Mills saw a single cohesive elite, Riesman saw many competing elites whose varied goals and interests prevent them from pooling their resources. As a result, social power is widely dispersed; no one group commands. While this plural-

Power is the ability to mobilize collective energies, commitments, and efforts. Although he never held elective office, Martin Luther King, Jr., wielded great social power by appealing to the nation's political and moral values. (Ernst Haas/Magnum Photos)

istic system protects us from dictatorship, in Riesman's view it also deprives us of effective leadership and decision-making.

More recently, G. William Domhoff (1967) has attempted to discover whether Mills's hypothesis that there is a ''power elite'' is valid. After a systematic analysis of the membership of the American upper class according to strictly defined socioeconomic criteria (wealth, education, club membership, and so forth), Domhoff identified a group accounting for about one two-hundredth of the U.S. population (approximately 11,000 people). This group was not quite the cohesive elite posited by Mills, but was clearly, in

Domhoff's view, a "governing class." The members of this class often belong to different political parties and economic or social groupings, but they are strikingly similar in that they are wealthy; hold a disproportionate number of high-level positions in government, business, or other important social organizations; and are tightly knit through intermarriage, school attendance, club membership, and civic affiliations. Domhoff concluded that as a result of their upper-class background or of socialization in upper-class institutions, the members of the American "governing class" share a concern for protecting and enhancing free enterprise, private property, and the right to make a profit. Key political decisions made by the members of this class tend to reflect that concern.

If Mills, Riesman, and Domhoff all take a somewhat different approach to the question of power in America, there is one implication that one draws with equal strength from the work of all three: the vast majority of Americans—the masses—have little personal or social power to speak of. As Mills wrote, most Americans can't control "great changes," but their behavior and outlook are affected by these changes.

Dimensions of Power But none of these theories can be proved or disproved unless power can be measured in some way. How do you calculate a person's or a group's sway over events? One measure of power is the offices people hold. We can reasonably assume that the president of a big corporation or the mayor of a large city has more power than ordinary people. But what about the people who work behind the scenes, who don't appear on official rosters? We can measure such influence by reputation. If people are asked to identify the influential members of their community, we can conclude that the individuals named on many different lists belong to the local elite. But

how do we verify the judges' opinions? Yet another measure of power is participation in key decisions. Who attends the crucial meetings? Who speaks for what groups? Who has lunch with whom? Who seems to have the final word? While this may seem the best method, in-depth analyses of key decisions require almost unlimited time and effort, and the combined skills of a psychologist and a detective (Dahl, 1963).

An equally important question in this context is whether people *feel* they are able to influence the decisions that affect them (regardless of whether they do in fact exercise power). This is what is meant by "political efficacy." Robert Dahl (1963) found that one's subjective sense of power rises with income, education, social status, and political participation. The more influential a person feels, the more likely he or she is to vote and to join organizations and attend meetings; and the more a person participates in political and community activities, the more likely he or she is to feel influential. Participation in such activities or lack of it is self-reinforcing. Like wealth and power, political efficacy is cumulative; the more you have, the more you get (Mills, 1956: 10). The same can be said of prestige.

Prestige

Consider the following advertisement:

We don't think anyone in this city can rival our assortment of chic wares from the world-famous House of Dior, each bearing the inimitable stamp of his renowned good taste.

Here is a random sampling of the exquisite *vendibles* you can find all around our store bearing the Dior label. We'll start with his signature luggage. Delectable. Noticeable at any airport. Woven in a tough, *take-it-on-the-chin* fabric, the pattern suddenly dawns on you. It's a design of C's and D's (Christian Dior, of course). (Trahey Agency)

After all, what good is carrying Dior luggage if nobody knows that it's Dior luggage? Dior luggage, like designer-initialed scarves, shirts, dresses, and underwear, is a status symbol. It shows that the individual has money and, more important, good taste.

Trivial as this example may seem, prestige is obviously one of the important dimensions of social stratification. People rank one another according to how they earn their money (their occupation), how they spend it (their ''consumptive class''), who they are (their ancestry), who they know, and how successful, well known, and respected they are.

For example, being listed in the *Social Register* or *Who's Who in America* is definitely a status symbol. These publications have long reigned as *the* guides to who counts in this country. The *Social Register* describes itself as a list of ''distinguished'' people—by which it means people who come from the right families, attend the right schools, belong to the right clubs, and live in the right neighborhoods. People who wish to be included in the *Social Register* are considered only if they bring recommendations from several people already on the list.

Prestige denotes the possession of attributes that are regarded as admirable, and perhaps enviable, by people in a specific social setting. In a society preoccupied with religion, holiness and zeal may be the most important attributes for prestige; in a military setting, physical courage is often what counts the most; people in the film or the fashion field often equate status with talent or good looks. In U.S. society as a whole, the main determinant of prestige appears to be one's occupation. Thus, the incessant scramble for a berth in the executive suite or the White House (and their more humble counterparts), or for entrée into such high-status, high-authority professions as medicine and law, is more than just a race for

Occupation appears to be the main determinant of prestige in American society as a whole. Medicine, especially surgery, ranks among the most respected professions, while street cleaning falls near the bottom of the occupational hierarchy. (Left, Charles Steiner / The Image Bank. Right, Jeffrey Foxx / Woodfin Camp & Associates)

riches and power; it is also a race for the social importance that comes with success.

Occupation Ratings   Probably the best measure we have of prestige in America is the Hatt-North scale of occupational prestige, which was designed for the National Opinion Research Center (NORC) in the 1940s. Paul Hatt and Cecil North (1947) compiled a list of ninety occupations and asked a cross section of Americans which term expressed their own personal opinion of each occupation's standing: excellent, good, average, somewhat below average, or poor. They then assigned a numerical value to each rating (100 for excellent, 40 for good, and so on), cal-

table 10:4   **PRESTIGE RANKING OF OCCUPATIONS IN THE UNITED STATES, 1963**

U.S. Supreme Court Justice	Mayor of a large city	Dockworker
Physician	Priest	Railroad section hand
Nuclear physicist	Head of a dept. in a state government	Taxi driver
Scientist	Sociologist	Farm hand
Government scientist	Accountant for a large business	Janitor
State governor	Public school teacher	Bartender
Cabinet member in the federal government	Author of novels	Clothes presser in a laundry
College professor	Owner-operator of a printing shop	Soda fountain clerk
U.S. Representative in Congress	Farm owner and operator	Share-cropper—one who owns no livestock or equipment and does not manage farm
Chemist	Reporter on a daily newspaper	
Lawyer	Bookkeeper	
Diplomat in the U.S. Foreign Service	Carpenter	Garbage collector
Dentist	Mail carrier	Street sweeper
Architect	Automobile repairman	Shoe shiner
County judge	Barber	
Psychologist	Garage mechanic	
Minister	Truck driver	
Member of the board of directors of a large corporation	Streetcar motorman	
	Singer in a nightclub	

SOURCE: Adapted from Robert W. Hodge, Paul M. Siegel, and Peter H. Rossi, "Occupational Prestige in the United States: 1925–1963," in Reinhard Bendix and Seymour Martin Lipset, eds., *Class, Status, and Power,* 2nd ed. (New York: Free Press, 1966), pp. 324–325.

culated the average rating for each occupation, and listed them accordingly. The job hierarchy shown in table 10:4 is what one might have expected. Supreme Court justices, doctors, scientists, governors, and cabinet members are at the top; garbage collectors, street sweepers, and shoe shiners at the bottom; schoolteachers, builders, farmers, and police officers in between. But there are some surprises. Americans are not as anti-intellectual as many intellectuals think: college professors rank eighth (well ahead of bankers). Oddly, movie stars and athletes were awarded no more prestige than welfare workers, farm owners, and undertakers![3]

These occupational rankings have proven to be highly stable. The NORC study was repeated in 1963 and in an expanded form in 1964 and 1965. Although blue-collar occupations gained prestige and three categories of white-collar work (managerial, clerical, and sales) dropped somewhat, there were very few real changes over the twenty year span. Indeed, parallel research conducted in other countries, both industrialized and underdeveloped, revealed striking uniformity in job ranking (Hodge, Treiman, and Rossi, 1966; Treiman, 1977). These studies conclude that people rank occupations according to their importance for society, the power and influence that accompany them, educational requirements, income, the nature of the work and dress (white versus blue collar), and the characteristics of the people who fill each occupation.

The Hatt-North scale is a limited tool. It doesn't tell us anything about how family names, connections, life style, or other intangibles affect a person's social standing. But it does show quite clearly that Americans

award prestige unequally, that we are conscious of prestige differences, and that there is some degree of consensus about who counts in this country.

Classes in America

When asked, most Americans identify themselves as middle-class. This is part of our reverse snobbism. American culture glorifies the common man, the "average Joe"; the idea that no one is any better than anyone else is a central part of our national creed. Yet we have seen that there are obvious inequalities in the distribution of wealth, power, and prestige in America. To deny this would be foolish. Even a child knows how to distinguish between her "own kind" and families that are above or beneath hers socially.

Still, sociologists have found it difficult to identify distinct social classes in America. In part, the difficulty is due to the use of different definitions. Analyses based on such economic criteria as property or income usually yield three classes—upper, middle, and lower. If other criteria are employed, however, such as club membership or ownership of consumer goods, analysis yields more than just two or three classes and often reflects subtle gradations that economic studies alone don't detect. For instance, in his study of Yankee City, W. L. Warner described a six-class model based on a composite ranking of wealth, life style, possessions, social pedigree, and participation in community life and private clubs (Warner, Meeker, and Eels, 1949). Warner's six classes broke down this way: upper-upper (1.4 percent), lower-upper (1.6 percent), upper-middle (10 percent), lower-middle (28 percent), upper-lower (33 percent), and lower-lower (25 percent). The current feeling

[3] These occupations appeared on an extended scale, and ranked forty-fourth (Tumin, 1973: 66).

among sociologists is that the division into upper, middle, and lower classes is probably the most useful for *general* descriptive purposes.[4] Adding more refined occupation- or income-based criteria yields a more accurate but also a more unwieldy scheme.

Contrary to public rhetoric, then, social classes *do* exist in America. Yet when asked to label themselves by class, many people are unclear about the meaning of class and their own position in the class system. And even among those with some awareness of class, most do not have a strong sense of shared class interests. Our class consciousness, in other words, is limited. Why?

The belief that America is the land of opportunity, and the feeling that no people are any better than anyone else—even if some are better off—tends to retard the development of class consciousness in this country. In addition, racial, ethnic, and religious affiliations cut across economic lines. As a result, Americans have multiple social identities that interfere with the development of a coherent class or rank consciousness (see Wrong, 1972).

Still, the factors that retard class consciousness may not be as widespread as some believe. In a study conducted a few years ago, three sociologists set out to take a closer look at one of the factors that inhibits class consciousness—namely, the idea of equal opportunity (Rytina, Form, and Pease, 1970). The authors of the study began with the hypothesis that the American ideology of equality of opportunity is generally accepted by all strata in the United States. But surely, they argued, "people must test public ideologies against their daily life experiences" (94). Thus, they wondered, would poor people see a gap between how things ought to be and how things really are? Would people in lower strata feel the same way about equal opportunity as people in higher strata?

To find out, the authors used a novel approach. First they asked a vague, general question like "Do you think America is a land of opportunity?" Then, to make sure people weren't simply going along with a familiar cliché, the authors asked a specific situational question linking opportunity with income—that is, "Does a poor boy have the same chances as a rich boy to make a given amount of money?" The general statement elicited many more positive responses than the specific, income-linked question. Over 80 percent of the whites who were interviewed, and nearly 60 percent of the blacks, thought that, in general, America was indeed a land of opportunity. But in response to the second question, there was much less agreement. Almost 60 percent of the rich white people in the study believed that the rich boy and the poor boy had an equal opportunity to make the same amount of money; among middle-income and poor whites, about half thought that both boys had the same chances; among middle-income and poor blacks, though, only 21 and 11 percent, respectively, thought that the poor boy had an equal opportunity to grow rich. No matter what questions the authors asked, the rich were consistently more likely to believe in the existence of equal opportunity. They were also more likely to attribute wealth to such favorable personal attributes as hard work, motivation, and ability, instead of to privilege or other injustices in the social structure. "The support of any ideology," the authors conclude, "is strongest among those who profit the most from the system which the ideology explains and defends" (99). In this case, of course, the strongest supporters were the rich.

---

[4]   Some sociologists today reject the term "class" altogether in favor of more neutral and less politically charged terms such as "strata" or "socioeconomic status."

table 10:5 **BELIEFS ABOUT LEGAL AND POLITICAL EQUALITY, BY INCOME AND RACE (percentage who perceive equality)**

INCOME AND RACE	VOTING INFLUENCES GOVERNMENT	RICH AND POOR INFLUENCE GOVERNMENT EQUALLY	LAW AND COURTS ARE FAIR	JAIL EQUALLY LIKELY FOR RICH OR POOR
Poor:				
Black	76	3	46	8
White	88	30	75	23
Middle:				
Black	89	15	27	20
White	89	30	59	20
Rich:				
White	94	55	75	22

SOURCE: Adapted from Joan Huber Rytina, William H. Form, and John Pease, "Income and Stratification Ideology: Beliefs About the American Opportunity Structure," *American Journal of Sociology*, vol. 75 (January 1970), table 3, p. 712.

Another area of ideology explored by Rytina, Form, and Pease is the impartial functioning of the American legal and political systems. Their findings support the hypothesis that belief in an ideology is strongest among those who have the most to gain from the system which the ideology defends—in this case, rich whites.

TWO THEORIES OF SOCIAL STRATIFICATION

Like knights in a jousting tournament, sociologists trying to explain the reason for the unequal distribution of wealth, power, and prestige in human societies tend to enter the fray from opposite sides. On one side are the functionalists, who argue that stratification is a necessary and perhaps inevitable piece of machinery that keeps societies functioning efficiently. On the other are the conflict theorists, who maintain that instead of being functional and inevitable, stratification is the result of the selfish struggle between individuals for scarce rewards, and that it persists in society because those who have are determined to preserve their advantage by dominating and exploiting those who have not. As we will see in the following discussion, strengths and weaknesses are distributed fairly equally on both sides of this intense and far-reaching debate.

Functionalist Theory

The idea that stratification serves an important function in society was first elaborated by Kingsley Davis and Wilbert E. Moore (1945, 1953) in the pages of the *American Sociological Review*. Davis and Moore reasoned as follows: If all the positions that have to be filled in a society were equally important and equally pleasant, and if all members of society were equally capable of doing these jobs, there would be no need for stratification. But this is not the case. Some tasks are clearly more essential than others, and some require a great deal more talent and training. For example, almost anyone can learn to dig ditches in a day or two, but it takes years of schooling to become a physician. Medical school is tedious and demanding. For a year or more, medical students devote all of their time to the business of memorizing the facts of human anatomy. As interns, young doctors are expected to work long hours, sacrificing their nights and weekends and social life. They earn very little for their efforts; many go into debt to finance their education. And the job of physician itself is trying. How many people would choose to spend their lives around the sick and dying if they did not know they would be amply rewarded in money and respect?

This is the key to Davis and Moore's argument. Societies must motivate people to seek socially important positions and to fill these positions conscientiously by awarding those who do so with more of the things that contribute to sustenance and comfort, humor and diversion, self-respect and ego expansion than they would otherwise receive. In other words, societies have to entice people into jobs that are essential and difficult to fill by rewarding them unequally.[5] Otherwise, many essential tasks wouldn't get done. Therefore, social inequality is both necessary and functional. The functionalists argue that since stratification serves the interests of the society as a whole, coercion is not required to maintain social stability. Rather, most members of a society accept the system and cooperate in preserving the existing distribution of rewards and opportunities. In the long run, the entire society benefits.

One Critique   But Melvin Tumin (1953) and others have challenged the functionalist position. Tumin argues that stratification doesn't facilitate but rather limits competition for socially important positions to those who can afford training, eliminating people who may be equally or better qualified for the job. Perhaps a few poor people make their way into satisfying and important careers, but the vast majority do not. Nearly 20 percent of all the physicians in this country and over 40 percent of all professionals followed in their fathers' footsteps. There is no way to calculate the number of potentially brilliant doctors, statesmen, teachers, and so on who were too poor to attend college. In a stratified society, the lower class's talents, energy, and potential are lost. Davis and Moore seem to overlook the role inheritance plays in recruitment to important positions.

Tumin charges that Davis and Moore also do not consider the motivation of "the masses," other than to suggest that most members of society accept the stratification system and believe they get what they deserve. (But as the riots of the sixties demonstrated so clearly, marked inequalities create distrust, hostility, and suspicion between different segments of the population—a condition that can hardly be called "functional.") People who are struggling to survive in a society that boasts hundreds of millionaires have little motivation to abide by society's norms, to respect the dictates of culture. And how many of the millionaires are actually performing socially useful work? Tumin drives his point home by criticizing the notion that doctors receive high incomes

---

[5]   Important jobs that are easy to fill don't call for such high rewards. In technological societies, for example, teachers may be as important as doctors, but more people have the talent, training, and desire to teach than to practice medicine. As a result, teachers receive more modest compensation than doctors.

because their jobs are both important and hard to fill. Doctors are scarce, not because the long years of training discourage people from pursuing a career in medicine, but because medical schools turn down hundreds of thousands of qualified applicants every year. Physicians—whose professional group, the American Medical Association, acts as one of the most powerful lobbies in the country—protect their incomes by limiting their numbers. Again, society as a whole loses.

Tumin concludes that even if some economic incentive is necessary to motivate people to fill certain essential roles, it is difficult to see how inequality as extreme as that which exists in this country is either functional or inevitable. He suggests that the functionalist theory of stratification is little more than a rationalization of the status quo. Stratification exists because the rich and powerful use their considerable resources to hold on to what they have.

Conflict Theory

As its name implies, conflict theory stresses the link between stratification and an ongoing struggle in society between competing groups and classes over a limited supply of rewards and resources. From this point of view, the winner takes all and remains firmly determined not to surrender any advantage. Thus, the rich stay rich or get richer while the poor stay poor or get poorer.

Marx and the Theory of Class Conflict As opposed to the functionalist perspective, which is a product of twentieth-century sociology, conflict theory derives ultimately from the nineteenth century, and particularly from the work of Karl Marx (1818–1883), one of the precursors of modern sociology. Marx was the first to suggest the significance of social class in capitalist societies. Of the various uses Marx made of the term "class" in his various writings, the best known and most widely accepted is that a class consists of a number of people who stand in the same relation to the means of production (land, factories, equipment, and so forth). According to Marx, there are only two such basic relations: ownership of the means of production, and nonownership. In modern capitalist societies, the owners of the means of production are the *bourgeoisie* (from a French word meaning "people who live in towns"); the nonowners, who must sell their skills to the owners, are the *proletariat*.

Since the members of the proletariat class far outnumber the members of the bourgeoisie, why does the apparently stronger class allow itself to be dominated by the apparently weaker one? The reason, Marx explained, is "false consciousness." Among the bourgeoisie, *objective class* (one's relation to the means of production) and *subjective class* (class consciousness) coincide: the owners realize they are in a dominant position as long as they maintain control over the means of production, and they use every device at their disposal to maintain their advantage. Members of the proletariat, on the other hand, understand that they aren't in the same class as the owners (subjective class), but they don't realize that as long as they don't own the means of production, they will never have true equal opportunity but will be exploited instead (objective class). Marx argued that the bourgeoisie imposes poverty, ignorance, and powerlessness on the workers through a combination of coercion and deception, fostering a false class consciousness among the workers. He saw the nation-state as an instrument of oppression, religion as a method of diverting and controlling the masses, and the family as a device for keeping wealth and education in the hands of the few. The basic thrust of

Marx's analysis, then, is that the fundamental dynamic in capitalist societies is a class conflict over limited rewards and opportunities, with the odds overwhelmingly stacked against the working class.

Updating Marx   Until recently, Marxist theory was largely ignored in the United States because virtually none of Marx's predictions ever became fact. Marx prophesied that capitalism was doomed to collapse because the lower classes would come to see that they were being exploited by a greedy minority. The ranks of the impoverished among the proletariat would swell, and class consciousness would lead to open warfare between the bourgeoisie and the proletariat. The proletariat would emerge victorious by virtue of superiority in numbers and would go on to create a utopian classless communist society in which everyone would have an equal stake in the means of production.

The lack of congruence between Marxist analysis and conditions in the United States also contributed to the apparent uselessness of Marx's perspective. A phrase like "exploitation by the ruling class," for instance, seemed to have nothing to do with the American belief in equal opportunity and upward mobility; nor did Marx's theories—forged during the most appalling years of the Industrial Revolution—seem to have much to do with an understanding of American society, particularly during the prosperous and occasionally booming years following World War II.

But these shortcomings, sociologists are beginning to argue, don't invalidate Marx's insight into the relationship between stratification and conflict over rewards and resources, or his perception of state power and ideology as the servants, justifiers, and defenders of the interests of the dominant class. Both of these Marxist notions are at the heart of a modern conflict theory that is now emerging in such works as *The Political Economy of Social Class* (1974), Charles H. Anderson's study of stratification in capitalist societies. Anderson speaks of a "ruling class" in the United States that consists, among others, of the heads of some very large businesses, and that exerts enormous and self-interested control over American domestic and foreign policy (281). The working class, Anderson finds, is neither as apathetic nor as well-integrated into society as "ruling-class ideology" suggests. Within the broad working class, feelings (and activities) of opposition run deep; the major source of inspiration and leadership in the raising of working-class consciousness has—and will continue to—come from minority groups, particularly blacks (290).

Combining the Two Theories   The differences between the functionalist and conflict theories would appear to be profound and in many ways irreconcilable. Perhaps the most fundamental problem at issue in both perspectives has to do with human nature in the social setting. The functionalists argue that people won't work for abstract goals; motivation must be provided in the form of rewards. According to the functionalists, members of society agree that some jobs are more important than others, and they therefore accept as legitimate a system that distributes rewards unequally. The conflict theorists argue that the present reward system is out of line—prestige, joy in one's work, and other such rewards are as important as material benefits. If society were structured differently, the conflict theorists hold, people would be more apt to cooperate rather than compete with their fellow citizens. They also insist that social stratification does not rest on widespread consensus among the members of a society but on outright coercion—that is, on the domination of the weak by the strong, of the poor by the rich, of the working class by the ruling class. The functionalist approach to stratification focuses on the needs of society; the conflict model is concerned with the privileges of a few and the unmet needs of many. Other differences between the two theories can be seen in table 10:6.

Although the two theories are almost wholly at odds with each other, both have obvious strong points. In his influential work *Power and Privilege* (1966), Gerhard E. Lenski has taken a major step toward a workable synthesis of the two perspectives. He begins with the postulate that "where important decisions are involved, most human action is motivated by self-interest or partisan group interests." At the same time, he argues, "most of these essentially selfish interests can be satisfied only by the estab-

lishment of cooperative relations with others" (Lenski, 1966: 44). If there were enough rewards available to satisfy all members of society, then human selfishness would not necessarily give rise to stratification. But many of the things humans most desire are in short supply, and in societies that produce a surplus—that is to say, more than the minimum amount of goods, services, or other commodities necessary for survival—conflicts and struggles for the control of that surplus will be inevitable (44). Since not all members of society are equally fit for the struggle, some will acquire more of the surplus than others, and social inequality will be the inevitable result. The factor that most influences the outcome of the conflict and the distribution of nearly all the surplus is power, not need. Lenski bridges one of

---

table 10:6 TWO VIEWS OF SOCIAL STRATIFICATION

THE FUNCTIONALIST VIEW	THE CONFLICT VIEW
1. Stratification is universal, necessary, and inevitable.	1. Stratification may be universal without being necessary or inevitable.
2. Social organization (the social system) shapes the stratification system.	2. The stratification system shapes social organizations (the social system).
3. Stratification arises from the societal need for integration, coordination, and cohesion.	3. Stratification arises from group conquest, competition, and conflict.
4. Stratification facilitates the optimal functioning of society and the individual.	4. Stratification impedes the optimal functioning of society and the individual.
5. Stratification is an expression of commonly shared social values.	5. Stratification is an expression of the values of powerful groups.
6. Power is usually legitimately distributed in society.	6. Power is usually illegitimately distributed in society.
7. Tasks and rewards are equitably allocated.	7. Tasks and rewards are inequitably allocated.
8. The economic dimension is subordinate to other dimensions of society.	8. The economic dimension is paramount in society.
9. Stratification systems generally change through evolutionary processes.	9. Stratification systems often change through revolutionary processes.

SOURCE: Arthur L. Stinchcombe, "Some Empirical Consequences of the Davis-Moore Theory of Stratification," in Jack L. Roach, Llewellyn Gross, Orville Gursslin, eds., *Social Stratification in the United States* (Englewood Cliffs, N.J.: Prentice-Hall, 1969).

the gaps between functionalist and conflict thought by noting that, on the one hand, stratification may actually serve a purpose in society along the lines suggested by the functionalists. But on the other hand, forms of stratification will tend to persist long after they have ceased to be functional, which supports many of the claims advanced by the conflict theorists.

LIFE CHANGES

Social stratification affects individual chances to survive on a very elemental level. While most Americans have access to such essentials as food, shelter, jobs, and education, those at the top and bottom of the social hierarchy—the rich and the poor—have their chances enormously increased or decreased simply by virtue of their class. Only the very rich, for example, can afford the medical, psychiatric, and legal care that might make the difference, if not between life and death, then at least between a merely tolerable life and an extremely pleasurable one. The poor, on the other hand, have a sharply decreased chance of reaching their first birthday, of getting an education, of being able to afford adequate nutrition, decent housing, and health care, and of rounding out their days in dignity and comfort.

Nutrition and Health

The poor spend a much greater proportion of their incomes on food than other Americans do (53 percent for families earning less than $3,000 per year, compared with 12 percent for families with incomes of $20,000 to $25,000 per year). Often the poor pay more for less: ghetto merchants justify high mark-ups on the grounds that they take high risks; small local groceries with high prices extend credit, but supermarkets do not; chain stores unload day-old bread and other leftovers in low-income neighborhoods (Caplovitz, 1963).

Millions of Americans (mostly children) live on rice, beans, peanut butter, bread, powdered milk, Kool-Aid, and one can of meat a month. When money runs short, many poor people turn to pet food. (Estimates are that one-third of the dog food sold in low-income areas is eaten by human beings [Parenti, 1977: 24–25].)

From 30 to 50 percent of poor children suffer from protein, iron, and vitamin deficiencies. Malnutrition stunts a child's growth and makes him or her more vulnerable to disease, but this isn't all. There is a growing body of evidence to suggest that severe protein deficiency during the first twelve to eighteen months of life causes irreparable damage to the brain and nervous system. In addition, undernourished children are apathetic, lethargic, unable to pay attention for more than very brief spells, and often irritable and agitated (Read, 1971). In short, hunger interferes with learning.

Hunger is not the only medical problem of the poor, however. They suffer from more chronic and infectious diseases, and are less able to pay for medical care, than the rest of the population. The mortality rate of children of laborers and service workers is 50 percent higher than that of children of professionals and managers (Kotelchuck, 1976: 6). (We will discuss health problems of the poor in more detail in chapter 16.)

Housing

The streets of Kenwood-Oakland, a poor section of Chicago, are lined with garbage.

The sidewalks are crumbling; many of the buildings are condemned and abandoned. One woman told Senate investigators she was afraid to go to sleep because faulty wiring had caused so many fires. Her roof leaked whenever it rained, and the sewage was backed up in her toilet. The winter before, she and her seven children had had no water for two weeks (U.S. Senate Select Committee on Nutrition and Human Needs, November 1969).

The poor spend proportionately more of their incomes on rent than others do (78 percent of households earning $3,000 or less per year paid over one-quarter of their income for rent, compared with 3.5 percent of those earning $20,000 to $25,000 per year). Yet as of 1973, 18 percent of Americans, or 12.8 million families (a disproportionate number of whom are black), lived in sub-standard housing.

The lure of easy credit in many poor neighborhoods can be a financial trap for those who can't qualify for credit cards in large department stores or banks. High interest rates may increase the cost of merchandise, thus adding to the extensive burdens of poverty. (Joel Gordon)

Criminal Justice

As we saw in chapter 9, the poor are also the losers in the criminal justice system. Residents of low-income neighborhoods are frequently arrested for drunkenness, gambling, and such ambiguous crimes as vagrancy, which together account for about 60 percent of all arrests. The poor, too, are less likely to be released on their own recognizance (although they are the least able to afford bail), and they are more likely to be sent to jail if convicted (Cratsley, 1972: 192). Yet people in low-income neighborhoods are more likely to be the victims of crime.

These facts do not square with the belief that America is the land of opportunity; that our society guarantees the right to "life, liberty, and the pursuit of happiness" to all. The distribution of life chances is blatantly unequal. Is the system to blame? Are the poor themselves? Is anything being done to bring life chances in line with our ideology? Can anything be done? In the next two sections we will examine the American system for answers to these questions.

THE LAND OF OPPORTUNITY: AN EVALUATION

Societies vary both in the degree of inequality they exhibit and in their rigidity. Caste systems are closed: individuals are born into their social positions and usually cannot change them, especially in an upward direction. Class systems such as ours are comparatively open, so social mobility *is* possible and even encouraged. This means that individuals are able to rise (but also to fall) on the social scale.

The belief that any person who gets an education, works hard, and takes advantage of opportunities can "get ahead" is a central part of the American dream (and one reason why American workers have failed to develop sharp class consciousness). But is this country truly a land of opportunity? Have we moved any closer to the ideal of equal opportunity in the last decade? Can we?

Social Mobility

The first step toward answering these questions is to determine the degree of social mobility in this country. By *social mobility,* we mean the movement of people from one social position to another. The term *vertical mobility* refers to upward or downward changes in a person's status. A living example of upward mobility is Leonard Stern, whose father came to this country from Germany several decades ago. When their textile business got into trouble, the elder Stern and a friend decided to import canaries. They were moderately successful, but then the canary business also fell into debt. Meanwhile, Leonard had gone to college and acquired an M.B.A. at record speed. He took over the business in 1959. The younger Stern built the family's Hartz Mountain Corporation into a $150-million-a-year enterprise, and by the time he was thirty-five he had amassed over a half a billion dollars (*Fortune,* September 1973: 172–173). This is the prototypical American success story. The term *horizontal mobility* refers to changes in position that do not appreciably alter a person's status, as when an oil company executive becomes the secretary of transportation, or when people move from one region to another.

Open and Closed Systems   In a truly *open class system* (if any such system existed; this is an ideal type), there are inequalities but few impediments to social mobility: positions are awarded on the basis of merit, and rank is tied to individual achievement. Family origins, race, creed, color, sex, and other ascribed (or inherited) characteristics don't matter. Anyone with talent and ambition can advance. Class lines are blurred in open systems, and there is little class consciousness (in the sense of political solidarity among people in similar economic situations). This is not to say that an open society is an equal society; there is a difference between equality of opportunity and equality of situation (when all members of a society have the

BLUE-COLLAR ARISTOCRATS

We tend to assume that all Americans want to get ahead—to climb as far up the socioeconomic ladder as they can. Not so, says E. E. LeMasters (1975), after spending five years as a participant observer at a working-class bar.

For the most part, the men who frequented "The Oasis" were skilled construction workers. Far from being alienated from work, they liked their jobs. The pay was good—twice what a schoolteacher would earn. Their jobs felt secure: they did not believe a good bricklayer or plumber could be replaced by a machine. And the work was challenging. Many operated expensive, complex equipment. The boss wasn't looking over their shoulders all day. Tired and dirty at the end of the day, they felt they had done an "honest day's work." And they could see what they had accomplished.

"I tell you . . . I get a hell of a kick when I drive around town and see a building I helped put up. You know that Edgewater Hotel down by the lake? I worked on that sonofabitch fifteen years ago and she's still beautiful. Sometimes I drive down there just to see the damn thing. . . ." (22–23)

These "blue-collar aristocrats," as LeMasters calls them, wouldn't trade their independence for any white-collar job, no matter how much it paid. The tension and responsibility weren't worth it to them. A man the regulars at the bar knew had cracked up after he'd been promoted to supervisor. "He's a helluva good man but I don't think he'll live over five years more. He developed ulcers the first year they promoted him. . . ." (29) Indeed, the blue-collar aristocrats looked down on people who earned a living by "shuffling papers" or "working with their mouths"—phrases they used to describe all white-collar work.

High salaries had not altered their life styles. For example, the blue-collar aristocrats didn't buy a new car every year to impress the neighbors. They shopped around for a used car they could work on, and then kept it for several years. They weren't imbued with the middle-class values that might have strained their incomes—for example, the idea that every child must be sent to college. They put their money into their homes and into the recreations they'd always enjoyed, chiefly hunting and fishing. In short, they didn't want or expect to climb the social ladder as individuals. But they did hope collective bargaining would improve their lot *as members of the working class.*

LeMasters found that the wives of these men saw things rather differently. Over half of these women worked as cashiers, bookkeepers, clerks, and the like. They were exposed to middle-class values on the job and through the media. Most wanted all of their children (daughters and sons) to go to college. And these women had accepted the middle-class ideal of egalitarian marriage. Whereas the blue-collar aristocrats believed men and women have different needs and interests, and preferred the company of other men, their wives sought "togetherness." They wanted their husbands to be companions as well as providers—something the men couldn't understand.

SOURCE: E. E. LeMasters, *Blue-Collar Aristocrats,* Madison: University of Wisconsin Press, 1975.

same standard of living). Open systems provide everyone with the opportunity to succeed or fail.

A closed or *caste system* (also an ideal type) is the opposite: status is determined at birth; people are locked into their parents' social position, and their opportunities are limited accordingly. In caste systems, ascribed characteristics outweigh achievements. Caste lines are clearly defined, and legal and religious sanctions are applied to those who attempt to cross them. The South African apartheid system (which is euphe-

South Africa is governed by apartheid, a policy that divides the nation into a rigid caste system where status is ascribed at birth. Blacks, those of mixed race, Asians, and whites live in separate areas, attend separate schools, and obey separate laws. Thomas D. W. Friedmann / Photo Researchers

mistically described as "separate development") exemplifies a rigid caste system. In South Africa, blacks, Asians, and whites live in separate neighborhoods, attend separate schools, obey separate laws, endure different punishments. It was in South Africa that Mahatma Gandhi began his crusade against caste systems, first attacking discrimination against overseas Indians and later trying to change his own people's attitudes concerning the untouchables (who once constituted India's lowest caste) as well as British colonialism. Today, the caste system is illegal in India, but the struggle against apartheid in South Africa continues.

Most societies, including the United States, fall between the two extremes of open and closed stratification systems. Forty or fifty years ago, the social structure of the South was more castelike than it is today. Jim Crow laws prevented blacks from crossing racial lines, and many preachers taught

that black skin was a curse. Today the law explicitly forbids racial discrimination, and there are signs that the Civil Rights Act of 1964 has worked to some extent. Surveying recent data, Richard Freeman (1976) concludes that black women and young black college graduates are earning as much as their white counterparts today, whereas twenty years ago they earned substantially less (perhaps 30–40 percent less) than whites with equivalent education.

Horatio Alger: Myth or Reality? The stories of Horatio Alger exemplify the American dream: a poor immigrant boy works hard, has some luck, and becomes rich. How much truth is there to this tale?

The history of mobility in America has been generally upward. Our labor market has grown dramatically since the turn of the century, with the total number of jobs more than doubling and the number of white-collar jobs skyrocketing. Much of the cause is industrialization. Mechanization at first eliminates many jobs, but in the long run it opens up whole new fields of employment (mechanics are needed to fix the machines, for example). These new jobs require specialized skills, and the demand for educated workers increases. Employers who need highly trained personnel can't afford to hire brothers and cousins first. As a result, the job market becomes more and more open—that is, more people are hired for *what* they know, not *who* they know.

Technology also contributes to geographic mobility: it becomes easier for people to move to areas where jobs are plentiful. An influx of unskilled and semiskilled laborers, such as occurred here during the late nineteenth and early twentieth centuries, frees experienced workers to move up the occupational ladder. (A man who once did all the work in his shop can hire assistants, use his own time to expand operations, become a

white-collar worker, and so on.) The fact that white-collar workers tend to have fewer children than workers in other categories further stimulates upward mobility. Quite simply, white-collar workers don't produce enough children to refill their ranks, which gives individuals from other groups a chance to move up.[6] Thus, changes in the birth rate, improved technology, the demand for more education, and migration have acted to expand and change the U.S. labor market.

But even though our trend in mobility is generally upward, the extent to which a given person rises in status is usually limited. Individual mobility is measured by comparing fathers' jobs with sons' (intergenerational mobility). Using this measure, Peter M. Blau and Otis Dudley Duncan (1967) conclude that Americans as a whole are upwardly mobile, but that most individuals move only a step or two up the ladder. Inheritance plays an important role in determining occupational status. As noted earlier, about 40 percent of the professionals in this country are sons and daughters of professionals. This is nearly five times as many as would be expected in a perfectly open society. (If a society was perfectly open, there would be no correlation between the occupation of a father and that of his sons or daughters, or between ascribed characteristics and status. [See Tumin, 1973: 127.])

Even though ours is not a perfectly open society, Americans have always believed that the opportunities for advancement are greater here than in any other nation. Is this true? Seymour Lipset and Reinhard Bendix (1959) think not. Comparing the number of people who move across the line between manual and nonmanual jobs, they found rel-

---

6   Changes in the death rate may have a similar effect. One reason why women in the U.S.S.R. have achieved more high-level positions than women have elsewhere is that so many Soviet men were killed in World War II.

atively little difference between the mobility rates for the United States, Europe, Scandinavia, and Japan—despite the fact that some cultures encourage mobility and others discourage it. The mobility rate in this country is about 34 percent, compared with 32 percent in Sweden; 31 percent in Great Britain; 29 percent in France; and 25 percent in both West Germany and Japan (Lenski, 1966: 41). Lipset and Bendix conclude that industrialization creates high social mobility rates in a culture, and that there is nothing special or distinctive about America.

S. M. Miller and others have questioned both Lipset and Bendix's data and their interpretation of this material. Is the fact that sons of blue-collar workers become clerks really evidence of great opportunities? Miller argues that statistics concerning the number of working-class people who rise to the elite are more significant.[7] About 10 percent of working-class people obtain elite status in this country, compared to 7 percent in Japan, less than 4 percent in France and Sweden, and 1.5 percent in West Germany (Fox and Miller, 1965; Blau and Duncan, 1967: 432–435). By this measure, the United States is considerably more open than other industrialized nations.

Reducing Inequality

The available data on social mobility suggest that most Americans can look back on and forward to slow but more or less steady improvement in their standard of living and occupational status, but with no less inequality than before. What can be done to reduce this inequality?

---

[7] By *elite* Miller means "professional, technical and kindred workers," such as lawyers, engineers, and other highly trained workers.

Education For years Americans have believed that the principal way to break the cycle of poverty was to close the education gap. During the 1960s, the government spent massive amounts on preschool programs and job training, the courts began to attack de facto school segregation, and a number of colleges instituted open enrollment of all high school graduates. College graduates do earn about $6,000 more a year than high school graduates. However, if we go back one generation, we find that parents' education, occupation, and income have a decisive impact on the amount of education their children obtain. Thus, education may merely reflect family background and *its* impact on economic success.

In a 1967 study Blau and Duncan found that a son does not inherit his occupational status directly. Rather, his father's occupation influences his level of education, and this in turn influences his occupation. Thus, a young person whose parents work in low-income, low-prestige jobs is the least likely to pursue the education that might enable him or her to escape poverty.

Another factor severely limiting the importance of education is the simple fact that as more and more people receive a college degree, it becomes less and less valuable. A B.A. today doesn't guarantee a high-paying job. Nor does it even ensure a job in the specific field one has prepared for. (We will return to the subject of education in chapter 14.)

Income Redistribution If Americans are serious about reducing inequality, Christopher Jencks (1972) argues that they won't focus on schools or even on individual mobility but on reducing overall inequality through income redistribution. This could be done by closing tax loopholes, providing an income floor below which no one will fall, and keeping the rich from passing on their wealth.

America already makes a modest effort with programs that redistribute some money to the poor. The federal government is spending almost $170 billion a year in cash transfers to rich and poor alike (U.S. Department of Commerce, 1978). Where does this money go?

Social Security accounted for $85 billion in 1977. Payments are based on the amount of money a person earned before he or she retired (with the poor receiving proportionately more than more affluent people). In 1977 the average monthly payment to a retired worker was $241 (U.S. Dept. of HEW, January 1977). Recipients are allowed to earn up to $65 a month without losing benefits; thereafter, the government deducts $1 for every $2 they earn.

Cash transfers also go to the blind and disabled, to retired veterans, government employees, and railroad workers, and to the unemployed (6.9 million in May 1976), who may receive income benefits for a maximum of twenty-six weeks (or thirty-nine weeks if the national unemployment rate is above 4.5 percent for three consecutive months).

The most controversial income benefit program is welfare, a popular term which may denote any of a number of federal programs for assisting poor people, but which

figure 10:2   Attitudes toward welfare[1]

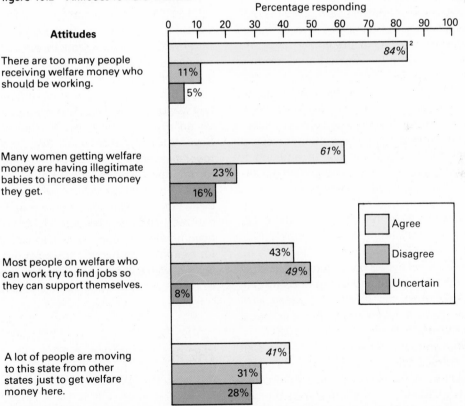

Percentage responding

Attitudes

There are too many people receiving welfare money who should be working.
84%[2]
11%
5%

Many women getting welfare money are having illegitimate babies to increase the money they get.
61%
23%
16%

Agree
Disagree
Uncertain

Most people on welfare who can work try to find jobs so they can support themselves.
43%
49%
8%

A lot of people are moving to this state from other states just to get welfare money here.
41%
31%
28%

[1]Data are taken from a 1969 nationwide survey of a cross-section of Americans, and represent the rank-and-file view.
[2]Italicized percentages reflect the traditional stereotyped position.

SOURCE: Adapted from Joe Feagin, *Subordinating the Poor* (Englewood Cliffs, N.J.: Prentice-Hall, 1975), p. 103.

usually refers to Aid to Families with Dependent Children (AFDC). In 1976, AFDC cost the government $5.7 billion. The general feeling is that those receiving such benefits are getting a free ride and are simply too lazy to work. But most welfare recipients are elderly or disabled or women with dependent children to care for, who can't work. The typical AFDC family is a mother with at least two children; only 13 percent of families receiving AFDC payments have fathers, and 68 percent of these fathers are disabled, while 32 percent are unemployed (*AFDC*, 1976). Contrary to popular myth, the majority of families receiving welfare are white, and most stay on the welfare rolls for less than two years.

Thus, cash transfers are administered through a hodgepodge of uncoordinated programs developed piecemeal over the years. There is no provision for the working poor—that is, for adults who work part or full time but who don't earn enough to support their families. In effect, the law discourages many from seeking employment. For example, in many states a single mother loses all benefits if she takes a job. In addition to these problems, welfare payments vary tremendously from state to state. Monthly benefits per person range from $14 in Mississippi to $97 in Massachusetts (U.S. Department of Health, Education, and Welfare, *Public Assistance Statistics*, 1977). In 1970, the number of people on welfare in New York exceeded the entire population of Baltimore. Even so, there are perhaps as many as 4 million poor families who receive no assistance whatsoever.

What can be done to "clean up the welfare mess"? The central problem now is to provide poor families with an income that would guarantee a minimum standard of living without destroying the incentive to work. Under the current system, families lose all financial assistance (and sometimes public housing, Medicaid, and the like as well) if the parents go to work. President Carter has proposed subsidizing the working poor (for example, with grants for housing), providing jobs and requiring welfare recipients who can work to take them, and implementing new procedures for identifying fraud.

Some would go a step further and provide a negative income tax. Each family would be guaranteed a minimum amount—say, $1,600 a year—by the federal government (plus whatever allotment states chose to provide). For every $2 earned, the guarantee would be reduced by $1. Thus, a family that earned $1,000 would lose $500 in federal payments, but its total income would be $2,100 ($1,600 − $500 + $1,000 = $2,100). The chief advantages of a negative tax are that it provides work incentive; it sets national standards; it would be less cumbersome and expensive to administer than existing programs; and it would eliminate the humiliations of welfare. This has been tried, on an experimental basis, in New Jersey. Seven hundred and twenty-five families in four cities received subsidies under negative income tax programs for a period of three years. The results, which are now being evaluated, are complex and not readily summarized. What has become obvious is that government intervention in just one area—for example, income and tax incentives—affects a whole range of problems, such as work patterns, housing, and education, in complex and interrelated ways.

THE PERSISTENCE OF INEQUALITY

All that we have said leads to the conclusion that America is a highly stratified society.

IN THE NEWS

Growth and Greater Equality Meet in Taiwan

TAIPEI, Taiwan—When Amy Hsu finished junior high school five years ago, near where her father has a small rice field, she went to work in one of the many electronics factories that have sprung up in Taiwan taking advantage of the island's cheap labor. She lived frugally in the factory dormitory, finishing high school in night classes.

Now, with the money she saved from her wages of about $150 a month, she has helped her parents buy a mechanical plow, harvester and rice thrasher for their two acres of land, and a color television set, electric refrigerator, gas stove and even a clothes dryer for their modest brick house. The next goal is to send her four younger brothers and sisters to college.

Amy Hsu's story is illustrative of the fact that, during the past two decades, the people of Taiwan have effectively been closing the gap between rich and poor, while their country has been growing economically. Most economists have found economic growth and social equality to be mutually exclusive. But during the 1950s, several government policies were implemented in Taiwan that have fostered the now-prosperous way of life. Among these were the institution of a free public education system, enabling many to attend universities; a land-reform program; and government control of such major industries as tobacco, oil, and liquor. The results are startling:

...In 1953, the bottom two-fifths of Taiwan's population received only 11 percent of the island's national income, while the top one-fifth got 61 percent. But by 1975, the share of the bottom two-fifths had risen to 22 percent, while the top one-fifth's share was reduced to 39 percent.

By contrast, in Brazil and Mexico, which have similar growth rates, the bottom two-fifths of the population earn 10 percent of income and the top one-fifth controls more than 60 percent. A similar gap exists in the Philippines.

Although these results are encouraging, the system is far from ideal, and there is still a big gap between the wealthy businessman who drives imported cars and the back-street vendor who sells his wares on foot. Yet there is more of a chance for the twain to meet here than in most other countries.

SOURCE: Fox Butterfield, "Taiwan Bridges the Income Gap While Maintaining High Growth," *The New York Times,* April 12, 1977, pp. 25, 26.

Drawing by Mary Petty; © 1953 The New Yorker Magazine, Inc.

The possibilities for social mobility have been exaggerated, and unlimited opportunity is a myth. The poorest fifth of Americans receive only 5.4 percent of the nation's annual income and own less than half of 1 percent of the nation's wealth, while the richest fifth receive 41.1 percent of the nation's annual income and control 77 percent of the wealth. Inequality is an undeniable fact.

There have been changes during the last fifty years, however. The New Deal (and subsequent programs) established a "floor" for poverty, beneath which one cannot sink. The government has set up as ideals full employment, social security, and the setting of minimum standards for income, housing, health care, and education. This represents a commitment to intervene in the corporate market on behalf of individuals and to cushion the impact of crises brought on by fluctuations in the world economy. As a result, the poor are not as poor as they once were, and everyone today receives at least some education. (Indeed, most Americans complete three years more schooling than their fathers did [Hauser and Featherman, 1976].)

Still, the gap between the rich and the poor is wide. Being poor in a country where most people are poor is one thing; being poor in an affluent society is quite another. *Relative deprivation* (having less than most people, less than one might reasonably hope for) may be worse than *absolute deprivation* (having as little as everyone else, and little hope for betterment). In addition to being deprived, the poor in America are also burdened with the knowledge that they are on the bottom.

The evidence suggests that inequality will persist. Attempts to wipe out stratification, to create a "classless society," have been only partially successful. In the U.S.S.R., for example, the director of a research institute earns 600 rubles a month; a typist, only 60 rubles (Yanowitch, 1969: 151). The elites in socialist countries live in better housing, eat better food, spend more on books and entertainment and travel, and make greater use of social services than average citizens do (Lane, 1971).

But although we can't hope to eliminate inequality, we can work to reduce the degree of inequality in American society by eliminating both excess privilege and abject poverty. Perhaps the first step is to recognize that the *system* (not the individual poor person) is responsible for most of the poverty that exists today.

SUMMARY

This chapter examines *stratification*: the way societies distribute desirable resources and rank their members. Property and wealth are only one dimension of stratification. As Weber pointed out, *class* (economic rank), *status group* (patterns of prestige), and *party* (degree of power) don't always overlap.

The first part of this chapter focuses on these three dimensions of stratification—income and wealth, power, and prestige. The distribution of income is unequal in this country: the poorest 20 percent of Americans earn only 5.4 percent of all income, while the wealthiest 5 percent account for 15.6 percent. Wealth is even more concentrated than income; 1 to 2 percent of the population dominates the ownership of corporate stock. The federal income tax is supposed to be *progressive* (increase with level of income) and thus to reduce inequality. In reality, tax laws favor the affluent; and many taxes are *regressive*, taking a greater proportion of poor people's income than of rich people's. Federal antipoverty programs have been unable to close the gap between poor and affluent Americans.

Power—the ability to mobilize collective energies, commitments, and efforts by means of *authority* (the legitimate prerogatives of office) and/or *influence* (informal, unofficial power)—is also distributed unequally in America. Mills argued that power is concentrated in the hands of a small, cohesive elite; Riesman contended that it is dispersed among many competing elites. But both agree that the majority of Americans are relatively powerless.

Prestige is a function of how people earn their money and how they spend it; who they are and what they know; and how successful, well known, and respected they are. The best measure we have of prestige is the Hatt-North occupational scale, which has shown that Americans award prestige unequally, are conscious of prestige differences, and agree about what jobs are and are not prestigious.

Social classes in America are difficult to identify due to the multidimensional nature of stratification, the lack of consistent definitions for these dimensions, and inconsistency between how people classify themselves and how they are classified by others. One reason for the confusion about social stratification in America is that the American ideal of equal opportunity inhibits class consciousness. However, the extent to which Americans endorse this ideal is itself an indication of class status. The rich are consistently more likely to believe in the existence of equal opportunity than are the poor.

Functionalists argue that societies have to entice people into jobs that are essential and difficult by rewarding them unequally. According to conflict theory, which derives from the work of Karl Marx, the poor are poor because the rich exercise a monopoly over society's resources and systematically deny opportunities to the poor. Lenski unites functionalism and conflict theory by asserting that while human action is motivated by self-interest, the achievement of personal and group ends requires cooperation.

Social stratification affects many Americans in an elemental way. The poor have limited access to medical, psychiatric, and legal care. Although they spend a greater proportion of their income on food than do most Americans, the poor suffer from inadequate diets. They spend a disproportionate amount of their income on rent, yet live in substandard buildings. Their crimes are more likely to be detected than are the crimes of the affluent, and they are more likely to be the victims of crime.

Is American society an open class system, one in which there are few barriers to social mobility, or a closed or caste society, where status is determined at birth? Most sociologists locate American society somewhere between these two extremes. The American dream of Horatio Alger, the poor boy who becomes rich, is a myth; studies show that although Americans as a whole are upwardly mobile, most move up only a step or two. Birth plays an important role in determining occupational status. However, some studies show that more people move from blue-collar to white-collar jobs in the United States than in other countries.

What can be done to reduce inequality? For some time we have assumed education was the key, but Blau and Duncan show that the relationship between education and income is complex. Jencks argues that we can't expect education to work miracles but must redistribute income to the poor. In the United States such redistribution programs, developed piecemeal over the years, have proved ineffective and tend to discriminate against the working poor. New programs are being designed in the hope of changing this. Still, the question remains as to whether it is possible to eliminate inequality. Perhaps not, but one step toward eliminating excess privilege and abject poverty is recognizing that the system, not the poor person, is responsible for poverty.

GLOSSARY

absolute deprivation having as little as everyone else, and little hope for betterment.

authority formal power; the prerogatives that legitimately go with an office or position.

bourgeoisie a term Marx used to denote the owners of the means of production.

caste system a class system in which status is determined at birth, and people are locked into their parents' social position.

class a term Weber used to refer to people who occupy the same rung on the economic ladder.

horizontal mobility a change in position that does not appreciably alter a person's socioeconomic status.

influence informal power based on know-how and know-who.

objective class Marx's term for class status as determined by one's relation to the means of production.

open class system a class system in which there are inequalities but few impediments to social mobility; positions are awarded on the basis of merit, and rank is tied to individual achievement.

party Weber's term for people who share interests and seek to further them by gaining access to power.

power the ability to mobilize collective energies, commitments, and efforts or to set policies for others to follow.

power elite Mills's term for a concentrated group occupying the command posts of society and determining its direction.

prestige status resulting from the possession of attributes that are regarded as admirable, and perhaps enviable, by people in a specific social setting.

progressive tax a tax that takes a larger share of a rich person's income than of a poor person's; the opposite of a regressive tax.

proletariat Marx's term for the people who must sell their skills to the owners of the means of production.

regressive tax a tax that takes a larger share of a poor person's income than of a rich person's; the opposite of a progressive tax.

relative deprivation having less than most people and less than one might reasonably hope for.

social mobility the movement of people from one social position to another.

status group Weber's term for people whose life style or patterns of consumption give them a distinct social identity.

stratification the division of a society into layers of people who have relatively more or less of any given scarce reward or resource.

subjective class Marx's term for class status as determined by one's class consciousness.

transfer payments welfare, Medicaid, workmen's compensation, and other government subsidies that are not drawn from a person's salary, as Social Security is.

vertical mobility upward or downward changes in a person's status.

REFERENCES

AFDC (Aid to Families with Dependent Children), *1975, Recipient Characteristics Study, Part One: Demographic and Program Statistics*, Office of Research and Statistics Pubn. no. (SSA) 77-11777. Washington, D.C. U.S. Government Printing Office, 1976.

Charles H. Anderson, *The Political Economy of Social Class*. Englewood Cliffs, N.J.: Prentice-Hall, 1974.

Peter M. Blau and Otis Dudley Duncan, *The American Occupational Structure*. New York: Wiley, 1967.

David Caplovitz, *The Poor Pay More: Consumer Practices of Low-Income Families*. New York: Free Press, 1963.

John Cratsley, "The Crime of the Courts," in Bruce Wasserstein and Mark J. Green, eds., *With Justice for Some*. Boston: Beacon Press, 1972.

Robert Dahl, *Modern Political Analysis*. Englewood Cliffs, N.J.: Prentice-Hall, 1963.

Kingsley Davis and Wilbert E. Moore, "Some Principles of Stratification." *American Sociological Review*, vol. 10 (April 1945): 242–249.

_____, Replies to Tumin, *American Sociological Review*, vol. 18 (1953): 394–396.

G. William Domhoff, *Who Rules America?* Englewood Cliffs, N.J.: Prentice-Hall, 1967.

Thomas Fox and S. M. Miller, "Intra-country Variations: Occupational Stratification and Mobility." *Studies in Comparative International Development*, vol. 1 (1965): 3–10.

Richard B. Freeman, *The Over-Educated American*. New York: Academic Press, 1976.

Edward Fried et al., *Setting National Priorities*. Washington, D.C.: Brookings Institution, 1973.

H. H. Gerth and C. Wright Mills, eds., *From Max Weber: Essays in Sociology*. New York: Oxford University Press, 1946.

Paul K. Hatt and Cecil C. North, "Jobs and Occupations: A Popular Evaluation." *Opinion News*, vol. 9 (September 1947): 1–13.

Robert M. Hauser and David L. Featherman, "Equality of Schooling: Trends and Prospects." *Sociology of Education*, vol. 49 (April 1976): 99–120.

Robert W. Hodge, Paul M. Siegel, and Peter H. Rossi, "Occupational Prestige in the United States: 1925–1963," in Reinhard Bendix and Seymour Martin Lipset, eds., *Class, Status, and Power*, 2nd ed. New York: Free Press, 1966.

Robert W. Hodge, Donald J. Treiman, and Peter H. Rossi, "A Comparative Study of Occupational Prestige," in Reinhard Bendix and Seymour Martin Lipset, eds., *Class, Status, and Power*, 2nd ed. New York: Free Press, 1966.

Christopher Jencks et al., *Inequality: A Reassessment of the Effect of Family and Schooling in America*. New York: Basic Books, 1972.

David Kotelchuk, *Prognosis Negative: Crisis in the Health Care System*. New York: Vintage, 1976.

David Lane, *The End of Inequality*. Middlesex, Eng.: Penguin Books, 1971.

Gerhard Lenski, *Power and Privilege: A Theory of Social Stratification*. New York: McGraw-Hill, 1966.

Seymour Martin Lipset and Reinhard Bendix, *Social Mobility in Industrial Society*. Berkeley: University of California Press, 1959.

Kurt Mayer, *Class and Society*. New York: Random House, 1955.

C. Wright Mills, *The Power Elite*. New York: Oxford University Press, 1956.

Michael Parenti, *Democracy for the Few*, 2nd ed. New York: St. Martin's, 1977.

Bob Reiss, "The Fifth Annual Salary Roundup: Who Gets the Most Money in Town?" *New York Magazine*, May 17, 1976, pp. 41-45.

David Riesman, *The Lonely Crowd*. New York: Doubleday, 1953.

Joan Huber Rytina, William H. Form, and John Pease, "Income and Stratification Ideology: Beliefs About the American Opportunity Structure." *American Journal of Sociology*, vol. 75 (January 1970): 703–716.

Philip M. Stern, "How 381 Super-rich Americans Managed Not to Pay a Cent in Taxes Last Year," in Jerome H. Skolnick and Elliott Currie, eds., *Crisis in American Institutions*. Boston: Little, Brown, 1970.

Donald J. Treiman, *Occupational Prestige in Comparative Perspective*. New York: Academic Press, 1977.

Melvin M. Tumin, "Some Principles of Stratification: A Critical Analysis." *American Sociological Review*, vol. 18 (August 1953): 387–393.

————, *Patterns of Society*. Boston: Little, Brown, 1973.

U.S. Bureau of the Census, *Current Population Reports*, Series P-60, no. 107, "Money Income and Poverty Status of Families and Persons in the United States: 1976 (Advance Report)." Washington, D.C.: U.S. Government Printing Office, 1977.

————, *Statistical Abstract of the United States, 1976*. Washington, D.C.: U.S. Government Printing Office, 1976.

U.S. Department of Commerce, Bureau of Economic Analysis, *Survey of Current Business*. Washington, D.C.: U.S. Government Printing Office, 1978.

U.S. Department of Health, Education, and Welfare, *Public Assistance Statistics, January 1977* (April 1977).

————, *Social Security Bulletin*, vol. 40, no. 1 (January 1977).

————, *Social Security Bulletin*, vol. 40, no. 12 (December 1977).

W. Lloyd Warner and Paul S. Lunt, *The Social Life of a Modern Community*. New Haven, Conn.: Yale University Press, 1941.

————, Marchia Meeker, and Kenneth Eels, *Social Class in America*. Chicago: Science Research, 1949.

Dennis H. Wrong, "How Important Is Social Class?" in Irving Howe, ed., *The World of the Blue-Collar Worker*. New York: Quadrangle, 1972.

Murray Yanowitch, "The Soviet Income Revolution." *Slavic Review*, vol. 32 (December 1963): 683–697. Also in Celia S. Heller, ed., *Structured Social Inequality*. New York: Macmillan, 1969.

FOR FURTHER STUDY

Welfare. Although we usually think of welfare as direct income subsidies for the poor, a variety of social programs, including education and job training, legal aid, and health care, have been developed with the stated goal of improving the welfare of poor people. Yet inequality and impaired life chances continue to prevail in the daily lives of the poor. This has led some social scientists both to question our ability to eliminate poverty and to analyze poverty's functions in our society. In *More Equality* (New York: Pantheon, 1973), Herbert Gans discusses the possible functions of poor people. John Lombardi and Carol Stack found evidence of these functions in their field work with poor people, who use the leftovers of our society's housing, food, and clothing; these authors elaborate on their findings in their article ''Economically Cooperating Units in an Urban Black Community,'' which appears in *Anthropology and the Public Interest,* edited by Peggy Reeves Sanday (New York: Academic Press, 1976). The problems of the war on poverty in official attempts to end poverty and provide a wide range of services to the poor are discussed by Peter Marris and Martin Rein in *The Dilemmas of Social Reform,* rev. ed. (New York: Atherton, 1972), and in *A Decade of Federal Antipoverty Programs: Achievements, Failures, and Lessons,* Robert H. Haveman, ed. (New York: Academic Press, 1977). In *Regulating the Poor* (New York: Pantheon, 1971), Frances Piven and Richard Cloward argue that welfare programs are used to ensure that poor people continue to carry out their functions: benefits are shrunk when low-wage labor is needed and then expanded in times of social unrest.

Mobility. A great American preoccupation is social mobility, particularly upward mobility. An investigation of the basis for this preoccupation may be found in Richard Weiss's *The American Myth of Success: From Horatio Alger to Norman Vincent Peale* (New York: Basic Books, 1969). Two sociological classics that focus on several facets of mobility are *Middletown* by Robert S. Lynd and Helen Lynd (New York: Harcourt Brace, 1937) and *Caste and Class in a Southern Town* by John Dollard (New York: Doubleday, 1957). A recent study of occupational mobility among American males that replicates the major work by Blau and Duncan (see References) and finds similar trends still prevailing is *Schooling and Achievement in American Society,* Robert M. Hauser and David L. Featherman, eds. (New York: Academic Press, 1976). A twenty-year mobility study by William H. Sewell et al., entitled *School Achievement* (New York: Academic Press, 1976), traces longitudinally the changes in one-third of the people who graduated from a Wisconsin high school in 1957.

Egalitarian Systems. Of course, the degree of mobility in a society depends on the degree of stratification; in a truly egalitarian system, mobility would no longer be a topic for study. An excellent book that explores how less rigid and less steep class-differences would affect American society is *Socialism* by Michael Harrington (New York: Bantam, 1973). This might be compared to one of the following descriptions of social relations in socialist countries: Donald Lane, *The End of Inequality? Stratification Under State Socialism* (Middlesex, Eng.: Penguin Books, 1971); Frank Parkin, *Class Inequality and Political Order: Social Stratification in Capitalist and Communist Societies* (New York: Praeger, 1971). The impact of egalitarian relations on socialization is closely studied by Melford E. Spiro in *Children of the Kibbutz* (New York: Schocken, 1965).

CHAPTER 11

Racial and Ethnic Minorities

"In pre-war Poland under the Czarist regime the Poles were a distinct ethnic minority. When they gained their independence at the end of the first World War, they lost their minority status but reduced their Jewish fellow Poles to the status of a minority. As immigrants to the United States the Poles again became themselves a minority" (Wirth, 1945: 347). The term "minority" is something of a misnomer, for often the so-called minority group actually outnumbers the majority. In South Africa, for example, nonwhites constitute 80 percent of the population, yet as a group they are treated as a minority by whites, who have the power of a majority. Louis Wirth defined a *minority* as "a group of people who, because of their physical or cultural characteristics, are singled out from the others in the society in which they live for differential and unequal treatment and who therefore regard themselves as objects of collective discrimination. The existence of a minority in a society implies the existence of a corresponding dominant group with higher social status and greater privileges. Minority status carries with it the exclusion from full participation in the life of the society" (1945: 351). In many societies, including our own, this definition applies to children (who have virtually no legal rights), the aged, and women (who make up 51 percent of the American population, but occupy few positions of power). Most societies also contain religious, ethnic, or racial minorities. All of these groups are "singled out . . . for differential and unequal treatment."

In this chapter we focus on racial and ethnic minorities in America. Many Americans feel uncomfortable talking about such differences because of the ideal of the "melting pot." Therefore, we begin with brief portraits of America's minorities, which include a description of each group's cultural orientation and relations with society as a whole. In the second part of the chapter we explore the roots of prejudice and discrimination and discuss the meaning of race. The third part of the chapter describes different patterns of discrimination and the way people respond to them. Finally, we look at the current state of race relations, paying special attention to institutionalized obstacles to racial and ethnic equality in the United States.

ETHNIC DIVERSITY IN AMERICA

Saturday being the Jewish Sabbath, Sunday is still the most important business day on Delancey Street in New York City's largely Jewish Lower East Side. Nearby lies Chinatown, with its own language and customs, temples and grocery stores. Little Italy is just across Canal Street, its streets lined with social clubs and funeral parlors, and on saints' days, with booths selling sausage and pastry from old-country recipes (and perhaps buttons reading "Kiss me, I'm Italian"). These are but three of the many ethnic groups that make up America.

An *ethnic group* is a group that is defined or set off by race, religion, or national origin, or some combination of these. This is not to say that race, religion, and national origin are equivalent, for they are not. Race refers to inherited physical characteristics, which have no connection with religion or nationality, both of which are cultural institutions. But these classifications are similar "in that all of them serve to create, through historical circumstances, a sense of peoplehood" (Gordon, 1964: 28); in fact, *ethnic* comes from the Greek word *ethnos,* meaning "people" or "nation." In other words, an ethnic group is a group of people whose ancestry and heritage make a difference—to them, and to the society in which they live—and whose destiny is affected by this very identification. Customs, language, religion, family names, social ties, food, dress, and appearance all play a part in defining ethnic groups.

Why haven't ethnic groups been quickly assimilated into our society? In part because established Americans have usually treated newcomers (and Indians, Mexican-Americans, and blacks) as foreigners and avoided them; in part because the groups themselves have an emotional investment in their ethnic communities and identities and have resisted assimilation. Portraits of the largest ethnic communities in this country follow,[1] and demonstrate how ethnic groups in varying degrees form the kinds of minorities Wirth talked about in the introduction to this chapter. Ethnic groups are held in lower esteem, are often spatially segregated, from the rest of the society and tend to suffer from more than the ordinary amount of social and economic insecurity.

Black Americans

The 25 million Americans who trace their ancestry back to Africa through 300 years of poverty, exploitation, and violence are this country's largest racial minority. As late as World War II, 80 percent of black Americans lived in the South, where they functioned in large part as farm workers. Today, 39 percent live in the North and 75 percent in metropolitan areas (U.S. Bureau of the Census, *Statistical Abstract,* 1977). Little is known about the specific origins of black Americans, although one man's recent attempt to discover his ancestry captured the public imagination (see the box). We do know that, in 1619, the first African immigrants settled in Virginia as indentured servants, and that by the end of the seventeenth century nearly all blacks and their descendants had been relegated to perpetual servitude under the law.

Slavery was abolished in 1865, but white terrorism and discrimination were not. *Jim*

---

[1] We use the term *community* advisedly. Not all Americans of black or Jewish or Indian heritage identify with their ethnic communities or consider their origins significant, but it is difficult to voluntarily "resign" from an ethnic group. So how one identifies oneself is closely related to how one is identified by the larger society.

Chinese, Mexicans, and blacks are just a few of the many ethnic and racial groups that add diversity to America's population. (Top Left, Alan L. Price. Top Right, Hella Hammid. Bottom, Hella Hammid)

Crow laws, which barred blacks from public facilities, and periodic lynchings kept blacks "in their place." That "place" meant continued economic exploitation and political exclusion.

Just before and during World War I, blacks began leaving the South in increasing numbers—some as soldiers in all-black regiments, others in search of work at factories in Chicago, Detroit, and other big cities. Harlem, Roxbury, and Chicago's South Side became cities within cities. Many of their resi-

ROOTS: THE IMPORTANCE OF ORIGINS

Roots, black American author Alex Haley's history of his family traced from its African origins, was presented as an eight-part television series in January 1977. The series, based on the book, drew the largest television audience in history. What compelled so many people to turn from their usual TV programs to this saga of survival and suffering? Why did *Roots* inspire a desire in both blacks and whites to search for their own origins?

Haley's book traces his ancestry back as far as 1750 to his great-, great-, great-, great-, great-grandfather, Kunta Kinte. Kunta is captured in Africa at the age of seventeen and sold into slavery in the United States. Both reader and viewer share Kunta's struggle against the restraints and cruelties of his captivity. He attempts to escape four times and is punished by having his foot cut off: "Kunta was screaming and thrashing as the ax flashed up, then down so fast— severing skin, tendons, muscles, bone—that Kunta heard the ax thud into the trunk as the shock of it sent the agony deep into his brain. . ." (244). Also painful to Kunta is the emotional torture of slavery: "These black ones seemed to have no concern in their lives beyond pleasing the toubob [white man] with his lashing whip. . . . Kunta couldn't fathom what had happened to so destroy their minds that they acted like goats and monkeys. Perhaps it was because they had been born in this place rather than Africa. . . . Kunta vowed never to become *like* them, and each night his mind would go exploring again into ways to escape from this despised land" (220).

Before he is captured, Kunta is shown traveling through the African forest with his father, training for adulthood, learning the traditions and history of his land. In this way *Roots* erased the long-held misconception that Africa is a wild, primitive continent whose people are without pride or dignity. Whites, too, are

dents were as poor as they had been in the South. But in the North, blacks fought back when they were attacked. The urban riots in the early part of this century were interracial.

A decisive battle against segregation began in the South during the 1960s with boycotts and nonviolent demonstrations. Blacks marched, picketed, and sat in at "white only" restaurants. Not long after, blacks began to win civil rights victories in the courts and in Congress. At the same time, the black migration north continued, and the ghettos grew. There arose a new generation of leaders, street-wise and uncompromising, who stopped looking to white America for answers.

Urbanization, social and economic mobility, and political awareness have made black Americans a growing force to be reckoned with. They still don't have their fair share of adequate housing, health care, and income, and they continue to be underrepresented in the higher levels of government and business, and in the professions. The ghettos of

shown in a more human light, rather than being simplistically depicted as cruel bigots.

The impetus to *Roots* was Alex Haley's need to discover his genealogy, but his thoughts when he discovered his link to Kunta Kinte show that his quest also had a wider meaning: "I remember the sob surging up from my feet, flinging up my hands before my face and bawling as I had not done since I was a baby. . . . The jet black Africans were jostling, staring. . . . If you really knew how we came in the seeds of our forefathers, captured, driven, beaten, inspected, bought, branded, chained in foul ships, if you really knew, you needed weeping. . ." (8). Haley's search became a vicarious one for many people. Though their individual histories may be lost forever, Haley provided black Americans with a link to ancient and distinguished African traditions.

Roots has been criticized for having many factual errors. Haley admits that this is true and that many incidents in the book are fictional accounts of what he believes took place. Yet a number of historians defend the book. They say that it stands as Haley's view on the meaning of slavery, and cannot be undermined by errors in factual detail. Haley defends himself by saying he intended the book as "a symbolic history of a people." Sometimes idealized, sometimes brutally realistic, *Roots* eased the pain of not knowing the past for black Americans. And being given a sense of their history helps them, as it does any ethnic group, see where they stand in relation to the rest of American society—today, as well as in the past.

SOURCE: Alex Haley, *Roots: The Saga of an American Family*, Garden City, N.Y.: Doubleday, 1976; Alex Haley, "My Furthest-Back-Person—the African," in Jim Watts and Allen F. Davis, eds., *Generations*, 2nd ed., New York: Knopf, 1978; and Robert D. McFadden, "Some Points of 'Roots' Questioned," *The New York Times*, April 10, 1977, pp. 1, 29.

the inner cities haven't disappeared. In fact, the gap between legal and social equality remains wide.

Jews

As the children of immigrants my brothers were aware of the fact that they represented the "undesirables," the "foreigners," as others had been "undesirables" in previous decades. They realized, too, that the only way to rise above undesirability was not merely to become desirable, but to become indispensable. This would require equal amounts of education and sacrifice. They filled every hour not devoted to study with part-time jobs as truant officers, book salesmen, teachers of English to foreigners—wearing out their eyes, their pants and their books, drinking black coffee to stay awake, postponing marriage, sharing clothes, colds, money and dreams. (Sam Levenson, in Freedman and Banks, 1972: 194–197)

Like Sam Levenson, thousands of contemporary American Jews grew up on the streets of New York, under the watchful eyes of parents who believed that by becoming educated, their children would "get ahead." Today, although only 29 percent of all Americans are college-educated, 58 percent of Jews hold college degrees (Gallup Opinion Index, 1978).

The first Jews came to America from Brazil in 1654, but it was not until the 1840s that Jews began arriving in the thousands, fleeing pogroms (periodic massacres of Jews) in Europe. Today there are more Jews in the United States—about 6 million—than in any other country in the world. (The Soviet Union is second, Israel a close third.) Nearly half live in or around New York City.

Urbanites and entrepreneurs throughout much of their past, Jews adapted to America with relative ease. Not that they didn't encounter discrimination—time and again they have been accused of disloyalty, of participation in international conspiracies, of unscrupulous business practices. Traditionally, many corporations, major law firms, banks, and private clubs didn't admit Jews (some still don't), and until World War II many universities maintained strict quota systems. Jews prospered nonetheless—in part by using Old World skills to start businesses (the garment industry, for example), in part by taking advantage of public education, and in part by continuing to some extent to see themselves as the "chosen people," no matter what the circumstances—a doctrine Jews share with Black Muslims. Of course, most Jews aren't wealthy, and many are poor, but as a group, Jews have prospered and are strongly represented in business and the professions: 43 percent of Jews earn $20,000 and over, compared with 21 percent of the total population, and 53 percent are in business and the professions, compared with 25 percent nationally (Gallup Opinion Index, 1978).

Mexican-Americans

The 6.6 million Catholic, Spanish-speaking Americans of Mexican descent constitute the second largest minority in this country. Before New England was colonized, the Spanish had settled in what is now the American Southwest, but not until 1848 did they and their land become part of the United States. Soon after, English-speaking settlers began edging the Hispanics out: if all else failed, they were "sent back" to Mexico. Except in New Mexico, where Hispanics were able to hold their ground, most withdrew to rural towns and mining camps. When they went into areas dominated by English-speaking settlers to work as migrant laborers, they were housed in segregated camps; when they moved into the big cities, they lived apart from other groups. The English speakers called them "greasers" and "spics"; they called the English speakers "Anglos" and "gringos." Many didn't want to send their children to Anglo schools, where they were slapped for speaking Spanish and often renamed (from "Jesús" to "Jesse," for example).

Hostilities between Mexican-Americans and Anglos reached a peak in Los Angeles in 1943, when police and restless sailors stormed the barrio (neighborhood), beating and then arresting some 600 of their victims in what came to be called the "zoot-suit riots." During the fifties, however, an influx of cold-war-related industries brought jobs to the Southwest, and by 1960, nearly half of the Mexican-Americans owned their own homes. (Still, the median income for Mexican-Americans remained about two-thirds that for the nation as a whole.) At about the same time, Mexican-Americans began to exercise their voting power, supporting John F. Kennedy and later George McGovern. César Chavez, a man appropriately compared to Martin Luther King, Jr., succeeded in organizing the grape pickers and other agricultural workers. And a new pride and militancy began to grow among the young: La Raza Unida was born.

Puerto Ricans

The United States acquired Puerto Rico in 1898, and in 1917, all Puerto Ricans were declared American citizens. Mainland companies began to open branches on the island, but were met with violent nationalist resistance. A compromise was reached, granting Puerto Rico aid in modernization and economic development as well as commonwealth status. Most Puerto Ricans didn't benefit from economic expansion, however, and when the airlines introduced low fares after World War II, increasing numbers left the island to seek their fortune in New York. Today there are about 1.8 million Puerto Ricans on the U.S. mainland, most of them in and around New York City.

In city ghettos Puerto Ricans are often forced to endure double discrimination—discrimination due to their language and due to their color (Puerto Ricans come in every shade from black to white, but they are usually labeled nonwhite). What makes the Puerto Rican situation unique is that immigration is a two-way street: the island is close enough for immigrants to return home, and most do, temporarily or permanently. As a result, there is less incentive to learn American ways and English.

In recent years, however, Puerto Ricans have begun to make rapid gains in prosperity. In 1969, median Puerto Rican family income was only half median white family income; by 1973, Puerto Ricans were earning almost two-thirds of what whites earned, despite barriers of language and color. In fact, by 1973, Puerto Rican families were better off than black families (Thurow, 1976: 5). Nonetheless, in 1976, one out of every three Puerto Rican families lived below the poverty line (U.S. Bureau of the Census, *Current Population Reports*, 1976).

American Indians

Indians are the poorest of the poor in America. Their past and present are stories of lies and abuse. The wars against the American Indians reached a peak toward the middle of the nineteenth century, when the eastern United States was becoming crowded and the transcontinental railroad made travel easier. During this period, gold was discovered in the Black Hills of Dakota and on other Indian lands, and adventurers could still make a profit from buffalo hides. Over 500,000 Indians died before the century was over. The 300,000 who survived war, disease, hunger, and bounties ($25 to $100 per scalp in many places) were forced onto inhospitable reservations that were administered by the notoriously corrupt Bureau of Indian Affairs (BIA).

Today about two-thirds of the 790,000 American Indians live on reservations under the trusteeship of the BIA. Despite the existence of the BIA, there are no comprehensive statistics on the economic status of American Indians, but one estimate places their median income at one-third that of whites, making Indians the poorest of American ethnic groups (Thurow, 1976: 6). Many of the

The 1973 occupation of Wounded Knee is one demonstration of the new militancy among American Indians, who are frustrated by the government's attitude toward conditions on the reservations. The Indians are the poorest of America's ethnic minorities, and the reservations are plagued by such problems as substandard housing, inadequate education, and alcoholism. (Camilla Smith/Rainbow)

reservations are more similar to Third World countries than to segments of the richest nation in the world. Only one out of every five adults on the 25,000-square-mile Navajo reservation, for example, has a high school diploma; the median educational level is 5.3 years (compared with 12.1 years nationally). The Navajo nation today numbers 137,000, and over half the adults are either unemployed or work only part-time. The per capita income is $1,000 (compared with $4,000

nationally).[2] Outsiders own 80 percent of the general stores on the reservation. Housing, generally built by outsiders, is substandard. Many Navajo rent one- or two-room houses, 80 percent of which have no running water or plumbing and 60 percent of which have no electricity.

During the early 1970s the rise of ethnic consciousness among blacks and Mexican-Americans began to affect Indians as well. In 1973, the newly organized American Indian Movement (AIM) returned to the scene of the 1890 massacre at Wounded Knee and occupied reservation headquarters. This was not simply theater. Once again the government had reneged on extravagant promises to protect Indian lands and resources; once

---

[2] "The budget of the Pine Ridge reservation, if divided among Indian families, would provide each with an income of $8,040, yet their median income is only $1,910" (Anderson, 1974: 250).

again it had subverted Indian efforts to achieve self-determination and reform the BIA (Collier, 1973).

Indians have also taken to the courts for redress. In 1977, a group of Maine Indians, represented by Archibald Cox, the former Watergate prosecutor and a Harvard law professor, and joined by the U.S. Justice Department, sued the state of Maine, claiming 5 million acres were taken illegally from their ancestors. Title to the whole northern quarter of the state is tied up in this suit. Other tribes are now employing the same tactics to improve their conditions.

Chinese- and Japanese-Americans

The Chinese began immigrating to the West Coast in the middle of the eighteenth century. Laboring on the railroad, washing, and cooking (women were scarce in the Old West), they earned a reputation as hard workers. But when the railroad was finished and unemployment began to rise, Occidental settlers turned on the Chinese. The Chinese Exclusion Act of 1882 halted further immigration, and in most places the Chinese were denied schooling, jobs, and housing. They withdrew to ethnic enclaves in coastal cities, keeping largely to themselves until anti-Chinese feelings started to subside. The border was reopened to the Chinese in the early fifties, and by 1970 there were about 435,000 people of Chinese ancestry in the country, an increase of 83.3 percent since 1960. Enclaves in four major U.S. cities—New York City, Los Angeles, San Francisco, and Boston—have absorbed this increase. The pressures of the influx of population have combined with the pressure of urban renewal on these strategically located Chinatowns, each

of which is located close to the financial heart of the city.

The traditional power structures in these communities are being challenged by assimilated second-generation Chinese-Americans and by younger, more militant immigrants and third-generation Chinese-Americans, who charge that little is being done to improve the substandard housing and education in the Chinese ghettos, or to bring down the high rate of unemployment in these areas. Under these pressures, the social order in the Chinatowns across the United States is crumbling, with crime and other indications of social pathology on the increase.

The Japanese came somewhat later, spreading out on farms all along the West Coast. But anti-Oriental sentiments ran high, and in 1924, all East Asian immigration was halted. Then, in 1942, 110,000 Japanese, including 70,000 who were American citizens, were rounded up and placed in "relocation centers," even though most had become American citizens and supported the Allies. During their internment, Japanese families lost an average of $10,000 each (Simpson and Yinger, 1972: 121). Despite this, the Japanese have prospered in the United States. Like the Jews, they emphasize the value of education and specialize in such middle-level professions as engineering, accounting, and management.

White Ethnics

White ethnics have been called by many names—the "silent majority" (by Richard Nixon), the "little man" (by George Wallace), the "man in the middle" (by sociologist David Riesman). Who are the white ethnics? They are the children, grandchildren, and great-grandchildren of eastern and southern European immigrants. The overwhelming majority of them (70 percent) are blue-collar workers who earn $10,000 to $12,000 a year and who own their own homes in communities such as Boston's Charlestown or Cleveland's West Side. Similar socioeconomic status and the tendency to live "with their own" explain why these ethnic groups often become interest groups (Levine and Herman, 1974).

White ethnics have never felt quite at home in this Protestant, Anglo-Saxon-dominated country. Indeed, the third and fourth generations tend to be more conscious of their ethnicity than their parents and grandparents were. The reason seems to be that they have become disillusioned with the American dream and turned inward (Levine and Herman, 1974).

During the late 1960s, white ethnics acquired a reputation for being archconservatives; the term "hard hat" became synonymous with "racist" and "hawk." But this image has proved to be incorrect. In fact, several surveys conducted during the Vietnam War indicated that white ethnics were more likely to be doves than white Anglo-Saxon Protestants. They are more likely than WASPS to support such liberal causes as a guaranteed annual wage and the fight against pollution. They are more sympathetic toward government efforts to help the poor (45 percent favor aid, as opposed to 19 percent of white Protestants). And a higher percentage of white ethnics than native-born white Protestants are prointegration (Greeley, 1974).

Social scientists know relatively little about white ethnics, in part because the Census bureau did not ask questions about ethnic identity until recently. In his analysis of a composite sample of twelve NORC surveys conducted between 1963 and 1974, which did contain such a question, Andrew Greeley (1976) found that there has been a general integration of many white ethnic groups into the American economy—in fact, Irish, Italian, German, and Polish Catholics have higher family incomes than all groups in American society except for Jews and two Protestant denominations. According to Greeley, the myth of the blue-collar middle-income white ethnic persists because society's elite is not willing to recognize that these groups have indeed "made it" (1976: 76).

table 11:1 **THE FIVE LARGEST ETHNIC GROUPS IN THE UNITED STATES**

ORIGIN	POPULATION (IN MILLIONS)	PERCENT OF TOTAL POPULATION
English, Scottish, or Welsh	26.0	12.6
German	20.5	9.9
Irish	12.2	5.9
Spanish	10.6	5.1
Italian	7.1	3.4

SOURCE: U.S. Bureau of the Census, *Statistical Abstract of the United States, 1976* (Washington, D.C.: U.S. Government Printing Office, 1976), table 41, p. 34.

RACE, PREJUDICE, AND DISCRIMINATION

The presence of varied ethnic and racial groups in the same society creates problems as well as opportunities. Diverse styles, languages, and traditions do enrich a culture, but they may also accentuate in-group/out-group tensions. In Great Britain, tension has developed over the "dark million," immigrants from Pakistan, the West Indies, and other Asian, African, and Caribbean nations who now make up 2 percent of the population of the British Isles. They are subject to treatment that some residents of Harlem or Watts might find familiar. In Uganda, the government confiscated the property of its Indian citizens and expelled all of them, despite the fact that many of these "Indians" had never lived outside of Uganda and were in fact second- or third-generation Africans. In America, of course, race has always served as a dividing line.

What Is Race?

Biologically, a *race* is a population that through generations of inbreeding has developed several distinctive physical characteristics that are transmitted genetically. In principle, it should be relatively simple to divide the human species into distinct categories and to assign each individual to a racial category. In reality, it is not.

Suppose we begin with the three groups most people identify as races—the white or Caucasian race, the yellow or Mongoloid race, and the black or Negroid race. Few of us have any difficulty telling Africans from Asians or Europeans. But where do we put the peoples of southern India, who have black skin but straight hair and Caucasian features? Do we classify the Bushmen of southern Africa, who have yellowish skin and epicanthic folds (which make the eyes appear slanted), as Mongoloid?

In an effort to define racial categories, physical anthropologists have long studied physical differences between groups of people. But studies of physical differences haven't led to clear and distinct definitions of racial categories. William Boyd (1950), for example, attempted to classify people according to blood types. He discovered, among other things, that a high percentage of the people who live in sub-Saharan Africa have the cDe gene. However, the gene is also found in Europeans, in Asians, and even in Navajo Indians. Moreover, blood types don't correlate with outward appearance. The Papuans of New Guinea look very much like Africans; they could easily disappear into the crowds of Nairobi or New York's Harlem. But the "Negroid gene," cDe, is exceedingly rare in New Guinea. In short, it is impossible to say biologically where one race stops and another begins. As Theodosius Dobzhansky points out, there is as much variation *within* one or another of the races as there is between them.

Nevertheless, people perceive and react to racial differences, and this is why sociologists study them—not because skin color, hair texture, or other physical characteristics are intrinsically significant. A sociological definition of *race* is a group of people whom others believe to be genetically distinct, and treat accordingly. For example, at one time in the United States a person with a single black parent (or grandparent) was legally defined as black, and subject to all the disadvantages American blacks suffered. Thus, the term "race" involves more than physical traits; it involves expectations about one's behavior, ability, and moral characteristics, indications of one's legal status, and so on. Pierre Van den Berghe terms this dimension "social race"—when a group is "socially defined but on the basis of physical criteria" (1967: 9).

Racial Myths

Numerous myths about racial and ethnic differences circulate in American society—for example, the notion that blacks have natural rhythm, or the belief that Jews have a talent for finance. And while there is no biological basis for these stereotypes, there are social explanations for them. People cultivate the talents they have the opportunities to use. Slaves were generally given only menial jobs to perform, but they *were* allowed to make music. Jews became traders and money-lenders because for centuries they weren't allowed to own land anywhere in the world.

Still, people who happen to note certain differences in achievement by race often conclude that the biology of race is responsible. As a result, there is a long list of works affirming or denying racial predisposition to cultural achievements, athletic ability, and intelligence. What truth is there to such claims?

Race and IQ In 1969, Arthur Jensen, an educational psychologist at the University of California at Berkeley, published an article on race, heredity, and intelligence in the *Harvard Educational Review*. The average score for black Americans on IQ tests, he reported, is ten to fifteen points lower than the average score for whites. Reviewing the literature on this subject, Jensen concluded that "it [is] a not unreasonable hypothesis that genetic factors are strongly implicated in the average Negro-white intelligence difference" (1969: 82).

Few researchers dispute the fact that there is a ten-to-fifteen-point difference between the average IQ for whites and that for blacks. The controversy centers rather on the *interpretation* of this finding, and few scientists agree with Jensen. Melvin Tumin (1973: 164–167), for one, attacks Jensen's conclusions on four grounds. First, he argues that racial comparisons would be meaningful only if we were able to assign each and every individual a clear racial identity, but we can't do this. Approximately 70 percent of black Americans have some white ancestry (and 20 percent of whites have some black ancestry [Hunt and Walker, 1974: 12]). How can we assume that "black genes" are creating an IQ difference? Second, the idea that IQ differences reflect *biological* differences is based on the assumption that IQ tests measure innate intelligence. This is not the case. The IQ test measures mastery of certain cultural skills, and while it has proven to be a relatively accurate predictor of achievement in school, there is no conclusive evidence that it measures a person's inborn abilities. Third, research indicates that environment has a substantial effect on intelligence—perhaps a greater effect than heredity. Jensen downplays the differences between black and white schools, neighborhoods, jobs, and experiences. He assumes that blacks and whites from similar socioeconomic backgrounds are alike in all respects but heredity.

Tumin argues that the high levels of prejudice and discrimination in this country make it impossible to equate blacks and whites, even if their incomes and educations are alike. If we could find people whose experiences were identical, only at that point could we make valid racial comparisons, concluding that whatever differences we found were innate. But we can't. Tumin concludes that there is no substantial evidence that the difference in IQ averages has anything to do with genetic endowment. In short, most social scientists have concluded that if there are differences between blacks and whites, Jews and gentiles, they exist largely because these groups haven't enjoyed and still don't enjoy the same opportunities. The significant differences are social, not biological.

Prejudice and Discrimination

The word "prejudice" comes from the Latin *praejudicium,* a pretrial that determined a defendant's social status in ancient Rome. The results of this trial determined how the court would treat the accused; and in contemporary usage, the word still indicates a prejudgment. *Prejudice* is an irrational and categorical like or dislike of a group of people because of real or imagined characteristics associated with their race, religion, ethnic group, sexual orientation, or perhaps occupation. When a person is so convinced that all members of a group are immoral, violent, and backward (or moral, brilliant, and creative) that he or she can't see them as individuals and ignores evidence that refutes his or her convictions, he or she is prejudiced.

Prejudice is an attitude; *discrimination* is an act—the act of disqualifying or mistreating people on grounds rationally irrelevant to the situation (Antonovsky, 1960). Granting people privileges on the basis of imagined characteristics that attach to race, religion, or sex is also discrimination. Discrimination is not necessarily an expression of one's own prejudice. For example, a black store owner may decide not to hire Jews, not because he himself is prejudiced against Jews, but because he believes his customers are. However, discrimination tends to create and support prejudice by keeping people apart and limiting opportunities to disprove rumors and stereotypes.

Prejudice exists on three levels. It is part of the socioeconomic system, reflecting and reinforcing the ways in which work and power are distributed in a society. It is also a cultural phenomenon, reflecting the traditions and history of a people. And it is a psychological phenomenon that seems to meet certain needs in individuals.

Prejudice and Stratification Prejudice and discrimination begin with *ethnocentrism*, the belief of an ethnic group that other ethnic groups are inferior to it. Ethnocentrism alone can't account for ethnic stratification or interethnic conflict, however. The groups must be in competition for the same scarce resources. And still another ingredient besides competition must be added—inequality of power, so one group can impose its will on other groups and thereby restrict their opportunities, hamper their effectiveness as competitors, and institutionalize the unequal distribution of rewards and opportunities.

Prejudice is used to justify both low and high social rank, as, for example, when some people argue that members of minority groups are poor because they don't want to work or because they aren't capable of learning skilled trades. The assumption underlying this argument is that minorities are naturally inferior; the competition for scarce jobs and the ability of employers to define minorities right out of jobs have been overlooked. Thus, ethnic stratification arises from ethnocentrism, competition, and unequal power (Noel, 1968).

Prejudice and Culture In ethnically stratified societies, prejudice is part of the culture, a social habit handed down from generation to generation. Children learn to value their whiteness or blackness and to avoid or defer to members of different races and ethnic groups, much as they learn their gender identity and sex role. Children learn from parents, siblings, friends, and of course television, which until recently indirectly taught young Americans that black people are like Amos and Andy, and that Indians are hostile, ignorant savages. A Southerner describes how he acquired his racial and religious prejudice as follows:

> I grew up just 19 miles from Appomattox. The teaching I received both in school and from my parents was hard-core South, with no chance of insight into the thinking and ways of other peoples. I was taught to look down upon Negroes, tolerate Jews (because we had to do business with them) and ignore Catholics.
>
> We celebrated Jefferson Davis's birthday, but ignored Lincoln's; the name Robert E. Lee was spoken with reverence and Appomattox was a shrine. The Golden Rule only applied to others who were either Methodist or Baptist, white and without a foreign-sounding name. (Letter to the Editor, *The New York Times*, May 16, 1963)

Today, racial and ethnic stereotypes still persist, even if they are couched in humor. One wonders whether the television show *All in the Family* has been popular because members of minority groups nearly always come out on top in the show, or because Archie Bunker has made bigotry respectable (Rose, 1974: 139).[3] In fact, two researchers who studied viewers of *All in the Family* concluded that "nonprejudiced viewers and minority group viewers may perceive and enjoy

[the program] as satire, whereas prejudiced viewers may perceive and enjoy the show as 'telling it like it is.' . . . By making Archie a 'lovable bigot' the program encourages bigots to excuse and rationalize their own prejudices" (Vidmar and Rokeach, 1974).

The Psychology of Prejudice Suppose a man works six or seven days a week in a factory, trying to support his family, but never seems to be able to make ends meet. If he analyzed his situation rationally, he would probably blame the well-to-do generally and his employers specifically for failing to pay him an adequate wage. But these people have the power to cut off his income; to oppose them openly would be self-destructive. He could also blame himself for his financial problems, but this too makes him uncomfortable. Instead, he looks to the Mexican immigrants who have begun working in his factory. He doesn't really know them, but he suspects they're willing to work for low wages and that many other Mexicans are eager to take his job. By a process of twisted logic, he blames the Mexicans for his poverty. Soon he is exchanging rumors about "them" with his cronies and supporting efforts to close the border. Hating Mexicans makes the man and his friends feel a little better.

This psychological portrait of prejudice is based on frustration-aggression theory. According to this view, people are goal-directed creatures who become angry and hostile when their desires are frustrated. If they don't know who or what is blocking their ambitions or believe the obstacle is too threatening and powerful to attack, they displace their hostility onto a substitute target, a scapegoat who is more accessible and, conveniently, too weak to retaliate.

Once a scapegoat is found, people justify their irrational feelings and behavior by

---

[3]   The same question could be asked about black comedian Redd Foxx's show *Sanford and Son*, which closely resembled *All in the Family*. (The character Foxx played had no use for Puerto Ricans, for example.)

''discovering'' evidence that the out-group is indeed wicked and inferior. In this way, people can maintain some feeling that they are reasonable and kind. The catch is that in verbally or physically attacking Mexicans, Jews, or representatives of any other group, prejudiced people avoid confronting their true enemy. Their situation doesn't change, and frustration and hostility grow.

Individuals vary in the intensity of their prejudice and of their need for scapegoating. Insecurity about one's own self-worth makes an individual especially prone to denigrate others (Adorno, 1950). Although highly frustrated or very insecure people are more likely to be bigots, a high level of frustration and insecurity alone won't predict a person's tendency toward racism and discrimination. The reason, according to Van den Berghe (1967), is that where racism pays, most people will act racist irrespective of their personality propensity for prejudice. . However, ''when social pressures and rewards for racism are absent, racial bigotry is more likely to be restricted to people for whom prejudice fulfills a psychological 'need' '' (1967: 20). The extent and intensity of an individual's need to put down others or to believe unfavorable stereotypes vary with his or her make-up, degree of psychological security, and level of self-esteem, but the fact of prejudice and the targets for it are determined by the ideologies, opportunities, and rewards offered by the society the individual lives in.

PATTERNS OF ETHNIC RELATIONS

Relationships between racial and ethnic groups in a heterogeneous society range from full integration—the elimination of majority/minority distinctions in a society that ranks people not by race or ethnic background but by individual characteristics— to the absolute intolerance that motivates extermination. Both of these extremes are rare, however, and intergroup relations are usually more complex than the everyday definitions of such words as integration and segregation imply. Nevertheless, it is possible to identify certain basic patterns.

Patterns of Acceptance

Amalgamation occurs when members of different ethnic and racial groups intermarry, and the groups fuse and disappear as separate entities. Perhaps a new hybrid culture may emerge, and a new ''race'' as well.[4] This is what Israel Zangwill had in mind when he described America as a melting pot: ''There she lies, the great melting pot—listen! Can't you hear the roaring and bubbling? Ah, what a stirring and seething—Celt and Latin, Slav and Teuton, Greek and Syrian, Black and Yellow—Jew and Gentile'' (1909: 198–199).

Acculturation means that immigrants give up their old ways and adopt the language, customs, religion, and dress of the country to which they've moved. For example, the American public school system was specifically designed to teach the waves of immigrants that began coming here in the nineteenth century the English language and English customs, to enforce what Stewart and Mildred Cole (1954: 135–140) call ''Anglo-conformity.'' (Later, public educa-

---

4   Perhaps the only place in the United States where biological amalgamation has occurred is Hawaii, where Polynesians, Chinese, Japanese, Europeans, and Americans have intermarried more or less freely.

IN THE NEWS

Becoming American

A Vietnamese woman who has been in this country several years compiled a list of comparisons between Americans and Vietnamese, which she plans to distribute in booklet form to new arrivals. Among the items on the list are these:

American	Vietnamese
1. AFFECTION	
a. Touching between members of the *same* sex is not acceptable.	One can see two men or women in the street holding hands.
b. A man and a woman may hold hands or touch in public.	People do not do this in public. It looks "ridiculous."
c. A man can touch a woman (put an arm around her shoulder, hold her arm, kiss her cheek, etc.).	A man cannot do this for affection or friendliness. It is "insulting" to a woman.
d. Kissing (between husband and wife, lovers) in public is usually acceptable.	It is a public offense. It has to be done in private quarters. No kissing in front of the children. Not at all, except babies.
2. FAMILY RELATIONSHIP	
a. The family relationship is not always close.	The family relationship is very close in Vietnam.
b. Two generations (parents and children) live in a home.	Three or four, sometimes five, generations live under one roof.
c. Sometimes old-aged parents live in nursing homes or by themselves.	Elders live with children and usually are well taken care of by members of the family.
d. Young children have a lot of freedom.	Children have to obey and respect their parents and do not have much freedom.
3. WORKING	
a. Workers are sometimes treated as machines.	Workers are more often treated as human beings.
b. Working conditions are often tense due to deadlines.	Working conditions are more relaxed.

tion was extended to blacks, Indians, and Mexican-Americans—for the same purpose.)

Is America the melting pot of Zangwill's dream? No, according to Milton Gordon (1964). Gordon makes the important distinc- tion between *behavioral assimilation* (immigrants adopting the language and behavioral patterns of the host culture) and *structural assimilation* (immigrants gaining admission to the host's government, businesses,

c. Educated people may not earn a much higher salary than less educated people.

Educated people are more highly paid than less educated people.

d. Educated people do not get automatic respect from others.

e. Skilled professions are highly paid.

Educated people get much respect from others.

Skilled labor is not appreciated or well-paid.

4. SOME NECESSITIES

a. Telephones are necessary. Almost everyone knows how to use [them].

[The telephone] is a luxury in Vietnam, and very few people know how to use it. Vietnamese should be taught to use it economically.

b. Many people know how to drive and own cars.

c. Credit cards are widely used.

Very few people know how to drive a car because it is a luxury.

Vietnamese have no idea what credit cards are. In Vietnam, to be in debt creates a bad reputation, unless a loan is made to invest in business.

d. Banks are popular and widely used.

Banks are for rich people. The majority of people do not know how to use banking services.

Through the eyes of this newest wave of refugees (there are now 150,000 Indochinese in this country), we can see the formidable adjustments they face. If they don't shed at least part of their native culture, they will be unable to get along here. But if they do "adjust," the price may be the loss of what in their eyes constitutes the basic meaning of family, work, and all aspects of life. This has always been the dilemma of the immigrant seeking to become "Americanized"; more and more, newcomers to this country and/or their children are looking to preserve rather than to give up their unique heritage.

SOURCE: Pamela Blafer Lack, "The Ways of Americans, Through Vietnamese Eyes," *The New York Times*, January 24, 1978, p. 31.

schools, churches, clubs, and ultimately families). While most ethnic groups have undergone behavioral assimilation and structural integration into secondary relationships in America, relatively little integration has taken place on the level of primary relationships (see chapter 7). In part this is because Americans of northern European descent intermarried among themselves and not with other immigrants, in part because later immigrants resisted complete assimilation to Protestant Anglo-Saxon culture.[5]

An alternative to integration is *cultural pluralism*, whereby different ethnic groups maintain their cultural identities and distinct ways, but no one group enjoys special privileges or is discriminated against. Cultural pluralism is based on the belief that ethnic diversity strengthens a society. In Switzerland, for example, Protestants and Catholics of German, French, and Italian descent have coexisted peacefully and equally. In America's large cities, with their Little Italies, Chinatowns, Germantowns, and other ethnic enclaves, there has also been pluralism, though not always of the most peaceful kind.

Patterns of Rejection

In a society that practices *segregation,* contacts between different groups are restricted by law and/or custom. Segregation is based on the premise that ethnic and racial groups are inherently unequal, and that the differences between them are permanent (hence the myths of racial inferiority). An individual's ethnic identity determines his or her social status; members of minorities are denied full participation in social institutions and are relegated to activities that benefit the majority (Hunt and Walker, 1974: 6–7). Clearly, segregation is an arrangement imposed and enforced by the majority.

In America, the civil rights movement has done much to reduce segregation. Today,

Until the Civil Rights legislation of the 1960s made segregation illegal, public facilities were rigidly segregated for Southern blacks and whites. (Bob Adelman/Magnum Photos, Inc.)

the United States is desegregated in the sense that *legal* barriers to interracial contacts have been removed. As Martin Luther King, Jr., once remarked, "The law may not make a man love me, but it can restrain him from lynching me, and I think that's pretty important" (in Rose, 1974: 103). But this is not yet a racially integrated society; there is no "easy and fluid mixture of peoples of diverse racial, religious, and nationality backgrounds in social cliques, families (i.e., intermarriage), private organizations and intimate

---

[5] Indeed, many immigrants never intended to become Americans. The Germans wanted to build a "new Germany" in Texas; the Irish petitioned Congress (unsuccessfully) for a territory of their own; and Scandinavians established colonies in the Northwest, beyond the reach of Americanization (Glazer, 1954).

friendships'' (Gordon, 1964: 246). Moreover, the white exodus to the suburbs has made most of America's big cities minority enclaves. Indeed, *de facto segregation*[6] may be increasing.

Expulsion (the forcible resettlement or deportation of a minority group) is another form of rejection of minorities. In 1972, for example, Uganda's General Idi Amin deported 27,000 Indians, many of whom were second- and third-generation Ugandans, with only a few months' warning, appropriating their homes, businesses, and savings (see Kramer, 1974). This country, too, has expelled minorities. In the 1830s, the Cherokees were forced to march from their homelands in Georgia to an arid reservation in Oklahoma. As many as 4,000 Indians died on what came to be known as the Trail of . Tears. As was mentioned earlier, during World War II the American government forcibly sent over 100,000 Japanese to ''relocation centers'' for the duration of the war.

The severest response to minority groups is *extermination,* the mass murder of a minority group. The Nazis murdered 6 million Jews between 1933 and 1945—as well as countless gypsies, communists, and members of other ethnic and political minorities. A century before, Americans slaughtered the Indians (a story that has been ''whitewashed'' for years). American Indians fought the European invaders, but to little avail. About two-thirds of the Indian population was wiped out. Some died in battle, but just as many died from the white man's diseases, against which they had no natural immunity, and from starvation, after white hunters killed off the buffalo.

---

[6] Unofficial segregation that results from social patterns, as opposed to segregation by law (*de jure segregation*).

Minority Responses

How do minorities respond to discrimination and abuse? How do people cope with a society that defines them as undesirable? Acceptance of the majority culture is one response. Some members of a minority will try to ''pass''—change their name, their appearance (with hair straighteners or skin bleaches, for example), and their way of life, thus shedding their minority identity. Passing means rejecting one's family and origins, and may leave a person stranded between two worlds, neither of which accepts him or her entirely. And there is always the possibility of ''discovery.''

For sheer psychological and physical survival, others play the role the majority assigns to them, obeying the etiquette of racism, deferring to one or another member of the majority in most interracial contexts. The classic example of this response to segregation is Uncle Tom, who smiled and shuffled and ''yes, ma'am''ed his way through Harriet Beecher Stowe's novel. Simpson and Yinger tell a revealing story about Uncle Toms:

> A Negro drives through a red light in a Mississippi town. The sheriff yells, ''Where you think you going?'' The Negro thinks fast and answers, ''Well, boss, when I see that green light come on an' all them white folks' cars goin' through, I says to myself, 'That's the white folks' light!' So I don' move. Then when that ol' red light comes on, I jus' steps on the gas. I says,''That mus' be the niggers' light!'' The sheriff replies, ''You're a good boy, Sam, but the next time you kin go on the white folks' light.'' (1972: 224)

It's obvious who had the last laugh here. Flattery, deference, and feigned stupidity can be effective forms of passive aggression—as when a slave pretended he was so simple-minded he couldn't understand a job he didn't want to do.

Psychological theory suggests, however, that if people are abused day after day, their anger will build until they find some way to vent it. Sociologists have speculated—but haven't demonstrated conclusively—that the relatively high crime rate in black ghettos is evidence of displaced aggression (see Simpson and Yinger, 1972: 224–225). Hitting back at whites is too dangerous, so blacks take out their hostility on one another.

An alternative to acceptance (real or feigned) or aggression (direct or indirect) is avoidance. For example, when anti-Chinese sentiment began to increase in the American West, Chinese families withdrew to cities on the Atlantic and Pacific coasts, shutting themselves off from the hostile society around them (Yuan, 1963). Not only does self-segregation provide insulation from aggression and slurs, but it also enables members of a minority group to maintain close family ties, to assist one another, to practice their own way of life, and to keep their culture alive.

The Psychological Consequences of Racism What does living in a society that preaches black inferiority do to a black person, inside? In *Dark Ghetto* (1965), psychologist Kenneth B. Clark argues that chronic social injustices ''corrode and damage the human personality, thereby robbing it of its effectiveness, of its creativity, if not its actual humanity. . . . Human beings who are forced to live under ghetto conditions and whose daily experience tells them that almost nowhere in society are they respected and granted the ordinary dignity and courtesy accorded to others, will, as a matter of course, begin to doubt their self-worth''

(63–64). Clark notes that black children often describe black dolls as ugly, dirty, or bad. Similarly, the preoccupation with hair straighteners and skin bleaches among the black bourgeoisie in the fifties and early sixties suggests that they accepted the white dislike of black physical traits.

Recent investigations, however, have shown that blacks have as much self-esteem as anyone else—perhaps more. For example, Morris Rosenberg and Roberta G. Simmons (1971) interviewed black and white children in predominantly black and in racially mixed schools in Baltimore. Many of the children weren't conscious of the low status assigned to blacks in the society at large, living as they did in nearly all black worlds. Others more or less accepted the white stereotype of blacks as slow and lazy, but didn't feel this image applied to them personally. And some attributed the negative evaluation of blacks to white irrationality. As for black children's feelings about themselves, Rosenberg and Simmons found that black children were *less* likely to consider poor grades or test scores evidence of personal inadequacy than were white youngsters. Thus prejudice may insulate a person from self-criticism. Curtis Banks (1977) found further that when blacks perceive those evaluating them as biased, they tend to discount these evaluations.

Most studies of the consequences of discrimination have been focused on the victims rather than on the victimizers. We don't know how to calculate the psychological and social costs of treating a whole group of people as less than human. What research there is in this area suggests that members of the dominant group in a segregated society suffer from insecurity and fear, particularly if that society respects rationality and democratic values. In South Africa, whites fear the possibility of a black revolution. Whites in small towns in the American South often own more than one firearm, and New Yorkers avoid the streets at night, shutting themselves in with three and four locks. "Thus a pattern of discrimination is supported only at the cost of much irrationality, moral confusion, arrogance, and fear" (Simpson and Yinger, 1972: 242).

PROTEST AND PROGRESS

On August 28, 1963, some 200,000 black and white Americans gathered jubilantly on the steps of the Lincoln Memorial in Washington and listened raptly as Martin Luther King, Jr., told the nation: "I have a dream. . . ."

The euphoria of that sunny afternoon was short-lived.[7] Just a month later, a bomb exploded in the basement of a black church in Birmingham, Alabama, killing four little girls. Congress began to move. The Public Accommodations Act was passed in 1964, the Voting Rights Act a year later. The legal obstacles to integration had been destroyed, but relations between blacks and whites became increasingly abrasive over the years. The Student Nonviolent Coordinating Committee (SNCC) expelled its white members, and its leaders began talking about black power.

The Watts ghetto riot of August 1965 set the pattern for the next three summers. Dr. King's assassination in April 1968 sparked a new round of destruction, a grim memorial to a man who had dedicated his life to nonviolence and brotherhood. The Kerner Commis-

sion, appointed to explain the riots to a frightened white America, issued an unexpected indictment that same year:

> What white Americans have never fully understood—but what the Negro can never forget—is that white society is deeply implicated in the ghetto. White institutions created it, white institutions maintain it, and white society condones it.

The commission went on to prophesy that

> our nation is moving toward two societies, one black, one white—separate and unequal. . . . To pursue our present course will involve the continuing polarization of the American community and, ultimately, the destruction of basic democratic values.

When the riots stopped, an uneasy quiet settled on the race issue. The leadership of the civil rights movement dispersed to deal with such issues as welfare and prison reform, and to conduct local political and economic campaigns. The gap between those blacks who could take advantage of newly opened opportunities and those whose lives continued to be encircled by poverty widened. But despite the erosion of black leadership and unity, despite setbacks and phantom hopes, much has changed since August 28, 1963.

One of the most significant achievements of the civil rights effort was the development of black pride. In a sense, blacks made ethnicity respectable. And they gave hope to other groups—to Mexican-Americans, American Indians, peace demonstrators, women, and homosexuals; even to those "white ethnics" who didn't want their children bused to schools in black districts—all of whom adopted the tactics and slogans of the civil rights movement. In short, the spirit of togetherness that motivated the March on

---

[7] This section is based in part on a series of four articles commemorating the tenth anniversary of the March on Washington that appeared in *The New York Times*, beginning August 26, 1973.

Washington has given way to a new pattern of race and ethnic relations based on ethnic pride.

Where Do We Stand?[8]

The picture of American race relations is uneven and contradictory. Blacks and Hispanics today are better educated, are better off financially, and have better job prospects than their parents (or even their older siblings) were or did, but they are still not even with whites in these areas. For example, in 1976, the percentage of all Americans between twenty-five and twenty-nine who attended college for at least four years was 24 percent, twice that for blacks. Blacks are still likely to attend racially imbalanced schools. Despite dramatic progress in the South, nationwide in 1972, over two-thirds of black students attended schools where blacks were in the majority, and about half of these students attended schools that were 95 to 100 percent black.

Economically, blacks have made gains, but they remain substantially worse off than whites. The ratio of black family income to white family income increased from 55 percent in 1965 to 59 percent in 1976. The gap between the median income of blacks and whites was still evident: on average, the white family earned $15,537; the black family, $9,242. About 29 percent of all blacks still live below the poverty level, as opposed to less than 10 percent of all whites.

Black poverty is in part a consequence of black unemployment; the unemployment rate for blacks has run around double that of whites since the Korean War. In August 1977, the black unemployment rate was

15.5 percent and stood at 40 percent for black teen-agers. If we count those blacks employed but earning less than the poverty-level income and those working part-time but wanting full-time jobs, we discover the subemployment rate, which is at least double the rate of those completely unemployed. In human terms, these figures are devastating, for they delineate a group of people who have little hope for a decent living, for whom jobs are a source of frustration rather than of satisfaction (Liebow in Anderson, 1974).

The most conspicuous gains for black

The 1970s have been a decade of economic growth for Hispanic Americans, due largely to the increasing participation of Spanish-heritage women, such as this factory worker, in the labor force. (Cary Wolinsky/Stock, Boston)

---

[8] Unless otherwise indicated, figures in this section are taken from *Statistical Abstract of the United States, 1977* of the U.S. Bureau of the Census.

Americans over the last ten years have been in politics. In Mississippi, for example, black voter registration leaped from 5.2 percent in 1960 to 60.7 in 1976. Between February 1970 and July 1977, the total number of blacks holding elective offices almost tripled.

Like blacks, Hispanic Americans are underrepresented in high-skill, high-income jobs, especially white-collar work, and are overrepresented in low-skill, low-paying jobs, though Hispanics have been more likely to be blue-collar or farm employees than blacks. Their unemployment rate has been high—in March 1977, 10.5 percent for men over sixteen, 13 percent for women—though not as high as blacks' (U.S. Bureau of the Census, *Current Population Reports,*

1977). They own fewer consumer durables than whites, though more than blacks. Income has been well below that of whites, but from 1969 to 1974 it rose from 58 to 69 percent of whites'. The improvement in the life situation of Hispanics is largely due to lower unemployment rates among Spanish-heritage males, and also to increasing participation in the labor market by Spanish-heritage women. The 1970s, then, have been relatively stagnant years for blacks and years of rapid economic gains for Spanish-Americans. But both groups have a long way to go to catch up with the white majority.

Black and White Attitudes Attitudes have changed since the beginning of the civil

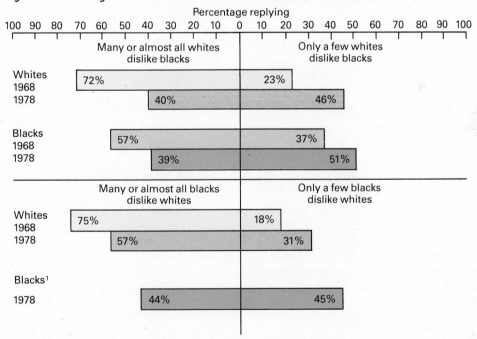

figure 11:1   Changes in racial attitudes in the urban North, 1968 and 1978

Percentage replying

| | 100 90 80 70 60 50 40 30 20 10 | 0 | 10 20 30 40 50 60 70 80 90 100 |

Many or almost all whites dislike blacks | Only a few whites dislike blacks

Whites
1968 — 72% / 23%
1978 — 40% / 46%

Blacks
1968 — 57% / 37%
1978 — 39% / 51%

Many or almost all blacks dislike whites | Only a few blacks dislike whites

Whites
1968 — 75% / 18%
1978 — 57% / 31%

Blacks[1]
1978 — 44% / 45%

[1]Question not asked of blacks in 1968.

SOURCE: Survey Research Center, University of Michigan; The New York Times/CBS News Poll.
Adapted from *The New York Times,* February 27, 1978, p. A14.

figure 11:2   Areas of discrimination against blacks as perceived by blacks and whites

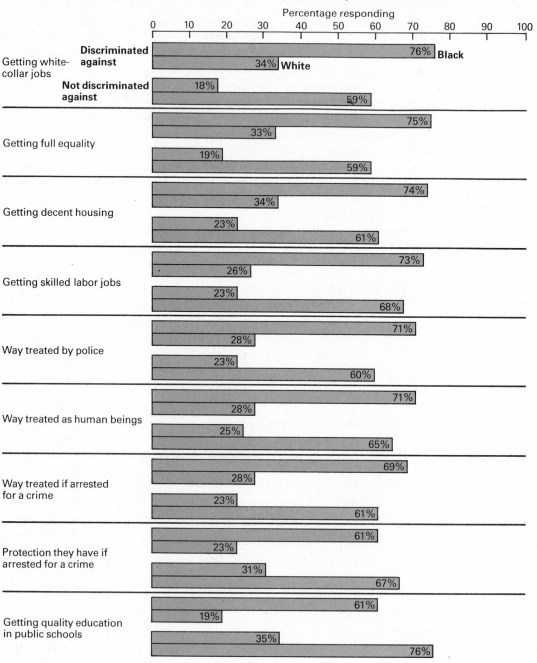

Percentage responding

SOURCE: Adapted from Louis Harris, ''Disagreement on Discrimination,'' *The Harris Survey*, September 12, 1977, p. 3.

rights movement, but not as much as one might expect. White Americans don't approve of discrimination, but neither do they want full integration. According to a 1976 Harris poll, only 12 percent favor "separation of the races," but only 28 percent favor "full racial integration." Forty-eight percent endorse "integration in some areas of life."

In a 1977 National Opinion Research Center survey, whites were presented with a number of possible "explanations" as to why blacks so often have "worse jobs, income, and housing" than whites. Only 39 percent attributed inequality to discrimination. Blacks could not disagree more. The majority of blacks believe they are being discriminated against in virtually all areas of life, from education and employment to humane treatment (see figure 11:2 on p. 324).

One point on which most blacks and whites agree is that people should help themselves. Ninety percent of whites and 64 percent of blacks reject the idea that the way to make up for past discrimination is to give women and minorities "preferential treatment" in college admission and jobs (Lipset and Schneider, 1977).

OBSTACLES TO FULL EQUALITY: INSTITUTIONAL RACISM

Full equality among the races may elude Americans unless we eliminate *institutional racism*. This term refers to the crystallization of habits of discrimination throughout a society, in institutional patterns of employment, schooling, housing, and government. Once this happens, individuals need not be "prejudiced" to discriminate; just by continuing to operate the way they always have, they perpetuate lines of discrimination. Given the

ambivalent attitudes most whites have concerning improvement of the status of blacks in America, it isn't surprising that the means for undoing institutional racism have been highly controversial. Three such controversies surround the issues of zoning, affirmative action, and busing.

Zoning

Can a suburb screen out low-income housing and thereby exclude blacks and other minorities? Since 1975, in New Jersey the answer to this question has been no, a suburb can't zone out low- and moderate-income housing. New Jersey's highest court ruled that the town of Mount Laurel was obligated to provide its "fair share" of low- and moderate-income housing. However, in 1977, the U.S. Supreme Court ruled that the nearly all white Chicago suburb of Arlington Heights could refuse to change zoning restrictions whose practical effect was to block construction of racially integrated housing for people with low and moderate incomes. To be unconstitutional, the Supreme Court said, there must be an "intent" to discriminate rather than simply to preserve such neighborhood characteristics as one-family dwellings or minimum lot sizes. Not only does this ruling cast doubt over the Mount Laurel decision, but it also may strike at the core of arguments for affirmative action in employment and education, since intent to discriminate must be proven.

Affirmative Action

If our institutions put up barriers to the advancement of minorities and women, and favor white males, then there must be some way to tear down the barriers and redress the

table 11:2 **HOW AMERICANS VIEW AFFIRMATIVE ACTION PROGRAMS, 1977 (by percent)**

Question: "Some people say that to make up for past discrimination, women and members of minority groups should be given preferential treatment in getting jobs and places in college. Others say that ability, as determined by test scores, should be the main consideration. Which point of view comes closest to how you feel on this matter?"

	GIVE PREFERENCE	ABILITY MAIN CONSIDERATION	NO OPINION
National			
Sex	11	81	8
Male	10	82	8
Female	12	80	8
Race			
White	9	84	7
Nonwhite	30	55	15
Education			
College	15	81	4
High school	9	84	7
Grade school	11	70	19
Region			
East	14	76	10
Midwest	8	87	5
South	9	79	12
West	15	82	3
Age			
Total under 30	15	79	6
30–49 years	10	84	6
50 and older	9	81	10
Income			
$20,000 and over	11	86	3
$15,000–$19,999	10	82	8
$10,000–$14,999	9	87	4
$ 7,000–$9,999	9	80	11
$ 5,000–$6,999	13	73	14
$ 3,000–$4,999	13	70	17
Under $3,000	20	70	10

SOURCE: Gallup Opinion Index, *How Americans View the Public Schools*, Report no. 151 (February 1978), p. 8.

historic imbalance. Civil rights advocates call such efforts affirmative action; many white males today brand them *reverse discrimination.*

Affirmative action has as its legal foundation the Civil Rights Act of 1964, which is aimed at eliminating discrimination based on race, religion, ethnic origin, or sex. According to its advocates, attacking discrimination involves more than just eliminating legal barriers, for if we ignore the deficits of skills and credentials suffered by minorities and women, little change is likely. Therefore, *affirmative action* — special consideration and preferential treatment — is necessary to eliminate the consequences of past discrimination.

Employers are asked to inventory all employees, and after they have identified areas of underutilization of minorities and women, they are then asked to set goals for the employment of members of such groups. Goals are a way of assessing an employer's commitment, but they are not quotas.

> The employer is not compelled to hire unqualified persons or to compromise genuinely valid standards to meet the established goal. If goals are not met, no sanctions are imposed, so long as the contractor can demonstrate that he made good faith efforts to reach them (U.S. Commission on Civil Rights, 1977: 6).

One problem, of course, is how to monitor and enforce affirmative action programs. The Equal Employment Opportunity Commission (EEOC) is the main arm. Its most notable success was the case in which AT&T agreed to set goals for sexual integration of its jobs and to give $38 million in back pay to women it had channeled into low-paying dead-end jobs. Despite such dramatic cases, most complaints to the EEOC languish for years.

Sluggish enforcement may be only a symptom of a greater problem—the feeling on the part of whites, especially white males, that affirmative action puts them at a disadvantage. Just such an issue was presented to the Supreme Court in the recent case of Alan Bakke, a white man who was twice rejected by a California medical school and who claimed that less-qualified people had been accepted under a special admissions program that reserved sixteen of the hundred places for minorities. Bakke contended that this policy denied him equal protection. In 1978 the Supreme Court ruled that Bakke be admitted. However, they also stated that race or ethnic background could be one—but not the only—factor in assessing applicants.

Busing

It has been nearly a quarter of a century since the Supreme Court ruled that separate public schools for blacks and whites are inherently unconstitutional. Yet in 1972, one-third of all black schoolchildren attended schools that were 95 to 100 percent black.

Residential patterns are the primary source of the imbalance, but the policies of certain school districts have intensified racial isolation.

After a decade of effort to get the Boston school board to rectify racial imbalance in its schools, a federal court ordered 81,000 pupils reassigned and 17,000 bused beginning September 12, 1974. The whites of Boston that fall were as gracious as the whites of Little Rock in the fall of 1956 about having blacks attending "their" schools.

At issue in the busing controversy are two

strongly held values—the elimination of discrimination against blacks, with special focus on the educational system, versus the tradition of sending students to schools in their own neighborhoods. So long as neighborhoods remain racially segregated, integration can't be attained without changing the method of pupil assignments. Busing is one means—and sometimes the only means—for implementing new assignments.

What about the prospects for achieving greater racial balance in the schools through increased residential integration? An assumption in busing cases has been that residential isolation of blacks is primarily due to economic factors—blacks supposedly can't afford to live where whites do, and special measures must therefore be taken.

A study of residential patterns in twenty-nine urban areas suggests that income is not the primary barrier to racial integration (Hermalin and Farley, 1973: 595–610). Instead, blacks are prevented from obtaining housing they can afford by a "web of discrimination" in real estate practices, mortgage policies, and the like. Eliminating these barriers to residential integration may ultimately be a less controversial and healthier means of integrating schools than busing. American whites have little objection to black neighbors *of the same class and income*, whereas in 1974, 65 percent of all Americans opposed busing to achieve racial integration (Gallup Opinion Index, 1974: 4). Perhaps more important, residential integration promotes contacts between blacks and whites that are generally more positive and go further toward reducing racial stereotypes than those resulting from the "induced" integration of busing.

Prospects

The Civil Rights Act of 1964 is a cornerstone in the attempt to achieve integration. But in neither affirmative action nor in school desegregation has the government kept pace with the need to enforce that law. Alexander Bickel, a noted constitutional scholar, observed in 1964 that merely passing a law can't change social relationships, that persuasion and inducement, from both the public sector and private groups, must be used to make it clear that the law embodies "minimal moral requirements" (1967: 462). If the law isn't supported by the majority of Americans, resistance to it will nullify it over the long run. As Bickel noted, "The limits of the law are the limits of enforcement" (1967: 451).

The majority of Americans support the principle of equal rights and opportunities for all, but it remains to be seen whether they can agree on ways to put that principle into practice.

SUMMARY

A *minority* is a group of people who are singled out for unequal treatment in the society in which they live because they are physically or culturally different from the majority. An *ethnic group* is any group that is defined or set off by race, religion, or national origin, or some combination of these. This chapter focuses on the numerous racial and ethnic minorities in America. Included are: 25 million blacks, who trace their history back through 300 years of discrimination to Africa; 6 million Jews, descendants

of those who came to America during the mid-nineteenth and early twentieth
centuries; 6.6 million Mexican-Americans, who have lived apart in the Southwest;
Puerto Ricans, of whom about 1.8 million live on the U.S. mainland; about 790,000
American Indians, the poorest of the poor in the United States; approximately 1 million
Americans of Chinese and Japanese descent; and white ethnics from southern
and eastern Europe.

Race and misconceptions about race have shaped ethnic relations in this country.
Biologically, a *race* is a population that through generations of inbreeding has
developed distinctive physical characteristics. Physical anthropologists who study these
characteristics haven't been able to agree on definite racial categories. Nevertheless,
people believe certain groups are genetically distinct and attribute what are actually
social differences to genetics. This confusion of biological and social explanations
creates racial myths that shore up the theories of such social scientists as Arthur
Jensen; Jensen maintains that blacks are innately less intelligent than whites—an
argument that rests on the erroneous belief that an IQ test is an objective measure of
innate or biological capacity. Most social scientists concur with Melvin Tumin's
assertion that social opportunities, not genetics, account for the differences between
the IQs of blacks and those of whites.

Prejudice is an irrational categorical like or dislike of a group of people because of
real or imagined characteristics associated with their race, religion, ethnic group, sexual
orientation, or occupation. *Discrimination* is granting or denying privileges on grounds
rationally irrelevant to the situation. Prejudice and discrimination may or may not go
together.

Prejudice is a combination of social, cultural, and psychological predispositions.
Ethnocentrism (an ethnic group's belief that other ethnic groups are inferior to it),
competition for scarce resources, and inequality of power all account for prejudice on a
social and cultural level. On a psychological level, prejudice may be the result of
people's venting their frustrations or projecting their own weaknesses onto a scapegoat.

Relationships between different racial and ethnic groups range from full integration
to absolute intolerance. *Amalgamation*, one route to integration, occurs when members
of different ethnic and racial groups intermarry, and the groups lose their separate
identities. *Acculturation* occurs when immigrants give up their ethnic identity and adopt
the ways of their new country. Assimilation into the American mainstream has
generally stopped at the level of secondary relationships—in part because the
Protestant Anglo-Saxon majority hasn't welcomed newcomers, in part because
immigrants have resisted Anglo-conformity. The term *cultural pluralism* refers to a
pattern whereby ethnic groups maintain their cultural identities and distinct ways but
coexist peacefully and equally. Switzerland and, to some degree, America's big cities
are examples.

Segregation, the restriction by custom and law of contacts between members of
different groups (usually ethnic and/or racial), is based on the belief that these groups
are inherently unequal. The history of racial segregation in the United States goes back
hundreds of years, and it still influences the structure of American society. Other forms
of rejection of minorities are *expulsion* (such as the forced march of the Cherokees) or
extermination (such as the slaughter of the Indians and the Jews).

Minorities cope with discrimination and abuse by trying to pass, by playing the
role assigned to them (often a form of passive aggression), or by avoiding the majority
(as the Chinese did). The psychological consequences of racism are still being studied.

Recent research indicates that despite white prejudice and discrimination, black children have high self-esteem. The response of the majority group to racism may be to fear the minority group that it discriminates against.

Racial and ethnic relations in America today are at a crossroads. The civil rights movement succeeded in destroying the legal barriers to equality and stimulated black pride. In the last decade, blacks have made significant gains in the fields of education, employment, and politics. But blacks are far from having achieved equality. A survey conducted in 1977 found that although only 39 percent of whites attributed black inequality to discrimination, the majority of blacks believe they are being discriminated against in all areas of life.

What lies in the future? *Institutional racism* (habits of discrimination that have become crystallized into the social structure, in patterns of housing, education, and so forth) still blocks the way to true ethnic pluralism. Attempts to combat institutional racism through zoning, affirmative action, and busing have been controversial and have achieved only limited success.

GLOSSARY

acculturation the adoption by immigrants of their new country's culture.

affirmative action an antidiscriminatory process in which special consideration and preferential treatment are given to members of minority groups.

amalgamation the intermarriage of members of different ethnic and racial groups and the disappearance of the groups as separate entities.

behavioral assimilation Gordon's term for the adoption by immigrants or minorities of the language and behavioral patterns of the host culture.

cultural pluralism the coexistence of different ethnic groups, each of which retains its cultural identity, without privilege or discrimination.

de facto segregation unofficial segregation that results from social patterns.

de jure segregation segregation by law.

discrimination granting or denying privileges on grounds rationally irrelevant to the situation.

ethnic group a group that is defined or set off by race, religion, or national origin, or some combination of these.

ethnocentrism the tendency to see one's own group and way of life, including behaviors, beliefs, values, and norms, as superior to the groups and ways of life of others.

expulsion the forcible resettlement or deportation of a minority group.

extermination the mass murder of a minority group.

institutional racism habits of discrimination that have become crystallized into the social structure, in institutional patterns of housing, schooling, employment, and so forth. These patterns persist despite an absence of conscious or deliberate discrimination.

integration the elimination of majority/minority distinctions in a society that ranks people according to individual characteristics, not race or ethnic background.

Jim Crow the legal and social barriers constructed in the South in the late nineteenth and early twentieth centuries to prevent blacks from voting, using public facilities, and mixing with whites. (Jim Crow was the name of a blackface minstrel character.)

minority a group of people who are singled out for unequal treatment in the society in which they live, and who consider themselves to be victims of collective discrimination.

prejudice an irrational categorical like or dislike

of a group of people because of real or imagined characteristics associated with their race, religion, ethnic group, sexual orientation, or perhaps occupation.

race biologically, a population that through generations of inbreeding has developed more or less distinctive physical characteristics that are transmitted genetically. Sociologically, a group of people who others believe are genetically distinct and whom they treat accordingly.

reverse discrimination discrimination against members of majority groups in favor of members of minority groups.

segregation laws and/or customs that restrict contact between groups. Segregation may be ethnic or racial, or based on sex or age.

structural assimilation Gordon's term for the admission of immigrant or minority groups into the educational, occupational, and social structures of the host culture.

REFERENCES

T. W. Adorno et al., *The Authoritarian Personality.* New York: Harper & Row, 1950.

Aaron Antonovsky, "The Social Meaning of Discrimination." *Phylon,* vol. 21 (Spring 1960): 13–19.

W. Curtis Banks et al., "Perceived Objectivity and the Effects of Evaluative Reinforcement upon Compliance and Self-Evaluation in Blacks." *Journal of Experimental Social Psychology,* vol. 13 (September 1977): 452–463.

Alexander M. Bickel, "The Limits of Effective Action," in Milton L. Barron, ed., *Minorities in a Changing World.* New York: Knopf, 1967.

William C. Boyd, *Genetics and the Races of Man.* Boston: Little, Brown, 1950.

Kenneth B. Clark, *Dark Ghetto.* New York: Harper & Row, 1965.

Stewart G. and Mildred Wiese Cole, *Minorities and the American Promise.* New York: Harper & Row, 1954.

Peter Collier, "Wounded Knee: The New Indian War." *Ramparts* (June 1973): 25–29ff.

Theodosius Dobzhansky, *Genetic Diversity and Human Equality.* New York: Basic Books, 1973.

Morris Freedman and Carolyn Banks, eds., *American Mix.* New York: Lippincott, 1972.

Gallup Opinion Index, *Religion in America, 1977–78,* Report no. 145 (May 1976).

_____, Report no. 113 (November 1974).

Nathan Glazer, "Ethnic Groups in America: From National Culture to Ideology," in Monroe Berger et al., eds., *Freedom and Control in Modern Society.* New York: Van Nostrand, 1954.

Milton M. Gordon, *Assimilation in American Life.* New York: Oxford University Press, 1964.

Andrew M. Greeley, *Ethnicity, Denomination, and Inequality.* Beverly Hills, Calif.: Sage Publications, 1976.

_____, "Political Attitudes Among American White Ethnics," in Charles H. Anderson, ed., *Sociological Essays and Research.* Homewood, Ill.: Dorsey, 1974.

Louis Harris, "Disagreement on Discrimination." *The Harris Survey,* September 12, 1977.

Albert I. Hermalin and Reynolds Farley, "The Potential for Residential Integration in Cities and Suburbs: Implications for the Busing Controversy." *American Sociological Review,* vol. 38 (October 1973): 595–610.

Chester L. Hunt and Lewis Walker, *Ethnic Diversity.* Homewood, Ill.: Dorsey, 1974.

Arthur R. Jensen, "How Much Can We Boost IQ and Scholastic Achievement?" *Harvard Educational Review,* vol. 39 (Winter 1969): 1–123.

Jane Kramer, "The Uganda Asians." *The New Yorker,* April 8, 1974, pp. 47–93.

Irving M. Levine and Judith Herman, "The Life of

White Ethnics," in Charles H. Anderson, ed., *Sociological Essays and Research.* Homewood, Ill.: Dorsey, 1974.

Seymour Martin Lipset and William Schneider, "An Emerging National Consensus." *The New Republic,* October 15, 1977, pp. 8–9.

National Opinion Research Center, *Cumulative Code Book for the 1972–1977 General Social Surveys.* Chicago: National Opinion Research Center, 1977.

Donald L. Noel, "A Theory of the Origin of Ethnic Stratification." *Social Problems,* vol. 16 (Fall 1968): 156–172.

Peter I. Rose, *They and We: Racial and Ethnic Relations in the United States,* 2nd ed. New York: Random House, 1974.

Morris Rosenberg and Roberta G. Simmons, *Black and White Self-Esteem: The Urban School Child.* Washington, D.C.: American Sociological Association, 1971.

George E. Simpson and J. Milton Yinger, *Racial and Cultural Minorities: An Analysis of Prejudice and Discrimination,* 4th ed. New York: Harper & Row, 1972.

Lester C. Thurow, "The Economic Status of Minorities and Women." *Civil Rights Digest,* vol. 8 (Winter/Spring 1976): 3–9.

Melvin Tumin, *Patterns of Society.* Boston: Little, Brown, 1973.

U.S. Bureau of the Census, *Current Population Reports,* Series P-20, no. 317, "Persons of Spanish Origin in the United States: March 1977." Washington, D.C.: U.S. Government Printing Office, 1977.

————, *Statistical Abstract of the United States: 1977.* Washington, D.C.: U.S. Government Printing Office, 1977.

U.S. Commission on Civil Rights, *Statement on Affirmative Action for Equal Employment Opportunities,* Clearinghouse Publication 54. Washington, D.C.: U.S. Government Printing Office, 1977.

Pierre Van den Berghe, *Race and Racism: A Comparative Perspective.* New York: Wiley, 1967.

Neil Vidmar and Milton Rokeach, "Archie Bunker's Bigotry: A Study in Selective Perception and Exposure." *Journal of Communication,* vol. 24 (Winter 1974): 36–47.

Louis Wirth, "The Problem of Minority Groups," in Ralph Linton, ed., *The Science of Man in the World Crisis.* New York: Columbia University Press, 1945.

D. Y. Yuan, "Voluntary Segregation: A Study of New York Chinatown." *Phylon,* vol. 24 (Fall 1963): 255–265.

Israel Zangwill, *The Melting Pot.* New York: Jewish Publishing Society of America, 1909.

FOR FURTHER STUDY

The references we have used in each section are among the best and provide an excellent beginning toward a fuller understanding of some aspects of ethnic relations. The most authoritative general text is *Racial and Cultural Minorities,* 4th ed., by George Simpson and Milton Yinger (New York: Harper & Row, 1972). A short and very readable account is Peter I. Rose's *They and We: Racial and Ethnic Relations in the United States,* 2nd ed. (New York: Random House, 1974).

Racial Myths and Science. Jensen's studies of IQ were not the first, nor the last, use of biology to rationalize discrimination policies. The science of eugenics, or selective breeding of humans, is also based on theories of the genetic superiority of certain groups. Richard Hofstadter examines the recurrence of genetic arguments in *Social*

Darwinism in American Thought, rev. ed. (San Diego, Calif.: Braziller, 1959). Marshall Sahlins analyzes biological explanations for social behavior in *The Use and Abuse of Biology: An Anthropological Critique of Sociobiology* (Ann Arbor: University of Michigan Press, 1976). Additional studies of the IQ test controversy include Leon Kamin, *The Science and Politics of IQ* (New York: Holstead, 1974); Samuel Bowles and Herbert Gintis, ''IQ in the U.S. Class Structure,'' *Social Policy,* vol. 3 (1972–1973): 65–96; and Richard Herrnstein, *IQ in the Meritocracy* (Boston: Atlantic Monthly Press, 1973).

Mexican-Americans. This ethnic group has a long history of struggle against discrimination. Several researchers have documented and analyzed their social conditions and political action, including Renato Rosaldo et al., *Chicano: The Evolution of a People* (Huntington, N.Y.: Krieger, 1976), and Gilberto López y Rivas, *The Chicanos: Life and Struggles of the Mexican Minority in the United States* (New York: Monthly Review Press, 1974). A popular study of the problems of this group and their growing militancy is Stan Steiner's *La Raza* (New York: Harper & Row, 1970). For a sociological overview of Mexican-Americans as an ethnic group, see Joan W. Moore, ed., *Mexican Americans,* 2nd ed. (Englewood Cliffs, N.J.: Prentice-Hall, 1976). A classic study of the migration of Mexicans to the United States and their communities in the Southwest is *North from Mexico* (Philadelphia, Pa.: Lippincott, 1949) by Carey McWilliams.

Blacks in America. Although we have suggested several books on the subject of the black American, there are many more. Two works which examine the ways that sociology has dealt with blacks are Stanford M. Lyman, *The Black American in Sociological Thought* (New York: Capricorn, 1972), and Joyce Ladner, *The Death of White Sociology* (New York: Random House, 1973). *Soul* (Chicago: Aldine, 1970), edited by Lee Rainwater, is a collection of articles describing aspects of black culture. Malcolm X's *The Autobiography of Malcolm X* (New York: Grove, 1966) takes you through his experiences and changing awareness as he becomes a spokesperson for black power. In *Tomorrow's Tomorrow: The Black Woman* (Garden City, N.Y.: Doubleday, 1972), Joyce Ladner analyzes the ability of black adolescent women to use their cultural resources in adapting to and struggling against the poverty and discrimination found in a big-city slum. Increasing opportunities available to some black Americans are explored in Richard Freeman, *Black Elite: The New Market for Highly Educated Blacks* (New York: McGraw-Hill, 1977). For an analysis of the political problems of racism, see William Wilson, *Power, Racism, and Privilege* (New York: Free Press, 1976).

CHAPTER 12

Power, Politics, and Economics

The idea of power is connected in most people's minds with that of politics and with those who are visibly in charge of running the country. It may therefore come as a surprise that a survey of over 1,000 key decision-makers in politics, business, and the professions list television and labor unions second and third only to the White House as the most influential on "decisions or actions affecting the nation as a whole." Big business ranked fifth, with the U.S. Senate and House sixth and eighth respectively (*U.S. News and World Report,* April 18, 1977).

Power is the ability to accomplish things, to overcome opposition, to dominate others—and it exists in all social institutions from the family to the highest levels of government. A parent has power over a child by virtue of traditions that support unequal family relationships and of his or her superior size, economic status, and perhaps knowledge. Children have power over their parents if their parents value their youngsters' happiness and well-being, want their admiration, and consider being good and loved parents essential to their self-esteem. As a result, homes can and do become sites of power struggles. Two areas where power is especially evident are politics and economics, and as we will see, even there, it is not always clear where the power of the government ends and that of business begins.

In this chapter we are concerned with the social structure of political and economic power. What is power? How is power channeled in the American economic and political systems? What changes are taking place in the exercise of power in this country today? This chapter addresses these questions.

WHAT IS POWER?

Power is, quite simply, the ability to control other people's behavior. An individual, group, or organization that can achieve its goals, regardless of what others might want, has power.

Struggles over control of the things people want and need and what they do take place at all levels of the social system—in families, in neighborhood play groups and adult social circles, in school, in sports, on the job, on the street, on the air (via radio and television), and especially in big business and government. Parents have power over children; teachers over students; employers over employees. On a different level, the media have power over public opinion; the government has power over the people it governs.

Power channeled through the government is *political power,* the ability to make and carry out binding decisions that affect the whole society. Power exercised by businesses is *economic power,* control of such resources as wealth, income, property, goods, and services. Although government and business appear to perform distinctively different functions, economic and political power are in fact shared by both. Governments set economic policy, regulate business, and control certain resources; businesses influence legislation through lobbying, and a government can be forced out of office by such economic crises as inflation or recession.

If power is the *ability* to control resources and other people's behavior, authority is the *right* to do so. When an individual justifies his or her decisions and actions in terms of moral beliefs, he or she is exercising authority (Andrain, 1975: 142). In other words, *authority* is power exercised in a way that peo-ple consider necessary and legitimate. Every year the Internal Revenue Service takes money from all working Americans. Although people grumble about taxes, few question the government's legitimate authority to collect them, and fewer still refuse to pay them. As Max Weber suggests, all organizations—particularly governments—depend on "a certain minimum of voluntary submission; [on] an interest (based on ulterior motives or genuine acceptance) in obedience" (Weber, 1947: 324). Power to which people willingly submit is authority.

Max Weber identified three types of authority: legal/rational, charismatic, and traditional. *Legal/rational authority* derives from a system of explicit rules or laws that define legitimate uses of power. Authority is vested in offices or positions, not in the people who temporarily occupy those posts. It is limited to "official business." For example, a boss has considerable authority over the way employees under his or her control spend their working days, but he or she doesn't have the authority to tell workers how to spend their weekends. In systems based on legal/rational authority, loyalty to the system largely replaces loyalty to a particular person.

Charismatic authority is the opposite of rational/legal authority. It derives from exceptional personal qualities that people perceive as a "gift of grace." People follow a charismatic leader because they are personally devoted to him or her. But as Weber observed: "The charismatic leader gains and maintains authority solely by proving his strength in life. If he wants to be a prophet, he must perform miracles; if he wants to be a war lord, he must perform heroic deeds" (1949: 249). The unique, irreplaceable qualities of a charismatic leader are not likely to appear twice in a row. For this reason, char-

As president of the United States, Richard Nixon was invested with legal/rational authority, which lies in the office, rather than in the person who holds it. The Watergate hearings revealed that he and his administration had overlooked this principle and had operated, instead, on the basis of personal loyalty. Many people feared that Nixon's abuse of his position might undermine the presidency as we know it, and the scandal led to his resignation. (Roland Freeman/Magnum)

ismatic authority is inherently unstable. Examples of charismatic leaders in recent history are Mahatma Gandhi, Martin Luther King, Jr., Malcolm X, and César Chavez.

Traditional authority lies somewhere between rational/legal authority and charismatic authority. In traditional societies, people tend to regard the way things have always been done as sacred; kings, queens, chiefs, priests, councils of elders, and the like are part of this sacred order. Although traditions may limit the authority of a king/queen or chief, he or she does have some personal latitude in making decisions. Positions are hereditary and people feel a sense of personal loyalty to the occupants. Thus, traditional authority is vested in *both* the office and the officeholder. A familiar example is the authority parents have over children.

In practice the three types of authority Weber identified may overlap. John F. Kennedy, for example, had rational/legal authority by virtue of his election to the presidency, the traditional authority that surrounds the office of the presidency, and charismatic appeal as well.

Whatever system of authority prevails, leaders or people in positions of power invariably try to *legitimize* their acts in terms of existing values, thereby attempting to establish authority. The legitimacy of an administration or system of government depends on its capacity "to engender and maintain the belief that existing political institutions are the most appropriate ones for the society" (Lipset, 1970: 40).

Influence is related, but not identical, to authority. We say people have *influence* when they are so highly respected, so well liked that they can change people's minds without resorting to compensation, threats, or manipulation. Although enhanced by official position, influence is ultimately a personal quality. Eleanor Roosevelt, for example, never held public office but she did hold much of the public's attention, respect, and admiration.

THEORIES OF POWER

There are essentially two schools of thought in regard to the origins and distribution of power. According to the *one-factor theory,* power is concentrated in the hands of a select few who dominate and manipulate the many. This position is evident in the writings of Karl Marx. Marx focused on economic interests, which he believed dictate power relations in a society. By contrast, Vilfredo Pareto and Gaetano Mosca focused on political power and governing elites. *Pluralists* such as David Riesman believe that a variety of groups and interests compete for power, with more or less success. Instead of one, there are many centers of power in society. This school of thought is a critical response to Marx's one-factor theory. We shall consider both here, beginning with Marx.

Marx: An Economic Theory of Power

Before Marx, political philosophers more or less assumed that social power resided in the state and in such related organizations as the military. Any discussion of power centered around government. In contrast, Marx argued that power is rooted in economics. The people who own the means of production (the factories, the raw materials, and so on) control society; the state (the official government) is little more than their servant (Olsen, 1970: 70).

According to Marx, each historical period is characterized by a predominant mode of production, a way of obtaining a livelihood, such as farming, commerce, or manufacturing. Each mode of production creates its own power hierarchy, or in Marx's terms, a ruling and an oppressed class. Under feudalism, the ruling class is made up of landowners; the oppressed class, of peasants. Under industrial capitalism, the ruling class is the bourgeoisie (the owners of industry); the oppressed class, the proletariat (propertyless wage earners). Because the bourgeoisie owns and controls the means of production, it directs not only economic activity but also the moral and intellectual life of the workers, including law, government, art, literature, science, and philosophy. The tension and conflict this inevitably creates between the haves and the have-nots culminates in a revolution and in the eventual creation of a classless society.

Pareto and Mosca: The Elitist View

Later political philosophers disagreed sharply with Marx's focus on economics and with his predictions about the coming of a classless society. Vilfredo Pareto (1848–1923) and Gaetano Mosca (1858–1941) saw inequalities of power as inherent in any social order. Pareto (1935) began with the simple observation that some lawyers are sharper, some royal mistresses more influential, some thieves more successful than others. These are the *elites* of their respective fields—members of that small minority who lead. The same holds true for any society as a whole. Throughout history, small governing elites, distinguished by talent and organization, have ruled the masses by virtue of their superiority.

By elite or ruling class, neither Pareto nor Mosca (1939) meant a strictly hereditary class; both believed that hereditary ruling classes, like families that have been inbred for too long, eventually degenerate. Such hereditary ruling classes, according to Pareto, become wily, manipulative, and decadent "foxes." At the other end of the scale are vigorous, ambitious individuals full of

MICHELS'S "IRON RULE OF OLIGARCHY"

Writing in the first decades of the nineteenth century, German economist and sociologist Robert Michels attempted to explain why power tends to fall into the hands of a small group of leaders in *all* organizations, whatever their goals and ideology. After studying the labor and socialist movements of his time, Michels concluded that as organizations grow in size and complexity, the need for leadership becomes more and more pressing. Informal decision-making in which all members participate becomes impractical: there are too many issues to resolve; the organization must present a united front to the outside. Leaders chosen for their special talents in administration and public relations gradually take command. In time, these leaders develop a vested interest in maintaining their positions. A combination of admiration and apathy in the rank and file accelerates this concentration of power in the hands of a few. Within the ruling clique, maintaining the organization becomes an end in itself. Leaders tend to become conservative, to seek compromises with enemies, to avoid taking risks, and to modify extreme and unpopular goals—in other words, to protect their positions. Nowhere is this process more obvious than in successful radical political movements; revolutions, Michels argues, are little more than the replacement of one elite by another. In Michels's view, "Who says organizations says oligarchy."

SOURCE: Robert Michels, *Political Parties* (1915), Glencoe, Ill.: Free Press, 1949.

confidence and convinced of their cause, the "lions" who unseat the foxes in an endless cycle or "circulation of elites." Underlying this idea is the assumption that the masses of people are neither desirous nor capable of leading or governing themselves.

Marx's economic heirs see a present dominated by economic *oligarchies*—small groups of powerful leaders—but believe the future holds the promise of a classless society. Pareto and Mosca's heirs believe political oligarchy is inevitable in any system.

C. Wright Mills: The Power Elite

I should contend that "men are free to make history," but that some men are indeed much freer than others. (Mills, 1958: 29)

Among American sociologists, C. Wright Mills took the lead in documenting the existence of an American *power elite,* that coalition of military leaders, government officials, and business executives which exists above and beyond the official political system. Mills began with the fact that many people who occupy high positions in government have also held high positions in corporations or the military and seem to move back and forth between these centers of power. America's governing elite, wrote Mills, is "a coalition of generals in the roles of corporation executives, of politicians masquerading as admirals, of corporation executives acting like politicians" (1959: 278). Tracing their personal histories, Mills found that by and large these people come from similar white Anglo-Saxon Protestant, old American backgrounds, attend the same Ivy League schools, belong to the same exclusive clubs, visit the same resorts, and so on. Thus if the president of an oil company doesn't know the federal "energy czar" personally, he surely knows someone who knows him (and can place a confidential call, if necessary). Through their social similarities, the power elite's coinciding interests are reinforced.

G. William Domhoff (1967) has collected concrete evidence that such an elite exists, although it isn't as unified or coordinated as Mills believed. The top .05 percent of the U.S. population controls a large share of the country's wealth and holds a disproportionate number of high-level positions in government and business. It is a tightly knit group whose members attend the same schools, belong to the same clubs and civic associations, and intermarry.

Mills argued that the different branches of the elite are interlocking. Congress approves billions of dollars in military appropriations every year, dollars that go more or less directly into corporate pockets. Why? In part for national defense; in part because military contracts create jobs; and in part because business leaders are important campaign contributors. Thus politicians tend to support big business, and business leaders often support politicians. (Ceilings on campaign contributions may now lessen the influence business has on government.) All three sectors—economic, political, and military—have a vested interest in what Mills calls "military capitalism."

Mills believed the trend toward centralization of power would continue unabated. "The top of modern American society is increasingly unified, and often seems willfully coordinated: at the top there has emerged an elite whose power probably exceeds that of any small group of men in world history" (in Olsen, 1970: 261).

The Pluralist View

But where is the evidence that America's political, military, and corporate chieftains are all of one mind or that they cooperate with one another? Isn't the reverse more likely—that is, that they see one another as rivals? This is the question pluralists ask. They agree with Mills that some people are freer to make history than others and that unorganized individuals (the masses) are powerless. But they don't see a single ruling clique, a power elite at the top of the power structure in this country (see figure 12:1). Rather, pluralists argue that social power is *dispersed* among a variety of competing interest groups—the oil industry and the coal industry, car manufacturers and ecologists, unions and business associations, hunters' lobbies and wildlife funds, and so forth. All these groups control resources and activities at different times with varying degrees of success, but no one group is in command. In most cases, they can do little more than veto programs that threaten their interests. In David Riesman's words, "Today we have substituted for [centralized, mercantile-aristocratic] leadership a series of groups, each of which has struggled for and finally attained a power to stop things conceivably inimical to its interests and, within far narrower limits, to start things" (1951: 242). (See also Dahl, 1961; Kornhauser, 1961; Keller, 1963.)

Mills believes that coinciding interests, reinforced by social similarity, bind America's leaders together into a single cohesive power elite. Riesman maintains that diverse, often conflicting interests preclude united policy or action. Mills argues that members of the power elite settle important questions among themselves, behind closed doors. Riesman disagrees, arguing that fundamental issues are decided through bargaining by

figure 12:1   Elitist and pluralist views of the American power structure

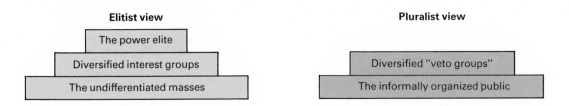

SOURCE: Adapted from William Kornhauser, " 'Power Elite' or 'Veto Groups'?'' in Seymour Martin Lipset and Leo Lowenthal, eds., *Culture and Social Character* (Glencoe, Ill.: Free Press, 1961), pp. 525–567.

The primary difference between elitists and pluralists is that the former see a unified elite at the top of the power structure and the latter do not.

and among interested parties, and that the parties who exercise power vary with the issue. (The National Rifle Association, for example, isn't interested in farm subsidies or the National Endowment for the Arts.) Mills laments the erosion of democracy, the loss of responsible and accountable centers of power, the alienation of the powerless many. Riesman deplores the dearth of leadership and the lack of direction in American politics.

In *The Power Structure* (1967), Arnold Rose concludes that both sides of this argument are correct in the case of the United States. Rose concedes that foreign affairs seem to be dominated by a small group of people who resemble Mills's power elite, but he suggests that the growth of the federal government and the emergence of new pressure groups (such as civil rights organizations) have undercut the power of big business[1] and that no such elite dominates domestic affairs. In his view, there are many power structures in America, not just one, and nationwide decisions are made through

a process of bargaining among them (the pluralist view). However, the power structures themselves (political parties, government agencies, legislatures, businesses, and so on) tend to be dominated by oligarchies (the elitist view). Rose also notes that senators, approximately one in five of whom are millionaires (what Mills calls social similarity), tend to vote according to their own, presumably upper-class convictions. In short, Rose sees the American power structure as a complex plurality of elites.

POWER IN THE ECONOMIC SYSTEM

All economic systems face the same basic problem: how to satisfy potentially unlimited human desires with limited resources. There is only so much land, water, fuel, money, labor, and talent. How resources get allocated and desires become shaped reflects

---

[1]   Rose was writing in 1967, *pre*-Watergate.

the distribution of power in the economic system.

Industrialization forces the development of complex economic systems. It involves a shift from muscle power (human and animal) to machines powered by fossil fuels; from reliance on traditional ways of producing goods to the application of technical and scientific knowledge. Whereas in nontechnological societies, families and villages are largely self-sufficient, in industrial society, all individuals are drawn into an intricate market economy. Work becomes separated from family life; people produce goods for the market rather than for their own use. Work also becomes more specialized: hundreds, even thousands, of individuals play small roles in creating a single product (such as a car). The more specialized the division of labor, the more interdependent members of a society become. Traditional methods of distributing goods and services, based on reciprocal obligations between family groups, no longer suffice.

There are four crucial questions that a modern economic system must answer if it is to function effectively: (1) What goods and services should be produced, and in what quantities (for example, private cars or public trains)? (2) How should these be produced? (3) How should goods and services be distributed? (4) What proportion of earnings should be spent now, and what proportion reinvested in production (building new factories, improving technology through research, and so on)?

Economic power is having the resources and the control over other people's actions to make these decisions. The ways in which economic power is acquired and used depend on the system. Here we will focus on the capitalist market economy, as exemplified by the United States.

The Organization of the American Economic System

The American economic system is based on an ideology of private ownership and a market economy. Privately owned firms decide what to produce, in what quantities, and how to distribute their products. Ideally, this gives consumers a free choice and the opportunity to influence production. The price consumers are willing to pay tells businesses how desirable a product is. If businesses compete freely to maximize profits and people consume selectively to minimize their expenses, needs should be met.

In contrast, the Soviet system is based on an ideology of public ownership and a planned economy. All economic activity is under government control. Central planning agencies make decisions about what goods to produce and how to distribute them, based on long-range plans and data on crops and inventories. Ideally, expenditures for such public services as education and transportation and reinvestment in production are higher in a planned than in a market economy. Opportunities for private consumption are limited, but are distributed more equally.

In reality, both the United States and the Soviet Union have "mixed economies." For example, most rural and half of all urban homes in Russia are privately owned. Doctors, lawyers, carpenters, tailors, and others conduct private practices. Such staples as milk and eggs are bartered at private farmers' markets. In the United States, a number of businesses (such as the Communications Satellite Corporation) operate under joint government/private ownership. Research and the defense, electronics, and oil industries are heavily dependent on government expenditures. (In effect, the government has become a silent partner.) Moreover, the government periodically "interferes" with the free market by instituting wage and price controls and price supports (Andrain, 1975: 166–169).

The National Power of Large Corporations Economic power derives from the particular system of production and distribution in a society, as indicated above. The corporation, with its roots in the joint stock companies of the sixteenth century, dominates modern technological capitalist societies. A corporation is an organization created by law that has an ongoing existence and powers and liabilities that are distinct from those of its members. Thus if you have an accident because the steering mechanism on your new car jammed, you sue General Motors (GM)—not the engineer who designed the car or the mechanic who neglected to tighten a bolt.

There is no disputing the fact that a small number of large corporations control a disproportionate share of the American economy. Of some 4.5 million businesses in the United States, only 13 percent are corporations. Yet the sales figures for the 500 largest corporations totaled $971.1 billion in 1976, for a combined profit of $49.4 billion (*Fortune*, May 1977: 364). Two hundred top corporations control $413 billion in assets, 40 percent of the national wealth. Twenty-eight giant corporations provide 10 percent of the jobs in this country. (Forty percent of Americans work for companies that employ 361 workers or more.) The seven largest laboratories employ 20 percent of all the technical and scientific experts in private industry, and account for 26 percent of the total expenditures for research and development in the country. In one six-year period, ten corporations were awarded contracts amounting to one-third of all defense expenditures—ten corporations, out of 4.5 million businesses (Kaysen, 1966: 232)!

Of course, wealth alone doesn't guarantee power. Are large corporations able to make choices that significantly affect others? Carl Kaysen (1966) thinks they are, for three basic reasons. First, a corporation that provides all or nearly all of a product or service is free from the restraints that exist in a competitive market. It can charge almost anything it wants for its product. And by advertising (associating a product with its brand name), taking out patents, controlling raw materials, and either convincing government to suppress competition or colluding with other corporations, it can prevent new firms from entering the market. It can also buy up other companies—competitors, suppliers, manufacturers of related or different products—and become a *conglomerate*, thus controlling huge amounts of resources and great numbers of jobs through subsidiaries. About 60 percent of manufacturing in this country is oligopolistic—that is, controlled by a very few corporations.

Second, corporations decide when and at what pace to invest, thus determining the rate of growth of different industries. For example, reluctance to expand steel production facilities in this country caused shortages in the 1950s and again in the 1970s. Our mills are outdated (in comparison with those of other nations), and we now import much of our steel—which affects employment rates, the price of anything made with steel, and even taxes (because steel is vital in the manufacture of defense equipment).

Third, corporations are free to decide what new technologies to explore through research and development, and what innovations will be translated into new products and services. Technology has a profound im-

table 12:1   THE 25 LARGEST INDUSTRIAL CORPORATIONS (ranked by sales)

RANK '76	RANK '75	COMPANY	SALES	ASSETS	RANK	NET INCOME	RANK	STOCKHOLDERS' EQUITY	RANK
1	1	Exxon (New York)	$48,630,817	$36,331,346	1	$2,640,964	2	$18,470,352	1
2	2	General Motors (Detroit)	47,181,000	24,442,400	2	2,902,800	1	14,385,200	2
3	4	Ford Motor (Dearborn, Mich.)	28,839,600	15,768,100	6	983,100	4	7,107,000	6
4	3	Texaco (New York)	26,451,851	18,193,818	4	869,731	9	9,002,077	4
5	5	Mobil (New York)[1]	26,062,570	18,767,450	3	942,523	5	7,651,811	5
6	6	Standard Oil of California (San Francisco)	19,434,133	13,765,397	7	880,127	8	7,007,013	7
7	8	Gulf Oil (Pittsburgh)	16,451,000	13,449,000	8	816,000	10	6,942,000	8
8	7	International Business Machines (Armonk, N.Y.)	16,304,333	17,723,326	5	2,398,093	3	12,749,287	3
9	9	General Electric (Fairfield, Conn.)	15,697,300	12,049,700	9	930,600	6	5,252,900	10
10	10	Chrysler (Highland Park, Mich.)	15,537,788	7,074,365	16	422,631	19	2,815,326	20
11	11	International Tel. & Tel. (New York)	11,764,106	11,070,078	11	494,467	15	4,574,256	13
12	12	Standard Oil (Indiana) (Chicago)	11,532,048	11,213,198	10	892,968	7	6,146,705	9
13	14	Shell Oil (Houston)	9,229,950	7,836,516	14	705,838	11	4,591,182	12
14	13	U.S. Steel (Pittsburgh)	8,604,200	9,167,900	12	410,300	21	5,129,000	11
15	15	Atlantic Richfield (Los Angeles)	8,462,524	8,853,334	13	575,178	14	4,091,133	14
16	17	E. I. du Pont de Nemours (Wilmington, Del.)	8,361,000	7,027,100	17	459,300	17	4,039,200	15
17	16	Continental Oil (Stamford, Conn.)	7,957,620	6,041,516	21	459,994	16	2,635,444	24
18	18	Western Electric (New York)	6,930,942	5,178,460	24	217,383	40	3,261,615	17
19	19	Procter & Gamble (Cincinnati)[2]	6,512,728	4,102,996	32	401,098	22	2,357,470	26
20	22	Tenneco (Houston)	6,389,236	7,177,100	15	383,500	23	2,651,000	23
21	21	Union Carbide (New York)	6,345,700	6,621,600	19	441,200	18	3,055,100	18
22	20	Westinghouse Electric (Pittsburgh)	6,145,152	5,318,342	23	223,217	39	2,138,435	30
23	23	Goodyear Tire & Rubber (Akron, Ohio)	5,791,494	4,336,125	29	121,967	88	1,861,911	36
24	26	Phillips Petroleum (Bartlesville, Okla.)	5,697,516	5,068,463	25	411,656	20	2,720,341	21
25	32	Dow Chemical (Midland, Mich.)	5,652,070	6,848,664	18	612,767	13	2,865,010	19

[1]A holding company created in 1976 as a successor to Mobil Oil, now a wholly owned subsidiary.
[2]Figures are for fiscal year ending June 30, 1976.

SOURCE: Adapted from "The Fortune Directory of the 500 Largest U.S. Industrial Corporations," *Fortune*, vol. 95 (May 1977), p. 366.

pact on all aspects of social life (as we'll see in chapter 19). If, for example, Ford and General Motors had put all of their assets into developing high-quality public transportation (such as electric trains) instead of private automobiles, this country's settlement patterns, dating habits, and even foreign policy (in particular, American relations with oil-producing nations) would be quite different from what they are today.

Kaysen concludes that each large corporation is run by a small group that makes choices affecting all aspects and all members of society, and that is "answerable ultimately only to itself" (237). Corporations wield considerable political power as well. On the state and local levels, national firms can promise to build or expand in a given area, or to withdraw from that area if legislatures don't pass the taxes, zoning regula-

tions, and road plans that suit them. Moreover, large firms operate as quasi-sovereign powers in much of the developing world. (The most highly publicized example of this was ITT's spending $1 million to overthrow Chile's socialist President Salvador Allende.)

The Global Power of Multinationals The multinational corporation is a mid-twentieth-century phenomenon. Crossing national boundaries to obtain raw materials and to market goods is an old tradition, one that dates back to the Phoenician glass merchants and even earlier. What is new about global corporations is that they no longer consider foreign factories and markets as adjuncts to home operations, but view the entire world as a single economic system. "The men who run the global corporations are the first in history with the organization, technol-

---

table 12:2 **RATING THE AMERICAN BUSINESS SYSTEM BY THE AMERICAN PUBLIC (by percent)**

	GOOD	AVERAGE	POOR
Developing new products	44	42	6
Providing products and services that meet needs	38	49	6
Hiring minorities	36	48	8
Paying good wages	33	50	10
Producing safe products	24	58	10
Being interested in customers	14	56	22
Communicating with employees	11	60	21
Dealing with shortages	11	49	32
Providing value for money	10	59	23
Controlling pollution	9	53	32
Honesty in advertising	7	52	33

SOURCE: Adapted from "Selected Summary Tables: Study of American Opinion, 1978," sponsored by *U.S. News and World Report* and conducted by Marketing Concepts, Inc., p. 7.

ogy, money, and ideology to make a credible try at managing the world as an integrated unit'' (Barnet and Müller, 1974: 13).

Multinational corporations are giant organizations with operations and subsidiaries in many countries. For example, Michael Fribourg heads a corporation with sales estimated at $3 billion per year, derived from real estate in Long Island, New York, Switzerland, France, and Morocco; 50,000 head of cattle in Argentina; hybrid grain produced in Latin America; ski resorts in Spain; a nail

factory in the United States; and the Overseas Shipholding Group, Inc.—among other holdings (Miller, 1973: 705). International Harvester assembles engines built in Germany and chassis built in America in factories in Turkey (Barnet and Müller, 1974: 41). Kodak Instamatic cameras are made in Germany, Sony televisions in the United States. The chairman of Nabisco anticipates a day when 2 billion people around the globe will munch Ritz crackers.

Global corporations are beyond the reach of national governments. By shifting assets and operations abroad, they are able to avoid government regulations, high taxes, and labor unions. (For example, by selling to their own divisions, they can take a loss in countries with high taxes and show a gain in countries with low taxes.) Moreover, global corporations are bigger than many national governments. GM's sales for 1973 were higher than the Gross National Products of

This gas station in Nigeria is representative of the rise of multinational corporations. Such organizations operate beyond the control of national governments, and they herald a new global power structure that may render political divisions obsolete. (Marc & Evelyne Bernheim/ Woodfin Camp & Associates)

Switzerland, Pakistan, and South Africa combined (Barnet and Müller, 1974: 15).

What all this means, in simple terms, is that a new global power structure is emerging, one that transcends the political power of nations. Increasingly, the managers of GM, IBM, Pepsico, GE, Pfizer, Shell, Volkswagen, Exxon, and perhaps a hundred other global corporations influence the prosperity, balance of payments, and political strength of the countries in which they operate. The decisions made by boards of directors are not *necessarily* any worse, or any better, than those politicians make. But "by what right do a self-selected group of druggists, biscuit-makers, and computer designers become the architects of the new world" (Barnet and Müller, 1974: 25)?

Who Controls the American Economy?

Who precisely are the druggists and biscuit-makers who apparently wield so much power in American society? Has the growth of giant corporations created a new breed of economic decision-makers?

Power Within the Corporation In a classic work entitled *The Modern Corporation and Private Property* (1932; rev. ed., 1968), Adolph A. Berle and Gardiner C. Means proclaim that

> the translation of perhaps two-thirds of the industrial wealth of the country from individual ownership to ownership by the large, publicly financed corporations vitally changes the lives of property owners, the lives of workers, and the methods of property tenure. (vii–viii)

In the "old days" (the early nineteenth century), owner-entrepreneurs ran their own businesses, made all key decisions, and reaped the profits or suffered the losses of their economic policies. With the rise of the corporation, however, ownership was divorced from management. The corporation collects wealth from small and large investors who are willing to take risks for a profit-making enterprise, and turns the actual operation of the firm (setting policy and making daily decisions) over to professional managers. As a result, ownership has become diffuse and passive. The thousands of people who own stock in IBM, for example, don't know one another or meet regularly. Moreover, they lack the technical and legal expertise necessary to make decisions for "their" company. So long as they make a profit, the managers (who have the cohesion and know-how shareholders lack) are free to do what they think best. Thus the owners don't manage, and the managers don't own (although they receive substantial salaries and may own some stock). According to Berle and Means, corporate responsibility—and power—are fragmented.

Charles H. Anderson (1974) is one of many social scientists who believe that the separation of ownership and management in modern corporations is an illusion. As noted in chapter 10, 1 percent of the American population owns four-fifths of all corporate stock. The few thousand investors who own the major share of the 500 top corporations in the country are in a position to exercise enormous economic power—to make choices that have a significant effect on others.

One-third of the top 500 corporations are identifiably in the hands of single individuals or families. Some stockholders may be "passive" owners, but others quite definitely are not. A study of 232 corporations revealed that 99 of their 2,784 directors and their families owned $13 billion or more worth of stock (Anderson, 1974: 203). Acting on behalf of individuals and families, the Morgan Guaranty Trust Company of New York has placed its officers on the boards of directors of over 100 corporations and directly or indirectly controls $70 billion in corporate assets (209). In Anderson's view, these active, wealthy owner-directors constitute a ruling capitalist class that operates America's corporations in its own interests.

The truth may lie somewhere between these two views. We don't have as much data on the rich as we do on the poor—in part because sociologists have only recently begun "studying up," and in part because corporations operate behind closed doors. But one sign of Americans' belief that business power is now too concentrated is the consumer movement.

The Rise of Consumerism The rise of mammoth anonymous corporations in America has been met by a rise in *consumerism*: a movement to protect buyers from dangerous, inferior, or useless products, misleading advertising, and unfair prices.

The consumer movement can be traced to the early 1960s and to two publications that sparked public awareness: the U.S. Surgeon General's *Report on Smoking* (1962), which declared cigarettes a health hazard, and Ralph Nader's *Unsafe at Any Speed* (1965), which took the auto industry to task for dangerously shabby engineering. The time was right. The buying public was better educated than ever before. For the first time, a great many people (not just the rich) were able to purchase such new, complex, expensive items as stereos and color TVs and had begun worrying about how these items would work. There was a growing feeling that no one was accountable to consumers for the quality of goods and services offered by banks, stores, manufacturers, or utilities.

Finally, the public was becoming aware that the environment was deteriorating rapidly. And so the consumer movement was born.

Much has changed as a result. Cigarette manufacturers are no longer allowed to advertise on radio or television, and must print a warning on every pack. Safety belts, headrests, and shatterproof glass are now mandatory equipment on all cars sold in the United States, and manufacturers are required to recall all cars thought to have defects. (Over a million were recalled between 1966 and 1976.) Safety standards have been raised, particularly on products designed for, or attractive to, children (such as toys and pill containers). A number of cities have extended truth-in-packaging regulations to include mandatory unit pricing (a supplementary system of pricing items by showing the prices in terms of standard units, such as price per pound) so that buyers can comparison-shop. Some food manufacturers now print full nutritional information on all packages. The Truth in Lending Act passed in 1968 requires banks and stores to inform consumers of the annual interest rate they pay for credit. If banks or stores refuse a person credit, they must reveal the sources of their information on him or her. A number of cities now require drugstores to display a price list of commonly prescribed medicines, along with their generic names. In some areas, lawyers are now permitted to advertise the cost of their services. And a number of companies have been required to print or broadcast retractions of misleading ads.

In addition, there are a number of organizations that provide consumer services. Better business bureaus offer free arbitration for disputes between businesses and consumers as an alternative to lengthy, expensive court procedures. Manufacturers and retail stores have established consumer service departments run by high-level executives, not by

table 12:3 **MAJOR FEDERAL CONSUMER LEGISLATION**

LEGISLATION	YEAR	MAJOR PROVISIONS
Food and drug		
Pure Food and Drug Law	1906	Forbade adulteration and misbranding of food and drugs sold in interstate commerce. Food and Drug Administration, under Agriculture Department, was made responsible for enforcement.
Meat Inspection Act	1907	Authorized the Department of Agriculture to inspect meat slaughtering, packing, and canning plants.
Federal Food, Drug, and Cosmetic Act	1938	Added cosmetics and therapeutic products to FDAs jurisdiction. Broadened definition of misbranding to include "false and misleading" labeling. The FDA was removed from the Department of Agriculture to the Department of Health, Education, and Welfare.
Kefauver-Harris Drug Amendment to Food and Drug Act	1962	Required manufacturer to test safety and effectiveness of drugs before marketing and to include the common or generic name of the drug on the label.
Wholesome Meat Act	1967	Updated and strengthened standards for the inspection of slaughterhouses of red meat animals.
Drug Listing Act	1972	Provided FDA with access to information on drug manufacturers.
Protection against misbranding and false or harmful advertising		
Wool Labeling Act	1939	Required fabric labeling, actual percentage of fabric components, and manufacturer's name.
Fur Products Labeling Act	1951	Required that furs name animals of origin.
Textile Fiber Products Identification Act	1958	Prohibited misbranding and false advertising of textile fiber products not covered in the Wool or Fur Labeling acts.
Federal Hazardous Substances Labeling Act	1960	Required warning labels to appear on items containing dangerous household chemicals.

powerless clerks. And there are hundreds of volunteer consumer groups at the state and local level that offer free advice and arbitration. The Nader forces are not alone.

Perhaps the most important advance has been in public awareness. According to a poll conducted by the Marketing Science Institute in 1976, Americans consider ''helping consumers to get a fair deal'' more important than reforming the federal bureaucracy, restoring integrity to government, or creating a national energy policy. Sixty-five percent of those polled said it was very difficult to get anything done when something they bought proved unsatisfactory. (Most had difficulty even reading a warranty.) Forty-six percent think most or all TV ads are seriously misleading. More than 40 percent believe food manufacturers, hospitals, and the medical profession need close supervision. Thirty percent express distrust of the oil industry, of car and pharmaceutical manufacturers, of electric utilities, and of auto repair shops. A large majority believe that business will help consumers only when forced to do so; 54 percent favor the creation of a federal consumer agency (Sentry Insurance, 1976).

Yet consumers are generally optimistic. Most Americans believe that products are safer and better labeled today than they were ten years ago, and that their own shopping skills have improved. Seventy-seven percent think the consumer movement is keeping business on its toes. (Businesspeople, in contrast, feel consumer activists don't understand how they operate.) Almost half the consumers polled anticipate continued improvement.

POWER IN THE POLITICAL SYSTEM

The political system in a society is responsible for ''making and carrying out . . . bind-ing policies related to crucial problems facing a society'' (Andrain, 1975: 49). All political systems, at all times and in all places, confront four basic problems. The first is *creating a common political identity.* The many civil wars that have erupted in sub-Saharan Africa, where regional tribal loyalties are often stronger than nationalism, suggest how difficult this can be. The second problem is *establishing power.* A government that is unable to implement its policies—to secure compliance from its citizens—is no government at all. The third problem is *establishing legitimate authority.* No political system relies exclusively on force. Leaders have to justify their decisions and gain acceptance for their policies. Fourth, there is the crucial problem of *producing and distributing goods and services,* which was discussed in the preceding section. In this section we will focus on the second and third problems, the establishment of power and authority, with emphasis on the American system.

Power and the State

The *state* differs from other organizations in a society, Weber wrote, in that it successfully ''claims the *monopoly of the legitimate use of physical force* within a given territory'' (1949: 78). Organized crime may use physical force to coerce people, but ordinarily not with social consent and approval. Only the state is conceded the legitimate right to forcibly arrest, jail, and in some cases kill people.

In *democratic states,* authority derives from the law, rooted in the consent of the people. Both the rulers and the ruled (ideally) believe in the principle of due process. The government has the power to implement its policies (opposition groups don't succeed in immobilizing the government), but that power is limited. Individuals or parties are granted only temporary authority. Other groups have the right and also the resources—including numbers of people, organization, knowledge, and private property—to challenge government decisions. The government guides but doesn't control the economy; private firms compete in a market system. Politics is based on the belief that power shouldn't be used in capricious or arbitrary ways, and on adherence to the democratic rules of the game. The state does not claim exclusive, unquestioning loyalty (Andrain, 1975: 191–197).

In contrast, in a *totalitarian state,* the centralized government doesn't recognize or tolerate parties of differing opinion. Authority rests on ideological and/or personal grounds. The leader justifies his or her right to rule by claiming that he or she embodies an ideological cause. Power tends to be concentrated in the hands of one ruling party, which is permanently identified with the government: the party and the state are one. The government (ideally) directs all economic activity. It also seeks to create ideological uniformity by controlling education, the mass media, and arts and literature. The power of authorities is so great that it may be exercised in capricious and apparently arbitrary ways. The resulting atmosphere of anxiety and insecurity compels citizens to demonstrate active loyalty to the state (Andrain, 1975: 214–218).

The contrasts between these two systems

In totalitarian states, power rests on ideological and/or personal grounds and is concentrated in one individual or party. The government attempts to direct all economic activity and to control education, the media, and the arts. Today, the Shah of Iran heads one of the world's most repressive totalitarian regimes. (G. Chauvel / Sygma)

are obvious, and we are accustomed to think of states as *either* democratic or totalitarian. However, as Andrain points out, many nation-states are neither one nor the other. The military rulers of Latin America and the hereditary rulers of some Arab states, for example, have neither the will nor the resources to establish total control over their societies. Their authority derives from personal charisma and from their position in a ruling family. Although they may be described (and see themselves) as absolute rulers, in reality they share power with the army, other members of the royal family, the landed aristocracy, and the clergy. Political goals are accomplished through a combination of consensus and coercion. However, power struggles usually take place in the capital city and have little or no effect on "the masses." Villages in the hinterlands are largely autonomous. The economy consists largely of subsistence agriculture (families producing for their own needs). There are few industries or cash crops for a leader or several leaders to control. Politics is based on ancestral ties and religion (Andrain, 1975: 228–242). The American system is quite different, but it too is not purely democratic.

"I don't feel like it, that's why. Why don't you exercise your power?" Drawing by Richter; © 1978 The New Yorker Magazine, Inc.

Political Power in America

Traditionally, political activity in America has centered around parties. In 1915, Robert Michels (1876–1936) defined a political party as a "society of propaganda and of agitation seeking to acquire power" (1949: 134). Although these aren't the words contemporary Americans might choose, this definition is essentially correct. *Political parties* are collectivities designed for gaining and holding legitimate governmental power. Parties perform several crucial functions in large, complex political systems. Ideally, they link the people and the government, transmitting public opinion up to where decisions are actually made, thereby converting public opinion into legislation. Parties also mobilize grass-roots support for policy decisions made at the upper level. Parties also serve as a link between different branches and levels of government (executive and legislative, federal and state) and between official (governmental) power structures and unofficial (nongovernmental) power structures. On the practical level, parties play a dominant role in recruiting personnel for elective office (Dowse and Hughes, 1972: 339–341).

The Two-party System Although we are accustomed to thinking in terms of two main parties, in some countries there are five or more parties, in others only one (and the struggle for power takes place within the party rather than between parties). Why is this? Why does the United States consistently generate two parties, while Italy consistently generates several? The answer lies in the structure of a country's electoral system.

French sociologist Maurice Duverger (1954) argues that two-party systems emerge when there can be only one candidate from each party and the winner of the election takes all. This simple-plurality system discourages third parties, because a vote for a minor party is in effect a wasted vote. There is almost no chance that the third-party candidate will win. In contrast, in proportional-vote systems like Italy's a party receives the same percentage of representation as of votes in the election. In this kind of electoral system, a vote for a minority-party candidate is not wasted, for even if the party receives only 10 percent of the votes, it receives a tenth of the seats in the legislature.

The simple-plurality system determines not only the number of parties in the United States, but also their character. To win state-wide and national elections, American parties must embrace diverse kinds of people and a wide range of interests. Differences of opinion must be settled *before* elections. Critics like Duverger argue that the American system forces parties into bland positions and prevents many groups from being represented. Both the Democratic and the Republican parties must lean toward the center and create policies that sound attractive to everyone and offend no one. Duverger's analysis suggests that politicians can't be blamed for political double talk; the social structure of American parties forces them to generate it. However, Duverger points out that the simple-plurality system is more stable than proportional representation, where coalitions must be formed issue by issue in the legislature.

There are signs that the party system in America is changing. The media—in particular, television news—have taken over some of the functions formerly performed by political parties: scouting for talent; informing voters about what candidates are saying; predicting which way the election will go. In some cases newscasters act as self-appointed public defenders, exposing the frailties of candidates and fixing blame for breakdowns in the system. Partly as a result, American voters are more independent than they once were. Parties can't organize and mobilize the electorate as effectively as they once did (Ladd and Hadley, 1975). The proportion of voters who identify themselves as Independents has grown steadily and is now larger than the proportion of voters who consider themselves Democrats, and twice the size of the proportion of voters allied with the Republican party (Nie et al., 1976 346).

The Power of Interest Groups In a sense, interest groups make up for the amorphous and tentative character of political parties in this country. An *interest group* is an organization created to influence political decisions that directly concern its members. They range from business associations (such as the National Association of Manufacturers) to labor unions (most notably the powerful AFL-CIO), agricultural groups (including the National Milk Producers Association), professional associations (the American Medical Association, the American Bar Association), civil rights groups (the National Association for the Advancement of Colored People, the American Civil Liberties Union), political groups (Americans for Democratic Action, the John Birch Society), and special-interest associations (such as the National Rifle Association). Corporations may form their own lobbies, the most notorious example in recent years being ITT's attempt to gain favorable settlement of an antitrust suit by offering to underwrite the 1972 Republican National Convention. In addition, agencies and departments within the government may lobby, using their resources and spokespeople to influence Congress. For example, members of the Defense Department regularly testify in favor of increased military spending. Foreign governments also place lobbies in Washington to look out for their interests (see Milbrath, 1963).

The activities of the National Rifle Association (NRA) illustrate the way interest groups work. The NRA has an annual budget of over $5 million and publishes the *American Rifleman* (circulation 900,000). In 1963, the year President Kennedy was shot, the House Judiciary Subcommittee on Juvenile Delinquency began to consider legislation that would forbid the mail-order sale of firearms to minors. The *American Rifleman* responded with articles characterizing the bill as irrational and emotional, and urged readers to write their representatives in Congress (even supplying their names). The subcommittee decided to defer action. In his message on crime given to Congress in March 1965, President Johnson called for strict gun control. The NRA sent an urgent letter to members, distorting the administration's bill and warning that "if the battle is lost, it will be your loss, and that of all who follow." This plea was successful, and in December the NRA thanked readers of the *American Rifleman* for letters that effectively prevented the passage of gun-control laws. No legislation reached the floor of the House or Senate in 1967, but the NRA continued its attacks, now focusing on individual legislators whom it called "do-gooders" and "fanatics." "All of these people would like to bury your guns. Some of them would like to bury us, also," read one editorial. Not until June 1968, when Robert Kennedy was as-

sassinated, did letters to Congress supporting gun control outnumber letters opposing it. In October of that year, Congress passed a law limiting interstate shipment of long guns (*Congressional Quarterly*, April–October, 1968).

Interest groups may negotiate directly with the executive branch (as ITT did), or may work through the courts (as the NAACP and the ACLU have done). Some support sympathetic candidates with endorsements, campaign funds, and campaign workers. In addition to pressuring lawmakers, lobbyists may direct public relations and propaganda campaigns to improve their constituent's image and to win popular support for their views.

In most cases lobbyists work for the elite of an organization; they are hired by the leaders of a union, for example, not by the rank and file, and they are accountable to those leaders. Still, the diversity of interest groups creates numerous crosscurrents. Many people are active in (or at least responsive to) different groups at the same time. For example, in her support of women's rights, a conservative Southern Democrat may find herself aligned with outspoken liberals. Seymour M. Lipset suggests that diverse and conflicting interests, which prevent the formation of solid political blocs, are essential to modern democracies. "Multiple and politically inconsistent affiliations, loyalties and stimuli reduce the emotion and aggressiveness involved in political choice. . . . The available evidence suggests that the chances for stable democracy are enhanced to the extent that groups and individuals have a number of cross-cutting, politically relevant affiliations" (1963: 77). If interests and affiliations didn't overlap, the country might split in half, as the United States did during the Civil War. The power of groups, however—that of the parties and that of interest groups—is partially offset by the power of individuals, as expressed in voting and in protest.

The Power of the People: Voting   The American political system is based on mass participation through periodic elections. Ideally the principle of one person, one vote offsets inequalities of class, sex, and race in our society. Surprisingly, a relatively small percentage of Americans use their ballot. Whereas in Western Europe 80 to 90 percent of the voters regularly turn out for elections, only 53.3 percent of Americans eligible to vote did so in the 1976 presidential election. The reasons for this are complex. We begin some years back.

The profile of voters that emerged from studies conducted during the 1940s and 1950s wasn't very flattering. American voters (it was alleged) paid little attention to political events, had little understanding of the issues, and felt removed from the political arena. They voted the way trusted members of their class voted—in particular, the way party leaders did. They were, to use Gerald Pomper's phrase, "dependent voters" (1975). Everybody knew the Republicans were for big business; the Democrats, for the underdog. Voting was an exercise in party loyalty, and party membership was determined largely by social class. By the 1960s, political observers were declaring "an end to ideology" in American politics.

Then, during the 1960s, a political storm developed. The so-called silent generation of the 1950s was replaced by a generation of student protesters; the "passive" Negro, by the militant black; the loyal partisan, by the concerned, issue-oriented independent (perhaps as a reaction to students and blacks) (Pomper, 1975: 5). For example, traditionally Democratic blue-collar workers (the so-called hard hats) first supported Democratic President Johnson, then Republican President Nixon, because of their stand on the war in Vietnam.

Studies conducted during the 1960s suggested that social class was no longer a decisive factor in American elections. In 1968, 47 percent of blue-collar workers voted for Democrat Hubert Humphrey, but so did 36 percent of white-collar workers. In 1972, Democrats attracted only 5 percent more blue-collar workers than Republicans did. The association between class and party seemed to have slipped. However, the 1960 and 1964 elections present a different picture. Given a choice between Johnson and Goldwater, 17 percent more blue-collar workers than white-collar workers voted for Johnson. This leads Pomper (1975, chapter 3) to conclude that Americans vote by class when, and only when, economic issues are at stake. In other words, Americans respond to the issues; they vote for a *candidate,* not for a party. As suggested earlier, there are more Independent voters than Democrats in America today, and there are twice as many Independents as Republicans (Nie et al., 1976: 346).

The 1960s also brought a number of new voters into the political arena. In large part because racial barriers to registration and voting were lowered, black Americans began to vote in increasing numbers. Blacks in the Deep South now vote almost as frequently as whites. Studies indicate a broad racial division in political attitudes. In 1972, for every eight whites who indicated they supported or trusted the political system, only five blacks so indicated. (The remainder described themselves as cynical or oppressed.) And this affects positions on the issues, evaluations of candidates, and votes. Black and white Americans respond differently to political choices (Pomper, 1975: 126, 140–

141). Women also began voting in greater numbers during this period (211).

The fact remains, however, that voter participation is declining. Turnout for presidential elections dropped from 60.1 percent of eligible voters in 1960, to 55.4 percent in 1972, to a low of 53.3 percent in 1976. Those under thirty, the poor, the poorly educated, and blue-collar workers were the least likely to vote (*The New York Times,* November 16, 1976, pp. 1, 33).

Several explanations of low voter turnout have been proposed. Some political observers have suggested that Americans are disillusioned and alienated; that *not* voting is a protest against Watergate and other scandals. However, only a few respondents to a 1976 postelection survey by *The New York Times* and CBS cited disillusionment as a reason for not voting.

Other observers have suggested that a majority of Americans feel that their votes don't matter, that things will go on much as they are whether or not they vote. The *Times*/CBS poll indicates that this is true, but that voters feel as politically powerless as nonvoters. Fifty-five percent of the nonvoters agreed with the statement "Politicians don't care much about what people like me think"—but so did 55 percent of the voters. Fifty-nine percent of the nonvoters concurred with the statement "The government is pretty much run for a few big interests." Fifty-eight percent of the voters also agreed

The American political system is based on mass participation through periodic elections. Voter turnout, however, is consistently low and appears to be declining. Apathy and feelings of individual powerlessness are partially responsible for this phenomenon, but its causes basically remain a mystery. (EPA–Documerica)

with it. Fifty-one percent of the nonvoters and 52 percent of the voters felt they could trust the government to do what's right only some of the time. Why did those who voted vote? Fifty-three percent said they went to the polls because it was their civic duty. Only one in seven felt strongly about their candidate. Only 17 percent voted because they thought it was a very important election. (Eighteen percent said they didn't vote because they didn't like either candidate.) In short, many Americans feel powerless, both those who vote and those who don't.

It may be that our system makes registration and voting too complicated. A University of California study suggested that voter turnout would increase by 10 percent (or 15 million voters) if registration were made easier (*The New York Times,* October 17, 1976). And most of the nonvoters in the *Times*/CBS survey said they didn't vote because they were physically unable to get to the polls. This may account for some voter apathy, but only for some. The cause of low turnout for American elections remains a mystery.

The Power of the People: Protest   Pomper (1975, chapter 10) feels the emphasis on voter turnout is misplaced. If one looks beyond the ballot box, there is evidence that political participation is increasing. Americans are detouring the polls and turning to an alternate form of political action: protest. A *protest movement* may be defined as the mobilization of a previously inactive, unorganized constituency to challenge established practices or policy.

Political protest was not an invention of the late 1950s and early 1960s. A scan of the years 1800 to 1945 reveals 400 to 500 protest movements ranging from the League of American Wheelmen (which sought to eliminate restrictions on bicyclists) to the German-American Bund (which sought to remake the American political system in the

image of German National Socialism, or Nazism).

William A. Gamson (1975) studied over fifty of these movements. Surprisingly, he found that the most successful groups used violence, strikes, and other disruptive tactics—but usually in contexts that evoked public sympathy and effectively neutralized counterattacks. A second, equally surprising key to success was bureaucratic organization. The ability to act quickly depends on having a cadre of workers ready to perform coordinated tasks: bureaucratic organization seems to promote "combat readiness."

The classic example of a protest movement in recent times is the civil rights movement. In *The Impossible Revolution?* (1975), Lewis M. Killian outlines the setting, strategy, and success of Dr. King's drive to achieve actual integration. On May 17, 1954, the day the Supreme Court declared the doctrine of separate but equal unconstitutional, it looked as if the battle against Jim Crow had been won. But within weeks it became clear that white Southerners were willing and able to use civil disobedience to maintain their privileges.[2]

At this early stage, the black population lacked both a strategy and a prophet. Martin Luther King, Jr., supplied both, at least for a time. He was, as Louis Lomax observed, "the first Negro minister I have ever heard who can reduce the Negro problem to a spiritual matter and yet inspire the people to seek a solution on this side of the Jordan, not in the life beyond death" (in Killian, 1975: 49). King preached that integration was right and segregation evil. He encouraged thousands with the belief that "right makes might." Inspired by the religious/political

---

[2]   The fact that during the 1950s whites were the first to threaten to use and then to employ civil disobedience in the South is often overlooked. If blacks were revolutionaries in that period, whites were counterrevolutionaries.

POOR PEOPLE'S MOVEMENTS

For nineteen years, from the time he was first elected to the House of Representatives in 1937, Lyndon Johnson had voted "no" on civil rights legislation 100 percent of the time. Then in 1957, Speaker of the House Johnson changed his mind and worked vigorously for the passage of the first Civil Rights Act since 1875. What had happened? Did this Southern politician suddenly see the moral rightness of racial equality? Not really.

What happened was the presidential election of 1956, in which Republican Dwight Eisenhower had done surprisingly well among black voters, who since the depression had been solidly Democratic. By the mid-1950s, 90 percent of blacks had migrated north to the cities of the ten most populous states—the key states in any presidential election. Johnson had his eye on the White House, and the defection of blacks from the Democratic party, largely because of its weak platform on civil rights, worried him. He knew that gaining favor with Northern blacks and their white supporters was more important than maintaining the loyalty of his fellow Southerners. So he marshaled his forces to help pass the Civil Rights Act of 1957. In short, Johnson's conversion was more political than moral.

In this scenario, Frances Fox Piven and Richard A. Cloward see the basis for the success of the civil rights movement, and in fact, for the success of any movement of weak against strong. The central principle in their book, *Poor People's Movements,* is that a powerful group will only grant concessions to a weaker group when the weaker group threatens the power of the stronger group (31). Thus, in the civil rights movement, migration of rural Southern blacks to the large cities of the key Northern states gave blacks a weapon they had never wielded before—their votes.

Piven and Cloward do not suggest that the powerful automatically yield to the weak when the strong feel threatened. Concessions come only after a struggle, often a violent one. In Piven and Cloward's analysis of the stages through which all poor people's movements progress, a key is social disruption: before the weak will even attempt to protest against the strong, extraordinary disturbances must occur in the larger society (14). The civil rights movement, with its boycotts by blacks followed by white reprisals, created a state of economic warfare in the

father of modern India, Mahatma Gandhi, King taught the nonviolent tactics of civil disobedience and nonviolent protest.

The latent power King mobilized in the black community during the late fifties and early sixties has since become a staple in American politics, a weapon for the power-

less. César Chavez's National Farm Workers' Association (which mobilized migrant farm workers in the mid-1960s), the antiwar movement of the 1960s and early 1970s, the women's liberation movement, the National Welfare Rights Organization, and gay liberation (to name a few) took the civil rights

South. Afraid of losing more black voters in the next election, the Democratic party, led by Lyndon Johnson in the House, became the champion of civil rights legislation. The strategy worked: John F. Kennedy was elected President in 1960, clearly with the help of black voters.

But the civil rights movement didn't end here—it intensified its efforts. The violent uprisings of Southern whites were beginning to embarrass national leaders. At this point, Piven and Cloward see another significant stage in any movement of weak against strong: the danger of being curtailed. "When government is unable to ignore the insurgents, and is unwilling to risk the uncertain repercussions of the use of force, it will make efforts to conciliate and disarm the protestors" (29). The Kennedy administration attempted to do this by shifting efforts from integration to voter-registration drives for blacks. But whites reacted violently against voter-registration drives, and fearing the loss of Southern white votes, the administration backed off (234). In the period that followed, the nonviolent discipline that had characterized the black movement began to give way. By June 1963, the administration was again feeling pressured to act, and one year later, the Civil Rights Act of 1964 was signed.

As in all poor people's movements, according to Piven and Cloward, there is one more stage: the co-opting of the movement's leaders. After making concessions to the protesters (such as the Civil Rights Acts), the government will try to absorb movement leaders. Thus, when black leaders joined President Johnson's War on Poverty in the 1960s, they left the battlefield of the civil rights movement for high-paying jobs in the federal bureaucracy (255).

Piven and Cloward's analysis of the civil rights movement doesn't end very positively. They admit that the decline of white violence against Southern blacks is no small gain, as is black political power, but they are doubtful of the movement's economic achievements. They conclude: "The question is whether the exercise of the franchise and the now virtually exclusive emphasis upon electoral strategies by southern black leaders will produce a meaningful improvement in the conditions of life of the southern black poor. We think not" (256).

SOURCE: Frances Fox Piven and Richard A. Cloward, *Poor People's Movements: Why They Succeed, How They Fail*, New York: Pantheon, 1977.

movement for a model. Each is an example of people who, although they lacked money, position, and other conventional sources of power, made themselves heard.

In the years since the civil rights movement, protest has become an accepted alternative to conventional political activities in American society. In 1968, about 33 percent of white Americans approved of demonstrations; by 1972, almost 50 percent approved of them. New voters and blacks of all ages approved of nonconventional tactics in the greatest numbers (Pomper, 1975: 127).

Pomper sees the growing approval and

César Chavez addressing farm workers in California. Chavez rose to national prominence in the late 1960s, when the grape boycott became a national cause célèbre. (Gerhard E. Gscheidle)

use of protest as a sign of decline in traditional authority—including that of political parties. Voters—and nonvoters—are more independent today. (Think how many polls say a vote will be decided by those who are uncommitted the day before the election.) In particular, black Americans, women, and the members of other minorities have become more self-aware and consequently more active. Increasingly, politics is becoming a leisure-time activity for the middle class. This infusion of "new blood" is not only expanding the political system but also changing it.

In addition, the American political scene is becoming more integrated in the sense that residential mobility, the mass media, and the corporate economy have created a uniform political culture in America. A decade ago, being a Democrat meant one set of values in the South, another in the North. Elections centered around racial issues in the South, economic issues in the North. Today racial issues are not confined to a Birmingham; the corporation is as influential in Arkansas as in Michigan.

As a result of these trends—on the one hand, new forms of political action, independence from class and party ties, and increased self-awareness; on the other, political integration—there is greater agreement about what the issues are, but a wider range of strong divergent opinions on how they should be resolved.

SUMMARY

Power is the ability to control other people's behavior. The most visible arenas in which the struggle for power takes place are business and government. *Political power* is the ability to make and carry out binding decisions that affect the whole society; *economic power* is the control of such resources as wealth, income, property, goods, and services. In reality, government and business each exercise both kinds of power: the government sets economic policy, and economic conditions influence the stability of governments.

Authority is power exercised in a way people consider right and legitimate. Weber identified three types: (1) *legal/rational authority,* which derives from a system of explicit rules and is vested in offices, not specific individuals; (2) *charismatic authority,* which derives from exceptional personal qualities; and (3) *traditional authority,* which derives from sacred traditions of loyalty to a king or chief. Influence derives from respect and affection and enables a person to effect decisions without resorting to threats or manipulation, or offering compensation.

Who exercises power in a society and why? What are the consequences? Breaking with tradition, Marx linked political power to economics, described capitalist societies as being divided into two hostile camps (the powerful owners and powerless workers), and predicted that revolution was inevitable. Pareto and Mosca disagreed, arguing that governing elites are and always will be a fact of history. They believed that elites, which are constant, renew themselves by recruiting people with new blood and novel talents.

Carrying on this debate, C. Wright Mills argued that America is governed by a *power elite*—people from prestigious families and schools who move back and forth between government, the military, and business, deciding important issues among themselves behind closed doors. Evidence for the existence of this elite has been provided by Domhoff. Agreeing that some Americans are more free and equal than others, David Riesman countered that power in America is dispersed among numerous competing elites, which function as veto groups, protecting their own interests (the pluralist view). Mills lamented the erosion of democracy; Riesman, the lack of leadership and direction. Arnold Rose suggested that while a power elite dominates American foreign policy, numerous competing elites have a say in domestic issues.

All economic systems face the basic problem of how to distribute scarce resources. In a capitalist market economy such as that of the United States, which is based on the ideology of free enterprise, in theory privately owned firms make the critical decisions. In fact, however, since ours is a "mixed" economy in which some resources and activities are owned or supported by the government, decisions are made by both government and business. In the business sector, a small number of corporations control a disproportionate share of the economy, and therefore wield a great deal of power and have a much greater voice in these basic decisions. Many traditional notions of the division of power between government and business are now being swept away by the multinational firms, who view the entire world as a single economic system and are largely beyond the reach of national governments.

The giant corporation controls the American economy. But who controls the corporation? Berle and Means argue that the nineteenth-century owner-entrepreneur system has given way to a system of managers who actually set policy and run the company, and a group of diffuse and passive owners who merely collect profits. Corporate responsibility and power are thus fragmented. Anderson, on the other hand, argues that since 1 percent of the population owns four-fifths of all corporate stock, and a significant number of this group actually function as corporate directors, American corporations are run by a ruling capitalist class. Because the monopoly power of large corporations puts them out of the reach of the forces of the free market, the rise of *consumerism,* a movement to protect buyers from dangerous products, misleading advertising, and unfair prices, has been seen as the attempt of the public to play a role in economic decision-making.

Political systems also face certain critical problems: how to create a common political identity, how to establish power and legitimate authority, and how to produce and distribute needed goods and services. The distribution of power and authority in the democratic American political system is complex. Parties, interest groups, individual voters, and social movements fill the gap between the top and bottom levels of the American power structure. A *political party* is a collectivity designed for gaining and holding legitimate governmental power. Because American parties must attract people with many different views, they must take pointedly unoffensive, bland positions. There are signs that the party system is changing because the media have usurped some of its functions and because voters are more independent than they once were. *Interest groups* (organizations created to influence political decisions that concern members) compensate for the tentative nature of American political parties. The National Rifle Association, for example, has successfully blocked gun-control legislation for years. Lipset believes interest groups create crosscurrents that prevent permanent splits in American society.

In the last few decades, traditional associations between voting, class, and party have weakened, so Americans now respond to issues and candidates far more than to parties when voting. But relatively fewer Americans are using the power of the ballot. In the 1976 presidential election, only 53.3 percent of those eligible voted. Pomper, however, feels that the emphasis on voting is misplaced; political participation is in fact increasing through an alternative form of political action: protest. The classic example of a protest movement in recent times is the civil rights movement. The latent power Martin Luther King mobilized in the black community in the 1950s and 1960s has since become a staple in American politics, a weapon for the powerless. In many ways, César Chavez modeled himself after King, but perhaps with less success, to mobilize the Chicano community.

There is some consensus now on the basic issues that face American society, but there is also a wider range of opinion as to how they should be resolved.

GLOSSARY

authority power exercised in a way people consider right and legitimate.

charismatic authority a type of authority (identified by Weber) that derives from exceptional personal qualities.

conglomerate a company consisting of a number of subsidiaries in a variety of unrelated industries.

consumerism a movement to protect buyers from dangerous, inferior, or useless products, misleading advertising, and unfair prices.

democratic state a state in which authority derives from the law, rooted in the consent of the people.

economic power control of such resources as wealth, income, property, goods, and services.

elite influential, expert, or powerful minorities.

influence the ability to affect collective decisions without resorting to compensation, manipulation, or threats.

interest group an organization created to influence political decisions that directly concern its members.

legal/rational authority a type of authority (identified by Weber) that derives from a system of explicit rules defining the legitimate uses of power. It is vested in positions, not in specific individuals.

multinational corporation a giant, usually diversified corporation with operations and subsidiaries in many countries.

oligarchy a small group of powerful leaders.

one-factor theory the view that power is concentrated in the hands of a single group who dominate and manipulate the many.

pluralism the view that the political power structure is composed of a variety of competing elites and interest groups.

political party a collectivity designed for gaining and holding legitimate governmental power.

political power the ability to make and execute binding decisions that affect the whole of society.

power the ability to accomplish things, to overcome opposition, and to dominate others.

power elite a coalition of military leaders, government officials, and business executives united by common interests and social affinity. In C. Wright Mills's view, this coalition rules America.

protest movement the mobilization of an unorganized constituency to challenge established practices or policy.

state according to Weber, the one organization in a society that has the authority to employ physical force.

totalitarian state a state in which the centralized government doesn't recognize or tolerate parties of differing opinion.

traditional authority a type of authority (identified by Weber) that derives from sacred traditions of loyalty to king, queen, chiefs, and priests.

REFERENCES

Charles H. Anderson, *The Political Economy of Social Class.* Englewood Cliffs, N.J.: Prentice-Hall, 1974.

Charles F. Andrain, *Political Life and Social Change: An Introduction to Political Science,* 2nd ed. Belmont, Calif.: Duxbury, 1975.

Richard J. Barnet and Ronald Müller, *Global Reach.* New York: Simon & Schuster, 1974.

Adolph A. Berle, Jr., and Gardiner C. Means, *The Modern Corporation and Private Property.* New York: Macmillan, 1932; rev. ed., New York: Harcourt Brace and World, 1968.

Robert A. Dahl, *Who Governs?* New Haven: Yale University Press, 1961.

G. William Domhoff, *Who Rules America?* Englewood Cliffs, N.J.: Prentice-Hall, 1967.

Robert E. Dowse and John A. Hughes, *Political Science.* New York: Wiley, 1972.

Maurice Duverger, *Political Parties,* trans. Barbara and Robert North. New York: Wiley, 1954.

William A. Gamson, *The Strategy of Social Protest.* New York: Irvington, 1975.

Carl Kaysen, "The Corporation: How Much Power? What Scope?" in Reinhard Bendix and Seymour Martin Lipset, eds., *Class, Status and Power,* 2nd ed. New York: Free Press, 1966.

Suzanne Keller, *Beyond the Ruling Class: Strategic Elites in Modern Society*. New York: Random House, 1963.

Lewis M. Killian, *The Impossible Revolution? Phase Two*. New York: Random House, 1975.

William Kornhauser, '' 'Power Elite' or 'Veto Groups'?'' in Seymour Martin Lipset and Leo Lowenthal, eds., *Culture and Social Character*. Glencoe, Ill.: Free Press, 1961.

Everett Carl Ladd, Jr., and Charles D. Hadley, *Transformation of the American Party System*. New York: Norton, 1975.

Seymour Martin Lipset, *Political Man*. New York: Doubleday Anchor, 1963.

———, ''Social Conflict, Legitimacy and Democracy,'' in Marvin E. Olsen, ed., *Power in Societies*. New York: Macmillan, 1970.

Karl Marx and Friedrich Engels, *Communist Manifesto* (1847). New York: Pantheon, 1967.

Robert Michels, *First Lectures in Political Science* (1915), trans. Alfred de Grazia. Minneapolis: University of Minnesota Press, 1949.

Lester W. Milbrath, *The Washington Lobbyists*. Chicago: Rand McNally, 1963.

R. L. Miller, *Economics Today*. San Francisco, Calif.: Canfield, 1973.

C. Wright Mills, *The Power Elite*. New York: Oxford University Press, 1959.

———, ''The Structure of Power in American Society.'' *British Journal of Sociology*, vol. 9 (March 1958): 29–41. (Also in Olsen, 1970.)

Gaetano Mosca, *The Ruling Class*. New York: McGraw-Hill, 1939. (Also in Olsen, 1970.)

Norman H. Nie et al., *The Changing American Voter*. Cambridge, Mass.: Harvard University Press, 1976.

Marvin E. Olsen, ed., *Power in Societies*. New York: Macmillan, 1970.

Vilfredo Pareto, *The Mind and Society* (1916), trans. A. Bongiorno and A. Livingston. New York: Harcourt Brace, 1935. (Also in Olsen, 1970.)

Gerald M. Pomper, *Voter's Choice*. New York: Dodd, Mead, 1975.

David Riesman, with Nathan Glazer and Reuel Denney, *The Lonely Crowd*. New Haven, Conn.: Yale University Press, 1951.

Arnold M. Rose, *The Power Structure*. New York: Oxford University Press, 1967.

Sentry Insurance, *Consumerism at the Crossroads*. Conducted by Louis Harris and Associates, Inc., and Marketing Science Institute, 1977.

Max Weber, *From Max Weber: Essays in Sociology* (1918), 2nd ed., trans. Hans H. Gerth and C. Wright Mills. New York: Oxford University Press, 1949.

———, *The Theory of Social and Economic Organization*, trans. Talcott Parsons. Glencoe, Ill.: Free Press, 1947.

FOR FURTHER STUDY

Political Protest. Periods of political protest and social upheaval show the relationship between politics and economics, since political protests often focus on economic concerns. For example, protests by older Americans in the Townsend Movement led to the enactment of the Social Security program. This protest and its results are described in *The Townsend Movement: A Political Study* (New York: Octagon Books, 1973) by Abraham Holtzman. Irving Bernstein discusses the protests of American workers during the Great Depression and the New Deal in *The Lean Years: 1920–1933* (Boston: Houghton Mifflin, 1972) and *The Turbulent Years: 1933–1944* (Boston: Houghton Mifflin, 1969). Another analysis of the American labor movement and its political aspects is Jeremy Brecher's *Strike!* (San Francisco, Calif.: Straight Arrow, 1974). Richard Cloward and Frances Piven analyze the protests of poor people during the 1960s and 1970s in their book *The Politics of Turmoil: Essays on Poverty, Race, and the Urban Crisis* (New York: Vintage, 1975). Two useful collections that give an overview of the uses of political protest for changing economic conditions are Joseph Gusfield's *Protest, Reform, and Revolt* (New York: Wiley, 1970) and Jerome Skolnick's *The Politics of Protest* (New York: Simon & Schuster, 1969).

Political and Economic Surveillance.   An important intersection between power, politics, and the individual is the area of surveillance. Those with power have been able to control the flow of information—collecting information about selected individuals (notably, individuals with political views disliked by those in power) while limiting access to information about their data-gathering practices. Two works that give detailed analyses of how the CIA works are *The CIA and the Cult of Intelligence* by Victor Marchetti and John D. Marks (New York: Dell, 1975), and *CIA File* by Robert Borosage and John D. Marks (New York: Grossman, 1976). *State Secrets* (New York: Holt, Rinehart and Winston, 1974), by Paul Cowan and others, contains essays on just what the FBI collects in its files. The government isn't the only agent of surveillance; business interests may also use the resources of credit bureaus to maintain files on individuals. An interesting study of how large credit agencies (for example, Master Charge and Visa) and national systems (for example, the driver-licensing system and National Health Insurance in Great Britain) use computers to gather vast amounts of confidential information about private individuals is James B. Rule's *Private Lives and Public Surveillance: Social Control in the Computer Age* (New York: Schocken, 1974).

Political Socialization.   The political attitudes held by adults and their participation in the political sphere may be understood in part through the process of socialization, which occurs in childhood. Richard E. Dawson and his co-authors provide a complete review of the methods, theory, and research of this field in *Political Socialization,* 2nd ed. (Boston: Little, Brown, 1977). A recent collection of the classic articles has been put together by Stanley A. Renshon and is entitled *Handbook of Political Socialization: Theory and Research* (New York: Free Press, 1977). Richard B. Niemi examines the process of developing political attitudes within the family and raises questions about our usual understanding of political socialization in his book, *How Family Members Perceive Each Other* (New Haven, Conn.: Yale University Press, 1974). Two works that explore political socialization and its consequences for particular groups are Paul R. Abramson's *The Political Socialization of Black Americans* (New York: Free Press, 1977) and Martha Githens and Jewel Prestich's *Portrait of Marginality* (New York: McKay, 1977), a study of women.

Social Institutions

To most Americans, the centers of political and economic power seem remote. Here, in part five, we turn to three major social institutions that are closer to home: the family, education, and religion. Surprisingly perhaps, these topics are as controversial as those we considered in part four.

Because we all have intimate experience of the family, it is particularly difficult to view this institution objectively. Chapter 13 uses cross-cultural comparisons and studies of family patterns at different levels of our own society to put the family, and changing family life styles, into perspective.

Education is of immediate concern to all readers of this book. Chapter 14 shows that there is a good deal more to education than teaching skills and transmitting knowledge. Do our schools fulfill the functions we expect of them? Is our faith in education, as individuals and as a society, justified?

We read, on the one hand, that traditional religion is dying, on the other, that nonconventional religions are enjoying a new popularity. Chapter 15 attempts to explain this paradox by examining the functions of religion in any and all societies. After reading this chapter you may view national holidays and other expressions of patriotism in a new light, as "civil religion."

CHAPTER 13

The Family

"Happy families are all alike; every unhappy family is unhappy in its own way." This is the sentence with which Leo Tolstoy began his novel *Anna Karenina.* But Tolstoy was wrong. Happy families are not all alike, not if we look at them from the sociological perspective. Throughout the world, both happy and unhappy families assume many different forms and fulfill many different functions. In Samoa, for example, a newly married couple doesn't move into its own home but becomes part of an already existing family. In *Coming of Age in Samoa* (1953), Margaret Mead wrote that "the young couple live in the main household, ... The wife works with all the women of the household and waits on all the men. The husband shares the enterprises of the other men and boys."¹

And even within one society happy families aren't all alike. In America, for example, the ideal happy family, as celebrated in the movies and on TV, consists of a devoted house-bound mother, a work-bound father, and two or more delightful children. Although many American families (happy and unhappy) may in fact fit this ideal, many—perhaps most— do not. In millions of American families

one or another of the ideal elements is missing: there are childless families and families with a dozen children; there are extended families (where grandparents or other kin live under the same roof with the mother, father, and their children) and families that are disrupted through death, divorce, separation, or desertion; there are families with working mothers and families with unemployed fathers; and with increasing frequency, there are new family forms altogether (like communes, group marriages, and unmarried parents).

In the first part of this chapter, we discuss the ways social scientists have defined the family, focusing on its four main functions. Next, we consider the family cross-culturally, discussing explanations for the variety of family forms found throughout the world. Then we focus on the American family—the meaning and reasons for the nuclear family, and the way social class affects both the form of the family and child-rearing. We also discuss both romantic love and divorce in America. Finally, we examine the changing American family and consider contemporary alternatives to traditional marriage.

DEFINING THE FAMILY

If it is true that different human groups devise different means for nurturing and training their young, how are we to come up with a single all-encompassing definition of the *family?* The most famous attempt at such a definition was made by social scientist George Peter Murdock after he had surveyed the family forms of 250 different societies. Murdock suggested that ''the Family is a social group characterized by common residence, economic cooperation, and reproduction; it includes adults of both sexes, at least two of whom maintain a socially approved sexual relationship, and one or more children, own or adopted, of the sexually cohabiting pair'' (Murdock, 1949: 2–3). But Murdock's definition does not cover the Nayar of southern India, for instance, whose families contain neither sexually cohabiting adults nor adults who reside or work together. (For details on the Nayar, see our discussion later in this chapter.) Kathleen Gough (1974), an anthropologist who studied this group, suggested that Murdock's definition be revised. For Gough, a family is a group characterized by the union of a man and a woman in which the children born to the woman are recognized as legitimate offspring of both parents. While according to Gough's definition, Nayar families could be called families, families in such tribes as the Nuer of East Africa could not. There, an older, wealthy, childless woman may marry a younger woman and claim her children as her legitimate heirs (Lévi-Strauss, 1956).

However the family is defined (and the issue has never been happily resolved), there seem to be four crucial *social functions* that are carried out by families throughout the world:

1. reproduction of new members of the society
2. child care
3. socialization of children to the values, traditions, and ranks or positions of the society
4. intimacy and support for family members

Thus, in all societies there is a reliable arrangement for producing, sustaining, and socializing succeeding generations. We call this institution the family.

The Family as a Biological and Social Unit

While it is clear that family arrangements involve important biological elements like heterosexual intercourse, conception and gestation, birth, and infant care, it would be a mistake to think of the family as merely a biological unit. The social contexts, the traditions and sentiments that surround and shape these biological givens, determine the form a particular family system will take.

The distinction between biological and social determinants of family life becomes clear if you consider the meaning of the word ''illegitimacy.'' A so-called illegitimate child surely has two biological parents and is therefore perfectly legitimate from a biological point of view. But a child (at least in America) who is conceived out of wedlock and whom no male acknowledges as his child and whom no male assumes responsibility for is illegitimate from a *social* point of view. A child is socially legitimate only if *some* male, even if he is not the actual biological father (or genitor, as social scientists call him), assumes social paternity and responsibility for him or her. Thus, at least with paternity, the biological and social bases of family life may be separate.

In the case of maternity, the separation is a little more complicated, since the biological

"First we were an extended family, then we were a nuclear family, and now we're divorced." (Drawing by Hamilton; ©1975 The New Yorker Magazine, Inc.)

connection between mother and child is so unmistakable: no woman can ever wonder whether or not she has carried and borne a particular child. Nonetheless, even with this strong biological connection, there are cases where biological and social maternity don't coincide. Consider, for example, the case of a child offered up for adoption by his or her natural mother, who later wants the child back. The adoptive mother, who has cared for the child from an early age and has formed great bonds of mutual attachment with him or her, is surely the child's psychological mother. In such cases, the biological and social bases of motherhood are clearly separable. In fact, in recent years the courts have begun to recognize the legitimacy of social motherhood, and in such cases sometimes allow adopted children to remain with their adoptive parents.

Once we recognize the distinction between social and biological parenthood, we can also begin to appreciate how closely the two are intertwined. In no society in the world is biological parenthood uncontrolled. As the British social scientist Malinowski once observed: ''The relation of mother to child, clearly dictated by natural inclinations, is yet not entirely left to them.'' Thus, everywhere, ''biological facts are transformed into social forces'' (Malinowski, 1964: 6, 8). By this, Malinowski means that all phases of procreation—conception, gestation, and infant maintenance—are everywhere governed by some social rules. The biological sex drive is always harnessed in some way. In our own society, for instance, we have many rules that limit the random expression of sexual desires, particularly if that expression is likely to lead to conception. We have rules about incest, marriage between kin, marriage between children, bigamous marriage, and even in some places still, marriage between members of different groups.

It is clear, then, that while family units are based on biological processes, these biological processes are universally channeled by social rules and traditions. Having a baby may be a biological fact, but creating a family is clearly a social one.

CROSS-CULTURAL PERSPECTIVES

It is intriguing to compare the different social forms of the family that have emerged at different times in different places. By comparing various family patterns we both broaden our cultural perspectives and also become aware, through contrast, of the precise nature of our own family patterns. Numerous forms of the family have been recorded by anthropologists and sociologists, and although many of them are very different from our own, none is more or less valid or correct than it.

The Nayar, the Dani, and the Israeli Kibbutzim

One of the more fascinating forms of family life is found among the Nayar of Kerala, India (Gough, 1974). During her adolescence a Nayar girl is encouraged to have several lovers. If she becomes pregnant, one or more of these lovers is obliged to acknowledge paternity and to pay the costs of delivering the baby, but beyond this, none of the lovers has any further obligations toward the girl or her child. The mother's kin are completely responsible for both care of the child and support for the mother. The Nayar do have a form of marriage, but it is simply a ritual that marks a girl's passage into adulthood; it is not a ceremony that heralds the beginning of a family as we know it. During the ritual marriage, the woman's tribe chooses a man to be her husband for three days. After these three days, husband and wife may never see each other again. Their only further obligations arise when the husband dies and the wife has to observe his funeral rites.

Once a Nayar woman is ritually married, her sexual relations with other men come under no social control whatsoever. If she gives birth to a child, some man of her own rank is assigned the status of biological father (whether or not he actually is the father). But this assigned father has no rights or obligations concerning the child. Thus, among the Nayar, social fatherhood (that is, acknowledged paternity) is totally unrelated to biological fatherhood. And yet the business of replicating the Nayar culture goes on just as smoothly as it does elsewhere; children are conceived, born, and socialized in an orderly, socially determined way, and family life is ordered according to regular and predictable expectations and rules.

The Dani of West Irian, Indonesia, have a family system that is equally different from the ones familiar to us. For the Dani, the family is not a very meaningful unit; in fact, the Dani language doesn't even have a word meaning ''family'' (Heider, 1972: 13). Social life is organized not around private, family households but around compounds that continually shift (sometimes as frequently as every three days). While the Dani do have a form of ritual marriage (and one man may ritually marry several women), husbands and wives don't necessarily live in the same compounds, and they rarely get together as a unit. There is some cooperation between spouses in regard to house-building and cooking, but family life is at best short-lived. Children, especially boys, spend much of their time away from their parents, and by the time they are ten years old, they generally move in with distant relatives.

The most striking feature of Dani life, for those of us raised in Western cultures, is the seeming indifference to sex. Men and women in Dani compounds generally sleep in separate quarters—men in the men's houses and women in the women's houses. The Dani also observe long periods of ritual sexual abstinence, particularly after the birth of a child. Husbands and wives may abstain from sexual relations for as long as four to five years after a baby is born, and there is no feeling among the Dani that this abstinence creates special hardship. ''Thus . . . both men and women remain celibate for long periods of time without discomfort . . . and this is accomplished without rigorous, overt mechanisms of social control'' (Heider, 1972: 15). Despite its strangeness to us, however, the Dani family system produces healthy, socialized children, just as families do everywhere.

The collective communes in Israel, called *kibbutzim*, provide yet another example of a

Among the Bedouins of the Middle East, women live together in huts, apart from their husbands. (Eve Arnold/Magnum)

family life style not familiar to us. On some kibbutzim many of the activities we have come to associate with family life are performed by the community as a whole. Men are not responsible for the economic support of their wives; instead, both men and women work for the community and are supported by it. Women are not exclusively responsible for the care of their children; instead, child care is the responsibility of the community as a whole (Talmon-Garber, 1962). While the biological mother of a child is responsible for nursing it during its first eight months of life, after this time children are cared for by communal nurses in separate children's houses. Since the children's houses are organized into homogeneous age groups, each child spends his or her childhood with the same group of peers. This group plays an enormously important role in each child's life.

On the kibbutz such household activities as food preparation, laundry, and recreation are all communally organized. The experience of the kibbutz has exploded a number of cherished myths about the indispensability of the small, intimate family and about the tight connection between biological and social parenthood. Psychological and sociological studies of kibbutz life have revealed that communal child-rearing has many virtues and does in fact provide a viable alternative to the traditional isolated nuclear family as we know it (Rabin, 1965; Bettelheim, 1971). *A nuclear family* is defined by social scientists as a husband and wife and their dependent children living apart from other relatives. It is the family form idealized in our own society.

Origins of Different Family Forms

Why do particular societies come to have their specific forms of family life? While it is true that attributing causes after the fact is always risky, because we can't study the beginnings of a process that is already completed, nonetheless many social scientists now agree that the form the family takes reflects the subsistence needs of the society. In agricultural and herding societies, where compliance and cooperation are crucial, the family structure is tightly organized and hierarchical. Individual members of such societies might endanger the limited food supply if they failed to adhere to established customs and rules for raising food. By contrast, in hunting and gathering bands, ever mobile in search of food, family life is more flexible, more egalitarian, and less tightly organized (Barry, Bacon, and Child, 1957).

In a study of family life in 549 different societies, two researchers discovered a close connection between the organization of the family and specific patterns of subsistence (Nimkoff and Middleton, 1960). In societies based on agriculture and fishing, family networks are large and cooperative, thereby assuring the survival of all through the cooperative labor of all. In hunting and gathering societies, where subsistence is based on individual enterprise and extensive mobility, family networks are small and tight in order to facilitate the groups' continual movement and to ensure the constant availability of a limited food supply.

Modern industrial societies, in which families are highly mobile, are more like hunting and gathering bands than like settled societies, and the small nuclear family, which permits its members a great deal of independence and individualism, tends to predominate. Winch and Blumberg (1953) concluded that the pattern of the nuclear family appears in both very simple and very developed societies, whereas the extended family appears in societies of intermediate complexity. In a

Among hunter-gatherers, like the !Kung Bushmen of the Kalahari Desert, frequent mobility necessitates small families. Similarly, in modern industrial societies where people are often on the move, the nuclear family is highly adaptive. (Top, Irven DeVore. Bottom, Elliott Erwitt/Magnum)

careful analysis of the connection between the modern nuclear family and modern forms of industrialization, sociologist William Goode (1963) suggested several reasons for the fit between the two.

Goode points out that the geographic mobility demanded by modern industrial societies (that is, the demand that people move to areas where work is available) requires a small family unit that can be moved readily. When a member of a family must move to increase economic or social opportunities, it is far simpler to take along a small nuclear family than to consult with and accommodate a large number of kin. In addition, small nuclear families can't build up the power and independence large family dynasties can, and therefore small families are subject to the whims of the marketplace rather than being able to control or oppose industry. For these and other reasons (for example, the lack of space in urban areas for large family homesteads), the small nuclear family is the ideal in contemporary American society.

The Nuclear Family as an Ideal

Although we can characterize the family as a reliable arrangement for carrying out the functions of producing, sustaining, and socializing succeeding generations, the manner in which these functions are carried out varies widely not only geographically but historically as well. In the nineteenth century, sex and reproduction were directly linked: people married mainly to have children. Today, by contrast, children are no longer necessary for the family's economic well-being, and contraception has weakened the link between sexuality and reproduction. Couples are more likely to marry for emotional fulfillment (or security), and to have children for much the same reasons. Emo-

tional support among family members has now become the dominant function of the family, while the family now has less of a role in socialization and has become basically a consuming unit rather than a producing one.

Once we recognize that family forms and functions represent adaptations to specific societal or environmental conditions, we can then begin to explore the *consequences* of various forms and functions for members of different societies. Consider, for instance, the modern isolated nuclear family. How is life structured in such a family? How does it differ from family life in the past? As we can see in table 13:1, there are a number of significant differences between the modern isolated nuclear family and the traditional extended form.

Isolation of the Family   In the traditional *extended family,* married couples from different generations—and their children, and often other relatives as well—typically lived and worked together in the same household. By contrast, the nuclear family is isolated, in the sense that each new couple sets up a household independent of either of their parents' homes. Husband and wife thus become extremely dependent on each other, both emotionally and physically. In the absence of large numbers of kin living under the same roof, the couple must rely on each other almost exclusively for protection and comfort; in addition, they must be self-supporting, and they must also take care of all household chores (including child care) by themselves. Thus, in place of the extensive and often intricate kinship relations that held the traditional family together and bound it to society, the mutual dependence of husband and wife characterize the nuclear family, which floats relatively free of other social bonds. Precisely because that mutual dependence is what keeps the nuclear family

table 13:1 **TRADITIONALISM VERSUS MODERNISM IN FAMILY FORM, FUNCTION, AND IDEOLOGY**

TRADITIONAL	MODERN
1. Kinship organizing principle of society.	1. Kinship differentiated from socioeconomic and political life; recruitment to jobs independent of one's relatives.
2. The extended family basic unit of residence and domestic functions.	2. Nuclear family basic unit of residence and domestic functions.
3. Most adults work at home.	3. Separation of home and work; household consumes rather than produces.
4. Low geographic and social mobility; sons inherit father's status and occupation.	4. High geographic and social mobility; individual mobility based on merit.
5. Dominance of parents over children, men over women.	5. Relatively egalitarian relations within nuclear family in ideals and practice.
6. High fertility and high death rates, especially in infancy; rapid population turnover.	6. Low, controlled fertility and low death rates, especially in infancy; death a phenomenon of old age.
7. Kinship bonds override economic efficiency and maximization of individual gain.	7. Advancement and economic gain of individuals prevail over kin obligations.
8. Ideology of duty, tradition, individual submission to authority and fate.	8. Ideology of individual rights, equality, freedom, self-realization.
9. Little emphasis on emotional involvement within nuclear family; marriage not based on love; predominant loyalty of individual to blood kin, rather than spouse; children economic rather than emotional assets, but subordination and dependency of children on parents may continue as long as parent lives.	9. Intense involvement of spouses, parents, and children with each other; ideologies of marital happiness and adjustment; great concern with child's development, current adjustment, and future potential, but sharp break with parental authority upon attaining adulthood.
10. Little or no psychological separation between home and community; broad communal sociability; no large-scale institutions.	10. Sharp line of demarcation between home and outside world; home a private retreat and outside world impersonal, competitive, threatening.

SOURCE: Adapted from Arlene Skolnick, *The Intimate Environment* (Boston: Little, Brown, 1973), table 1, p. 97.

intact, society has institutionalized love— once an almost irrelevant feature of marriage—as the social glue to replace the structural supports that fastened the traditional family to its social surroundings. Paradoxically, the prevalence of love as a bond in marriage correlates with high divorce rates, since it justifies breaking up a marriage when the couple no longer feels in love.

The Division of Labor Another important consequence of the isolated nuclear family is that the division of labor between husband and wife is such that one member must always be at home during the child-rearing years. By way of comparison, in societies where grandparents, cousins, aunts, and uncles all live together, there is always at least one competent adult around to care for the children or to perform other important domestic functions. But when the family structure consists of an isolated nuclear family, the child-rearing tasks as well as the breadwinning tasks must be divided between only two adults. Until recently, the American ideal has been for the husband to earn the money and the wife to keep the home fires burning (although we must remember that between this ideal type and the actual reality, there has always been much disparity).

No matter who is the breadwinner and who raises the children, though, the great dependency of husband and wife on each other makes the nuclear family extremely fragile. In traditional extended families, for instance, the death or departure of one member was not likely to have a crippling effect on the family. But when an isolated nuclear family loses one member (through death, separation, or divorce), the disruption can be enormous. And even if there are no such disruptions, the nuclear family is still programmed, in a sense, to eventually self-destruct once the children leave home. Children used to remain subordinate to, and dependent on, their parents for as long as their parents lived; today, children are encouraged to strike out on their own as soon as they reach maturity. Later, when the parents grow old and are less capable of at-

tending to their own needs, the ideal of the nuclear family inhibits them from moving in with their grown children. They must either manage on their own or be turned over to institutions specifically designed to care for the aged. Thus, while the isolated nuclear family may in fact snugly fit the economic system, it also causes problems for individuals in societies where it prevails.

THE AMERICAN FAMILY

One of the great American myths is that most families consist of a loving husband and wife and their well-adjusted, happy children. Generations of schoolchildren learned to read from textbooks describing such a family and their dog, Spot, living in their own home behind a white picket fence. In these books, minority groups with somewhat different life styles and family structures simply did not exist.

Sociologists have also perpetuated the myth that there's only one type of family in the United States. The people who study and write about family life most frequently describe young white, native-born, middle-class families with children (Heiskanen, 1971). And since these types of families most closely approximate the American ideal, it is not surprising that the myth continues to exist.

Family Types

Social scientists are now writing with an increased awareness of other family types. In an analysis of the relationship between societal complexity and family forms, Robert F. Winch and Rae Lesser Blumberg (1968)

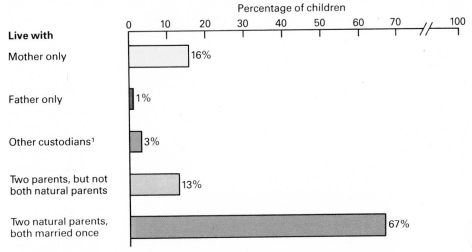

figure 13:1   Living arrangements for children under eighteen

Percentage of children

Live with

Mother only — 16%

Father only — 1%

Other custodians[1] — 3%

Two parents, but not both natural parents — 13%

Two natural parents, both married once — 67%

[1] Relatives or nonrelatives.

SOURCE: *Population Reference Bureau.* Adapted from *The New York Times,* November 27, 1977, p. 1.

identified three different types of family that may be found in the United States: a nuclear family embedded in a network of extended kin; an isolated nuclear family of the type discussed above; and a mother/child nuclear family that sometimes extends to include other female relatives, particularly grandmothers.

This third form, that of the single-parent family headed by a woman, is now a sizable and rapidly growing proportion of all families (15 percent in 1974). In fact, during the past ten years, the number of such families has increased almost ten times as fast as the number of two-parent families. Single-parent families have been formed through separa-

---

table 13:2   **THE CHANGING SOCIAL ATTITUDES OF SINGLE PARENTS (by percent)**

	SINGLE PARENTS	OTHER PARENTS
Would welcome		
More acceptance of the rights of children to be different	75	65
Less emphasis on parents sacrificing to give children the best	44	37
More acceptance of the rights of unmarried women to have children	43	23
More emphasis on sexual freedom	33	16
Less emphasis on respect for authority	31	20

SOURCE: Yankelovich, Skelly, and White, Inc., *The General Mills American Family Report, 1976–77, Raising Children in a Changing Society,* chart 21, p. 79. Copyright ©1977 General Mills, Inc.

RAISING CHILDREN IN A CHANGING SOCIETY

Sexual freedom, the new emphasis on self-fulfillment, the blurring of male and female roles, and the ethic of openness and frankness may be fine for adults. But what about children? How do parents raise children in a rapidly changing society like ours, in which traditional values are under attack and the future is uncertain? Have parents changed?

In 1976 and 1977, after a series of intensive workshops, Daniel Yankelovich and his colleagues conducted a survey of 1,230 American households with one or more children under thirteen. One parent was interviewed in each household, plus the second parent or a child between the ages of six and twelve in about 900 of the families. The results of this survey left no doubt: the 1970s had produced a New Breed of parent.

New Breed parents have rejected many of the traditional values by which they were raised. They don't consider religion, patriotism, saving and thrift, success, or the institution of marriage very important. These parents are self-oriented. They aren't prepared to sacrifice for their children—for example, to endure an unhappy marriage for the sake of the children or to give up things they enjoy in order to spend more time at home. They take a somewhat laissez-faire attitude toward their children. They don't push them to excel. They believe children should be allowed to dress as they like, eat what they want, and do pretty much as they please. They think boys and girls should be raised alike. They are permissive, but not doting. The New Breed parents saw having children as an option, not a social responsibility—and nine out of ten would do it again if given the chance to start over. Forty-three percent of the parents surveyed fit this pattern.

Yankelovich contrasts the New Breed to the Traditionalists (57 percent of all parents). Traditionalists consider religion, saving, hard work, and financial security very important. They value the institution of marriage and having children, and tend to be child-oriented. Although they believe parents are entitled to lives of their own, they are ready to give up things they want for their children. At the same time, they demand more of their children (achievements in studies and

tion, divorce, death, the bearing of illegitimate children, and the creation of separate households away from relatives. In their study of this phenomenon, Ross and Sawhill (1975) see this form as a transitional one in most cases, since it usually evolves from a two-parent form or later into a two-parent form or into yet another pattern. The primary cause of the current great increase is the changing economic and social condition of

women—their greater independence due to possibilities of income and social support outside traditional arrangements (5). Jobs and welfare benefits (in the form of money and available services) have made women freer to change their living arrangements and more able to seek personal satisfaction and fulfillment. Although the isolated nuclear family remains the ideal type in America, the increasing prevalence of this single-parent

sports, popularity, and good manners). They believe that parents should make decisions for their children; raise boys and girls differently; and be moderately or very strict. In short, they believe a traditional upbringing is still best.

Thus the survey revealed two groups of parents with very different values and attitudes. Surprisingly, Yankelovich found that *both* New Breed and Traditional parents strive to instill in their children the most basic American values: duty before pleasure; my country right or wrong; the only way to get ahead is through hard work; and everybody should save money even if it means doing without something right now. It is easy to see why Traditionalist parents would emphasize these values. Yankelovich speculates that New Breed parents pass on values they no longer endorse in part because they're uncertain themselves, in part to prepare their children for a society that hasn't yet caught up with the parents' ideas.

What about the children? By and large, Yankelovich found that the children of the 1970s are Traditionalists. For example, they believe it is their mother's, not their father's, job to cook and clean. These children say they like their mothers because their mothers are good homemakers and do nice things; their fathers because their fathers take them places and earn money for the family. They don't believe parents should separate just because they are unhappy, or should even take a vacation without their children. And they think it is all right for parents to spank children. There are some differences among the youngsters. Children of the New Breed parents are more relaxed: they realize their parents don't push them as hard as other parents do their children. And they are more tolerant of racial and other differences. When it comes to complaints about their parents, however, children of New Breed and Traditionalist parents are in almost total agreement—not being allowed to eat what they like and being forced to turn off the TV head the list.

SOURCE: Yankelovich, Skelly, and White, Inc., *The General Mills American Family Report 1976–77: Raising Children in a Changing Society*, Minneapolis: General Mills Consumer Center, 1977.

form of the family shows that in reality there is considerable variation in American family life, as well as considerable change.

Social Class Differences

Of all the factors that tend to influence the nature of family life, social class is one of the most important. No matter how social class is defined (by income, education, occupation, or family background), it invariably affects the organization of family life. Of course, on the superficial level, this statement is self-evident. A family's resources clearly influence the quality of the food it consumes, the number and kind of leisure activities it enjoys, the amount of space it has to live in, and the schools its children will attend (see chapter 10). But beyond these obvious options that money will buy, there are other class differences in family life.

Demographic Factors   Some of the most important are demographic. That is, both the number of children born to each family and death rates tend to vary with social class. Families lower in the social hierarchy are more likely to have (and desire) more children. The death rate is substantially higher

Social standing is an important influence on family life. Families lower in the social hierarchy, for example, tend to desire and have many children. Disciplinary attitudes also correlate with socio-economic status: studies confirm a relationship between social class and parental values.   (J. Albertson/Stock, Boston)

among lower-class families, which means that people in the lower social strata are likely to die at a younger age than people in higher strata. Of course the death rate is related to such other class variables as health care, nutritional variety, living conditions, and occupational hazards. In addition, lower-class families are more likely than upper-class ones to be disrupted by illness, early death, desertion, and divorce.

Types of Discipline   Families from different classes also appear to raise their children in somewhat different ways. Sociologist Melvin Kohn (1959), who has studied the relationship between social class and child-rearing, argues that in order to understand why different classes raise their children differently, we must know what the parents value and

want for their children. Kohn suggests that one of the most significant value differences between middle- and working-class parents is in the realm of obedience to authority versus inner controls. "Working-class parents want the child to conform to externally imposed standards, while middle-class parents are far more attentive to . . . internal dynamics" (Kohn, 1974: 283).

Kohn suggests that these differences in values stem in large part from differences in occupational conditions. Working-class parents anticipate that as adults their children will have to follow orders. Conformity and obedience, then, become highly valued traits. Middle-class parents tend to envision their children in professional careers, where initiative and self-discipline bring success. Recently, James D. and Sonia R. Wright (1976) carried out a partial replication of Kohn's 1959 survey, and they were able to confirm the strong relationship between social class and parental values; specifically, they found that the tendency to value self-direction—"internal standards for behavior"—increased with social class. The Wrights argue, however, that Kohn has exaggerated the importance of occupation. Instead, they say, more emphasis should be placed on level of education to explain the relationship between social class and the kinds of values parents inculcate in their children, because level of education is more important in determining how much self-direction a person exercises at work.

What differences do these values make in terms of actual family behavior and child-rearing practices? Apparently, a considerable amount. One of the early reviews of child-rearing techniques in relationship to social class concludes that "in matters of discipline, working-class parents are consistently more likely to employ physical punishment, while middle-class families rely more on reasoning, isolation, appeals to guilt and other

methods involving the threat of loss of love" (Bronfenbrenner, 1958). The difference between the two classes in punishment behavior seems to hinge on different conceptions of what constitutes punishable behavior. For working-class parents, acts with negative *consequences* are punishable (for instance, marking up the furniture with crayons), whereas for middle-class parents, acts with negative *intentions* are punishable (for instance, deliberately knocking down a sibling's pile of blocks). Often, of course, an act has both negative intentions *and* consequences (for example, stealing candy from the neighborhood drugstore), and in such cases, parents of either class would punish.

Parent-child Relationships Discipline, of course, is not the only area in which differences in values are reflected in differences in behavior. Differences show up not only in behavior toward children but also in the kinds of relationships parents have with their children. Middle-class fathers are expected to be supportive and considerate of their children. Since such behavior is also expected of middle-class mothers, the differences between the roles middle-class mothers and middle-class fathers play are not so vast: both concentrate their energies and efforts on the inner development of the child.

In working-class families, however, where constraint and obedience are the keynote of upbringing, the mother is more likely to be the supportive parent and the father is usually the constrainer. But although the mother generally has full charge of the girls, the father will assume control of the sons once they are beyond infancy and early childhood, for he considers it his job to socialize his boys into the role of a man (LeMasters, 1975: 111ff.). This sharp division of labor is becoming blurred as the forces of social change (for example, women's liberation, increased occupational opportunities for women, and rising levels of education) begin to influence young working-class people. But for the time being, the values and practices of each class will continue to perpetuate themselves, if only because people tend to raise their children much as they themselves were raised.

Love and Marriage

In any society, when two people marry, their union binds many other people together as well. Nowhere in the world is marriage a simple, unguided act of commitment involving just two people in love. Every society has patterned means for guiding its young people toward "appropriate" marriages. In societies such as our own, the guidance is subtly concealed. In others, it is codified into systems of arranged marriages. Because so many people are involved in the outcome, it is risky to leave such an important decision to the discretion of the impractical young.

Arranged Marriages Although systems of arranged marriages seem cruel and unusual to those of us raised with values of individualism and free choice, it's easy to understand why such systems develop and flourish. Think, for instance, of societies in which newlyweds move into the husband's family's household. In such cases, the husband's family will have an important stake in the type of woman the son brings home. Will she share the family's ideas about what is good and worthwhile? Will she readily adjust to the family's codes of behavior? Will she pull her weight in the household? If a new wife is to live in her husband's household forever, it is reasonable for the members of that household to have some say about the new addition.

But over and above these positive reasons for arranged marriages, there are also cogent reasons for actively discouraging romantic love as a basis for marriage between young people in societies where the newlyweds live with either the bride's or the groom's family. Romantic love, in such situations, would have an enormous potential for disruption. The bond of love between the two might create jealousy and competition for attention among other household members. In addition, if the husband were strongly devoted to his wife, he might form a coalition with her against other household members and thereby threaten customary relationships. For these reasons, at least, traditional societies don't leave affairs of the heart to the discretion of the young, but rather attempt to control such affairs through arranged marriages.

Subsurface Controls Our own society has a different set of requirements that affects the nature of our patterns of mate selection. Since newlyweds in the United States typically set up their own households, that a new spouse be acceptable to one's family is not so important, although a person can't totally ignore the wishes of his or her family. Since an "inappropriate" marriage may "scandalize the family," whereas an "appropriate" one might bring glory and pride, parents and the rest of society subtly shape children's marriage aspirations from a very early age. (Recall Peter Berger's passage about love on p. 57.)

Parental choices of residential neighborhoods and school districts influence the kinds of peers children will have to choose from for playmates and later for dates. Such intangibles of family life as the development of a sense of "we" and "they," of "our kind" and "their kind," influence young people's ideas concerning whom they will consider attractive. A family's choice of recreational activities, selection of vacation spots, and style of celebrating holidays and special occasions will all influence the kinds of potential mates that young people from that family will meet or eventually seek on their own.

These kinds of subsurface controls effectively direct a young person's love interests toward an appropriate pool of eligible mates. And, in fact, the effectiveness of these subtle influences shows up in the marriage statistics. Although religious intermarriage in the United States appears to be increasing, marriages between people of different races and nationalities are relatively rare, particularly among those who belong to the higher strata of the society (Udry, 1971). Once young people have learned what sorts of people swim in their pool of eligibles, then they are encouraged to allow the impulses and emotions of romantic love to take over.

Romantic Love   Romantic love is idealized and exalted in American society. Much of our youthful energy and emotion is devoted to the quest for love, and many a psychiatrist's couch groans under the burden of those who have failed in this culturally exalted quest. There are good reasons why romantic love has become an important basis for marriage in our society (just as there are good reasons why a system of arranged marriages has developed in more traditional societies). When a man and woman in the United States marry and set up a new household (as more than 2 million American couples did in 1978), the new family unit is relatively independent (at least geographically) of other kin. As a result, husband and wife are free to love each other without creating tensions, jealousies, and competition among other household members. Also, since the two will depend on each other for a wide range of emotional and physical supports, they will be better able to meet each other's needs if they are guided by love rather than by strictly de-

fined rights and obligations. Romantic love also helps weaken the strong emotional ties that bind young people to their own families, and enables them to move more comfortably out of the familial nest into their own independent world.

But as the basis of marriage, romance has its limitations. In some ways, romance is completely antithetical to the daily demands of married life. Romance thrives on mystery, distance, and uncertainty, while married life can be described as anything but mysterious. When romance fades, all too often the marriage fades with it. Thus, by celebrating romance so avidly, we may be simultaneously undermining the very relationships we hope to promote: stable, enduring, child-producing marriages. Since marriage is a business partnership as well as a romantic fairy tale (it involves, among other things, compromises, division of labor, specialization, communication systems—all the trappings of an institution), to bill it as a flower-strewn paradise is to risk its eventual demise.

Divorce

That American society has been successful in promoting marriage as a way of life is clear from American marriage statistics. Nine out of ten people in America get married at least once in their lives (*Population and the American Future*, 1972: 67)—and they do it early in life. The median age for marriage among women is slightly over twenty years, and for men, it is between twenty-two and twenty-three. But what happens to all of those marriages that start out with so much love and so many high hopes? Unfortunately, it's very difficult to know for certain what *does* happen.

To start with, it is almost impossible to come up with a satisfactory definition of what constitutes a happy or unhappy mar-

Romantic love is idealized and exalted in American society, but all too often it cannot withstand the demands of married life. (The Bettmann Archive)

riage. If we can't define "good" and "bad" marriages, we can hardly expect to come up with figures concerning how many of each kind occur. But even if we rely on information that does seem to be measurable—for instance, the number of marriages that end in divorce—we soon see how complicated the task is (see the accompanying box).

Explaining Divorce Rates Although it is difficult to calculate current divorce rates, they do seem to be going up. Besides psychological reasons, the major explanations are social factors, all involving change—in values, in institutions, and in the position of women.

The major change in values involves a shift from a philosophy of self-sacrifice to one that emphasizes individual happiness. The principal reason for getting married today is to satisfy one's psychological needs ("romantic love"); failure to have these needs met now leads to dissolution of the marriage rather than to an attempt to stay together "for the children's sake." Institutions affecting family life have also changed. For instance, most churches now recognize divorce. In addition, the legal apparatus for obtaining divorces is less complex than formerly: twenty-six states now have some form of no-fault divorce laws, and free legal aid is available for those wishing to obtain a divorce (Glick, 1975). Finally, the change in the position of women has contributed to increasing divorce rates in two ways: (1) it has made women less economically dependent on men, and therefore freer to opt out of marriage (Kephart, 1977: 479); and (2) in promoting the general equality of the sexes, "it has helped ease the social adjustments of people who are not married" (Glick, 1975).

PUZZLE: MEASURING DIVORCE

Measuring the divorce rate would seem to be an easy job. Just count up the number of divorces granted in any one year and compare that statistic with the number of marriages performed in that year. For example, in 1976 there were 1,077,000 divorces and 2,133,000 marriages (*Monthly Vital Statistics Report*, March 8, 1977), for a divorce rate of roughly 50 percent. Simple? Not really.

The problem is that you are comparing the wrong things. The number of marriages and the number of divorces in a year are both straightforward statistics, but comparing them to get an annual divorce rate is another matter. Think about the 1976 data again. That 50 percent divorce rate means that half the people who married in 1976 were divorced that same year. But in reality, very few of the couples who were divorced in 1976 were also married that year. So simply comparing marriages and divorces for a single year tells us nothing about the *rate* of divorce. It's as if you compared the number of births in a single year with the number of deaths in that same year in order to find the national death rate. Instead, you must compare the *total* number of people living in a year with the number who die. Similarly, a valid divorce rate must compare the number of divorces in one year with the *total number of marriages that exist in that year*. For example, when you compare the more than 50 million marriages existing in 1976 with the 1 million divorces in that year, the divorce rate turns out to be only *2 percent*. This presents another problem, because it tells us nothing about the even lower divorce rates of other eras. In short, what seems like a low rate for 1976 may be alarmingly high when compared to the divorce rate for 1876, for example.

Also, the 2 percent rate reveals nothing about the marriages that ended in that year. How many lasted less than three years? How many more than ten? More than twenty? Comparing these figures would tell us something more about the stability of marriage than we learn from the simple 2 percent figure.

How, then, should we measure divorce? One method that would solve some of these problems is the longitudinal study: a researcher could follow a representative sample of Americans from the year they marry to the end of their lives. Such a study would yield several kinds of data: average age at marriage; average duration of the group's marriages; rate of remarriage; and so forth. A number of such studies done over different periods of time would reveal a great deal more about divorce in America than a simple annual "rate" statistic can ever tell us.

Of course, personal factors also enter into any explanation of divorce. The most common reasons for divorce are sexual incompatibility, personality problems, infidelity, excessive drinking, financial difficulties, and in-law relationships. Middle-class people tend to emphasize psychological reasons, whereas lower-class people tend to accentuate financial problems and such factors as physical abuse (Kephart, 1977: 480).

Whether the percentage of marriages that end in divorce will increase, decrease, or remain constant is of course a matter of speculation. But whatever else divorce does, it doesn't seem to sour people on the institution of marriage. One-fourth of the people who get divorced are remarried within the year, and within nine years of divorce a full 75 percent are married again. Thus, while marriage may be difficult to sustain, it is certainly not going out of style. Almost everybody gets married (and gets remarried when necessary).

THE CHANGING AMERICAN FAMILY

The relative ease with which present-day marriages may be dissolved is only one of the recent changes in American family life. Another involves the amount of time a couple spends in married life and the number of years they devote to raising children. In 1920, the average American lived fifty-four to fifty-five years. Today the average man lives sixty-eight (68.2 years), and the average woman, seventy-six (75.9 years). Thus, a couple who marries young and stays married can now expect almost fifty years of togetherness—a long stretch of time encompassing many different life-cycle changes. The most crucial of these changes are perhaps the ones that revolve around children.

Child-rearing

When the first child is born to a couple, drastic life-style changes occur. Husband and wife are no longer free to come and go as they please, but must make arrangements for every outing, excursion, or supermarket trip. If the mother has been working, she must either quit her job or make complicated arrangements for child care. Usually the couple must move to larger quarters, perhaps to a neighborhood where there are likely to be other young children. In addition,

the love, attention, and leisure time two people once shared must now be spread out among three or more individuals. These changes can be very trying, and with the birth of a first child a couple finds itself in a whole new social framework.

Drastic changes in one's life style also occur at the end of child-rearing. As their grown children leave home, husband and wife are once again thrown back on their own resources, and after all the years of activity, commotion, demands, and scheduling, the couple may find the new regime as unsettling as was the birth of the first child eighteen or so years earlier.

While this sequence of events concerning the child-rearing aspects of marriage hasn't changed much over the decades, the duration of the sequence has: the number of child-oriented years of marriage has been reduced. Over the past twenty-five years, women in general have gradually been marrying later, having children later, and having fewer children. One possible explanation is that expanded educational opportunities and increasing acceptance of nontraditional living arrangements provide women with alternatives to such traditional life choices as early marriage (Van Dusen and Sheldon, 1976: 175).

When the abridged child-oriented years of marriage are linked with the greater longevity for both sexes, we can see that one of the crucial changes in married life is the amount of time the couple will spend alone together at the end of their lives (and due to the fact that women generally live longer than men, it also increases the amount of time that a woman is likely to be a widow).

Women in the Work Force

Even before the current late-marriage, late-childbearing trend began, changes in family life-cycle schedules (notably the reduction in the average number of child-oriented years of marriage) had already provided women with substantially more free time, particularly in their middle years. As the labor-market statistics show, women are using this time to enter (or reenter) the occupational world. In 1960, women represented 37.8 percent of the labor force. By April 1977, this figure had risen to 47.7 percent. Today, women are not only entering the labor force *after* their children have grown, but they are also remaining in jobs even *during* their childbearing years. As of 1976, 56.9 percent of women in the twenty-five-to-thirty-four age bracket were in the work force. In 1960, this rate was only 35.8 percent (U.S. Bureau of the Census, 1977, tables 570, 571). Again, this can be explained in part by the increased availability of educational opportunities for women; related to this is the fact that women who have earned jobs and inde-

pendence are increasingly reluctant to give them up. Yet another factor is that there are times during the family life cycle when expenses are high and women must work to supplement the family income; this is especially true just after a couple has gotten married and when their children reach adolescence (Van Dusen and Sheldon, 1976).

The more women work (particularly when they are in satisfying and responsible occupations), the more pressure they'll bring to bear on the traditional roles in family life (see chapter 6). They will balk at traditional divisions of labor and at traditional patterns of authority. As political scientist Andrew Hacker has said:

In the past and until very recently, wives were simply supplementary to their husbands, and not expected to be full human beings. Today, women are involved in much

figure 13:2　Percent distribution of individuals answering the question, "Do working women make better or worse mothers than nonworking women?"

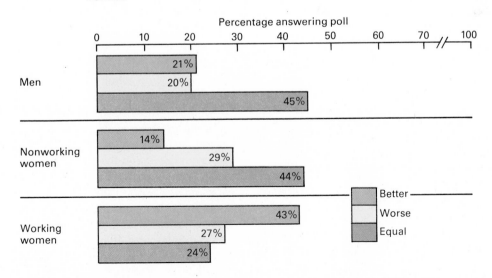

SOURCE: *"The New York Times / CBS News Poll," The New York Times,* November 27, 1977, p. 74.

greater expectations and frustrations. . . . The trouble comes from the fact that the institution we call marriage can't hold two full human beings—it was only designed for one and a half. (1970: 34–39)

As Hacker's "half" becomes more of a social and psychological whole, there are likely to be a series of profound reorganizations in that much-beleaguered institution called the isolated nuclear family.

Alternative Forms of Marriage

One of the reorganizations, already in its formative stage, may be the attempt to rewrite the marriage script. Instead of expecting a man and a woman to be legally linked in a male-oriented, monogamous, isolated household, a new set of expectations and arrangements may arise (as they have already begun to do). Rapid changes have already occurred in regard to monogamy and sex outside the context of marriage. With the development of an easy, efficient, accessible, inexpensive contraceptive, these changes are likely to become even more marked.

If in fact extramarital sex becomes solely a matter of private conscience and not public taboo, and if sexual relations come to occupy two separate spheres—recreational and procreational—then it is likely that some of the powerful motives for getting married will lose their force. Clearly, attitudes toward the recreational aspects of sexual relations are changing, as every study on the subject indicates. The use of birth control is now generally accepted, as is making birth-control information available to everyone—including unmarried teen-agers. This is a far cry from the national attitudes that showed up in a Gallup poll in 1936. In that study, 70 percent of the American people opposed the legali-

zation of distribution of birth-control information, even to married people (Wattenberg, 1973).

Such enormous changes in attitudes (and in sexual behavior) may have far-reaching effects. Couples will feel increasingly free to live with each other before marriage, or after an earlier marriage has ended. As women come increasingly to determine their own childbearing histories, they will in all likelihood make greater demands on their mates for more equal unions and for greater work opportunities, and they will determine for themselves the number of children they wish to raise.

Two-career Marriages There are already in this country several types of innovative marriages, which are being pursued by a substantial number of couples. With increasing frequency, for instance, Americans are undertaking *two-career marriages*—typically, a marriage in which both partners pursue careers and share family responsibilities equally. Two-career or dual-career marriages occur most commonly among such upper-middle-class professionals as lawyers or academics. The main problem that arises in marriages of this type stems from the need of each partner to somehow mesh the demands of a job with the demands of a family. This is particularly true when both husband and wife have rigid (nine-to-five or later) work schedules: if they have children, they must arrange for them to be looked after; they must make sure that necessary domestic tasks get done; and they must also try to set aside time simply for being together. Professions in which work schedules are relatively flexible, such as college teaching, make it somewhat easier to juggle a job and family, but careful organization of tasks and responsibilities is still important. And not all conflicts can be predicted or avoided: husband or wife may have to attend an unexpected

table 13:3 A PILOT STUDY OF THE PROBLEMS OF UNMARRIED STUDENTS WHO LIVE TOGETHER[1]

PROBLEM AREA	NUMBER INDICATING		AVERAGE RATING GIVEN BY THOSE INDICATING SOME PROBLEM
	NO PROBLEM	SOME PROBLEM	
Emotion problems			
Overinvolvement (loss of identity, lack of opportunity to participate in other activities or with friends, overdependency)	14	21	2.7
Jealousy of partner's involvement in other activities or relationships	14	15	3.1
Feeling of being trapped	18	15	2.9
Feeling of being used	19	13	2.6
Guilt about living together			
—at beginning of relationship	20	9	3.7
—during relationship	25	5	3.8
—at end of relationship	15	2	4.0
Lack of feeling of "belonging" or of being "at home"	22	9	3.4
Sexual problems			
Differing degrees or periods of sexual interest	10	23	3.4
Lack of orgasm	11	21	3.6
Fear of pregnancy	15	15	3.1
Impotence of partner	23	6	3.0
Problems related to living situation			
Lack of privacy	15	17	3.4
Lack of adequate space	19	13	3.0
Did not get along with apartment- or house-mates	20	6	2.2
Lack of sufficient money	26	6	3.3
Disagreement over use of money, sharing of money, etc.	27	4	3.5

[1] This table is based on interviews with junior and senior women at Cornell University. Respondents were asked to rate each problem from 1 to 5, with 1 = great deal of problem, 5 = no problem (no other points defined). The last category (5 = no problem) has been separated, because it may be qualitatively different from the other rating categories. Average ratings are therefore based on ratings from 1 to 4; thus, the lower the average rating, the greater the problem for those experiencing it.

SOURCE: Adapted from Eleanor D. Macklin, "Heterosexual Cohabitation Among Unmarried University Students," *Family Coordinator*, vol. 21 (October 1972), p. 42.

meeting, or the baby sitter may not show up, or vacation schedules may not jibe, just to name a few typical problems. How are these conflicts settled? In theory, the demands of both the husband's and the wife's jobs are given equal weight when decisions have to be made. But in practice, one study suggests, a wife accommodates to her hus-

IN THE NEWS

Living Alone—and Liking It

The freedom to come and go as one pleases, the right to clean up after oneself only when one feels like it—these are just a couple of the day-to-day reasons more and more people under thirty-five find living alone an attractive alternative to marriage. Though many of these young people see marriage as a possibility in the future, they are wary of settling down for the present. So for now most are quite satisfied with the freedom of their solitary life style:

At 29, Eleanor Holmes is ambitious and single. She lives in a comfortable one-bedroom apartment amid a mixture of chrome modern and old attic furniture, just a stone's throw from Lake Washington. She shares the place with nobody but her seven-toed cat, Alfred, and she likes that just fine.

Miss Holmes and a growing legion of young Americans choose to live quite alone, without roommate or spouse. "I would consider marriage if the right person comes along, but I would not give up my career for it," she said. She is a legislative aide to a City Councilwoman.

Miss Holmes's situation speaks volumes about some sweeping changes in the way young men and women are living throughout the country. Last month, the Census Bureau reported that the number of adults under 35 who live alone had more than doubled since 1970 despite an uncertain economy. This is far greater than the expansion of this age group in the population, which was less than one-fifth.

The trend toward single living is a reflection of several other shifts in American family and social life in recent years: the tendency to postpone or even forgo marriage, the growing career ambitions of women, the easing of salary and credit discrimination against women, the mounting divorce rate, a general independence of young people from their parents and a wide new tolerance for unconventional living arrangements generally.

The tendency for the young to leave home early and to marry late is leading to a prolonged phase of isolation in the lives of many, according to Arthur Norton, a Census Bureau expert in matters of marital status and living arrangements. . . .

Many link their solitary living to a new wariness about marriage. At 24, Greg Beaumont of Euclid, Ohio, is already past the median age of marriage for men, but he has no plans to take the plunge soon. "I have seen too many people broken up by bad marriages," said Mr. Beaumont, who is a store manager. "When I get married I would like it to be permanent."

Others say that they are having too good a time to settle down. Ward M. Wilson, a 35-year-old stockbroker who has a whole house to himself in Binghamton, N.Y., takes ski trips to Colorado and winter holidays in Puerto Rico. He said that he wanted "very much" to have children someday, but for the moment he did not want to be "hampered" by a wife or family.

Drawbacks to living alone can be the increased cost and occasional feelings of loneliness. Yet nearly all the men and women interviewed agreed that the advantages far outweighed these disadvantages.

SOURCE: Robert Reinhold, "Trend to Living Alone Brings Economic and Social Change," *The New York Times,* March 20, 1977, pp. 1, 59.

band's career more often than a husband accommodates to his wife's career; the woman's time is considered to be less valuable than the man's; and despite the egalitarian philosophy of the two-career marriage, the domestic realm is—at least at the moment—ultimately defined as the woman's responsibility. Thus, in an analysis of twenty two-career marriages, Lynda Lytle Holmstrom concluded that "despite their great deviation from middle-class norms, most professional couples were still a great distance from equality of the sexes" (1972: 155).

Perhaps the greatest strain in two-career marriages arises over the issue of geographic separation due to career commitments—that is, when both the husband's and the wife's participation in a career requires that they work in different locations. One increasingly popular solution to this problem is the so-called commuter marriage, in which marriage partners spend some of the time living in separate residences—from a few miles to a continent apart—while remaining married. The drawbacks of this arrangement are strained communication, occasional sexual problems, and an often sharply reduced social life. Many couples report being satisfied with commuter marriage, however, because it allows both partners increased autonomy, gives them diverse experiences to share, minimizes the kinds of trivial conflicts that often arise when people live together day after day, and also makes marriage—at least that part which husband and wife spend together—more romantic (Gerstel, 1976).

Contract Marriages Two-career and commuter marriages that succeed do so because of informal understandings between husbands and wives as to their respective duties within the marriage. But some people want a more explicit statement of marital rights and obligations, and such people may write up a formal marriage contract. Arguing in favor of such *contract marriages*, feminist writer Susan Edmiston explains:

> First we thought marriage was when Prince Charming came and took you away with him. Then marriage was orange blossoms and silver. But most of us never even suspected the truth. Nobody ever so much as mentioned that what marriage is, at its very heart and essence, is a contract. . . . When you say "I do" you are subscribing to a whole system of rights, obligations and responsibilities many of which may be antithetical to your most cherished beliefs. (1972: 2)

Important areas covered by the contract include not just the division of labor in the household but also the number and timing of children—if the couple decides to have any at all.

Childless Marriages Increasing numbers of couples, particularly among the college-educated, are deciding to remain childless (Pohlman, 1974: 276). According to an exploratory study of fifty-two voluntarily childless couples, in about one case out of every three, the decision not to have children was made by the couple before they are married, and then was explicitly stated in a marriage contract. The rest of the time, childlessness was the result of repeated decisions to postpone parenthood until it was either too late or clearly no longer desirable to have children (Veevers, 1973). While a great deal has been learned over the past few decades about the factors involved in a couple's decision to have children, relatively little is known of the factors that promote what sociologists now call "negative fertility attitudes." Preliminary research suggests that the typical childless couple is likely to live in a large metropolitan area, to have been married about five years, to be about thirty years old, to claim no religious inclinations, and to

This man and woman—young, urban, educated, and well-off—are typical of the growing number of married couples choosing to remain childless. (Camilla Smith)

be of higher-than-average socioeconomic status (Gustavus and Henley, 1971). Particularly when childlessness is the result of repeated postponements, the many social, economic, and personal advantages of non-parenthood exert a strong influence on a couple's deision (Veevers, 1973). But these aren't the only reasons for childless marriages. In a study of couples seeking help in obtaining voluntary surgical sterilizations, the two most frequently mentioned reasons for wanting to remain childless were health considerations and concern with overpopulation (Gustavus and Henley, 1971).

Open Marriage Another model that has gained considerable attention (at least if media coverage is any measure of public interest) is known as the *open marriage*. In a best-selling book about the virtues of open marriage, a husband/wife team of social scientists contrast their flexible marriage arrangement with the more traditional, or closed, marriage. In conventional marriages, claim Nena and George O'Neill (1972), husband and wife feel that they possess each other and conform to rigid marital roles, which include, among other things, absolute fidelity. An open marriage, by contrast, stresses more flexible roles and more consideration of each partner's needs, talents, and desires, and a considerable amount of autonomy for husband and wife.

While the open marriage does not depart drastically in structure from marriage as we know it, other more radical—and less popular—departures in structure have been attempted. There are, for instance, a variety of plural mating arrangements in which several individuals or couples share housekeeping duties, child-rearing, income, and even bed. These arrangements meet with varying degrees of success, depending on the personalities of the individuals involved and the attitudes of the surrounding community (Constantine and Constantine, 1970).

In *The Marriage Premise* (1977), however, Nena O'Neill, in examining the reasons why people are still choosing to marry despite the existence of socially acceptable alternatives, has concluded that there has been a return to some of the traditional constants, such as sexual fidelity—although from choice rather than from duty or obligation as before. "It seems to me that marriages today are turning back, not to the old closed coercions and external pressures, but to new combinations and a reappraisal of what marriage can still offer. . . . As the old order gives way to the new, we are coming to realize that many of the old foundations of marriage are still firm, and that we can still build on them" (27, 28).

All these explorations into innovative forms of marriage are earnest attempts at retaining commitment and permanence while maximizing individual freedom and growth. No one can predict how these experiments will succeed; what is certain is that marriage is likely to display a different profile as future generations arrive at new solutions to the age-old tension between individual freedom and social responsibility.

SUMMARY

Although there are a variety of ways to define the family, social scientists generally agree that families everywhere fulfill four crucial *social functions*: (1) reproduction of new members; (2) child care; (3) socialization of children to the values, traditions, and norms of the society; and (4) intimacy and support for members. The family is not just a biological unit, since social forces, not personal desires, strongly influence both the choice of marriage partner and the form the family will assume.

The isolated nuclear family that predominates in most Western industrialized countries is only one of many possible forms of the family. Cross-cultural research has revealed numerous other patterns, such as those of the Nayar of India, the Dani of Indonesia, and the *kibbutzim* of Israel. Many social scientists suggest that the form of the family is determined by other aspects of the society's social structure—in particular by subsistence needs. Family arrangements are thus determined both by the geography the society inhabits and by the kinds of work people in the society perform in order for it to survive. In modern industrial societies, where due to frequent job changes families must be highly mobile and often must live in confined urban spaces, the small nuclear family, with its emphasis on independence and individualism, predominates because it fits society's economic needs.

The modern nuclear family now has the dominant function of providing emotional support for its members, as well as the new economic function of consuming rather than producing. It also has several consequences for its members. Husband and wife become very emotionally and physically dependent on each other. Further, one or the other must always be at home during the child-rearing years. The great dependence of husband and wife on each other makes the American family very fragile, and since children leave home early, the nuclear family is a short-lived unit.

There is not just one type of family in America, however; social scientists have discovered important variations, such as the single-parent family. Families also differ according to social class. A couple's social class affects the number of children they will decide to have, if any, and also the likelihood of disruption of the family by illness, death, desertion, or divorce. Social class also influences the way families raise their children, particularly the values parents transmit to children and the kinds of relationships parents and children have. Melvin Kohn has suggested that these differences in values—conformity and obedience, or initiative and self-direction—stem in large part from differences in occupational conditions.

Every society has patterned means for guiding its young people into "appropriate" marriages. In many societies, marriages are arranged, particularly if the couple will live with one spouse's parents. By selecting the mate in advance, the family can avoid the problem of gaining an unacceptable member. In America, marriages are not arranged, but from an early age children learn about the kinds of people who will be acceptable marriage partners. And parental choice of residential neighborhood and school district determines whom children play with and later date. Americans idealize romantic love, but as a basis for marriage, romance has its limitations. The familiarity that comes with marriage often brings an end to romantic illusions—and sometimes to the family unit.

Although most people are aware that divorce rates are rising, calculating the current rate, as well as monitoring changes in rates, is very difficult. Social reasons for the growing number of divorces include more career opportunities for women, easier divorce procedures, less stigmatization, and a growing awareness that a divided family may be better for children than a conflict-laden one.

The American family has been changing in a number of ways over the past few decades, particularly in ways that concern children. Many women marry later, have children later, and have fewer children. Since people now live longer, they may expect to be married for a longer time. And since children leave home at about age eighteen, married couples have many more years alone together. Role changes are also occurring as more women find satisfying careers outside the home.

Changes in the family and in attitudes toward sex have sparked a number of suggestions for alternative forms of marriage. Some couples form *two-career marriages*; others draw up a formal *marriage contract*. Still others choose to remain childless. New models such as *open marriage* and plural mating arrangements have also appeared. It is clear that marriage as we know it has been subjected to enormous pressures and is likely to display a different profile in the future.

GLOSSARY

contract marriage a marriage in which the couple designs their own marriage contract, specifying rights and obligations of each spouse concerning domestic and economic activities, division of labor, and the number and timing of children.

extended family a household consisting of married couples from different generations, their children, and other relatives.

family the social institution that provides a reliable arrangement for producing, sustaining, and socializing succeeding generations.

kibbutzim collective settlements in Israel where individuals work for and children are raised by the community as a whole.

nuclear family a husband and wife and their dependent children living apart from other relatives.

open marriage a marriage that involves flexible roles, consideration of each partner's needs, talents, and desires, and a considerable amount of autonomy and independence for husband and wife.

two-career marriage a marriage in which the work requirements of both the male and the female are given serious consideration before such family decisions as geographic location, vacation schedules, and the number and timing of children are made.

REFERENCES

H. Barry, Margaret K. Bacon, and I. L. Child, "A Cross-Cultural Survey of Some Sex Differences in Socialization." *Journal of Abnormal Psychology,* vol. 55 (1957): 327–332.

Bruno Bettelheim, *Children of the Dream.* New York: Avon, 1971.

Urie Bronfenbrenner, "Socialization and Social Class Through Time and Space," in Eleanor Maccoby, Theodore Newcomb, and Eugene L. Hartley, eds., *Readings in Social Psychology.* New York: Holt, Rinehart and Winston, 1958.

Larry L. and Joan M. Constantine, "Where Is Marriage Going?" *The Futurist,* vol. 4 (April 1970): 44–46.

Susan Edmiston, "How to Write Your Own Marriage Contract." *Ms.,* vol. 1 (Spring 1972): 66–74.

Naomi R. Gerstel, "The Feasibility of Commuter Marriage," in Peter J. Stein, Judith Richman, and Natalie Harmon, eds., *The Family.* Reading, Mass.: Addison-Wesley, 1977.

Paul C. Glick, "A Demographer Looks at American Families." *Journal of Marriage and the Family,* vol. 37 (February 1975): 15–26. (Also in Skolnick and Skolnick, 1977.)

William J. Goode, "The Role of the Family in Industrialization." *Social Problems of Development,* vol. 7, The U.S. Papers Prepared for the UN Conference on the Application of Science and Technology for the Benefit of the Less Developed Areas. Washington, D.C.: Government Printing Office, 1963.

E. Kathleen Gough, "Nayar: Central Kerala," in David Schneider and E. Kathleen Gough, eds., *Matrilineal Kinship.* Berkeley: University of California Press, 1974.

Susan O. Gustavus and James R. Henley, Jr., "Correlates of Voluntary Childlessness in a Select Population," in Ellen Peck and Judith Senderowitz, eds., *Pronatalism.* New York: Crowell, 1974.

Andrew Hacker, "The American Family: Future Uncertain." *Time,* December 28, 1970, pp. 34–39.

Karl G. Heider, *The Dani of West Irian.* Andover, Md.: Warner Modular Publications, 1972.

Veronica Stolte Heiskanen, "The Myth of the Middle-Class Family in American Family Sociology." *The American Sociologist,* vol. 6 (February 1971): 14–18.

Lynda Lytle Holmstrom, *The Two-Career Family.* Cambridge, Mass.: Schenkman, 1972.

William M. Kephart, *The Family, Society, and the Individual,* 4th ed. Boston: Houghton Mifflin, 1977.

Melvin L. Kohn, "Social Class and Parental Values." *American Journal of Sociology,* vol. 64 (January 1959): 337–351.

———, "Social Class and Parent-Child Relationships: An Interpretation," in Robert F. Winch and Louis W. Goodman, eds., *Selected Studies in Marriage and the Family,* 4th ed. New York: Holt, Rinehart and Winston, 1974.

E. E. LeMasters, *Blue-Collar Aristocrats.* Madison: University of Wisconsin Press, 1975.

Claude Lévi-Strauss, "The Family," in Harry L. Shapiro, ed., *Man, Culture, and Society.* New York: Oxford University Press, 1956.

Bronislaw Malinowski, "The Principle of Legitimacy: Parenthood, the Basis of Social Structure," in Rose Laub Coser, ed., *The Family: Its Structure and Functions*. New York: St. Martin's, 1964.

Margaret Mead, *Coming of Age in Samoa*. New York: Modern Library, 1953.

George Peter Murdock, *Social Structure*. New York: Macmillan, 1949.

M. F. Nimkoff and Russell Middleton, "Types of Family and Types of Economy." *American Journal of Sociology,* vol. 66 (November 1960): 215–225.

Nena O'Neill, *The Marriage Premise*. New York: M. Evans, 1977.

———— and George O'Neill, *Open Marriage*. New York: Evans, 1972.

Edward Pohlman, "Changes in Views Toward Childlessness: 1965–1970," in Ellen Peck and Judith Senderowitz, eds., *Pronatalism*. New York: Crowell, 1974.

Population and the American Future. Washington, D.C.: Government Printing Office, 1972.

Albert I. Rabin, *Growing Up in the Kibbutz*. New York: Springer, 1965.

Heather L. Ross and Isabel V. Sawhill, *Time of Transition: The Growth of Families Headed by Women*. Washington, D.C.: The Urban Institute, 1975.

Arlene S. Skolnick and Jerome H. Skolnick, eds., *Family in Transition,* 2nd ed. Boston: Little, Brown, 1977.

Y. Talmon-Garber, "Social Change and Family Structure." *International Social Science Journal,* vol. 14, no. 3 (1962): 468–487.

J. Richard Udry, *The Social Context of Marriage*. Philadelphia: Lippincott, 1971.

U.S. Bureau of the Census, *Statistical Abstract of the United States, 1976*. Washington, D.C.: Government Printing Office, 1976.

Roxann A. Van Dusen and Eleanor Bernert Sheldon, "The Changing Status of American Women: A Life Cycle Perspective." *The American Psychologist,* vol. 31 (February 1976): 106–116. (Also in Skolnick and Skolnick, 1977.)

J. E. Veevers, "Voluntarily Childless Wives: An Exploratory Study." *Sociology and Social Research,* vol. 57 (April 1973): 356–365. (Also in Skolnick and Skolnick, 1977.)

Ben J. Wattenberg, "A Family Survey: Is the Family Really in Trouble?" *Better Homes and Gardens,* vol. 51 (March 1973): 2, 30, 31, 33.

Robert F. Winch and Rae Lesser Blumberg, "Societal Complexity and Familial Organization," in Robert F. Winch and Graham B. Spanier, eds., *Selected Studies in Marriage and the Family,* 3rd ed. New York: Holt, Rinehart and Winston, 1968. (Also in Skolnick and Skolnick, 1977.)

James D. Wright and Sonia R. Wright, "Social Class and Parental Values for Children: A Partial Replication and Extension of the Kohn Thesis." *American Sociological Review,* vol. 41 (June 1976): 527–548.

FOR FURTHER STUDY

Experiments in Marriage.   Given the changes described in this chapter, many people are trying out new patterns of getting and staying together, but they often find that the old problems of compatibility and possessiveness don't simply disappear as a result of new life styles. Satisfying human relationships demand sustained attention whether the marriage is conventional or communal. In *The Mirages of Marriage,* William J. Lederer and Don D. Jackson (New York: Norton, 1968) explore the false assumptions people have about marriage, and suggest ways to reach more realistic expectations. Possible choices other than marriage are discussed by Roger W. Libby and Robert N. Whitehurst in *Marriage and Alternatives: Exploring Intimate Relationships* (Glenview, Ill.: Scott, Foresman, 1977).

The Black Family. Until recently, the black family has been discussed largely by white social scientists, who tended to judge it by white middle-class standards. This has been corrected by a number of black social scientists, who have pointed out that there can be no single model of the black family. Indeed, social class must be taken into account among blacks as well as among whites, and the typical family is adapted to the social class of its members. A good collection of readings representing various points of view was edited by Charles V. Willie and is entitled *The Family Life of Black People* (Columbus, Ohio: Merrill, 1970). Another book that focuses on cultural understanding of black families and domestic units is *Afro-American Anthropology: Contemporary Perspectives* (New York: Free Press, 1970), edited by Norman Whitten and John Szwed. Herbert C. Gutman gives an excellent historical account of changes in the black family in his book *The Black Family in Slavery and Freedom: 1750–1925* (New York: Pantheon, 1976). In *The Strength of Black Families* (Washington, D.C.: National Urban League, 1972), Robert Hill examines the structure of contemporary black family life.

Divorce. In *Marital Separation* (New York: Basic Books, 1975), Robert Weiss uses his experiences as the leader of a series of seminars for the separated to discuss the importance of attachment and the sense of loss experienced by people in the process of divorce. Another timely issue is the implications of the growing divorce rate for children. Heather L. Ross and Isabel V. Sawhill explore the changes involved for parents and children in single-parent families in their book, *Time of Transition: The Growth of Families Headed by Women* (Washington, D.C.: Urban Institute, 1975). Studies dealing with the responses of children to divorce include: Judith S. Wallerstein and Joan B. Kelly, ''The Effects of Parental Divorce: Experiences of the Child in Later Latency,'' in Arlene S. Skolnick and Jerome H. Skolnick, eds., *Family in Transition,* 2nd ed. (Boston: Little, Brown, 1977); and Gail Howrigan, *The Effects of Divorce and Separation on Children* (Cambridge, Mass.: Center for the Study of Public Policy, 1975).

The Plight of Children. Childhood, it has been said, is a rather recent invention. Its special status implies both privileges and constraints. Setting children up as a special group with special needs exempts them from some of the obligations of adulthood, but it also deprives them of the rights adults enjoy, while children's lives are limited by adults' decisions concerning marriage or divorce. Their welfare is determined by public policies written and implemented by adults. The demand for children's rights is the thrust of a recent movement to win autonomy for children, freedom from subjection to parents, school, and community. Several books deal with this issue, including the following: Beatrice Gross and Ronald Gross, eds., *The Children's Rights Movement* (New York: Anchor Books, 1977); David Gottlieb, ed., *Children's Liberation* (Englewood Cliffs, N.J.: Prentice-Hall, 1973); and Albert E. Wilkerson, ed., *Rights of Children: Emergent Concepts in Law and Society* (Philadelphia, Pa.: Temple University Press, 1973). A study by the National Research Council, *Toward a National Policy for Children and Families* (Washington, D.C.: National Academy of Sciences, 1976), examines government programs and suggests new policies for adequate income and health and social services for children. Within families, the rights of children usually depend on parental behavior; an interesting guide to parental effectiveness is Thomas Gordon's *PET in Action* (New York: Wyden Books, 1976). For a sensitive view of the lives of children and parents in a variety of social contexts, see Thomas Cottle's *A Family Album: Portraits of Intimacy and Kinship* (New York: Harper & Row, 1975), which is based on the personal accounts of family members.

CHAPTER 14

Education

In small, nontechnological societies, children learn everything they need to know by observing and imitating adults. There is little or no formal schooling. Eskimos, for example, don't hold formal classes in hunting. Rather, when they kill a bear, they give small children spears and encourage them to stab at the animal as the youngsters have seen adults do. By the time children are old and strong enough to hunt, they have thoroughly rehearsed this skill (Pettitt, 1946). In modern societies, informal education is not enough. There are simply too many things to learn, too many skills to master. People from very different cultural and economic backgrounds must learn to live and work, if not together, then at least side by side. Over the last fifty years, schools have become a vital link between the individual and society.

As these examples suggest, education is closely related to socialization. Normally, when we use the word "education," we're referring to school programs for teaching skills and values. But even in modern societies, much education—for example, "learning the ropes" of a new job —takes place outside formal institutions. For this reason, sociologists define *education* as formal or informal efforts to teach the knowledge, skills, and values of one's culture.

Americans have always put great faith in *schooling*—formal instruction in a classroom setting. In colonial times, one of the things that distinguished this country from European nations was the Founding Fathers' belief that no democracy could survive without an educated electorate. A century later, industrialists reaffirmed the need for mass education—this time to provide the nation with an educated labor force that could take advantage of technological breakthroughs. In the 1950s, civil rights leaders saw integrating schools as the key to integrating our society. Generations of American parents raised their children to believe that getting an education was the way to get ahead.

Is our faith in education justified? In the first section of this chapter, we examine the functions of education and ask how and how well American schools are performing them. Next, we look at the social structure of higher education in both four- and two-year colleges. In the last part of the chapter, we explore some aspects of education as a lifelong process.

THE SOCIAL FUNCTIONS OF EDUCATION

As a student, you are a natural expert on education. You spent much of your youth in school (some 12,000 hours by the time you graduated from high school). You've been graded and disciplined; exposed to subjects that interested you and subjects that didn't; had good and not so good teachers; learned how to deal with the system and play the role of student. However, a sociologist's training permits him or her to look at an institution differently than a student might. Viewing education from the sociological perspective—examining what latent and manifest functions education performs for society and how well it performs them—will very likely cause you to reexamine your own experiences.

We immediately think of learning and job preparation as the functions of the school system—and these in fact are its manifest functions (those it is openly set up to perform). But schools have equally significant latent functions (indirect and sometimes unrecognized results), including social and political integration and preparation for life in the larger society. We will see that functionalist and conflict theorists interpret the workings of our educational system somewhat differently.

Schools as Agents of Political and Social Integration

The rise of mass public education in America coincided with the spread of industrialization and with the arrival of waves of immigrants who came to this country in search of jobs. The school system served in part to Americanize these immigrants and their children, to fit them into American society.

One of the functions of formal education is political and social integration into the mainstream culture: teaching students what it means to be American or English or Russian or Chinese. Such socialization is both direct (classes in civics and history, and student government) and indirect. Classes are conducted and students are evaluated in ways designed to socialize them to their culture. In the Soviet Union, for example, students are divided into "links" (groups) and are graded according to how well the group performs, not on the basis of individual effort. An exceptionally bright student is rewarded only if he or she helps others in the group who aren't as quick (Bronfenbrenner, 1970). The American grading system, in contrast, stresses individuality. If the teacher discovers that several students are helping one another solve a math problem during an exam, they are punished for cheating.

The results of this effort to integrate children into the cultural mainstream can be evaluated in different ways. Conflict theorists point out that the dominant cultural group forces Americanism on students from minority groups. Observation of schools in black and Mexican-American communities and on Indian reservations supports this view. For example, approximately one-third of all Indian youngsters attend boarding schools run by the white-dominated Bureau of Indian Affairs. These schools were first instituted in the nineteenth century for the express purpose of separating children from their "savage" parents so that the youngsters might learn to be "Americans." Visits to and from parents are discouraged. As many as 16,000 Indian children don't go to school at all because their parents refuse to send them away, and every year hundreds run away from school.

In China, as in our country, formal education helps to integrate children into the mainstream culture. (Jody Reston / Photo Researchers, Inc.)

Indians aren't the only Americans whose heritage is ignored or denigrated in school. Until the late 1960s, Texas law forbade teaching in any language but English. In one school, students from extremely poor Mexican-American families were fined a penny every time they used Spanish words; in another, they were forced to kneel and beg forgiveness for the same "offense" (Silberman, 1971: 94). Most textbooks still give only brief consideration to Indian, Mexican-American, and black history—if these peoples are mentioned at all. The assumption in our schools has always been that minorities must be assimilated—for their own good—and that they won't become "Americanized" unless they abandon their different ways.

In the past ten to fifteen years, as a result of the civil rights movement, courses geared to minorities—black English and black history, for example—have been set up, and in some places, bilingual education is required by law. Still, some are left stranded: too Americanized to feel comfortable in the communities in which they were born, yet not wholly accepted as Americans. Cultural bias accounts in part for the high dropout rate among students from strong, distinctive ethnic groups.

The Hidden Curriculum

A second function of schools is to integrate children by weaning them from the private world of family, where rules are bent to fit the occasion and the individual (it's Johnny's birthday; Mary doesn't feel well) and where status (as daughter/sister, son/brother) is guaranteed, and socializing them to a public world, one which ideally applies universal rules to all and grants status on the basis of achievement. What matters at school is what you do (how you behave and perform in class), not who you are (as at home). In school, children learn to accommodate themselves to a hierarchical institution in which power and privileges are distributed impersonally and unequally (Parsons, 1975).

Put in concrete terms, to advance from grade to grade, to survive academically and socially, youngsters must learn to be quiet, to line up, to wait, to act interested even when they aren't, to please their teachers without alienating their peers, to come to grips with the inevitability of school—in short, to play the role of student. Conflict theorists argue that this *hidden curriculum*—the set of unwritten rules of behavior that prepare children for the world outside and that they must master to succeed in school—(Jackson, 1968) pushes children into unthinking acceptance of the system's demands.

Kindergarten is the child's initiation into the student role. On the surface, most kindergarten activities seem purposeless. But the children *are* learning—learning to do what the teacher wants, when she wants it done. In kindergarten there is a story time, a nap time, a pick-up time—in short, an official routine. Day after day kindergarten children are shown the rituals of school, including the raising of one's hand and lining up. They are taught behavior and attitudes teachers believe to be essential, and are drilled in these patterns. Harry L. Gracey compares kindergarten to boot camp: it is "successful" if youngsters learn to follow routines and obey orders without question, even if the orders are trivial (1972: 251).

The teacher is the child's first boss. Learn-

"For what it's worth, Jane, I, too, found first grade a drag. But I hung in there, and now, needless to say, I'm mighty glad I did."
(Drawing by Opie; © 1977 The New Yorker Magazine, Inc.)

ing to accept orders from a boss, to cope with contradictory evaluations from superiors and peers, and to tolerate frustrations, delays, and being in a crowd are the very qualities students need if they are to function effectively on an assembly line or in a large corporation when they leave school. In effect, the hidden curriculum is designed to mold students into good workers. Individuals who are obedient and eager to please may not make great inventors or artists, but they do presumably make good employees.

Interestingly, most Americans agree that the hidden curriculum is necessary and desirable. When asked by Gallup pollsters what qualities were important in the development of a child, nearly as many adults responded "the ability to get along with others" as "learning to think for oneself." When asked how to improve the overall quality of education, as many people responded "enforce stricter discipline" as answered "devote more time to teaching basic skills." Indeed, most Americans consider discipline the biggest problem with our schools (Gallup Opinion Index, 1978).

A number of educators and parents would disagree, however. Critics of the school system argue that the obsession with rules and regulations keeps youngsters in a chronic state of dependency, and that the assumption that students can't be trusted is harmful and unfounded.

The Open Classroom The *open classroom*—or open education, as this practice is sometimes called—is a direct attack on the distrust and regimentation that characterize traditional education. It is a concerted effort to *de*institutionalize education by letting youngsters learn what they want to learn, when and how they want to learn it. The practice of fighting students' natural inclinations and curiosity and forcing education on them according to an imposed schedule and plan is banished. It is an educational environment that aims to increase learning by decreasing regimentation and encouraging children to develop their own interests.

Abandoning the traditional arrangement of desk-rows and "performances" by individual children, the open classroom strives for flexibility—for students as well as for teachers. (Bruce Roberts/Rapho/Photo Researchers)

In a typical open classroom, the uniform rows of desks, all facing front, are eliminated. Instead, seating is flexible, changing as groups come together and move apart for instruction. The room is organized around various interest areas—science, art, reading, and so on. Teachers don't direct from the front but walk around assisting students who need help with their projects. Instead of dividing time into rigid blocks, teachers base their plans on what children need at a given moment.

Outwardly an open classroom may look chaotic: in one corner two children are tending their soybeans; a girl is working with Cuisenaire rods in another spot, while a group sings a song in the middle of the room. To keep classrooms from degenerating into mere playgrounds, the teacher must plan carefully, maintaining some kind of structure and direction. Such a system imposes heavy demands on teachers, but frees them from their usual roles as "timekeeper, traffic cop, and disciplinarian" (Silberman, 1971). The assumption is that if children are busy and happy, they won't need to be disciplined.

In many ways, open classrooms reflect new trends in the organization of work (see pp. 000–000), sharing goals and attitudes with factories where workers are given the initiative and responsibility for solving problems with the resources available.

Schools and Learning

A third basic function of schools is, of course, to educate. This involves teaching basic skills (reading, writing, and arithmetic); developing students' ability to think (to apply skills to new and varied problems); and providing knowledge that will be useful for their careers (both general and specific preparation).

A 1976 Gallup poll reflects these values.

Over 50 percent of the respondents think "devoting more time to teaching basic skills" would do the most to improve our schools. Twenty-six percent believe learning to think for oneself is more important than getting along with others, willingness to accept responsibility, high moral standards, eagerness to learn, or desire to excel. And 80 percent would like to see high schools put more emphasis on careers (Gallup Opinion Index, 1976).

Do Schools Teach Basic Skills and the Ability to Think?   The answer to this would have to be, in many cases, no. In 1975, over 14 percent of the seventeen-year-olds in a nationwide survey were found to be functionally illiterate. They could not read at a fourth-grade level. Some groups suffer more from poor schooling than other groups do. Twenty-one percent of the students from inner-city ghettos, 20 percent of the students in the Southeast, and 42 percent of blacks (many of whom live in ghettos or the Southeast) couldn't perform such everyday tasks as reading a newspaper or the instructions on a can (NAEP, 1977).

Few seventeen-year-olds could organize their thoughts effectively in writing. Short, childish sentences and incoherent paragraphs were common. The majority of seventeen-year-olds could perform basic arithmetic skills, but couldn't apply them to practical situations. Less than half could figure out the most economical size of a product; only 45 percent could read a federal income tax table; a mere 1 percent could balance a checkbook. Overall, American students seem to have trouble applying the skills and facts they know to new situations (NAEP, 1975).

There are signs that teachers and students are getting back to basics, with good effect. Nine-year-olds today have a better grasp of elemental skills than nine-year-olds did seven years ago. Still, our educational standards fall below those of other industrialized nations. (Many American universities allow British and French college-level students, for example, to enter as sophomores.) Indeed, some critics argue we have no real standards. Students may be promoted simply because they show up more or less regularly. In 1973, Peter W. Doe sued the San Francisco school district for $1 million, for although he had been promoted regularly and had received a high school diploma, he could not read (*The New York Times,* September 16, 1973). As we have seen, he is not alone. Nationwide tests that would require students to demonstrate their knowledge and skills on standardized questions before receiving a diploma would eliminate this possibility. The fact that today 65 percent of Americans favor such tests (compared with 50 percent in 1958) marks a growing concern over whether students are learning basic skills. (Gallup Opinion Index, 1976).

Do Schools Prepare Students for Jobs? The data on seventeen-year-olds in the preceding section suggest that by and large, high school doesn't prepare young people for jobs. More than half of those surveyed had difficulty filling out a standard job application. Less than half had ever taken an aptitude test (which might suggest what type of career suited them), and only 16 percent of those surveyed had discussed the results with a counselor (NAEP, 1976).

What about college graduates? Not long ago, a college degree guaranteed an American a good job with a decent income. With the economic recession of the 1970s and a flood of college graduates glutting the job market, this is no longer true. When only 6 percent of Americans went to college, graduates were an elite minority and could command high salaries. Today, about 40 percent of Americans go on to college, and a B.A. isn't the badge of distinction it once was. Add to this a decline in the number of available jobs, and the result is an inflationary spiral in educational requirements. It takes a B.A. to get a mundane, relatively low-paying job today.

According to the Department of Labor, 4,300 new jobs for psychologists opened up in 1975. That same year colleges turned out over 58,000 graduates with degrees in psychology. Of thirty psychology majors who graduated from Vassar, an elite college, in 1972, only five had jobs even remotely related to psychology a year later. The others were working as delivery truck drivers, dietary technicians, claims adjusters, secretaries, typists, and waitresses. An estimated 104,000 graduates in communications and letters competed for about 14,000 jobs in journalism, radio, television, and public relations that year; 45,000 graduates in the fine arts and anthropology vied for 7,000 museum jobs. Fewer than 10 percent of the 18,200 graduates in education in New York found work in the state's public schools (*The New York Times,* May 1, 1977). Competition for professional schools is also stiff: over 3,000 students apply for 65 places in Mount Sinai's School of Medicine each year; 8,000 apply for 500 places in Harvard Law School. From an employer's point of view, it's a buyer's market. Corporations that used to court graduates can now pick and choose among hundreds of qualified applicants.

Who Needs College? If success is defined purely in monetary terms, college may be a bad investment (Bird, 1975). The majority of men who earned $15,000 or more in 1970 didn't have college degrees, and the majority of men with college degrees didn't earn $15,000. Caroline Bird calculates that if a young person bound for Princeton in 1972 put the $34,000 it would have cost to obtain a B.A. in a savings account earning 7.5 percent interest, compounded daily, at sixty-four the nongraduate would have $528,200 more than a graduate could expect to earn between the ages of twenty-two and sixty-four (168, 63).

Why doesn't a degree "pay off"? Bird suggests that successful people are those who come up with a new idea that solves a problem for many people; who have "a burning ambition to put that idea over"; and who possess extraordinary physical energy—and luck. College can't teach any of these qualities.

Howard Bowen (1977) contends that the value of a college education can't be measured solely on the basis of monetary gains to individuals. He argues that college significantly improves the quality of people's lives. The studies he cites show that college brings about many desirable changes in the individual: for example, increased cognitive abilities through the acquisition of verbal and mathematical skills, promotion of logica thinking, increase of knowledge and intellectual curiosity, and stimulation of interest in and responsiveness to the arts. College has an even greater impact on the student's emotional and moral development. It decreases a person's materialism (studies show that seniors place more emphasis on nonmaterialistic rewards than freshmen do), and it helps students achieve a secure and positive sense of self—one researcher reported that 86 percent of the students in a group of diverse colleges and universities felt that college heightened their sense of self-awareness. A college education improves the individual's financial state by increasing his or her earnings while limiting the size of his or her family.

Further, Bowen finds that the benefits of a college education aren't confined to individuals; college improves the quality of life for society as a whole. Colleges tend to instill such values as a sense of social responsibility and a belief in human equality—values that lead to constructive social changes. Colleges provide a place where scholars and scientists can conduct research in an atmosphere relatively free of political pressure. In the long run, Bowen asserts, the increasing availability of college education may reduce inequality: "As the number of persons with higher education steadily increases relative to the number with less education, the earnings and status of the more educated can be expected to fall and the less educated to rise" (357).

Nevertheless, as a result of the decline in the number of jobs for college graduates in the 1970s, the proportion of young people enrolling in college has dropped for the first time; students are moving out of academic and scientific fields into business and vocational programs, and graduate enrollment is dropping. Some colleges have closed, some have cut back on staff or put a freeze on hiring, and others are orienting courses toward careers (Freeman, 1976, chapter 2).

Selecting Talent: The Screening Function

A fourth function of education is selecting talent. In small, nontechnological societies, a boy nearly always enters his father's occupation, and a girl simply learns the household roles of her mother. But modern-day technological societies can't afford to rely on sons and daughters following in their parents' footsteps. The need for skilled personnel is too great. Ideally, according to functionalist theory, the school system identifies those students with the particular tal-

table 14:1 **PREFERENCES FOR LIFETIME GOALS AND JOB CHARACTERISTICS, BY LEVEL OF EDUCATION (by percent)**

	EDUCATION OF FAMILY HEAD[1]			
	0–11 GRADES	HIGH SCHOOL GRADUATE	COLLEGE, NO DEGREE	COLLEGE GRADUATE
Percentage of respondents giving first rank to following life goals:				
Prosperous life	40	30	30	16
Secure life	46	55	51	32
Important life	8	10	8	30
Exciting life	6	5	11	22
	100	100	100	100
Percentage of respondents giving first rank to following job characteristics:				
Income steady	39	39	24	8
Income high	24	10	16	8
No danger of being fired	19	9	11	1
Hours short	1	1	1	1
Advancement good	7	18	23	18
Work important	10	23	25	64
	100	100	100	100

[1]Based on a 1971 random sample of 574 male heads of family, most of whom were under 40 years of age.
SOURCE: Howard R. Bowen, *Investment in Learning: The Individual and Social Value of Higher Education* (San Francisco, Calif.: Jossey-Bass, 1977), table 19, p. 110; B. Strumpel, *Economic Means for Economic Needs* (Ann Arbor: Institute for Social Research, University of Michigan, 1976), pp. 34, 35.

ents society needs and trains them to fill important positions.

The idea that schools should screen out individuals with lesser talents goes against the American ideal that all people are created equal. The solution to this conflict is to give every individual an equal opportunity to display his or her talents. Ideally, the right people will be selected for the right jobs, regardless of who they are or where they come from.

Yet conflict theorists point out that the American school system perpetuates economic and class differences. Most obviously, some school districts are wealthier than others. Typically, the children of well-off parents go to gleaming new schools with the latest laboratory equipment, and are taught by highly paid teachers; the children of the poor attend aging schools with outdated equipment, and often are instructed by poorly trained, underpaid teachers. Thus advantages are heaped on advantages; disadvantages on disadvantages. This crack in the myth of equal opportunity has led to campaigns to upgrade inner-city schools and to divide the funds for schools more equally between inner-city schools and those in the more affluent suburbs.

However, there is some evidence that simply upgrading schools won't in and of itself provide equal opportunity. During the 1960s, James Coleman and a team of sociologists undertook a study of 570,000 students and 60,000 teachers in 4,000 schools (1966). Halfway through the research Coleman told an interviewer that ''the study will show the difference in quality of schools that the average Negro child and the average white child are exposed to. You know yourself that the difference is going to be striking'' (Hodgson, 1973: 37).

The final results were not at all what Coleman expected. He found relatively little difference between predominantly black schools and predominantly white ones in expenditure per pupil, building age, library facilities, number of textbooks, teacher characteristics, and class size. For example, 98 percent of the white schools and 94 percent of the black schools had chemistry laboratories. Even more surprising, Coleman found that modern buildings, up-to-date texts and curricula, and higher expendi-

---

table 14:2 ESTIMATES OF THE RELATIVE PROBABILITY OF ATTENDING COLLEGE FULL-TIME, BY INCOME (by percent)

INCOME OF FAMILY (IN DOLLARS)	ESTIMATED PROBABILITY 1969	1973
Less than $3,000	16	13
$ 3,000–4,999	22	17
5,000–7,499	31	22
7,500–9,999	40	27
10,000–14,999	45	33
15,000+	62	50

SOURCE: Adapted from Richard B. Freeman, *The Overeducated American* (New York: Academic Press, 1976), table 2, p. 37; U.S. Bureau of the Census, ''School Enrollment,'' *Current Population Reports*, Series P-20, nos. 206, 272.

The American school system perpetuates economic and class differences. Although the probability of attending college decreased at all income levels between 1969 and 1973, children of middle- and upper-income families are still far more likely to be college bound than are their poorer counterparts.

tures per pupil had *no* discernible effect on achievement test scores. Neither did the quality of teachers. The government and most educators have always assumed a cause-and-effect relationship between school resources and student performance: the more money you spend on pupils, the better their education will be. Further, Coleman found that blacks who attended integrated schools for an extended period did only slightly better on achievement tests than blacks who attended segregated schools. Coleman concluded that

> schools bring little influence to bear on a child's achievement that is independent of his [or her] background and general social context. . . . This very lack of independent effect means that the inequalities imposed on children by their home, neighborhood, and peer environment are carried along to become the inequalities with which they confront adult life at the end of school. (Coleman, in Silberman, 1971: 71)

In other words, the quality of the school affects a student's achievement test scores only to the extent that it reflects the wealth of the community in which the student lives.

Coleman discovered that the family, not the school, is the major educational institution—even in modern society. Differences between families strongly affect children's chances for equal educational opportunities. Traditionally, equality of opportunity has meant trying to give all children access to the same kinds of educational *inputs*—teachers, facilities, and so on. This is roughly equivalent to giving someone who has never played golf and an experienced player identical sets of clubs and balls and pointing them toward the same green. There is little doubt who will win. Coleman argues that to achieve true equality of opportunity, we must treat individuals differently, much as we give a handicap to a beginning golfer. Just as we come up with a fair handicap by calculating the average number of strokes it takes a beginner to complete a golf course so that with this handicap he or she will come out about the same as the more experienced player, so we should measure educational opportunity by *outcome*. Equal opportunity in education exists when the average scores of graduates from different schools (not per-pupil expenditures, facilities, and the like) are about the same. Parallel studies of students in nineteen other countries confirm Coleman's findings.

Tracking In some respects, the American school system is more open than the systems of other countries. In Western European nations, all students are given stiff qualifying examinations at about junior high school age. The 20 percent or so who pass earn the right to academic training; the remainder are diverted into vocational programs. In contrast, the American system is designed to give students an almost unlimited number of chances to display their talents—in elementary school, in junior and senior high school, in junior college, and even later. We provide more school for more students for more years than any other nation. Nevertheless, there is some official, and much unofficial, tracking in American schools.

The screening process begins in elementary school, when children are divided into slow, average, and bright groups on the basis of aptitude and achievement tests and teachers' recommendations. *Tracking*, as grouping children according to their test scores is called, is based on the assumption that students will learn more if they don't have to compete with students who are much brighter than they are, and if they don't have to wait for students who are slower. It is designed primarily to move above-average children ahead more quickly and to give below-average children the extra attention they need.

In practice, tracking tends to segregate students along socioeconomic and racial lines—white middle-class youngsters being assigned to the college-preparatory track, nonwhite lower-class children to the "general" and vocational tracks. According to one study of 467 Southern school districts, 60 percent of racial segregation in elementary schools and 35 percent in high schools was justified in terms of tracking ("Testing and Tracking," 1973: 15).

The Self-fulfilling Prophecy   Tracking also influences teacher expectations. Low expectations tend to become self-fulfilling prophecies. (See the discussions of labeling and socialization to deviance in chapter 9.)

> A fourth-grade math teacher writes a half-dozen problems on the board for the class to do. "I think I can pick at least four children who can't do them," she tells the class, and proceeds to call four youngsters to the board to demonstrate, for all to see, how correct the teacher's judgment is. Needless to say, the children fulfill the prophecy. (Silberman, 1971: 139)

Rosenthal and Jacobson (1968) tested this proposition experimentally by giving elementary school teachers a list of students and telling them to expect great progress from these students. Supposedly these youngsters had very high IQs, but they'd actually been selected at random. At the end of the school year the IQ scores of this group had increased significantly more than the scores of students who hadn't been selected. A study by Leacock (1969) confirmed Rosenthal and Jacobson's findings, with an added twist. In middle-class schools, teachers treated students *better* if the children were supposed to be bright. But in the lower-class black school, teachers *rejected* bright children as smart alecks and wise guys.

Although tracking does seem to improve the performance of good students, it doesn't help poor students. In fact, Coleman found ghetto youngsters did best in racially and economically mixed classes. Tracking merely widens the gap between good and poor students, stigmatizing those who are placed in the "dummy" programs.

THE SOCIAL STRUCTURE OF HIGHER EDUCATION

Despite the recent drop in college enrollment, about 40 percent of Americans have had some higher education. Twenty years from now the figure may well be 50 percent. Junior and community colleges have reached out to attract new students. Adults are going back to school, for professional and recreational reasons. In short, going to college has become an integral part of the American way of life.

The College Experience

Going to college involves major life changes. For many, it means leaving the highly regimented, routinized life of high school for life in college, an institution that provides the student with the freedom to organize his or her day and to choose among a variety of courses and extracurricular activities. For many students, starting college involves leaving home for the first time. Among other things, entering freshmen have to learn how to make decisions without first consulting their parents, how to budget their own time, and how to handle their own money. Rather suddenly, the student is treated as an adult, not as a child.

The college years are a time to grow. Major developmental tasks to be tackled during this period include: achieving confidence in one's ability to cope; learning to manage one's emotions (becoming aware of one's feelings and learning to trust them); becoming autonomous by freeing oneself from the pressing needs for reassurance, affection, or approval; establishing one's identity, or sense of inner and outer continuity; developing intimate personal relationships; acquiring a sense of purpose; and developing the integrity to make one's own decisions without unnecessary debate or equivocation (Chickering, 1969: 8–19).

Needless to say, it can be an exciting—and confusing—time.

Expectations and Realities Some students enroll in college for the express purpose of training for a career. Others hope to "find themselves." But the majority are simply doing what society expects them to do. For this group, going to college is a matter of course, not the result of a conscious decision. Nevertheless, entering freshmen have high hopes.

Many students are disappointed. Most report they're as free as they'd hoped to be. But they have major complaints. There is less contact with the faculty than they had hoped for. There are fewer opportunities to become active. Classes are unexpectedly and disappointingly large and may be taught by graduate students who are serving as teaching assistants. The opportunity to take a variety of courses is limited by the college's requirements (Goodman and Feldman, 1975).

Peer Groups In college, students often devote more time to social activities than to academic pursuits. When asked how they spent their time, Berkeley college students listed reading, spectator and participant

Relations with peers are an important part of the college experience. In fact, many students devote more time to social activities than to academic pursuits. (Owen Franklin/Stock, Boston)

IN THE NEWS

Racism Persists on Campus

Both the black and white students could tell he was a visitor on campus because he sat at the wrong table. Blacks seldom ate in that part of the cafeteria. They usually carried their trays to the "black section," in an adjacent room.

There were no printed signs, no written rules to alert him to the practice. The visitor could be forgiven for his ignorance. He would learn in time.

That is the way things are done at Duke University in Durham, N.C., at Cornell University in Ithaca, N.Y., and at many other predominantly white campuses across the country, where 72 percent of the nation's 948,000 black college students attend school.

In contrast to the open racial strife that characterized them during the 1960s, campuses today seem calm. But it is a strained and separate peace, rather than true racial harmony, since integration on college campuses throughout the country rarely goes beyond the classroom. Prejudice and pride on both sides help separate the groups socially. Blacks often show black solidarity in the form of their own study programs, associations, newspapers, and social events. White fraternities, sororities, and campus clubs stay all-white, in keeping with what members call tradition. And peer pressure to stay segregated is great. Those who cross racial lines often find themselves ostracized by members of their own racial group. Many students find this lack of communication between blacks and whites on an individual level disturbing:

At Duke, [black] student T. C. Adams says he is troubled by the segregation that exists outside the classroom setting. . . .

"I've missed dealing with people on a very basic level. We've experienced knowledge [in class] together, but out-

sports, and movies before lectures. When asked what was important to them, about 15 percent gave curiosity and knowledge a high rank; about 25 percent focused on intellectual and artistic activities; and 73 percent of the men and 89 percent of the women spoke of emotional well-being, love, and affection, of maintaining one's self-respect, and of being accepted and liked (Katz, 1968: 23, 31). Clearly, then, peers are an important part of the college experience.

Typically college offers a choice of four types of peer groups with four distinct life styles: the collegiate subculture, which revolves around parties, drinking, football, fraternities, and fun; the vocational subculture, which centers around working hard to get into a good graduate or professional school or into a good business position; the academic subculture, which focuses on exploring ideas simply for the sake of exploring them; and the nonconformist subculture, which focuses on rebelling for the sake of rebelling. A student may become deeply in-

side of that atmosphere, casually talking, that's what I've missed. It's that kind of experience that gives you an idea of what people are all about."

When they are not socially oblivious to one another, blacks and whites on campus are often divided by anger. On many campuses, white liberal students and black student leaders have taken opposing stances on the issue of reverse discrimination, a polarization brought about by Allan Bakke's Supreme Court case claiming he was denied entrance to a medical school because he is white. Racial tension is also evident in other ways. At the University of California at Los Angeles, for instance, the office of black student officials has been vandalized several times during the year. At Cornell, black and white students, administrators, and faculty warn that a dispute over even a minor issue, such as failure to book black artists for school concerts, could end the deceptive peace.

Perhaps what is most disturbing about the divisiveness on campus is what it says about racial harmony in America's future. As black sociologist Kenneth Clark notes:

"These students are being trained to take their racial views with them into society. They're being trained to carry on a segregated society. Rather than trying to learn to counter the status quo, they're being trained to keep it going."

SOURCE: Warren Brown, "Prejudice and Pride: The Wall Between Black and White on Campus," *Dallas Times Herald*, November 20, 1977, pp. G1, G7.

volved in one of these subcultures, or may explore several (Katz, 1968: 23).

The Impact of College   Studies indicate that although students change over their college years, comparatively few go through the identity crisis Erikson predicted would be experienced at this stage (see pp. 117–119). About a third of the Berkeley and Stanford students Joseph Katz (1968) interviewed during their senior year felt they had developed more self-confidence, poise, and independence. Their philosophies were more clearly defined at this point, and they had more emotional control and tolerance than they'd had as freshmen. They were willing to stand up for themselves. Almost half attributed these changes to personal relationships. Contacts with a variety of people, dating, and falling in love were also mentioned. A fourth said that courses and professors had been an important influence. A small number mentioned the challenge of aca-

figure 14:1 Benefits of college as perceived by junior and senior students (by percent)

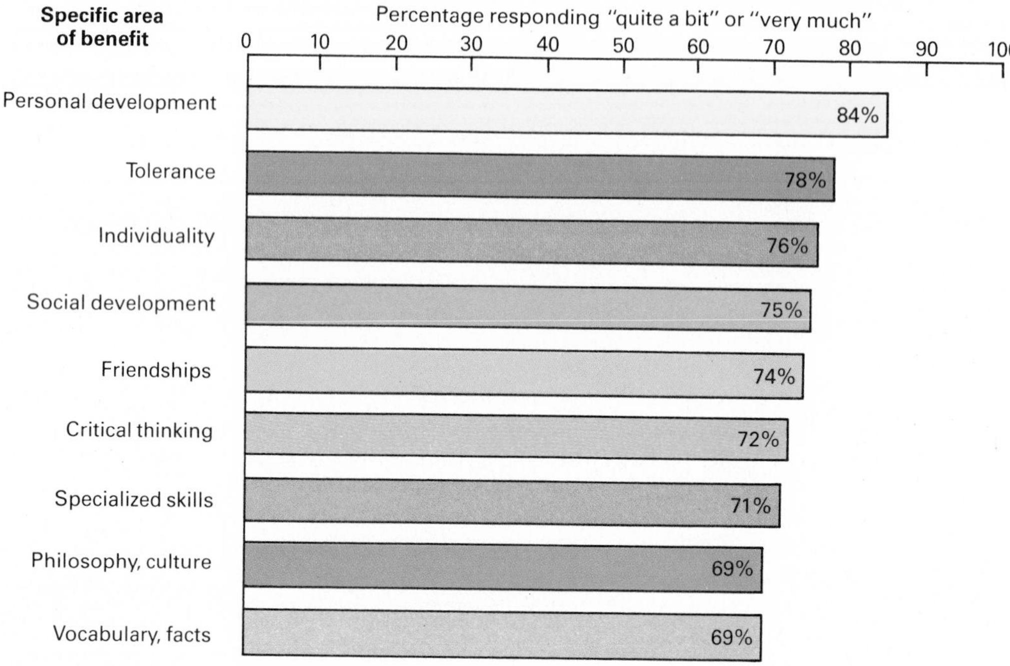

Specific area of benefit	Percentage responding "quite a bit" or "very much"
Personal development	84%
Tolerance	78%
Individuality	76%
Social development	75%
Friendships	74%
Critical thinking	72%
Specialized skills	71%
Philosophy, culture	69%
Vocabulary, facts	69%

SOURCE: Adapted from data in Howard R. Bowen, *Investment in Learning* (San Francisco, Calif.: Jossey-Bass, 1977), pp. 228–229.

demic work, and an even smaller number brought up political activities.

It seems that relatively few students develop a strong sense of direction in college. Most are unsure about what they want to do with their lives. Students rarely describe careers in terms of intrinsic interest, self-fulfillment, or social usefulness. They see careers as a means by which to establish a desired life style, not as an end in themselves. Katz suggests several reasons why. First, our educational system fails to connect work with pleasure or to develop a respect for good workmanship. Second, college itself encourages students to focus on their performances (on getting good grades), not on participating in activities that are satisfying in themselves or useful to others. Third, although most students have done some kind of work, they haven't had exposure to sustained work. This makes it difficult for them to make realistic occupational plans and decisions.

One promising alternative is the federal University Year for Action program, established in 1971. Students receive academic credit for spending a year off-campus as a volunteer in health, legal, economic development, education, or housing projects. About 2,000 students, most of them sociology, psychology, and education majors, are currently enrolled in the programs. Participants report that they've learned more working as a volunteer than they would have in a traditional academic program, and that they are better able to make career choices when they complete their schooling.

College does seem to produce an overall change in attitudes, however. Entering freshmen tend to be somewhat authoritarian in outlook: to be conventional and anti-intellectual; to think in terms of stereotypes; to exhibit an intolerance of ambiguity, and hostility toward people they consider different (Sanford in Chickering, 1969: 10). By their senior year, students generally are less rigid and dogmatic, less prejudiced, more open to new and complex situations, and more sensitive. The trend is toward flexibility and openness in thinking. Whether this is a direct result of the college experience or simply a matter of growing up is debatable. Young people who don't attend college undergo similar (if less marked) changes (Feldman and Newcomb, 1969: 362–338).

Junior and Community Colleges

Whereas enrollment in four-year colleges has been dropping, enrollment in two-year insti-

---

table 14:3 **CHANGES IN THE VALUE PATTERNS OF COLLEGE STUDENTS (by percent)**[1]

	DARTMOUTH COLLEGE			UNIVERSITY OF MICHIGAN, ANN ARBOR		
	1952	1968	1974	1952	1969	1974
It's unwise to give people with dangerous social and economic viewpoints a chance to be elected.	36	12	14	42	18	13
Only people whose loyalty to the government has been proved should run for public office.	42	15	6	52	12	6
People who talk politics without knowing what they are talking about should be kept quiet.	31	14	15	27	20	20
Religions that preach unwholesome ideas should be suppressed.	18	5	5	19	5	8
Steps should be taken right away to outlaw the Communist party.	30	5	4	36	11	2
Americans must be on guard against the power of the Catholic church.	30	8	13	20	13	12

[1]The sample was composed of male students in all cases.
SOURCE: Dean R. Hoge, "Changes in College Students' Value Patterns in the 1950s, 1960s, and 1970s," *Sociology of Education*, vol. 49 (April 1976), table 6, p. 162.

The values of American college students have shifted significantly since the 1950s. At both small private colleges, such as Dartmouth, and large state universities, such as the University of Michigan, there has been a broad trend toward more liberal attitudes regarding political and religious toleration. The 1970s, however, have seen a general turn away from political commitment back toward career orientation.

tutions for both full-time and part-time students surges ahead year after year. Over one-third of this country's undergraduates (over 4 million students) attend junior and community colleges (AACJC, 1977a).

The first junior colleges in this country were designed to provide students who couldn't attend four-year schools with an opportunity for higher education. The first community colleges were an extension of the public school system on the local level. Both junior and community colleges served to round out education for students who otherwise would have left school after graduating from high school; to prepare students for enrollment in four-year colleges; to train semi-professionals; and to provide continuing education for adults.

Who Attends for What?   Today, junior and community colleges usually offer three types of programs: vocational training (in such fields as health services, mechanics, and business technologies—for example, computer programming, social work, and police work); "transfer" programs (which emphasize the liberal arts and prepare students to transfer to four-year colleges); and community education (special-interest courses in the general areas of civic and cultural affairs and recreational activities). Three out of four students in two-year schools cite getting a better job as their primary reason for attending school. Enrollment in vocational training programs rose from 13 percent in 1965 to 30 percent in 1970. However, about half the students who enter junior college go on to four-year institutions. In addition, 3.2 million Americans were enrolled in community education courses or programs that didn't lead to a degree (AACJC, 1977b).

Surveys reveal a number of significant differences between students who attend two-year colleges and those who attend four-year

schools. About 75 percent of those who postpone college for five or more years after graduating from high school enroll in junior or community colleges. Over half of the students in two-year schools are twenty-one or older (for an average age of thirty in some schools). Twice as many are married (30 percent). Almost half (43 percent) attend school part-time. As many as 70 percent hold full- or part-time jobs. Close to one-fifth of the freshmen in two-year schools are members of minority groups. (Indeed, the number of black students enrolling in college increased 80 percent between 1970 and 1975 [AACJC, 1977b].) Clearly, junior and community colleges have helped to open up a system that once "selected" only middle- and upper-class students for higher education.

THE FUTURE OF EDUCATION

Education is a lifelong process, beginning at birth and continuing into old age. Human beings are naturally curious at all ages, not just during the years our society sets aside for formal schooling. In recent decades social scientists have begun to focus on two neglected areas: infant and adult (post-college) education.

Infant Education

There is abundant evidence that the first three years of life are crucial to a child's cognitive development; that despite the many years we spend in school, we get our fundamental education at home. According to Burton L. White, director of Harvard University's Pre-School Project, "To begin to look at a child's educational development when he [or she] is two years of age is already much too late. . ." (1975: 4).

In the early 1970s, Harvard Pre-School Project researchers rated a group of three- to six-year-olds on their mastery of seventeen specific intellectual and social skills (the ability to plan and carry out projects, the ability to attract and hold an adult's attention, and so forth). Using teachers' reports and their own observations, the researchers divided the children into two groups: an "A" group of very competent children, and a "C" group of those less able to cope.

The researchers then turned their attention to toddlers, aged one to three. They found that children with "A" skills had received special attention from their mothers (or fathers or other adults) during a critical age period: from ten months to one and a half years. The adults involved provided plenty of toys and other objects, and gave children considerable physical freedom. Baths and other such ordinary events often became the occasion for an informal lesson: "Show me your knee. Now where are your toes?" These adults answered questions and provided information when asked for it, although none had really tried to teach their children in any formal way (Pines, 1971).

The "good" mothers didn't hover over their children: in fact, many worked outside the home. Some were well-educated and well-off, but others had only a high school education and were in a low economic bracket. The difference lay in the kind of attention they paid their children. In a warm, relaxed way, they constantly stimulated and challenged the children.

Lifelong Learning

The average age of Americans is rising (as indicated in chapter 16). So is the average level of education, and it seems that the more education people have, the more they want. Moreover, technological innovations now force many workers to seek retraining at least once in their lives. As a result, the demand for adult education is growing.

For example, about a fourth of California's 15 million adults are enrolled in school—most (78 percent) in community colleges. According to a survey conducted by the Educational Testing Service, over three-fourths of California's adults would like to continue their education. Almost half are interested in studying a vocational subject; about a quarter, an academic subject; an eighth, a hobby. Many (43 percent) would like to attend conventional classes; some (32 percent) would prefer to study independently, in consultation with an instructor. The most commonly cited obstacles to continuing education for

Education is now understood as a lifelong experience. The demand for adult education— both traditional liberal-arts studies and occupational training—is growing steadily, as the average age of Americans rises and as technological change forces workers to retrain. (Camilla Smith)

adults are cost (43 percent), home responsibilities (36 percent), job responsibilities (27 percent), and scheduling (25 percent) (Peterson, 1976).

The programs designed for these nontraditional students vary from occupational training to traditional studies, including the liberal arts. Many of the newer programs include field work and cooperative work-study, and provide extensive counseling.

The problem is to overcome the obstacles on both sides: to bring would-be adult students and institutions together. The Educational Testing Service recommends providing a central source of information on learning opportunities in a given region;

more counseling; economic assistance for adults; education for groups with special problems (such as the aged); off-campus programs at convenient times and locations; individualized degree-oriented programs; and techniques for evaluating academic or occupational competence acquired without formal schooling.

In conclusion, schools are major social institutions that now engage us from childhood to old age. Each type of school reflects both the people it serves (who aren't necessarily just the students) and the people who run it. As our culture shifts and new needs gain attention, the shape of education will shift with them.

SUMMARY

One of the functions of formal education is political and social integration—teaching students what it means to be a member of their own culture. American educators have always assumed that in order to become Americanized children from minority groups must abandon their different ways. During the past decade, though, courses focusing on minorities have been added to the curricula of many school systems.

A second function of schools is to wean children from the private world of the family into the more impersonal public world, where, ideally, status depends on achievement. Conflict theorists argue that in learning to play the role of a student, children are guided by a *hidden curriculum*; they must learn to deal with absolute authority, to live in a crowd (but to act as if alone), and to withstand constant evaluation by peers. Critics claim that this hidden curriculum stifles initiative and creativity and fosters dependency. Open classrooms, where education is structured around children's natural curiosity rather than around imposed schedules, provide an alternative to the regimentation of traditional schools.

A third function of schools is to educate. This involves teaching basic skills, developing cognitive abilities, and providing knowledge that will be useful in careers. It seems that schools are performing this function poorly; millions of seventeen-year-olds are functionally illiterate, and more than half those surveyed had difficulty in filling out a standard job application.

Even colleges and universities often fail to prepare their students to function in the world. While more students are going on to college, fewer jobs are available, with the result that many college graduates must take jobs that are unrelated to their educations. Measuring the value of college in monetary terms, Caroline Bird believes that young people would be better off putting the cost of a college education in a savings account than spending it on going to college. Howard Bowen and others argue that college offers many nonmaterial rewards for both individuals and the society as a whole; these rewards more than compensate for the expenses of college.

A fourth function of schools is selecting talent. The American ideal is that all people should have an equal opportunity to develop and display their talents; theoretically, schools should provide that opportunity. However, conflict theorists argue that schools are at least partly responsible for inequality. Evidence, such as that collected by James Coleman, indicates that the family, not the school, is the educational institution with the power to ensure equal opportunity. Yet studies also suggest that such school procedures as *tracking* (grouping according to test scores) tend to create self-fulfilling prophecies that perpetuate economic and racial inequality.

Attending college has become an integral part of education for many Americans. Students often have high expectations as they enter college, but they may be disappointed by the reality of large classes and curriculum restrictions. College is a time when young people seek identity through involvement with peer groups, of which there are four types—collegiate, vocational, academic, and nonconformist. Evidence suggests that college helps students gain a stronger sense of self, although it provides few with a sense of career direction.

Junior and community colleges now account for more than one-third of undergraduate enrollment. Junior and community college students are more likely to be married, to hold a job, and to belong to a minority group than are four-year college students. Whether two-year colleges reduce inequality or simply extend tracking is a subject of debate.

Recently, social scientists have become interested in the education of infants and of post-college-age adults. Some hold that infants who receive special informal lessons from adults develop advanced social and cognitive skills. Many adults past the traditional age for college now wish to continue their educations, and this too has prompted specialists to try to develop programs appropriate to these students' needs.

GLOSSARY

education both formal and informal lessons in the skills, knowledge, and values of one's culture.

hidden curriculum a set of unwritten rules of behavior needed to prepare children for the world outside and that they must master to succeed in school.

open classroom an educational environment that aims to increase learning by decreasing regimentation. Children are encouraged to develop their own interests, rather than being tied to inflexible routines.

schooling formal instruction in a classroom setting.

tracking grouping children according to their scores on aptitude and achievement tests.

REFERENCES

AACJC (American Association of Community and Junior Colleges), "Enrollment in Two-Year Colleges." May 1977a.

———, "Students in Two-Year Colleges." May 1977b.

Caroline Bird, *The Case Against College.* New York: McKay, 1975.

Howard R. Bowen, *Investment in Learning.* San Francisco, Calif.: Jossey-Bass, 1977.

Urie Bronfenbrenner, *Two Worlds of Childhood.* New York: Russell Sage Foundation, 1970.

Arthur W. Chickering, *Education and Identity.* San Francisco, Calif.: Jossey-Bass, 1969.

James S. Coleman, "Equal Schools or Equal Students?" *The Public Interest,* no. 4 (Summer 1966): 70–75.

Kenneth A. Feldman and Theodore M. Newcomb, *The Impact of College on Students.* San Francisco, Calif.: Jossey-Bass, 1969.

Richard B. Freeman, *The Over-Educated American.* New York: Academic Press, 1976.

Gallup Opinion Index, *How Americans View the Public Schools.* Report no. 151 (February 1978).

———, Report no. 135 (October 1976).

Norman Goodman and Kenneth A. Feldman, "Expectations, Ideals, and Reality: Youth Enters College," in Sigmund E. Dragastin and Glen H. Elder, eds., *Adolescence in the Life Cycle: Psychological Change and Social Context.* New York: Halsted, 1975.

Harry L. Gracey, "Learning the Student Role: Kindergarten as Academic Boot Camp," in Dennis H. Wong and Harry L. Gracey, eds., *Readings in Introductory Sociology.* New York: Macmillan, 1972.

Godfrey Hodgson, "Do Schools Make a Difference?" *Atlantic,* vol. 213 (March 1973): 35–46.

Philip W. Jackson, *Life in Classrooms.* New York: Holt, Rinehart and Winston, 1968.

Joseph Katz et al., *No Time for Youth: Growth and Constraint in College Students.* San Francisco, Calif.: Jossey-Bass, 1968.

Eleanor Leacock, *Teaching and Learning in City Schools.* New York: Basic Books, 1969.

NAEP Newsletter (National Assessment of Educational Progress) "Basic Reading Skills Improve, but . . . ," vol. 10 (February 1977): 1–2.

———, "1975: Education 'Portrait' Taking Shape," vol. 8 (December 1975).

———, "Survey Studies 'Job Readiness,'" vol. 9 (December 1976): 1–2.

Talcott Parsons, "The School Class as a Social System: Some of Its Functions in American Society." *Harvard Educational Review,* vol. 29 (Fall 1959): 297–318. (Also in Holger R. Stub, ed., *Sociology of Education: A Source book,* 3rd ed. Homewood, Ill.: Dorsey, 1975.)

Richard E. Peterson, "California Makes Plans for Lifelong Learning." *ETS Findings,* vol. 3 (1976): 1–4.

G. A. Pettitt, *Primitive Education in North America.* Berkeley: University of California Press, 1946.

Robert Rosenthal and Lenore Jacobson, *Pygmalion in the Classroom.* New York: Holt, Rinehart and Winston, 1968.

Nevitt Sanford, *American College: A Psychological and Social Interpretation of Higher Education.* New York: Wiley, 1962.

Charles E. Silberman, *Crisis in the Classroom: The Remaking of American Education.* New York: Vintage, 1971.

"Testing and Tracking: Bias in the Classroom." *Inequality in Education,* no. 14 (July 1973): 1–66.

Burton L. White, *The First Three Years of Life.* Englewood Cliffs, N.J.: Prentice-Hall, 1975.

FOR FURTHER STUDY

Becoming a Teacher.   Although the teaching profession attracts many college students, they rarely know much about it. Charles E. Silberman's *Crisis in the Classroom* (New York: Vintage, 1971) is a study of teaching that describes what happens in American classrooms, reforms that have failed, and reforms that work. In *Life in Classrooms* (New York: Holt, Rinehart and Winston, 1968), Philip W. Jackson examines the complex interactions between teachers and students. An interesting exploration of the uncertainties a teacher must face in a sometimes isolated profession is Dan C. Lortie's *Schoolteacher: A Sociological Study* (Chicago: University of Chicago Press, 1975). Robert J. Havighurst and Daniel U. Levine include good materials on teaching in *Education in Metropolitan Areas* (Boston: Allyn & Bacon, 1971). A classic study of teaching that continues to be useful is Willard Waller's *The Sociology of Teaching* (New York: Wiley, 1939).

Adult Education.   More and more adults every year are going back for additional schooling or for training in new careers. An overview of the current boom in programs for adults may be found in Fred H. Harrington's book, *The Future of Adult Education* (San Francisco: Calif.: Jossey-Bass, 1977). K. Patricia Cross and her co-authors report the findings of their national survey of courses offered to adults, and of courses desired by adults, in *Planning Non-Traditional Programs* (San Francisco, Calif.: Jossey-Bass, 1974). In addition to courses designed for adults, some universities offer students credit for nonacademic experience. An analysis of these programs and the controversies surrounding them is provided by Morris T. Keeton and Associates in *Experiential Learning: Rationale, Characteristics, and Assessment* (San Francisco, Calif.: Jossey-Bass, 1976). Alexander Astin raises questions about the impact of college education and analyzes educational policy in his study entitled *Four Critical Years* (San Francisco, Calif.: Jossey-Bass, 1977). An interesting analysis of the historical variations in adult education is Malcolm S. Knowles's *The Adult Education Movement in the United States* (New York: Holt, Rinehart and Winston, 1976).

Roots of Schools Today.   Many of the institutional arrangements and educational practices today can't be understood unless one finds out the history of their origins. A group of historians have given us a bounty of lively books that do just this: Michael B. Katz, *Class, Bureaucracy and Schools* (New York: Praeger, 1971); Carl F. Kaestle, *The Evolution of an Urban School System: New York 1750–1850* (Cambridge, Mass.: Harvard University Press, 1973); Raymond E. Callahan, *Education and the Cult of Efficiency* (Chicago: University of Chicago Press, 1962); and Diane Ravitch, *The Great School Wars: New York City 1805–1972* (New York: Basic Books, 1974). No student interested in educational reforms should miss *Transformation of the School* (New York: Knopf, 1961), Lawrence Cremin's history of the first progressive movement. In *American Education: The Colonial Experience 1607–1783* (New York: Harper & Row, 1972), Cremin has written about education before the development of what we now know as public schools.

CHAPTER 15

Religion

This nation was founded by people who came to America to escape religious persecution in Europe, where government and religion were intertwined. Our Constitution includes a firm commitment to the separation of church and state. Yet an outsider familiar with neither our Constitution nor our history might well receive the opposite impression.

In his 1976 inaugural address, President Carter declared:

> In this outward and physical ceremony we attest once again to the inner and spiritual strength of our nation. . . .
>
> Here before me is the Bible used in the inauguration of our first President in 1789, and I have just taken the oath of office on the Bible my mother gave me just a few years ago, . . .

Nearly every U.S. president has invoked God to help us in our national mission. George Washington, in his first inaugural address, rejoiced that the revolution had succeeded but warned that "the propitious smiles of Heaven can never be expected on a nation that disregards the eternal rules of order and right which Heaven itself has ordained. . . ."

An outsider might well conclude that our inaugurals are religious ceremonies; our presidents, high priests of a nation of believers; our national mission, making the world safe for the practice of democratic rituals and converting others to a way of life based on technological innovation and semifree enterprise. Every Thanksgiving and Fourth of July we rededicate ourselves to the principles of freedom, hard work, family solidarity, and national unity with what might seem —at least to this outsider—religious fervor.

In one sense, the outsider would be wrong. Our presidents aren't high priests. Yet in another sense—the sociological sense—the president does function as a kind of religious leader.

As this brief discussion of "civil religion"(which we will examine more closely in the chapter) suggests, sociology looks beyond theology and belief to explain religious experiences in terms of their social context. In this chapter we will investigate what religion is, examine its functions for society and the individual, and explore its role in social change. We will also discuss the different forms of religious expression, and then look at trends in American religion today.

THE BASIC ELEMENTS OF RELIGION

When the Mbuti Pygmies of the Ituri Forest are faced with sickness, poor hunting, or other misfortunes, and when all practical remedies have failed, they hold a special festival, or *molimo*, to restore order and harmony to their temporarily troubled world. And so it is when a member of the band dies: instead of mourning the deceased in any formal manner, the Mbuti perform a number of relatively informal ritual acts in a special death *molimo* that is intended to honor the memory of the deceased, comfort the bereaved, and emphasize that nothing evil or out of the ordinary has happened. The Mbuti close all the paths leading from the forest to the homes of their Bantu neighbors; they wear clothes made of leaves, feathers, flowers, and vines; they eat foods that come from the forest rather than from their villages; and they sing especially fervent songs of praise to the forest. At the core of the death *molimo* is the wish of the Mbuti to identify themselves with the forest's life-giving power, a wish that is also expressed in the Mbuti creed: "The Forest is the Mother and Father, because it gives us all the things we need. . . . We are the children of the forest. When it dies, we die" (Turnbull, 1965: 312).

Of course the contrasts are striking between the *molimo* and the kind of religious observance we are likely to find in our own society, such as a mass or a synagogue service. Yet both the *molimo* and the mass or synagogue service embrace what Durkheim identified as the basic features of religion: the glorification of sacred beings or sacred things; the affirmation of deeply held beliefs through specific practices, or *rituals*; and a special community of worship.

Émile Durkheim: The Sacred and the Profane

Sociologist Émile Durkheim believed that all aspects of human experience could be defined in terms of two diametrically opposed categories: the sacred and the profane. Religion is associated with the *sacred*, that which is ideal and transcends everyday existence; it is extraordinary, powerful, potentially dangerous, awe-inspiring. The *profane* is human experience that is mundane and ordinary, matter-of-fact. Almost anything can be considered sacred—a cross, a lizard, an odd-shaped stone—but the quality of sacredness is not inherent in those objects. Rather, sacredness is bestowed upon objects or people by a community. Something one society considers sacred, therefore, may be regarded elsewhere as mundane.

The sacred may be a supernatural being or beings. For the Mbuti, the forest, personified as Mother and Father, Life-Giver, and occasionally Death-Giver, is sacred. Monotheists, like the world's 951 million Christians, 14.5 million Jews, and 538 million Muslims,[1] believe in a single deity called "God," "Yahweh," or "Allah." Polytheists worship several deities; today's 519 million Hindus, most of whom are found in India, have a pantheon of five gods, who are in turn reflections of a higher, more sacred principle of *Brahman*, or "Oneness." Sacred ghosts or ancestor spirits, who are imbued with supernatural powers but spring from a human rather than a divine origin, may also be objects of veneration: to the 61 million mostly Japanese followers of Shintoism, family ancestors are sacred beings.

[1] Data on members of the major world religions from *Information Please Almanac, 1978*, 32nd ed. (New York: Information Please Publishing, 1978), p. 351. See also table 15:1.

table 15:1 **POPULATIONS OF THE MAJOR WORLD RELIGIONS**

RELIGION	N. AMERICA[1]	S. AMERICA	EUROPE	ASIA	AFRICA	OCEANIA[2]	TOTAL
Total Christian	228,479,000	161,872,500	358,732,600	86,358,000	98,326,000	17,290,000	951,058,100
Roman Catholic	130,789,000	151,017,000	182,087,000	44,239,500	31,168,500	3,230,000	542,531,000
Eastern Orthodox	4,121,000	55,000	62,145,600	1,786,000	16,335,000	360,000	84,803,200
Protestant	93,569,500	10,800,500	114,500,000	40,332,500	50,822,500	13,700,000	323,724,500
Jewish	6,356,675	675,000	3,960,000	3,186,460	274,760	80,000	14,532,895
Muslim	248,100	197,800	8,277,000	427,035,000	101,889,500	66,000	537,713,400
Shinto	600,000	92,000	–	61,004,000	–	–	61,156,000
Confucian	96,100	85,000	25,000	175,440,250	500	42,000	175,688,850
Buddhist	155,000	195,300	220,000	244,212,000	2,000	16,000	244,800,300
Hindu	80,000	547,000	330,000	516,713,500	473,650	650,000	518,794,150
Totals	236,283,425	163,676,600	371,547,600	1,543,430,010	200,966,940	18,144,000	2,533,256,275

[1] Includes Central America and the West Indies.
[2] Includes Australia and New Zealand, as well as islands of the South Pacific.
SOURCE: *Information Please Almanac, 1978*, 32nd ed. (New York: Information Please Publishing, 1978), p. 351.

This stone shrine in the Arizona desert is a sacred place to the Navajo Indians. Symbolic sacrifices are offered today, as they were generations ago, to secure divine favor. (New York Public Library)

Three Asian religions—Buddhism, Confucianism, and Taoism—regard moral or philosophical principles as sacred. The world's 245 million Buddhists, for instance, are less concerned with the god Buddha than with achieving the ethical and spiritual ideals that he set forth in his message of the "four noble truths." *Totems*, worshiped by primitive peoples the world over, are also sacred objects. A symbol or repository of deep-seated group sentiments or feelings, a totem may be a sacred animal, such as a kangaroo or a bear, or a sacred vegetable, such as corn, or an object, such as the special trumpet used in the death *molimo* by the Mbuti. Even a supernatural force may be sacred, though it lacks shape or permanence. The Melanesians use the word *mana* to describe such a force: it may reside in a warrior's accurate spear or in a tree growing near a particularly fertile field or—who knows?—in the rabbit's foot or other lucky charms that Americans like to carry in their pockets. In sum, be it a force, a god, a ghost, a moral principle, or a totem, a sacred thing gives the members of a religion a shared sense of the reality of the supernatural, or of what is sometimes called "the holy."

Beliefs

Sacred things derive their meaning from the beliefs that sustain or underlie them. To regard a cross as sacred, for instance, presupposes a belief in the Resurrection. By the same token, the Ten Commandments are sacred because they are believed to have been given directly by God to Moses atop Mount Sinai. But not all who profess a certain religion accept all its beliefs unequivocally. While Gallup polls have found that about 94 percent of Americans believe in God—a high

percentage compared with that in other industrialized nations—there is considerable difference in level of belief from one religion to another. Nearly all Southern Baptists believe unswervingly in God; about four-fifths of all Catholics do; and less than half of the Congregationalists are completely certain (Glock and Stark, 1965: 90–91).

Rituals

While beliefs are the conceptual aspect of religion, practices and rituals are its visible expression. Although the range of possible rituals is tremendous—from following special dietary laws to using drums, drugs, and magic—ritual activities play a part in every religion. A ritual can recall an aspect of religious belief, honor the sacred, or establish a relationship between the believer and the sacred. Ritual is usually highly symbolic, often condensing several elements of belief into a single activity and striking a responsive chord deep in the participants. Its power transcends theology. For example, the Lord's Supper (the Eucharist) has had many theological interpretations applied to it over the centuries, and indeed, it is a pre-Christian ritual taken over and retheologized. The theology of the Catholics is not the same as that

The Catholic Mass and the Jewish seder are religious rituals. They are similar in form—both are commemorative meals—but the seder is celebrated by families at home, while the Mass is celebrated by a congregation in church. (Top, Ray Ellis/Rapho/Photo Researchers, Inc. Bottom, Hanna Schreiber/Rapho/Photo Researchers, Inc.)

of the Lutherans or of the Reform or Orthodox Jews, yet the ritual of the Last Supper is age-old and has continuing power for each of these religious groups.

As with beliefs, people who profess a religion don't necessarily observe all its rituals. Not all Protestants who believe in Christ go to church, and not all those who do go to church take part in the Eucharist. In 1976, a nationwide survey found that of the 42 percent of the populace who did attend religious services regularly, Catholics went most often (55 percent); Protestants next most often (40 percent); and Jews least often (23 percent) (Gallup Opinion Index, 1977: 27). (See table 15:2.)

Attendance at church or synagogue is not, however, an absolute indicator of personal involvement in religion. Some people stay away from religious services for nonreligious reasons (for example, they don't want to get up early on Sunday or don't want to get dressed up), while others attend religious services out of habit rather than piety. Moreover, not all religions encourage church or synagogue attendance equally. More than one-third of American Jews, for instance, perform rituals at home often enough for their household to be categorized as "traditional" (Goldstein and Goldsheider, 1968: 196).

The Community of Worship

Religion, however, is more than just a distinctive cluster of sacred objects, beliefs, and rituals. It is also a social phenomenon—in Durkheim's term, a *moral community* composed of those who share common beliefs and practices. For Durkheim, the foundation of religion was the moral community: "The idea of society is the soul of religion" (1965: 419). He felt community and religion were inseparable for two reasons—because religion both celebrates and creates community.

Durkheim also maintained that religion and community are inseparable because religion sustains community. To him, a religion is born when a number of people worship together in a common faith. Close social contact encourages similar sets of values and thus unites persons in a community which has its own beliefs and rituals. In addition, participation in the moral community can lead to feelings of belonging and to the development of friendships. These ties of communal involvement are a significant dimension of religious behavior (Lenski, 1961), as we shall see below.

table 15:2	CHURCH ATTENDANCE DURING AN AVERAGE WEEK, 1976 (by percent)
National	42
Catholic	55
Protestant	40
Jewish	23
Men	37
Women	46
White	42
Nonwhite	42
College	43
High school	40
Grade school	45
18–29 years	32
30–49 years	42
50 and over	48
East	41
Midwest	45
South	46
West	30

SOURCE: Gallup Opinion Index, *Religion in America, 1977– 78.* Report no. 145, p. 27.

THE FUNCTIONS OF RELIGION

The remains of flowers found among the skeletons of a Neanderthal burial site, indicating some kind of funeral rite, suggest that human religiosity may extend as far back as 60,000 years. The massive slabs of Stonehenge in England, the temple ruins of Greece from Rhodes to Corfu, the monumental heads carved from volcanic rock on the slopes of Easter Island—all attest to the existence of religious behavior among different peoples in different times.

Indeed, throughout history, there have been few—if any—societies in which some form of religion did not exist. The obvious suggestion is that religion is a crucial part of social life. But why is it so critical—and so pervasive? What purposes does religion serve for societies and individuals?

Social Functions

The concept of the moral community points to one possible answer. By providing a context in which relationships develop, by establishing norms of "right behavior" (and sanctions against antisocial conduct) within a community, and by offering ways of atoning for infractions through prayers, fasting, or penance, religion enhances security in the community by acting as a kind of social cement.

In our own society, for example, every week rabbis, priests, and ministers deliver sermons that translate religious themes into guidelines for practical everyday action. Precepts like "love thy neighbor," "thou shalt not steal," or "turn the other cheek" are more than pious abstractions or sermon topics: they are norms aimed at promoting stability (or discouraging conflict) in the community.

In many primitive societies, too, religion offers a code of conduct. In the Manus society of the South Pacific, families place the skull of an ancestor in a wooden bowl, which they keep and worship in their homes. This ancestor, referred to as "Sir Ghost," is believed to keep a careful eye on the behavior of his descendants. If someone transgresses, particularly through sexual looseness or economic irresponsibility, Sir Ghost may cause a person (not necessarily the offender) to fall ill, have poor fishing, or suffer some other misfortune. The ancestor's potentially harmful displeasure thus acts as a sanction against misbehavior (Pelto and Pelto, 1976: 378).

Legitimation Religion may also help legitimize the fundamental social structure of a community. Consider the current debate in the United States (and elsewhere) over sexual equality—and over the role of women in general. This is in many ways a religious controversy, since traditional male and female roles in society are based to a large extent on the patriarchal philosophy and mythology of Judeo-Christian religions. For example, the Garden of Eden legend, in which Eve is created out of one of Adam's ribs and later encourages Adam to sin by eating the forbidden apple, has been used for centuries as a "proof" of the moral and physical superiority of men over women. Biblical concepts of fatherhood, motherhood, and sexuality have also served to reinforce male dominance in many countries. And although there are now women rabbis and women ministers, the Vatican administration of the Roman Catholic church remains firmly committed to an all-male priesthood, and by implication, to a male-dominated society. A recent decree endorsed by the Pope declared that only men may be priests because Jesus Christ ''was and remains a man,'' and besides, Christ chose only men to be apostles (*Time,* February 7, 1977, p. 65).

A strong connection between religion and social structure can also be seen among so-called primitive peoples. In a comparative study of fifty primitive societies, Guy E. Swanson found that people are likely to worship ancestor spirits when kin groups are important decision-making units (Swanson, 1969: 97–108). The belief in ancestors who are actively concerned about their living descendants tends to reinforce the authority of the kin groups. Swanson also found that religion supports the hierarchy in societies in which wealth is unequally distributed, for in those societies, the gods tend to intervene in human affairs mainly to discourage behavior that might upset the status quo (1969: 153–174). Functionally, these interventions serve to minimize the social disorder that might ordinarily result from widespread inequalities in wealth, privilege, or both.

Social Adaptation   Religion may provide a cushion against the rough edges of a different and perhaps suspicious culture, a haven where ''back-home'' customs and beliefs reaffirm one's roots. In a nation of immigrants, argues sociologist Andrew Greeley (1972), American churches large and small have derived much of their vitality from the struggles of different ethnic groups to adapt to American life. It is too simple to regard ourselves as a nation of Protestants, Catholics, and Jews. Rather, American religion is made up of German Lutherans, English Presbyterians, and Southern Baptists; Irish, Italian, and Polish Catholics, Russian and German Jews—to mention only a few examples. Greeley calls America ''the denomina-

tional society'' because the religious practices of each group are distinct and reflect members' backgrounds.

This social function of religion began with the first settlements. The Puritanism of the Massachusetts Bay Colony, for instance, was modeled closely after the Congregationalism practiced in many English villages. The Anglicanism of the Southern tobacco planters was a link with the urban aristocratic society they had known at home; and the African-derived slave religions served the same function for blacks suddenly torn from their societies.

During the colonial period, Protestantism was the religion of the vast majority of Americans; Catholics and Jews accounted for less than 2 percent of all worshipers. But beginning in the 1820s, waves of Catholic immigrants began to arrive; by 1900, Catholicism was the religion of 25 percent of Americans. All immigrants had to deal with the same problem: ''What am I, and where do I belong?'' For the Catholics, the answers came chiefly from two sources—shared national heritage and shared religion. These provided the basis for both fellowship and self-definition.

But Greeley maintains that besides helping immigrants anchor themselves in a new environment, religion can also exert a strong influence on the ways in which they adapt. For example, although Jews did not come to America in great numbers until the early 1900s, within fifty years they had managed to surpass both Protestants and Catholics in terms of wealth, cultural sophistication, and political and social power. Why did Jews adapt so much more quickly and successfully than other groups?

The reason, according to Greeley, has to do with Jewish self-definition, which was based partly on a regard for learning, especially practical learning; Jews were encouraged to take advantage of the educational opportunities America offered. It was also based on the development of intellectual and emotional adaptability, which had been crucial to the survival of the Jews as a persecuted minority in Europe (195). Catholic self-definition, in contrast, has much less to do with making the most of the opportunities American society offered; it was based primarily on intense loyalty to the church, and on an equally intense fear of "Protestantization" (188). The Catholic church pulled its members inward by trying to make itself both the center and the boundary of life: Catholics worshiped, were educated, and conducted their social lives in an atmosphere almost exclusively Catholic.

Individual Functions

Many psychologists agree that for the individual, religion serves to reduce anxiety and uncertainty. Sigmund Freud, for instance, explained religion as a neurotic solution to an unresolved Oedipal conflict: torn between guilt-provoking sexual desire for his mother, on the one hand, and fear and hatred for his father, on the other, man creates a god in his father's fearful image, in order to keep those sexual impulses under control.

Reducing Anxiety Although Freud's idea that religion is based on sexual repression may seem extreme, it serves to point up a major function of religion—reducing anxiety. According to most religions, human life is part of a divine scheme, and like it or not, that is why we are all here, spinning through the universe. By obeying rules laid down by the gods, believers are assured that they will be at least virtuous and at best successful.

Even if your life is fraught with sorrow and hardship, religion again serves to reassure you that sorrow and hardship are really not very important after all, because a far better existence awaits you in the hereafter. This comfort in times of distress—particularly in the face of death—is an especially important function of religion. Many religions maintain that the soul lives on after death; some even provide detailed descriptions of its progress once it leaves the body.

As Freud and other psychologists have suggested, the reassurances offered by religion have a powerful effect on the human psyche. In a study of primitive culture on the Trobriand Islands in the Southwest Pacific, Malinowski found that religion helped lessen the anxiety of fishermen heading out to the high seas. The islanders were excellent fishermen who sought their catch both in a calm lagoon and in the occasionally dangerous open ocean. Malinowski observed that before the men went fishing in the lagoon, they performed no special ceremonies; but when they were about to leave for the open sea, they invoked the help of their gods through a variety of rituals. Malinowski concluded that when the Trobriand Islanders were confident of their skills and their safety—as in the lagoon—they felt religion was expendable; but when they faced a dangerous situation, like the open sea, they felt the need for religion and divine aid (Malinowski, 1954). This example suggests that the reassurances offered by religion can have a specific survival value: in this case, religion gave the Trobriand Islanders the confidence they needed to carry on important food-gathering activities.

Consecrating Life Events Along with reducing anxiety, religion can also serve to interpret and consecrate life's most important experiences for the individual. Birth, maturity, marriage, and death—universal features of the human life cycle—are celebrated and explained by practically all religions. Many religions have ceremonies to celebrate victory in war or the succession of a new head of the state or community, and many also have puberty rites of one sort or another to mark the transition from childhood to adulthood. The beliefs and rituals surrounding such impor-

In this Shinto wedding ceremony a Japanese bride pledges her vows by drinking sake. Religion serves to consecrate and interpret this important personal experience. The beliefs and rituals surrounding such events also provide social cohesion for the community in general. (F. A. Heiniger/Photo Researchers, Inc.)

tant events in life as birth, puberty, marriage, and death illustrate how religion simultaneously provides both an interpretation of these events for the individual and social cohesion for the community. Among the Northern Shoshone Indians, when a girl menstruated for the first time, she was isolated from the rest of the tribe for the period of her flow. Since whatever she did at that time was believed to have a lifelong influence, the girl would have to keep very busy in order not to turn into a lazy woman later on. During her isolation she could eat no meat, and she could scratch herself only with a special stick. When the isolation ended, her mother would bring her new clothes— the garments of an adult woman (Hoebel, 1972: 382).

In the Andaman Islands, when his friends

and relatives decided that a boy was old enough, he underwent an extraordinary (and painful) ritual of transformation. the boy would kneel down and put his elbows on the ground in front of him. An older man then took a sharpened arrowhead and began making horizontal cuts on the boy's back. The cuts were made in three rows, with twenty to thirty cuts to a row. After the cutting was over, the boy had to sit with his back to a fire until the bleeding stopped. He had to remain silent throughout the entire procedure (Radcliffe-Brown, 1964: 93). Other puberty rites involve circumcision for boys and girls; in the Jewish religion, thirteen-year-old boys and girls are welcomed into the adult community by being invited to read from the Torah, or law, during a Sabbath synagogue service.

RELIGION AND SOCIAL CHANGE

Religion is created by society, yet it may also help shape society. An issue that causes much debate today is how involved churches should get in social movements and social change. Should the clergy lecture the laity on civil rights, on women's liberation, on grape and lettuce boycotts? Some members of the laity grumble that they aren't in church to hear about grapes. Conversely, others want the church to speak out—on birth control, on political corruption, on the minimum wage, on imperialistic wars. The interplay between religion and society has been described in different but not contrasting ways by two important theorists: Marx and Weber.

Repressing Change: Marx

Karl Marx believed that all religious institutions inhibit social change and revolution by legitimizing the status quo. Marx hoped in vain that the working classes would rise up against their oppressors, and he felt that one reason they didn't revolt was that religion defused rebellion against the existing social order. For example, consider the elaborate caste system in India, in which people receive an unchanging social status depending on what caste they are born into. According to the Hindu belief in reincarnation, which forms a basis for the caste system, if a person fails to perform the obligations that go along with membership in a particular caste, he can expect to live his next life as a member of a lower caste, or if he belongs to the lowest caste, as an animal. The Hindu religion therefore contains strong sanctions against disrupting the social order, no matter how oppressive that order may be. If a certain religious group has become established in a society and has acquired significant property or wealth, it may also block change. Under such circumstances, that group has a vested interest in maintaining the status quo. Marx argued that, in general, the dominant religion in any society develops as a justification for the material conditions in which one class grows wealthy at the expense of another.

In analyzing the repressive nature of religion (and, for that matter, of all social institutions), Marx drew heavily on the concept of *alienation*, his term for a condition in which humans mistakenly come to regard values and institutions of their own making as elements of an unchanging natural order. "Man makes religion, religion does not make man," Marx explained (1964), meaning that religion arises when humans falsely project

FROM RITUAL TO POPULAR EXPRESSION: MODERN AND RELIGIOUS CHANGE IN INDIA

In Kapileswar, a village in eastern India, stands a Hindu temple which for centuries was the religious, social, and economic center of village life. Daily, worshipers performed the ancient rituals of bathing, clothing, feeding, and entertaining the temple deity. Annual festivals marked events in the deity's life, and services were conducted for pilgrims who visited the temple. In return, the villagers received temple lands on which they raised their own food. The distribution of property was controlled by the Mallias, a temple servant caste.

Today this traditional way of life has nearly disappeared. Young villagers don't know the ancient rituals, daily temple attendance has dropped 50 percent since 1920, and few people celebrate even the holiest annual festivals. Nor is the temple anywhere near as important economically as it used to be: by 1971, 80 percent of Mallia males earned their income outside the temple, 25 percent in government jobs (124).

But these changes don't mean that the people of Kapileswar have turned away from religion. They have simply turned to more popular forms of religious expression (127). An annual fire-walking ceremony attracts many villagers who willingly tread the hot coals as proof of their faith in the curative powers of the goddess Kali. As recently as 1962, another public religious festival, Durga Puja, the festival of the goddess Durga, wasn't celebrated by the villagers out of loyalty to Kali, their patron goddess. By 1971, however, Durga Puja had become an important event. The festivities, which last for three days, include "chanting by priests, personal offerings and prayers, feasts, musical performances, and a final celebration in which a singing, dancing crowd [gather] all of the images and [throw] them into a small river" (129).

In his discussion of the way religious worship has changed in Kapileswar,

their own power and self-consciousness onto hypothetical divine beings. They then worship these beings, thinking of them as superhuman and forgetting that their gods are man-made and can therefore be changed.

Among the lower classes, Marx believed, religion grows out of the need to understand the reasons for social oppression and the need to cope with it somehow. "Religion is the sigh of the oppressed creature," he wrote, "the sentiment of a heartless world, and the soul of soulless conditions. It is the opium of the people" (1964). Although religion ministers to real needs, it provides an illusory happiness. By promising the working classes a better life in the world to come, it blinds them to the possibilities of creating a better world on earth.

Inspiring Change: Weber

In *The Protestant Ethic and the Spirit of Capitalism* (1930) and other writings, Max Weber (1864–1920) extended Marx's insight. He observed that just as material con-

James M. Freeman contrasts the vitality of these public rituals with the "obliga-tory services of the Kapileswar temple" (128). He suggests several reasons why the growth of popular religion happened when it did. The first is economic. During the past century the population of Kapileswar grew so large that the temple landholdings could no longer support the village's families. To make things worse, the region was regularly struck by natural disasters that destroyed both crops and property. Inevitably, Mallias and other temple workers looked for jobs outside the temple. These jobs were available in the neighboring capital city, which had only been built in the 1950s. Naturally, the villagers' economic de-pendence on the temple decreased as their ability to find secular jobs increased.

A second reason for the decline of the temple, according to Freeman, was government interference in its management, whereas popular religious activities were free of such control. Third, the caste-controlled rituals of temple life were out of step with the democratic ideals of independent India. The popular religious festivals, by contrast, were more egalitarian. Finally, the temple simply couldn't afford to sponsor large spectacles, so the villagers turned instead to popular festivals.

In his conclusion, Freeman argues that Weber was wrong about religion yielding to modernization. The people of Kapileswar didn't lose their religious world view; they simply shifted their style of religious activity from temple ritual to expressions of popular religion (131). In short, religion didn't die with urban-ization—but adapted to it.

SOURCE: James M. Freeman, "Religious Change in a Hindu Pilgrimage Center," *Review of Religious Research*, vol. 16 (Winter 1975), pp. 124–133.

ditions can influence ideas, so ideas, under certain circumstances, can influence mate-rial conditions. Struck by the development of modern industrial society, Weber was at-tempting to find the source of what he termed the "Spirit of Capitalism."

Weber began his investigation with a fact: capitalism had emerged in Europe, not in Asia or Africa. And in the Germany of his day, predominantly Protestant areas were more likely to be industrialized than largely Catholic areas. Protestants were more likely to be industrial millionaires than Catholics

were. Why should this be so? Weber exam-ined a variety of religious ideas, not as they appeared in abstract theological debates but as they influenced social and economic be-havior. The search led him to seventeenth-century Calvinism, at the heart of which was the concept of predestination, the idea that a person's fate after death—salvation or dam-nation—is determined from the very first moment of life. The practical effect of this idea was that people tried to prove they were among God's chosen by doing good works, which meant paying meticulous attention to everyday affairs. Hard work was a duty to God that carried its own intrinsic reward.

Thus Calvinism contained a built-in incentive to hard work and self-denial. The ideal Calvinist, anxious to prove his faith in his own salvation, put aside frivolity and pleasure to pursue that all-important sign of being chosen—success. Profits were not to be spent but to be reinvested in one's business or enterprise, or to be given to the church. What is more, since Calvinist doctrine held that every individual stood alone before God, hard work and frugality were the means of expressing one's dedication to that one-to-one relationship with the divinity. But what Weber had constructed was an ideal type—a standard against which to measure the concrete examples encountered in the real world; his Calvinist—sober, ceaselessly industrious, and dedicated to the pursuit of profit as a sign of divine favor—could be found in varying degrees in early capitalist societies.

The Protestant Ethic Today Today the phrase *Protestant ethic* has become synonymous with dedication to hard work and pursuit of profit; the term is also used to explain why people so often feel guilty about loafing when they could be doing some "useful" task instead. But is there really such a thing as a "Protestant ethic"? If there is, it is not particularly Protestant: in the United States, Catholics have a higher income on the average than Protestants do, and Jews are the most successful of all. In addition to those who say that the Protestant ethic doesn't exist, there are those who claim that there used to be a Protestant ethic, but that it has pretty much disappeared by now. In an investigation of the recent upsurge of experimentation with alternative life styles and social arrangements in the United

States, Robert Wuthnow found that some of the attitudes lying at the heart of the Protestant ethic are less widely accepted now than they used to be. For example, in the San Francisco Bay area, Wuthnow found that for people over thirty, the dominant meaning of existence was either that God governed life and had a specific purpose for every person, or that the individual was solely responsible for his or her own success. People under thirty, however, were much less Calvinist in their thinking: they explained the meaning of life either in terms of the influence of inexorable social forces or in terms of mysticism— the idea that life may be understood only from an intuitive standpoint, through intense personal experiences that allow the individual to alter time and space and create his or her own reality (Wuthnow, 1976: 3–4, 155, 161). Some of the "decline" of the Protestant ethic may also be related to the fact that religious beliefs can now be expressed in forms other than Calvinism.

FORMS OF RELIGIOUS EXPRESSION

There are many possible outlets for religious beliefs or feelings, including organized churches (with which we are all familiar); sects; what sociologists call "invisible" or private religion; and the "civil religion" described and analyzed by Robert Bellah. The existence of a variety of forms may be part of the explanation for the fact that although religious belief among Americans is stable and even rising, church attendance and membership seem to be declining.

table 15:3 CHURCH AND SECT

CHARACTERISTIC	CHURCH	SECT
Size	Large	Small
Relationship with other religious groups	Tolerant	Rejects; feels it has sole truth
Wealth	Extensive	Limited
Religious services	Limited congregational participation; formal; intellectual emphasis	Extensive congregational participation; spontaneous; emotional emphasis
Clergy	Specialized; professional	Unspecialized; little training; part time
Doctrines	Liberal interpretation of scriptures; emphasis upon this world	Literal interpretation of scriptures; emphasis upon other world
Membership	By birth or ritual participation; social institution embracing all socially compatible	By conversion; moral community excluding unworthy
Social class of members	Mainly middle class	Mainly lower class
Relationship with secular world	Endorses prevailing culture and social organization	Renounces or opposes prevailing cultural standards; requires strict adherence to Biblical standards

SOURCE: Adapted from Glenn M. Vernon, *Sociology of Religion* (New York: McGraw-Hill, 1962), p. 174; supplemented with material from Leonard Broom and Philip Selznick, *Sociology*, 5th ed. (New York: Harper & Row, 1973), p. 411.

Church and Sect

Ernst Troeltsch, a sociologist of the early twentieth century (1865–1923), views religious institutions as being basically either churches or sects (Troeltsch, 1957); these, he says, differ from each other in size and in attitudes toward religiosity and society. (Church and sect are ideal types; a given group may not conform to the type in every respect.)

Troeltsch describes the *church* as a large, conservative, universalist religious institution. Most members are born into it. The church promises its members grace, but makes few demands on them. Because it is large, it tends to acquire a certain amount of social and political power, which it more often than not retains by becoming associated with the government or the ruling classes. The church thus accommodates itself to the claims of other powerful sociopolitical institutions and tends to support the status quo. The Church of England or the Catholic church in Spain would come close to fitting this ideal type.

The *sect* is a small, exclusive, uncompromising fellowship of individuals seeking spiritual perfection. Members are voluntary converts, and their lives are pretty much controlled by the sect. Sects are usually characterized by asceticism, and their attitude toward society tends to be either indifferent or hostile. Most sects are concerned strictly with religious values and withdraw as much as possible from society; a few, however, are quite critical of the social order and have definite ideas about how to improve it.

All the fundamentalist groups we shall discuss later in the chapter are really sects, as are the groups focused on mysticism. Fundamentalists tend toward extreme orthodoxy and a fairly literal interpretation of the Bible. Their doctrines emanate from the belief that the troubles of the world are results of human sinfulness, and that the human condition can't be improved until the Second Coming of Jesus. They feel the need for and seek personal salvation in Christ, and they view religious participation as a means of redemption through faith.

The strong demands sects make on their members are themselves a major reason why people turn to them. Everybody has a basic need to find some meaning in life, and people are often not satisfied by abstract concepts or theologies. Only when they make personal sacrifices for the sake of a belief can they feel they have found something compellingly meaningful—something worth living and struggling for.

Invisible or Private Religion

Many people who say that they belong to no church or sect or that they have no religion are in fact religious: they practice what Thomas Luckmann has described as *"invisible"* or *private religion*. Like everyone else, these people must grapple with life's great issues; but instead of accepting the formulations of established religion, they choose certain themes and private experiences and construct from them an individual "sacred cosmos" that gives meaning to their lives (Luckmann, 1967: 104–106).

Luckmann's formulation has been supported by the work of other investigators. In a study of 208 households in a white working- to middle-class area in the South, for example, Machalek and Martin (1976) found a wide array of beliefs and behaviors, a variety of what they called "ultimate concerns" and "coping strategies." Only 25 percent of this group used churchlike coping strategies; 67.5 percent relied on such private humanistic strategies as informal discussion groups to help them with such ultimate concerns as interpersonal relationships, world problems, economic security and survival, and peace of mind and happiness. The issues traditional religion concerns itself with—the relationship between human beings and God, life after death, the nature of God—were mentioned by only 18 percent of the people interviewed in this investigation.

Civil Religion

There are also those who claim that a set of national beliefs binds together individual and denomination alike. At almost every American state or political occasion, says sociolo-

The Stars and Stripes is one of the key symbols of America's civil religion—those extrareligious beliefs, such as patriotism, which help give legitimacy to our national community. (John Lei)

gist Robert Bellah, God plays an important role. He is mentioned in the Pledge of Allegiance, in legislative invocations, in all oaths of office, at party conventions, in courtroom procedures, and in political speeches— including every presidential inaugural address save one (Washington's second, which was only two paragraphs long). The nation's currency proclaims "In God We Trust." And Bellah points to the traditional feeling in the United States that this nation was established "under God," from whom the gov-

ernment derives its ultimate legitimacy. These elements of faith are for Bellah parts of a national or *civil religion,* a collection of potent beliefs, symbols, and rituals that exists outside the church and that pervades and helps legitimize the national community (Bellah, 1970: 168–186).

The God of American civil religion is a unifying figure in a pluralistic society. Universal rather than sectarian, sufficiently impartial so that no religious group is offended, he is not concerned with such personal ends as salvation. Instead, God devotes his attention to law, justice, order, and other matters of interest to the entire community.

The flag, the American eagle, and the monuments in Washington, D.C., and in many town squares are the symbols of the American civil religion; its hymns are "The Star-Spangled Banner" and "America, the Beautiful." Among the high priests of the civil religion are George Washington and Thomas Jefferson; among the martyrs are Abraham Lincoln and John F. Kennedy. The rituals of the civil religion include the Fourth of July, which, like Christmas, commemorates a significant birth; Memorial Day, which honors the sacrifices of military men; and Thanksgiving Day, which commemorates the successful voyage across an alien sea and the founding of a new promised land. According to Bellah, the idea of a civil religion simply indicates the links between religion, morality, and politics that exist in all societies (Bellah, 1973: 20).

But the precise distinction between civil and church religion is somewhat ambiguous. Using a sophisticated statistical method, Ronald C. Wimberley and his co-workers (1976) found empirical evidence that civil religion is indeed a distinct dimension of religious commitment; but other sociologists using different methods haven't been as successful. Whether or not the empirical evidence is strong, it seems clear that currently, at least, civil religion—and for that matter, invisible religion—are realities. That does not mean, though, that they are healthy. In a highly praised book entitled *The Broken Covenant* (1975), Bellah examined the roots of both civil and invisible religion; he found civil religion to be "an empty and broken shell" (142), a victim of the eroding away of transcendent meaning by economic and technological advances. As for inner spiritual sensitivity, Bellah feels there is a general decline of belief in all forms of moral obligation: to one's occupation, family, country, and self (x). America, according to Bellah, is facing a severe crisis: "I am convinced that the continued and increased dominance of the complex of capitalism, utilitarianism, and the belief that the only road to truth is science will rapidly lead to the destruction of American society, or possibly, in an effort to stave off destruction, to a technical tyranny of the 'brave new world' variety" (1975: xiv). The only hope, says Bellah, is a mending of the broken covenant of virtue, the development of a basis of genuine human sympathy from which to view our technical rational accomplishments, and another religious "Great Awakening." Perhaps, in the context of civil religion, the election to the presidency of Jimmy Carter, a devout evangelical Baptist, is a first symbolic step in that direction.

TRENDS IN RELIGION

Hare Krishna, Hare Rama is now as familiar a sound on the streets of most major American cities as the noise of passing traffic; no one even turns to stare at the saffron robes and shaven heads of devotees any more. The pope bans artificial birth-control devices, but many American Catholics ignore the ban. All these are current trends in religion—reflections of the interplay between religion and society and the changes in both.

Between the time that Marx wrote and Weber's day, the pace of change in society increased steadily, and between Weber's day and our own, that pace has quickened still more. The questions before us, then, are: How has social change influenced religion? How has religion influenced social change? And what guesses can we make about the future?

Secularization

Weber himself observed that the spirit of capitalism laid the groundwork for an economic order that eventually eliminated the ethical and religious dimension of work. The shift Weber was describing is often referred to as *secularization*, "the process by which sectors of society and culture are removed from the domination of religious institutions and symbols" (Berger, 1967: 107). During the Middle Ages, for example, education and religious education were one and the same, since faculty and students were all members or aspiring members of religious orders; gradually, however, formal learning was secularized, removed from ecclesiastical authority. By the same token, secularization can be seen in the decrease in the number of religious ideas and symbols in philosophy, literature, and art; in the doctrine of separation of church and state; and particularly in the rise of the scientific world view, according to which life is seen in totally nonreligious terms (Berger, 1967: 107).

The end result of secularization is that increasing numbers of people no longer understand the world, or their lives, through the medium of religious doctrine, and church religion becomes increasingly peripheral to society. For instance, Peter Berger notes that in Europe church-related religion is strongest in areas and among people at the farthest remove from industrialization (1967: 107); and in general, church attendance is more of a rural than an urban phenomenon (Hill, 1973: 254).

Among the young, three-quarters of the college students in the United States say that their religious beliefs are very or fairly important, and more than six out of ten college students say they believe in life after death (Gallup, 1976: 66). Though they appear to be highly religious, however, young Americans are also highly critical of organized religion. A survey of American youth in Dayton, Ohio, revealed that many feel that the church is "materialistic," "apathetic," "out of step with the times," and "failing to meet the needs of the people" (Gallup Opinion Index, 1976: 5).

Trends in the Major Faiths

Two functions religions have traditionally performed—the conservation of beliefs and the prophetic function of serving as a social conscience—are today a source of increasing conflict. The voice of the clergy has become more and more strident as congregations challenge both dogma and institutional structures. At the same time, the churches themselves played a large role in the civil rights movement, in the opposition to the war in Vietnam, and in the movement to pressure corporations to become socially responsible. The exercise of this prophetic function always creates tension, since not having social problems brought to their attention keeps congregations comforted and stable, whereas becoming involved shakes

people up by forcing them to confront not only the problems but also themselves.

Among Protestants, the civil rights movement unleashed conflict over the purposes and authority of the church, as well as over beliefs (Hadden, 1969: 3–33). The main split is between the clergy and the laity. Many church members want the church to comfort them; many of the clergy want the church to offer challenges to its people. This clash divides many churches and has led to a decline in contributions to the church and to a weakening of support by church members of church leaders when leaders attack the status quo. Protestantism is threatened not simply by secularization but also by crises of purpose, belief, and authority.

Large changes are disrupting the Catholic church as well. The church is reassessing its separation from Protestant churches and is trying to deal with the burgeoning spirit of individualism and contemporary ferment within its own ranks. In an effort to achieve greater Christian unity, Catholic and Anglican theologians have reached agreement on the nature of the priesthood and the ministry; Catholics recognize the legitimacy of the Anglican clergy, and the sharing of communion between the two churches is now possible. Catholics and Lutherans have also reached accord on the issue of papal primacy, a major issue in the Protestant Reformation four centuries ago. A joint study has declared that papal primacy is no longer a barrier to the reconciliation of the two churches and envisions the day when they will be part of one "larger communion."

All these fraternal moves on the part of the Catholic church are the legacy of Vatican II, the Catholic ecumenical council called by Pope John XXIII to reexamine the doctrine and rituals of the Catholic church. The council, which met from 1962 to 1965, brought about sweeping changes within the church,

table 15:4 **PROFILES OF AMERICAN RELIGIONS (by percent)**

CHARACTERISTICS	PROTESTANTS				CATHOLICS	JEWS
	Methodists	Episcopalians	Baptists	Total		
Percentage of population	11	3	21	60	28	2
Education						
College	30	45	18	27	28	58
High school	57	50	58	55	58	34
Grade school	13	5	24	18	14	8
Occupation						
Professional and business	24	43	15	22	26	53
Clerical and sales	10	11	6	8	10	15
Farmers	4	1	3	4	2	1
Manual	46	25	52	41	44	11
Income						
$15,000+	38	60	22	35	43	59
$10,000–$14,999	20	17	24	23	23	21
$7,000–$9,999	12	11	11	11	10	4
$5,000–$6,999	11	6	16	11	10	7
$3,000–$4,999	11	3	13	10	7	5
Under $3,000	8	3	14	10	7	4
Community Size						
1,000,000+	9	32	13	13	28	52
500,000–999,999	8	16	9	10	15	16
50,000–499,999	27	25	20	25	28	16
2,500–49,999	18	13	21	17	15	5
Under 2,500 (rural)	38	14	37	35	14	11
Politics						
Republican	30	38	17	27	17	8
Democrat	45	27	57	44	53	56
Independent	23	32	24	27	28	36

SOURCE: Gallup Opinion Index, *Religion in America, 1977–78*. Report no. 145, pp. 57 and 60.

A recent Gallup poll conducted among American adults indicates some interesting trends in religion, and points to possible relations between religious beliefs and other sociological characteristics. There continues to be an affinity between religion and politics in this country. As the poll revealed, Jews and Catholics are predominantly Democrats, while Protestants show a more even split between the Republican and Democratic parties. The percentage of individuals from all religious faiths who are Independents has increased markedly in the last decade. The pattern of educational and occupational attainment shows that Jews rise to notably higher levels than do either Protestants or Catholics.

such as the vernacular mass, but it also led to a crisis of authority. Many among the clergy and the laity are no longer prepared to accept the will of the pope. Lay persons are more and more asserting their right to share in decision-making, and priests and nuns are questioning the role of celibacy and their own role in the church.

One of the most conspicuous current crises in Catholicism involves the pope's 1968 ban on the use of artificial birth control. A ten-year study of Catholic attitudes in the United States, completed in 1976, con-

cludes that the pope's firm stand on the matter has led to a drastic decline in religious devotion—as measured in terms of daily prayer and of attendance at weekly mass and monthly confession—as well as to a drop of as much as $1 billion a year in contributions made by Americans to the Catholic church. According to sociologist Andrew Greeley, who is also a priest, the ban has also caused many Catholics to question the pope's credibility: between 1963 and 1976, the percentage of Catholics agreeing that "Jesus invested the church's leadership in the Pope" dropped from 70 to 42 percent (Greeley, McCready, and McCourt, 1975).

In Judaism, there is mounting concern over the decline in Jewish religious belief and over the possible weakening of communal ties as the children and grandchildren of immigrants have become Americanized. Much of the blame for the divisions within the family over the issue of Jewishness lies with the parents, says one editor of a Jewish monthly, because they have failed to impress upon their children the importance of the Nazi holocaust and of the creation of the state of Israel. "To most American Jews, being a Jew is like being a stamp collector. It's an avocation," says a student supporter of the Radical Jewish Union, who sees Jewishness as a totality. "It encompasses a political ideology, a set of values, a general philosophy, a religion, customs, diet, language—a whole way of life" (*Newsweek*, March 1, 1971, pp. 61–62).

Some Jewish religious leaders are not particularly worried over the decline in orthodox belief because they feel that heterodoxy has always been a part of Jewish tradition. Moreover, though they note a decline in regular synagogue attendance, they are pleased with the stability in synagogue membership. And they have found the increased interest in Jewish education gratifying. Such training

figure 15:1　Catholics and contraception, 1965–1975

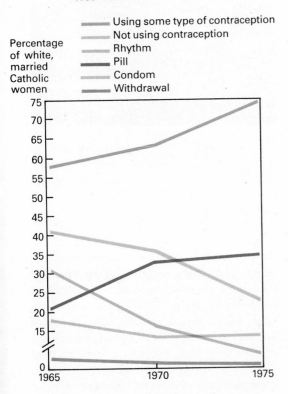

Percentage of white, married Catholic women

Using some type of contraception
Not using contraception
Rhythm
Pill
Condom
Withdrawal

SOURCE: Adapted from Charles F. Westoff and Elise F. Jones, "The Secularization of Catholic Birth Control Practices," *Family Planning Perspectives*, vol. 9 (September–October 1977), table 3, p. 204.

through the synagogue and Hebrew schools reinforces the sense of Jewishness that persists despite the decrease in formal religious belief. In the 1970s, there has also been a countertrend among educated young Jews in the form of a return to Jewishness through new communal groups, programs of Jewish studies, and even traditional Orthodoxy.

The Fundamentalist Revival

If participation in formal organized religion is declining, more and more people each year are participating in another traditional form of religious experience. The revivalists, the evangelists, and the fundamentalists have grown steadily since the late 1960s. Young people predominate in the fundamentalist revival. The Assemblies of God, Pentecostal groups, Evangelists, Mormons, and Seventh-day Adventists have all had steady increases in membership. The Southern Baptist Convention, a large, relatively conservative denomination, has expanded by more than 2 percent a year since 1975, and the Jehovah's Witnesses have increased annually by 5 percent since 1958, more than doubling their membership (Kelley, 1972: 21). Even Catholicism, usually leery of evangelicism, has been reached by *Pentecostalism:* nearly a quarter of a million Catholics have experienced a personal spiritual encounter known as "baptism in the Holy Spirit," speak in tongues, practice miraculous healing by prayer, and regard themselves as charismatics. The evangelical movement, Kelley concludes, has attracted more and more of a following because it exacts commitment and thereby creates meaning (26).

The Jesus People are also part of the evangelical revival, although their membership is comprised almost exclusively of mid-

While participation in organized religion is declining, fundamentalist and evangelist groups are growing steadily. Young people predominate in this revival. (Myron Wood/Photo Researchers, Inc.)

dle-class white teen-agers, often former drug users. Sometimes tagged "Jesus Freaks," they seek personal salvation through the teachings of Christ. They attend prayer services and go through baptism rituals. Some live and work together in communes, where the life style is ascetic and a strict code of morality is followed. Emphasis is placed on the experience of religion, the experience of knowing God's will and performing it. Intellectualism and independent thought are not encouraged.

IN THE NEWS

Converting to Health

"We believe that Christ will return to Earth, but we should be in the best state of health when he does."
—Lorenzo Paytee, Seventh-day Adventist, executive secretary of the Southern California Conference.

Out of its conviction that the body is the temple of God, the Seventh-day Adventist church has for years preached the benefits of good nutrition and physical fitness. And for years, few people listened. Recently, though, Americans have become more concerned about diet and preventive medicine, and the Seventh-day Adventist church is growing.

With a current membership of 525,000, the church has had an average growth rate of 3.3 percent a year, placing it among the most rapidly expanding denominations in the nation. Church officials say that perhaps as many as 20 percent of the new members are initially attracted to the church by the medical services it provides, including free blood pressure tests and stop-smoking clinics.

The church believes that people are always interested in health matters, so it staffs its mobile "health on wheels" units with medical personnel who can discuss physical problems. People who enter the mobile units aren't pressured to discuss religion, but many do become interested in finding out more about the church.

Many Adventists have been drawn to the church by the stop-smoking program, which has enrolled 12 million Americans. Anna Roddy of Simi Valley, Calif., for example, broke a 38-year habit in the course and then began talking to Adventists about religious questions. She joined the church four years ago and said she "hasn't missed a Sabbath since."

Dr. Samuel DeShay, a physician who is head of all church health ministries, said an informal poll by the church three years ago indicated that nearly 10 percent of new members had become involved through a health program. But Dr. DeShay believes that the percentage is at least twice as high.

"There can no longer be a dichotomy between religion and medicine," said the Rev. Edward Bryan, chaplain of the Glendale Adventist medical center. "Neither can afford to be without the other."

SOURCE: Kenneth A. Briggs, "Adventists' Emphasis on Health Attracting Members," *The New York Times*, February 26, 1978, p. 24.

The Rise of Mysticism

"I've been looking for something like this for years. It answers all the questions I've been asking" (Rice, 1974: 23).

That brief comment, spoken by an enthusiastic member of the Reverend Sun Myung Moon's Unification Church, sums up an attitude that is shared by a growing number of Americans, young and old, who have joined a variety of mystical groups in search of truth, fulfillment, and not infrequently, an escape route from a culture that is seen as obsessed with technology, material success, and the accumulation of possessions (Judah, 1974: 113). Although these mystical groups are often lumped together in the category of counterculture movements, they actually range from the highly structured Unification Church and Hare Krishna movements, whose members can be seen chanting or soliciting donations on street corners in many American cities, to the more diffuse and individualized transcendental meditation groups, and from Zen Buddhism to dozens of cells formed around gurus and yogis.

Although these groups have been proliferating since the 1960s, their participants represent but a small percentage of the total population. In the San Francisco Bay area, for instance, Robert Wuthnow found that only 2.6 percent of a large survey sample claimed a strong attachment to any of these movements, and that only 4.3 percent had ever taken part in one (1976: 33). Data on the Jesus People revealed a similar picture of lack of familiarity and participation (35). But despite the lack of mass open participation, the very existence of such groups, according to Charles Glock (1976), is a visible sign of fundamental, far-reaching change in a society traditionally defined as materialistic.

In the same San Francisco survey, Wuthnow found that for a significant number of people, the dominant meaning of life was mystical, grasped as much by intense peak experiences as by more rational or intellectual perceptions, such as that God, the individual, or social forces are the chief determinants of human destiny (Wuthnow, 1976: 142). In the twenty-one to thirty group, 30 percent described their dominant meaning system as mystical, as compared to 15 percent of those aged thirty-one to forty, 18 percent of those forty-one to fifty, and 19 percent of those fifty or older (Wuthnow, 1976: 155).

The Hare Krishna Movement What lies behind this growing preference for mysticism? A study of the Hare Krishna movement by religion scholar J. Stillson Judah (1974) gives some insights. Judah observes that one of the reasons that Hare Krishna participation predominates among young people is that they are relatively mobile; older individuals often have jobs, families, and other commitments that make it difficult to adhere to the rigid discipline of the movement. But to old and young alike, Judah found, the Hare Krishna movement offers an opportunity to satisfy three needs that Philip E. Slater (1976) says must be met in order to have a stable culture: community, meaning a life of close fellowship and cooperation with others; engagement, the chance to deal directly with social and interpersonal problems; and dependence, or sharing with others the responsibility for controlling one's impulses and guiding one's life (Judah, 1974: 102–103). Judah argues that the emphasis on individualism in our technological society has led to the suppression of community, engagement, and dependence, and that the Hare Krishna movement can be seen as part of a larger counterculture revolution of social values.

Most of the Hare Krishna devotees Judah studied were former hippies (98). Many of them came to Hare Krishna as the counter-culture changed from a large, loosely unified protest movement, which was what it was during the 1960s, to a search for a unified philosophy with which to achieve a common culture. Some of these former hippies had already experimented with other countercul-ture life styles, such as living in communes and practicing yoga techniques for spiritual realization; others had previously sought meaning through involvement with drugs (135). Disenchantment with such specific es-tablishment values as the emphasis on ma-terial success through competitive labor, and disillusionment with civil and parental au-thority that favors the status quo, war, and hypocrisy, especially in regard to civil rights, are other bases for Hare Krishna involvement (16).

Looking to the future, Judah saw a limited but nonetheless strong future for the Hare Krishna movement. Although its ability to satisfy the needs for community, engage-ment, and dependence has given the move-ment a substantial amount of internal stabil-ity, the conditions that during the 1960s gave rise to the initial interest in Hare Krishna have changed: hippiedom is on the wane, the day of the "big protest" is behind us, and the counterculture in general seems to have lost much of its original momentum (182–183).

The Sun Myung Moon Church It is interest-ing, and not too surprising, that many of the patterns that Judah found to be true of the Hare Krishna movement are also true of Sun Myung Moon's Unification Church, which had attracted or recruited 300,000 followers by 1974. For instance, many members come to the Moon church after experimenting with other cults, communes, or counterculture al-ternatives (Rice, 1974: 25). And just as Hare Krishna devotees spend every waking mo-ment trying to further their own and others' Krishna consciousness, so the "Moonies"

work feverishly in the service of the cult's "New Messiah," whose place and date of birth—Korea, 1920—happen to be the same as those of South Korean industrialist Sun Myung Moon. Both the Moon and Hare Krishna movements are also similar in the total conformity they impose upon members.

The striking rise of interest in mysticism during the 1960s and early 1970s does not necessarily portend that America is about to become a society of mystics. By the same token, the fact that the values of traditional religion are not quite as dominant as they used to be doesn't mean that these values have lost their meaning. In San Francisco, where the counterculture began and where it has reached a relatively high level of devel-opment, Robert Wuthnow found that 47 percent of his survey sample had a "high" or "medium high" likelihood of holding a theistic meaning system, which focuses on "God as the agent who constructs reality and makes life meaningful" (Wuthnow, 1976: 138). Wuthnow also determined that 36 percent had a "high" or "medium high" likelihood of subscribing to a meaning sys-tem based on individualism (141), the idea that "individuals themselves are primarily in charge of their own destinies" (139).

Thus, the twin pillars of Calvinism—an all-powerful God and individuals with free will—can hardly be said to have vanished from religion in America. But as Wuthnow notes, it is conceivable if not desirable that the rise of newer meaning systems may help revitalize some of the key elements in the American tradition: a growing awareness of the influence of social factors on present-day life, for example, may lead to the realization of Robert Bellah's hope that people become aware of their interdependence and mutual responsibility. Thus, the basic elements and functions of religion with which we began this chapter live on, but their forms change as our technology and the shape of our lives change.

SUMMARY

The basic elements of religion identified by Émile Durkheim, the first sociologist of religion, are the glorification of *sacred* beings or sacred things; the affirmation of deeply held beliefs through specific *rituals;* and a special community of worship. According to Durkheim, religion both promotes social solidarity and celebrates the common sentiments of a society. Religion and community are inseparable because religion sustains community.

Nothing is inherently sacred; it becomes sacred when a community designates it so. Gods, ghosts, spirits, moral principles, totems, and natural forces are examples of sacred "things" worshiped by different societies. These sacred things derive their meaning from the beliefs that sustain or underlie them. The beliefs, in turn, are expressed in rituals. Just as the forms of the sacred vary, so do the degree of belief in them and the level of ritual or communal involvement.

Religion serves a variety of functions for society and for the individual. For society, religion creates and reinforces a sense of community and consensus. It discourages antisocial behavior and offers a means for reintegrating transgressors. It serves to legitimize secular authority. In American society, which is made up of immigrants from many cultures, it serves to help people adapt to a new way of life.

For the individual, religion serves to reduce anxiety and uncertainty. It offers an explanation of and rules for life; it is a source of comfort in times of distress, particularly in coping with death. The universal milestones in each human life—birth, maturity, marriage, death—are also interpreted and celebrated by religion.

The interplay between religion and the society at large—the role of religion in social change—has been described in various ways in sociology. To Marx, religion was an essentially conservative institution that provided comfort for suffering but no impetus to relieve its causes. Religion inhibited social change by legitimizing the status quo. To Weber, religion was a primary shaper of capitalism and the social changes it induced. Both Protestant (particularly Calvinist) doctrines about economic activity and the *Protestant Ethic*—the values of hard work, individualism, and competition—were readily translated into capitalism.

The expression of religious beliefs is not limited to one particular form in any time or place. We are all familiar with the organized church, but there are also such forms as the sect, private or "invisible" religion, and civil religion. Ernst Troeltsch identified two polar forms of religious organization—church and sect. The *church* is universal and often allied with the status quo. Most people are born into a church, and it places few demands on them. Small and exclusive, the *sect* is composed primarily of converts. It controls members' lives and tends to be either indifferent or hostile to society. Thomas Luckmann has described and analyzed a form he calls *invisible* or *private religion,* which is characterized by individuals choosing for themselves the basic life issues with which they will be concerned and the ways in which they will deal with them. Robert Bellah believes that the United States has developed a *civil religion* with its own symbols, hymns, high priests, and martyrs, which binds together our pluralistic society.

We can see the interaction between social change and religion in such trends as *secularization,* the removal of sectors of society and culture from the domination of religious interpretations. People no longer see themselves or the world through the eyes of a particular religion. Change can also be seen within the major religious denominations in the United States. Among Protestants, there is division between clergy and laity over the purposes of the church; among Catholics, the most conspicuous issue is the pope's ban on artificial birth-control devices, which has led to a drastic decline in religious devotion and in the pope's credibility. Jews are concerned over declining belief and the weakening of communal ties as descendants of immigrants become thoroughly Americanized. Finally, change is reflected in contemporary religious trends, particularly the fundamentalist revival and the rise of mysticism. Young people predominate in the steady growth of revivalists, evangelists, and fundamentalists since the late 1960s. The rise of mysticism can be seen in the growth of such groups as the Hare Krishna movement and Sun Myung Moon's Unification Church, in which the emphasis is on engagement, community, and interdependence. Thus religion in America continues to perform its traditional functions, but in different forms and sometimes with different means.

GLOSSARY

alienation Marx's term for a condition in which humans mistakenly come to regard values and institutions of their own making as elements of an unchanging natural order.

church a large, conservative, universalist religious institution, which makes few demands on its members and accommodates itself to the culture of a society.

civil religion Bellah's term for a collection of religious beliefs, symbols, and rituals that exists outside the church and that pervades and helps legitimize a community.

invisible (private) religion a set of individual themes and experiences that many people substitute for the beliefs of organized religion.

mana a Melanesian term for a benign supernatural force that has no shape of its own but inhabits living or inanimate things.

moral community a group of people who share common beliefs and practices.

Pentecostalism an evangelical movement marked by belief in personal spiritual en-

counters and miraculous healing by prayer.

profane human experience that is ordinary and mundane (Durkheim).

Protestant ethic a phrase, originally used by Weber, which has come to mean dedication to hard work and the pursuit of profit.

religion a unified system of beliefs and practices that pertains to sacred things, and that unites adherents into a moral community (Durkheim).

ritual a specific practice through which sacred beings or things are glorified.

sacred human experience that is ideal and transcends everyday existence (Durkheim).

sect a small, exclusive, uncompromising fellowship that makes heavy demands on its members and sets them apart from the larger society.

secularization the process by which sectors of society and culture are removed from religious domination.

totem a sacred object, plant, or animal that is worshiped in a primitive religion.

REFERENCES

Robert N. Bellah, *Beyond Belief*. New York: Harper & Row, 1970.

———, *The Broken Covenant*. New York: Seabury Press, 1975.

———, "American Civil Religion in the 1970s." Unpublished paper given at Drew University, March 1973.

Peter Berger, *The Sacred Canopy*. New York: Doubleday, 1967.

Émile Durkheim, *The Elementary Forms of Religious Life* (1912), trans. Joseph Ward Swain. New York: Free Press, 1965.

Gallup Opinion Index, *Religion in America, 1976*. Report no. 130 (May 1976).

———, *Religion in America, 1977–1978*. Report no. 145 (August 1977).

Charles Y. Glock, "Consciousness Among Contemporary Youth," in Charles Y. Glock and Robert N. Bellah, eds., *The New Religious Consciousness*. Berkeley: University of California Press, 1976.

——— and Rodney Stark, *Religion and Society in Tension*. Chicago: Rand McNally, 1965.

Sidney Goldstein and Calvin Goldsheider, *Jewish Americans: Three Generations in a Jewish Community*. Englewood Cliffs, N.J.: Prentice-Hall, 1968.

Andrew M. Greeley, *The Denominational Society*. Glenview, Ill.: Scott, Foresman, 1972.

———, William McCready, and Kathleen McCourt, *Catholic Schools in a Declining Church*, new ed. Mission, Kan.: Sheed, Andrews & McMeel, 1975.

Jeffrey Hadden, *The Gathering Storm in the Churches: The Widening Gap Between Clergy and Laymen*. New York: Doubleday, 1969.

Michael Hill, *A Sociology of Religion*. London: Heinemann, 1973.

E. Adamson Hoebel, *Anthropology*, 4th ed. New York: McGraw-Hill, 1972.

J. Stillson Judah, *Hare Krishna and the Counterculture*. New York: Wiley, 1974.

Dean M. Kelley, *Why the Conservative Churches Are Growing: A Study in the Sociology of Religion*. New York: Harper & Row, 1972.

Gerhard Lenski, *The Religious Factor: A Sociological Study of Religion's Impact on Politics, Economics, and Family Life*. New York: Doubleday, 1961.

Thomas Luckmann, *The Invisible Religion*. New York: Macmillan, 1967.

Richard Machalek and Michael Martin, " 'Invisible' Religions: Some Preliminary Evidence." *Journal for the Scientific Study of Religion*, vol. 15 (December 1976): 311–321.

Bronislaw Malinowski, *Science, Magic and Religion*. New York: Anchor Books, 1954.

Karl Marx, *Selected Writings in Sociology and Social Philosophy* (1848), T. B. Bottomore and Maximilian Rubel, eds. Baltimore, Md.: Penguin, 1964.

Gretel H. and Pertti J. Pelto, *The Human Adventure*. New York: Macmillan, 1976.

A. R. Radcliffe-Brown, *The Andaman Islanders* (1922). New York: Free Press, 1964.

Berkeley Rice, "The Pull of Sun Moon." *The New York Times Magazine*, May 30, 1974, pp. 8ff.

Philip E. Slater, *The Pursuit of Loneliness*, rev. ed. Boston: Beacon Press, 1976.

Guy E. Swanson, *The Birth of the Gods*. Ann Arbor: University of Michigan Press, 1969.

Ernst Troeltsch, "Church and Sect," in Milton J. Yinger, ed., *Religion, Society, and the Individual: An Introduction to the Sociology of Religion*. New York: Macmillan, 1957.

Colin Turnbull, "The Mbuti Pygmies of the Congo," in J. L. Gibbs, Jr., ed., *People of Africa*. New York: Holt, Rinehart and Winston, 1965.

Max Weber, *The Protestant Ethic and the Spirit of Capitalism* (1920). London: Allen & Unwin, 1930.

Ronald C. Wimberley et al., "The Civil Religious Dimension: Is It There?" *Social Forces*, vol. 54 (June 1976): 890–900.

Robert Wuthnow, *The Consciousness Reformation*. Berkeley: University of California Press, 1976.

FOR FURTHER STUDY

The Priesthood.   One specific way to explore the changes taking place in religion in America is to examine what is happening to the Catholic priesthood. What is the social role of the priest today? What is his relation to the church, to the laity, to society? Some books that explore these questions are Andrew Greeley's *Uncertain Trumpet: The Priest in Modern America* (New York: Sheed and Ward, 1968), Charles E. Rice's *Authority and Rebellion* (Garden City, N.Y.: Doubleday, 1971), and David J. O'Brian's *The Renewal of American Catholicism* (New York: Oxford University Press, 1972). An important point of confrontation between the Catholic church and the secular world is over the issue of priestly celibacy. Richard A. Schoenherr and Andrew Greeley analyze the importance of kelibacy in commitment to or rejection of the priestly role in their article "Role Commitment Processes and the American Priesthood," *American Sociological Review,* vol. 39 (June 1974): 407–426.

Religion in Japan.   While the United States has the highest number of religious believers in the industrialized world, Japan has the lowest. To understand the differences, students may be interested in Kiyomi Morioka's *Religion in Changing Japanese Society* (Forest Grove, Ore.: International Scholarly Book Service, 1975) and in Edward Norbeck's *Changing Japan,* 2nd ed. (New York: Holt, Rinehart and Winston, 1976). Both of these works describe the cultural changes in modern Japan that have led to religious change. Another analysis of modern religion in Japan is Ted J. Solomon's "The Response of Three New Religions to the Crisis in the Japanese Value System," *Journal for the Scientific Study of Religion,* vol. 16 (March 1977): 1–14, which discusses the trends toward modernization in Japan since World War II and the attempts of new religions to combine such traditional values as nationalism and veneration for elders with the influences of industrial society. An interesting account of the transport of religion from Japan to the United States, primarily to the West Coast, may be found in *The Eagle and the Rising Sun: Americans and the New Religions of Japan* (Philadelphia, Pa.: Westminster, 1974) by Robert S. Ellwood, Jr.

Death.   In recent years there has been a renewed interest in death, particularly in finding what people in the Middle Ages called the "good death"—that is, when a person prepares for death by bringing together his or her family and friends and perhaps enemies, and by putting as much as possible in order before dying. Although not heavily laced with theology, this is certainly a religious movement of large proportions. To understand the meaning of death in American life, see Jessica Mitford's *The American Way of Death* (New York: Fawcett, 1969) and Elisabeth Kübler-Ross's classic *On Death and Dying* (New York: Macmillan, 1970). Diana Crane analyzes the decisions of doctors in the treatment of critically ill patients—decisions that often depend on such social factors as the roles a patient will be able to continue performing if he or she is kept alive—in *The Sanctity of Life* (New York: Russell Sage Foundation, 1975). A sociological study of how hospitals and their staffs "handle" terminal patients is David Sudnow's *Passing On* (Englewood Cliffs, N.J.: Prentice-Hall, 1967). In *The First Year of Bereavement* (New York: Wiley, 1974), Ira O. Glick and his co-authors examine the grief experiences of young widows and their adjustments to the deaths of their partners.

Changing Society

It has become almost a cliché to say that the world is undergoing rapid, drastic change at a rate unprecedented in human history. The goal of part six is to look beyond the cliché, to pinpoint the ways in which our society is changing and suggest why.

Chapter 16 introduces demography—the study of patterns of birth, death, and migration and their consequences, particularly for health. Has modern technology eliminated some health problems, only to create others? Chapter 17 considers the effects of urbanization on both our physical and social environments. Suburban sprawl and industrial pollution caught us unaware. Can we plan better for the future? Chapter 18 examines the effects of crowds and of sudden social change on individual behavior. Are social movements a break with the ordinary—exceptions to the rules of social behavior—or simply part of a continuous, ongoing process of social adjustment? Chapter 19 deals directly with social change, emphasizing the role technological innovation plays. There are a number of theories of social change. Each contributes something to our understanding of the past and our ability to predict and plan for the future.

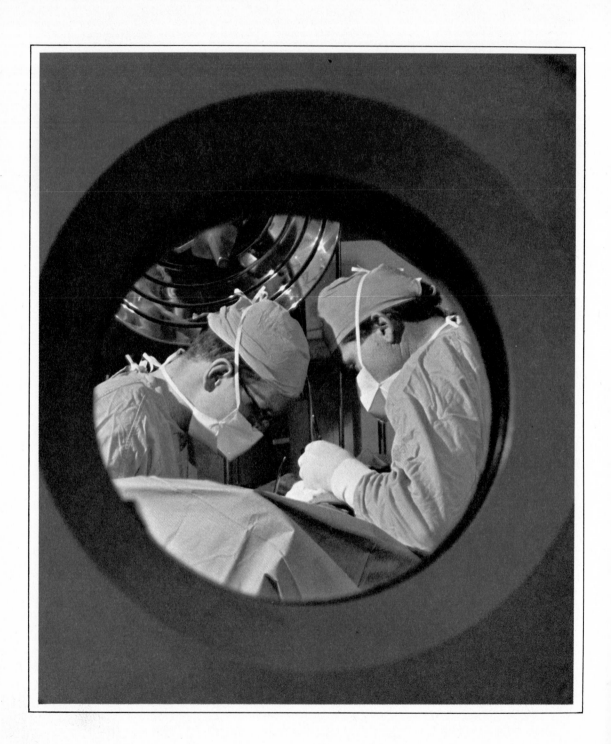

CHAPTER 16

Population and Health

The year of your birth has a definite impact on your life. Between World War II and 1958, America experienced a sudden increase in the number of babies born. Local governments struggled to keep pace with the demand for more teachers and classrooms. As the bumper crop of kids got older, they created a ''youth market'' in the 1970s that transformed industries like television, food processing, and tourism. Meanwhile, starting about 1960, birth rates began to drop. America went from a ''baby boom'' to a ''birth dearth.''

If you were born in 1960 or later, you will find life opening up before you. Schools are less crowded and better staffed and equipped than they were ten to fifteen years ago because there are fewer of you. It will be easier for you to get into college and graduate and professional schools; universities that in the 1960s turned away hundreds of qualified applicants every year are now advertising for students.

After you graduate from college, however, things may get rough. The postwar babies are now in their thirties. They are starting to fill the top positions in business, government, and the professions, establishing their seniority. You may get a good first job, but find the route to promotion blocked. You will be pushing against a solid population wall.

With fewer babies being born, our society as a whole is aging. According to government calculations, by the year 2000, 12 percent of the population will be over sixty-five. To keep pace, the manufacturer of Gerber baby foods is now producing a new line of single-serving products for the elderly. In September 1977, the House voted to extend the age for mandatory retirement from sixty-five to seventy. Delayed retirement for the elderly may mean delayed promotions for the young.

This chapter deals with *demography*, the study of such changes in population and their effects on society. After discussing the components of population growth, we will describe the world crisis in population and health. Turning to the United States, we will consider our own population projections and trends in the use of contraception and abortion. The final section will discuss another aspect of demography, the health of the population. We will focus on the diseases of the affluent and on problems relating to the distribution of health care.

STUDYING POPULATION

The study of population centers on three *demographic variables*: the birth rate, the death rate, and (*net migration*) the difference between immigration and emigration. Together, they not only produce increases or decreases in population but determine the very shape of society—the size of the labor force, the demand for food and shelter, the proportion of young and old people, the ethnic composition.

Demographers (those who study population) are concerned with the changes in the three demographic variables, with the causes of such changes, and with the consequences. They continually ask such questions as: Is the birth rate increasing? Did the baby boom after World War II occur because parents wanted larger families or were there simply more families with parents of childbearing age? As the crop of baby-boom adults grows old, will their predominance turn us into a nation of aged conservatives? To find answers, demographers rely upon information in government and community records, the census, and vital statistics.

Counting Population

In the periodic head count called the *census*, a mass of data about each citizen is collected: his or her sex, age, occupation, and much more. Compilations of *vital statistics*—computations done at frequent intervals of births and *immigration*, movement to a country for permanent settlement, deaths and *emigration*, movement out of a country to settlement in another—ensure that the census picture stays up to date.

According to our Constitution, the government must take a census every ten years to determine congressional representation and taxes. (Starting in 1985, the cycle is going to be shortened to five years.) Due to the use of computers, ours is one of the most complete and accurate censuses in the world. Yet in 1970, about 1.9 million blacks and 3.4 million whites were not counted, for a net undercount rate of 2.5 percent (U.S. Bureau of the Census, *User's Guide*, 1970: 5). More recently, researchers have estimated the black undercount to be 8 percent (Coale and Rives, 1973). This error means that federal allotments to cities may be less than they should be, depriving many people of needed services.

Modern societies could not do without the census. As societies become more complex, census data become more varied. So do the uses to which this information is put: to discover where and when new schools will be needed, to anticipate tax revenues, to figure out the potential market for a new soft drink (see the box). And demographers must rely upon the census for data about population growth or decline.

Population Growth

To determine population growth, demographers study the interaction of birth rates, death rates, and net migration. *Crude birth rate* represents the number of births per 1,000 people during a given year. In 1947, during the postwar baby boom, our crude birth rate soared to 27 per 1,000. At its low points—during the depression and in the mid-1970s—it plummeted to 14.7 per 1,000. Meanwhile, our *crude death rate* (deaths per 1,000 people during a given year) has fallen and remains well below the birth rate. In 1900, the death rate was about 17 per 1,000, in contrast to 8.9 per 1,000 in

THE CENSUS: A CONTINUOUS COUNT

A newly appointed parks and recreation director for a city of about 100,000 people was given the following assignment by the mayor: choose the location for a new playground to be built in a low-income area. At General Motors, a group of executives must decide how many cars to manufacture in a variety of sizes and price ranges. And at Whirlpool, managers wonder how many households will be buying washing machines in the years to come.

The source of information for each of these problems is the federal Bureau of the Census. From its surveys, the parks director can learn where in the city low-income families with children live, and the GM and Whirlpool planners can consult data on family size, income, and suburban versus urban living patterns.

But the most frequent user of census data is the government itself. How Americans are taxed, how legislatures are apportioned, and how revenue sharing is distributed are all determined with the help of information supplied by the bureau. To turn the data compiled by its census takers into usable form, the bureau employs 7,800 workers and spends much of the $100 million the government budgets annually for statistics.

The amount budgeted for statistics is used to cover considerably more than the cost of the national population count taken once each decade. Regular surveys reach over 50,000 homes a month, and the bureau monitors almost every aspect of the nation's social and economic health. Every five years, for example, "a census of retail, wholesale and service businesses tells how much the average American spends in the supermarkets; in gas stations, and in restaurants." And from the agriculture census, the government learns "how many bushels of soybeans and peanuts are harvested yearly, who runs the farms, where they are, and how they are financed."

The main focus of the bureau's work, however, is the population count. Their most difficult problem is accuracy of numbers. Because 7.7 percent of blacks were overlooked in the 1970 census, officials are trying to ensure that the 1980 census gives an accurate count of blacks and others who live in the nation's inner cities. Advisory committees of blacks and Spanish-speaking groups are attempting to educate minority groups about the advantages of cooperating with census takers. Because census information is used to determine congressional representation, to calculate how money should be divided up among over 100 federal programs, and to implement revenue sharing, underrepresentation means an undeniable loss of both power and money.

SOURCE: U.S. Department of Commerce, Bureau of the Census, *Case Study: The Location of a Playground*, Washington, D.C., U.S. Government Printing Office, 1976.; Robert Reinhold, "The Census, All Year Round," *The New York Times*, November 30, 1975, Section 4, p. 7.

1976 U.S. Bureau of the Census *(Statistical Abstract*, 1977: 26). Population growth reflects the excess of births over deaths (U.S. Bureau of the Census, *Current Population Reports*, 1977). In 1976, for example, America's crude birth rate was 14.3 and its crude death rate was 8.9, for a growth rate of 5.4 per 1,000. (Compare this with the high world growth rate of 18.)

But population growth also depends upon migration. The United States has traditionally attracted more people than it has lost.

figure 16:1   The key demographic variables

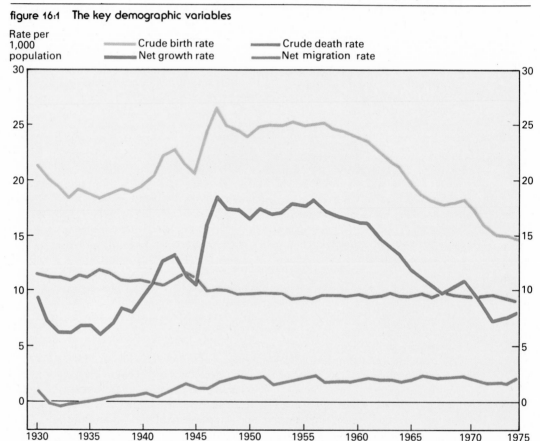

Rate per 1,000 population

Crude birth rate ······ Crude death rate ▬▬▬
Net growth rate ▬▬▬ Net migration rate ▬▬▬

SOURCE: U.S. Bureau of the Census, *Current Population Reports,* "Population Estimates and Projections," Series P-25, no. 632 (Washington, D.C.: U.S. Government Printing Office, 1976), figure 1.

$NGR = (CBR + NMR) - CDR$. *The* net growth rate *of a population can be expressed as the sum of its* crude birth rate *(number of births per 1,000 people in a given time span) and* net migration rate *(the difference between the number of immigrants and the number of emigrants) minus the* crude death rate *(number of deaths per 1,000 people in that time span). In the United States today, variations in the growth rate mirror changes in the birth rate. The death rate is relatively low and stable because many of the forces that carried off large numbers of people—such as influenza or widespread crop failures—have been tamed. While immigration now represents only a small component of American population growth, earlier in this century it played a much larger role.*

In demographic terms, immigration (or in-migration) to the United States has exceeded emigration (out-migration) from it, resulting in a net increase in population. The rate of population growth is the amount by which the crude birth rate and immigration together exceed the crude death rate and out-migration (see figure 16:1).

Birth Rate   A number of factors affect a nation's birth rate. From menarche (first menstruation) to menopause (the permanent cessation of menstruation), the average women's fertile period lasts about thirty years. But biological potential for reproduction, or *fecundity*, is only one aspect of a society's birth rate at a given time. No society has ever reached, or has even come near, its theoretical biological potential for reproduction. The *fertility rate* shows the number of children actually produced per 1,000 women between the ages of fifteen and forty-four.

The number of fertile women in a population at any one time will influence the birth rate, but won't determine it. Another factor that must be taken into account is the *sex ratio*, or the number of men per 100 women in a population. Twice during this century war has decimated the population of marriageable males in Germany and Russia, with a corresponding decrease in birth rates.

Because most children are born to married parents, the proportion of the population who are married also affects the birth rate. For example, during World War II many American couples put off getting married until the conflict was over; after the war when the proportion of married persons in the population rose significantly, so did the birth rate.

Birth control is yet another factor affecting the birth rate. Some societies control births by placing a taboo on intercourse while a mother is still nursing a child—sometimes for a period as long as three years. Other societies use abortion, sterilization, or infanticide to limit fecundity. Today most birth control consists of contraception.

How do these factors—fecundity, fertility, the sex ratio, the proportion of married couples, and birth control—combine to affect the birth rate? In one example, the postwar baby boom, Thomlinson (1976) divides the responsibility as follows: the larger number of women (24 percent), which increased fecundity (or birth potential) and the sex ratio; the larger proportion of women who married (30 percent); increased fertility due to the higher percentage of wives who bore children (34 percent); and the higher rate of births per mother (12 percent) (1976: 194).

These figures represent an intelligent guess, not a certainty. The causes and consequences of a country's birth rate remain elusive, especially when someone attempts to manipulate it. In 1966, for example, the Romanian government was worried that its population was shrinking. Cheap legal abortions were a major form of birth control, so in order to raise the birth rate, officials suddenly outlawed abortion. Unable to get abortions and lured by government incentives to have larger families, Romanian women had tripled the birth rate only eleven months after the law went into effect! Two years later, however, previous cultural patterns began to reassert themselves. Women found other means of limiting births, and the birth rate declined once more (Clark, 1973).

A statistic as important as crude birth rate and fertility rate is the net reproduction rate (NRR). This is an average of the number of female children born per woman of childbearing age—that is, the rate at which a woman replaces herself by producing a female child to bear children in the next generation. An NRR of 1.0 would indicate that, on the average, each woman produces one daughter.

Kingsley Davis coined the term *zero population growth* (ZPG) in the late 1960s to indicate a population that is stable, neither increasing nor decreasing in numbers. ZPG occurs in a population when the crude birth rate is equal to the crude death rate. An NRR of 1.0 may eventually bring about ZPG. However, even if an NRR of 1.0 is reached, it will take several decades to achieve constant population in the United States because of the large number of women of childbearing age and because of the age composition of the population as a whole (Davis, 1973).

Death Rate and Life Expectancy *Life span*, the maximum number of years a human being can possibly live, hasn't changed substantially over the centuries. But *life expectancy*, the average number of years of life remaining for an individual of a given age, has increased dramatically in the last seventy-five years or so. An infant born in 1920 had a life expectancy of 54.1 years; by 1976, the life expectancy at birth was 71.9 years (see table 16:1).[1]

The crude death rate does not fully explain the reasons for the change in life expectancy; age-specific mortality rates are more revealing. The *infant mortality rate*, or deaths per 1,000 children one year of age or younger in a year, shows clearly that most of the gain in life expectancy has come because of fewer infant deaths. The crude death rate dropped slightly between 1935 and 1976, from 10.9 to 8.9 deaths per 1,000. But the infant mortality rate dropped dramatically from 55.7 to 15.1 per 1,000 (U.S. Bureau of the Census, *Statistical Abstract*, 1977: 55).

The chances of dying in the first year of life

table 16:1 LIFE EXPECTANCY AND AGE-SPECIFIC MORTALITY RATES, 1975

AGE	LIFE EXPECTANCY[1]	MORTALITY RATE
Under 1	72.5	16.06
5	68.9	.44
10	64.0	.25
15	59.1	.75
20	54.4	1.30
25	49.8	1.38
30	45.1	1.40
35	40.4	1.78
40	35.8	2.68
45	31.4	4.25
50	27.1	6.57
55	23.1	10.02
60	19.6	15.56
65	16.0	21.95
70	12.8	33.21

[1]Note that the longer a person survives, the greater the total number of years he or she can expect to live. Thus, if a person lives to sixty, he or she can look forward to living to seventy-eight, whereas an infant can expect to live only seventy years.

SOURCE: U.S. Bureau of the Census, *Statistical Abstract of the United States, 1977* (Washington, D.C.: U.S. Government Printing Office, 1977), table 96, p. 66.

are still quite high. Age-specific tables show that after the first year the mortality rate drops quite sharply until the later years of life. An infant under one year is now about as likely to die as a person in his early sixties.

A Close Look at Immigration Since the discovery of the New World, one of Europe's big exports has been people; 45 million of them to North America, 20 million to Latin America, 10 million to Australia and South Africa combined. This movement of people from one country to another is called *international migration*.

Why do people migrate? William Petersen (1975) suggests four basic reasons: (1) in-

---

[1] The figures can be broken down to show differences in life expectancy by sex and race. In 1975, for example, a man could expect to live 68.7 years; a woman, 76.5. Life expectancy for the white population was 73.2 years; for all others it was 67.9 years (Rice, 1977: 3).

ability to cope with natural forces; (2) government action; (3) the desire for novelty or improvement; and once migration starts, (4) group momentum. All four brought people to this country. The potato famine of the 1840s—a natural force—started a wave of Irish immigration. Political action (genocide) sent Jews to this country during World War II. The desire for economic betterment attracted immigrants from southern and eastern Europe in the 1880s. Word of their relative success filtered back to their native lands, creating a social momentum that brought an influx of 6 million of their countrymen by 1910.

Immigration patterns may have an immense impact on a country. Israel, for example, became a homeland for many European Jews after World War II. From 1948 to 1951, the period immediately after the establishment of Israel, the new country grew by 24 percent a year. Ninety percent of this growth was due to immigration! For some years after 1952, the growth rate slowed to 3 percent, of which half was still due to immigration. By 1970, fewer than half the Jews in Israel were native-born, or sabras (a name derived from that of a native desert plant); 28 percent were of European and 26 percent of Afro-Asian origin (Friedlander and Sabatello, 1972).

The United States, too, is a nation of immigrants—including some 10 to 20 million slaves who came against their will. Between 1820 and 1975, more than 46 million people came to the United States. People left the country, too—a comparative trickle in most years, though during the depression more people left the United States than came here for the first and only time. Until the 1920s, immigration was almost unrestricted; the United States welcomed newcomers to help settle and industrialize the nation. During the 1920s, however, laws were passed setting limits on the number of immigrants, espe-

cially those from non-European countries. Objections to the discriminatory aspects of this immigration policy led to its modification in the Immigration Act of 1965. Each year nearly 400,000 people enter the United States legally. Illegal immigration also takes place: in 1977 alone, over 1 million illegal aliens were apprehended at the time they entered the country (Bureau of Immigration, 1978; *Intercom,* 1977). The Population Reference Bureau (*Intercom,* 1977) estimates that there are 6 to 12 million illegal aliens now living and working in the United States.

Internal Migration Movement within a country, or *internal migration*, can have as much impact on a society as movement in or out of that country. Americans have always been

Migration frequently occurs within the borders of the United States. Florida attracts so many of the nation's elderly that they form a distinct subculture there. Many retirees have settled into the leisurely lifestyle offered by the state. (Sylvia Johnson / Woodfin Camp & Assoc.)

IN THE NEWS

Blacks Move South Again

Cristy Brown quit a well-paying job as a television news artist in Baltimore to move to Miami—a part of what she considers the land of opportunity....

For the first time since the Civil War, more blacks are moving South and fewer are leaving for the North, according to a U.S. Census Bureau report on black migration trends.

The figures themselves are startling. From 1955–60, 394,000 blacks left the South and only 117,000 moved back from the North. That figure turned around drastically between 1970 and 1975—only 288,000 blacks left the South but 302,000 moved back from the North.

More and more blacks are looking to the South as the land of opportunity. This striking reversal of trends can mainly be attributed to the availability of jobs and professional opportunities, which are decreasing in the North. Career opportunities, less discrimination, a better quality of life—these are the characteristics of the South luring blacks now, the same characteristics that produced the black migration to the North after World War I.

In the 1970s, a big construction boom began in the South. At the same time, businesses began to expand and relocate into the South, lured by the lack of unions, low taxes, and cheap labor. All of this came on the heels of legislation abolishing job discrimination due to color, and blacks have taken advantage of the changes. When federal legislation made it mandatory that government agencies and some private industries hire members of minority groups, there was suddenly an abundance of jobs for professional and semiprofessional blacks. Blacks began to consider where they wanted to relocate, and most of them returned to the state of their birth (or the state of their parents' birth).

a people on the move. In 1790, the colonial population was concentrated in the narrow strip of land along the coast of the Atlantic. Then people began to move west, toward the Pacific. By 1850, a quarter of the nation's population lived in the Northwest Territory (a region north of the Ohio River, between Pennsylvania and the Mississippi); by 1900, a third lived in even newer territories. This westward migration continues. The Sunbelt states (California, Florida, and the South) are experiencing the highest growth rates in America today. A combination of good climate and readily available space and resources has drawn new and relocating businesses to those states. Not only economic but also political power has shifted from traditional centers in the Northeast to the Sunbelt. Of the last four presidents, three (Johnson, Nixon, and Carter) were from the South or West.

During the nineteenth century another trend emerged: the migration from rural to urban areas. Industrialization, which began in earnest after the Civil War, had a push-pull effect. The mechanization of agriculture

Tony and Beatrice Crapp, both 24, liked the idea of raising their two sons near their Miami grandparents—and where the boys could attend Mount Zion Baptist Church, which Tony attended as a youth.

"I like the old people in church," said Beatrice. "They're all like family."

"Like grandmothers, aunts and uncles," adds Tony. "That's the kind of feeling I have there."

The Crapps also were glad to leave the North for another reason—problems with discrimination and desegregation in the North that were faced, though not necessarily solved, years before in the South.

The Crapps saw racial problems developing in the desegregation of South Boston schools, when Tony studied at Harvard.

Bea described the atmosphere as "blatant and overt tension. . . . We don't want to raise them any place there's tension."

Along with the new jobs, cleaner air, and less discrimination comes a substantial cut in salaries. But this has not posed much of a problem because the cost of living is so much less, and taxes are lower.

Right now middle-class blacks are the ones reaping the benefits of these new jobs, which usually require highly educated workers. Sociologist Alvin Rose questions whether employment gains for blacks in the South may be temporary. "As soon as the quotas are reached, opportunities will be no better [for blacks]," he feels. "Maybe worse than for whites."

SOURCE: Gayle Pollard, "Jobs Lure Blacks Home to South," *Miami Herald*, April 16, 1977, pp. 1, 6.

pushed farm workers out of rural areas; factories and the demand for industrial labor pulled them to the city. In 1900, 60 percent of the population lived on farms; today, only 25 percent live in rural areas (towns of 2,500 or less) (Taeuber, 1977).

However, many cities in the Northeast and the Midwest are losing population to adjacent suburbs. Demographers first noted this trend during the 1940s. The fact that this movement seemed to coincide with an influx of rural blacks from the South leads some demographers to describe the phenomenon as "white flight." Whether or not such a correlation exists, black Americans are becoming urbanized. In 1900, 90 percent of black Americans lived in the rural South. Today, 58.5 percent live in big cities (compared with 28.2 percent of white Americans). But not all blacks live in big Northern cities; new growth in the Sunbelt is drawing middle-class blacks back (see the box). Although blacks constitute only 11 percent of the total population, our big cities are about one-quarter black. Far more significant than racial composition per se is the concentration of the disadvantaged in our decaying inner cities (Taeuber, 1977).

Another movement away from the cities began in 1970: not only are people moving out of cities into nearby suburbs, but they are moving to distinctly remote rural areas. Two-thirds of all *non*metropolitan counties, which for years registered losses in net migration, are now showing gains (more people moving in than moving out) (Population Reference Bureau, *Population Bulletin*, 1976).

THE POPULATION EXPLOSION

Terms such as ''population explosion'' have become frighteningly familiar in recent years. One of the first people to sound a warning about population growth was a gentleman-scholar named Thomas Robert Malthus (1766–1834). In 1798, his theories appeared in ''An Essay on the Principle of Population, or A View of Its Past and Present Effects on Human Happiness, with An Inquiry into Our Prospects Respecting the Future Removal or Mitigation of the Evils Which It Occasions.'' He stated simply that people require food, and people will continue to have children. Population, he maintained, increases in a geometric progression (2, 4, 8, 16), while food supplies increase only arithmetically (2, 3, 4, 5). No population can continue to grow indefinitely, because people will simply run out of food. Increase the standard of living and reduce the number of deaths, and the population will simply increase, thereby wiping out whatever gains have been made. The standard of living will fall and mortality will again rise.

To Malthus, the only solution to the problem was to marry late and have fewer children (he did not approve of birth control or abortion). Otherwise, population growth would inevitably be checked by drastic means: starvation, pestilence, or war.

As Malthus predicted, when the death rate declines and fertility remains high, the population grows very quickly. From 1650 to 1850, world population doubled, going from 500 million people to 1 billion. But it took only eighty years—from 1850 to 1930—for the population to double again. In 1976, world population was increasing at about 1.8 percent a year and doubling every thirty-five years (U.S. Bureau of the Census, *Statistical Abstract*, 1977: 6, 7). Just like interest in a savings account, population increases by compounding. The total number of people on earth is now estimated at over 4 billion (Population Reference Bureau, *World Population Data Sheet*, 1976).

Is human population reaching the limits of growth predicted by Malthus? (See chapter 17 for more discussion of this question.) Some demographers are haunted by the Malthusian specter of starvation, plague, and war. Others believe that humanity may be able to avert such a disaster. Some evidence suggests that we can achieve a population with low mortality and fertility, or even zero population growth. In fact, industrialized countries have gone through the demographic transition, which has brought their rapid rate of population growth down, and world population growth as a whole now shows signs of declining.

The Demographic Transition

The term *demographic transition* describes four stages of the population dynamics in Europe and America during the last two centuries. Initially, there was a high, steady birth rate and a high death rate, which peaked during famines and epidemics. Then, during the second phase, the death rate gradually declined. This decline was due less to medical advances than to sanitary water and sewage systems, soaps and disinfectants, better and faster ways of shipping foods, and more productive farming techniques. Because the birth rates remained high, the rapid population growth Malthus had predicted began. In the third phase, the birth rate slowly declined as people realized they needed to bear fewer children in order for the same number to survive into adulthood. Nevertheless, the widening gap between the two rates meant that population continued to grow faster than at any time in human history. Toward the end of this phase, the death rate leveled out.

Today the industrialized nations are in the fourth and final phase, with a low, steady death rate and a low but fluctuating birth rate. Population growth in these countries is no longer so explosive.

In the developing nations, death rates have been dropping more rapidly than they did during the demographic transition in the West. In just five years, from 1945 to 1950, the average drop in the rate of these nations has been a staggering 24 percent. The words of a Calcutta man reveal the radical change:

"When I was a boy, they took away forty or fifty bodies after a cholera epidemic. It happened every five or ten years. Now they

figure 16:2   The demographic transition

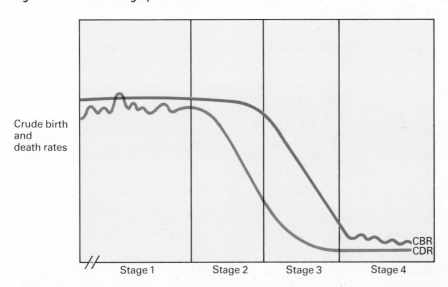

Crude birth and death rates

Stage 1　　Stage 2　　Stage 3　　Stage 4

CBR
CDR

This schematic graph shows the differences in behavior of birth rates and death rates during the demographic transition in the industrialized nations. The gap between births and deaths in stages 2 and 3 produced rapid population growth. Today, the gap has narrowed, although jumps in the birth rate may produce spurts of population growth, as in our postwar baby boom. Even though its population is not growing as fast as that of the developing nations, the industrialized world still must be concerned with population growth because of the heavier demands its people place upon the environment. The United States, for example, has one-sixteenth of the world's population but consumes over one-third of the world's resources.

come and vaccinate our children. I have lived here almost seventy years. The biggest change in my time has been health. We've learned how to keep from dying.'' (Thomlinson, 1976: 29)

United Nations and government agencies contribute to these rapidly falling death rates by providing sanitation and preventive medicine and by implementing public-health measures.

In developing nations such as India, the decline in the death rate—due largely to improved sanitation and public health programs—has led to tremendous increases in population growth. There are signs, however, that the demographic transition toward a lower birth rate and a stabilized population may bring the population problem under control. (François Lochon / Gamma / Liaison)

With death rates—especially infant mortality—lower, population grows at an astounding rate. For example, the annual growth rate in Indonesia was 2.1 percent in 1975 (compared to 0.6 percent in the United States). At this rate, the population would double in thirty-three years. Indonesian officials attribute this boom almost entirely to improved health conditions (Simons, 1977).

But although the problem of overpopulation is pressing, there are signs that it may become less so. In the last decade, according to the Population Council, the crude birth rate has begun to drop significantly in the developing countries, the areas where it has been the highest. For all of Asia, for example, there was a drop of 17 percent from 1965 to 1975, contrasted with only a 2 percent decline during the preceding fifteen years. The rate of world population growth, which was the subject of so many gloomy predictions in the 1960s, seems to have peaked and may

stabilize sooner than had been expected. Of course, population will still continue to grow during this century and much of the next, but there is at least a chance that it may come under control (Population Council, 1978).

Why Birth Rates Are High Three main variables seem to control fertility in the developing nations: social values governing marriage, number of children, and contraception; the resulting age structure of the population; and the lack of economic development that might make lower birth rates both possible and more advantageous. These combine to produce the Malthusian nightmare of runaway population.

Marriage in developing nations is universal—and early. Take Africa and Asia, for example. Here, the average woman marries before she is twenty. And most women want children. In one study, nearly half of the rural Moroccan women questioned desired more children than they already had. On the average, they wanted 4.6 children. In order to ensure that at least four or five children survive, a woman might have to bear eight or nine. Moroccan values clearly favor fertility, not contraception (Latham, 1970).

To Westerners, it may seem totally irrational for people who are poor and struggling to have so many children. However, from the point of view of the individual family in Indonesia or Mexico or Nigeria, having as many children as possible may be the only hope of improving their standard of living. In developing nations, families work together. "All but the very young and the very old make some productive contribution to the economy of the household" (Mamdani, 1972: 129). Thus, the more children a couple have, the better their chances are. In addition, children are a couple's only source of economic security in old age; a childless couple is condemned to living on handouts.

A large family also provides physical security in the absence of police or other forms of organized law enforcement (Mamdani, 1972: 133). Some experts argue that reducing childhood mortality through child-health programs would eliminate an important incentive for large families.

The Burdens of High Birth Rates

The high birth rates that result from such social values produce a large population of young people, which leads to a large *dependency ratio*, or proportion of people of nonproductive age (under fifteen or over sixty-five) in the total population. In Mauritius, 47 percent of the people are in the dependent age group; therefore the dependency ratio is 47. Developed countries have very different ratios. Japan's, for example, is only 39.

This large population of young people means a continuing cycle of high fertility, as they have their own babies. We have seen the effects of our limited postwar baby boom—but imagine what would happen if the boom were continuous!

Lack of economic development also contributes to the high birth rate. Some experts point out that economic development helped the Western nations bring down their birth rates by making it advantageous to have fewer children, and that such development could do the same for the developing nations. No longer would parents need a huge brood to ensure that enough offspring survive to support them in their old age, for example. Ironically, however, one of the greatest obstacles to economic development is overpopulation itself.

Overpopulation and Economic Development Increased population is quite likely to eat up any economic gains a nation makes, but there are other aspects to the problem.

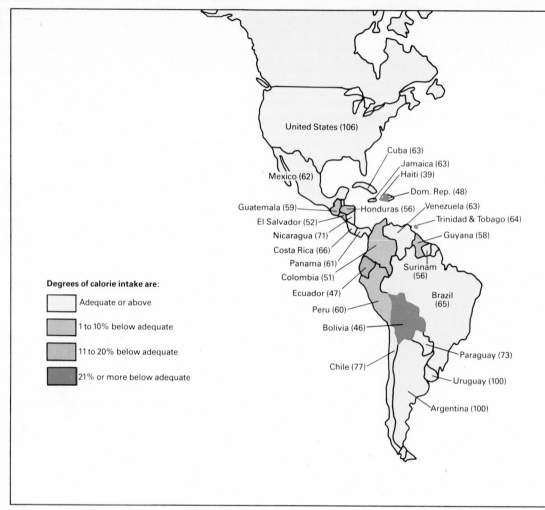

figure 16:3   The geography of hunger

SOURCE: Figure from Boyce Rensberger, "Experts Ask Action to Avoid Millions of Deaths in Food Crisis," *The New York Times*, July 26, 1974, p. 35. Data in caption from Emma Roths-child, "The Politics of Food," *The New York Review of Books*, May 16, 1974, pp. 16–17.

Based on 1974 data from the Food and Agricultural Organization of the U.N.

Two kinds of food deficiency are represented on the map. Shading denotes adequacy of calorie, or food energy, consumption while numbers in parentheses denote daily per capita consumption of protein in grams. Protein quality varies. Thus, some experts consider the adequate protein level to vary from 40 to 60 grams.

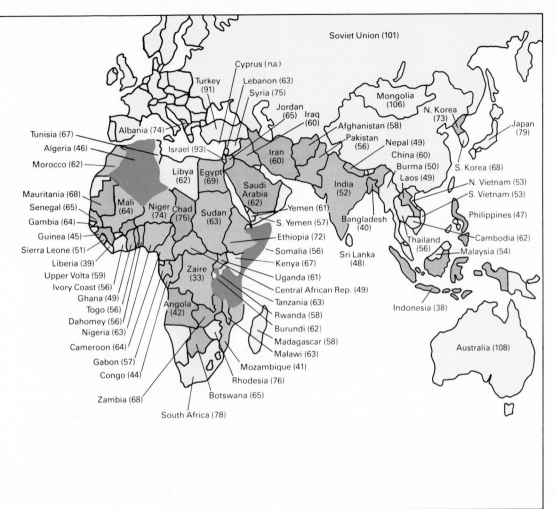

When population grows, the number of jobs must grow, too, or there will be greater unemployment or underemployment.

Economists estimate that investment in machinery, factories, and so forth must increase annually at a rate two or three times greater than the increase in the labor force if *per capita income* (the income available to each citizen if the total income of the country were divided equally) is not to fall. A work force increasing at a rate of 3 percent annually would thus require an increase in capital investment of from 6 to 9 percent just to maintain productivity. Furthermore, a work force needs training and education, and providing this requires another large investment. Where can this much capital come from in those countries just beginning to develop more than a subsistence economy? The land base and income levels are so low that taxing the citizens would accomplish little. Thus, overpopulation and slow economic growth form a vicious circle.

Overpopulation and Hunger These abstract figures on economic development can be translated into something more elemental:

the lack of enough food to provide sufficient calories (undernourishment) or sufficient nutrients (malnutrition). A study conducted by the Food and Agriculture Organization of the United Nations in 1974 estimates that at least 400 million people are undernourished. The number of people suffering from protein malnutrition is much higher. Most of the malnourished people—over 300 million—live in eastern and southern Asia. It has been estimated that half of all young children in developing nations have inadequate diets. In some Latin American countries, nutritional deficiencies are responsible for more than half of all the deaths of children under five years old (Moulik, 1977: 10–11). In the United States, a Public Health survey uncovered 10 to 15 million chronically hungry Americans, a large proportion of them children. Another 10 to 15 million had such low incomes that malnutrition was inevitable (Ehrlich and Ehrlich, 1972: 94). In other words, from 20 to 30 million Americans suffer from nutritional problems like those of people living in developing countries.

Why should malnutrition and undernourishment be so widespread? There have always been famines; they are disastrous, but temporary and limited in extent. Famine is not a primary cause of the world's food problems. Distribution is. According to food economist C. Peter Timmer, we produce enough food now to provide every member of the human race with 65 grams of protein and 3,000 calories every day. Moreover, food production increased at a rate of about 2.8 percent per year throughout the 1950s and 1960s (Cochrane, 1969: 66)—just ahead of population growth. "But hunger and malnutrition afflict . . . people, because of the mechanisms for determining access to food. Distribution, not production, is the key" (Timmer, in Rensberger, 1976).

A look at Brazil suggests why the world food gap is widening. A decade ago, experts

predicted that Brazil would steadily develop itself out of its "poor country" status, but it has not. While the population of Brazil increased 20 to 30 percent, food production remained at a standstill. The main reason is that Brazil has massive foreign debts. One way to pay these off is to grow cash crops for export. The land now being used to pro-

It has been estimated that one half of all young children in developing nations have inadequate diets. This West African child is a victim of a famine brought on by a severe drought. However, the effects of such disasters are limited and temporary; most malnutrition results from uneven distribution of available foods. (J. M. Bertrand / Black Star)

duce 10 million tons of soybeans for Japan each year once produced food for Brazilians (Rensberger, 1976).

Like Brazil, most developing nations export soybeans, fish-meal products, and the like (high-protein foods that might raise their standard of nutrition) to the developed nations, who feed them to livestock. Rich, meat-eating nations consume more than their share of protein. And the developing nations end up having to depend on the United States and other industrialized food-producing nations for the grain imports necessary to survival. In fact, in the not-too-distant future the United States may find itself in the uncomfortable position of having to decide who in the world will eat and who will not (*The New York Times*, December 7, 1975, Section 4, p. 2).

People in the developing nations are hungry for more than food. Even in the remotest village, modern forms of communication are awakening people everywhere to an important fact: other people live better. Other people have cars, hospitals, bicycles, and plenty of food. Aware of such things, the poor have learned to want and even to expect them. Cochrane sees 1948 as the turning point in a "revolution of expectations" (1969: 3). Armed with new wants, the have-nots may create social unrest as they struggle to catch up with their more affluent neighbors. The question remains: What is to be done?

Bringing the Birth Rate Down

To attack the problem directly, many countries attempt to use family planning programs as a means of persuading citizens to limit their families. The experience of Costa Rica reveals just how complicated it can be to stem the tide of births. This Central American nation was a classic example of population gone wild. Before 1950, the birth rate was 45 per 1,000 and the death rate slightly over 15 per 1,000. This meant a net increase in population of 3 percent annually, or a doubling every twenty-three years. The 1950s brought economic and social development, including better health standards. These helped reduce the death rate to 10 but also increased the birth rate to 50, a net rate of growth of 4 percent, or a doubling of the population every seventeen years! (To determine the time it takes for populations—or your savings account—to double, divide the percent into sixty-nine.)

Then cultural values and family practices started to change, and the birth rate began to decline. In 1967, Costa Rica started a family planning program. The program worked, but in large part because it was started *after* values supporting small families had taken hold. The birth rate declined 28 percent in the 1960s.

Nevertheless, Costa Rica's problems continue. The economy faces the task of absorbing young adults born during the period of high fertility. Since these young people will have families of their own—even if they limit births—the decline in birth rates will be less rapid during the next decade. A work force of 534,000 in 1970 will expand to nearly twice that by 1985. It will be a long time before zero population growth comes to Costa Rica (Sanders, 1973).

As we have seen from this example, the key to lowered fertility is motivation, shaped by social values. If fertility is to decline, three conditions must be found together. First, the community and the individual must accept the idea of smaller families. And once men and women have decided that having fewer children gives them certain economic and social advantages, they must be able to find effective means of birth control. Birth control, then, must be acceptable, advantageous, and available (Coale, 1973: 65).

This billboard in Calcutta, India, is representative of family planning campaigns that have been instituted in many countries. Such programs aim to reduce the motivation to have large families by making birth control available and also socially acceptable. (Santosh Basak/Gamma/Liaison)

2000, about 80 million more than in 1970 (U.S. Bureau of the Census, *Statistical Abstract*, 1977: 6–7). More people call for more food, more energy, and more resources— and create more pollution. If we want to continue to enjoy our comfortable way of life, then some feel we had best halt population growth.

POPULATION GROWTH IN AMERICA

The developing nations may outstrip us in population growth, but we will still have about 283 million Americans by the year

Contraception

Americans now use more effective contraceptive devices than ever before. About three out of every four married couples using contraception in 1975 favored the most ef-

figure 16:4 Projections of U.S. population from 1975 to 2025, assuming 2.7 children, 2.1 children, and 1.7 children per woman

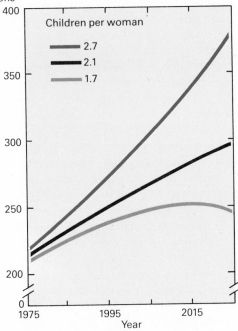

Population, in millions

Children per woman
— 2.7
— 2.1
— 1.7

Year

SOURCE: U.S. Bureau of the Census, *Current Population Reports*, "Projections of the Population of the United States, by Age and Sex, 1975 to 2000, with Extensions of Total Population to 2025 (Advance Report)," Series P-25, no. 541. (Washington, D.C.: U.S. Government Printing Office, 1975), p. 1.

fective methods—the pill, the IUD, and sterilization. Use of these methods increased from 38 percent in 1965 to 74 percent in 1975 (Westoff and Jones, 1977). Catholics, despite religious prohibitions, are using birth control much the way their compatriots are (see the chart on p. 475).

Although the pill is the most popular method of birth control, there is increasing concern about possible side effects, and its use appears to have stabilized, while the popularity of sterilization has increased substantially. Whereas the pill is still the favorite method of contraception for young people, sterilization is the most popular method for couples who have been married for ten years or longer. Westoff and Jones feel that this increase in the use of sterilization as a form of contraception is an indication that "couples are more willing to accept [the] irreversibility of the decision to terminate childbearing" (1977: 155).

Abortion

Until the past few years abortion was illegal in the United States. However, in 1973 the Supreme Court ruled (in *Roe* v. *Wade*) that abortion during the first twenty-four weeks of pregnancy was a private matter between a woman and her physician; state statutes could not interfere with it.

The Court's ruling seemed to reflect public opinion. A substantial majority of people approve of abortion if the mother's health is in danger, if she has been raped, or if her child is likely to be born deformed. About 50 percent approve of the procedure if the woman is unmarried (and doesn't want to marry), if a family can't afford more children, or if the woman doesn't want more children. In general, education goes hand in hand with approval of abortion. People with more than a high school education are most likely to approve of abortion under various circumstances. Race and religion influence attitudes, too: more white non-Catholics than nonwhites or white Catholics approve of abortion (Evers and McGee, 1977).

However, those who oppose abortion (on the grounds that a fetus is a potential person with a right to protection by the state) maintain a powerful lobby. In 1977, tempering its original decision, the Supreme Court ruled that states don't have to provide public funds for "nontherapeutic" abortions (that is to say, abortions in which the mother's life is not endangered by pregnancy). Reaction to this ruling was swift. Critics pointed out that the decision discriminates against the poor, who once again may face a choice between unwanted babies and unsafe illegal abortions. The New York Civil Liberties Union argued that "exactly when a human life begins is a theological decision," and that the Court's ruling violated the principle of the separation of church and state (NYCLU memorandum, 1977).

How many states will decide to deny funds to poor women who want abortions, and how this will affect the birth rate, remain to be seen. After abortion first became legal, the birth rate dropped sharply, but only half of this drop was a result of abortions (Tietze, 1973). The rest was due to new attitudes. Like every other country with legal abortion, the United States has found that abortion reduces unwanted babies, a burden not only to families but to society. Legal abortions also improve maternal health by replacing hasty, often dangerous backroom procedures with sanitary, medically supervised ones.

The Birth Dearth: Will It Last?

After running its course, the postwar baby boom was followed by a baby bust. After the boom peaked in 1958, the crude birth rate fell steadily throughout the 1960s and into the 1970s. Our birth rate reached a low of 14.7 per 1,000 in 1976. If this decline continues, we can achieve zero population growth much faster than people even five years ago had hoped.

But population growth may not be over yet. As the boom generation moves into its own childbearing years, an echo boom is expected to take place. To some extent the recent decline occurred because the women bearing children were part of the unusually small group of depression babies. In 1965, there were just a few more women of prime childbearing years than there were in 1935 (11.1 million as compared to 11 million), although the total population had grown by over 50 million people during those years. But this age group has been growing steadily, to more than 16 million in 1976 (U.S. Bureau of the Census, *Current Population Reports*, 1977: 19).

Thus, the current low rate of births may still result in large crops of babies because there are so many more mothers. Will twice as many mothers mean twice as many children? Probably not, according to most indicators. Young women today are having their children later. Furthermore, they are planning to have smaller families. Women now in their late thirties have, on the average, 3 children; but in 1975, married women aged eighteen to twenty-four expected to have an average of 2.2 children per family, though experience shows that families usually end up larger than people expect them to be (U.S. Bureau of the Census, *Population Characteristics*, 1976). According to Charles F. Westoff (1976), 29 percent of all births between 1966 and 1970 were wanted but unplanned (usually mothers wanted another child but not just yet), and 14 percent were both unwanted and unplanned.

In late 1972, births fell below *replacement level* (the point at which a population replaces itself but doesn't grow) for the first time. Optimists hailed this as zero population growth. One called the day of the announcement ''a milestone . . . a day as historic as the Fourth of July, the birth date of any President, or the termination date of any war'' (Kahn, 1974). But had we really achieved a constant population? On the contrary. Even if we hold to replacement-level fertility—a big if—it will still take from sixty-five to seventy-five years for population growth to end, because of the age structure of the population.

HEALTH IN AMERICA

In the last twenty to thirty years, modern medicine has virtually eliminated a host of dangerous diseases: smallpox, polio, rubella (German measles), tetanus, diphtheria, and even mumps and measles. By and large, Americans avoid the most common causes of death in developing nations: infections, parasites, and nutritional deficiency (Twaddle and Hessler, 1977: 70). But we have our own way of dying. In a sense, Americans *choose* to die: many of our health problems result from the way we spend our money, on the ''good life.''

The Diseases of Affluence

Americans like nothing better than rich, red, juicy steaks. If we don't have meat at least once a day we feel deprived. We consider a cholesterol-rich breakfast of fried eggs, bacon, and buttered toast ideal. It is no coincidence that the most common cause of death in America is heart attacks.

Cancer is the second leading cause of death in America, and seems to be on the rise. The major causes of our growing cancer rate seem to be environmental—exposure to radioactivity, bad diet, and especially smoking. There is no doubt that cigarettes cause cancer. In the fifteen years since the Surgeon General of the Public Health Service officially reported on the hazards of smoking cigarettes, about 29 million people have quit. Still, about 52 million Americans smoke, including a large number of young people (3,000 teen-agers begin smoking every day) (Brody, 1974). For some, smoking cigarettes is a habit, something done unthinkingly; for others, it is a psychological addiction. Smokers feel they need cigarettes to relax or to perk up. Sociological factors (such as pressure at work, or, among the young, pressure from peers) also help to explain smoking.

Americans are now smoking new types of cigarettes, with less tar and nicotine—the substances considered harmful. Nevertheless, the Public Health Service estimates that 300,000 people die annually as a direct result of complications from smoking, such as lung cancer and heart disease. Smokers miss 40 percent more working days than nonsmokers do, visit doctors more often, spend more time in hospitals, and require surgery more often (Brody, 1974: 1, 8).

Americans apparently like drugs. In 1976, we spent about $1.5 billion on prescriptions alone (IMS Research Group, 1977). To that must be added the incalculable cost of the grass, cocaine, and heroin consumed by members of the so-called drug culture, and of the over-the-counter drugs (including alcohol) used to relieve tension, insomnia, headaches, depression, and the like. Legal and illegal drugs are not only the direct or indirect cause of many deaths. More important, drugs are a symptom of our fast-paced, stress-inducing way of life and a contributor to our third major cause of death—strokes.

Finally, fatal accidents are far more common in rich countries than in poor ones. Quite simply, developing nations don't have the number of cars and high-powered machines we have. Accidents are the fourth leading cause of death in America.

Health of the Disadvantaged

Of course not all Americans have equal access to the means of preventing and treating the diseases of our affluent society. Disadvantaged Americans don't enjoy the same standard of medical care as other citizens do. And for this reason, we are among the least healthy of the affluent nations.

The American people have the highest incomes in the world, and they spend more than anyone else on health care, nearly 8.6 percent of the Gross National Product (U.S. Bureau of the Census, *Statistical Abstract*, 1977: 94). Nevertheless, the crude death rate and the infant mortality rate are higher in the United States than in a number of other developed nations. Socioeconomic factors help to determine mortality rates in America. As one demographer puts it, "the relatively high mortality of the United States compared with other advanced nations is undoubtedly in large measure a reflection of the high mortality of the disadvantaged in the nation—the lower socioeconomic groups of whites and the even more disadvantaged minority groups" (Kitagawa, 1972: 106). Kitagawa's studies show, for example, that those with the lowest incomes have higher overall mortality rates, higher infant mortality rates, and a greater incidence of infectious and chronic diseases. Levels of education also correlate with mortality rates: the higher the level of education, the lower the mortality rates. Differences between the races in terms of mortality rates are particularly marked. From 1959 to 1961, for example, nonwhite females had a death rate 34 percent higher than that of white females. The rate for all nonwhite males was 20 percent higher than that for white males at all ages (Kitagawa, 1972).

These statistics led Kitagawa to ask: How many people die unnecessarily in the United States today? To find out, she devised an index of excess mortality, which in simple terms measures the deaths that would *not* have occurred if every subgroup had the same relatively low death rate as whites aged twenty-five years and over with at least one year of college. In 1960, this figure was 292,000, or 19 percent of all deaths, 17 percent of deaths among whites, and 36 percent of deaths among nonwhites (Kitagawa, 1972). These deaths must be considered preventable, partly through changing our social structure so that more people can share the advantages of a middle-class life, and partly by improving health care.

Health Care in America

There really isn't any health-care *system* in America. Individual doctors have traditionally been highly independent, deciding on what they want to specialize in, practicing where they want to in the manner they want, and charging whatever they want to patients who want (and can afford) to see them. This individualism has its dark side, for it means that such sociological factors as class, family background, and education determine who gets good health care.

Our relatively high infant mortality rate and relatively low life expectancies (compared with those of the other developed nations) are concrete evidence that this "non-system'' isn't working. Basically there are three problems, all related to the delivery of health care: the availability, the quality, and the cost of care.

Availability of Service Physicians in America are unevenly distributed, both geographically and professionally. One hundred and thirty-five counties and 5,000 towns in America have no doctor at all. There are 260 doctors for every 100,000 people in Westchester County, New York, but only 82 per 100,000 in Mississippi. The shortage of doctors is as acute in urban ghettos as it is in rural areas. The reason is obvious: doctors would rather practice among the affluent. As a result, poor Americans and those who live in rural areas have to spend more time searching for doctors than other Americans

do. Rather than lose working time, many pay no attention to health problems until they become acute.

Doctors are also badly distributed professionally. Seventy-two percent of the nation's physicians are specialists (Margolis, 1977: 13). This country needs an estimated 133 general practitioners per 100,000 population for quality medical care, but the national average is about 59 per 100,000 (*America's Children*, 1976: 42). As a result, even middle-class families in affluent communities have trouble finding personalized care for general medical problems. Americans are

American blacks at all income levels visit doctors less often than whites. One quarter of all blacks receive medical care in hospital clinics or emergency rooms. (Dennis Stock/Magnum)

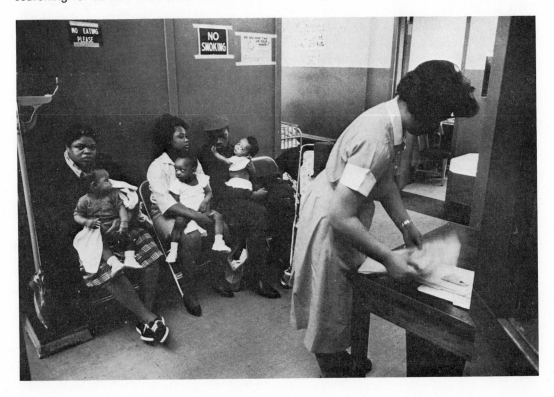

better off contracting a rare skin disease than the flu.

Quality of Care   Nothing beats the best of American medical care, but in reality the quality of care varies greatly. Malpractice suits are becoming more common, with courts more often deciding that the doctor or hospital made a mistake. Reports of the overprescription of drugs, unnecessary tests, and unnecessary surgery are widespread (Marmor, 1977: 76). This reflects the values of the medical profession, which has stoutly resisted any system of quality control or of continuing education to keep doctors up-to-date with medical advances. Now, however, under heavy federal pressure, physicians are being required to take refresher courses and to have their work reviewed by their peers.

A major but overlooked problem in terms of the quality of medical care arises out of the profession's emphasis on cure rather than prevention. Both doctors and the public prefer the drama of open-heart surgery to the practicality of a low-fat diet that would prevent the heart attack from ever having taken place. Nowhere does the neglect of prevention take its toll as with children. About 40 percent of American children under fifteen (20 million of them) have not been immunized against one or more contagious diseases (*The New York Times*, April 7, 1977, p. 14). A 1975 survey found one-fourth of the children in the United States to be anemic (Kennedy, 1976). Only about 10 percent of children with mental health problems receive care, and child abuse was legally unrecognized until just a few years ago. As a nation, we spend less on pediatrics than on any other medical specialty, and fewer children than members of any other age group are covered by health insurance (Miller, 1976: 26).

The children of the poor suffer the most. The infant mortality rate for blacks, more of whom are poor, is twice that for whites (Miller, 1976: 22, 25). Poor children are doomed before they start. One-third of the women who give birth in public hospitals receive no prenatal care (Kennedy, 1976), and many are malnourished. (Food stamps provide less than two-thirds the calories and protein needed for fetal development.) Low birth weights are linked to various birth defects, including mental retardation (*America's Children*, 1976: 34, 40, 41). These children grow up malnourished, and they are exposed to special environmental dangers as well, such as lead poisoning, worms, and rat bites (*America's Children*, 1976: 36). They receive little or no medical attention in childhood: only 10 percent ever visit a pediatrician (Hurley, 1970: 91–93). Low birth weight, malnutrition, disease, and lack of care eventually take their toll—often showing up in the form of behavior problems and low school achievement. Thus, health problems contribute to educational deficiencies, which reduce earning potential; and the cycle of poverty begins again.

Federal programs to break the cycle of poverty have had mixed results. The secretary of Health, Education, and Welfare has pressed for funds to raise immunization levels to 90 percent. As of 1975, 25 million children were enrolled in school lunch programs (42 percent at little or no cost); 1.9 million in breakfast programs (*America's Children*, 1976: 47). Still, on the national level only half the children who are eligible for Medicaid (and in the South, only one-tenth) are receiving benefits. Many believe that the solution to the problem of providing adequate medical care for children lies in a comprehensive national health program for all Americans.

figure 16.5 Prevalence of nutritional deficiencies among American children

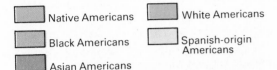

☐ Native Americans   ☐ White Americans

☐ Black Americans   ☐ Spanish-origin Americans

☐ Asian Americans

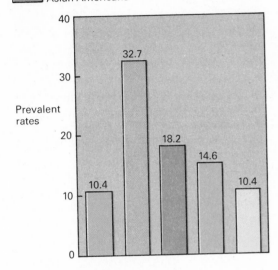

The general nutritional level of American children is satisfactory compared with those of other countries. However, nutritional deficiency is a significant problem among all ethnic groups in the United States.

SOURCE: *America's Children 1976*. Washington, D.C.: National Council of Organizations for Children and Youth, 1976, p. 36.

Costs and Insurance   The total bill for health care in America is rising about 20 percent a year. In 1960, health care cost $26 billion; in 1977, it cost $160 billion (*U.S. News & World Report*, October 17, 1977, p. 56). This came to $725 for every man, woman, and child, as compared with $142 in 1960. Hospital bills have been rising even faster.

Why is our health bill so high? First, be-cause the medical profession has empha-sized care by specialists, which costs much more than primary care, and the cure rather than the prevention of illness. There is also a lot of profiteering in medical care. Drug companies and firms that make and supply hospital equipment have among the highest profit margins in American industry.

Costs are also high because Americans demand care that is often unnecessarily ex-pensive. We demand to see a physician or a specialist, when a nurse-practitioner or our family doctor could easily handle the prob-lem. We want a semiprivate room when we go into the hospital, and we are impressed with shiny new equipment.

Finally, costs are high because this is the only industrialized nation with no national health insurance regulations on what doctors and hospitals can charge. A major reason for this is the medical profession, which has steadfastly opposed any national insurance program or any regulation of its fiercely in-dependent members. When the first step to-ward national insurance was finally taken during the 1960s, it was insurance without cost controls. Congress passed Medicaid (for the poor) and Medicare (for the elderly) to cover the major medical expenses of these groups, but the American Medical Associa-tion made sure that no cost controls were included. What happened is not hard to imagine. Overnight millions of people who hadn't been patients or who had been char-ity patients could pay, and they arrived in droves. Demand so exceeded supply that prices soared, and ironically, the very physi-cians who had opposed this federal insur-ance made handsome profits.

On a personal level, the burden of these costs varies according to family income. The poor have Medicaid (and Medicare if they are elderly too), while almost everyone else has voluntary insurance through an employer or on his or her own. A family earning an average or higher-than-average income finds insurance covers about half its medical expenses. But the real test of insurance occurs when a family faces catastrophic medical expenses. Because insurance policies limit what they will cover, one family in eight must lay out 15 percent or more of their personal income for major expenses. Again the poor get hit the hardest; for them it's one family in three.

Future Trends

Great changes are underway in health care, largely because the federal government has become concerned. Because of federal initiatives, primary care is receiving great attention both in medical training and in the organization of services. Insurance compa-

nies as well as the government are now implementing controls on cost. Under government pressure, professional societies have organized a wide network of courses to keep physicians and other health workers abreast of their fields, and forms of quality control in offices and hospitals are spreading rapidly. Medicaid and Medicare foreshadow a comprehensive national insurance plan, which will probably be passed in the next few years (Margolis, 1977). Preventive care is enjoying new popularity, and the federal government is strongly behind efforts to reduce pollution, to make companies obey safety regulations, to make cars and trucks safer, to ensure that most people are immunized against contagious diseases, and to teach people better health habits. Americans are eating better and exercising more. As a result, the infant mortality rate has dropped, heart attacks are down, and the population, it seems, is getting healthier.

SUMMARY

Demography, the study of population, concerns the patterns of birth, death, and migration that determine the size and composition of a society's people. The *census,* which is a periodic counting of the population and a collection of data about them, and compilations of vital statistics give demographers their major sources of data.

Population growth depends on the relationship between three demographic variables: births, deaths, and net migration. The rate of population growth is the extent to which births and immigration exceed deaths and emigration.

Thomas Malthus was the first scholar to analyze population growth and to worry about its consequences for humankind. He felt that increases in food supply could never keep pace with population growth. Malthus thought that the only way to halt population growth was by voluntary abstinence from sexual relations; otherwise, population would be checked drastically by war, pestilence, or starvation.

The basic model of population change in the West over the past two centuries is known as the *demographic transition.* In stage one, a high, steady birth rate and an equally high death rate, which peaked during epidemics and famines, kept the rate of population growth low. In the second phase, the death rate began to decline as public hygiene and sanitation improved, and better food supplies became available.

Populations grew rapidly. Next, the birth rate began to decline, and the death rate continued to drop. Finally, as in the industrialized nations of today, the death rate is low and steady, while the birth rate is low but fluctuates with social trends.

Malthusian growth still haunts the less developed parts of the world. There, the demographic transition has taken a different form because more advanced medical practices, better hygiene, and increased agricultural productivity have greatly reduced the death rate within just a few years. The birth rates in these countries, although they have recently begun to decline, remain high, as does population growth. As population growth strains available resources, hunger, unemployment, and social unrest result. Birth-control programs help only if they reinforce cultural trends toward smaller families, whether or not economic development is taking place.

Even in the United States, population growth may eventually threaten our way of life. Although birth rates have dropped from the heights of the baby boom—reinforced by legalized abortion and widely available contraceptives—zero population growth is many decades away. Even if women continue to bear children at the new low rates, the enormous numbers of women in the baby-boom generation may produce an echo boom.

Quality of life is as important as quantity. The leading causes of death in this country are, in large measure, diseases of affluence. America has fallen behind other industrialized nations in health care. High costs, uneven distribution, and poor-quality care all affect medical services. The poor and the young in particular are not getting the care that is theoretically available. But government pressure for greater attention to primary care, cost controls, and quality controls, as well as public pressure for a comprehensive national insurance plan, seem to point to an overall future improvement of health in America.

GLOSSARY

census a periodic counting of the population, in which facts on age, sex, occupation, and so forth are also recorded. In the United States the census is taken every tenth year and provides a wealth of statistical data for both demographers and social planners.

crude birth rate the number of births per 1,000 people in a given year.

crude death rate the number of deaths per 1,000 people in a given year.

demographer one who studies population.

demographic transition a four-stage process in which a population shifts from a high birth rate and high death rate to a low birth rate and low death rate.

demographic variables births, deaths, and net migration.

demography the statistical study of changes in population and the effects of these changes on society.

dependency ratio the proportion of people under fifteen and over sixty-five in the total population.

emigration the movement of people out of one country to settle in another.

fecundity the biological potential for reproduction.

fertility rate the number of births per 1,000 women between the ages of fifteen and forty-four.

immigration the movement of people into a country for permanent settlement.

infant mortality rate the number of deaths per 1,000 children one year of age or younger in a year.

internal migration the movement of people from one place to another within the same country.

international migration the movement of people from one country to another.

life expectancy the average number of years of life remaining to a person of a given age.

life span the maximum number of years of a human life.

net migration the difference between immigration and emigration.

net reproduction rate (NRR) an average of the number of female children born per woman of childbearing age.

per capita income income available to each citizen if the total income of the country were divided equally.

replacement level the point at which a population replaces itself with new people but does not grow.

sex ratio the number of men per 100 women in a population.

vital statistics computations between census years of births, deaths, immigration, and emigration.

zero population growth (ZPG) when a population reaches a point at which it is neither increasing nor decreasing, because the crude birth rate is equal to the crude death rate.

REFERENCES

America's Children 1976. Washington, D.C.: National Council of Organizations for Children and Youth, 1976.

Jane E. Brody, "Decade's Warnings Fail to Cut Smoking." *The New York Times,* January 11, 1974, pp. 1, 8.

Leon E. Clark, "Baby Boom by Fiat: The Effects of Population Policy on Fertility in Romania; An Inquiry Teaching Module." *Teaching Notes on Population,* vol. 3 (Spring/Summer 1973): 24–28.

A. J. Coale, "The Demographic Transition Reconsidered," in *International Population Conference.* Liège; n.p., 1973.

———— and N. W. Rives, Jr., "A Statistical Reconstruction of the Black Population of the United States 1880–1970." *Population Index,* vol. 39 (January 1973): 3–36.

Willard W. Cochrane, *The World Food Problem.* New York: Crowell, 1969.

Kingsley Davis, "Zero Population Growth: The Goal and the Means." *Daedalus,* vol. 102 (Fall 1973): 15–30.

Paul Ehrlich and Ann H. Ehrlich, *Population Resources Environment.* San Francisco, Calif.: Freeman, 1972.

Mark Evers and Jeanne McGee, "The Trend and Pattern in Attitudes Toward Abortion: 1965–1976." Paper presented at the annual meetings of the American Sociological Association, Chicago, September 1977.

Dov Friedlander and Eitan Sabatello, "Israel," in *Country Profiles.* Washington, D.C.: Population Council, 1972.

Roger Hurley, "The Health Crisis of the Poor," in Hans Peter Dreitzel, ed., *The Social Organization of Health.* New York: Macmillan, 1970.

IMS Research Group, Fifteenth Annual Edition of the National Prescription Audit General Information Report. © Copyright 1977, IMS America Ltd., Ambler, Pa., 19002.

E. J. Kahn, *The American People: The Findings of the 1970 Census.* New York: Weybright and Talley, 1974.

Edward M. Kennedy, Address to the National Council of Organizations for Children and Youth, Bicentennial Conference on Children,

Washington, D.C., February 3, 1976.

Evelyn M. Kitagawa, "Socioeconomic Differences in Mortality in the United States and Some Implications for Population Policy," in Charles F. Westoff and Robert Parke, Jr., eds., *Demographic and Social Aspects of Population Growth,* vol. 1. Washington, D.C.: Commission on Population Growth and the American Future, 1972.

Robert J. Latham, "Morocco: Family Planning Knowledge, Attitudes, and Practice in the Rural Areas." *Studies in Family Planning,* vol. 1 (October 1970): 1–22.

Mahmood Mamdani, *The Myth of Population Control.* New York: Monthly Review Press, 1972.

Richard J. Margolis, "National Health Insurance—The Dream Whose Time Has Come?" *The New York Times Magazine,* January 9, 1977, pp. 12ff.

Theodore R. Marmor, "Rethinking National Health Insurance." *The Public Interest,* vol. 46 (Winter 1977): 73–95.

C. Arden Miller, Address to the National Council of Organization for Children and Youth, Bicentennial Conference on Children, Washington, D.C., February 2, 1976.

Moni Moulik, *Billions More to Feed.* Rome: Food and Agriculture Organization of the United Nations, 1977.

NYCLU (New York Civil Liberties Union) memorandum, Emergency Campaign to Save the Right to Abortion in New York State, 1977.

Population Council, *Studies in Family Planning,* vol. 9 (April 1978).

Population Reference Bureau, *Population Bulletin: Rural Renaissance in America?* vol. 31 (October 1976).

———, *World Population Data Sheet 1976.* Washington, D.C.: U.S. Government Printing Office, 1976.

Boyce Rensberger, "Serious World Food Gap Is Seen Over the Long Term by Experts." *The New York Times,* December 5, 1976, pp. 1, 67.

Dorothy P. Rice, *Statement Before the Senate Health Subcommittee.* Washington, D.C.: U.S. Department of Health, Education, and Welfare, March 31, 1977.

Thomas G. Sanders, "Costa Rica, Population Perceptions and Policy," in Harrison Brown et al., eds., *Population Perspective, 1973.* San Francisco, Calif.: Freeman, Cooper, 1973.

Lewis M. Simons, "Indonesia: Prepare for the Worst." *The Washington Post,* March 25, 1977, p. A25.

Irene B. Taeuber, "The Changing Distribution of the Population of the United States in the Twentieth Century," in Louis K. Loewenstein, ed., *Urban Studies: An Introductory Reader,* 2nd ed. New York: Free Press, 1977.

Ralph Thomlinson, *Population Dynamics,* 2nd ed. New York: Random House, 1976.

Christopher Tietze, "Two Years' Experience with a Liberal Abortion Law: Its Impact on Fertility Trends in New York City." *Family Planning Perspectives,* vol. 5 (Winter 1973): 36–41.

Andrew C. Twaddle and Richard M. Hessler, *A Sociology of Health.* St. Louis, Mo.: Mosby, 1977.

U.S. Bureau of Immigration, *Annual Report of Immigration and Nationalization Service.* Washington, D.C.: U.S. Government Printing Office, 1978.

U.S. Bureau of the Census, *Current Population Reports,* Series P-25, no. 643, "Population Estimates and Projections." Washington, D.C.: U.S. Government Printing Office, 1977.

———, *Population Characteristics,* Series P-20, no. 301, "Fertility of American Women, June 1975." Washington, D.C.: U.S. Government Printing Office, 1976.

———, *Statistical Abstract of the United States, 1977.* Washington, D.C.: U.S. Government Printing Office, 1977.

———, *User's Guide.* Washington, D.C.: U.S. Government Printing Office, 1970.

"U.S. Says Aliens May Stay, But . . . ," *Intercom,* vol. 5 (August 1977): 1, 6.

Charles F. Westoff, "The Decline of Unplanned Births in the United States." *Science,* vol. 191 (January 1976): 38–41.

——— and Elise F. Jones, "Contraception and Sterilization in the United States, 1965–1975." *Family Planning Perspectives,* vol. 9 (July/August 1977): 153–157.

FOR FURTHER STUDY

Occupational Health.   The dangers to health arising from one's work are often ignored because it may be quite a long time before one develops measurable symptoms. Several books document the dangers of working with specific materials or in particular industries. For example, Jeanne Sellman and Susan Daum have written a handbook of occupational hazards, which also discusses measures to prevent these hazards, in *Work Is Dangerous to Your Health* (New York: Pantheon, 1973). In *Bitter Wages,* Joseph Page and Mary-Win O'Brien (New York: Grossman, 1973), members of the Ralph Nader group, report on diseases and injuries related to working conditions. Rachel Scott discusses a broad range of occupational hazards in *Muscle and Blood* (New York: Dutton, 1974). In *Expendable Americans* (New York: Viking, 1974), an interesting occupational-health case study, Paul Brodeur thoroughly investigates the problems of asbestos workers at Johns-Manville Corporation.

Sterilization.   Charles Westoff and N. B. Ryder report the increase in sexual sterilization as a method of contraception in *The Contraceptive Revolution* (Princeton, N.J.: Princeton University Press, 1977). For some people, this form of birth control is a very liberating alternative; however, sterilization does have the potential for abuse. Allan Chase's *The Legacy of Malthus* (New York: Knopf, 1977) is an impassioned but thoroughly researched attack on sterilization as a racist policy implemented during the early twentieth century. Another examination of the problems of sterilization abuse is Morris E. Davis's "Involuntary Sterilization: A History of Social Control," *Journal of Black Health Perspectives,* vol. 1 (August–September 1974): 46–60. Gena Corea discusses the issues of sterilization and women's health in *The Hidden Malpractice* (New York: Morrow, 1977). Both India and Puerto Rico have had widely publicized sterilization programs that some analysts consider to be politically motivated. An account of sterilization practices in Puerto Rico, along with case studies from other Latin American countries, may be found in *Population Target: The Political Economy of Population Control in Latin America* (Brampton, Ontario: Charters, 1976) by Bonnie Mass. A discussion of the problem in India is available in M. Henry's "The Inevitable Failure of Shortcut Policy—Compulsory Sterilization in India: Is Coercion the Only Alternative to Chaos?" *Hastings Century Report,* vol. 6 (April 1976): 13–15.

Health Care.   The inequities of health care and their relation to life and death are of great concern today. Probably the best and most interesting material comes from the hearings on health care that Senator Edward Kennedy conducted. Reports of the committee are available in libraries. Robert Alford discusses the political aspects of America's health-care problems in "The Political Economy of Health Care: Dynamics Without Change," *Politics and Society,* vol. 2 (Winter 1972): 127–164. An important issue in health care is the condition of nursing homes. An excellent work that examines the profits from abuse of the elderly is *Tender Loving Greed* by Mary Adelaide Mendelson (New York: Knopf, 1974). Claire Townsend explores the social conditions in nursing homes in her book *Old Age, The Last Segregation* (New York: Grossman, 1971). For an analysis of the interpersonal relations of staff and patients in a nursing home, see the ethnography *Living and Dying at Murray Manor* by Jaber F. Gubrium (New York: St. Martin's, 1975).

Food. Another crucial area for population and health is food—its quantity and nutritional content. The world situation can be assessed in various documents published by the United Nations. See also "The Politics of Food" by Emma Rothschild, *The New York Review,* May 16, 1974, pp. 16–18. Frances M. Lappé and Joseph Collins discuss the politics of food production and distribution as the basis of world food problems in *Food First: Beyond the Myth of Scarcity* (Boston: Houghton Mifflin, 1977). In *The Politics and Responsibility of the North American Breadbasket* (Washington, D.C.: Worldwatch Institute, 1975), Lester Brown analyzes world dependence on United States agribusiness and the need for new food policies. Not all countries are tied to the production and distribution system of American food; Virginia Li Wang explores one exception in her article "Food Distribution as a Guarantee for Nutrition and Health: China's Experience," *Milbank Memorial Fund Quarterly,* vol. 54 (Spring 1976): 145–165.

CHAPTER 17

Urban Life and the Environment

An inquiring reporter stopped passers-by on a city street and asked their opinion of contemporary American urban culture.

Said the balding taxi driver, "Lousier every day. It isn't just the traffic jams and the well-dressed muggers. The wife and I used to look at a lot of TV, but what's happened to wrestling?"

Said the prosperous young developer, "How could it be any better? The population's growing, isn't it? And all those babies have to live somewhere."

Said the suburban commuter, "I see nothing but threats. It isn't just the developers. A lot of people want to put high-rises in my town. What will happen to our way of life if a lot of old people and childless families move in?"

Said the engineer from the Highway Department, "Our main job is to give the people what they want at a cost they can afford. What they want is more lanes going more places. Most of them don't want all this prettification that the planners and architectural nuts write about."

Said the lean young man in a lumber jacket, "I'm afraid there isn't much hope. As soon as we get a piece of the wilderness declared a preserve, too many humans start wanting to go there. It's too easy, with highways and all. Too many humans mean too few birds."

Said the Ford worker, "This is a great culture and it's getting better. The union's going to get us all a $25,000 guaranteed annual wage. How can you beat that? Of course there'll be a lot of spare time, but let the sociologists worry about that."

Said the mayor, "I look for great things from the federal government next year."

City life has left us all like blind men trying to describe an elephant. What we think about the urbanization of America depends on where we sit.[1]

In this chapter we step back a bit, to look at our urban way of life from the sociological perspective. We'll describe the rise of cities, the shapes they've taken in modern times, the life styles of people inhabiting them today, and the problems cities face. Then we'll look at what urbanization and industrialization have done to our environment and suggest why correcting and preventing environmental abuse is so problematic.

---

[1] Adapted from Burchard, 1977: 432–457.

THE URBAN TRANSFORMATION

Cities are such a familiar part of our lives that we often forget how much of human culture depends on their existence. Human beings first began to form permanent settlements some 8,000 to 10,000 years ago, and their effect upon social organization was enormous. Stationary residence encouraged the development of written language, the calendar, organized scientific inquiry, complex stratification systems, an organized priesthood, institutionalized religion, and the state, among many other important social institutions. Indeed, civilization as we know it is very much a product of urban society.

The Birth of the City

For at least the first three-quarters of human history, human beings were nomadic creatures who traveled about in small families or bands, hunting, fishing, and foraging for food. Because the bounty of nature in most parts of the world was not plentiful enough to support more than a few persons in any one spot, humans would settle in one place for only a short time, and then move on. Without adequate means of storing supplies, people were unable to accumulate a surplus and therefore faced a rather precarious existence (Childe, 1952).

The Neolithic Revolution At the dawn of the neolithic period, some 10,000 years ago, people began to discover techniques for cultivating plants and domesticating animals. People developed simple tools for use in gardening and made pots for storage; these technological innovations were a way of multiplying nature's bounty enough to allow early groups of humans to forgo nomadic wandering for a rooted residence. The earli-est villages were small by today's standards, housing only 200 to 400 residents. This form of village organization prevailed for the next 4,000 to 5,000 years (Childe, 1952).

The First True Cities In about 6000 to 5000 B.C. in the alluvial plains of the Nile, Tigris-Euphrates, and Indus river valleys, there emerged settlements more than ten times the size of any previous ones. Housing between 7,000 and 20,000 persons, these first true cities developed largely because innovations in agricultural and transportational technologies enabled these societies to take advantage of the valleys' exceptionally fertile soils. Agricultural output increased with the domestication of new kinds of plants and with the development of the ox-drawn plow, irrigation, and metallurgy. Storage facilities for grain were improved, and enough food was produced to support all farming families and a large population of nonfarmers as well. This relative abundance permitted the emergence of a complex division of labor, which has been characteristic of all human societies since.

The first cities reached their zenith about 3000 B.C. and then faded away. The next flowering of urban life occurred some 2,500 years later, in classical Greece and Rome. Roman urban life attained a remarkable degree of sophistication, from magnificent public architecture to such conveniences as water pipes and steppingstones for crossing muddy streets. But with the fall of Rome these classical cities also declined. Urban development did not begin again in Europe until the rise of the feudal city during the Middle Ages.

The Preindustrial Feudal City Feudal technology was such that no more than about 100,000 persons could inhabit a city. Agricultural techniques were productive enough to allow about 10 percent of an area's total population to live in an urban setting. However, the technological base limited the growth of cities beyond this point. Transportation methods were poorly developed, and it was therefore difficult to bring in the bulky goods needed for construction and manufacturing. Without large-scale manufacturing, job opportunities were limited. Poor communication methods made it hard to govern a large adjacent hinterland. And sanitation methods and medical techniques were so primitive that dense urban settlements bred disease and death.

The Industrial Revolution and the Urban Explosion The Industrial Revolution brought with it technological innovations that reduced the constraints on the size and density of the city. The mechanization of agriculture increased food production dramatically. Chemical and biological advances also produced new ways of raising animals, new insecticides, new herbicides, new fertilizers, and new plants, which also resulted in food surpluses. Because of increased productivity, fewer workers were now needed on the farms. Displaced farmers and their families streamed into the cities in search of jobs, which were increasing as a result of the surge of growth in factory production—again the consequence of the revolution in machine technology. Techniques for overcoming the obstacle of distance also aided in the explosive growth of cities. The spread of the railroads allowed the city to reach the far-away resources needed for growth. The development of cheap steel and the invention of the elevator made possible skyscrapers, which met the residential and office needs of an increasingly dense urban population. And innovations in public hygiene and in medical facilities cut the health risks that had plagued preindustrial cities.

In America, within a matter of decades, well-nigh the whole nation had moved from the hinterlands to metropolitan areas. In 1850, only 15 percent of the population of the United States lived in urban areas; by 1900, the proportion was almost 40 percent. The turning point came around 1920, when more than half of all Americans were urban dwellers. Fifty years later, more than 70 percent of the population was urbanized, by which the U.S. Bureau of the Census means living in towns or cities larger than 2,500 persons (Hauser, 1969). Within a generation, America shifted from a rural base to an urban one. (See figure 17:1.)

World Urbanization

Nor was the United States the only nation that refused to stay "down on the farm." America's rush to the cities was part of a worldwide phenomenon of *urbanization,* in which increasing percentages of the population moved to urban settlements and came under the predominating influence of urban ways. Between 1800 and 1950, a period in which total world population expanded about 2.6 times, the number of people living in cities with 20,000 or more inhabitants swelled almost 23 times, going from about 21.7 million to about 502.2 million (Breese, 1966:14). What caused this great demographic shift? First, the increase in population must be taken into account; cities grew, at least in part, because of a growth in population as a whole. A more significant influence, however, was the change in patterns of employment. As farming methods grew more efficient, fewer people were needed in agriculture. A tremendous expansion in the number of industrial and service jobs took place, and since these jobs were located chiefly in the cities, they tended to draw large numbers of people to the metropolitan areas (Hall, 1966: 11–12).

figure 17:1   World urbanization, 1950 to 2000[1] (by percent)

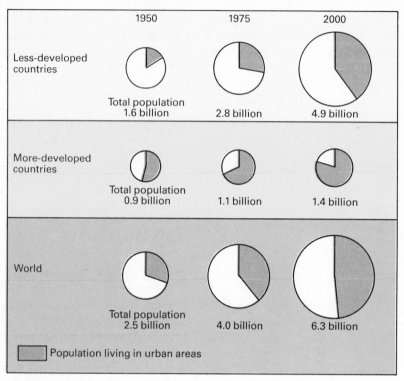

[1] Includes temperate South America, North America, Japan, Europe, Australia, New Zealand, and the Soviet Union.

SOURCE: From *Environmental Quality–1977*, the eighth annual report of the Council on Environmental Quality (Washington, D.C.: U.S. Government Printing Office), figure 72, p. 312; George J. Beier, "Can Third World Cities Cope?" *Population Bulletin*, vol. 31 (1976), p. 2, based on United Nations Population Division, "Trends and Prospects in Urban and Rural Population, 1950–2000 as assessed in 1973–1974," ESA/P/WP.54 (New York, 1975), table C, medium variant. Courtesy of the Population Reference Bureau, Inc., Washington, D.C.

In many ways, the cities have grown too fast—particularly in the developing countries, where too many people crowd into the city without there being the employment, services, and facilities to sustain them. Calcutta, India's largest city, is an excellent example of such a "premature metropolis" (Bose, in Schwirian, 1977: 53). Most of the people in this city live in slums, many on the streets. Sanitation, health conditions, and transportation are all inadequate, while the primitive, disorganized urban economy shows little sign of generating the necessary capital to effect significant change. Nevertheless, the population of Calcutta—and the populations of similar urban centers in most of the developing countries—continues to grow, often at a rate exceeding that of cities in the industrialized world.

The movement from a rural to an urban

With modernization, millions of the poor have migrated to cities like Rio de Janeiro, often clustering in vast slums on the outskirts of the city. Because the technological and economic bases cannot support such large concentrations of people, much suffering and squalor have resulted from this "overurbanization." (Paolo Koch/Rapho/Photo Researchers)

environment all over the world has had tremendous effects on social structure. Describing the character of the social life of the modern city has been a persistent challenge to sociologists, as we shall see in the next section.

MODERN URBAN LIFE

The striking contrasts between the intimacy and neighborliness of village life and the anonymity and self-interestedness of life in the city formed the major focus of early urban sociology. Much of the pioneering work in this field was done during the 1920s and 30s by social scientists at the University of Chicago. This was a period in which migration to the cities was particularly heavy and in which

it seemed that Americans by the hundreds of thousands were trading the primary relationships of their rural lives for the impersonality of existence in a large city. One classic study that reflects these assumptions about life in large and small communities is Louis Wirth's "Urbanism as a Way of Life" (1938). Like many of us, Wirth saw the *city* as the prototype of mass society, in which the traditional bases of social solidarity and control—

kinship and the neighborhood—are undermined; the individual is thus left atomized and depersonalized, and is more often subject to mental breakdown, suicide, delinquency, crime, corruption, and disorder. Wirth believed that urbanism fosters sophistication, rationality, and a utilitarian approach to interpersonal relations. These traits in turn lead to reserve, indifference, and a blasé outlook, and to anonymity and depersonalization. Wirth understood that the peculiar kind of social relationship fostered by city living is determined by three factors: the size, density, and heterogeneity of the city population. According to his view, larger populations tend to be more diversified and heterogeneous than small ones. Although a city dweller may have an enormous number of encounters with others, these encounters are likely to be segmented and superficial, impersonal and transitory. In place of sustained and intimate relations with relatives and close neighbors, a person encounters the butcher, the taxi driver, the waitress, the news vendor, yoga teachers, and co-workers on the job. In other words, a person's social relations are secondary rather than primary (see chapter 7).

These impersonal and anonymous social relations give people who live in the city a sense of increased personal freedom. Freedom is not an unmixed blessing, however, for it can mean that some people are free to prey on others—con artists or muggers, for example. With the waning of traditional social constraints, the urban society must maintain order through formal mechanisms of control—law and its supporting agencies, the police and the courts. But because these mechanisms of control are rarely as effective at keeping order as tradition and custom, the urban society is more prone to personal and social disorganization, more prone to alienation. In Tönnies's terminology, the social

relations of an earlier rural age have been replaced in urban society with *Gesellschaft*-like relations. (See chapter 7 for the *Gemeinschaft-Gesellschaft* distinction.)

Is the City Alienating?

Does the city necessarily destroy intimate social bonds? There is much recent evidence to show that Wirth and his school failed to observe a great deal of the actual social life of urban communities and hence drew a very one-sided and overly negative picture. Those who studied urban communities during the 1960s—spearheaded by Herbert J. Gans, whose book *The Urban Villagers* was published in 1962—have departed from Wirth's thesis that population density is related to social disorganization and alienation. Gerald Suttles, for example, who lived for three years in the Addams area, one of the oldest slums in Chicago, found that rather than being marked by a lack of social cohesion, this neighborhood was in fact intricately organized along ethnic lines. Moreover, instead of the normlessness posited by the members of Wirth's school, Suttles found that conventional morality was not flouted by the slum residents, but was interpreted differently according to their particular needs (Suttles, 1968: 3). Richard Sennett, who also studied Chicago (1971), discovered that the pressures of city life did not disrupt family connections, but instead caused the family to become a refuge from the disorder members felt existed in the outside environment. Sennett did note, however, that certain changes appeared in the family structure. Bonds between fathers and sons, for example, tended to weaken over the years. But these changes may be interpreted as an attempt to evolve new patterns to cope with urban life, rather than as evidence of the breakdown of family ties in general.

What a person does for a living or how long he or she has lived in a neighborhood may determine how much that person feels an integral part of his or her surroundings. Focusing on several working-class neighborhoods in New York City, John Esposito and John Fiorillo found that residents in certain areas tended to have similar occupations. These included such fields as construction, textiles, transportation, public administration, and insurance. Shared employment tended to generate a sense of cohesiveness in the neighborhood—far more so, in fact, than ethnic identity, since most of the communities studied exhibited a high degree of ethnic diversity (Esposito and Fiorillo, 1974: 324–325). In a British study, residents of both rural and urban communities were asked such questions as: How many people do you know in your neighborhood? How many friends and relatives live within a ten-minute walk from your home? How glad or sorry would you be if you had to move away from your neighborhood? The responses showed that regardless of the population size and density of the community in which they lived, individuals who'd spent a longer time in a neighborhood tended to have more extensive social networks and a greater number of relatives living nearby. The investigators also found that the social bonds of members of large urban communities were *more numerous* than those of rural residents (Kasarda and Janowitz, 1974).

On the basis of these studies, it must be concluded that the city is *not* intrinsically alienating. Wirth's contrast between the cozy, intimate village and the cold, impersonal city appears to be overdrawn, probably because Wirth himself was influenced by what he saw in Chicago at the time he conducted his research—an influx of vast numbers of foreign-born immigrants who had not yet become thoroughly integrated into the community. Recent research indicates that population size may even have an effect directly opposite to that described by Wirth. Claude S. Fischer (1975) has suggested that size *is* an important factor in urban life, but that it leads not to weakened ties but to a diversity of subcultures, within each of which there is strong cohesion. According to Fischer, urban population density fosters a rich social life within subcultures by ensuring that unconventional individuals and members of ethnic groups can find others like them. People, it seems, can enjoy the intimacy, loyalty, and cooperation that characterize life in a closely knit community, regardless of how large or small or densely or sparsely populated that community happens to be.

Life in the Suburbs

But whatever opportunities the inner city may offer for rewarding social attachments, there are still a number of highly attractive elements that it usually can't provide. These include home ownership, with a private outdoor space that may be used for gardening, barbecuing, sunbathing, or any number of other activities; a sense of security and physical safety; and the feeling of belonging to an attractive, well-regulated community populated by congenial neighbors who share many of the same goals and values as oneself. Driven by such motivations, millions have already left and each year many more flee the inner city to settle in the surrounding suburbs. In fact, this move from city to suburb represents a major factor in shaping the urban area as we know it today and in forming the expanding "megalopolis," which we will discuss later in the chapter. The postwar baby boom also contributed to the strong desire for a healthy environment in which to raise children. By 1970, 38 percent of the total population of the United States lived in the suburbs, comprising 54 percent of all city dwellers (Commission on the Cities in the Seventies, 1972: 71).

The Price of Suburban Life   In the 1950s, America's dissatisfaction with the suburbs was exemplified by the film *Rebel Without a Cause,* which starred James Dean as an inarticulate misfit surrounded by uncomprehending suburban conformists. The 1960s saw Dustin Hoffman in *The Graduate* escaping to the bottom of his swimming pool to get away from his parents' hollow and oppressive suburban neighbors. This critical attitude was also reflected in such sociological works as William F. Whyte's study of a Chicago suburb called Park Forest, which was then a home for middle-level "organization men" and their families (in Stein, 1960). As Whyte saw it, conformity governed nearly every aspect of the residents' lives. Houses tended to resemble one another both inside and out; adults were supposed to look happy and to be friendly with neighbors; and children were expected to be "well adjusted" and to participate enthusiastically in all the recommended activities. The goal of "getting ahead" dominated people's lives: although they were expected to make friends in the community, those friendships were not supposed to interfere with upward mobility. However, just as Wirth and those of his school presented an overly negative image of life in the cities, early critics of the suburbs tended to dwell exclusively on the more unpleasant features of suburban living. The result was a caricature that didn't do justice to the complexity of the original.

The Variety of Suburbs   The suburbs are far from being all alike; life in them differs largely on the basis of the inhabitants' social

class and point in the life cycle (Gans, 1968: 132–140). Most of the postwar suburbs have been settled by members of the lower-middle class, often with young families, and consequently their way of life has commonly been identified as the suburban one. But sociologists have found that lower-middle-class life styles are much the same in the suburb as they are in the city. In general, the social life of the lower-middle class centers around friends and neighbors rather than around distant relatives. The major source of recreation is the home and child care; indeed, the home is the vital center of life here. Lower-middle-class people swell the membership in churches and in other sorts of voluntary organizations—the Elks, PTA, and the like.

Other studies have shown upper-middle-class suburbanites to be quite different from less affluent suburban dwellers (Gans, 1968). Being better educated and more cosmopolitan in their interests, they put less emphasis on the home as the center of life. These people tend to be extensively and intensively involved in community activities—social, cultural, and civic. They participate in many shared activities with friends, such as partying, and they are even less likely than lower-middle-class persons to have strong ties with relatives. And again, this life style is characteristic of the upper-middle class in general, both in the suburb and in the city.

While it is misleading to lump all suburbs together, regardless of their socioeconomic make-up, it is nonetheless true that suburban communities as a whole do have certain features in common. Just as the large population of a city may encourage a diversity of subcultures by ensuring that there are enough of any particular group to create a sense of community, the relatively small size of a suburb often has the opposite effect: suburbs may encourage conformity simply because their size relegates nonconformists

to an insignificant minority. But suburbs may
enforce conformity more directly than this.
Because most suburbs are politically autonomous, they can maintain considerable influence over the composition and life style of
their populations. By means of zoning laws,
licensing, school boards, business associations, and the local police department, a suburban community can effectively dictate who
is allowed to live in it, as well as how those
people must conduct their lives. The conformity fostered by these means tends to be
self-perpetuating, since individuals who migrate to the suburbs are usually those who
already approve of and share suburban values. The suburbs offer the promise of a settled, comfortable life style centered around
home, family, and friends—in short, the values upheld by middle-class America. Thus,
while there are differences *between* suburbs
of different class and ethnic groups, *within*
each one are found similar forces toward
conformity with the community's values.

Urban Ecology

The metropolis is divided not only into city
and suburb but also into specialized areas of
manufacturing, commerce, and housing.
Major cities typically have areas that corre-
spond to Wall Street, skid row, the Gold
Coast, Watts, and Broadway. But how does
this organization develop?

During the 1920s and 1930s a number of
sociologists, again at the University of Chicago, established the study of *urban ecology*,
feeling that urban land specialization could
best be explained by analogy to the ecologi-

cal model in biology. They saw the urban environment as a product of competition and natural selection. The urban ecologists, as the group came to be known, hypothesized that established land uses usually resist displacement, and since dissimilar uses are usually incompatible with one another, a single area typically harbors one kind of development (for example, factories *or* low-cost housing *or* entertainment facilities). When competition for the limited urban space becomes particularly intense, however, the land use of the greatest economic significance generally wins out.

Ecological Succession

That neighborhoods go through changes is all too obvious, especially to long-time residents. Some neighborhoods deteriorate, while others are reclaimed and renovated. Industries move to the residential suburbs and provoke zoning battles in the councils of city government. Change is visible enough, but is there a pattern to these changes? The urban ecologists described an *invasion cycle,* which they felt constituted a general pattern (Park, Burgess, and McKenzie, 1925). The invasion cycle begins before it is recognized by the area's inhabitants. One brownstone or dilapidated urban mansion in a rundown area is bought and refurbished by an architect, for example. Next, more professionals buy houses nearby, and the area's inhabitants notice and oppose the invasion. As land values and taxes and rents go up, the older and poorer residents protest that they can no longer afford to live there and have nowhere else to go. If opposition is unsuccessful, a general influx of newcomers into the area begins. A tip point is reached as the old inhabitants are forced out or no longer wish to remain in the area. The invasion reaches the climax stage when the new inhabitants completely occupy the area. This is how a slum becomes a George-town, or a Georgetown a slum. The neighborhood may stabilize or it may undergo further succession.

The Shape of Cities

Urban ecologists believed that not only could the *dynamics* of city growth and change be generally described, but that similar outcomes in the overall *structure* of the city could also be detected. Focusing mainly on *economic* criteria—such as competition for land or the prices of things in a particular area—they tried to anticipate the shape a developing city would take.

On the basis of evidence at hand, Ernest W. Burgess proposed in the 1920s that cities are laid out according to a *concentric zone model* (Park, Burgess, and McKenzie, 1925: 47–62). At the center is the business district, made up of shops and offices. Adjacent and outward from the business district is an area of transition, which is characterized by residential instability, high crime rates, and various forms of vice. Beyond the transitional ring are the various residential zones. The innermost is inhabited by working-class people, the next by the middle class, and the outermost by the upper class. Each of these zones reflects a group's capacity to compete for space in terms of its resources and its acceptance by the settled inhabitants. While concentric zone patterning is by no means typical of all or even most urban areas, as Burgess first conjectured, it can be seen in certain cities like Chicago, which developed very rapidly in the period after the Industrial Revolution and before the development of the automobile.

In the 1930s, Homer Hoyt proposed a system of urban patterning that emphasized the importance of transportation routes—highways, railroad lines, and waterways—in shaping the growth of cities (1943). It features the same type of outward movement,

figure 17:2   Models of urban space

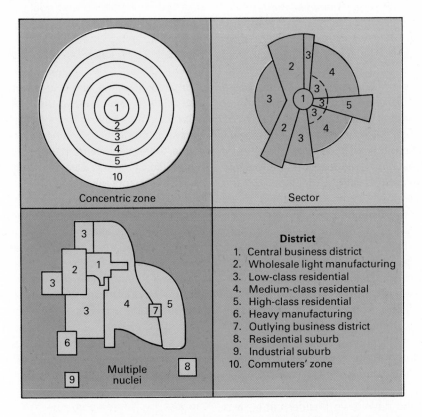

Concentric zone

Sector

Multiple nuclei

District
1. Central business district
2. Wholesale light manufacturing
3. Low-class residential
4. Medium-class residential
5. High-class residential
6. Heavy manufacturing
7. Outlying business district
8. Residential suburb
9. Industrial suburb
10. Commuters' zone

SOURCE: Chauncy D. Harris and Edward L. Ullman, "The Nature of Cities," in Paul K. Hatt and A. J. Reiss, Jr., eds., *Cities and Society* (Glencoe, Ill.: Free Press, 1957). Courtesy of Professor Harris.

Attempts to describe the structure of cities produced the three alternative models shown here. A newer approach to the analysis of urban structure is called social area analysis. Analysts, using the census and other social indicators, attempt to explain residential patterns by correlating broad social categories, such as social rank, family structure, and ethnicity. With the advent of the computer, even more factors are being taken into account in models of urban land use and social structure.

but in sectors rather than concentric zones. According to Hoyt's *sector model,* a business district occupies the center of the city; beyond that, development occurs in sectors that tend to be distributed along major transportation routes radiating out from the city's center. As land uses expand, they tend to remain within their respective sectors, but extend outward toward the edge of urban development. San Francisco and Minneapolis are two examples of this type of development.

Yet another design of urban ecological development, the *multiple nuclei model,* was proposed by Chauncy D. Harris and Edward L. Ullman (1945). Land uses, costs, and interests cause a city to develop in a series of nuclei, each with its specialized activities. For example, a nucleus of car manufacturing might develop in an area on the outskirts of town with lots of space, low rents, and good transportation facilities. Manufacturing interests requiring less space might cluster in a nucleus closer to the center of the city, while residential centers might develop on the other side of town. As the city grows, nuclei proliferate and become specialized.

The ecological approach to cities has one basic weakness, however; it tends to minimize the fact that cities are inhabited by people, and that people's behavior can often be complex and unpredictable. For one thing, the different zones of cities not only reflect the workings of market forces, but are also based to a great extent on the values and personal preferences of the people who live and work there. The historic Boston Commons, a forty-eight-acre park in the middle of the downtown business area, is a good example of sentimental attachment overriding economic considerations. The Commons, which in colonial days served as a grazing area for livestock, continues to be protected by a special provision of the city charter even though it occupies extremely valuable territory and causes traffic delays (Firey, 1961: 257). These and similar examples in other cities show that the use of space is governed not only by utilitarian factors but by emotional and symbolic ones as well.

Megalopolis

During the past decade and a half, a number of observers have noticed a new pattern of urban development, one that is regional. A number of American metropolises are growing so large that they are growing together, forming what Jean Gottman (1964) has called a *megalopolis,* a word that literally means "great city." The most prominent megalopolis is the one that exists along the northeastern seaboard of the United States. Municipalities having more than 100 people per square mile are stretched along a continuous 500-mile belt from Kittery, Maine, to Quantico, Virginia. Over 40 million people live in this sprawling belt (Tunnard, 1967). And there are other emerging megalopolises as well: Los Angeles-San Diego; Palm Beach-Miami; Dallas-Fort Worth; Pittsburgh-Youngstown-Canton-Akron-Cleveland; Milwaukee-Chicago-Detroit; and perhaps even Seattle-Tacoma. Because this trend seems to be the wave of the future, we must give up the idea that a city is a tightly settled and organized territory in which people, activities, and riches are crowded into a small area distinctly separated from its nonurban surroundings. The unplanned growth that has created these megalopolises—called urban sprawl by some—continues unabated. Indeed, this is an essential part of what is often called the crisis of the cities.

The spread of cities has caused some striking changes. Shopping malls now stand on fields where corn grew only a decade ago. Row upon row of tract houses cover the ground where cows used to graze, and six-lane highways bisect once-deserted marshlands. Ugliness and pollution have made their appearance now that 32 percent of suburban communities have become industrial. The desire for better services and low tax rates is being thwarted by the ever-increasing cost of schooling and other municipal services. In many suburbs rising crime rates, juvenile delinquency, and other social disorders typical of the cities make the suburbanite's dream of personal safety and security seem increasingly remote. Attempts have been made to find some workable solution to these problems, but while the problems are common to the megalopolis as a whole, they can be dealt with only by individual local governments administering tiny segments of a huge metropolitan area.

In some instances, large central cities have attempted to annex adjoining suburban areas in an attempt to widen their tax base and thus to provide more funds with which to attack problems common to both cities and suburbs. But such moves have usually resulted only in legal battles between suburban and city governments. A more effective strategy is to use federal money to fight local problems. In order to dispense federal funds to the cities and suburbs, a special agency has been created—the Metropolitan Area Planning Council—which is the first important attempt to deal with problems on the regional rather than on the local level (Miller, 1975: 344). But the powers of the council are limited. If present trends continue, some wider form of government that has jurisdiction over cities and suburbs—in effect, over all parts of the megalopolis—would appear to be imperative.

THE URBAN CRISIS

In several large cities of the Northeast during the 1960s, five or more people moved from the city to the suburbs for every one person moving in the opposite direction—a trend that continues nationwide today. It is clear that the suburbs, not the central cities, are the scenes of metropolitan growth in the United States at the present time. At first glance, a drop in population in the inner cities might seem like a cause for rejoicing; fewer people should mean more resources to go around, more housing, more room on public transportation, a less burdened bureaucracy. But in actuality, the cities' loss of population is anything but reassuring. It is a sign of crisis, and one for which there is no ready solution.

Why should lack of growth plunge cities into crisis? The answer to this question is that most of the people who are moving out of the inner cities and into the suburbs are white and belong to the middle and upper income brackets, while most of those who remain in the cities are nonwhite and poor. As a result, the central core of the cities is left to those who can least afford to finance its upkeep. Although there is some migration into the cities, it is not enough to offset the flow outward. Moreover, the majority of these city-bound migrants are relatively poor, and their arrival does little to pull the city out of its downward spiral. The movement of blacks from the Southern countryside into the Northern cities, for example, made ghettos of the inner cities. Even though blacks constitute only one-tenth of the total population in America, nineteen of the nation's thirty largest cities are more than 30 percent black. Four are more than 50 percent black. Moreover, four-fifths of all urban blacks live in the inner city, whereas only two-fifths of urban whites live there. This trend shows no signs of letting up.

During the last ten years, the average economic and educational levels of blacks migrating to the Northern urban centers have been higher than those of resident blacks and in some cases those of resident whites (Farley, 1976: 27–28). However, this trickle of highly qualified blacks has had little effect on the growing poverty of the cities, nor can it do much to avert the ills poverty brings.

The most serious of these ills is a decline in

IN THE NEWS

Families May Leave, but the City Still Thrives

Seattle, Washington, has "begun to think the unthinkable." After years of worrying about the loss of white middle-class families, some city officials are beginning to say the trend is not so bad.

An iconoclastic study . . . released by the city's Office of Policy Planning has provoked sharp debate by saying, in effect, that there is little the city can do to attract more families with children, that it can get along without them and that it might as well encourage the mounting tide of young single people and childless couples.

While to Eastern eyes Seattle, with its immaculate streets and bustling downtown, seems relatively healthy, it has not been immune to the ills that have ravaged places like Detroit and Newark—unemployment, racial friction, housing decay, the flight to suburbia. It has also been deeply affected by the demographic shifts that are transforming many American cities, such as the declining birth rate, the postponement of marriage, the trend toward living alone or sharing homes with unrelated people.

People have been particularly concerned about the loss of children in the city; single people and childless couples have been moving into the private homes once owned by families. "Only about a quarter of the households [now] include children, a proportion well below the national average, [and] one-third of the households have only one person." School enrollment dropped from 100,000 in 1962 to 93,000 in 1977, and is expected to fall to 90,000 in the 1980s.

At the same time, the proportion of people aged twenty to thirty-four has risen from 19 to 29 percent of the population. Many of these people are professionals or skilled workers earning high salaries. While these people don't require such public services as the maintenance of play-

the quality of public services and housing. Cities raise their money for public services—education, mass transportation, hospitals, police, sewers, and so forth—through taxes. Poor populations yield less tax money. Whereas one in fourteen suburban residents had an income that fell below the poverty line in 1971, one in seven inner-city dwellers was listed as officially poor. And blacks generally are poorer than whites. Nonwhite income for 1976 averaged only two-thirds of white income for that year (U.S. Bureau of the Census, *Statistical Abstract,* 1977: 407).

Unemployment rates are also high in the inner-city slums. In 1966, which was a good year for the national economy (3.7 percent unemployment nationwide), some slums had as much as five times the national unemployment rate. But unemployment figures are not the best indicators of insufficient

grounds and schools, they encourage the opening of such new businesses as restaurants and stylish clothing and furniture shops. A number of city officials feel this new group is putting more into the city than they are taking out. In the words of the head of the Office of Policy Planning: ''[It's time to examine the] urban mythology that says if you lose children the city will die.''

Far from dying, Seattle can become more vigorous, says the report, if its recommendations are followed. The study urges that apartments be built to accommodate the growing childless population and that more office towers be built to satisfy the new business/service economy.

Not everyone agrees with the report's conclusions and recommendations:

"It is true that these young people have lots of spending money," says [one city official]. "But you change more of the city than you can afford to. It leads to an anonymous locked-door type of city."

And another official thinks that new office towers will add little to the city's income base, because most of the people who will work in them live in the suburbs.

Through all the controversy, Seattle's mayor retains a philosophical outlook. ''Most mayors,'' he says, ''wring their hands about the loss of the white middle class, but a city is a living organism that changes every 20 to 30 years.''

SOURCE: Robert Reinhold, ''Seattle's Families Are Pulling Out, but the City May Learn to Like It,'' *The New York Times*, March 28, 1977, pp. 31–32.

employment opportunities or substandard wages. In a special study, the Department of Labor determined the ''subemployment'' rates in several inner-city slums throughout the nation. These figures included all those persons who didn't show up in the official unemployment statistics but who made wages inadequate to live on. These subemployment rates were 45 percent in New Orleans's slums, 24 percent in Boston's Roxbury section, 31 percent in New York's Harlem, 47 percent in San Antonio's East and West sides, and 34 percent in North Philadelphia (Matza, 1971: 605). Unemployment seems to hit black teen-agers the hardest. In 1977, teen-age joblessness in America's black urban ghettos soared to more than 40 percent.

One of the reasons for urban poverty is the steady decrease in job opportunities in the

The widespread movement of middle- and upper-class families from the cities to the suburbs has helped to create blighted inner-city areas, such as New York's South Bronx.
Because the poor who remain pay lower taxes, less revenue is available for public services and housing, and the quality of these facilities declines. (Bernard Guillot)

inner cities. Industry and commerce once located in the inner cities are moving to the suburbs. This means that fewer jobs are available to the inner-city resident. New York City, once a major producer of consumer goods, has declined drastically as a manufacturing center, with a quarter of a million jobs being lost between 1970 and 1974 (Stern, 1974: 1). Its garment industry has lost out to foreign manufacturers, while other businesses have been discouraged by the

deterioration of its rail system and by the difficulties involved in transporting goods through the congested New York streets. Even New York's attraction as a prestigious business address may be on the wane now that improved communication systems allow corporations to relocate elsewhere and still remain "in touch" (Starr, 1976: 100–101).

Because of deteriorating conditions in the inner cities, there is a strong demand for public services which can't be met by the cities' inadequate tax revenues. Widespread unemployment means that more money must be spent on welfare. Because crime and poverty are so closely associated, more money must be spent on police services. Health, education, and mass transit get the short end of the budgetary stick. In New York's rich neighborhoods, there is 1 private doctor for every 200 persons; in some poor inner-city neighborhoods, there is 1 for every 10,000 persons. Inner-city schools spend two-thirds as much per pupil as some suburban schools do. Rural- or suburban-dominated state legislatures allocate more money to highway construction than to mass transit. Because inner-city buildings are older, more money must be spent on fire protection. In some cases, inner-city buildings are falling apart and being abandoned. Estimates of abandoned buildings in New York City go as high as 100,000 (Commission on the Cities in the Seventies, 1972:43–80). And New York City is not alone in its problems; this is the condition of most of America's older cities.

City governments can't reverse this decline because they have no way to make the suburban dweller pay for his or her use of the city. Suburbanites commute into the city for work and entertainment and thereby use the city's transit, fire, police, and other public services. Increasing toll fees on commuter routes into the cities involves the risk of losing even more of the commuters' business.

Because the suburbanite is getting a good deal, he or she is not going to put more money into the city's coffers voluntarily. And because the city government seldom has control over the entire metropolitan region, no unified local government exists that can enforce a more equitable taxation scheme. (The average number of separate governing units for the typical metropolitan area is ninety-one!)

"Unslumming" the City

The causes of urban disorganization and inner-city decline are numerous, and there are many proposals for reversing these trends. Some of these concentrate on improving the inner cities, while others involve coping with sprawling urban growth.

One strategy that has been popular in the past is urban renewal. This has the advantage of presenting an impressive appearance of improvement. As disreputable slums collapse beneath the wrecking ball and spanking new high-rise apartment buildings appear in their place, casual onlookers can't help but receive the impression that the city is taking a new lease on life. The truth is that such face-lift measures may save particular areas of a city, but not the city itself. At its worst, urban renewal merely provides the city's existing middle class with better places to live as it squeezes the poor into a smaller area. On the other hand, when applied to tourist areas, face-lifting methods may make the city more attractive to visitors.

Many present-day observers argue, therefore, that truly significant improvements in the cities can result only from somehow increasing the income of inner-city residents. Sociologist Herbert J. Gans maintains that the most effective way to transform the cities from poor to middle-class communities is not to lure the middle class back from the suburbs but to transform the poor themselves into middle-class citizens. He argues that poor, nonwhite inner-city dwellers aren't inherently attached to unhealthy, violence-ridden life styles—quite the contrary. They would live middle-class lives if only they had the chance. Gans suggests that the federal government give them that chance by instituting ''a revival of the war on poverty, but this time it should be a major war, rather than a minor skirmish'' (Gans, 1977: 21).

Other proposed solutions to the urban problem are based on the premise that radical change is inevitable and that the best we can do is to prepare for it in such a way as to avert outright catastrophe. Some have championed the idea of building *new towns,* carefully and comprehensively planned communities, usually near a larger metropolis, which would take care of urban growth in a systematic fashion. Ebenezer Howard began an English new town, Letchworth, back in 1902, and according to its 1966 census, Great Britain had over 150,000 people living in such developments. In the United States, Columbia, Maryland, and Reston, Virginia, are perhaps the best-known new towns (Schaffer, 1970: 22–25). But this strategy, affecting only small minorities, offers only a partial and gradual solution to the urban crisis.

Still other observers have suggested that our shrinking cities would operate far more efficiently if residents of deteriorating neighborhoods were induced to relocate in more economically viable areas where public funds could be concentrated (Starr, 1976: 105). In a similar vein, some commentators have suggested that the best way to cope with the flight from the cities is not to work against it but to concentrate on opening up the suburbs. Under such a plan, the suburbs would cease to be the exclusive haven of the

THE PLIGHT OF THE CITIES: WHO IS RESPONSIBLE?

City planners have been lauded as miracle workers who can turn decaying city neighborhoods into clean, well-designed centers of community life. They have also been criticized for creating uninteresting, homogeneous environments where vital neighborhoods once stood. Below, Jane Jacobs and Herbert Gans, two vigorous spokespeople for city life, discuss the role of planners in the cities of modern America.

In *The Death and Life of Great American Cities*, Jane Jacobs argues that a city neighborhood's vitality comes from the diversity of its inhabitants and the variety of services it provides. For her, Boston's North End and New York City's Greenwich Village are models of vital, thriving city neighborhoods. In these neighborhoods, low-level residential buildings, where both low- and high-income residents live, coexist with small businesses. This combination generates a bustling, round-the-clock street life, which in turn promotes neighborhood safety, because the residents watching the streets and the people on the sidewalks discourage criminal activity.

An active street life also provides residents and storekeepers with an opportunity for socializing. Jacobs describes the street life of Boston's North End this way:

Mingled all among the buildings for living were an incredible number of splendid food stores, as well as such enterprises as upholstery making, metal working, carpentry, food processing. The streets were alive with children playing, people shopping, people strolling, people talking. Had it not been a cold January day, there would surely have been people sitting. . . . The general street atmosphere of buoyancy, friendliness and good health was so infectious that I began asking directions of people just for the fun of getting in on some talk.

All cities, she argues, should have neighborhoods and street life like this. People want diversity, and where it exists, they join in community life, generating vitality.

But over the past few decades, neighborhoods like Greenwich Village and the North End have become scarcer and scarcer. Gone are the low-rise residential buildings that shared the streets with small shops. In their place are architecturally bland high-rise apartment buildings whose tenants are either rich and white or poor and black. The small stores are also gone, replaced by shopping centers full of chain stores.

This new kind of city building has serious social consequences. The stores of small merchants no longer line the streets; the area is no longer alive with children playing and people stopping to talk. The streets have ceased to be the center of neighborhood communication.

Who is to blame for the destruction of vital city neighborhoods and community life? According to Jacobs, city planners are.

Concerned more with theory than with human needs, the planners have substituted homogeneity for cultural variety. And as their theories have influenced policy makers and bankers, less and less money has been available for revitalizing older neighborhoods that don't conform to their ideals. In short, city planners have inadvertently been planning the destruction of American cities.

In *People and Plans,* Herbert Gans attacks Jacobs's theory. First, Gans asserts, the neighborhoods Jacobs maintains are models of vital, thriving areas are not diverse, but are actually quite homogeneous. They simply seem diverse because the people who live in them are primarily from the working class. Since in working-class culture the home is reserved for family life, much social life takes place on the streets. Second, Gans counters, Jacobs uses a working-class neighborhood as her ideal and assumes that neighborhoods that differ from her model are inferior to it. He contends that although the street life of working-class neighborhoods makes them appear more vital than middle-class ones, "visibility is not the only measure of vitality" (29). In middle-class families, most socializing takes place in the home, so although street life doesn't exist, vital social relations still do.

Gans claims that Jacobs is also mistaken in blaming the ills of cities on city planners. The new styles of residential neighborhoods reflect not so much the ideas of city planners as the preferences of the middle-class people who inhabit many of these neighborhoods. Middle-class families don't want working-class neighborhoods. They value privacy more than "visible vitality," status more than convenience. And since to them status means quiet residential streets, they would rather drive to shopping centers than walk to shops down the street. Shopping centers haven't been imposed by planners; they have been built to answer a need.

Finally, the factor responsible for the plight of the cities is not their lack of diversity but "the overcrowding of already old buildings by poverty-stricken and otherwise deprived nonwhites, who have no other place to go" (31). Slum landlords would rather see their buildings overcrowded than rehabilitate them, simply because it is more profitable. It is not city planners who are responsible for the deterioration of the cities, but private enterprise (which profits from the city's impoverished residents) and the middle class (who chooses to ignore them).

SOURCE: Jane Jacobs, *The Death and Life of Great American Cities,* New York: Vintage, 1961; Herbert J. Gans, "Urban Vitality and the Fallacy of Physical Determinism," in *People and Plans: Essays on Urban Problems and Solutions,* New York: Basic Books, 1968, pp. 25–33.

class and would become open to low- and moderate-income housing. Besides improving conditions in the ghettos, and allowing workers employed by suburban companies to live near their jobs, this plan would help to prevent future confrontations between the disadvantaged inner city and the privileged suburbs (Downs, 1973: 26).

Whatever plan or plans our society opts for, one thing is clear: the problems of cities are so massive that a national policy is needed to help solve them. Tinkering separately with transportation, urban renewal, employment, education, health services, and the rest does not work. Comprehensive plans for monitoring cities and devising strategies for dealing with their problems are imperative.

THE ENVIRONMENT

When June comes to the farmlands around Edwardsville, Illinois, residents know they can count on the weather to soon turn foul. Every summer, as though by a design of fate, the Edwardsville area is subjected to abnormally heavy thunderstorm activity, rain, and hail. Why does it get 90 percent more rain and 80 percent more hail than the surrounding area? The not-so-obvious answer is that the industry of St. Louis twenty-one miles to the southeast has caused marked changes in the climate to the northeast, and the winds concentrate the effects on Edwardsville.

The Edwardsville story illustrates just one facet of the direct and indirect effects cities have on the natural environment (Clawson and Hall, 1973: 226). The direct effects, for the most part, involve modifying the environment through various uses of land, such as building schools, homes, factories, and

shopping centers, and paving roads and highways. The indirect effects are often less visible, but they are no less serious. For example, cars carrying commuters from their homes to jobs in the city are a major source of air pollution. The airplanes that carry intercity travelers also cause air pollution, and the noise they create is another kind of pollution. Indirect effects result from the manufacturing of cars for commuters and planes for travelers, since these industrial activities create enormous demands for such materials as rubber, steel, and glass, and for oil and other natural resources—none of which exists in unlimited quantities. Still more pressures on resources result from the unremitting rate at which urban dwellers use up food, textiles, and a wide variety of other goods. Consumption leads in turn to the disposal of waste products, which can pollute both air and water. The acres of garbage dumps on the outskirts of large cities attest to the persistence of this urban consumption/pollution cycle.

The Ecosystem: How Much Will It Sustain?

The impact of urbanization on air, water, land, climate, natural resources, and people is only one sign of the environmental crisis that we now face. It is fashionable to blame the crisis on such isolated factors as the spread of cities, overpopulation, and industrialization, but while these are certainly contributing factors, they are ultimately only symptoms of more basic difficulties. A major cause of the crisis is an approach to nature that is derived from an idea of it as an inexhaustible, indestructible, "free source of supply for whatever human purposes man can conceive" (Murphy, 1971: 63). By contrast, ecologists have proposed that we look at the environment as a delicate and intricately interconnected whole, an *ecosystem*—a term ecologists use to mean a system formed by the interaction of a community of living things with their environment. For example, the great plains of East Africa support one of the largest animal populations on earth. The predators (such as lions and hyenas) depend on the vast herds of grass-eaters (wildebeest, zebras, and so on) for food; the herbivores depend on the predators to remove weak and sick individuals and to keep the size of their populations under control. All—from the ant to the elephant—are interdependent.

Environmentalists identify two processes that threaten this delicate balance. One is *pollution,* which occurs when the amount and kind of wastes produced by human activities exceed the environment's capacity to absorb them. Much of our air is polluted, as

is most of our water—by one estimate, for example, a third of the drinking water in this country fails to satisfy standards set by the federal government (Bredemeier and Getis, 1973). The other side of the problem is *resource depletion,* which involves using up the earth's nonreplaceable resources, such as fossil fuels. The oil crisis has made us aware that such supplies are not inexhaustible, and that practical and safe new energy sources are needed to supplement dwindling oil reserves.

Pollution—one by-product of urbanization and industrialization—threatens to destroy nature's delicate ecosystem. Many people believe that the continuation of human life depends upon a new ethic that stresses cooperation with, rather than conquest of, the environment.
(EPA-Documerica)

Throughout history, of course, people have been changing the face of the environment. The process began slowly with fishing, hunting, and gathering, which had only a negligible impact on the landscape; then came herding, which involved a growing ability to control nature, and which was followed by the systematic cultivation of land (Dansereau, 1970: 631). But no development in humankind's relatively short sojourn on earth has had a greater or more negative effect on nature than urbanization and industrialization, both of which entail increasing power not only to manipulate the environment but also to destroy it. Ecologist Pierre Dansereau suggests that there are only two ways left to accelerate our ''mastery'' over the environment: the first is to control the climate, and the second is by means of ''exobiological escape,'' or mass exodus into outer space.

As long as we stay on earth, however, the problems of pollution and dwindling resources are inescapable. In fact they are forcing us, at the last possible moment, to develop a new attitude about nature in order to survive. Many believe that the continuation of human life on earth requires nothing less than a new ''global ethic'' of conservation, cooperation, and harmony with, rather than conquest of, nature.

Limits to Growth The earth's capacity to support a growing human population and economy was the subject of a study called *The Limits to Growth* (Meadows et al., 1972), sponsored by the Club of Rome, an informal international organization. The conclusions reached in the study were ominous. According to the report, both the population and the economy are growing at an exponential rate—doubling in size every so often. But there are limits to the earth's ability to sustain exponential growth—to provide food, raw materials, and fossil and nuclear fuels—and limits to the planet's capacity to absorb wastes and recycle matter. If present growth trends persist in population, industrialization, food production, resource depletion, and pollution, warned the Club of Rome, the earth's upper limits of tolerance will be reached within the next 100 years.

The only solution, according to the Club of Rome, is an immediate drop in the birth rate (by about 40 percent); stabilization of resource consumption; and at least a 20 percent cut in investments in new industry and agriculture (put another way, a significant cut in our standard of living). Decisions, the group argued, must be based on hard facts, on ''value-free'' computer analysis. Nor will a piecemeal approach, centered around local problems only, work. The solution is to design a cooperative global strategy that takes the world and all its parts into account.

Needless to say, the reports sponsored or endorsed by the Club of Rome have stirred heated debate. Critics argue that predicting imminent doom is counterproductive, for it suggests that taking small steps to correct environmental problems is futile. Indeed, fatalism (the feeling that nothing can be done) could lead to an orgy of consumption and waste. Others do not accept the club's assumption that we have reached the limits of our technological ingenuity. There may yet be technological solutions to the problems technology has created. Morever, critics feel the Club of Rome underestimates the political, cultural, and practical difficulties of implementing a global plan. Traditions, attitudes, hopes, dreams, and other variables that can't be computerized do make a difference.

Ultimately, whether one accepts the Club of Rome's pessimistic view depends on whether one is predisposed to see Western industrial civilization as doomed, or to con-

figure 17:3   Ecology and the escalation of human impact on the environment

SOURCE: Pierre Dansereau, ''Ecology and the Escalation of Human Impact,'' *International Social Science Journal*, vol. 22, (1970), figure 1, p. 631. Published by UNESCO, Paris, France.

The steps in human control of the environment, and a tentative characterization of their impact: (1) virgin land; (2) gathering; (3) hunting and fishing; (4) herding; (5) agriculture; (6) industry; (7) urbanization; (8) climate control; (9) exobiological escape.

tinue to have faith in humanity's capacity for reason and ability to adapt. But there is general agreement that there are, indeed, limits to growth; that we can't count on technology to overcome these limits, as it has in the past; and that therefore human beings must change their ways.

Environmental Problems in Sociological Perspective

In a 1977 address to the nation, President Carter urged Americans to accept the necessity of energy conservation as being "the moral equivalent of war," and he warned that a failure to do so could easily result in a national catastrophe. The White House also prepared a comprehensive energy plan that included such provisions as higher taxes on gasoline, the use of insulation in new houses and buildings, and a reduction in the annual growth rate of energy demand. However, to date, only small portions of the plan have been implemented.

As yet unanswered is the question of why, when the problems of pollution and resource depletion are so obvious, so little is being done. Sociology doesn't have all the answers, but it can point out obstacles to environmental action in the social system. Here we will use the 1969 Santa Barbara oil spill to show what the sociological perspective reveals about environmental problems.[2]

On January 28, 1969, an oil well off the coast of Santa Barbara, California, erupted. For the next ten days oil poured into the ocean. The well was finally brought under control on February 7, only to erupt again on February 12. This fissure was closed on March 3, but seepage continues to this day. Damage to this town, which prided itself on its physical environment, was severe.

_____

[2] The description of the Santa Barbara incident is based on Molotch, 1977.

In testimony before the county board that February, one engineer after another said there was no way to prevent such accidents in the future. Nevertheless, on April 2 the Department of the Interior announced that selective drilling would be resumed "to relieve pressures." (Geological or political pressures? queried the local newspaper.) The government did issue what it called tough new standards for offshore drilling. (Oil companies are now financially responsible for cleaning up after a spill.) The government also invited local officials to participate in hearings on reopening the wells. (They refused because they felt the hearings were a sham.) But there was nothing Santa Barbarans could do to prevent further drilling.

Such powerlessness came as a shock to residents of this wealthy upper-middle-class community. Having never had reason to oppose the government or big industry, they had believed the establishment was on their side. At first they thought they would be able to stop the drilling through court action. They could not. Even so, Santa Barbarans assumed they had the resources, spare time, and contacts with national leaders in government and industry to get something done. They did not. Drilling was resumed. Today the question residents of Santa Barbara ask is not whether the channel will be polluted but how polluted it is.

Attitude Change   The Santa Barbara oil spill and similar incidents make headlines for a week or two, but fail to capture the national imagination. Some social scientists would attribute the lack of sustained interest in environmental problems to the attitude we have already discussed—that exponential growth is necessary for social happiness and stability. This feeling is central to what Kenneth Boulding calls the "cowboy economy," a reckless and romantic way of life dedicated to maximum production and maximum consumption. Boulding recommends a transition to a "spaceman economy," in which the earth is seen as a spaceship with limited reservoirs of everything (Boulding, 1970: 96). E. F. Schumacher, in *Small Is Beautiful* (1973), argues that the solution to most contemporary ills is decentralization and a life style emphasizing frugal living.

Resistance in the Social System Not all environmentalists and social scientists, however, believe spendthrift attitudes are the only—or even the major—problem. Instead, they point to a collusion of government, business, and the communications media (and even universities and scientists) in resisting limitations on industry. The Department of the Interior based decisions about the Santa Barbara channel on data provided by the oil companies. As if this weren't suspicious enough, the government refused to release these data to the public because they belonged to the oil company. The information was "proprietary." Morever, when Santa Barbarans did obtain "facts," these were often contradictory. Estimates of the rate of seepage during the spill ranged from 630 gallons per day (the U.S. Geological Survey) to 8,400 gallons per day (an independent research company). Later, residents discovered that many of the local experts depended on grants from oil companies for their research. The odds against local protesters being able to resist joint actions by government, industry, and the universities are pitifully small.

Harvey Molotch (1977) cites a number of subtle ways in which the establishment can diffuse local opposition and disorient the public. The government has the resources to stage "pseudo-events"—that is, to stage events so that prearranged consequences will follow. Examples in Santa Barbara were President Nixon's "inspection of the beach" (a short stroll, far from demonstrators and from the areas of worst damage) and public hearings. Although the hearings gave the impression that the public was participating in the decision-making process, the hearings themselves had no effect on subsequent decisions. Their sole function was to allow the public to blow off steam—steam that might have been harnessed for the opposition. Pseudo-events are empty ceremonies.

The government can also arrange what Molotch calls "creeping events." By dribbling information out piecemeal, over a period of time, it can prevent local people from realizing an event is taking place until it has already happened. For example, authorization to resume drilling at different wells was announced on April 1, June 12, July 2, August 2, and so on. Hence there was no particular point in time when the government permitted drilling in the channel to resume—an event that might have incited strong protest.

Add to this the fact that the media are not set up to cover events like the Santa Barbara oil spill, except in the barest outline. Media news is largely anecdotal. The complexity of environmental issues requires more time on the air, and more research behind the scenes, than journalists have at their disposal. Whether the oil companies exercise direct control over the media by threatening to withdraw advertising is difficult to say. A Metromedia crew spent several days filming in Santa Barbara, but the project was suddenly dropped. No reasons were given.

All of this makes it extremely difficult to mobilize opposition to activities that degrade the environment. Thus, resistance to change is built into the social structure.

The Costs and Benefits of Pollution Allan Schnaiberg (1977) takes this analysis of structural resistance to environmental programs a step farther. Environmentalists have long assumed that pollution of the air and water is a universal problem that affects rich, poor, and middle-class people alike. Through cost-benefit analysis (a technique borrowed from economics), Schnaiberg shows this is not the case.

The costs of environmental decay are far higher for the poor than the rich. Many of the poor are trapped in inner cities, where air and water pollution are the most severe. They can't afford to move to the suburbs or to take long vacations. In rural areas, migrant farm workers—not farm owners—are the most likely to be exposed to such harmful agricultural chemicals as DDT.

Not only are the well-off able to escape pollution, but they actually benefit from it. As producers and stockholders, they reap the profits from industries that pollute the air and

water without paying the costs of environmental degradation. As the largest consumers, they also benefit from prices lower than would be expected if strict standards were enforced. Not surprisingly, the upper class resists environmental legislation. (Santa Barbara was an exception: the residents' upper-class homes were under direct attack.)

As things stand, steps to improve the environment would cost the poor as much as environmental neglect does. As consumers, the poor pay as much for mandatory pollution-control devices on cars as the rich do—but the cost of such devices represents a higher percentage of their incomes. As employees, the poor are the first to be fired when plants are shut because environmen-

figure 17:4 Reordered national goals in an environmentalist framework

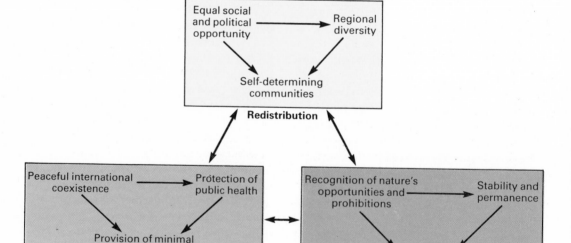

SOURCE: T. O'Riordan, *Environmentalism* (London: Pion Limited, 1976), figure 1.2, p. 26.

Under our present system, many citizens at all socioeconomic levels benefit from environmental abuse. Environmentalists feel that any effective means of improving our environment will require substantial changes in both our social structure and values.

tal-protection standards make them unprofitable. Not surprisingly, the poor are extremely wary of programs that raise the cost of living and also threaten jobs.

What we have, then, is a surprising "alliance" between the rich and the poor *against* correcting environmental abuse. This need not be. Schnaiberg suggests that the rich might well be convinced to accept a system of environmental controls that passes the cost on to the poor and middle classes, but that this would result in *"social environmental* degradation [that] may far outweigh any gain in the *physical* environment" (476). The alternative is to distribute costs and benefits proportionately. Schnaiberg cites by way of example a project in the Chicago area.

Newspapers are collected in middle- and upper-class white suburbs and delivered to an organization in a poor black inner-city neighborhood, which sells them to paper companies for recycling. In this project, everyone benefits.

As we've emphasized throughout this section, environmental problems are extremely complex. Experts can't agree on the parameters of the problem, or on the length of time we have to solve them. New technology may provide some of the answers. But there are sure to be changes in values and in the social structure as well if we are to reverse current trends. When and how change will take place, and what form it will take, are open questions.

SUMMARY

With the Industrial Revolution of the nineteenth century and its technological innovations, the rapid growth of cities began—not only in this country but worldwide. Villages grew into towns, towns into cities, cities into metropolises, and metropolises into megalopolises.

The relative anonymity and impersonality of urban social relations has created images of alienation and loneliness in the city. Research has shown that this notion of life in the city is largely a myth. The urban environment may foster close family and neighborhood ties and may also allow for a range of subcultures, each of which is a closely knit community. Heavily urbanized areas rarely offer space for private homes and gardens or a sense of security, however, so the flow of people to the suburbs has increased steadily in recent years. Suburban life is often regarded as oppressively conformist, but this is also a caricature. Suburbs are far from being all alike, although within each community, there is a tendency toward shared values and life styles.

Describing the modern city has been a persistent challenge to sociologists. Much of the pioneering work in the study of urban organization—physical and social—was done during the 1920s and 30s. Attempts to explain patterns and changes within cities relied on *urban ecology,* which applies biological principles of competition and natural selection to the city. Since dissimilar uses of land are often incompatible, a single area usually harbors only one kind of use. When competition for the limited urban space becomes intense, however, the land use of greatest economic significance usually prevails. Changes occur in a predictable succession, described as an *invasion cycle.* The results of these processes have been described by several models of urban structure: the *concentric zone, sector,* and *multiple nuclei* models. The major weakness in the ecological approach is its minimization of the influences that residents' often complex and unpredictable behavior can have on a city's development.

In most large metropolitan areas, the number of people moving to the suburbs far exceeds the number of those relocating in the central city. Since most of the people who leave for the suburbs belong to the middle class, and those who stay are poor, these cities are in a state of crisis. Because poor populations pay lower taxes, there is less money available for adequate public services and housing. Business and industry are also relocating to suburban areas, so unemployment and underemployment rates in the inner city are high. Several methods have been proposed to reverse these trends. Besides urban renewal, they include upgrading the socioeconomic status of the urban poor, building new towns, relocating residents of blighted areas in more economically viable neighborhoods, and opening the suburbs to lower-income people.

The impact of urbanization on air, water, land, climate, natural resources, and people is only a part of the environmental crisis we now face. A prevalent disregard for the fact that we are part of an *ecosystem,* a delicate network of interactions between a community of living things and their environment, is largely responsible for this situation. Two processes threaten this ecosystem—*pollution* and *resource depletion.* Several studies, including one sponsored by the Club of Rome, have emphasized that there are limits to our growth that demand prompt attention.

In addition to the need for a change in values, it is apparent that there are many obstacles to environmental action built into our social system. Molotch's report on the 1969 oil spill off the coast of Santa Barbara, California, points to the collusion of government, industry, and other forces against environmental improvement. Schnaiberg emphasizes that different classes pay for and benefit unequally from environmental abuse. The problem of the quality of the environment is a highly complex one, and one of the few certainties is that any effective solution is bound to alter both our values and our social structure.

GLOSSARY

city   as Wirth defines it, a relatively large, dense, and permanent settlement of socially heterogeneous individuals.

concentric zone model   a model of urban structure proposed by E. W. Burgess; according to it, cities are laid out with the business district at the core, surrounded by a transitional ring of residential instability and high crime rates, beyond which are the various residential zones.

ecosystem   a system formed by the interaction of a community of living things with their environment.

invasion cycle   a general pattern of change in urban land use that begins imperceptibly. Once change is recognized, opposition de-

velops and continues until a tip point is reached, when the new users succeed in starting to drive out earlier users. Once the new use is established, the cycle has reached its climax phase.

megalopolis   a recent urban form in which once-distinct cities grow together, forming a functional unit.

multiple nuclei model   a model of urban structure proposed by Harris and Ullman; according to it, land uses, costs, and interests cause a city to develop in a series of nuclei, each with specialized activities.

new town   a comprehensively planned city, usually near a larger metropolis, built to absorb urban growth in a systematic fashion.

pollution a condition that occurs when the amount and kind of wastes produced by human activities exceed the environment's capacity to absorb them.

resource depletion using up the earth's nonreplaceable resources.

sector model a model of urban structure proposed by Hoyt; according to it, cities are composed of sectors around a central business district, distributed along major transportation routes radiating outward from the center.

social area analysis a method for describing the social characteristics of subareas in terms of such broad social categories as social rank, family type, and ethnicity.

urban ecology the study of urban patterns and their changes based on a biological model of competition and natural selection.

urbanization the increase in the percentage of a population that lives in urban settlements and the consequent extension of influence of urban ways over the populace.

REFERENCES

Kenneth E. Boulding, "The Economics of the Coming Spaceship Earth," in Garrett de Bell, ed., *The Environmental Handbook.* New York: Ballantine, 1970.

Harry C. Bredemeier and Judith Getis, eds., *Environment, People, and Inequalities.* New York: Wiley, 1973.

Gerald Breese, *Urbanization in Newly Developing Countries.* Englewood Cliffs, N.J.: Prentice-Hall, 1966.

John Burchard, "The Culture of Urban America," in Louis K. Loewenstein, ed., *Urban Studies,* 2nd ed. New York: Free Press, 1977.

V. Gordon Childe, *Man Makes Himself.* New York: New American Library, 1952.

Marion Clawson and Peter Hall, *Planning and Urban Growth.* Baltimore, Md.: Johns Hopkins University Press, 1973.

Commission on the Cities in the Seventies, *State of the Cities.* New York: Praeger, 1972.

Pierre Dansereau, "Ecology and the Escalation of Human Impact." *International Social Science Journal,* vol. 22 (1970): 628–647.

Anthony Downs, *Opening Up the Suburbs.* New Haven, Conn.: Yale University Press, 1973.

John Esposito and John Fiorillo: "Who's Left on the Block? New York City's Working Class Neighborhoods," in Hans Spiegel, ed., *Citizen Participation in Urban Development.* Fairfax, Va.: Learning Resources Corporation/NTL, 1974.

Reynolds Farley, "Components of Suburban Population Growth," in Barry Schwartz, ed., *The Changing Face of the Suburbs.* Chicago: University of Chicago Press, 1976.

Sylvia Fleis Fava, "Beyond Suburbia." *Annals of the American Academy of Political and Social Science,* vol. 422 (November 1975): 10–24.

———, ed., *Urbanism in World Perspective: A Reader.* New York: Crowell, 1968.

Walter Firey, "Sentiment and Symbolism as Ecological Variables," in George A. Theodorson, ed., *Studies in Human Ecology.* Evanston, Ill.: Row, Peterson, 1961.

Claude S. Fischer, "Toward a Subcultural Theory of Urbanism." *American Journal of Sociology,* vol. 80 (May 1975): 1319–1341.

Herbert J. Gans, *People and Plans.* New York: Basic Books, 1968.

———, "Why Exurbanites Won't Reurbanize Themselves." *The New York Times,* February 12, 1977, p. 21.

Jean Gottman, *Megalopolis: The Urbanized Northeastern Seaboard of the United States.* Cambridge, Mass.: MIT Press, 1964.

Peter Hall, *The World Cities.* New York: McGraw-Hill, 1966.

Chauncy D. Harris and Edward L. Ullman, "The Nature of Cities." *Annals of the American Academy of Political and Social Science,* vol. 242 (November 1945): 12.

Philip Hauser, "Applications of the Ideal-Type Constructs to the Metropolis in the Economically Less Advanced Areas," in Sylvia Fleis Fava, ed., *Urbanism in World Perspective: A Reader*. New York: Crowell, 1968.

————, "The Chaotic Society." *American Sociological Review*, vol. 34 (February 1969): 1–19.

Homer Hoyt, "The Structure of American Cities in the Post-War Era." *American Journal of Sociology*, vol. 48 (January 1943): 475–492.

John D. Kasarda and Morris Janowitz, "Community Attachment in Mass Society." *American Sociological Review*, vol. 39 (June 1974): 328–339.

David Matza, "Poverty and Disrepute," in Robert K. Merton and Robert A. Nisbet, eds., *Contemporary Social Problems*, 3rd ed. New York: Harcourt, Brace, Jovanovich, 1971.

Donella Meadows, Dennis L. Meadows, Jorgen Randers, and William Behrens, III, *The Limits to Growth: A Report for the Club of Rome's Projection on the Predicament of Mankind*. New York: Universe Books, 1972.

Delbert C. Miller, *Leadership and Power in the Bos-Wash Megalopolis*. New York: Wiley, 1975.

Harvey Molotch, "Oil in Santa Barbara and Power in America," in John Walton and Donald E. Carns, eds., *Cities in Change*, 2nd ed. Boston: Allyn & Bacon, 1977.

Earl Finber Murphy, *Man and His Environment: Law*. New York: Harper & Row, 1971.

Robert E. Park, Ernest W. Burgess, and Roderick D. McKenzie, eds., *The City*. Chicago: University of Chicago Press, 1925.

Frank Schaffer, *The New Town Story*. London: MacGibbon & McKee, 1970.

Allen Schnaiberg, "Politics, Participation and Pollution: The 'Environmental Movement,'" in John Walton and Donald E. Carns, eds., *Cities in Change*, 2nd ed. Boston: Allyn & Bacon, 1977.

E. F. Schumacher, *Small Is Beautiful*. New York: Harper & Row, 1973.

Kent P. Schwirian, *Contemporary Topics in Urban Sociology*. Morristown, N.J.: General Learning Press, 1977.

Richard Sennett, *Uses of Disorder: Personal Identity and City Life*. New York: Random House, 1971.

Social Indicators, 1973. Washington, D.C.: U.S. Government Printing Office, 1974.

Roger Starr, "Making New York Smaller." *The New York Times Magazine*, November 14, 1976, pp. 32ff.

Maurice R. Stein, *The Eclipse of Community: An Interpretation of American Studies*. Princeton, N.J.: Princeton University Press, 1960.

Michael Stern, "Continued Job Declines Threaten City Economy." *The New York Times*, July 21, 1974, pp. 1, 40.

Gerald D. Suttles, *The Social Order of the Slum*. Chicago: University of Chicago Press, 1968.

Christopher Tunnard, "America's Super Cities," in H. Wentworth Eldredge, ed., *Taming Megalopolis: What Is and What Could Be*, vol. 1. New York: Doubleday Anchor, 1967.

U.S. Bureau of the Census, *Statistical Abstract of the United States, 1977*. Washington, D.C.: U.S. Government Printing Office, 1977.

Louis Wirth, "Urbanism as a Way of Life." *American Journal of Sociology*, vol. 44 (July 1938): 1–24.

FOR FURTHER STUDY

Urban Revitalization.   A small but growing trend toward a return to the central cities, notable in Boston, Washington, and Detroit, might lead to new urban residential patterns and the preservation and renovation of neighborhoods and historic landmarks. In *How Cities Are Saved* (New York: Universe Books, 1976), Herbert R. Lottman discusses the problems of cities and successful strategies to rebuild them. Rachelle Warren and Donald I. Warren examine neighborhood preservation in *The Neighborhood Organizer's*

Handbook (Notre Dame, Ind.: University of Notre Dame Press, 1977). An important aspect of revitalization is adequate housing for a city's residents. In *Housing by People* (New York: Pantheon, 1977), John F. C. Turner describes the efforts of local groups in North and South America to control the process of building construction and renovation; policies to encourage personal involvement in solving city housing problems are also suggested. In addition, several timely articles in the journal *Design and Environment,* vol. 7 (Summer 1976), deal with downtown renovations.

Urban Migrants—Coping with City Life.　After leaving the traditional order of rural areas, migrants to cities often appear to lead disorganized lives. However, social scientists have discovered that migrants may bring support systems to the city through family and friendship networks that help them create their own social order. An excellent study of Micmac Indians who live in the Northeast Maritime region and travel to Boston, Massachusetts, in search of employment is Jeanne Guillemin's *Urban Renegades: The Cultural Strategy of American Indians* (New York: Columbia University Press, 1975). In her book *All Our Kin: Strategies for Survival in a Black Community* (New York: Harper & Row, 1974), Carol Stack examines urban black households made up of migrants from the rural South. She finds these groups survive through a generalized reciprocity in which relatives and friends constantly exchange goods and services in order to spread irregular income throughout the community. In *Gypsies: The Hidden Americans* (New York: Free Press, 1975), Ann Southerland describes the ability of gypsies to manipulate the regulations of urban bureaucracies in order to maintain traditional cultural patterns and family ties.

The Environmental Crisis.　The environmental crisis created by our technological, urban society first received widespread attention with the publication of Rachel Carson's *The Silent Spring* (Boston: Houghton Mifflin, 1962). It remains an extraordinary book. More recently, John Fuller reports and discusses a series of crises that have already occurred, not just those we may expect in the future, in *The Poison That Fell from the Sky* (New York: Random House, 1978). Environmental factors from food production and distribution to the dumping of industrial wastes contribute to growing problems of world health. In his book *The Picture of Health: Environmental Sources of Disease* (Washington, D.C.: Worldwatch Institute, 1977), Erik Eckholm analyzes the spread of environmental diseases and the need for changes in social conditions to improve life chances. Clearly, the crisis in the environment is related to our use of energy sources. In *The American Energy Consumer* (Cambridge, Mass.: Ballinger, 1975), Dorothy K. Newman and Dawn Day discuss the different types of energy sources available.

CHAPTER 18

Collective Behavior
and Social Movements

On a Wednesday afternoon in June 1962, eleven workers in a textile mill in a small Southern town were hospitalized for severe nausea, weakness, and numbness in the limbs. The incident was reported on the evening news, along with rumors that all eleven had been bitten by insects, "June bugs," contained in a shipment of cloth from England. The next day another forty workers were stricken.

Two entomologists from a nearby state college searched the plant from top to bottom. They collected one black ant, a housefly, and several gnats, but none of the mysterious "June bugs." Public health officials were baffled. As far as they could tell, there was nothing physically wrong with the victims. Although they hesitated to use the words, clearly they attributed the epidemic to mass hysteria, fed by rumors and the media. Local people—particularly the victims—were skeptical; when the outbreaks stopped about three weeks later they could conclude only that "whatever has been here ain't here now" (Kerckhoff and Back, 1968: 7). If it was mass hysteria, why did the June bug hit these particular people at this particular time?

Why were some workers susceptible, others "immune"?

Mass hysteria is not the only form of seemingly inexplicable collective behavior. Why do ordinarily law-abiding citizens participate in lynchings, join in the burning and looting involved in riots, lose all semblance of self-control at revival meetings? In short, why do people behave differently in crowds than they do in small numbers? How can we explain the rise, fall, and subsequent resurrection of feminism in this country?

Psychologists and sociologists have long pondered the riddles of mass hysteria, fads, rumors, mobs, the rise of social movements, and the fluctuations of public opinion. While psychologists have focused on why individuals become caught up in the mood of the crowd, sociologists have concentrated on the social conditions that seem to precipitate collective behavior and on the social consequences of such behavior.

In this chapter we will look at various forms of crowd behavior (including mass hysteria, panics, and riots), social movements (the women's movement in particular), and public opinion as related forms of collective behavior.

COLLECTIVE BEHAVIOR: AN OVERVIEW

Collective behavior refers to the actions of relatively temporary, unstructured groups of people who more or less spontaneously focus on the same thing and react to one another's behavior. This definition encompasses a wide range of collective activities: crowds, riots, panics, fashions, crazes, social movements, public opinion. What do these varied phenomena have in common? They seem to take place outside ordinary social convention. They reflect no clearly defined rules or role expectations. Anything can happen. Participants improvise, picking up behavioral cues from one another. It is this sense of unpredictability and novelty that makes rock audiences different from history classes, protest movements different from established political parties.

Preconditions of Collective Behavior

Panics, such as the stock market crash that drove many to bankruptcy and precipitated the Great Depression in 1929, appear at first glance to be totally illogical and unpredictable. Fads, such as goldfish swallowing in the late 1930s or skateboarding in the 1970s, crop up spontaneously and spread of their own momentum. In its formlessness, collective behavior appears to be the opposite of normal, organized social behavior. But despite this impression, collective behavior doesn't simply erupt, any time, any place. There are several preconditions that make collective behavior more likely.

Structural Conduciveness The theory of *structural conduciveness* suggests that pre-

"Of course, I didn't know George was a Trekkie when I married him." (Drawing by Ziegler; © 1976 The New Yorker Magazine, Inc.)

conditions for collective behavior are built into a society's social structure. For example, the possibility of financial panics is inherent in open, fluid money economies, where people are able to speculate and to acquire or dispose of assets on short notice, and where wealth is considered personally and socially important. Such panics cannot occur in traditional societies, where property is acquired only through inheritance and marriage. Thus money economies are conducive to financial panics; traditional societies are not (Smelser, 1962: 15).

Similarly, the concentration of minorities in urban ghettos, where high unemployment and substandard housing encourage people to spend much of their time outdoors, is conducive to other forms of collective behavior: social movements as well as civic disorders. But the potential for collective behavior alone doesn't explain its occurrence.

The Unanticipated Event Sudden, unexpected events may create a state of *normlessness:* people don't know what they can or should do, and there are no cultural guidelines to direct them. For example, when a tornado struck Judsonia, Arkansas, and the surrounding towns in 1952, people had only a minute's warning. One moment people were heading home for dinner. The next moment 600 buildings had been leveled and 800 severely damaged; 46 people had been killed and more than 600 injured; electricity, telephone, and gas lines had been wiped out; and the nearest radio tower stopped broadcasting.

The worst problem for police in the hours that followed was traffic. Hundreds of cars poured into the area with people seeking relatives, offering help, or just sightseeing, mindless of the fact that they were blocking roads needed for emergency vehicles (Barton, 1969: 3–10).

When people are unexpectedly deprived of the world they take for granted, when catastrophic events such as the Judsonia tornado throw their ability to cope into doubt, *doing* becomes more important than thinking and planning. There is a need to define the situation, to restructure the social world, to reaffirm one's sense of mastery—in short, a need to act (Turner and Killian, 1972: 72–73).

Frustrated Social Concerns The free speech movement of 1964—a semester of sit-ins, strikes, and rallies—clearly illustrates the role of frustrated social concerns in collective behavior. Many of the Berkeley activists had participated in the civil rights movement during the previous summer, working for the rights of black Americans in the Deep South. When they themselves were denied such basic rights as peaceful assembly and free speech on their own campus, they erupted. Similarly, women who worked in the student movement of the 1960s found themselves denied both responsibility and respect—and so the women's liberation movement was born. There were no established, institutionalized channels through which either group could express its concerns.

The business district of Judsonia, Arkansas, after a tornado struck the town in 1952. Sudden and unexpected disasters such as this often create a state of normlessness in which it becomes more important to act than to think or plan. (UPI)

Frustrated social concerns, unanticipated events, and built-in sources of instability (structural conduciveness) create a sense of acute disorientation. Existing channels for self-expression seem inadequate; consciously and unconsciously people seek to define their unrest, to determine what is happening, who or what is responsible, how they should act. This urge to act, in the absence of clear cultural guidelines, sets the stage for collective behavior.

CROWD BEHAVIOR

Crowds are temporary collections of people, gathered around a person or event, who are conscious of and influenced by one another's presence. The primary difference between crowds and other social groups is that crowds are ephemeral; they lack a past and future, and they are relatively unstructured. For example, the people who collect around an accident will stop interacting as soon as they leave the scene. In his classic essay "Collective Behavior," first published in 1939, sociologist Herbert Blumer labeled such spontaneous congregations *casual crowds* whose "members come and go, giving but temporary attention to the object which has awakened the interest of the crowd, and entering into only feeble association with one another" (1951: 178). Blumer also identified three other types: conventional, expressive, and acting crowds.

Passengers on a plane, shoppers in a store, the audience at a concert are usually *conventional crowds*. These people are gathered for a specific purpose and behave according to established norms. For example, booing is expected at a football game, but would be considered extremely bad form at a concert of classical music or at a funeral.

There is relatively little interaction in a conventional crowd, where members individually pursue a common goal, a destination, a bargain, an entertainment.

The people at rock festivals, revival meetings, and carnivals (such as those held in New Orleans and in South American cities) are *expressive crowds:* members may behave in ways they would consider unacceptable in other settings. The legendary Woodstock Music and Art Fair, held in New York's Catskill Mountains in August 1969, is an example of such a crowd. An impressive array of rock stars drew over 300,000 young people to the farm where the festival was held. Because the focus was on individual, subjective experience, and because some conventional norms were suspended (police did not make arrests for drug possession or use, for example), and because of the peaceful, cooperative way the crowd behaved under these adverse circumstances, Woodstock became a legend.

An *acting crowd* is an excited, volatile collection of people who are focused on a controversial event that provokes their indignation, anger, and desire to act—a rape, for example, or an incident of real or imagined police brutality. The difference between an acting crowd and an expressive crowd is that an acting crowd is angry and purposeful. The difference between an acting crowd and a conventional crowd is that the members of an acting crowd are aroused to the point where established norms carry little weight with them.

Mobs

A *mob* is a crowd whose members are emotionally aroused and are engaged in or ready to engage in violence (Hoult, 1969: 206). In short, an acting crowd is a mob. Mass uprisings and destructive orgies have for cen-

A mob is a crowd whose members are emotionally aroused and prepared for violence. Infected by spontaneous mass excitement, they act with a sense of invincible power. During the Civil War, rioters in New York City, protesting conscription, battled the military. In 1968, young demonstrators in Prague, Czechoslovakia, attacked invading Soviet tanks with their fists and sticks. (Top, Culver Pictures. Bottom, Magnum Photos)

turies been the nightmare of people in power. Mob action was common in eighteenth- and nineteenth-century Europe: in town and country, throngs of armed men and women took over markets and warehouses, demanding rollbacks in prices and sometimes appropriating goods. In England angry bands of craftsmen burned factories and destroyed the machines that threatened their livelihood. On July 14, 1789, Parisians stormed the ancient Bastille in the most famous confrontation of the French Revolution.

Violent, unruly crowds have also figured importantly in American history. The nineteenth century was marked by farmers' revolts, miners' rebellions, bloody battles between unions and police, lynchings, and urban riots. The Civil War Draft Riot of 1863, which raged for four days, was probably one of the worst riots in this country's history. Mob action has also arisen in the twentieth century, one of the most recent examples being the civil disorders of the 1960s. The following brief account of the Detroit riot of July 1967 is based on the *Report of the National Advisory Commission on Civil Disorders* (1968). Although the report falls short of completely explaining the disorders, it does portray the dimensions of the Detroit uprising in concrete terms.

Riot in Detroit   *Riots* occur when crowds of people collectively engage in destructive behavior. In the summer of 1967, black ghettos in twenty-three cities exploded in violent public disturbances. Civil rights legislation had raised hopes but delivered little in the way of concrete improvements. The National Advisory Commission on Civil Disorders, which had been appointed by President Johnson, found that 70 percent of the rioters believed they deserved better jobs and blamed their problems on racism, not on lack of training, ability, or ambition.

Still, crowds don't become mobs unless they develop a generalized belief about who or what is responsible for their problems (Smelser, 1962). Anger must be focused. In the ghetto, stores that tantalize with the goods America seems to promise, and police who harass and sometimes abuse residents but seem unable to protect them, are ever-present reminders of white dominance. Anger and frustration were widespread. All that was needed was a spark to set it off.

On Saturday night, July 22, the Detroit vice squad conducted gambling raids on five social clubs. This mass arrest was the precipitating incident. By the time police hauled the last of the party-goers away on Sunday morning, a crowd of 200 had gathered on the street. A bottle hurled from the crowd crashed through the window of the last retreating patrol car. That was the beginning.

By 8:00 A.M., the crowd on 12th Street had grown to 3,000. Outnumbered, police withdrew. For a few hours the street became a carnival. However, by noon police reinforcements had moved quietly into surrounding streets. Soon rumors were spreading. A black man, it was said, had been bayoneted just blocks away.

The crowd's mood shifted from revelry to anger; people began stoning police and setting fire to stores. Firemen tried to control the fires. But at 4:30 Sunday afternoon, exhausted, they abandoned the area. At this point, the mayor proclaimed a curfew and summoned the National Guard.

As the number of fires and lootings declined, reports of snipers increased. These reports, reaching a peak of 534 on Wednesday, July 26, created panic and confusion. By Wednesday police were breaking into homes on the slightest excuse and arresting anyone found to have a weapon. Although it would be exaggerating to say the police rioted in Detroit, they were not acting in a routine manner. There is nothing routine about a riot; both the rioters and the police were caught up in collective behavior.

Before the end of the week, 7,200 people had been arrested. Forty-three people had been killed, thirty or more by police and soldiers, two by store owners, two or possibly three by rioters. Included among the dead were one National Guardsman, one fireman, and one policeman (killed accidentally by a fellow officer). Thirty-three of the victims were black, ten white. Property damage was estimated at $22 million.

The 1960s riots were not instigated or carried out by criminals; they were generally directed at property, not at people; their aim was to benefit from, not overthrow, the American social system (Allen, 1970). In short, they were "spontaneous protests against unjust social conditions" (Campbell and Schuman, 1968). They also proved to be an effective means of protest. They brought results that decades of peaceful protest had failed to bring. As one observer put it: "Reporters and cameramen rushed into ghettos; elected and appointed officials followed behind; sociologists and other scholars arrived shortly after. The President established a riot commission; so did the governors" (Fogelson, 1970: 146).

Explanations of Crowd Behavior

Why do riots break out? An explanation that appeals to many people is the riffraff theory—that only criminal types (hoodlums, drifters, bums, drug addicts) participate in riots, that a hard core of agitators incites violence against the strong disapproval of the vast majority of ghetto dwellers.

The Kerner Commission disproved this and other myths. The average Detroit rioter was better educated, better informed, and more involved in the community than the nonrioter, and he had a job (albeit one he thought beneath him). Nearly 40 percent of ghetto residents in Detroit either participated in the riot or identified themselves as bystanders—hardly a deviant minority. The commission thus confirmed what sociologists have long believed: that the crowd itself generates a collective excitement that influences people's behavior. There are several theories explaining how this comes about.

Emotional and Social Contagion In a now-classic work originally published in 1895 (*The Psychology of Crowds*, 1960), French sociologist Gustave Le Bon (1841–1931) argued that the transformation of individuals into a crowd "puts them in possession of a collective mind" that makes people think, feel, and act quite differently than they would if they were alone. Being part of a crowd gives people a sense of invincible power: they "will undertake the accomplishment of certain acts with irresistible impetuosity," wrote Le Bon. The crowd gains control over the individual much as the hypnotist gains control over his subjects. Individuals become highly suggestible; they are no longer conscious of their actions. Waves of emotion sweep through the crowd, infecting one person after another as though excitement were actually contagious. The thin veneer of civilization falls away, allowing unconscious motivations and antisocial impulses to rise to the surface. "The age we are about to enter," Le Bon wrote, "will be in truth the *era of crowds*." He meant this as a warning.

Clearly, Le Bon believed an untamed, destructive creature lurked behind the social masks people ordinarily present to one another. Despite his obvious distaste for "the masses," there is some truth to Le Bon's theory. The anonymity of a crowd does weaken conventional norms by shifting moral responsibility from the individual to the group. And a large number of excited people in close proximity does create the impression of unanimity and invincible power. Moreover, emotions and behavior do seem to spread through crowds, as if they were contagious.

In his essay on collective behavior, Herbert Blumer (1951) refined Le Bon's ideas. He traced contagion to an "exciting event" that creates unrest in a crowd. People begin milling about, "as if seeking to find or avoid something, but without knowing what it is they are trying to find or avoid" (173). As people search for clues, excited behavior or rhetoric catches their attention. Instead of interpreting and judging these actions, as they ordinarily would, people respond immediately and directly. Their reactions reinforce the original actors, making them still more excited (what Blumer calls the *circular reaction*).

As excitement builds, people become more and more inclined to give immediate expression to their feelings, to act on impulse. This, in Blumer's view, explains "the relatively rapid, unwitting and nonrational dissemination of a mood, impulse or form of conduct" (1951: 176) through a crowd. Like Le Bon, then, Blumer emphasized the irrational nature of collective behavior and implied that people are not quite themselves in crowds.

Emergent Norms and Social Relationships More recently sociologists have questioned the idea that people necessarily behave in an unreflecting, irrational way in crowds (Turner and Killian, 1972). Wasn't looting a rational solution for ghetto residents who felt entitled to goods they could not afford and who saw the police caught momentarily off guard? Don't demonstrations obtain desired goals? Turner and Killian also question the implicit assumption that

social conformity fails to operate in a crowd. They suggest that crowd members act in deviant or unusual ways precisely because everyone around them is acting that way, and they are moved to join.

The transformation of a crowd of bystanders (a casual crowd) into a mob (an acting crowd) can be explained by the development of new norms (this is called the *emergent norm theory*). In ambiguous, undefined situations, one or more innovators suggest a course of action—either with words or with direct action (for example, throwing a bottle). Others follow. The crowd begins to define the situation, to develop a justification for acts that would in other circumstances seem questionable. In this way a new set of norms emerges, and people need not entirely share the crowd's mood to go along with its undertakings.

In other cases, the transformation of a casual crowd into a mob can be explained in terms of emergent social relationships. For example, lynching was an institutionalized form of social action in the early American West and South. There were established rules for behavior among crowd members; one lynching was much the same as the last. However, for a lynching to occur, bystanders had to improvise a system of social relationships, including a division of labor in the lynch mob itself.

Thus collective behavior may involve emergent norms, emergent social relationships, or both. (Weller and Quarantelli, 1973). The important point here is that crowds are neither normless nor totally lacking in social organization. Collective behavior often originates within an established group, often follows established norms, and always expresses divisions that exist within the society at large. Thus to understand crowd behavior you have to analyze the specific historical, social, and cultural setting—the ideas and images people bring to the scene—as well as collective processes (Lang and Lang, 1961: 561).

SOCIAL MOVEMENTS

A *social movement* is an ongoing collective effort to promote or resist change. Social movements arise when people develop new conceptions of themselves—new ideas of their rights and privileges—that don't conform to the positions they occupy in life. This gap breeds discontent where none existed before. Unrest is not enough, however: ideology and organization are needed to transform discontent into a social movement. Movements combine dissatisfaction with current conditions and a yearning for a better system. Although amorphous in the beginning, social movements gradually acquire organization, leadership, a division of labor, a body of traditions, a philosophy, a set of rules and expectations (Blumer, 1951; Gusfield, 1968).

There are essentially two types of social movements: revolutionary movements, which aim to tear down existing norms and values and substitute new ones; and reform movements, which blame social defects on a breakdown in existing norms and values and attempt to reinforce them (Blumer, 1951).

Whether reform or revolutionary, social movements go through certain predictable stages. The first stage is characterized by generalized restlessness. An agitator who stirs and excites people, pries them loose from their customary ways of thinking, and gives focus to their impulses may play an important role at this stage. In the second stage, more definite ideas emerge about what is wrong, who or what is to blame, and what can be done to rectify the situation. A prophet or reformer may take the lead in sharpening the movement's objectives. The third stage is characterized by formalization: the development of organized rules, policy, tactics, and discipline. This is the time for a statesman or a skilled negotiator/spokesperson. In the fourth and final stage, the movement becomes institutionalized: an accepted, routine part of the social order. Leadership becomes a question of administration or carrying through (Blumer, 1951).

The success of a social movement ultimately depends on how well it expressed the "feelings, resentments, worries, fears, concerns, and hopes" of a large number of people, as well as whether it is seen as a vehicle for the solution of wide-ranging problems (Milgram and Toch, 1969: 585). The women's movement, which touches everything from interpersonal relations to business, education, and politics, illustrates this.

Women's Liberation: A History and an Explanation

Feminism, which gained strength as a social movement in the early 1970s, has a long and often overlooked history. As early as 1792 an English feminist named Mary Wollstonecraft was protesting women's frivolous existence and "slavish obedience" to men. She offered men "rational fellowship" and demanded legal rights and educational opportunities for women. In this country women not only fought for suffrage but were in the front ranks of the abolitionist, labor, and temperance movements in the late nineteenth and early twentieth centuries (Firestone, 1973). In the 1940s and 1950s, however, women as a group were generally silent about feminist issues.

Then in 1963, Betty Friedan's *Feminine*

KEEPING THE FAITH OR PURSUING THE GOOD LIFE

When the Montgomery, Alabama, bus boycott began in December 1955, marking the start of the civil rights movement, white faces were not seen among the protesters. But two years later, white students joined with blacks in a second bus boycott. By 1960, white students were participating in lunch-counter sit-ins, and during the next few years, hundreds of young whites helped to organize black voter-registration drives.

Since those turbulent years, much has been written about the civil rights movement—its origins, its achievements, its failures—and its leaders have been analyzed and reanalyzed. But what about the young activists who participated in it? What has happened to them? This question interested sociologist James M. Fendrich. Specifically, he wanted to "examine the adult politics of former students who were part of the early 'radical probe' of the student rebellion in the 1960s" (145). Fendrich also wondered whether there would be any differences for whites and blacks.

He found that there are indeed clear differences between the two groups. The 100 former activists (28 white and 72 black) he surveyed were asked "to identify themselves politically on a continuum from right to left. For whites, 21 percent are political moderates, 25 percent are liberals and 54 percent are radicals. For blacks, 13 percent are political conservatives, 52 percent are moderates, 25 percent are liberal and 10 percent are radicals. Moreover, 75 percent of the whites participated in political demonstrations as adults compared to 47 percent of the blacks. . . ." Clearly, whites tended to be further to the left than blacks "and more willing to continue to engage in protest politics" (154).

To explain these differences in adult politics, Fendrich looked to the motivations that each group started with. The white students had nothing material to gain by participating in the civil rights movement: their commitment, says Fendrich, was purely ideological, and as adults they retained their "leftist" political outlook. In contrast, black activists would benefit directly by the movement's achievements—they were motivated more by self-interest than by political ideology. "And, because of the relative success of the movement for young college-educated blacks, they are now able to reap the benefits of that struggle" (154).

So, concludes Fendrich, it is not fair to say that blacks have been co-opted by the system. Simply put, this group of blacks fought for the right to enter the mainstream of American life, and though still committed to civil rights issues, they are not interested in fighting anybody else's battles. The white group of adults started out as political radicals and have stayed that way.

SOURCE: James M. Fendrich, "Keeping the Faith or Pursuing the Good Life: A Study of the Consequences of Participation in the Civil Rights Movement," *American Sociological Review*, vol. 42 (February 1977): 144–157.

Mystique was published, a book that helped to launch a decade of change in America. The private grievances of women whose careers had been thwarted, of isolated suburban matrons, of abandoned mothers with no means of supporting themselves or their children became a public outcry. Friedan played the role of agitator in the early stages of the movement.

Three social forces contributed to the rise of collective efforts to improve the status of women. First, the civil rights movement stimulated protest in a wide variety of groups and provided a model for activism. Second, a growing number of women, including mothers, had begun participating in the labor force, some but not all out of necessity. Finally, dutiful suburban wives and mothers were finding their nests empty at midlife. In earlier times, when three or more generations lived together and there were fewer devices to simplify housekeeping, women whose children had grown were kept busy with grandchildren and household chores. Now they had nothing substantial or socially useful to do (Dixon, 1971: 419–433).

These changes hit educated, economically secure middle-class women the hardest. Trained from childhood not to be self-reliant, achievement-oriented, or autonomous, and having devoted their lives to serving others, many found themselves dependent, isolated, and beset by "the problem that has no name" (Friedan, 1963: 281–295). Women's liberation gave a name to the problem that faced conventional women whose children, successful husbands, and surburban dream houses had not saved them from feeling superfluous.

The movement also appealed to women who weren't happy with full-time domesticity and opted for careers in fields marked "for men only," as well as to women who tried to combine home and work. Although not systematically discouraged from pursuing an education, women typically ran head on into an invisible bar of prejudice and discrimination when they left school and attempted to find a job in a "man's world" (Bird, 1971). Both these groups of women fanned the demands for new patterns of earning, new marriage and divorce laws, new opportunities for living and learning.

During 1963, commissions to investigate the status of women were organized in fifty states. These commissions brought large numbers of politically active women into contact with one another. But they did more; they created a climate of expectations. Three years later, on June 29, 1966, a small group of women attending the Third National Conference of Commissions on the Status of Women met in Betty Friedan's hotel room to discuss the possibility of founding a civil rights organization for women. They decided to call themselves the National Organization for Women (NOW). With Friedan as president, NOW began to attract women in the professions, labor, government, and the communications industry. However, it was not until 1969, when several national news stories on women's liberation appeared, that NOW's membership reached into the thousands.

NOW's goal, stated in 1966, is "to bring women into the mainstream of society." Through its national board and 800 or more local chapters, NOW has used legal suits, lobbying, demonstrations, boycotts, and other methods to press for such goals as educational reform, nonstereotyped portrayal of women in the media, repeal of anti-abortion laws, lesbians' rights, and enhanced roles for women in religion, politics, and sports. In addition to NOW and WEAL (Women's Equity Action League, a national organization which focuses on legal questions), the women's movement has generated hundreds of special-interest groups, such as the National Black Feminist Organization, and local organizations, such as Chicago's Women Employed, which deals with the problems of white-collar women working in Chicago's Loop (Carden, 1977).

From its inception, NOW has concentrated on concrete, short-range goals such as the equal rights amendment to the Constitution, the repeal of laws limiting abortion, and day care. Despite efforts to attract poor and minority women and career housewives, most of NOW's membership consists of upper-middle-class white women who work.

A second, more radical branch of women's liberation began to gather momentum in the 1960s. Thousands of young women under thirty were deeply involved in the student movement in that period. Like their male counterparts they had lived in an atmosphere of questioning, confrontation, and change ever since entering college. They identified with the radical community and thought of themselves as movement people. More often than not, however, they found themselves relegated to such traditional and unrewarding jobs as typing and cooking. Rejecting formal structure and leadership of any kind, the radical branch of the women's movement focused on changing the entire structure of human relations—not just on opening the system to women. The rap session was designed to change women's identities as well as their attitudes.

The radicalism of the late 1960s—in politics as well as feminism—has subsided. But the effects remain, in the form of altered consciousness.

Jo Freeman argues that neither branch of the women's movement would have materialized without the communications networks developed through the commissions on the status of women and the student movement. Women's opportunities in this country were as limited in 1945 or 1955 as they were in 1965. "What changed was the organizational situation. It was not until a communications network developed between like-minded people beyond local boundaries that the movement could emerge and develop

The climate of turmoil and change during the 1960s facilitated the growth of the women's liberation movement. Although the broad objectives of this movement are now widely accepted, we still cannot be sure whether it will follow the classic stages of a social movement and eventually become an institutionalized part of the social order. (Owen Franken / Stock, Boston)

past the point of occasional, spontaneous uprising'' (1973: 804).

We can't be sure at this time whether the women's movement will follow the classic stages of a social movement, eventually becoming an institutionalized part of the social order. Although the broad objective of equality for women is agreed upon, there is conflict within the coalition of groups that make up the movement as to the best means of achieving this goal. And while the visible part of the movement has pressed for changes and seems to be causing them, the less visible part is a response to changes occurring in society as a whole—notably the large numbers of women entering the labor force and the trends toward later marriage and fewer children (see chapter 13 for more on these changes).

Nevertheless, the example illustrates the origins and development of social movements. Structurally, they begin when people find that existing institutions are not answering a need. If the need is pervasive, grievances and frustrations accumulate, as does the pressure to bring about change. In time leaders develop; so does an organization focused on specific programs. A movement then takes on some trappings of permanence.

Professional Movements

The classical model of social movements depends on a groundswell of uneasiness and frustration in the early stages and on grassroots organization in the later stages. At least two sociologists—John D. McCarthy and Mayer N. Zald (1973)—believe this model does not accurately describe the current state of affairs.

McCarthy and Zald argue that social movements have become professionalized in recent years. The professional movement is organized by leaders who work full time for the cause; obtain funds from foundations and private donors who have little control over their activities and may be only indirectly involved in the issues; have only a small membership or one that exists only on paper; and use the media to mobilize sentiment without the direct contact characteristic of traditional social movements. Leading—indeed, creating—a social movement has become an accepted career.

Ralph Nader is a characteristic professional advocate. Nader's first attempts to expose the auto industry were from within the system, from positions in an insurance company and later in the federal government. When these attempts failed, he decided to publish the results of his studies independently. *Unsafe at Any Speed* (1972, orig. 1965) was an instant success. Foolishly, General Motors hired detectives in the hope that they could unearth information to discredit Nader. When this came to light, Nader became a hero overnight. It was a replay of the biblical story of David (Nader) versus Goliath (General Motors). And it was good copy for the media.

From an out-of-court settlement of a suit against GM for invasion of privacy, from the royalties on his book, and from lecture fees, Nader amassed $425,000. He used this money to set up a nonprofit law firm called Public Interest Research Group. And everywhere he lectured he encouraged young people to come to Washington to join ''Nader's Raiders,'' as his youthful investigative teams came to be known (Faber, 1972).

Thus Nader did not emerge as a spokesperson for the discontented; he *created* the discontent, largely by means of the media, and created a funding agency that enables him and his staff to decide which issues are important. (See chapter 12 for more on the consumer movement.)

COMMUNICATION AND COLLECTIVE BEHAVIOR

Collective behavior depends heavily on the kind of communication available to people. Daily newspapers, which became available early in the eighteenth century, and radio and television, which are products of the twentieth century, have created new forms of collective behavior. When millions of people are frightened or angered by the same broadcast, they act very much like people in a crowd who have been ignited by an incident or a speech. Even though the members of the audience are in their own homes, they are reacting to a common stimulus. And they carry their excitement to friends, relatives, and neighbors, setting off the circular reaction Blumer observed in crowds.

A historic example of the powerful impact of radio was Orson Welles's 1938 broadcast of *War of the Worlds.* The play began innocuously enough; then the action was interrupted for bulletins about an invasion from Mars. The story came across so realistically that people panicked, jamming telephone lines with calls to bid loved ones farewell, rushing into the streets for help, and gathering in excited crowds in bars and other public places. After a few hours the confusion died down, but newspapers continued to print stories about the night of panic for a week (Cantril, Gaudet, and Herzog, 1947: 47–55).

Some of this extreme reaction can be attributed to the skill of the dramatist and to the use of "expert testimony," which lent credibility to increasingly terrifying descriptions of a Martian invasion. Yet how could so many people believe, even briefly, that Martians were climbing out of a spaceship on a New Jersey farm? The study of rumors provides important clues.

Rumors

A *rumor* is an unverified story that circulates from person to person, most often by word of mouth, and is accepted as fact, although its sources may be vague or unknown. Rumors proliferate in tense and ambiguous situations, when people are unable to learn the facts or when, for one reason or another, they distrust the information they receive. When the Japanese bombed Pearl Harbor, for example, many Americans believed our entire fleet had been wiped out. There were rumors that the Japanese had occupied Hawaii. President Franklin D. Roosevelt's radio broadcast only partially dispelled these stories. Nearly half the college students interviewed shortly afterward were convinced that Roosevelt was covering up the truth (Allport and Postman, 1947).

A rumor may begin as an accurate report but become distorted and exaggerated in the process of transmission. After studying rumor transmission in the laboratory and in the field, Allport and Postman (1947) discovered a basic pattern. A person hears a story that strikes him as interesting. He repeats the story—what he remembers of it—to a friend. The friend talks to others: "Did you hear . . . ?" Gradually, the original story is reduced to a few essential details that are easy to tell. This is what Allport and Postman mean by *leveling:* "As a rumor travels, it tends to grow shorter, more concise, more easily grasped and told. In successive versions, fewer words are used and fewer details are mentioned" (75). As a result of leveling, certain details gain in importance, and the rumor is *sharpened*—people remember and pass on only part of the original story. And as a rumor circulates, people tend to ''correct'' details so as to make the story more plausible and more coherent.

Public Opinion

A *public* is a scattered group of people who share a common interest, concern, or focus of attention. (A theater audience, environmentalists, and college students are all publics.) The formation of publics is greatly aided by the mass media, which can give frequent national exposure to an issue, product, team, or politician. The media also influence the ebb and flow of *public opinion*—that is, the prevailing interests (what people define as an issue), attitudes (predispositions to react positively or negatively toward certain people, groups, or events), and opinions (specific judgments of specific issues) of a public.

Obviously, there have always been publics, and publics have always had opinions. But modern polling techniques have made it possible to collect these opinions, to bring the views of scattered individuals together into a new form of collective behavior more powerful than a crowd or protest. A shouting crowd may not represent general opinion, but a poll does. A simple table reflecting widespread support for free, safe abortions for all women, for example, would speak louder than a demonstration in Washington.

The Media and Public Opinion The media not only report news, they *make* news. The civil rights movement, the student movement, and the women's liberation movement would have had little impact on American society if journalists had not decided they were worth reporting. ''News, if unreported, has no impact. It might as well have not happened at all. Thus the journalist is the important ally of the ambitious, he is a lamplighter for stars. . . . Each day, undaunted by history, plugged into the *instant*, journalists of every creed, quality, and quirk report the news of the world as they see it, believe it, understand it. Then much of it is relayed through America, millions of words a minute'' (Talese, 1970: 1–2). In choosing to report and headline some stories instead of others, newspaper publishers and television news editors affect the flow of information.

In addition, the media carry considerable prestige: people tend to believe what they read in the papers or see on the evening television news (Jarrell, 1961). This legitimating power of the media makes it hard to distinguish news from propaganda. During the 1960s, for example, films on Vietnam from communist news sources were called propaganda by network newscasters, who emphasized how low-angle shots and other filming techniques were used to create certain impressions. However, when the networks showed films made by the Pentagon with the same techniques and using selected footage, they were treated as factual, and their source was not given (Cirino, 1971: 180–181).

How much do the media influence opinion? To the extent that they are the only source of information, their influence is bound to be considerable. When researchers try to *change* people's opinions, however, the picture becomes more complex. Sum-

The media not only report news, they make news. In choosing to report and headline some stories instead of others, newspapers and television networks affect the flow of information. (John Lei)

marizing the research on opinion change, Raymond Bauer states, ''The audience selects what it will attend to. Since people generally listen to and read things they are interested in, these usually are topics on which they have a good deal of information and fixed opinion. Hence the very people most likely to attend to a message are those most difficult to change; those who can be converted do not look or listen'' (Bauer, 1972: 235).

Moreover, the media work through the social networks that characterize everyday life. Studies by Elihu Katz and Paul F. Lazarsfeld (1955) indicate that mass media influence people *if* their social background predisposes them to accept a report as fact and a particular course of action as legitimate; *if* one viewpoint or another is associated with groups they consider significant (their reference groups); and *if* individuals whose opinion they respect (that is, opinion leaders) call their attention to the issue. Thus social background, reference groups, and interpersonal influence seem to be the deciding factors in the creation of issues and formation of public opinions. The media serve to amplify existing trends.

Manipulating Public Opinion

Lincoln once said, ''You may fool all the people some of the time; you can even fool some of the people all the time; but you can't fool all of the people all the time." The wisdom of this epigram has not prevented many people from trying. There are essentially two ways to attempt to sway public opinion: restricting the flow of information by means of censorship or presenting information in a way that is calculated to gain uncritical acceptance of a partisan point of view—that is, through propaganda and public relations.

Censorship The restriction of information reaching an audience—or *censorship*—is essentially a device for preventing collective behavior that might foster social change. Popular American wisdom has it that censorship is something that foreign (especially communist) governments employ, but not our own. The fact that *all* governments practice censorship, including our own, is rarely mentioned.

During the early 1970s, however, an instance of government censorship in this country attracted the public's attention. In June 1971, the government went to court to prevent *The New York Times* and the *Washington Post* from publishing the Pentagon Papers, a secret 7,000-page report on the origins of the war in Vietnam, prepared within the Pentagon and leaked by Daniel Ellsberg. On July 1, 1971, the Supreme Court decided in favor of the publishers, but it was not the landmark decision journalists had hoped for. The decision was split six to three, and three justices rejected the government's suit only because they didn't believe it had proved that publication of the Pentagon Papers was a threat to national security. The government's right to censor the press was neither approved nor rejected.[1]

---

[1] In a related decision the Supreme Court ruled that local communities had a right to establish their own standards of decency and to ban films, books, and magazines that violate these standards.

Public opinion on this issue was divided. Of the people Louis Harris polled in August 1971, 41 percent thought the newspapers had been "more right" than the government in this instance, and they supported the Supreme Court decision by nearly two to one. But although 54 percent thought it was time the American public was told the truth about the war, and 47 percent believed we would not learn the truth if newspapers had to get permission to print inside information, 70 percent agreed that "if there is any doubt about violating the national security in publishing documents such as the Pentagon Papers on Viet Nam, then the documents should not be published" (Harris Poll, August 12, 1971).

Propaganda and Public Relations Censorship is a way of manipulating collective behavior; propaganda and public relations are methods for inspiring certain kinds of collective behavior, such as voting for a particular candidate, buying American-made cars, demonstrating for or against a piece of legislation.

Propaganda appeals to people's emotions and prejudices, not to their critical abilities. This is the main difference between propaganda and simple persuasion through rational arguments. Name calling, the invocation of authorities ("Doctors recommend...") and sacred values, appeals to fear, and shows of strength are some of the more obvious tools of propaganda (Lee and Lee, 1939).

Adolf Hitler was a genius at propaganda. His rhetoric, his symbols (the swastika, uniforms, the Nazi salute), his storm troopers, who "protected" Nazi rallies and broke up opposition gatherings, all served to convince his followers that they belonged to an irresistible movement. Once in office Hitler created a superagency for "public enlightenment'' that controlled the press, the arts, and education (Holborn, 1969: 719, 738–739).

Political propaganda is also used widely in this country.[2] Every election year political candidates are packaged by experts in mass persuasion and sold with posters, buttons, straw hats, television spots, articles planted in popular magazines, and ''news items'' about the candidates that reporters use because the stories have already been written for them.

Closely linked to propaganda is *public relations,* another means of manipulating public opinion. Public relations is a form of indirect advertising—including press releases *(The New York Times* receives some 5,000 press releases weekly from the business community); briefings for businesspeople, community leaders, and politicians; junkets (all-expenses-paid trips); gifts; and entertain-

ment. The main purpose of public relations is to present a favorable image of the client to the public.

Public relations techniques are not the exclusive province of politicians and corporations. Many groups advocating social change, such as civil rights organizations and groups fighting discrimination against women or minorities or religious sects, have effectively used public relations campaigns to gain public support. The aim of these campaigns is generally to present information that the public would otherwise not be aware of. Persuasion through education is their goal.

The mass media not only stimulate collective behavior but also permit us to learn—through television and newspapers—of expressions of collective behavior taking place in society today. The social energy that may be released when an idea or a fashion catches on is a tremendous force in modern society—and a continuing challenge to sociologists to understand its workings more clearly.

---

[2]   Today the Defense Department spends nearly $3.5 million annually on public relations (Fulbright, 1970: 32).

SUMMARY

Collective behavior refers to the actions of relatively temporary, unstructured groups of people who focus on the same thing and react to one another's behavior. Although it appears spontaneous, collective behavior does not erupt any time, any place. Social structures that encourage people to value unstable things, unanticipated events that create a state of normlessness, and frustrated social concerns are preconditions for collective behavior.

A *crowd* is a temporary collection of people gathered around an event who are conscious of and influenced by one another's presence. Herbert Blumer distinguished between *casual crowds* (spontaneous congregations), *conventional crowds* (groups who gather for a specific purpose and are abiding by established norms), *expressive crowds* (congregations that encourage unconventional behavior), and *acting crowds* (volatile collections of people who are focused on a controversial event that inspires their desire to act). *Mobs*, crowds whose members are ready for violence, have been common since the eighteenth century. *Riots* occur when crowds of people collectively engage in destructive behavior. The riot in Detroit was an example of mob action.

The Detroit rioters were not "riffraff," as many people supposed. How, then, do sociologists explain their behavior? The nineteenth-century French sociologist Le Bon characterized mobs as hypnotized masses of people acting out unconscious motives under the delusion of invincible power. Blumer, too, believed people behave irrationally in crowds: an exciting event catches their attention, they begin milling about, and they respond directly and unreflectively to rhetoric (setting off the *circular reaction*). More recently, sociologists have focused less on the individual in the crowd and more on the overall structure of collective behavior. The *emergent norm theory* is based on the idea that in ambiguous situations, innovators suggest a course of action, the crowd begins to develop new norms, and bystanders are pressured into conformity (as they are in other groups). Other mob actions, such as lynching, can be explained by the theory of emergent social relationships: bystanders develop a system of social relationships that becomes institutionalized.

A *social movement* is an ongoing collective effort to promote or resist social change. Although social movements may be reformist or revolutionary, they go through certain predictable stages. To be successful, they must be seen as a way of solving a wide range of problems. The women's movement is an example. It gave a name to the isolation, dependency, and prejudice that have confronted both housewives and career women, transforming private grievances into a public outcry. The 1960s gave women a climate that encouraged change, communications networks, and the stimulation of opposition and ridicule.

Recently a new kind of movement—the professional movement—has become prominent. Best exemplified by Ralph Nader's consumer advocates, this kind of movement is organized by leaders who work full time for the cause, is funded by foundations and private donors, has a small membership, and effectively uses the media to mobilize support.

Mass media have created new forms of collective behavior: daily, millions of people read the same headlines, watch the same television shows, and at times react like members of a crowd. For example, rumors of an invasion from Mars—sparked by Orson Welles's broadcast of *War of the Worlds* in 1938—created mass panic. A *rumor* is an unverified report that circulates from person to person and is accepted as fact. Rumors proliferate in tense and ambiguous situations. In the course of transmission, rumors become *leveled* and sharpened; people "correct" the details for themselves.

Mass media help to create *publics* (scattered groups of people who share a common interest, concern, or focus of attention). Reference groups and opinion leaders influence public opinion, and the media amplify existing trends. As the ability to measure public opinion through polls has grown, so have attempts to manipulate it. *Censorship* is a method for preventing the expression of collective behavior seeking change. *Propaganda* and *public relations* (behind-the-scenes advertising) are ways of inspiring and directing collective behavior.

GLOSSARY

acting crowd Blumer's term for an excited, volatile group of people who are focused on a controversial event that provokes their indignation, anger, and desire to act.

casual crowd Blumer's label for a spontaneous gathering whose members give temporary attention to the object that attracted them and then go their separate ways.

censorship restricting information before it reaches its audience.

circular reaction Blumer's term for a phenomenon of crowd behavior in which people react immediately and directly to an action, thereby encouraging the original actors to continue their behavior.

collective behavior the actions of relatively temporary, unstructured groups of people who are focused on and reacting to the same event, rumor, person, group, or custom.

conventional crowd Blumer's term for people gathered for a specific purpose who behave according to established norms.

crowd a temporary collection of people gathered around some person or event who are conscious of and influenced by one another's presence.

emergent norm theory the principle that crowds develop new norms in order to define an ambiguous situation.

expressive crowd Blumer's label for a crowd that gives people license to express feelings and behave in ways they wouldn't consider in other settings.

leveling the reduction of a complex story to a few simple details, as with rumors.

mob a crowd whose members are emotionally aroused and are engaged in, or are ready to engage in, violent action.

normlessness a condition in which people don't know what they can or should do, and have no cultural guidelines to direct them.

propaganda information that appeals to people's emotions and prejudices and is used to inspire certain kinds of collective behavior.

public a scattered group of people who share a common interest, concern, or focus of attention.

public opinion the prevailing interests, attitudes, and opinions of a group of people who share a common interest, concern, or focus of attention.

public relations a form of indirect advertising that aims to present a favorable image of an organization to the public.

riot a violent public disturbance, particularly when a crowd of people collectively engage in destructive behavior; it may be caused by an intolerable gap between what people believe they are entitled to and what they actually have.

rumor an unverified story that circulates from person to person, usually by word of mouth, and is accepted as fact, although its sources may be vague or unknown.

social movement an ongoing collective effort with focused goals and articulated tactics to promote or resist social change.

structural conduciveness the principle that preconditions for collective behavior are built into a society's social structure.

REFERENCES

Vernon L. Allen, "Toward Understanding Riots: Some Perspectives." *Journal of Social Issues,* vol. 26 (Winter 1970): 1–18.

Gordon W. Allport and Leo Postman, *The Psychology of Rumor.* New York: Holt, 1947.

Allen H. Barton, *Communities in Disaster.* Garden City, N.Y.: Doubleday, 1969.

Raymond Bauer, "The Obstinate Audience," in Alan Wells, ed., *Mass Media and Society.* Palo Alto, Calif.: National Press Books, 1972.

Carolyn Bird, "The Invisible Bar," in Elsie Adams and Mary Louise Briscoe, eds., *Up Against the Wall, Mother . . .* Beverly Hills, Calif.: Glencoe, 1971.

Herbert Blumer, "Collective Behavior," in Alfred McClung Lee, ed., *New Outline of the Principles of Sociology.* New York: Barnes & Noble, 1951.

Bertram S. Brown, U.S. Department of Health, Education, and Welfare, *How Women See Their Roles: A Change in Attitudes.* Washington, D.C.: U.S. Government Printing Office, 1976.

A. Campbell and H. Schuman, "Racial Attitudes in Fifteen American Cities," in *Supplementary Studies for the National Advisory Commission on Civil Disorders.* Washington, D.C.: U.S. Government Printing Office, 1968.

Hadley Cantril, with Hazel Gaudet and Herta Herzog, *Invasion from Mars.* Princeton, N.J.: Princeton University Press, 1947.

Maren Lockwood Carden, *Feminism in the Mid-1970s.* New York: Ford Foundation, 1977.

Robert Cirino, *Don't Blame the People.* Los Angeles, Calif.: Diversity Press, 1971.

Marlene Dixon, "Why Women's Liberation?" in Elsie Adams and Mary Louise Briscoe, eds., *Up Against the Wall, Mother . . .* Beverly Hills, Calif.: Glencoe, 1971.

Doris Faber, *Enough: The Revolt of the American Consumer.* New York: Farrar, Straus and Giroux, 1972.

Shulamith Firestone, "On American Feminism," in Peter I. Rose, ed., *The Study of Society,* 3rd ed. New York: Random House, 1973.

Robert M. Fogelson, "Violence and Grievances: Reflections on the 1960s Riots." *Journal of Social Issues,* vol. 26 (Winter 1970): 141–163.

Jo Freeman, "The Origins of the Women's Liberation Movement." *American Journal of Sociology,* vol. 78 (1973): 792–811.

Betty Friedan, *The Feminine Mystique.* New York: Dell, 1963.

J. William Fulbright, *The Pentagon Propaganda Machine.* New York: Liveright, 1970.

Joseph Gusfield, "The Study of Social Movements," in *International Encyclopedia of the Social Sciences,* vol. 14. New York: Macmillan, 1968.

Hajo Holborn, *A History of Modern Germany, 1850–1945.* New York: Knopf, 1969.

Thomas Ford Hoult, *A Dictionary of Modern Sociology.* Totowa, N.J.: Littlefield, Adams, 1969.

Randall Jarrell, "A Sad Heart at the Supermarket," in Norman Jacobs, ed., *Culture for the Millions.* Princeton, N.J.: Van Nostrand, 1961.

Elihu Katz and Paul Lazarsfeld, *Personal Influence.* New York: Free Press, 1955.

Alan C. Kerckhoff and Kurt W. Back, *The June Bug: A Study of Hysterical Contagion.* New York: Appleton-Century-Crofts, 1968.

Kurt and Gladys Lang, *Collective Dynamics.* New York: Crowell, 1961.

Gustave Le Bon, *The Crowd: A Study of the Popular Mind* (1895). New York: Viking, 1960.

Alfred M. Lee and Elizabeth Lee, *The Fine Art of Propaganda.* New York: Farrar, Straus, 1939.

John D. McCarthy and Mayer N. Zald, *The Trend of Social Movements in America: Professionalization and Resource Mobilization.* Morristown, N.J.: General Learning Press, 1973.

Stanley Milgram and Hans Toch, "Collective Behavior: Crowds and Social Movements,'' in Garner Lindzey and Elliot Aronson, eds., *The Handbook of Social Psychology,* 2nd ed., vol. 4. Reading, Mass.: Addison-Wesley, 1969.

Ralph Nader, *Unsafe at Any Speed* (1965), rev. ed. New York: Grossman, 1972.

Report of the National Advisory Commission on Civil Disorders. Washington, D.C.: U.S. Government Printing Office, 1968.

Neil J. Smelser, *Theory of Collective Behavior.* New York: Free Press, 1962.

Gay Talese, *The Kingdom and the Power.* New York: Bantam, 1970.

Ralph H. Turner and Lewis M. Killian, *Collective Behavior,* 2nd ed. Englewood Cliffs, N.J.: Prentice-Hall, 1972.

Jack M. Weller and E. L. Quarantelli, ''Neglected Characteristics of Collective Behavior.'' *American Journal of Sociology,* vol. 79 (November 1973): 665–685.

Alan Wells, ed., *Mass Media and Society.* Palo Alto, Calif.: National Press Books, 1972.

FOR FURTHER STUDY

Witch Hunts and Repression of Dissent. Social movements and protest often bring about a unified negative response toward those who have challenged the existing order. Albert James Bergesen examines this response cross-culturally in his article, ''Political Witch Hunts: The Sacred and the Subversive in Cross-National Perspective,'' *American Sociological Review,* vol. 42 (April 1977): 220–233. This kind of reaction has appeared at several stages in American history; for example, Kai Erikson documents the response of early Americans to a perceived evil in *Wayward Puritans* (New York: Wiley, 1966). Later, the McCarthy Era provided another example, which is discussed by Lawrence Wittner in *Cold-War America: From Hiroshima to Watergate* (New York: Praeger, 1974) and Eric Bentley in *Thirty Years of Treason* (New York: Viking, 1973). More recently, the protests of the 1960s social movements led to widespread repression and reprisals. Black Americans were imprisoned in many cases; one notable example is the story of George Jackson, which has been investigated by Eric Mann in his book *Comrade George* (New York: Harper & Row, 1974). Students and professors have also been defined as the enemy and have suffered reprisals for their involvement in social movements. Several personal accounts by social scientists discuss the issues involved in the repression of dissent. Two of these works are Michael Parenti's ''Repression in Academia: A Report from the Field,'' *Politics and Society,* vol. 1 (August 1971): 527–537 and David Colfax's ''Repression and Academic Radicalism,'' *New Politics,* vol. 10 (Spring 1973): 14–27. Of course, the methods available to harrass dissenters have changed since witch burning; the techniques used in the 1960s and 1970s are described by Theodore Becker and Vernon Murray, eds., in *Government Lawlessness in America* (New York: Oxford University Press, 1971).

Torture. More extreme measures of repression have been and are being used to eliminate social movements in some countries. The organization Amnesty International has published several studies of torture and extended confinement of political prisoners. Among their studies are *A Report on Torture* (New York: Farrar, Straus, and Giroux, 1975); *Torture in Greece; The First Torturers' Trial* (New York: Amnesty International, 1977), which includes testimony from the trial giving the viewpoint of the torturers; and

Evidence of Torture: Studies by the Amnesty International Danish Medical Group (New York: Amnesty International, 1977), a report using case studies of torture victims in four countries. *Time Magazine* provides an account of torture practices in several countries in its cover story on the subject of August 16, 1976. In addition, the UN has sponsored several studies of torture in Chile and South Africa through its Human Rights Commission in Geneva.

Revolutions.   At times, social movements may transform a society. The study of revolutions is exciting and rewarding, because the structure of a society becomes more clear when under attack. The most comprehensive and profound book on the subject is *The Natural History of Revolutions* by Lyford Edwards (Chicago: University of Chicago Press, 1970). Implicitly, it raises an important question: What are the relations between revolution and modernization? While revolutions can be analyzed as social events in their own right, they must also be considered in the larger perspective of social change in the societies where they occur. The following books provide interesting materials for considering these questions: Howard F. Cline, *Mexico: From Revolution to Evolution* (New York: Oxford University Press, 1962); Charles C. Cumberland, *The Meaning of the Mexican Revolution* (Boston: Heath, 1967); and John Womack, *Zapata and the Mexican Revolution* (New York: Vintage, 1970). An excellent comparative analysis of the long-range results of revolution is Susan Eckstein's *The Impact of Revolution* (Beverly Hills, Calif.: Sage Publications, 1976), which investigates the revolutionary experience in Mexico and Bolivia. For a more literary view of the Mexican Revolution, students may be interested in *Autumn of the Patriarch* (New York: Harper & Row, 1976) by Gabriel Garcia Marquez. Finally, for an exploration of revolution in several countries, see Eric Hobshawm's *Revolutionaries* (New York: Pantheon, 1973).

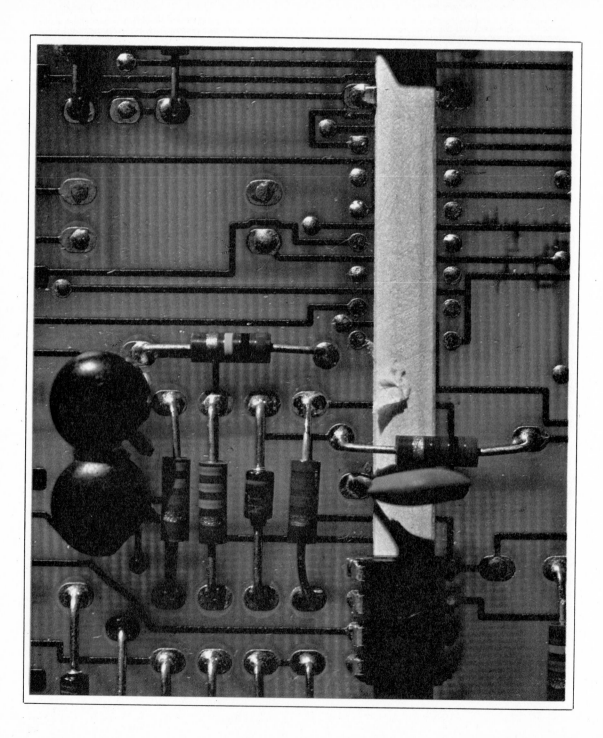

CHAPTER 19

Social Change and Technology

We are still in control, but the capabilities of computers are increasing at a fantastic rate, while raw human intelligence is changing slowly, if at all. Computer power is growing exponentially; it has increased tenfold every eight years since 1946. . . . In the 1990s, . . . the compactness and reasoning power of an intelligence built out of silicon will begin to match that of the human brain (Jastrow, 1978: 59).

There has always been technological change, but the rate of change today is staggering, and the challenges of coping with it are enormous. Sociologists don't focus on every single change that occurs, but only on *social change*, an alteration of the patterns of social organization over time. The socialization of a child certainly represents a profound change in this child's life, but it doesn't change the basic organization of the family. Creating communal child-care centers in which to house, feed, and teach the young (as in the Israeli kibbutz), on the other hand, represents a social change. The child is socialized in a different way, and this affects the organization of the family. Similarly, an invention is of no importance to sociologists if the inventor uses it solely for his own purposes; but when it becomes as widespread as the computer, it begins to affect the patterns of our daily life and the structure of such basic institutions as the schools.

This chapter will begin with some of the more ambitious attempts to understand and explain social change, and will then examine sources of change. After a look at *modernization*—the process by which developing nations are attempting to catch up with the already industrialized ones—we will explore the effects of technological change in one important area, the workplace. Finally, we will take a glimpse at what tomorrow's society may be like.

APPROACHES TO SOCIAL CHANGE

During World War II the U.S. Air Force established numerous resupply bases on several islands in the South Pacific. Many of these islands were inhabited by peoples barely out of the Stone Age; what were they to make of these huge silvery birds dropping from the sky into their midst? White-skinned men wearing bizarre clothes moved about their strange vehicles, coaxing these enormous birds open, taking out fantastic things. One day these white-skinned men suddenly left, and the gift-bearing birds flying overhead never descended again. On the island of Tana in the New Hebrides, many of the natives belong to a cult centered around the old GI jacket of John Frumm, about which nothing is known except that he was one who had powers over the cargo planes. For decades now the devotees of this cult have awaited the return of these silvery birds. Like others who belong to the many cargo cults that have developed throughout the South Pacific, John Frumm cult members have constructed a primitive landing strip in the highlands, complete with bamboo control towers, grass-thatched cargo sheds, torch-lit markers on the edges of the strip, and even tin-can microphones and earphones to coax the birds to the ground again. The arrival of the Americans deeply affected the ancient society of Tana, leading to the development of a new religion that integrated many of the disturbing new elements by reinterpreting them as signs of redemptive hope for the islanders (Harris, 1971: 566).

Sociologists have always looked at change—at what happens within societies as ideas come and go and as circumstances are altered. Although in a sense this whole book is about change, we look at change here as a separate topic, because since World War II it has been rapid and continuous. It is part of all of our lives, no matter how small or remote our community. People alive now have grown up not just in different generations, but in different worlds. In all kinds of societies, the pace and scale of change have been enormous: tribal peoples have become a part of industrial society, and industrial societies have themselves been transformed. Yet although change is the modern condition, it is difficult to describe and even more difficult to account for and predict. Because it is so central a part of our experience, many approaches have been tried. We will describe the most important ones here. There is no single, overarching explanation; each of the perspectives we will look at captures a *part* of what is involved in change, because different thinkers have focused on different aspects. For some, change is evolutionary; for some, it is cyclical. Others see it in terms of equilibrium, and still others in terms of conflict.

The Evolutionary Perspective

The nineteenth century was the Age of Progress. Europeans immodestly considered themselves the most highly civilized—the most *advanced*—people on earth. Things seemed to be getting better and better: there was no apparent end to economic development or to the wonders science and technology could perform. Social theorists of the day elevated the idea of progress to the stature of a natural law.

Herbert Spencer (1820–1903), in England, and Émile Durkheim, in France, were leading exponents of the idea of social evolution, or the *evolutionary perspective*. From simple beginnings, they reasoned, societies evolve into more and more complex forms.

Simple societies have a relatively undifferentiated social structure, with minimal division of labor among members of the same society. People share a common set of values, and these values provide the chief source of solidarity among members. As we learned in chapter 7, Durkheim (1947) called this kind of moral cohesion ''mechanical solidarity.''

As the population grows, resources become scarcer and there is a greater division of labor in order to exploit these scarce resources efficiently. The society becomes differentiated into increasingly specialized units, which are more dependent upon each other—a kind of cohesion Durkheim called ''organic solidarity.'' Social differentiation multiplies, common values decrease, and the fragmented social order then requires more formal means to hold it together. Civil law and a central government are among the institutions that evolve in the face of growing change and diversity.

According to Spencer (1974), the driving forces in the evolution of societies were the ''struggle for existence'' and the ''survival of the fittest'' (phrases Darwin borrowed from Spencer, not vice versa). Capitalism and the spirit of free enterprise were ''only natural.''

Governments and popular opinion interpreted Spencer and Durkheim to mean that small, tribal societies in such places as New Guinea represented early stages in social evolution. Europe had, if not a divine right to rule the world, at least an ''evolutionary prerogative'': it was the white man's burden.

Social Darwinism, as this position became known, was self-serving. No social scientist today maintains that all societies are evolving toward the Western form. However, many believe that modernization is inevitable and that this involves social transformations like those pointed out by Spencer and Durkheim. For example, Neil Smelser (1973) suggests that all modernizing societies shift from simple traditional technology to the application of scientific knowledge; subsistence agriculture to the growing of cash crops; the use of human and animal power to the utilization of fossil fuels; rural to urban settlement patterns.

The Cyclical Perspective

The onslaught of World War I caught off guard those who believed Europeans were too civilized to engage in the mass slaughters of the savage past. Were societies in fact advancing? The *cyclical perspective* on change develops out of the idea that every society has a natural life span. Societies may grow and develop, but eventually they begin to decay, to grow old; at some point they must die and be replaced by a ''new generation'' of societies. In *The Decline of the West* (1926–1928), Oswald Spengler announced this theme, which had an immediate impact. In Spengler's view, cultures are destined to follow a course of growth and decline in much the same way that the lives of individuals do. But Spengler's explanation was more poetic than scientific. He appealed to cosmic destiny rather than finite causes.

Arnold Toynbee's multivolume *A Study of History* (1946) is, on the other hand, a detailed and concrete comparative history of civilizations. While fault has been found with his analyses on many points, Toynbee's significant contribution is his method, which applies key specific questions to each of the twenty-one major civilizations of past and present that he chose for study.

> Toynbee's volumes ask four main questions, each with numerous subquestions. The first concerns the genesis of civilization: What are the conditions which allow or stimulate the rise of civilizations—the conversion of what

had been preliterate, simple, more or less lethargic peoples into the kinds of civilization of which the classical, the Indian, the Chinese, and the Mayan are notable types? Second, what are the factors involved in the expansion and development, in what Toynbee calls the "growths" of these civilizations? Third, what accounts for the breakdowns of civilizations, that is, the conversion of what had been for centuries a highly dynamic, innovative, intrepid, and enterprising people into one characterized by mere routinization and repetition of the old? Fourth, what leads to the disintegration of historical civilizations, the passing into nothingness or atavistic primitivism of civilizations? (Nisbet, 1970: 353)

In answering these questions for individual cultures, Toynbee developed several partial explanations. A key one for social change was his concept of challenge and response: a civilization's accomplishments are its particular reponses to the specific physical and social challenges posed by its environment. When a civilization can no longer respond to challenges, it rigidifies and atrophies.

Cyclical approaches have an intrinsic appeal. They seem to cover all eventualities (the rise *and* fall of civilizations). But they don't really *explain* change. Why, for example, does a society that has successfully responded to social and physical challenges suddenly become rigid? For an answer, one has to turn to other approaches.

The Equilibrium Perspective

Yet another perspective on social change, the *equilibrium perspective*, is based on the biological concept of homeostasis (equilibrium). This theoretical approach actually focuses on how to keep a system in balance despite the changes that are continually oc-curring. Each of the specialized parts of an organism is continually active, but all the different changes within the parts are coordinated and integrated so that the total organism is relatively the same from one day to the next. A change in one part sets off compensatory changes in other parts until equilibrium is restored.

Parsons (1951, 1966) applied this concept to society, which he sees as a system made up of parts or subsystems (institutions) that each perform a special function, but in concert with all the others. Change in a political, cultural, or economic subsystem therefore affects not just that particular subsystem but the others as well. The subsystems also tend to change at different rates. The slowest to change is the cultural subsystem, which incorporates the basic values of a society. Because of the differential rate of change, one or another part of the system can therefore act as a brake. Changes in the economic and political systems, for example, tend to be slowed down as they impinge upon the more steadfast cultural system, the crucial force for ensuring the continuity of a society.

William F. Ogburn (1964) coined the term *cultural lag* to describe the problems that arise when one part of the social system changes too rapidly for the other parts to adapt, thus creating disequilibrium. Material culture (technology, medicine, and other such *things*) changes far more readily than nonmaterial culture (beliefs and values). A classic example of cultural lag comes from Australia. Gifts of steel axes to aborigines whose entire network of social relations centered on the ceremonial exchange of stone axes created chaos (Arensberg and Niehoff, 1964: 50). Cultural lag abounds in societies such as ours as well. We have the technology to perform genetic engineering, but are neither morally nor socially prepared to tamper with life on this level.

Technology changes far more rapidly than beliefs or values, often resulting in cultural lag. In America, for example, we have embraced the automobile wholeheartedly, but have been unable to alter our way of life to bring its potential to destroy human life and the environment under control. (Stella Gosman)

Ogburn suggests that major social change occurs when leaps in technology or other material changes force us to adjust culturally, which in turn lays the foundation for further changes in material conditions.

The Conflict Perspective

The approaches described thus far emphasize the integrative and stabilizing processes at work in social systems. In direct opposition to these is the *conflict perspective*, an approach based on the belief that social systems are inherently unstable, that struggle and conflict are the norm, that change (indeed, violent change) is unavoidable.

By far the most articulate and influential advocate of the conflict perspective was Karl Marx. ''Without conflict,'' Marx wrote, ''no progress: this is the law which civilization has followed to the present day'' (Dahrendorf, 1959: 27). In particular, Marx focused on class struggle. He postulated that with the advent of capitalism, society would begin to break up into two classes: the exploiters (the bourgeoisie) and the exploited (the proletariat). These two classes would become increasingly polarized as the proletariat was systematically stripped of dignified means of supporting itself and the wealth was concentrated in the hands of a very few. As greater and greater differences developed between the two classes, each class itself would become more and more homogeneous. Inevitably the conflict would boil over; the oppressed would seize power, and a new society would emerge. Marx went on to predict that the revolution of the proletariat would ultimately create a classless society, eliminating the sources of conflict once and for all.

Much of what Marx predicted has not come to pass. Capitalist societies haven't broken down into two hostile camps. Rather, society has become increasingly differentiated, with countless factions and interest groups. Although great wealth may be concentrated in the hands of the few, the workers have not been pauperized. Instead of polar opposites, we find gradations. Marx failed to consider the role social mobility would play in defusing class conflict. And he did not foresee the separation of ownership and technical expertise in modern capitalist ventures (Applebaum, 1970: 92–93).

Year	500,000 B.C.	20,000 B.C.	500 B.C.	300 B.C.
Required time to travel around the globe	A few hundred thousand years	A few thousand years	A few hundred years	A few tens of years
Means of transportation	Human, on foot (over ice bridges)	On foot and by canoe	Canoe with small sail or paddles, or relays of runners	Large sailboats with oars, pack animals, and horse chariots
Distance per day (land)	15 miles	15–20 miles	20 miles	15–25 miles
Distance per day (sea or air)		20 miles by sea	40 miles by sea	135 miles by sea
Potential state size	None	A small valley in the vicinity of a small lake	Small part of a continent	Large area of a continent with coastal colonies

Communications	Word of mouth, drums, smoke, relay runners, and hand printed manuscripts prior to A.D. 1441	① 1441 The Gutenberg printing press	② 1863 The rapid print Web newspaper press

figure 19:1   Shrinking of our planet because of increased travel and communication speeds around the globe

The German sociologist Ralf Dahrendorf is a contemporary thinker who agrees with Marx that sources of conflict and change are built into the social structure. Rather than adhere to the view that society is relatively stable and based on consensus (the equilibrium view), Dahrendorf proposes that:

1. Every society is subjected at every moment to change; social change is ubiquitous.
2. Every society experiences at every moment social conflict; social conflict is ubiquitous.
3. Every element in a society contributes to its change.
4. Every society rests on constraint of some of its members by others. (1973: 103)

Like Marx, Dahrendorf sees the unequal distribution of power and authority as the fundamental source of conflict in a society. Those persons or groups with power want to preserve the status quo. This puts them in conflict with the subordinate groups, whose interest is to change the status quo. Organized interest groups struggle over nu-

merous issues. This conflict can lead to various changes in the society's structure if dominance relations are changed. But the nature, speed, and depth of the conflict and the resulting change depend on numerous variable conditions. Change needn't be cataclysmic.

SOURCES OF CHANGE

The evolutionary, cyclical, equilibrium, and conflict perspectives on change, while not explaining change in any definitive way, do show how multifaceted a process it is. But where, specifically, does change come from? What prompts people to alter their way of life? The sources of change are many. Consider Japan, a feudal nation that transformed herself into a modern one in the years following World War II. A combination of population pressure (always a problem for this island people), new ideology (shifting from a

A.D. 1500	A.D. 1900	1925	1950	1965
A few years	A few months	A few weeks	A few days	A few hours
Big sailing ships (with compass), horse teams, and coaches	Steamboats and railroads (Suez and Panama canals)	Steamships, transcontinental railways, autos, and airplanes	Steamships, railways, autos, jet and rocket aircraft	Atomic steamship, high speed railways, autos and rocket-jet aircraft
20–25 miles	Rail, 300–900 miles	400–900 miles	Rail, 500–1,500 miles	Rail, 1,000–2,000 miles
175 miles by sea	250 miles by sea	3,000–6,000 miles by air	6,000–9,500 miles by air	408,000 miles by air
Great parts of a continent with transoceanic colonies	Large parts of a continent with transoceanic colonies	Full continents and transoceanic commonwealths	The globe	The globe and more

③ 1876 The Bell telephone	④ 1895 The Marconi telegraph	⑤ 1920 First commercial radio broadcast	⑥ 1950 National television	⑦ 1965 Transcontinental TV with the introduction of Early Bird satellite

SOURCE: John McHale, *World Facts and Trends* (New York: Macmillan, 1972), p. 3.

military to an economic orientation), and social strain (inequalities under the feudal system) prompted Japan to borrow new technology and a new system of government (democracy) from the Western nations that had defeated her. Japan was under both internal and external pressure to change.

Internal Sources of Change

Demography It is impossible to overestimate the importance of numbers. Indeed, most scholars attribute the shift from hunting and gathering (living off the land) to food production (gardening and raising animals) in about 10,000 B.C.—surely the most profound revolution in human existence—to population pressure (Pfeiffer, 1977). As we saw in chapter 16, the postwar baby boom in the United States affected the need for services (such as schools), the size and shape of the labor force, the demand for consumer goods (creating the "youth market"), and even traffic flow and settlement patterns.

From the point of view of individual families, the decision to have a third child may have seemed minor, but the aggregate impact on society was profound (Moore, 1974: 74).

Ideology Ideas are at least as powerful as numbers, and shifts in *ideology* are a second internal source of change. It would be safe to say that most people in most times have looked at nature with a sense of awe. We needn't detail the wave of changes set off by the shift from a magical to a rational orientation toward the environment—to a new emphasis on humanity's mastery over nature (a shift that began in the Middle Ages).

Inequality As explained in chapter 10, those in power generally try to protect the system that gives them privileges. However, it is not necessarily those at the bottom of the social scale who instigate change, for the very poor tend to be fatalistic. But when people have reason to believe their situation is improving, when they experience a period of rising expectations, a sudden and unexpected reversal is intolerable. Relative deprivation (a gap between expectations and reality), not absolute deprivation, sets off revolutions.

Technology We have saved perhaps the most obvious internal source of change for last: new *technology,* knowledge directed toward practical applications in the material and social aspects of life. Discoveries (exploration or investigation that produces new knowledge about things already in existence) and inventions (new combinations or applications of knowledge) affect not only the material aspects of life but social arrangements as well. The automobile is a classic example. In a very short time, the Model-T Ford changed the way Americans worked (it rolled off the first assembly line) and the way they courted (for the first time couples had mobility and privacy). Our economy, our residence patterns, the air we breathe—all have been affected by the dominance of the car.

John Diebold (1973) has compared the invention of computers to the invention of writing, printing, and the radio (5). Just as in the 1890s mechanized printing made it possible for individuals to own their own books, so in the 1980s microelectronics will make it possible for individuals to own their own notebook-sized computers (Kay, 1977). (Most people already have pocket calculators.) Although it once took a trained person to operate a computer, these machines are now being programmed to ''read'' and ''write'' and even to ''speak.''

Already, computers are changing our lives. For example, the people who check out your groceries at the supermarket don't have to figure out your change: a computerized cash register does the job for them. The bills you receive are virtually untouched by human hands. If you don't already own credit cards, you undoubtedly will soon. (Fifteen years ago only businessmen—and we mean men—flashed American Express

cards. Forecasters predict a cashless society in the very near future.) Somewhere, all of your vital statistics are recorded in retrievable form on magnetic tape. (And a proliferation of committees and commissions are trying to balance society's need for data with your right to privacy.) When you register for classes, the bursar's office may know immediately if you have a library book overdue. If you decide to go to graduate school, you will probably be able to substitute a course in computer programming for a language requirement—and undoubtedly will be able to use a computer to sort through data for your dissertation (even if your field is English literature).

As for the macro-level of social structure, computers have eliminated some jobs and created others. Labor unions, which used to fight exploitation through regulation of wages, hours, and working conditions, are now fighting to ensure that their members aren't replaced by machines. There is a

The computer chip, a recent technological advance, allows information to be stored and retrieved far more efficiently than ever before. This innovation, only .040 square inches, may enable the computer—already a pervasive influence in our society—to become a common household appliance. (Erich Hartmann / Magnum)

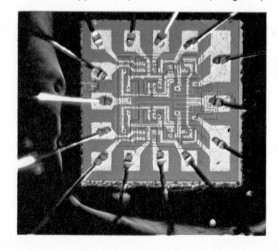

table 19:1 STAGES OF TECHNOLOGY

DOMINANT AGES	MODERN CRAFT, 1000–1781	MACHINE AGE, 1785–1869	POWER AGE, 1870–1952	ATOMIC AGE, 1953–
Power	Human and animal muscle, wind and water	Multiple horse teams and steam engines	Gasoline engines and electric motors	Atomic energy and fossil fuel burning equipment used to produce electric power and heat = fuel cells
Tools	Hand-wrought iron and wooden	Machine-wrought iron and steel	Multiple machine tools and automatic machines	Cybernated factories with computer closed feedback control loops
Work Skills	All-around skilled craftsmen and unskilled manual workers	Subdivided manufacturing processes replace skilled craftsmen with semi-skilled machine operators	Human feeder or tender replaced by skilled inspector-mechanics	Highly trained engineer-designers and skilled maintenance technician systems specialists and programmers
Materials	Wood, iron, and bronze	Steel and copper	Alloyed steels, light alloys, and aluminum	Plastics and super alloys (32 new metals used, notably magnesium and titanium)
Transportation	Walking, use of animals by dirt road or via waterways by sailboat	Horse and buggy, steam trains via steel rails, and steam ships via ocean ways	Automobile via paved highways, diesel trains and ships, and airplane via world airways	Rocket and jet vertical takeoff aircraft, atomic ships, helicopters, and automobiles
Communication	Word of mouth, drum, smoke signals, messenger, and newspaper	Mail by train and ship, mechanically printed newspaper, telegraph, and telephone	A.M. and F.M. radio, movies, television, magnetic tape, transoceanic telephone and microfilm	Video-phone, data phone, Telstar & Syncom, world-wide communications satellites, graphic computers

SOURCE: John McHale, *World Facts and Trends* (New York: Macmillan, 1972), p. 53.

whole new class of white-collar workers who specialize in designing computer models, simulating changes in supply and demand, and applying game theory to the conduct of business. The traditional division of companies into separate departments is being replaced by interdepartmental task forces. Computerization has accelerated the growth of multinational corporations, owned and operated by people who come from different countries but speak the same computer language.

Perhaps the most profound effects of computers are being felt in education. The first attempts to put computer technology to work in the classroom were motivated by the belief that our educational system is failing to teach students the most basic skills, much less the way to learn, independence of thought, or the use of one's imagination.

Computers would allow a student to experiment with problem-solving strategies and to get immediate feedback on the consequences of different plans. And computers might be a boon to students with a record of academic failure, for the machines "can exhibit infinite patience in the face of error without registering disappointment or disapproval—something no human teacher can ever manage" (in Diebold, 1973: 221).

Looking ahead to the time when many people have home computer terminals, Diebold (1973: 13–14) foresees executives working at home (an end to absentee fatherhood and split careers for mothers); doctors making "home visits" via two-way TV screens; D.A.'s and lawyers summoning up records and precedents in minutes, thus unclogging the court system; housekeepers ordering groceries within a set budget; and readers requesting a specific book review, political profile, or ball score (not having to take whatever newspaper and magazine editors think they should give them). Other side benefits include the leisure time to pursue a lifelong education, and a revival of the arts. (Imagine if composers could hear a passage they've just written immediately, via computer simulation.)

We've shown how new technology (here the computer) can set off waves of social change. This brings us to a more fundamental question. What factors give rise to inventions? Moore (1974) suggests an answer: persistent environmental challenge. No society enjoys a "frictionless" relationship with its natural setting. As long as natural forces remain out of control, as long as physical survival is uncertain, people will look for better ways of coping.

External Sources of Change

Human beings rarely stay in one place for very long. So for a society to be totally isolated for more than a generation is extremely unusual. And contact between cultures invariably leads to change, in one or both societies.

The term *acculturation* refers to social changes that result from extended contact between two cultures. Soldiers, colonial administrators, missionaries, migrants, traders, visiting scholars and artists, exchange students, and even tourists are agents of acculturation. (An "invasion" of free-spending tourists who dress and act as they would at home can have as much impact on their hosts as an invading army.)

Contact between societies may result in a cultural "takeover." For example, Dutch colonials transformed Indonesian society from a collection of subsistence horticulturists who lived in small, egalitarian villages into a competitive, stratified society oriented toward the world market (Plog, Jolly, and Bates, 1976: 470). At the other extreme, contact may prompt people to withdraw and cling to their traditions. Although the Sumu Indians of Nicaragua have been trading with neighboring groups for centuries, until recently they shut their doors when strangers entered their villages, kept their ways secret, and married only among themselves. Between these extremes are numerous examples of societies borrowing foreign traits selectively and modifying them to suit their needs. For example, the Haitians wove myths and rituals from Catholicism and the West African religions together in a new religio-magical system, voodoo.

Diffusion is the spread of traits from one society to another, irrespective of contact. For example, the Chinese "invented" thin round noodles; Marco Polo introduced them to Italy, where they were called spaghetti; Italians brought spaghetti here, where it has become a favorite low-cost meal. The Incas of Peru discovered quinine and then passed it to their Spanish conquerors, who shared it with other Europeans, who in turn used it in Africa to offset malaria attacks. (Were it not for the Inca, Europeans might never have colonized Africa.)

Although technology spreads more easily than systems of values and beliefs or forms of social organization, these too may diffuse widely. Examples are the world's great missionary religions, Buddhism, Christianity,

Diffusion occurs when one culture adopts elements—either material, such as the motorbike, or nonmaterial—from another culture. Today, both America's technology and its life style have an important influence on cultures throughout the world. (Georg Gerster/Rapho/Photo Researchers)

and Islam; and the Napoleonic code (the basis for law in France and in all its former colonies). We shall look at the diffusion of modernization in the next section, after we say a word about conservatism.

Every society has forces that operate to resist change, that focus instead on conservation and preservation. Geographic barriers, lack of the resources needed for a new technology, vested interest in the status quo, reverence for the past, fear of the unforeseen consequences of innovation, the pressure of tradition and habit, and selective forgetting (remembering the past as brighter than it was) can all act as brakes on change. In Nisbet's view, cultural elements don't change until all these forces have been "satisfied"—until the substitutes or innovations have been tested and have proven to have more utility for the society than the elements they will replace (Nisbet, 1970: 71).

MODERNIZATION

In the last fifty years, societies around the globe have been swept up in the process of modernization. *Modernization* means change toward the type of society found in the advanced industrial nations. Diffusion, acculturation, raw technology, new inequalities, new ideology, and demographic shifts have all contributed to this wave of social change.

In all but the most remote corners of the world, people are hungry for the fruits of an industrial economy and are pushing for a rapid—even revolutionary—transformation of their society. Up until the past few centuries hundreds, and perhaps thousands, of local societies went about their business pretty much the same way day after day. Most of these societies had subsistence economies, living either by nomadic hunting and gathering or by sedentary agriculture. But the societies created by the bourgeois revolutions in North America and Western Europe have been expansive ones. In their desire for prestige, their search for resources to fuel their economic development, and their sense of mission in spreading ''civilization,'' they have penetrated these once-traditional and isolated societies and have introduced them to the trappings of modern life. Much of the non-Western world has been colonized and brought into the world-wide market system, although those who lived in the colonies (mostly ex-colonies now) held to many of their traditional ways while supplying raw materials for Western industrial development. From a distance many of these people saw the riches that industrialism produced. And the native elites in these colonies and former colonies often had a chance to see modern capitalist societies from the inside when they came to London, Paris, or New York for their education. Their appetites whetted for manufactured riches and comforts, different peoples all over the world began trying to transform their nations into modern societies. This effort has had profound social, political, and psychological implications.

Political Modernization   Modernization is the consolidation of policy making in a centralized state bureaucracy (Black, 1968). The state expands its activities and absorbs functions once carried out by other traditional structures, such as the family and the church. In America and Western Europe, political centralization and the development of democratic traditions went together. Societies that have more recently embarked on a crash course of industrialization have had a difficult time promoting rapid social transfor-

mation within a democratic political structure. But even in those nondemocratic states undergoing modernization, there is a need for the state to seek popular legitimacy rather than to rely on more traditional forms of legitimation (such as appealing to the divine right of kings). Popular legitimation is usually sought and created through the organization of mass political parties (Eisenstadt, 1966).

Social Modernization   Modernization also means the following changes in social structure: intensive urbanization; the growth of large-scale and often bureaucratic organizations; equalization of income, education, and opportunity; extension of literacy; extension of communication systems and mass media; improvements in health care; and *social mobilization,* which is the process whereby commitments to traditional economic, political, and social roles are loosened. This makes the individual susceptible to new values, new socialization patterns, and new commitments. In the political sphere this usually means the replacement of local allegiances with an allegiance to the nation as a whole (Deutsch, 1953).

Psychological Modernization   Modernization involves psychological changes as well. In strongly traditional societies, an individual's life (where he or she will live, what he or she will do, whom he or she will marry) is largely predetermined by custom; the self is subordinated to the demands of the kinship group, the village, and the tribe. Any number of so-

The meaning of modernization depends upon the model a developing nation is following. The United States and the Soviet Union each offer a pattern, and in recent years, China has become an important model as well. (Audrey Topping/ Rapho/Photo Researchers)

cial scientists have suggested that modernization is an unsettling, often traumatic experience for people who have grown up in the confines and safety of traditions. However, Inkeles and Smith (1974) found that for most people, working in a factory or even going to school is a liberating experience. Individuals begin to seek freedom of choice in residence, religion, marriage partners, friends and enemies. Fear of strangers and fear of change give way to tolerance of human diversity and a readiness to try new things. Individuals break through passivity and fatalism, and express the active desire "to take charge of their individual lives and their collective destiny" (5). Seventy-six percent of the factory workers Inkeles and Smith interviewed in Argentina, Chile, India, Israel, Nigeria, and Bangladesh exhibited these modern personality traits, compared with only 2 percent of individuals who had no experience with modern organizations. This is not to say that modernization comes easily, however.

Strains and Adjustments

When modernization occurs slowly over a long period of time, as it did in America and Western Europe, new political systems, new value systems, new economic systems, and new personalities have a chance to adjust to one another gradually. These changing patterns reinforce one another, replacing the traditional way of life with new and (more important) integrated patterns of social organization.

However, the leaders of developing nations can't afford the luxury of slow development. Their people want the fruits of modernity *now*. Rapid, overnight modernization tends to produce social disintegration. Inevitably, some elements of social life change faster than others. For example, the birth rate in the Third World has continued to climb, although the death rate has fallen off. A nation prepares for the future by sending young people abroad to universities, but doesn't have appropriate jobs for them when they return. The ties that bind a traditional society together loosen. Governmental coordination and control of these large-scale changes become all the more necessary. Because the armed forces of these societies are often the institutions most capable of planning and organizing large-scale efforts, many modernizing societies experience takeovers by their armies. Given such drastic imbalances, it is no wonder that modernization so often produces feelings of rootlessness and anomie, outbreaks of mass hysteria, violence, and civil war (Eisenstadt, 1966).

The disruptive effects of modernization are often exaggerated, however. New technology and ideology don't necessarily *replace* old forms. Magic and medicine can exist side by side, as alternate means of curing illness. Modern modes of communication, mobility (easy travel), and literacy may serve to spread and intensify traditions as well as new ideas. (More people can read holy books, make pilgrimages to far-off shrines, and so on.) Often it is the most highly educated members of a society (the intellectuals) who work to preserve and develop what is unique about the indigenous or native culture (Gusfield, 1967).

Ultimately the growing pains a developing society experiences depend on its readiness, the rate of change, and the desirability of change. When people believe that the situation is under control and that they are heading in a direction they have chosen or at least accept, the stress of even rapid change will be lessened (Lauer and Lauer, 1976: 521). One of the major effects of change, whether it is controlled or uncontrolled, is on the kinds of work people do and the structure of jobs; appropriately, the symbol of modern-

IN THE NEWS

Amish Farmers Resist Modernization

In 1977, a new state law designed to control the bacteria count in milk went into effect in Indiana, making it mandatory that milk for public sale be cooled to fifty degrees within two hours of milking. The Amish farmers there, whose existence depends heavily on the weekly sale of milk, were faced with a dilemma that threatened their well-being and tested their religious convictions. The Amish are a clan of Mennonites (an evangelical Protestant sect) whose religion dictates a style of life that precludes the use of modern technological devices for any reason. For most Amish farmers, dairy products provide the largest part of the family income, and the milking of cows and the preparation of milk for sale are affairs participated in by the whole family. For instance, a day in the life of the Freeman M. Yoder family could be described this way:

Each morning at 5:30 the Yoder girls and boys join their father in milking in the barn, which is lighted by a kerosene lamp. After the work, which lasts an hour, the milk is poured through strainers into 10-gallon pails and then immersed in well water. Milk buckets are sterilized, and then the family has breakfast. The same job is repeated in the late afternoon, followed by dinner.

The hand-milking of cows and the use of hand-carried kerosene lanterns are characteristic of life in most Amish farms in this area. Water is pumped by windmills, no electric power is used and there are no radios or television or other modern devices.

Religious beliefs aside, Amish farmers also worried about the cost of modern cooling systems—over $2,000, a stiff price for small farmers—which could have led to the need for other means of income and resultant larger farms. Fortunately, this time around, a bill allowing a temperature range that the Amish could achieve without mechanical devices was passed, and the 1977 law was repealed.

However, modernization is a continual threat to the Amish. As Roy Miller, a bishop in an Amish congregation, states:

"It wasn't just the fine line between water cooling and mechanical cooling that bothered me.... Next, there will be mechanical milking, then larger herds, expanded expenses and more mechanization to operate more efficiently.

"Soon, instead of having family farms, we will have super farms," he said, adding that the Amish do not want big farms.

"That's what I'm interested in," he said, "seeing the family farm preserved, and this [kind of measure] really endangers it."

Asked what would happen if [such] regulation[s] were enforced, Mr. Miller said:

"We'd face some hard decisions on which way to go. I'm just not sure. It would disrupt our church. Some of our people just couldn't accept this."

SOURCE: Reginald Stuart, "Amish Farmers in Indiana Are Facing Tough Choice Between Economic Needs and Religious Principles," *The New York Times*, March 2, 1977, p. A12.

ization has long been that of the tractor supplanting the ox, or the factory the hand loom.

TECHNOLOGY AND WORK

The technological innovations that are so much a part of modernization imply changes in the world of work far beyond the building of factories and the installation of machines: whole new social organizations must grow up to support and utilize the new devices, and living patterns must be altered accordingly. A computer, for example, calls for engineers, programmers, and service technicians. The organization that has installed the computer will often change its ways of doing things to accommodate the new machine. People who once performed the functions taken over by the computer will be reassigned or may have to seek new jobs. Let us look first at what technological changes have meant for the kinds of work people do and then at how these changes have affected attitudes toward that work.

Technology and the Occupational Structure

The transformation of the content of work brought about by technological change has also been accompanied by a transformation in the occupational structure. The advances of the Industrial Revolution, for example, turned many a farmer into the operator of a machine in an urban factory. Statistics show this clearly. In 1820, about 70 percent of the American population worked the farm. This proportion fell to about 40 percent in 1900 and is currently just over 3 percent (U.S. Bureau of the Census, 1977: 406).

In time, fewer workers were needed for manual labor, and more were needed for servicing, distributing, and coordinating. This has meant an enormous rise in paperwork, again reflected in aggregate figures. Whereas clerical workers constituted only 0.6 percent of the labor force 100 years ago (Mayer, 1956), they are now the largest occupational group, comprising 1 out of every 5 people (U.S. Bureau of the Census, 1977: 406). Furthermore, as the coordination and administration of work has become more complex, the proportion of nonfarm managers and administrators has risen from less than 6 percent of the 1900 labor force to over 10 percent in 1977, an increase of over 80 percent (Thomlinson, 1976: 397; U.S. Bureau of the Census, 1977: 406).

Another significant shift is the increase in demand for specialized technical and professional workers. The growth of science and technology during the past few centuries has produced an explosion of knowledge. This in turn has created new occupations that require mastery of a complex body of specialized knowledge and skills. Agricultural societies, with their low level of technological development, needed only a small professional class. Precise figures on the size of this group in preindustrial America are not available, but if one can judge from its size in other preindustrial societies, it must have been small. During the 1940s Mexico had only 1 percent of its work force in the professions, and during the 1920s Greece had only 3 percent. In contrast, America had over 15 percent of all workers in professional and technical occupations in 1977 (U.S. Bureau of the Census, 1977: 406).

The point of all these statistics is that Americans—and others—are again living in the midst of a radical shift in the occupational structure. Within the past two decades, America has become the first society with a majority of workers engaged in *service occupations*—jobs that involve activities of-

THE ARTIST'S SHIFTING IMAGE

Reminiscing about his life as an artist, Marcel Duchamp said: "One became a painter because one didn't want to go to the office every morning" (in Adler: 361). In one sentence, Duchamp expressed a great deal about the traditional role of artists in Western society.

To be an artist meant to live and work outside of the commercial market place. Artists were drawn to a life style that rejected the ordinary values of their time and glorified individual development and expression. They were considered immune from the "alienating aspects of work in advanced industrial society: the molding of the work and worker to meet the market's shifting demand, rapid occupational change and the consequent early obsolescence of work skills" (362–363). This image of the artist as a stranger to the technological world that the rest of us live in is, argues Judith Adler, no longer true.

Far from being exempt from the pressures of the market place, Adler claims that artists are even more subject to them than the rest of us are. In a society where innovation and change are among the dominant values, artists feel pressed to come up with new models of their own. Last year's "in" aesthetic becomes as dated as last year's Ford. The only tradition left in the arts, states Adler, is the tradition of breaking tradition (367).

If this obsession with change makes things difficult for the working artist, it makes things almost impossible for the art teacher. Studying aesthetic traditions seems pointless to students who want to be in the vanguard of the art market. The development of skills also has little appeal to young artists. Why spend years perfecting your drawing when you can think of a route to success that doesn't require drawing at all? Even the teacher's practical experience in entering and working in the art world seems useless to young artists who face a constantly shifting set of rules.

With their authority so weakened, art teachers find themselves predicting trends in the art market and helping students to become good at self-promotion. Any young artist who persists in an idealized image of the artist as a member of a noncommercial, "purer" world than the rest of us live in is quickly disabused of such notions.

Adler concludes that this new, realistic picture of the artist is a useful one. Instead of imagining artists as having greater integrity than we do and as living in a world without commercial pressures, the true picture of the art world provides a vivid lesson in the pressures and compromises that everyone who works in the modern world must face.

SOURCE: Judith Adler, "Innovative Art and Obolescent Artists," *Social Research*, vol. 42 (Summer 1975): 360–378.

fered for sale—rather than in the production of foods and goods. A growing service economy means that there will be a growth in such areas as health, education, research, and government.

Industrialization and Alienation

According to a long tradition of sociological thought, people become alienated from work under the impact of industrialization and the division of labor it produces. Karl Marx developed this theme over a century ago, when industrialization was just beginning, and it has been a cornerstone of social criticism ever since. In *The Communist Manifesto* (1848), Marx and Friedrich Engels declared:

> Owing to the extensive use of machinery and to division of labor, the work of proletarians has lost all individual character and, consequently, all charm for the workman. He becomes an appendage of the machine, and it is only the simplest, most monotonous, and most easily acquired knack that is required of him. (1959: 14)

The propertyless worker suffers from *alienation:* he is separated from his work because the ownership of the tools of production and the product itself has been appropriated by another. The worker isn't paid to "express himself"; the boss is interested only in getting the work done. The worker is thus reduced to his mere labor power, which has a market value. His labor power becomes a commodity, a thing to be bought and sold. Man thereby becomes alienated from himself, for his labor power is no longer an inextricable part of his essential self. Work becomes separated from play; work becomes separated from self-expression; work has no intrinsic meaning and is only self-sacrifice undertaken to earn money for leisure-time pursuits.

Are Workers Alienated Today?

Determining whether workers are satisfied or alienated would seem to be a relatively simple task. Why not just ask them if they are happy with their work? A number of such studies are reported in *Work in America* (1973), a special task-force report for the Department of Health, Education, and Welfare. One is a Gallup poll revealing that 80 to 90 percent of those questioned felt that their work was satisfying. In a representative cross section of American workers, about 80 percent indicated that they would continue to work even if they inherited enough money to live without working. Another finding was that as people's income and wealth increased, they didn't reduce the amount of time and energy expended at work.

A better indicator of job satisfaction may be whether or not workers would choose the same line of work again if they were given the chance to start over. A study reported in *Work in America* indicates that 41 percent of skilled steelworkers and only 16 percent of unskilled auto workers would choose their jobs again. About twice as many white-collar workers as blue-collar workers are satisfied with their work, but in both groups the percentage satisfied was less than half. Only among professionals was satisfaction really high: 83 percent of the lawyers surveyed, 89 percent of the physicians and biologists, and 97 percent of the urban university professors would choose the same line of work again (*Work in America,* 1973).

What Makes Work Satisfying?

A twenty-eight-year-old truck driver explains why he likes his work:

> There's a good feeling when I'm out there on the road. There ain't nobody looking over

figure 19:2   Job satisfaction

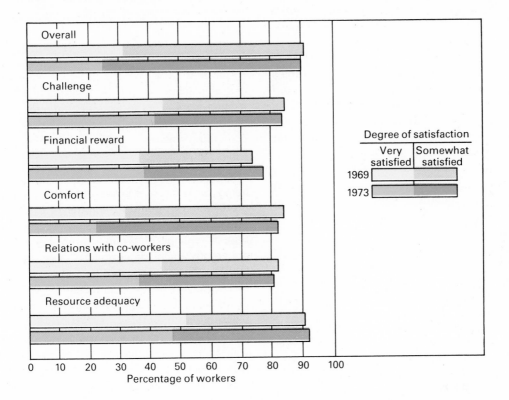

SOURCE: U.S. Bureau of the Census, *Social Indicators, 1973* (Washington, D.C.: U.S. Government Printing Office, 1974), p. 123.

In 1969 and 1973 the Survey Research Center of the University of Michigan asked a sample of workers to rate twenty-three aspects of their jobs. Analysts then grouped the answers into various dimensions. The overwhelming majority of Americans expressed some degree of satisfaction with their jobs, but the percentage that were very satisfied was significantly lower. Not surprisingly workers seemed most displeased about their wage compensation. These findings support the conclusion of Work in America *that American workers are dissatisfied only if the group "somewhat satisfied" is taken to indicate a large pool of people with reservations about their work.*

your shoulder and watching what you're doing. When I worked in a warehouse, you'd be punching in and punching out, and bells ringing all the time. On those jobs, you're not thinking, you're just doing what they tell you. Sure, now I'm expected to bring her in on time, but a couple of hours one way or the other don't make no difference. And there ain't nobody but me to worry about how I get her there. (Rubin, 1976: 157)

Unlike most blue-collar (or white-collar) workers, a long-distance truck driver is free of close supervision. The work demands strength, skill, and most important, initiative—the making of independent judgments. On the road, the driver is in control.

Degree of Control Any number of studies show that job satisfaction is directly related to the degree of control a worker exercises over his or her activities. The closer individuals are to the top decision-making level of a hierarchical organization, the more contented and motivated they will be. Alienation is rare in nonhierarchical work groups in which all members participate in setting goals and defining policy (Tannenbaum et al., 1974: 162).

This has been demonstrated on the job. As was mentioned in chapter 8, the SAAB automobile plants in Sweden have abandoned the assembly-line type of operation. *All* an auto's parts are conveyed to a work space, where a small group of workers assembles the entire car. Working as a team, the group itself decides who will do what, thus allowing for day-to-day variation. Workers have more contact with each other, have a stronger identification with the product of their labors, and apparently receive direct satisfaction from their work. Absenteeism has decreased dramatically, and productivity has remained high. When Texas Instruments turned maintenance over to self-directing teams of janitors, plant cleanliness rose 65 to 85 percent; job turnover dropped from 100 percent to 9.8 percent per quarter; and the company saved about $103,000 the first year (*Work in America,* 1973: 96–100). General Foods Corporation found that the team approach not only increased productivity but also improved safety records (Dickson, 1975: 156–160). Such programs have been so successful that American industry now supports a private foundation—the Work in America Institute—which serves as a clearinghouse for pilot projects in worker participation.

Meaningful Work The examples of self-bossed work teams also illustrate two other sources of job satisfaction. The first is doing meaningful work. Work on a traditional assembly line is fragmented and repetitious. Recall Marx and Engels's assertion that the use of machinery and the division of labor robbed work of its individual character and charm. The teams we've described produce something meaningful (an automobile; a clean plant).

Being on a Team Second is the intrinsic gratification of being a member of a team. The formation of friendships and the generation of feelings of group responsibility are apparently major determinants of job satisfaction.[1] This is supported by a study of factory workers which revealed that 65 percent of workers integrated into work groups were pleased with the *intrinsic* and secondary aspects of their work (that is, the pay, working conditions, and the like), while only 28 percent of isolated workers expressed a similar degree of satisfaction (*Work in America,* 1973).

Work Hours The formation of work groups has been paralleled by flexibility in working hours, another source of job satisfaction. According to a 1977 survey, about 13 percent of American businesses have instituted "flexitime." Employees must still work

---

[1] *Work in America* identifies several related determinants of job satisfaction. These include the status of the work, its prestige as compared with other jobs; job content, the degree to which it is repetitious or challenging; supervision, the degree to which the worker is free to make his own decisions and regulate his work; wages (high pay and high satisfaction tend to go hand in hand); mobility, the availability of opportunities for promotion; working conditions, the length and time of day of working hours and the comfort and pleasantness of surroundings; and job security, the degree to which the employee is susceptible to layoffs or to being fired (1973: 94).

seven hours a day, but they may distribute two of those hours before or after a required core period, such as 9:00 A.M. to 3:00 P.M. In some companies, workers can distribute work time over days in a week. The original idea behind flexitime was to alleviate traffic jams by staggering work hours, but it has turned out to have other benefits. Workers can more easily take care of such personal responsibilities as child care, housekeeping, and errands. And flexitime encourages workers to take the responsibility for managing their own time and their own jobs (*The New York Times,* November 9, 1977). Very likely more and more businesses will adopt this program. Change, not just in work but in all facets of social life, is a certainty of the future.

CHANGING WORLD DIRECTIONS

What lies ahead? Where are global modernization and related changes in politics, social forms, and individual psychology taking us? Different prophets foresee different futures.

Daniel Bell (1973) believes change is already upon us: we have entered the postindustrial age. Whereas early inventions of the Industrial Revolution were typically produced by craftspeople or tinkers, new technologies depend increasingly upon specialized knowledge. The development of the machine was the central force in industrial society. In *postindustrial society,* the central force will be the organization of theoretical knowledge. Energy production drove industrial society; information production drives the postindustrial society. Economic growth was the goal of industrial society; advancement of theoretical knowledge is the new goal.

The class structure of postindustrial society will be based on access to information and control of decision-making rather than on ownership of property. Thus the lower class will be defined not by their poverty but by their lack of the knowledge that would give them access to dominant organizations. The primary value of technological society is efficiency, which means greater output for less cost. In order to promote efficiency, Bell argues, human activities are likely to be more bureaucratized. Postindustrial society will not be without its conflicts, Bell contends. The political system will stress the values of equality and popular participation, which go against the values of hierarchy and subordination found in bureaucratic organizations.

French sociologist Jacques Ellul (1964) believes we are doomed. Technology, writes Ellul, is like a virus. A virus perpetuates its strain by invading a cell, taking over its chemistry of reproduction, and causing it to stop producing its own kind and begin producing viruses. Similarly, "technique," or technology, takes over society and "dissociates the sociological forms, destroys the moral framework, . . . explodes social and religious taboos, and reduces the body social to a collection of individuals" (126).

This occurs because technology always seeks the most efficient way of performing tasks, not taking into consideration that it might thus make work less satisfying to the individual or foul the environment or disrupt the social fabric. Trying to curb pollution (or to correct other defects of technological progress) with new technology only compounds the problem, since the criterion is still efficiency and the new technology has its own imperatives that may lead to equally unfortunate side effects. One of these imperatives is a tendency toward self-perpetuation and immunity from human control, so technology may proliferate if unchecked.

Because of the importance of efficiency in a technological society, Ellul maintains there will be an increasing effort to limit human error and human interference in technological progress. As a result, techniques will be developed to manipulate behavior through education, propaganda, and psychology. Ellul suggests that although people will be unhappy about these encroachments on their freedom, they won't revolt, for unhappiness is just another technical problem. Instead, technology will devise one last ignominy, a human technology that will manipulate people into happiness—or at least complacency. Thus, technology will become a tyrant, ruling human society with absolute power.

Willis W. Harman's analysis (1977) is less dramatic, but no less sobering. Harman believes the problems we are experiencing today derive from the *successful* solution of problems we faced in the past. Modern societies are struggling with four basic dilemmas:

1. *The growth dilemma:* Unless we continue to grow economically, unemployment and alienation will rise to intolerable levels. But the environmental costs of continued growth are unacceptably high.
2. *The control dilemma:* We need to control technological development. Technology has reached the point where *everything* in our environment and in our physical make-up and behavior is subject to human intervention. (Just think of genetic engineering.) The dangers are enormous unless there is some kind of guiding intelligence. But we fear centralized control.
3. *The distribution dilemma:* The gap between the rich nations and the poor ones is widening at a dangerous rate. Yet we have no suitable mechanism, no philosophy, for distributing wealth. The problem can't be solved through the development of the poor nations. The

planet simply couldn't support all the people alive today consuming and polluting at the United States level.

These dilemmas all relate to what Harman calls the "new scarcity" (of fossil fuels and minerals, of fresh water, of productive land, of living space, and of places to dispose of waste), and to limits to the resilience of the earth's life-support ecosystems. Our modern problems are the product of technological solutions for the problems of the "old scarcity" (of food, clothing, shelter, and the like). We can't resolve them through more of the same.

4. *The work-role dilemma:* Modern societies are increasingly unable to provide meaningful social roles. The only legitimate roles in our society are related to work: holding a job, being married to someone who holds a job, or studying in preparation for a job. Yet millions are unemployed. Being jobless means being useless in our society: individual self-respect, effective citizenship, and ultimately even national security are endangered. Creating jobs—make-work—won't solve problems of self-respect. (Harman considers this perhaps the most serious dilemma, because for the most part we try to ignore it.)

Harman believes the future is indeed bleak *unless* we reexamine the pathogenic premises on which we now operate, including each and every one of the following ideas: any technology that can be developed should be; the sum total of the knowledge of specialized experts is wisdom; people can be treated in dehumanizing ways; individuals are essentially separate, and so have little responsibility for faraway people or future generations; nature is to be controlled and exploited, rather than cooperated with; ever-increasing economic growth is possible and desirable; the future can be left safely in the hands of autonomous nation-states; "the disbelief that 'what ought to be' is a meaningful and achievable concept" (1977: 8).

*The master control room of the computerized
Bay Area Rapid Transit (BART) system in
Oakland, California. According to Willis M.
Harman, the application of such advanced
technology to every aspect of our environment
is one of the basic problems confronting modern
societies. (Tom McHugh/Photo Researchers)*

For Harman, the main hope lies in massive
and effective reeducation in the values of
frugal living so that micro-decisions (what to
buy, who to hire) add up to sensible macro-
decisions (a controlled rate of growth, clean
air). Treading the line between optimism and
pessimism, Harman concludes that "industrial society . . . . will transform itself into
something different, probably involving a
wrenching and traumatic transition period"
(1977: 11).

To Harman's analysis we must add a
promising footnote. The 1960s saw the
emergence of what was called a counterculture; a rejection of materialism and competitive life styles; a move "back to nature" and
a reemphasis of human relationships. Most
observers viewed these developments as a
youthful, idealistic fling; a rebellion among
the overindulged and pampered, something
they would outgrow. Viewed another way,
however, this movement anticipated many

of the changes Harman forecasts: limited
growth; global interdependence; a shift from
a work-centered to a people-centered world
view.

Charting out these trends and projecting
them into the future affords us only general
predictions—perhaps more correctly called
hunches. The forces of affluence, of scarcity,
and of the new values are all at work on
American society, but perhaps some other
forces, only dimly perceived today, will
emerge in the future. Whatever forces have

greatest power, however, it is likely that there will be conscious attempts to guide their impact, for social change is increasingly subject to measurement and planning. This active approach to social change may itself represent the most fundamental break with the past and the central theme for social development in the future.

SUMMARY

General approaches to social change fall into four main categories. Those who see social change from the point of view of the *evolutionary perspective* stress the progressive differentiation and complexity of social structures, although the reasons for this process are in dispute. Those who operate from the *cyclical perspective* view societies and civilizations as passing through inevitable stages of development and decay. Theorists who view social change from the *equilibrium perspective* stress the adjustments that maintain social stability; social change is generally seen as harmonious. Directly opposed to this point of view is the *conflict perspective,* which stresses the prevalence of conflict and change. Society, according to conflict theories, rests on the constraint of one group by another; social change is generally seen as discontinuous as power shifts from group to group.

Demographic shifts, changes in ideology, inequality (in particular, relative deprivation), and new technology are internal sources of social change. A discussion of computer technology suggests how machines affect our social lives.

Acculturation (social changes that result from contact between societies) and *diffusion* (the spread of traits from one society to others) are external sources of social change.

Internal and external pressures have forced most societies to get involved in the process of *modernization:* change toward the type of society found in the advanced technical nations. Modernization affects politics, social forms, even individual psychology. Whether modernization creates strain depends on what the rate of change is, whether change is uneven, and whether people believe change is desirable and controllable. (Not all societies find modernization traumatic.)

Technology has led to profound changes in the structure of the workplace, first in the movement of people off farms and into factories, and in this century, in the transition to *service occupations*—those involved with the performance of activities offered for sale, rather than in the direct production of food or goods. Technology has also meant increased specialization, and with it has the specter of the alienated worker. Today, dissatisfaction with work appears to be fairly widespread, even among white-collar workers. However, many organizations are adopting practices that have been shown to increase job satisfaction: increased control over the job, a sense of doing meaningful work, and a feeling that one is working on a team.

Looking ahead, all forecasters see dramatic change for society as a whole. Harman sees our current problems (the growth, control, distribution, and work-role dilemmas) as the product of successful solutions to the problems of the past. He believes that we can't resolve these dilemmas with more of the same, but that we must reexamine the basic premises of modernization and industrialism.

GLOSSARY

acculturation social changes that result from extended contact between two cultures.

alienation Marx's term for a condition resulting from machine-age technology that requires only simple, repetitive tasks of workers, whose labor is purchased like any other commodity.

conflict perspective the view that social systems are inherently unstable and that struggle and conflict are the norms.

cultural lag Ogburn's term for the discontinuity that occurs when one part of the culture changes more rapidly than another.

cyclical perspective the view that every society has a natural life span; it grows and develops, but eventually decays.

diffusion the spread of traits from one society to another, irrespective of contact.

equilibrium perspective the view that a society struggles to keep itself in balance by attempting to integrate the changes that occur.

evolutionary perspective the view that societies evolve from simple, traditional structures into increasingly complex and differentiated forms.

modernization change toward the type of society found in advanced industrialized nations; it has profound social, political, and psychological implications.

postindustrial society Bell's term for a society in which advancement of theoretical knowledge is the goal.

service occupations jobs that involve activities offered for sale (or offered in connection with the sale of goods) rather than the production of foods or goods.

social change an alteration of the patterns of social organization over time.

social mobilization the process whereby commitments to traditional economic, political, and social roles are loosened, making the individual susceptible to new values, new socialization patterns, and new commitments.

technology knowledge directed toward practical applications in the material and social aspects of life.

REFERENCES

Richard P. Applebaum, *Theories of Social Change*. Chicago: Markham, 1970.

Conrad M. Arensberg and Arthur H. Niehoff, *Introducing Social Change*. Chicago: Aldine, 1964.

Daniel Bell, *The Coming of the Post-Industrial Society*. New York: Basic Books, 1973.

Cyril Black, *Dynamics of Modernization*. New York: Harper & Row, 1968.

Ralf Dahrendorf, *Class and Class Conflict in Industrial Society*. Stanford, Calif.: Stanford University Press, 1959.

_____, "Toward a Theory of Social Conflict," in Amitai Etzioni and Eva Etzioni-Halevy, eds., *Social Change: Sources, Patterns, and Consequences*. New York: Basic Books, 1973.

Karl A. Deutsch, "The Growth of Nations: Some Recurrent Patterns of Political and Social Integration." *World Politics*, vol. 5 (January 1953): 168–195.

Paul Dickson, *The Future of the Workplace*. New York: Weybright and Talley, 1975.

John Diebold, *The World of the Computer*. New York: Random House, 1973.

Émile Durkheim, *The Division of Labor in Society* (1893), trans. George Simpson. Glencoe, Ill.: Free Press, 1947.

S. N. Eisenstadt, *Modernization: Protest and Change*. Englewood Cliffs, N.J.: Prentice-Hall, 1966.

Jacques Ellul, *The Technological Society*. New York: Knopf, 1964.

Joseph R. Gusfield, "Tradition and Modernity: Misplaced Polarities in the Study of Social Change." *American Journal of Sociology,* vol. 72 (January 1967): 351–362.

Willis W. Harman, "The Coming Transformation." *The Futurist,* vol. 11 (February 1977): 5–12.

Marvin Harris, *Culture, Man, and Nature.* New York: Crowell, 1971.

Alex Inkeles and David Horton Smith, *Becoming Modern: Individual Change in Six Developing Countries.* Cambridge, Mass.: Harvard University Press, 1974.

Robert Jastrow, "Toward an Intelligence Beyond Man's." *Time,* February 20, 1978, p. 59.

Alan C. Kay, "Microelectronics and the Personal Computer." *Scientific American,* vol. 237 (September 1977): 230–244.

Robert H. Lauer and Jeanette C. Lauer, "The Experience of Change: Tempo and Stress," in George Zollschan and Walter Hirsch, eds., *Social Change.* Cambridge, Mass.: Schenkman, 1976.

Karl Marx and Friedrich Engels, *The Communist Manifesto* (1848), in Lewis Feuer, ed., *Basic Writings of Politics and Philosophy.* New York: Anchor, 1959.

Kurt Mayer, "Recent Changes in the Class Structure of the United States," in *Transactions of the Third World Congress of Sociology.* London: International Sociological Association, 1956.

Wilbert E. Moore, *Social Change,* 2nd ed. Englewood Cliffs, N.J.: Prentice-Hall, 1974.

Robert Nisbet, *The Social Bond.* New York: Knopf, 1970.

William F. Ogburn, *On Culture and Social Change.* Chicago: University of Chicago Press, 1964.

Talcott Parsons, *The Social System.* New York: Free Press, 1951.

———, *Societies: Evolutionary and Comparative Perspectives.* Englewood Cliffs, N.J.: Prentice-Hall, 1966.

John Pfeiffer, *The Emergence of Society.* New York: McGraw-Hill, 1977.

Fred Plog, Clifford J. Jolly, and Daniel G. Bates, *Anthropology: Decisions, Adaptation, and Evolution.* New York: Knopf, 1976.

Lillian Breslow Rubin, *Worlds of Pain: Life in the Working-Class Family.* New York: Basic Books, 1976.

Neil Smelser, "Toward a Theory of Modernization," in Amitai Etzioni and Eva Etzioni-Halevy, eds., *Social Change: Sources, Patterns, and Consequences.* New York: Basic Books, 1973.

Herbert Spencer, *The Evolution of Society: Selections from Herbert Spencer's "Principles of Sociology,"* ed. Robert L. Carniero. Chicago: University of Chicago Press, 1974.

Oswald Spengler, *The Decline of the West* (1918–1922). New York: Knopf, 1926–1928.

Arnold S. Tannenbaum et al., *Hierarchy in Organizations: An International Comparison.* San Francisco, Calif.: Jossey-Bass, 1974.

Ralph Thomlinson, *Population Dynamics,* 2nd ed. New York: Random House, 1976.

Arnold Toynbee, *A Study of History.* New York: Oxford University Press, 1946.

U.S. Bureau of the Census, *Statistical Abstract of the United States, 1977.* Washington, D.C.: U.S. Government Printing Office, 1977.

Work in America: Report of a Special Task Force to the Secretary of Health, Education, and Welfare. Cambridge, Mass.: MIT Press, 1973.

FOR FURTHER STUDY

Technological Society. The sociology of our technological society is powerfully analyzed by Jacques Ellul in *The Technological Society* (New York: Knopf, 1964). Another major figure studying technology is Lewis Mumford, who has written many books on the subject, among them *The Myth of the Machine,* 3 vols. (New York: Harcourt Brace Jovanovich, 1970). Alvin Gouldner and Richard A. Peterson examine the social consequences of change in *Notes on Technology and Moral Order* (New York: Irvington Publishers, 1977; orig. 1962). E. F. Schumacher conveys the possibility for alternatives to our present direction in technology in his work *Small Is Beautiful* (New York: Harper & Row, 1976).

Changing Work for Women. Changes in technology combined with changing social values have led to new work roles for women. In order to understand these changes, we depend on historical analysis to clarify developments over time. Two books that discuss the changes in women's work are Rosalyn Boxandall et al., eds., *America's Working Women: A Documentary History—1600 to the Present* (New York: Random House, 1976) and Ann Oakley, *Women's Work: The Housewife Past and Present* (New York: Pantheon, 1975). Philip S. Foner presents a case study of women mill workers through their own words in *The Factory Girls* (Urbana, Ill.: University of Illinois Press, 1977). In her book *Pink Collar Workers* (New York: Putman, 1977), Louise Howe shows that despite change, some work remains "women's work," with the accompanying problems of low wages and job insecurity. An interesting analysis of new trends among women working as criminals is *Sisters in Crime: The Rise of the New Female Criminal* (New York: McGraw-Hill, 1975) by Freda Adler, in which the author demonstrates that more educated middle-class women have become involved in prostitution and drugs and that more women have also entered the area of white-collar crime.

Social Change in the Third World. Social change is particularly evident in areas of the world that are undergoing a transition from a traditional to an industrial economy. This transition, with its social and political consequences, has been studied intensively in Latin America. Two excellent books on this topic are James D. Cockcroft et al., *Dependence and Underdevelopment* (Garden City, N.Y.: Doubleday, 1972) and Dale Johnson, *The Sociology of Change and Reaction in Latin America* (Indianapolis, Ind.: Bobbs-Merrill, 1973). Eric Wolf analyzes the process of change in several third-world countries, including Mexico, Algeria, Cuba, and Vietnam in his book, *Peasant Wars of the 20th Century* (New York: Harper & Row, 1970). A classic study of American foreign policy as an agent of change in other countries is Harry Magdoff's *Age of Imperialism: The Economics of U.S. Foreign Policy* (New York: Monthly Review Press, 1969).

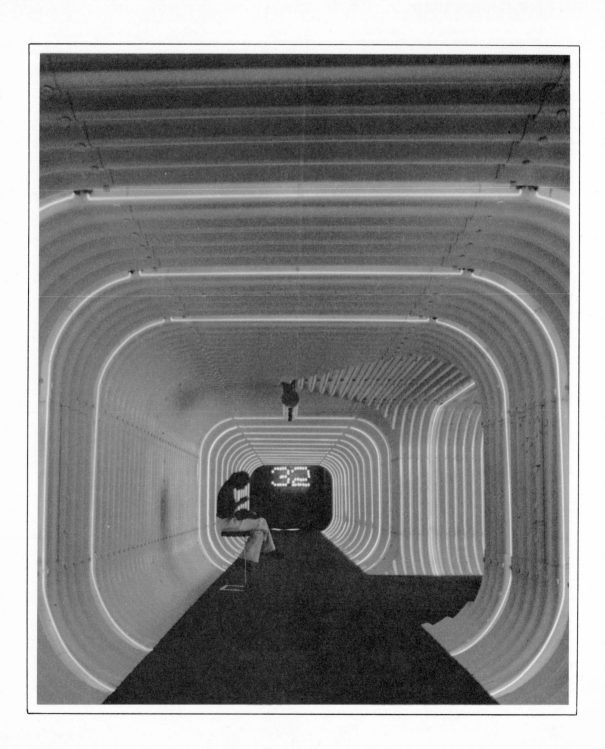

CHAPTER 20

Epilogue

Americans are sports fanatics. As a nation, we spent $12 billion on sports equipment in 1976 alone. That same year the television networks provided 1,000 hours of sports competition. Monday-night football has given us a three-day weekend. Top athletes like basketball center Bill Walton and tennis player Chris Evert earn as much as any top executive (including our chief executive, the president, whose salary is $200,000 a year), and considerably more than most scientists, senators, and poets.

Sports help to illustrate the point of view we have presented in this book, the sociological perspective. Like players on a team, we are all members of groups that are larger than ourselves. Group norms and values influence even our most personal choices, such as what career to pursue or whom to marry. We cooperate and compete according to rules. We inherit these rules, learn how to use them, and in the process change them. Innovation is part of the game. Like players on a team, we are all interdependent. Whether our teams "win" or "lose" depends not only on how well each individual plays but on how well we play *together*.

American culture tends to divert attention away from the collective aspects of life. From early childhood we are taught to worry about our *own* needs, our *own* ambitions, our *own* lives; to take care of ourselves and let others take care of themselves. We idealize self-made and self-directed men and women. Not content to compare our heroes to stars, we invented superstars. But superstars are a social phenomenon: they are made, not born. If Muhammad Ali had been born in 1900 instead of in the 1940s, he might have become a local hero. But he wouldn't have been able to draw crowds in such faraway places as Africa and Southeast Asia. If Walter Cronkite were a schoolteacher instead of a TV anchorman, his impact on world events—on the way millions of Americans perceive them—would be negligible. Superstars like Ali and Cronkite are products not just of their own talents and ambitions but also of the social system in which they live.

Team sports illustrate the sociological perspective. Like these basketball players, each of us belongs to several teams (social groups) with rules that govern personal conduct, competition, and cooperation. The success or failure of our teams depends upon not only how we play individually, but also how we work together. (Peeter Vilms/Jeroboam)

Social forces operate on two levels. Our lives are shaped not only by the micro-dynamics of group interaction (the norms applied to the roles we play), but also by the macro-structures of American society (our socioeconomic status and the like). This is precisely what writer John McPhee had in mind when he wrote *Levels of the Game* (1969). In it, McPhee describes a tennis match between Clark Graebner and Arthur Ashe, stroke for stroke. He then goes on to show how the particular circle of family, friends, and coaches in which each player moves (the micro-level of social structure) and their respective locations in the American social structure (the macro-level) influence each player's game. "A person's tennis game begins with his nature and background and comes out through his motor mechanisms into shot patterns and characteristics of play" (3). Clark Graebner put it this way:

> "I've never been a flashy stylist like Arthur. I'm a fundamentalist. Arthur is a bachelor. I am married and conservative. It affects the way you play. I've never seen Arthur discipline himself. He's an underprivileged type who worked his way up . . . an average Negro from Richmond, Virginia. Negroes are getting more confidence. They are asking for more and more and they are getting more and more. They are looser. They're liberal. In a way liberal is a synonym for 'loose.' And that's exactly the way Arthur plays."

Arthur Ashe replied:

> "Clark is tall, strong, white, Protestant, middle-class, conservative. He's tight with his money, and he wants to see the poor work for their money . . . he probably doesn't see all the ramifications. He's high-strung and can be very demanding. He's accustomed to instant gratification. He's a damn smart player, a good thinker . . . his game is predictable." (i)

Like the men on Tally's corner (pp. 52–54), these players are shaped by forces beyond their control.

"FINDING THE HANDLE"

All in-groups use language to enhance their sense of identity (as shown in the discussion of the jazz subculture, p. 99), and people in sports are no exception. When a basketball player fumbles badly, sportscasters say that he or she "couldn't find the handle." The dynamics of social life are far more difficult to grasp than a basketball passed behind a player's back to a spot toward which his or her teammate is moving. But sociology provides conceptual handles for analyzing the pattern of social events and our role in them. Here we will review some of the points made in earlier chapters.

Organizations

Everyone who reads this book has had, and will have, to cope with organizations, again and again. Sociology can't help you avoid red tape, but you might find it less frustrating if you understand the workings of bureaucracies. For example, why can't the clerk who sells you stamps at the post office also sell you a money order? Why all those separate windows and separate lines to stand in? As we saw in chapter 8, the post office, like any bureaucracy, employs a complex division of labor, which increases the efficiency of the organization overall (though it may annoy individuals from time to time). The wait would be even longer if one person was trying to handle every task.

Sociology can help you operate within a bureaucracy as well. Suppose you go to work for a large organization—for example, you become a doctor and are employed in a hospital. You will be responsible for a certain number of patients, and you can legitimately expect nurses on the wards to carry out your instructions. But unless you recognize the informal social structure in the hospital—the procedures ward personnel have worked out to solve problems not covered by the rules, to eliminate unpleasant and unnecessary work, and to protect their own interests—you will be continually frustrated. Nurses can use the rules against you. To get anything done, you will have to learn the informal social order—and negotiate. The same is true in any organization, including colleges and universities.

Deviance

The presence on city streets of derelicts, pimps and prostitutes (of both sexes), and "shopping-bag ladies" (whose paper bags hold all their worldly possessions) is disturbing to everyone. Labeling theory provides insights into why they are there. As likely as not, the derelict is an individual who years before got caught breaking minor social rules and didn't have the power to get away with misdemeanors. Most people who commit deviant acts are not labeled deviant. But this person was stigmatized and effectively pushed outside respectable society. He is where he is in part because you and others treat him as an outcast. From this perspective the real issue at hand is not why this person is flaunting convention but why most people can get away with deviant acts. The answer, as we suggested in chapter 9, lies in the social structure.

Groups

The discussion of groups in chapter 7 has direct application to our personal lives. For example, when we're in a group, why do we so often "play to the crowd" and make rude, cutting remarks about people we basically like? As we saw, one of the ways in which groups establish and maintain an identity, a sense of "we-ness," is to set up boundaries between insiders and outsiders. This principle explains much of our behavior in groups. Consider locker-room talk. Here men constitute the in-group, women the out-group, and joking about women in stereotyped ways helps ensure that.

The changes in dynamics that occur when a dyad becomes a triad or perhaps a group of four, five, or more (pp. 183–185) explain other forms of group behavior. Indeed, many of the experiences we associate with romance may be attributed to the simple fact that a couple is a dyad. A dyad is an all-or-nothing proposition. If one party loses interest in a conversation, the interaction dissolves; if one loses interest in the relationship, it will end. The addition of a third party—a friend who drops in—takes some of the responsibility off the other two. But a third party opens the door to divisions of two against one. Perhaps this is why we say two's company, but three's a crowd.

Social Stratification

In chapter 10 on social stratification we examined the American dream and concluded that opportunity is never unlimited. As much as we would like to think social positions in our society are based solely on achievement, in fact sex, age, race, and who you know all matter a great deal. Knowing this helps you predict and prepare for obstacles. We pointed out that Americans tend to romanticize the role education plays in social mobility. In fact, the level of education you are likely to reach reflects the level your father

attained and his social position. Schooling is important, but *how* you use your education—including how you apply your understanding of groups, organizations, and so on—is equally important.

How can you, in fact, as an individual, prepare for the changes you are likely to encounter in all areas of your life? If one thing is certain, it is that we are in a period of rapid change. Sociology can help you see what kinds of changes are taking place, and can thus prepare you to cope with them.

PREPARING FOR CHANGE

In 1971, astronaut Alan B. Shepard, Jr., surprised audiences by pulling a golf club from his spacesuit, in full view of TV cameras recording the moon landing. It was (forgive the pun) a brilliant stroke. At the time, space exploration was shrouded with incredulity. A surprising number of people believed broadcasts from the moon were an elaborate hoax—not unlike the radio broadcast of Orson Welles's *War of the Worlds* in 1938, which created a night of panic (p. 534). Astronaut Shepard's prank cut through disbelief and tension. He made the fact that humans were on the moon a little more believable and a little less threatening, and at the same time demonstrated that scientists are not altogether humorless.

Space flights have become old hat, just another news item. But would it surprise you to learn that any number of scientists are seriously working on plans for space colonies—permanent satellites that could house up to 10,000 people for extended periods?

Princeton physicist Gerard K. O'Neill virtually stumbled onto the idea. In 1969, he

asked an introductory physics class to design space colonies, just as a hypothetical problem. To his surprise, students had little trouble overcoming such practical difficulties as creating gravity or finding raw materials. He began to take the project seriously himself. O'Neill has calculated that the technology being developed now for space shuttles would enable us to begin constructing orbital colonies in seven to ten years, for occupation in the year 2000. By the end of the twenty-first century, self-supporting space colonies could provide three times the land area available on earth.

As a measure of O'Neill's seriousness, 100 scientists, engineers, international lawyers, and social scientists met at Princeton in May 1975 for a three-day conference on feasibility. Most left convinced the idea is eminently practical.

According to Princeton physicist Gerard K. O'Neill, we will have the necessary technology to begin building space colonies—permanent satellites that could house up to 10,000 people—within seven to ten years. Life in a space colony will present challenges not only to engineering but to human relations as well. (G. K. O'Neill/Princeton University)

Note that the conference included social as well as physical scientists. Colonizing space is a challenge to human relations as well as to engineering. "The task will call upon the unique capacity of the human species to adjust and adapt to complex sets of future conditions never before experienced. Creative imagination and scientific projection will have to be exercised and applied [to realities previously seen] as only remote possibilities by authors such as Jules Verne, Isaac Asimov, and Arthur C. Clarke. . . ." (Shurley, Natani, and Sengel, 1977: 1).

Life on a space colony will demand adjustments in everything from our concepts of what is food and what is waste (everything, including air, will have to be imported or manufactured) to our notions of freedom and privacy and our definitions of the purpose of life.

The space colonists of the future will be able to transport some institutions from earth to their new home, but only some. For example, for a society to exist in space, there will have to be some form of government and some legal system for arbitrating disputes and settling conflicts. Yet it is impossible to foresee all the influences an unprecedented and alien environment will have on behavior. Orderly mechanisms for *changing* the rules as new circumstances develop will clearly be as important as mechanisms for enforcing rules.

Without question, a self-perpetuating space colony will need both sexes. What sorts of men and women will apply for life on space colonies? Will they be carrying excess baggage in the form of stereotypes about one another? Will we want to re-create the division of labor by sex in space that we have on earth now? the same kinds of families?

We know from data on remote polar stations, desert expeditions, submarine crews, and the like that life in a closed, isolated environment is hard. Sheer monotony and the lack of escape routes tend to promote the formation of cliques and to exacerbate conflicts both within and between groups. This could spell doom on a space station. What can be done? One possible solution would be to set up a system of role rotation to prevent the formation of cliques, entrenched inter-

ests, and intolerance. "Nothing enables one to see the world from another's point of view like operating from another's position, even in 'role playing,' for variable periods of time. An organized program of role rotation could uncover apparent idiosyncratic behaviors that are actually due to environmental variables and encourage mutual problem solving" (Shurley, Natani, and Sengel, 1977: 6). To pick an obvious example, taking a six-month turn in the nursery would give men an entirely new perspective. But think what rotation would do to our whole notion of specialization and of careers in general.

The effort to foresee problems that might develop in space colonies and to devise solutions is not just a game, a sophisticated diversion for imaginative scientists. It has practical applications in the here and now. Change has become part of our social structure. The adjustments each of us makes in our lives reflect and at the same time subtly reshape the macro-structures of society. One of the central messages of sociology is that we needn't plunge blindly ahead. Identifying and analyzing the forces for change is the first step toward harnessing those forces. Where are we heading?

The Family

The chances are that the family will mean something rather different to you than it did to your parents and grandparents. Not terribly long ago, the family was the foundation of social structure—an almost self-sufficient, multi-generational group of people who worked, studied, prayed, and played together for most of their lives. As the functions of the family have changed, the number of choices you face in arranging your own family life has increased. You may postpone marriage to establish a career; forgo traditional marriage (but live with someone); choose to remain single; marry but not have children; have children but not marry; marry, divorce, and remarry or not. And no one will be terribly shocked by these departures from standard family life.

In effect, we have added two new stages to our life cycles: singlehood (a period of living independently, outside the context of a family), and the post-parent years (a return to being a couple, a state once reserved for newlyweds). These stages are largely without precedent and therefore somewhat troubling. With few models to go on, we are having to redesign our lives as we go along. At the same time, our society is less preoccupied with sorting everyone into families. We are freer to explore diverse ways of creating intimacy and rearing children than our parents were.

Sex Roles

Partly because being a wife and mother is no longer a full-time, lifelong job, gender stereotypes are breaking down. With the rest of their lives an open book, women are preparing for new careers. And when half of society changes, the other half (the male half) must too. For example, the old division of labor in the family—men handling the finances and women minding the family's emotional needs—is not well suited to working wives and housekeeping husbands. We are in the process of redefining what it means to be a man or a woman and the relationship between the two. This is both confusing and liberating for everyone involved.

Assume for the moment that you do get married one day and that both you and your spouse want to work. Will you decide to have children or not? If you do have children, who will care for them? Would you feel comfortable about leaving a baby at a day-care center or with a baby-sitter all day? If you are a woman, how would you feel about your husband working only part-time or taking a year or two off to devote to the family while you work full-time? If you are a man, what would you do if your wife left you with one or more small children to care for? What do the answers to these questions tell you about the need for new social institutions that take changing family patterns and sex roles into account?

Education

The meaning of education has changed as well. For generations, Americans identified education with security. To get a good job, you had to go to college; if you graduated from college, you were practically guaranteed a good job. Simply put, a diploma was money in the bank. This is no longer the case, and not just because the number of people with college diplomas has increased. It is no longer possible to prepare for a career, once and for all. Technology changes year by year (requiring further training); so do management and decision-making strategies. The chances are you will go back to school at several points in your career, to study technology, better ways to handle interpersonal relations, or both. In addition, you may find you have more leisure than your parents had, and you may use it to pick up interests you had set aside. Taking courses has become a major form of recreation. For you, then, education will be a lifelong process.

Religion

Reports that religion was dying—widespread in the 1960s—seem to have been greatly exaggerated. But religion is changing. No longer is a faith passed intact from generation to generation in the belief that one's religion is as vital and immutable a part of one's identity as one's race or sex. On the one hand, we find secularization (the replacement of a religious world view with a scientific perspective), and invisible religion (a private set of beliefs drawn from personal experience). On the other, we see an increase in fundamentalist, evangelical churches and in such "exotic" religions as the Hare Krishna movement, which meet a search for meaning and provide a sense of community for small but active groups of Americans. In a sense we have become religious "consumers," examining different faiths until we find one that fits. Here again, you have a freedom of choice that would have been unimaginable a decade or two ago.

Population

Perhaps the most profound change occurring at this time is in the composition of society itself. The United States—birthplace of the "youth culture" of the 1960s—is slowly but surely becoming middle-aged. If current trends continue, the median age of Americans in the year 2050 will be thirty-seven. (The median age in 1900 was twenty-three; in 1800, sixteen.) Seventeen percent of the population will be over sixty-five, and there will be 50 Social Security recipients for every 100 workers. (Today, with 10 percent of the population over sixty-five, there are 35 pensioners per 100 workers.) The "graying of America" (a phrase used by Dr. Robert Butler of the National Institute on Aging) reflects declines in both fertility and mortality rates.

What does this mean for you as an individual? Very likely the notion that youth is the prime of life (and anyone over thirty is over the hill) will give way to a new emphasis on adults in the media and the arts. You may have a somewhat easier time finding a job than people five or ten years older than you did, but a harder time earning promotions, since higher-level positions likely will be filled by members of the "boom" generation born during the 1940s. The job market has changed. For example, the fact that people are having fewer children means that we need fewer teachers. And more of your income will go to providing for the elderly, via Social Security. By the time you reach old age, facilities for retired people may be far superior to those that exist today. Why? Because there are enough older people in our society today to command attention.

What does this shift in age composition mean for society as a whole? Will an older population be as productive as the current population? more so? Will it be as creative? as innovative? Will older people come to dominate institutions, shutting the young out? Will society be wiser? calmer? How will we care for twice the number of old people we have today? To date, our record on care for the elderly is extremely poor.

Then there is the problem of sheer numbers. The world is badly overcrowded today, with a human population of 4 billion (4,000 million). A conservative estimate forecasts a population of 6.5 billion for the year 2000. There will then be as many people in Asia as there were in the entire world in 1970 (O'Neill, 1977: 24–25). We are using up the resources that fuel our technology and way of life. Even if we could put all our arable land under cultivation, there would still not be enough food to go around—unless we make drastic changes in our social structure. Signs of change are beginning to appear. There is no going back to older ways of life, and we can no longer afford to let the future design itself. We are doomed only if we fail to see that micro-decisions have macro-consequences and to plan. The designs for space described earlier in this section may be one source of inspiration for planning the future on earth.

REFERENCES

John McPhee, *Levels of the Game.* New York: Farrar, Straus and Giroux, 1969.

Gerard K. O'Neill, *The High Frontier: Human Colonies in Space.* New York: Morrow, 1977.

Jay T. Shurley, Kirmach Natani, and Randal Sengel, "Ecopsychiatric Aspects of a First Human Space Colony." Paper presented at the Third Princeton/AIAA Conference on Space Manufacturing Facilities, Princeton, New Jersey, May 9–12, 1977.

APPENDIX

If you're like most college students today, you've already given considerable thought to your career. Where might sociology fit into your plans? What does sociology contribute to your education in general? The purpose of this section is to give you a brief overview of career opportunities for majors in sociology, or for people who go on to get an advanced degree in the discipline.

CAREERS IN SOCIOLOGY[1]

Job opportunities for sociologists with advanced degrees fall into three main categories: teaching, research, and policy administration.

Almost eight out of ten sociologists teach. The students they teach are not only undergraduates and future sociologists (in graduate programs) but also students enrolled in medical, educational, engineering, and other professional programs. Sociology is also a popular course in high schools and in continuing education programs for adults.

Teaching offers the reward of guiding students combined with considerable job security. The demands of teaching sociology depend largely on the setting. Typically, an instructor at a state community college teaches four or five courses a semester. Teaching itself—preparing lectures and conducting classes—is only one of an instructor's responsibilities. He or she often spends as much time meeting with students outside class as within. Counseling is part of the job. Every instructor spends considerable time keeping up with developments in the field, by reading research journals, professional books, and attending academic conventions and meetings. After three to five years as a successful teacher, an instructor will usually receive tenure—a guarantee of a job (unless the teacher engages in some form of unacceptable behavior or the school has severe financial problems).

Professors in university sociology departments usually begin their careers as teaching or research assistants. This not only supports them while they complete requirements for the Ph.D., it is also part of their training. As full faculty members they will teach both undergraduate courses and graduate seminars. Doing research and writing are at least as important to a university professor's career as teaching. Scholarly publication enhances the individual's chances of receiving tenure and promotions. (This is where the expression "Publish or perish" comes from.) The opportunity to do original research and the company and stimulation of colleagues are what attract sociologists to universities.[2]

The second most common career for sociologists is full-time research in government agencies, business and industry, or at a research institute. In these settings a sociologist may be called upon to do anything from analyzing census data to conducting experiments. Today, many sociologists are engaged in "evaluation research"—that is, assessing the impact of a particular program or policy. No longer do government agencies launch programs and hope for the best. For example, a sociologist may be asked by a highway department to project population

[1] This section and the following are drawn largely from *Careers in Sociology* (Washington, D.C.: American Sociological Association, 1977).

[2] Readers who consider college or university careers should be aware that the demand for teachers is not as great as it once was, because quite simply there are now fewer students to teach. See chapter 14.

shifts into and out of a city. Such data take much of the guesswork—and some of the political jockeying—out of government decisions.

Careers in research range from running a personnel department to working on the staff of a health center (where one of the sociologist's main problems may be convincing other professionals that his or her data are useful) to designing and carrying out research for a consulting firm. Full-time research combines the rigors of the scientific discipline with action—seeing one's data and ideas put to work in government or business projects.

Hiring sociologists as policy administrators, the third major category, is something relatively new. Ordinarily a policy administrator in, say, a public assistance or law enforcement agency does not teach (although he or she may conduct workshops) or do research (although he or she may commission and oversee research). Instead, an administrator acts as a liaison between the scientific community and the business community or government—keeping up with ongoing research in sociology and related fields, and working out useful applications of social-science findings. Typically, an administrative position involves drawing up budgets, allocating work, making personnel decisions, and other responsibilities for which a sociologist has no specific training. Some policy administrators have worked their way up from low-level staff positions; others were hired from the outside, because of the reputations they earned at a research institute or university. It is challenging work, particularly for sociologists who have a professional as well as personal interest in people, social problems, and the shape society will take in the future.

This by no means exhausts the kinds of work sociologists do, but it should give you an idea of the range of careers available.

Advanced Degrees in Sociology

How can you prepare for such careers? Should you major in sociology or consider graduate work? What can you do with a degree in sociology?

A B.A. in sociology is excellent preparation for general employment in a wide variety of fields. Depending on what you plan to do, certain courses will be especially useful. For example, if you're attracted to the business world you should give particular attention to courses in industrial sociology, organizations, and social psychology. A basic working knowledge of research methods and statistics will be useful for almost any career you pursue. (The arts may be the only area left today that does not depend heavily on statistics.) An associate or bachelor's degree will not qualify you to be employed as a professional sociologist, but it will certainly be useful in any job within a large organization or corporation, or in any type of work that involves direct contact with a wide variety of people.

There are two basic graduate degrees, the master's (an M.A. or M.S.) and the doctorate (a Ph.D.). A master's takes from one to three years study beyond the B.A., depending on the program. The courses are somewhat similar to advanced undergraduate courses, though more demanding, with an emphasis on theoretical issues and research methods. A thesis written on a specific topic or issue may or may not be required. An M.A. or M.S. is adequate preparation for most jobs in public agencies and private business, and for teaching in high school or two-year colleges.

Work toward a Ph.D. picks up where the

M.A. leaves off. Usually seminars replace lecture courses, and the emphasis shifts from learning about the field to actually *doing* sociology. In most programs, a Ph.D. candidate is required to take comprehensive written or oral examinations in the field as a whole or in a special area; demonstrate competence in two foreign languages (sometimes this includes a "computer language"); write a dissertation—a book-length study based on original research; and defend the dissertation before a faculty panel. A Ph.D. is the highest degree sociology offers, and takes at least four or five years of study beyond the B.A.

If you are considering an advanced degree in sociology our best advice is to talk with your sociology teachers. Graduate programs vary widely: look for the ones that suit your particular interests and skills.

Sociology and Your College Career

What if you do not go on to major in sociology or seek advanced training?

Undoubtedly some topics covered in this course sparked your interest. One might have been sex roles: figuring out what kind of man or woman you want to be in a world where cultural norms are changing rapidly. Perhaps the subject of deviance—who we consider deviant, why, and how the law treats them—captured your attention. Understanding how organizations work may have appealed to you. If so, *pursue your interest.* There is no better reason to choose a course than that it interests you. Most colleges offer courses in the sociology of sex roles or the family, the sociology of deviance or the law, and the sociology of organiza-

tions. The purpose of a survey course, in sociology or any other field, is to teach you the basic concepts and to provide you with a general overview of the discipline. Once you go beyond the introductory level to study more specialized topics and areas, you will begin to get a sense of the power of sociology as a perspective for better understanding social phenomena.

A few well-chosen courses in sociology can be an important supplement to a major in many fields—history, economics, political science, and others. These disciplines also study social life, yet no other discipline trains you to look at group and institution patterns in the way that sociology does. Many undergraduates today choose programs in such professional areas as business, health, law, social services, and education. As we hope this book has demonstrated, sociology provides important tools for looking beneath the surface of professional activities to understand the social patterns and forces that shape those activities. To take just one example, by 1990 there will be about 2.37 physicians for every 1,000 Americans—1.37 more per 1,000 than we need (Enthoven, 1978: 717). This surplus will affect many other careers in the health field, as physicians scramble to maintain their power and jobs. It may alter relations with nurses, physicians' associates, and other health workers. Learning to spot a trend and figure out its impact is one of the most useful tools of sociology.

One last word. We cannot overemphasize the importance of learning about sociological methods. The techniques for identifying social patterns too large or too complex for personal observation are invaluable tools in other disciplines as well as in many—if not most—lines of work.

Glossary

absolute deprivation, page 296
acculturation, pages 330, 569
achieved status, page 75
acting crowd, page 540
affirmative action, page 330
aggregate, page 199
alienation, pages 451, 569
amalgamation, page 330
anomie, page 258
ascribed status, page 75
authority, pages 296, 362

behavioral assimilation, page 330
bourgeoisie, page 296
bureaucracy, page 227

case study, page 46
caste system, page 296
casual crowd, page 540
category, page 199
censorship, page 540
census, page 483
charisma, page 199
charismatic authority, page 362
chromosome, page 170
church, page 451
circular reaction, page 540
city, page 516
civil religion, page 451
class, page 296
cognitive development, page 138
collective behavior, page 540
competition, page 75
concentric zone model, page 516
conflict, page 75
conflict orientation, page 19
conflict perspective, page 569
conformity, page 258
conglomerate, page 362
consumerism, page 362
contract marriage, page 396
contractual cooperation, page 75
control group, page 46
conventional crowd, page 540
cooperation, page 75
cross-sectional research, page 46
crowd, page 540

crude birth rate, page 483
crude death rate, page 483
cultural integration, page 105
cultural lag, page 569
cultural pluralism, page 330
cultural relativity, page 105
cultural transmission, page 258
cultural universals, page 105
culture, page 105
cyclical perspective, page 569

de facto segregation, page 330
de jure segregation, page 363
democratic state, page 363
demographer, page 483
demographic transition, page 483
demographic variables, page 483
demography, page 483
dependency ratio, page 483
dependent variable, page 46
deviance, page 259
deviant career, page 259
diffusion, page 569
directed cooperation, page 75
discrimination, page 330
dyad, page 199

economic power, page 363
ecosystem, page 516
education, page 421
ego, page 138
elite, page 363
emergent norm theory, page 540
emigration, page 483
equilibrium perspective, page 569
ethnic group, page 330
ethnocentrism, page 105
ethnomethodology, page 75
evolutionary perspective, page 569
exchange, page 75
experiment, page 46
experimental group, page 46
ex post facto research, page 46
expressive crowd, page 540
expulsion, page 330
extended family, page 396
extermination, page 330
external environment, page 227

family, page 396
fecundity, page 483
fertility rate, page 483
folkways, page 105
formal organization, page 227

formal social controls, page 259
formal structure, page 227

Gemeinschaft, page 199
gender, page 170
gender differentiation, page 170
generalized other, page 138
Gesellschaft, page 200
group, page 75
group dynamics, page 200

hidden curriculum, page 421
hierarchy, page 227
horizontal mobility, page 296
hormones, page 170
hypothesis, page 46

id, page 138
identity, page 138
identity crisis, page 138
immigration, page 484
independent variable, page 46
individual mobility, page 296
infant mortality rate, page 484
influence, page 363
informal social controls, page 259
informal structure, page 227
in-group, page 200
innovation, page 259
institution, page 75
institutional racism, page 75
integration, page 330
interest group, page 363
internal environment, page 227
internalization, page 259
internal migration, page 484
international migration, page 484
interview, page 46
invasion cycle, page 516
invisible (private) religion, page 451

jargon, page 105
Jim Crow, page 330

kibbutzim, page 396

labeling, page 259
language, page 105
latent functions, page 75
laws, page 105
legal/rational authority, page 363
leveling, page 540
life expectancy, page 484
life span, page 484
longitudinal research, page 46

looking glass self, page 139

machismo, page 171
macro-level of social structure, page 75
mana, page 451
manifest functions, page 75
master status, page 75
mean, page 46
mechanical solidarity, page 200
median, page 46
megalopolis, page 516
micro-level of social structure, page 75
minority, page 330
mob, page 540
mode, page 46
modernization, page 569
moral community, page 451
mores, page 105
mortification, page 227
motor intelligence, page 139
multinational corporation, page 227
multiple nuclei model, page 516

negotiated order, page 227
net migration, page 484
net reproduction rate (NRR), page 484
new town, page 516
normlessness, page 540
norms, page 105
nuclear family, page 396

objective class, page 296
object permanence, page 139
oligarchy, page 363
one-factor theory, page 363
open classroom, page 421
open class system, page 296
open marriage, page 397
organic solidarity, page 200
out-groups, page 200

Parkinson's Law, page 227
participant observation, page 46
party, page 296
Pentecostalism, page 451
per capita income, page 484
Peter Principle, page 227
plea bargaining, page 259
pluralism, page 363
political party, page 363
political power, page 363
pollution, page 517
population, page 46
postindustrial society, page 569
power, pages 296, 363

power elite, page 296
prejudice, page 330
prestige, page 296
primary deviance, page 259
primary group, page 200
profane, page 451
progressive tax, page 296
proletariat, page 296
propaganda, page 540
Protestant ethic, page 451
protest movement, page 363
public, page 540
public opinion, page 540
public relations, page 540

race, page 331
random sample, page 46
rational-legal authority, page 227
rebellion, page 259
reference group, page 200
regressive tax, page 297
relative deprivation, page 297
reliability, page 46
religion, page 451
replacement level, page 484
resource depletion, page 517
retreatism, page 259
reverse discrimination, page 331
riot, page 540
ritual, page 451
ritualism, page 227
role, page 75
role conflict, page 75
role set, page 75
role strain, page 75
rumor, page 540

sacred, page 451
sample, page 46
schooling, page 421
secondary deviance, page 259
secondary group, page 200
sect, page 451
sector model, page 517
secularization, page 451
segregation, page 331
service occupations, page 569
sex, page 171
sex ratio, page 484
sex role, page 171
significant others, page 139
significant symbols, page 139
social area analysis, page 517
social change, page 569
social control, page 259
social-emotional leadership, page 200

social group, page 200
socialization, page 139
social indicators, page 19
social mobility, page 297
social mobilization, page 569
social movement, page 540
social structure, page 75
sociological perspective, page 19
sociology, page 19
spontaneous cooperation, page 75
state, page 363
status, page 75
status group, page 297
stratification, page 297
stratified random sample, page 46
structural assimilation, page 331
structural conduciveness, page 540
structural-functionalism, page 20
subculture, page 105
subjective class, page 297
superego, page 139
survey, page 46
symbol, page 105
symbolic interactionist orientation, page 20

task leadership, page 200
technology, page 569
theory, page 46
total institution, page 227
totalitarian state, page 363
totem, page 451
tracking, page 421
traditional authority, page 363
traditional cooperation, page 75
transfer payments, page 297
triad, page 200
two-career marriage, page 397

urban ecology, page 517
urbanization, page 517

validity, page 46
values, page 105
variable, page 46
vertical mobility, page 297
vital statistics, page 484
voluntary association, page 227

zero population growth (ZPG), page 484

NAME INDEX

Adler, Judith, 561
Adorno, T. W., 315
Ali, Muhammad, 573
Alland, Alexander, Jr., 81
Allen, Vernon L., 527
Allende, Salvador, 345
Allport, Gordon W., 124, 534
Amin, Idi, 319
Anderson, Charles H., 269, 282, 322, 347–348
Andrain, Charles P., 336, 343, 350, 351, 352
Antonovsky, Aaron, 313
Applebaum, Richard P., 549
Aramoni, Aniceto, 165
Arensberg, Conrad M., 95, 548
Ashe, Arthur, 574
Asimov, Isaac, 578
Askenasy, Alexander, 247

Back, Kurt W., 521
Backman, Carl W., 188, 189
Bacon, Francis, 11
Bacon, Margaret K., 374
Baird, Leonard L., 158
Bakke, Alan, 327, 415
Bales, Robert, 188–189
Ball, Donald W., 101
Balswick, Jack O., 162
Bandura, Albert, 239
Banks, Carolyn, 305
Banks, Curtis, 320
Bardwick, Judith M., 146
Barnes, Harvey Elmer, 10–11
Barnet, Richard J., 346, 347
Barry, H., 374
Barton, Allen H., 523
Barton, Eugenia, 210
Bates, Daniel G., 554
Bauer, Raymond, 18, 536
Baumrind, Diana, 124–125, 128, 130–131
Becker, Howard S., 42–43, 243, 245
Bell, Daniel, 565
Bell, Derrick A., Jr., 252
Bell, Robert, 438, 441, 442, 449
Bendix, Reinhard, 289–290
Berger, Peter L., 57, 68–69, 384, 442, 443
Berk, Bernard, 70–71
Berkman, Lisa, 197
Berle, Adolph A., 347
Bernard, Jessie, 154
Berne, Eric, 83
Bettelheim, Bruno, 103, 375

Bickel, Alexander M., 328
Bird, Caroline, 407–408
Black, Cyril, 556
Blau, Peter M., 9, 14, 62, 63, 207, 211, 215, 289
Blau, Zena, 136–137
Bloch, Albert A., 254
Bloomgarden, Zachary T., 58
Blumberg, Rae Lesser, 374, 378–379
Blumer, Herbert, 69, 73, 523, 528, 529
Bose, 492
Boulding, Kenneth, 512–513
Bowen, Howard, 408, 409, 416
Bowlby, John, 111n
Boyd, William, 311
Bredemeier, Harry C., 509
Breese, Gerald, 491
Briggs, Kenneth A., 447
Brim, Orville G., Jr., 115
Brody, Jane E., 477
Bronfenbrenner, Urie, 383, 402
Broom, Leonard, 439
Brown, Warren, 415
Bryan, Edward, 447
Bryant, Anita, 65
Burchard, John, 489n
Burgess, Ernest W., 498
Burridge, Kenelm O. L., 86
Butler, Robert, 580
Butterfield, Fox, 293

Campbell, A., 527
Camus, Albert, 83
Cantril, Hadley, 36, 534
Caplovitz, David, 284
Caplow, Theodore, 185
Carns, Donald E., 196
Carroll, John B., 92
Carter, Jimmy, 96, 234, 270, 292, 425, 442, 464, 512
Carter, Richard, 32
Cater, Douglass, 126, 128
Chagnon, Napoleon A., 92
Chambliss, William J., 244–245
Chavez, César, 337, 358
Chickering, 413
Child, I. L., 374
Childe, V. Gordon, 490
Church, Joseph, 124, 125
Churchill, Winston, 90
Cirino, Robert, 535
Clark, Kenneth B., 320, 415
Clark, Leon E., 461
Clark, Mary Jo, 158
Clarke, Arthur C., 578
Clausen, John A., 110
Clawson, Marion, 508
Cloward, Richard A., 358-359
Coale, A. J., 458, 473
Cochrane, Willard W., 472, 473

Cohen, Albert K., 232, 238, 239, 240
Cole, Mildred, 315
Cole, Stewart, 315
Coleman, James, 410–411
Collier, Peter, 309
Comte, Auguste, 11, 29
Constantine, Joan M., 395
Constantine, Larry L., 395
Cooley, Charles Horton, 112–113, 191
Coolidge, Calvin, 97
Coser, Lewis A., 65, 182
Cronkite, Walter, 573

Dahl, Robert A., 274, 340
Dahrendorf, Ralf, 550
Dansereau, Pierre, 510
Darwin, Charles, 11, 110
Davids, A., 130
Davis, Allen F., 305
Davis, Fred, 135
Davis, Kingsley, 13–14, 109, 111, 128, 279–280, 462
Dean, James, 496
Descartes, René, 11
DeShay, Samuel, 447
Deutsch, Karl A., 556
Deutsch, Morton, 63
Dickens, Paul, 564
Dickson, Paul, 223, 224
Dickson, William, 34
Diebold, John, 552, 554
Dixon, Marlene, 531
Dobzhansky, Theodosius, 311
Doe, Peter W., 407
Domhoff, G. William, 273–274, 340
Dornbusch, Sanford, 26–27
Douvan, Elizabeth, 146
Downs, Anthony, 508
Dowse, Robert E., 352
Dragastin, Sigmund E., 131
Dreitzel, Hans Peter, 17
Duchamp, Marcel, 561
Duncan, Otis Dudley, 289
Durham, Michael, 254
Durkheim, Emilé, 8, 9, 10, 12, 24–28, 30, 195, 232, 239, 426, 430, 546–547
Duverger, Maurice, 353

Edgerton, Robert B., 246
Edmiston, Susan, 393
Eels, Kenneth, 277
Ehrhardt, Anke, 145, 147
Ehrlich, Ann H., 472
Ehrlich, Paul, 472
Eifler, Deborah, 146
Eisenhower, Dwight D., 96, 134, 358
Eisenstadt, S. N., 556, 558
Elder, Glen H., Jr., 128, 131
Ellsberg, Daniel, 537

Ellul, Jacques, 565–566
Ember, Carol R., 83
Ember, Melvin, 83
Engels, Friedrich, 149, 562
Engen, T., 130
Erikson, Erik H., 117–119
Erikson, Kai, 23, 25, 236, 250
Esposito, John, 495
Evers, Mark, 475
Evert, Chris, 573

Faber, Doris, 533
Farley, Reynolds, 328, 501
Featherman, David L., 294
Feldman, 413
Fendrich, James M., 530
Ferree, Myra Marx, 152–153
Ferrero, 237
Field, Mark G., 150
Fiorillo, John, 495
Firey, Walter, 500
Fischer, Claude S., 495
Flynn, Karin I., 150
Fogelson, Robert M., 527
Form, William H., 278
Fox, Robin, 94
Fox, Thomas, 290
Freedman, Morris, 305
Freeman, James M., 437
Freeman, Richard B., 159, 289, 408, 410
Freud, Sigmund, 101–102, 115–117, 235n, 238, 433
Fribourg, Michael, 346
Fried, Edward, 272
Friedan, Betty, 143, 529, 531
Fromm, Erich, 196
Frumm, John, 546

Gagnon, John H., 241
Gamson, William A., 357
Gandhi, Mahatma, 288, 337, 358
Gans, Herbert J., 35, 36, 54, 494, 496, 505, 506, 507
Garfinkel, Harold, 72–73
Gaudet, Hazel, 534
Geis, Gilbert, 254
Gelman, David, 167
George, Katherine, 94
Gerstel, Naomi R., 393
Gerth, H. H., 206, 266
Getis, Judith, 509
Gibbons, Don C., 239
Gilligan, Card, 122
Glick, Paul C., 386
Glock, Charles Y., 428, 448
Gmeich, George, 101
Goffman, Erving, 70, 71–72, 83, 219–220, 245, 247
Golding, William, 177, 185, 188, 189, 190
Goldner, Fred H., 218
Goldsheider, Calvin, 430

Goldstein, 234
Goldstein, Sidney, 430
Goldwater, Barry, 355
Goode, William J., 59, 211, 376
Goodman, 413
Goodwin, John, 196, 198
Gordon, Milton M., 302, 316, 319
Goring, Charles, 238
Gottman, Jean, 500
Gough, Kathleen, 370, 372
Gouldner, Alvin, 42, 208
Gove, Walter R., 156, 246
Gracey, Harry L., 404
Graebner, Clark, 574
Greeley, Andrew M., 310, 432, 445
Griffiths, Martha W., 160
Gubbels, Robert, 160
Gusfield, Joseph R., 529, 558
Gustavus, Susan O., 394
Gutek, Barbara A., 210

Hacker, Andrew, 389–390
Hadden, Jeffrey, 443
Hadley, Charles D., 353
Hagedorn, Robert, 32
Haley, Alex, 304–305
Hall, Peter, 491
Hall, Richard H., 208
Hare, A. Paul, 185
Haring, Douglas, 92
Harlow, Harry F., 110–111
Harman, Willis W., 566–567
Harris, Chauncy D., 499, 500
Harris, Marvin, 546
Hartnett, Rodney T., 158
Hatt, Paul K., 276–277, 499
Hauser, Philip, 491
Hauser, Robert M., 294
Heider, Karl G., 373
Heiskanen, Veronica Stolte, 378
Henley, James R., Jr., 394
Hennessy, Bernard, 32
Hennig, Margaret, 162
Henry, Jules, 85
Hermalin, Albert I., 328
Herman, Judith, 310
Herzog, Herta, 534
Hessler, Richard M., 477
Hill, Michael, 443
Hilton, I., 125
Hirschi, Travis, 239, 240, 242
Hitler, Adolf, 537–538
Hodge, Robert W., 276, 277
Hodgson, Godfrey, 410
Hoffman, Dustin, 496
Hoge, Dean R., 417
Holborn, Hajo, 538
Holmstrom, Lynda Lytle, 393

Holter, Harriet, 147
Homans, George, 180, 186–188
Horner, Matina, 157–158
Horowitz, Irving Louis, 43
Hoult, Thomas Ford, 523
Howard, Ebenezer, 505
Hoyt, Homer, 498–499
Huber, Joan, 160
Hughes, John A., 352
Hull, Raymond, 211
Humphrey, Hubert, 355
Hunt, Chester L., 312, 318
Hunter, Catfish, 573
Hurley, Roger, 480
Hutchinson, Anne, 235–236

Inkeles, Alex, 558

Jackson, Philip W., 404
Jackson, Reggie, 100
Jacobs, Jane, 506–507
Jacobson, Lenore, 412
Janowitz, Morris, 495
Jardim, Anne, 162
Jarrell, Randall, 535
Jastrow, Robert, 545
Jefferson, Thomas, 441
Jencks, Christopher, 290
Jensen, Arthur, 312
John XXIII, Pope, 443, 445
Johnson, Alvin, 214–215
Johnson, Lyndon Baines, 65, 271, 354, 355, 358–359, 464
Jolly, Clifford J., 82, 554
Jones, Elise, 475
Jones, Joseph F., 239
Judah, J. Stillson, 35, 448, 449

Kahn, E. J., 477
Kahn, Robert L., 210
Kanter, Rosabeth Moss, 180–181
Kasarda, John D., 495
Katz, Daniel, 210
Katz, Elihu, 536
Katz, Joseph, 414, 415
Katzenbach, Nicholas deB., 252
Kay, Alan C., 552
Kaysen, Carl, 343, 345
Keller, Suzanne, 340
Kelley, Dean M., 446
Kennedy, Edward M., 480
Kennedy, John F., 134, 307, 337, 359, 441
Kennedy, Robert, 354
Kephart, William M., 386, 387
Kerckhoff, Alan C., 521
Killian, Lewis M., 357, 523, 528
King, Martin Luther, Jr., 273, 307, 318, 321, 337, 357–358

Kinsey, Alfred, 243
Kitagawa, Evelyn M., 478
Kluckhohn, Clyde, 93
Kohlberg, Lawrence, 122
Kohn, Melvin, 124, 382–383
Komarovsky, Mirra, 17, 150–151, 165, 182
Kornhauser, William, 340
Kotelchuck, David, 284
Kramer, Jane, 319

Labovitz, Sanford, 32
Lack, Pamela Blafer, 317
Ladd, Everett Carl, 353
Lane, David, 294
Lang, 529
Lang, 529
La Rochefoucauld, 62
Latham, Robert J., 469
Lauer, Jeanette C., 558
Lauer, Robert H., 558
Lazarsfeld, Paul F., 536
Leacock, Eleanor, 412
Lear, Martha Weinman, 167–168
Le Bon, Gustave, 527
LeMasters, E. E., 287, 383
Lemert, Edwin M., 243–244
Lenski, Gerhard G., 266, 283–284, 290, 430
Levenson, Sam, 305
Levine, Irving M., 310
Levinson, Daniel J., 120
Lévi-Strauss, Claude, 370
Lewis, Michael, 145
Liebenstein, Harvey, 15
Liebow, Elliot, 35, 52–54, 59, 60, 62, 63, 322
Lincoln, Abraham, 441, 536
Linton, Ralph, 81, 95
Lipset, Seymour Martin, 66, 289–290, 325, 337, 354
Little, Roger, 191
Lomax, Louis, 357
Lombroso, Cesare, 237–238
Lorber, Judith, 248
Luckmann, Thomas, 440
Lynch, James, 197
Lynd, Helen M., 36
Lynd, Robert S., 36, 44

McCarthy, John D., 533
Maccoby, Michael, 134, 221
McCourt, Kathleen, 445
McCready, William, 445
McGee, Jeanne, 475
McGovern, George, 307
McGregor, Douglas, 223
Machalek, Richard, 440
McKay, Henry, 240
McKenzie, Roderick D., 498
McPhee, John, 574

Malcolm X, 337
Malinowski, Bronislaw, 101, 371–372, 433
Malthus, Thomas Robert, 466
Mandani, Mahmood, 469
Margolis, Richard J., 482
Marmor, Theodore R., 480
Marshall, S. L. A., 60
Martin, Michael, 440
Marx, Karl, 12, 149, 150, 281–282, 338, 435–436, 549, 562
Massey, Grace Carroll, 27
Mayer, Kurt, 266, 565
Mayo, Elton, 34–35
Mead, G. H., 121
Mead, Margaret, 136–137, 148–149, 369
Meade, George Herbert, 113–115
Meadows, Donella, 510
Means, Gardiner C., 347
Meeker, Marchia, 277
Melville, Keith, 18
Merton, Robert K., 13, 56, 59, 69, 178, 209, 239–240
Meyer, Marshall W., 9, 207, 211, 213
Mezzrow, Mezz, 99
Michels, Robert, 339, 352
Middleton, Russell, 374
Miles, Betty, 146
Milgram, Stanley, 33–34, 44, 529
Miller, C. Arden, 480
Miller, Jerome, 255
Miller, R. L., 346
Miller, S. M., 290
Mills, C. Wright, 5, 206, 266, 273–274, 339–341
Mitford, Jessica, 249, 252, 253
Molotch, Harvey, 513
Money, John, 145, 147
Moon, Sun Myung, 198, 448, 449
Moore, Wilbert E., 279–280, 551
Moreno, J. L., 186
Mosca, Gaetano, 338–339
Moulik, Moni, 472
Müller, Ronald, 346, 347
Murdock, George Peter, 93, 370
Murphy, Earl Finber, 508
Myrdal, Gunnar, 29, 42, 96

Nader, Ralph, 348, 350, 533–534
Natani, Kirmach, 578
Newcomb, T. M., 37, 183, 187
Newman, Graeme, 233
Nie, Norman H., 353, 355
Niehoff, Arthur H., 95, 548
Nimkoff, M. F., 374
Nisbet, Robert, 62, 63, 548, 555
Nixon, Richard M., 17, 309, 355, 464, 513
Noel, Donald L., 313
North, Cecil, 276–277
Norton, Arthur, 392

Ogburn, William F., 548–549
Okner, Benjamin, 270
Olsen, Marvin E., 338, 340
O'Neill, George, 394
O'Neill, Gerard K., 576–577, 580
O'Neill, Nena, 394, 395
O'Riordan, T., 514

Parenti, Michael, 284
Pareto, Vilfredo, 338–339
Park, Robert E., 498
Parkinson, C. Northcote, 211
Parsons, Talcott, 404, 548
Pavlov, Ivan, 110
Paytee, Lorenzo, 447
Pease, John, 278
Peek, Charles W., 162
Pelto, Gretel H., 431
Pelto, Pertti J., 431
Peter, Laurence F., 211
Petersen, William, 462–463
Peterson, 420
Pettitt, G. A., 401
Pfeiffer, John, 551
Phillips, J. L., Jr., 121
Piaget, Jean, 119–122
Pines, Maya, 419
Piven, Frances Fox, 358–359
Plath, Sylvia, 72
Pleck, Joseph, 162, 164
Plog, Fred, 82, 554
Pohlman, Edward, 393
Pollard, Gayle, 465
Pomper, Gerald, 355, 357, 359–360
Postman, Leo, 534
Prescott, D., 158
Presthus, Robert, 221–222

Quarantelli, E. L., 528

Rabin, Albert I., 374
Radcliffe-Brown, A. R., 435
Rainwater, Lee, 17
Read, Merrill S., 284
Reinhold, Robert, 392, 503
Reiss, Albert J., Jr., 249
Rensberger, Boyce, 472, 473
Reuben, David, 144
Rice, Berkeley, 448
Riesman, David, 128, 273, 274, 309, 338, 340–341
Riley, Matilda White, 135
Ritti, R. R., 218
Ritzer, George, 44
Rives, N. W., Jr., 458
Robbins, Edward, 158
Robbins, Lillian, 158
Roethlisberger, F. J., 34
Rokeach, Milton, 314
Roman, Paul Michael, 246

Roosevelt, Eleanor, 337
Roosevelt, Franklin D., 534
Rose, Arnold, 341
Rose, Peter I., 314, 318
Rose, Sanford, 270
Rosen, Marjorie, 148
Rosenbaum, David E., 16
Rosenberg, Morris, 320
Rosenberger, Boyce, 470
Rosenthal, Robert, 412
Ross, Heather L., 380
Rossi, Peter H., 276
Rubin, Lillian Breslow, 563
Ruesch, Hans, 92
Ryan, William, 285
Rytina, Joan Huber, 278

Saint-Simon, Henri de, 11
Sanders, Thomas G., 473
Sapir, Edward, 91–92
Sawhill, Isabel V., 380
Scarf, Maggie, 144
Scheff, Thomas J., 16
Schnaiberg, Allan, 513–515
Schneider, William, 325
Schumacher, E. F., 513
Schuman, H., 527
Schur, Edwin M., 235n
Schwartz, Morris S., 17
Schwirian, Kent P., 492
Secord, Paul F., 188, 189
Selznick, Philip, 439
Sengel, Randal, 578
Sennett, Richard, 494
Shaw, Clifford, 36, 240
Shaw, George Bernard, 231
Sheldon, Eleanor Bernert, 388, 389
Shepard, Alan B., Jr., 576
Sherif, Muzafer, 67
Shils, Edward A., 17, 192
Shurley, Jay T., 578
Siegel, Paul M., 276
Silberman, Charles E., 125, 403, 406, 411, 412
Simmel, Georg, 62, 65, 67, 180, 182, 184
Simmons, J. L., 238
Simmons, Roberta G., 320
Simon, William, 241
Simons, Lewis M., 468
Simpson, George E., 309, 319, 320, 321
Skolnick, Arlene S., 377, 379
Skolnick, Jerome H., 379
Slater, Philip E., 102–103, 156, 448
Smelser, Neil J., 522, 526, 547
Smith, David Horton, 558
Smith, Hedrick, 88–89, 94, 150, 248
Snow, C. P., 24
Solzhenitsyn, Alexander, 41
Spencer, Herbert, 11–12, 29, 546–547
Spengler, Oswald, 547

Spitz, R. A., 111n
Srole, Leo, 243
Stanton, Alfred H., 17
Stark, Rodney, 428
Starr, Roger, 504, 505
Stein, Maurice R., 496
Stern, 250
Stern, Leonard, 286
Stern, Michael, 504
Stern, Philip M., 270
Stoller, Robert, 147
Stone, L. Joseph, 124, 125
Stowe, Harriet Beecher, 319
Strauss, Anselm, 213
Strickland, Stephen, 126, 128
Strodtbeck, Fred L., 189
Stuart, Reginald, 559
Sullerot, Evelyn, 149
Sullivan, Harry Stack, 113
Sumner, William, 179
Sutherland, Edwin, 240
Suttles, Gerald, 494
Swanson, Guy E., 432

Taeuber, Irene B., 465, 466
Talese, Gay, 535
Talmon-Garber, Y., 374
Tannenbaum, Arnold S., 223, 564
Temin, Howard, 236
Terkel, Studs, 203
Thomas, W. I., 70
Thomlinson, Ralph, 461, 468, 565
Thompson, James D., 215
Thurow, Lester C., 307
Tietze, Christopher, 476
Timmer, C. Peter, 472
Toch, Hans, 529
Tocqueville, Alexis de, 204
Tolstoy, Leo, 369
Tönnies, Ferdinand, 195
Toynbee, Arnold, 547–548
Tracy, Lane, 211
Treiman, Donald J., 277
Tresemer, David, 158
Trice, Harrison M., 246
Troeltsch, Ernst, 439
Tucker, Patricia, 147
Tudor, Jeannette F., 156
Tumin, Melvin, 280–281, 289, 312
Tunnard, Christopher, 500
Turnbull, Colin M., 63, 65, 426
Turner, Ralph H., 66–67, 523, 528
Twaddle, Andrew C., 477

Udry, J. Richard, 385
Udy, Stanley H., Jr., 208
Ullman, Edward L., 499, 500

Van den Berghe, Pierre, 312, 315

Van Dusen, Roxann A., 388, 389
Vanek, Joann, 161
Van Maanen, John, 135
Veevers, J. E., 393, 394
Verne, Jules, 578
Vernon, Glen, 439
Vidmar, Neil, 314
Vladimirov, Leonid, 89

Waldman, Elizabeth, 160
Walker, James, 90
Walker, Lewis, 312, 318
Wallace, George, 309
Wallace, Walter A., 73
Waller, Willard, 72
Walters, Richard H., 239
Walton, Bill, 573
Walton, John, 196
Warner, W. Lloyd, 277
Washington, George, 441
Watson, John B., 110
Wattenberg, Ben J., 390
Watts, Jim, 305
Webb, Eugene, 35
Weber, Max, 12, 29, 70, 206–211, 214, 266–267, 336, 350, 436–438
Weick, K. E., 215
Weitzman, Lenore J., 146
Weller, Jack M., 528
Welles, Orson, 534, 576
Westoff, Charles F., 475, 476
White, Burton L., 418–419
Whiting, J. W. M., 94
Whorf, Benjamin Lee, 91–92
Whyte, William Foote, 35, 36, 496
Whyte, William H., Jr., 218
Williams, Robin, 96, 97, 98
Wilson, James Q., 213
Wimberley, Ronald C., 441
Winch, Robert F., 374, 378–379
Wirth, Louis, 301, 302, 493–494, 496
Witkin, Herman A., 238
Wolfe, Bernard, 99
Wollstonecraft, Mary, 529
Wright, James D., 383
Wright, Sonia R., 383
Wrong, Dennis H., 278
Wuthnow, Robert, 438, 448, 449

Yankelovich, Daniel, 97, 380–381
Yanowitch, Murray, 294
Yinger, J. Milton, 309, 319, 320, 321
Yuan, D. Y., 320

Zald, Mayer N., 533
Zangwill, Israel, 315
Zimbardo, Philip, 33, 44
Zimmerman, R. Z., 111

SUBJECT INDEX

Abortion, 461, 475–476
Abstract reasoning, 122
Acculturation, 315, 554
Achieved status, 55
Acting crowds, 523; see also Mobs
Adaptation, 94, 432–433
Adolescence, 94, 119, 122, 128–131
Affirmative action, 325–327
Age: church attendance and, 430; creative output and, 132; life expectancy and, 462; at marriage, 94, 469; -specific mortality rates, 462
Aggregates, 178
Aggression, 92, 115, 116, 126–128
Alcoholism, 246
Alienation, 131, 435–436, 494–495, 562
Amalgamation, 315
American economic system, 342–350
American education system, see Colleges; Education; Schools
American family, 378–395; changes in, 388–395; child-rearing in, see Child-rearing; divorce and, 94, 133, 378, 380, 385–388; love and, 68, 69–70, 377–378, 384, 385, 386; marriage and, see Marriage; single-parent, 379–381; social class and, 381–384; types of, 378–381
American Indians, 302, 307–309, 316, 319, 321, 402
American Medical Association, 281, 353, 481
American sex roles, 151–168; changes in, 143, 151, 153; female, 152, 154–162; future of, 165–168; history of, 151, 154; male, 162–165
Amish farmers, 559
Andaman Islanders, 434–435
Anglo-conformity, 315
Anomie, 131, 239
Apartheid, 288
Arapesh society, 148
Ascribed status, 55
Asylum, 219
Attitude scale, 31
Authority, 273, 336, 383; types of, 336–337
Autonomy, 118, 156–157, 392

Balance theory, 187
Banaro society, 92
Behavioral assimilation, 316, 317
Beliefs, 428, 430, 434
Biology: deviance and, 237–238; family structure and, 370–372; sex roles and, 144–145; socialization and, 110–112
Birth control, 165; abortion and, 461, 475–476; in America, 474–476; changing attitudes toward, 390; contraception and, 445, 461, 469, 474–475; in Costa Rica, 473; Roman Catholics and, 442, 445, 475
Birth rates: in America, 474–476; crude, 458, 460–462, 467, 468; during demographic transition, 466–469; in developing nations, 469; factors affecting, 461; lowering of, 473; overpopulation and, 469–473; social class and, 382
Black Americans: attitudes of, 278, 279, 323–325; busing and, 327–328; education and, 316, 322, 402, 406, 410, 411, 412, 414; health care and, 479, 481; historical background of, 302–305; housing discrimination and, 325; income of, 268, 322, 502; infant mortality rate of, 480; intelligence tests and, 312–313; internal migration of, 464–465, 501; political gains of, 322–323; poverty and, 271; protest by, 321–322, 357–358; responses to discrimination and abuse, 319–321; rioting by, 526; segregation and, 304, 318–319, 411, 414; unemployment and, 503; U.S. census and, 458, 459; voting by, 355, 358–359; see also Civil rights movement; Race; Racism
Bourgeoisie, 281, 338
Buddhism, 427, 428, 555
Bureaucracy, 205–211, 575; attitudes toward, 210; growth of, 206, 221; problems of, 208–209, 211, 221–222; as social fact, 8–9; Weber's model of, 206–208; see also Organizations
Busing, 327–328

Calvinism, 437–438, 449
Cancer, 477
Case study, 36
Caste system, 288
Casual crowds, 523
Categories, 7–8, 178
Cause and effect, rule of, 121
Censorship, 537
Charisma, 188
Charismatic authority, 336–337
Cherokee society, 319
Child-rearing: changes in, 388; impact of, 130–131; New Breed parents and, 380–381; in nuclear vs. extended families, 378; organizational personality, 221; sex roles and, 145–148; social class and, 124, 382–384
Chinese-Americans, 309
Chromosomes, 144
Church, 439–440; attendance, 430, 443, 445; characteristics of, 439; social adaptation and, 432; see also Religion
Cigarette smoking, 477
Circular reaction, 528
City life, see Urban life
Civil rights movement, 304, 318, 325, 327–328, 357–360, 443, 530, 531
Class, see Social class

Cloning, 88
Cognitive development, 119–122
Collective behavior, 521–539; communication and, 534–538; defined, 522; preconditions of, 522–524; social movements, see Social movements
Colleges: community, 417–418; junior, 417–418; relative probability of attending, 410; social structure of, 412–418; value of, 407–408, 415–417
Comanche society, 95
Communal society, 103
Communication: collective behavior and, 534–538; symbolic, 90, 91
Community: religion and, 430, 431; search for, 196–198
Community colleges, 417–418
Competition, 63, 67–68
Computers, 552–554
Concentric model, 498, 499
Conflict, 65–67; cooperation and, 65; female role and, 161–162; group, 182–183, 184; between individual and society, 101–102; interethnic, 313; male role and, 164–165; between norms and values, 88; problem definition and, 65; re-socialization and, 135; resolution of, 66–67; social change and, 65–66
Conflict theory, 14–15, 116, 281–284, 402, 404, 409, 549–550
Conformity, 69; crowd behavior and, 527–528; deviance and, 239–242; suburban life and, 496–497
Confucianism, 427, 428
Conglomerate, 343
Consumerism, 348–350
Contraception, 445, 461, 469, 474–475
Contractual cooperation, 63
Control group, 34
Conventional crowds, 523
Cooperation, 62–65
Copping a plea, 252
Corporate careers, 134
Corporate crime, 250, 285
Corporations: control of, 347–348; global power of, 345–347; lobbies formed by, 353–354; multinational, 216, 345–348; national power of, 343–345
Counterculture, 567
Courts, 249, 251–253
Courtship behavior, 68–69, 82
Crime, see Deviance
Crime rate, as social fact, 8
Criminal justice, social stratification and, 285–286
Cross-cultural studies, 37, 148–150, 233, 247, 372–378
Crowd behavior, 521, 524–529
Cultural lag, 548–549
Cultural pluralism, 318
Culture, 81–104; adaptation and, 94; American,

95–103; defined, 81; diversity in, 92–95; elements of, 82–92; ethnocentrism and, 94–95, 313; evolution of, 82; integration in, 95; language and, 90–92; norms and, see Norms; against people, 101–103; prejudice and, 313–314; relativity of, 94; subcultures, see subcultures; symbols and, 89–90, 91; universals of, 93; values and, see Values
Cyclical perspective, 547–548

Dani society, 372
Data: analysis, 27–28; gathering, 26–27; interpretation, 38–42
Death: leading causes of, 477–478; religion and, 434
Death rate: crude, 458, 460, 461, 462, 467, 478; during demographic transition, 466–469; life expectancy and, 462; race and, 478; sex differences in, 144; social class and, 382, 478
Decision-making, group, 189
De facto segregation, 319
Delinquency, 239, 241–246
Democracy, 96–97
Democratic states, 350–351
Demographers, 458
Demographic transition, 466–469
Demographic variables, 458, 460
Demography, see Health; Population growth
Dependency ratio, 469
Dependent variable, 26
Deviance, 231–258, 575; attitudes toward, 233; biological explanations of, 237–238; cultural transmission of, 240–241; labeling and, 243–246, 248, 257, 575; nature of, 232, 234–235; psychological explanations of, 238–239; social control and, 232, 245–257; social functions of, 235–236; sociological explanations of, 239–243
Diffusion, 554–555
Directed cooperation, 63
Disapproval, as social control, 247–248
Discipline, 382–383
Discrimination: affirmative action and, 325–327; racial, 288–289, 302–307, 313–315, 318–321, 324–328, 415; sexual, 147, 159–161
Divorce, 94, 133, 378, 380, 385–388
Drug use, 232–235, 241, 477
Dyads, 183–185, 576

Ecological succession, 498
Ecology, urban, 497–500
Economic development, 469, 471
Economic power, 336, 341–350
Economic stratification, 226–272, 279–286
Economic systems, 548, 558
Ecosystem, 508–512
Education, 401–421; of American Indians, 402; of Black Americans, 316, 322, 402, 406, 410, 411, 412, 414; changes in, 579; computers and,

Education *(Continued)*
  553–554; death rate and, 478; defined, 401; future of, 418–420; income and, 268, 409–410; of Jews, 445–446; of Mexican-Americans, 402, 403; religion and, 442, 444; sex roles and, 158–159; social class and, 409–410; social functions of, 402–412; social mobility and, 290; social structure of higher education, 412–418; *see also* Schools
Ego, 115, 116–117, 238
Elitist view, 273, 274, 338–340
Emergent norms, 528
Emergent social relationships, 528
Emigration, 458, 460, 461
Emotional contagion, 527–528
Environment, urbanization and, 508–515
Equal rights amendment (ERA), 166–167
Equilibrium perspective, 548–549
Eskimo society, 92
Ethnic group, defined, 302; *see also* Minorities; Race
Ethnocentrism, 94–95, 313
Ethnomethodology, 72–73
Evolutionary perspective, 546–547
Exchange, 62–63
Experimental group, 34
Experiments, 33–35
Ex post facto study, 37–38
Expressive crowds, 523
Expulsion, 319
Extended family, 374, 376
Extermination, 319

Fads, 522
Family, 369–395; American, *see* American family; as biological and social unit, 370–372; changes in, 578–579; cross-cultural perspectives, 372–378; defined, 370–372; extended, 374, 376; as institution, 61; nuclear, 61, 191, 374, 376–378, 379; origins of family forms, 374–376; social functions of, 13, 61, 370; socialization and, 123–125; urban life and, 494; *see also* Child-rearing
Family planning, 473
Fecundity, 461
Female role, 152, 154–162
Fertility rate, 461; *see also* Birth rate
Field experiments, 34–35
Fiji Island society, 92
Folkways, 86
Formal organizations, 204–205, 211, 212
Formal social controls, 249–257
Freedom, 96
Free enterprise, 87
Free speech movement, 523
Free will, 68–73
Frustrated social concerns, 523–524
Frustration-aggression theory, 314–315
Functionalist theory, 279–284

Fundamentalist revival, 446–447

Gay liberation, 358–359
Gemeinschaft, 193–196
Gender identity, 145–148
Generalized other, 114–115
Geographic mobility, 376
Gesellschaft, 193–196
Global corporations, 345–348
Goals: anomie and, 239; conflict with means, 239–240; group, 178
Governing class, 274
Groups, 60–61, 177–199, 575–576; boundaries of, 179–183; decision-making in, 189–191; defined, 178; dynamics of, 185–188; interest, 353–355; leadership in, 188–189; primary, 191–196; search for intimacy and community and, 196–198; secondary, 192–196; size of, 183–185; structure of, 178–185
Group therapy, 255

Hare Krishna movement, 198, 448–449, 580
Hausa society, 93–94
Hawthorne effect, 35
Health, 284, 477–482
Heredity: criminal behavior and, 238; sex differentiation and, 144–145
Hidden curriculum, 403–406
Higher education, social structure of, 412–418
Hindus, 426, 427, 435, 436–437
Homosexuality, 147, 233, 235, 241, 242, 243, 321
Hopi Indian society, 92
Horizontal mobility, 286
Hormones, 144–145
Housing, 284–285, 325, 502
Hunger, 470–473
Hypothesis, 25, 26

Id, 115, 116
Identity: group, 178; socialization and, 112–122
Ik society, 64–65
Immigration, 458, 460–463
Income: of American Indians, 307, 308; of Black Americans, 268, 322, 502; education and, 268, 409–410; inequalities, 267–272; of Jews, 306, 438; life chances and, 284–286; of Mexican-Americans, 306–307; of Puerto Ricans, 307; redistribution of, 290–292, 294; religious affiliation and, 444; sex differences in, 160–161, 268, 269
Independent variable, 26
Industrialization, 342, 508–515, 562
Industry, 118–119
Inequality, *see* Social stratification
Infant care, 145
Infant education, 418–419
Infant mortality rate, 462, 468, 478, 480, 482
Influence, 273

Informal organization, 211, 213–214, 575
Informal social controls, 246–248
In-groups, 179–180, 576
Innovation, 240
Institutional racism, 54, 325–328
Institutions, 61
Insurance, health, 481–482
Integration: cultural, 95; racial, 315, 317–318, 325, 328
Intelligence, 312–313
Interest groups, 353–355
Internalization, 245
Internal migration, 463–466
International migration, 462–463
Interviewing, 36–37
Intimacy, 196–198
Invasion cycle, 498
Islam, 555
Isolation, 110–111, 136

Japanese-Americans, 309
Jargon, 99
Jesus Freaks, 446
Jews, 312, 313, 432; education and, 445–446; historical background of, 305–306; immigration of, 463; income of, 306, 438; Nazi extermination of, 319; profile of, 444; puberty rites of, 435; social adaptation by, 432–433; synagogue attendance by, 430, 445; world population of, 426, 427
Jim Crow laws, 288, 302–303
Job satisfaction, 223, 562–565
Junior colleges, 417–418

Kibbutzim, 103, 223, 373–374

Labeling, 243–246, 248, 257, 575
Language, 90–92, 121
Law, 61, 86
Leadership, 188–189
Learned behavior, 110
Learning: infant education and, 418–419; lifelong, 419–420; in schools, 406–407; see also Education
Legal/rational authority, 336, 337
Life chances, 284–286
Life expectancy, 462
Life span, 462
Longitudinal study, 37
Looking-glass self, 112–113
Love, 68, 69–70, 154, 156, 377–378, 384, 385, 386

Macro-level of social structure, 52, 54–55
Madagascan society, 95
Male role, 162–165
Malnutrition, 284, 472
Manus society, 431
Marijuana, 232, 234, 235, 238
Marriage, 133–134; alternative forms of, 390–395;
arranged, 384; birth rate and, 469; childless, 393–394; child-rearing and, see Child-rearing; contract, 393; cultural differences in, 93–94, 372–378; in extended families, 374–376; love and, 377–378, 384, 385; in nuclear families, 374, 376–378; open, 394–395; religion and, 434; in Samoa, 369; subsurface controls in, 384–385; see also Family
Mass hysteria, 521
Master status, 55–56, 245
Mbuti Pygmy society, 426
Mechanical solidarity, 195
Mechanization, 206
Media: influence of, 538; public opinion and, 535–536; socialization and, 125–128
Medicaid, 480, 481, 482
Medical profession, 276, 280–281, 479–481
Medicare, 481, 482
Megalopolis, 495, 500–501
Mental illness, 16–17, 219–220, 237, 246
Mexican-Americans, 302, 306–307, 316, 321, 402, 403
Micro-level of social structure, 52–54, 61
Migration, 458, 460–466
Minorities, 301–330; defined, 301; ethnic diversity, 302–311; patterns of ethnic relations, 315–321; see also Race; specific minority groups
Mobs, 523–527
Modernization, 555–560
Monotheists, 426
Moral community, 430, 431
Moral development, 122
Mores, 86
Mortification, 219
Motor intelligence, 121
Multinational corporations, 216, 345–348
Multiple nuclei model, 499, 500
Mundugumor society, 148–149
Muslims, 426, 427
Mysticism, rise of, 448–449

National Organization for Women (NOW), 531, 532
Navajo society, 308
Nayar society, 370, 372
Nazis, 319, 445, 537
Negative income tax, 292, 294
Negotiated order, 213–214
Neolithic revolution, 490
Net growth rate, 460
Net reproduction rate (NRR), 461
New towns, 505
Nonconforming behavior, 69
Normlessness, 522–523
Norms, 83–86; conflict and, 65; defined, 83; deviance and, 232; emergent, 528; folkways, 86; group dynamics and, 186–187; informal social control and, 246–248; internalization of, 245–246; laws and, 86; mores, 86; relation between values and, 87–88; transmission of, 240–241

Northern Shoshone Indian society, 434
Nuclear family, 61, 191, 374, 376–378, 379
Nutrition, 284, 480, 481

Obedience, experiments on, 33–34
Objective class, 281
Objectivity, 29, 42–44
Object permanence, 121
Occupation: as achieved status, 55; income distribution by, 268; prestige and, 275–277; religious affiliation and, 444; sex roles and, 165–166; social stratification and, 290; technological change and, 560, 562; urban life and, 495
Occupational socialization, 134–135
Occupational subculture, 100–101
Oglala Sioux society, 89–90
Oligarchies, 339
One-factory theory, 338
Open classroom, 405–406
Operational definition, 25
Organic solidarity, 195, 547
Organizations, 203–227, 575; external environment of, 215–216; formal, 204–205, 211, 212; future of, 221–225; informal, 211, 213–214, 575; internal environment of, 216–219; organizing, process of, 214–215; problem solving in, 214–221; total institutions, 219–221; see also Bureaucracy
Out-groups, 179, 181–182
Overpopulation, 466–473

Parents, 133–134, 370–372, 383–384; authoritarian vs. permissive, 124–125; New Breed, 380–381; see also Child-rearing; Family
Parkinson's Law, 211
Participant observation, 35–36
Party, 266
Peer groups: in college, 413–415; socialization and, 128–130
Peter Principle, 211
Physicians, see Medical profession
Plea bargaining, 252
Pluralists, 338, 340–341
Police, 213, 249, 251, 252
Political modernization, 556
Political parties, 352
Political power, 336, 350–360; in America, 345, 352–360; elitist view of, 338–340; Marxist theory and, 338; pluralist view of, 340–341; the state and, 350–352
Political systems, 548, 558
Pollution, 509, 512–515, 565
Polytheists, 426
Population growth, 457–477, 580–581; in America, 474–477; birth rate, see Birth rate; census and, 458, 459; death rate, see Death rate; demographic transition and, 466–469; determination of, 458, 460–466; family planning and, 473;

migration and, 458, 462–466; social change and, 551; world crisis in, 466–473
Positivism, 11
Postindustrial society, 565
Poverty, 270–272, 294, 332; health care and, 480; housing and, 284–285; nutrition and, 284; urban deterioration and, 501–503; wealth and, 284; welfare and, 291–292, 294
Power, 335–362; defined, 273, 335, 336–337; economic, 341–350; organizational, 215–216; political, see Political power; prestige and, 215, 216; social stratification and, 266, 272–274; theories of, 338–341
Power elite, 273, 274, 339–340
Preindustrial feudal city, 490–491
Prejudice, 313–315
Prestige, 215, 216, 266, 267, 274–277
Primary deviance, 243
Primary groups, 191–196
Prisons, 33, 219, 220, 252, 253–257
Problem solving in organizations, 214–221
Profane, the, 426
Professional ethics, 43–44
Professional movements, 533–534
Progress, 98
Progressive tax, 270
Project Camelot, 43–44
Proletariat, 281, 549
Propaganda, 537–538
Prostitution, 13–14, 15
Protest, 321–322, 357–360
Protestant ethic, 438
Protestants, 310, 430, 432, 437, 438, 443
Psychoanalytic theory: criminal behavior and, 238–239; socialization and, 115–117
Psychological development, 112–119
Psychological modernization, 556, 558
Puberty rites, 434–435
Public opinion, 535–538
Public policy, 17–18
Public relations, 538
Puerto Ricans, 307

Questionnaire, 31, 32

Race: attitude toward abortion and, 475; death rate and, 478; defined, 302, 311–312; discrimination and, 54, 288–289, 302–307, 313–315, 318–321, 324–328, 415; as group boundary, 179; income and, 268, 269; myths about, 312–313; political attitude and, 355; prejudice and, 313–315; prison sentences and, 252; psychological consequences of, 320–321; see also Minorities; specific racial groups
Racism, 54, 96, 320–321, 325–328, 414
Random sample, 30–33
Rebellion, 240
Recruitment, 216, 218

Red tape, as social fact, 8–9
Reference groups, 183
Relativity, cultural, 94
Religion, 425–451; American, 432, 440–442, 444; attitude toward abortion and, 475; basic elements of, 426, 428–430; beliefs and, 428, 430, 434; changes in, 580; church, *see* Church; civil, 440–442; community and, 430; diffusion of, 555; education and, 442, 444; forms of religious expression, 438–442; fundamentalist revival in, 446–447; individual functions of, 433–435; as institution, 61; invisible or private, 440; mysticism in, 448–449; populations of major religions, 427; rituals and, 428–430, 434–435; sects, 439, 440; secularization and, 442–443, 580; social change and, 435–438; social functions of, 431–433; trends in, 442–449
Religious movements, 198
Research design, 26–27; defining the problem in, 24–25, 26
Resocialization, 134–135
Resource depletion, 509
Retirement, 136
Retreatism, 240
Riots, 65, 526–527
Ritualism, 209, 240
Rituals, 428–430, 434–435
Role conflict, 59–60
Role confusion, 119
Roles, 56–60; group, 60–61, 178; the individual and, 56–57; institutional, 61; leadership, 188–189; marital, 133–134; occupational, 218; for older people, 135–137; sex, *see* Sex roles; "sick person," 9–10; socialization and, 113–115; statuses and, 57
Role set, 56
Role strain, 59
Roman Catholic church, 431–432, 433, 440, 443, 445
Roman Catholics: abortion and, 475; belief in God and, 428; birth control and, 442, 445, 475; church attendance by, 430; immigration of, 432, 433; income of, 438; profile of, 444; world population of, 427
Romance, 385
Rules, 9–10, 72–73, 204, 208, 209, 433
Rumors, 534–535

Sacredness, 426, 428
Samoan society, 369
Samples, 30–33
Santa Barbara oil spill, 512, 513
Sapir-Whorf hypothesis, 91–92
Scapegoating, 314–315
Schools, 218, 219; as agents of political and social integration, 402–403; gender training in, 146–147; hidden curriculum and, 403–406; inner-city, 504; learning and, 406–407; screening function of, 408–412; socialization and, 125; tracking in, 411–412
Science: deviance in, 236, 237; nature of, 24–28; sociology and, 28–30
Scientific method, 23–28, 42
Secondary deviance, 243–244
Secondary groups, 192–196
Sect, 439, 440
Sector model, 499
Secularization, 442–443, 580
Segregation: of races, 304, 318–319, 411, 414; of sexes, 161
Self: presentation of, 71–72; sense of, 112–119
Self-help groups, 205
Semi-structured interview, 37
Sentencing, 252–253
Service occupations, 560, 562
Sex differences, 144–148; biological evidence, 144–145; in church attendance, 430; in income, 160–161, 268, 269; socialization and, 145–148; *see also* Sex roles
Sex drive, 372
Sex hormones, 144–145
Sex ratio, 144, 461
Sex roles, 133, 143–170; in America, *see* American sex roles; biology and, 144–145; changes in, 579; cross-cultural variation in, 148–150; socialization and, 145–148; society and, 148–151; stereotypes, 127, 146, 151, 168; subcultural variation in, 150–152
Sexual behavior, 133, 165, 390
Shintoism, 426, 427, 434
Significant others, 113
Significant symbols, 113
Simple-plurality system, 353
Singlehood, 196–198, 392
Single-parent families, 167, 379–381
Siriono society, 266
Situational self, 115
Slavery, 302
Social-bond theory, 242–243
Social change, 545–568; approaches to, 546–550; conflict and, 65–66; defined, 545; deviance and, 236; future, 565–568; modernization and, 555–560; religion and, 435–438; sources of, 550–555
Social class, 266, 277–279; conflict theory and, 281–284; death rate and, 380, 478; divorce and, 387; education and, 409–410; elections and, 355; family life and, 381–384; group membership and, 182; open and closed systems of, 286, 288; in postindustrial society, 565; sex roles and, 150–152; socialization and, 114; suburban life and, 496; urban crisis and, 505–508; *see also* Social stratification
Social contagion, 527–528
Social control, 232, 245–257
Social Darwinism, 547

Social-emotional leadership, 189
Social facts, 7–9
Social groups, see Groups
Social indicators, 17–18
Socialization, 109–138; adult, 131–137; agents of, 123–130; biology and, 110–112; cognitive development and, 119–122; culture and, 110–112; defined, 109; family and, 123–125; gender identity and, 145–148; identity and, 112–122; media and, 125–128; moral development and, 122; occupational, 134–135; organizational, 218–219, 221; peer groups and, 128–130; psychological development and, 112–119
Social mobility, 286–290, 294, 556
Social modernization, 556
Social movements, 529–534; civil rights, 304, 318, 325, 327–328, 357–360, 443, 530, 531; professional, 533–534; women's liberation, 102–103, 155–156, 529, 531–533
Social pressure, 68–69
Social race, 312
Social relationships: emergent, 528; patterns of, 62–73
Social roles, see Roles
Social stratification, 265–296, 576; conflict theory of, 281–284; dimensions of, 266–279; functionalist theory of, 279–284; income and, 266–272; life chances and, 284–286; persistence of, 294; power and, 266, 272–274; prejudice and, 313; prestige and, 266, 267, 274–277; reduction of, 290–294; social change and, 551–552; social class and, 266, 277–279; social mobility and, 286–290, 294; wealth and, 267, 269
Social stress theories, 239–240
Social structure, 51–75, 431–432; components of, 55–62; defined, 51; impact of, 68–73; levels of, 52–55; patterns of social relationships, 62–73; religion and, 431–432
Sociograms, 186
Sociological perspective, 5–11
Sociology: development of, 11–12; ethical issues in, 42–43; methods of, 30–42; public policy and, 17–18; science and, 28–30; theoretical orientations of, 12–15; uses of, 15–17; value free,

193, 219, 303
eration, 63
147, 162, 163

tratification, 266,
roles; Women

17
22
3–14, 68–69
37

Subcultures, 98–101; sex roles and, 150–152; transmission of deviance in, 240–241
Subjective class, 281
Suburban life, 495–497
Success, 97
Suicide, 10–11, 24–28, 30, 237, 239
Superego, 116, 239
Survey research, 30–33
Symbolic interactionists, 15, 69–73, 90
Symbols, 89–90, 91, 113

Tables, interpretation of, 39, 40
Taboos, 93–94, 157, 162, 461
Tangu society, 86
Taoism, 428
Task leadership, 169
Taxation, 270, 292, 294
Tchambuli society, 149
Teachers, 6–7, 404, 406, 411, 412
Team membership, 564–565
Technology, 343, 345; cultural lag and, 548–549; geographic mobility and, 289; modernization and, 555–560; in postindustrial society, 565–566; social change and, 552–565; work and, 560–565
Television: as agent of socialization, 126–128; prejudice and, 314; sex roles and, 146, 151, 168
Tepoztlan Indian society, 83
Theoretical orientations, 12–15
Theory X, 223, 224–225
Theory Y, 223–225
Tokenism, 180
Totalitarian state, 351
Totems, 428
Tracking, 411–412
Traditional authority, 337
Traditional cooperation, 63, 64
Transfer payments, 270
Triads, 183–185
Trobriand Islanders, 433
Two-career marriages, 390–391, 393
Two-party system, 352–353

Unanticipated events, 522–523
Undernourishment, 472
Unemployment, 322, 323, 502–504
Union of Soviet Socialist Republics: culture in, 88–89; economic system of, 342; education in, 402; informal social control in, 248; Jews in, 306; social stratification in, 294; women in, 149–150
Universals, cultural, 93
Unstructured interview, 37
Urban ecology, 497–500
Urbanization, 464–466, 491–493, 508–515, 556
Urban life, 489–516; modern, 493–501; urban crisis and, 501–508; urban transformation and, 490–493; see also Urbanization
Urban renewal, 505

Values, 86–89; American, 96–98, 417; conflict and, 65; defined, 86; group, 178; in high-crime neighborhoods, 241; informal social control and, 246–248; internalization of, 245–246; relation between norms and, 87–88; social class and, 382–384; in sociology, 42–43; of students, 87, 417
Variable, 25–26
Vertical mobility, 286
Vietnam War, 182–183, 192, 193, 310
Vital statistics, 458
Voluntary associations, 204–205
Voting, 355–360

Wealth, 267, 269, 290
Welfare, 16, 291–292, 294
White ethnics, 309–310
Widowhood, 136
Women: church attendance by, 430; as heads of family, 379–380; income of, 268; sex roles of, 152, 154–162; in U.S.S.R., 149–150; voting by, 356; on welfare, 292; workers, 150–152, 156, 159–161, 217, 388–390; see also Child-rearing; Family; Marriage
Women's movement, 102–103, 155–156, 529, 531–533
Work: meaningful, 564; technological change and, 560–565; value of, 97
Workers: alienation of, 562; blue-collar, 287, 355, 356, 562–564; group membership and, 180–181; humanizing organizations and, 223–224; job satisfaction and, 223, 562–565; white-collar, 289, 553, 562, 563; women, 150–152, 156, 159–161, 217, 388–390; see also Occupation
Work furlough programs, 254

Yankee City study, 277

Zero population growth, 462, 476–477
Zoning restrictions, 325

(Continued from the copyright page.)

Ch. 1: Adapted from Kingsley Davis, "The Sociology of Prostitution," *American Sociological Review*, vol. 2 (1937), by permission of the American Sociological Association and the author. From an article by David E. Rosenbaum, *The New York Times*, May 22, 1977. © 1977 by The New York Times Company. Reprinted by permission. Excerpt from Keith Melville, "A Measure of Contentment," *The Sciences*, vol. 13 (December 1973), by permission of the New York Academy of Sciences.

Ch. 2: Adapted by permission from Grace Carroll Massey, Mona Vaughn Scott, and Sanford M. Dornbusch, "Racism Without Racists: Institutional Racism in Urban Schools," *The Black Scholar*, vol. 7 (November 1975). From Gunnar Myrdal, "How Scientific Are the Social Sciences?" *Bulletin of the Atomic Scientists*, vol. 29 (January 1973). Reprinted by permission of the Bulletin of the Atomic Scientists. Copyright © 1973 by the Educational Foundation for Nuclear Science. From John B. Williamson, "Beliefs about the Motivation of the Poor and Attitudes Toward Poverty Policy," *Social Problems*, vol. 21 (June 1974), from Alvin W. Gouldner, "Anti-minotaur: A Myth of a Value-free Society," *Social Problems*, vol. 9 (1962), and from Howard S. Becker, "Whose Side Are We On?" *Social Problems*, vol. 14 (Winter 1967). Reprinted by permission of the Society for the Study of Social Problems and the authors.

Ch. 3: From TALLY'S CORNER: A STUDY OF NEGRO STREET-CORNER MEN by Elliot Liebow, by permission of Little, Brown and Co. Copyright © 1967 by Little, Brown and Company (Inc.). From Zachary T. Bloomgarden, M.D., "The End of the Line," *The New York Times*, January 18, 1977. © 1977 by The New York Times Company. Reprinted by permission. From Bernard Berk, "Face-Saving at the Singles Dance," *Social Problems*, vol. 24 (June 1977). Reprinted by permission of the Society for the Study of Social Problems and the author.

Ch. 4: From an article by Pamela Hollie, *The New York Times*, October 23, 1977. © 1977 by The New York Times Company. Reprinted by permission. From THE RUSSIANS by Hedrick Smith. Reprinted by permission of Quadrangle/The New York Times Book Co. Copyright © 1976 by Hedrick Smith, as quoted in J. W. M. Whiting, "Effects of Climate on Certain Cultural Practices," *Explorations in Cultural Anthropology*. Reprinted by permission of McGraw-Hill Book Company. © 1969. From Katherine George, "The Civilized West Looks at Primitive Africa: 1400–1800, a Study in Ethnocentrism," by permission of David H. George. From REALLY THE BLUES by Milton Mezzrow and Bernard Wolfe. © 1946, 1973 by Milton Mezzrow and Bernard Wolfe. Reprinted by permission of Harold Matson ˙any. From George Gmelch, "Baseball Magic," *Transac-* 8 (June 1971), by permission of Transaction Periodi-

˙d Flast, "Survey Finds that Most Children
ᵗ Fear World," *The New York Times*,
ᵇᵧ The New York Times Company.
Warren Boroson, "In Defense of
ᵐber 1969). Reprinted by
˙ Baumrind, "Early So-
© 1975 by Hemi-
D.C. Reprinted by
oration.

'The Confused Ameri-
September 1976. Re-
ᵍazine. Copyright © 1976
ᵑ Alice Rossi, "Equality Be-
oposal." Reproduced by per-

mission of DAEDALUS, Journal of the American Academy of Arts and Sciences, Boston, Mass., Spring 1964. From Paul Starr, "Hollywood's New Ideal of Masculinity," *The New York Times*, July 16, 1978. © 1978 by The New York Times Company. Reprinted by permission.

Ch. 7: From MEN AND WOMEN OF THE CORPORATION, by Rosabeth Moss Kanter. © 1977 by Rosabeth Moss Kanter, Basic Books, Inc., Publishers, New York. Reprinted by permission of Coward, McCann & Geoghegan, Inc. from LORD OF THE FLIES by William Golding. Copyright © 1954 by William Gerald Golding. From Harry Nelson, "Study Links Social Ties, Mortality Rate," *Los Angeles Times*, December 11, 1977. Reprinted by permission of *Los Angeles Times*. © 1977 UPI. From "Be My Life's Companion" by Hillard and Delugg. Copyright © 1951 by Edwin H. Morris & Company, a Division of MPL Communications, Inc. Used by permission.

Ch. 8: Adapted from Daniel Katz, Barbara A. Gutek, Robert L. Kahn, and Eugenia Barton, *Bureaucratic Encounters* by permission of Survey Research Center, Institute for Social Research, University of Michigan. From *The Washington Post*, December 27, 1977. © The Washington Post. Reprinted by permission.

Ch. 9: From Kai T. Erikson, EVERYTHING IN ITS PATH. Reprinted by permission of Simon & Schuster. From Gerald M. Stern, THE BUFFALO CREEK DISASTER. Reprinted by permission of Vintage Books, a Division of Random House, Inc. From Nathaniel Sheppard, "A Lesson in Prison Life, Taught by Experts," *The New York Times*, January 25, 1977. © 1977 by The New York Times Company. Reprinted by permission.

Ch. 10: From Bob Reiss, "The Fifth Annual Salary Roundup: Who Gets the Most Money in Town?" *New York*, May 17, 1976. Copyright © 1976 by the NYM Corp. Reprinted with the permission of *New York* Magazine. From E. E. LeMasters, *Blue-Collar Aristocrats*. Reprinted by permission of the University of Wisconsin Press. From Fox Butterfield, "Taiwan Bridges the Income Gap While Maintaining High Growth," *The New York Times*, April 12, 1977. © 1977 by The New York Times Company. Reprinted by permission.

Ch. 11: Adapted from ROOTS by Alex Haley. Copyright © 1976 by Alex Haley. Used by permission of Doubleday & Company, Inc. Adapted from Alex Haley, "My Furthest Back Person—the African," by permission of Paul R. Reynolds, Inc. From Robert D. McFadden, "Some Points of 'Roots' Questioned," *The New York Times*, April 10, 1977. © 1977 by The New York Times Company. Reprinted by permission. Selections by Sam Levenson in Morris Freedman and Carolyn Banks, eds., THE AMERICAN MIX. © 1972 by Sam Levenson. Reprinted by permission of Harold Matson Company, Inc. From Pamela B. Lack, "The Ways of Americans Through Vietnamese Eyes," *The New York Times*, January 24, 1978. © 1978 by The New York Times Company. Reprinted by permission.

Ch. 12: Adapted from Robert Michels, *Political Parties*, by permission of The Free Press. Adapted from Frances Fox Piven and Richard A. Cloward, POOR PEOPLE'S MOVEMENTS: WHY THEY SUCCEED, HOW THEY FAIL, by permission of Pantheon Books, Inc.

Ch. 13: Adapted from Yankelovich, Skelly, and White, Inc., *The General Mills American Family Report 1976–77: Raising Children in a Changing Society*, by permission of General Mills Consumer Center, General Mills, Inc. From Andrew Hacker, "The American Family: Future Uncertain," *Time*, December 28, 1970. Reprinted by permission from *Time*, The Weekly Newsmagazine. Copyright Time Inc., 1970. From Robert Reinhold, "Trend to Living Alone Brings Economic and Social Change," *The New York Times*, March 20, 1977. © 1977 by The New

York Times Company. Reprinted by permission. From Susan Edmiston, "How to Write Your Own Marriage Contract," *Ms.,* vol. 1 (Spring 1972). Copyright © 1972. Reprinted by permission of Ms. Magazine Corp.

Ch. 14: From Warren Brown, "Prejudice and Pride: The Wall Between Black and White on Campus," *Dallas Times Herald,* November 20, 1977. © 1977 by the Dallas Times Herald. Reprinted by permission.

Ch. 15: Adapted from James M. Freeman, "Religious Change in a Hindu Pilgrimage Center," *Review of Religious Research,* vol. 16 (Winter 1975), by permission of the Religious Research Association. From K. A. Briggs, "Adventists' Emphasis on Health Attracting Members," *The New York Times,* February 26, 1978. © 1978 by The New York Times Company. Reprinted by permission.

Ch. 16: From Robert Reinhold, "The Census, All Year Round," *The New York Times,* November 30, 1975. © 1975 by The New York Times Company. Reprinted by permission. From Gayle Pollard, "Jobs Lure Blacks Home to South," *Miami Herald,* April 16, 1977. Reprinted by permission of the Miami Herald.

Ch. 17: From Robert Reinhold, "Seattle's Families Are Pulling Out, but the City May Learn to Like It," *The New York Times,* March 28, 1977. © 1977 by The New York Times Company. Reprinted by permission. Adapted from Jane Jacobs, THE DEATH AND LIFE OF GREAT AMERICAN CITIES, by permission of Vintage Books, a Division of Random House, Inc. Adapted from PEOPLE AND PLANS: Essays on Urban Problems and Solutions, by Herbert J. Gans, © 1968 by Basic Books, Inc., Publishers, New York.

Ch. 18: Adapted from James M. Fendrich, "Keeping the Faith or Pursuing the Good Life: A Study of the Consequences of Participation in the Civil Rights Movement," *American Sociological Review,* vol. 42 (February 1977), by permission of the American Sociological Association and the author.

Ch. 19: From Robert Jastrow, "Toward an Intelligence Beyond Man's," *Time,* February 20, 1978. Reprinted by permission from *Time,* The Weekly Newsmagazine. Copyright Time Inc., 1978. From Reginald Stuart, "Amish Farmers Are Facing Tough Choice," *The New York Times,* March 2, 1977. © 1977 by The New York Times Company. Reprinted by permission. Adapted by permission from Judith Adler, "Innovative Art and Obsolescent Artists," *Social Research,* vol. 42 (Summer 1975).

Ch. 20: From Jay T. Shurley, Kirmach Natani, and Randal Sengel, "Ecopsychiatric Aspects of a First Human Space Colony." Courtesy of the AIAA.

Table 2:1. Permission granted by the Gallup Poll; table 5:1. Courtesy of the *Journal of Gerontology;* table 7:1. Copyright © 1962, the Free Press; table 9:1. Reprinted by permission of Elsevier-North Holland Publishing Co., Inc. Copyright © 1976; table 9:2. Reprinted by permission of Mouton Publishing Co., B. V. Copyright © 1974; table 10:4. Copyright © 1966, the Free Press; table 10:5. Reprinted by permission of the *American Journal of Sociology,* the University of Chicago Press, and the authors. Copyright © 1970; table 10:6. Reprinted by permission of Prentice-Hall, Inc.; table 11:2. Permission granted by the Gallup Poll; table 12:1. Adapted by permission from *Fortune,* May 8, 1978; table 12:2. Adapted by permission from *U.S. News and World Report;* table 13:1. Copyright © 1973 by Little, Brown and Company (Inc.). Reprinted by permission; table 13:2. Reprinted by permission of General Mills Consumer Center, General Mills, Inc.; table 13:3. Copyright 1972 by the National Council on Family Relations. Reprinted by permission; table 14:1. Reprinted by permission of Jossey-Bass, Inc., Publishers. Copyright © 1977; table 14:2. Reprinted by permission of Academic Press, Inc. Copyright © 1976; table 14:3. Reprinted by permission of *Sociology of Education.* Copyright © 1976; table 15:1. Reprinted by permission of Encyclopedia Britannica from *Britannica Book of the Year, 1977* (Chicago, 1977). Compiled by Franklin H. Littell; table 15:2. Permission granted by the Gallup Poll; table 15:3. Adapted by permission of McGraw-Hill, Inc. Copyright © 1962; table 15:4. Permission granted by the Gallup Poll; table 19:1. Reprinted by permission of Macmillan, Inc. Copyright © 1972.

Fig. 5:2. Adapted by permission of Alfred A. Knopf, Inc. Copyright © 1978; fig. 6:3. Copyright by JDR 3rd Fund for Edna McConnell Clark Foundation, Carnegie Corporation of New York, Hazen Foundation, Andrew W. Mellon Foundation; fig. 7:2. Adapted by permission of Holt, Rinehart and Winston. Copyright © 1976; fig. 13:1. © 1977 by The New York Times Company. Reprinted by permission; fig. 13:2. © 1977 by The New York Times Company. Reprinted by permission; fig. 14:1. Adapted by permission of the Carnegie Commission on Higher Education. Copyright © 1974; fig. 15:1. Adapted by permission from *Family Planning Perspectives,* vol. 91 (September–October 1977); fig. 16:3. © 1974 by The New York Times Company. Reprinted by permission; fig. 16:5. Courtesy, National Council of Organizations for Children and Youth; fig. 17:3. Reprinted by permission of UNESCO; fig. 17:4. © 1976 Pion Limited. Reprinted by permission; fig. 19:1. Reprinted by permission of Macmillan, Inc. Copyright © 1972.

(Joseph Crilley)

ABOUT THE AUTHORS

Donald Light, Jr. was born in Massachusetts in 1942. After graduating from Stanford University in 1963, he worked in Boston to implement President Kennedy's plan for equal employment opportunities. He did graduate work in sociology at the University of Chicago and at Brandeis University, receiving his Ph.D. in 1970. Professor Light has taught at Princeton University, and is now on the faculty of the City University of New York. He has written a number of articles on youth and on the nature of higher education, which have appeared in *Daedalus, Sociology of Education,* and the *Yearbook of Education, 1974*. Recently, he completed a detailed study of how psychiatrists are trained. Articles on this work have appeared in the *American Journal of Sociology* and in the *International Social Science Journal*. The entire study will soon be published by W. W. Norton as a book. Currently, he is conducting research on the structure of mental health services in several countries.

Suzanne Keller is currently Professor of Sociology at Princeton University, where she has served as Chairperson of the Department of Sociology. She was born in Vienna, Austria, and came to the United States as a child. After college she spent several years in Europe, mainly in Paris and Munich, where she worked as a survey analyst and translator. She received a Ph.D. in sociology from Columbia in 1953. In 1957, she became an Assistant Professor at Brandeis University, where she taught courses in social theory, stratification, and the sociology of religion. A Fulbright Lectureship in 1963 at the Athens Center of Ekistics marked the beginning of her interest in architecture and community planning. At the completion of her Fulbright in 1965, Professor Keller joined the Center, where she remained until 1967. That year she came to Princeton University as a Visiting Professor, and in 1968 she was the first woman to be appointed to a tenured Professorship there. She has also been Vice-President of the American Sociological Association.

Today, Professor Keller is pursuing her interests in teaching, writing, research, public lectures, and world-wide travel. A Federal Grant is currently permitting Professor Keller and an interdisciplinary team to investigate methods for the assessment of a planned environment. She is also active in the women's movement. The author of numerous articles and two books, she has just completed a module on sex roles for General Learning Corporation.

A NOTE ON THE TYPE

This book was set by computer in Univers typeface, a style comparable to the face designed by Adrian Frutiger. Univers was designed to produce an even series of integrated designs from the blackest extended to the lightest condensed. It is probably the most rational large type series ever executed. All versions were planned and executed according to a single original master plan.

This book was composed by New England Typographic Service, Bloomfield, Inc., Ct. It was printed and bound by Rand McNally & Co., Indianapolis, Indiana.